Hi Marcus!

Have a nice summer.

Nori

John Andrews   Architect of Uncommon Sense

john ar

Paul Walker

With contributions by
Mary Lou Lobsinger,
Peter Scriver, Antony Moulis,
Philip Goad, Paolo Scrivano,
and Noritaka Minami

architect of ur

drews

Published by
Harvard Design Press
at the Harvard University
Graduate School of Design

Distributed by
Harvard University Press,
Cambridge, Massachusetts,
and London, England

common sense

8		INTRODUCTION
20	01	EARLY LIFE
48	02	SCARBOROUGH COLLEGE Mary Lou Lobsinger
76	03	OPEN FORM AND DESIGN THINKING IN ANDREWS'S EARLY PRACTICE, 1964–1967 Peter Scriver and Antony Moulis
104	04	GREENFIELDS AND URBAN SYSTEMS: BUILDINGS FOR EDUCATION Philip Goad
136	05	METRO CENTRE: THE "VERY OBVIOUS JOB" THAT WAS NEVER BUILT Paolo Scrivano
164	06	MIAMI SEAPORT TERMINAL
184	07	GEORGE GUND HALL
212	08	THE CAMERON OFFICES AND THE RETURN TO AUSTRALIA
240	09	ANDREWS AS A PUBLIC ADVOCATE FOR DESIGN
264	10	ENVIRONMENTALISM AND THE QUEENSLAND PROJECTS Antony Moulis
288	11	TOWERS
312	12	INTELSAT: A KIND OF CULMINATION
336	13	CONVENTION CENTERS
360	14	FINALE
380		CONCLUSION
396		CODA Noritaka Minami

Contents

492	MAJOR PROJECTS
494	INDEX
502	IMAGE CREDITS
504	CONTRIBUTORS
506	ACKNOWLEDGMENTS

intro-
duction

by   Paul Walker

John Andrews was the architect of a remarkable series of buildings, beginning with Scarborough College in Toronto's outer suburbs in 1965 and ending with the Intelsat Headquarters in Washington, DC, in 1988. In between came buildings he designed in Canada, the United States, and his native Australia, including Gund Hall for the Harvard University Graduate School of Design (GSD); the CN Tower in Toronto, which held the title of the world's tallest inhabited built structure for more than 30 years; the Miami Seaport Terminal; major urban projects in Toronto and Adelaide, and, related to these, the Cameron Offices, a vast bureaucratic complex for the Australian federal government intended as part of a new urban assemblage in Canberra; and office and hotel towers, of which the best known is the remarkable King George Tower in Sydney.

These are all major buildings of international significance and achievements for which Andrews wished to be known. More than anything, he was proud of what he built. Andrews saw himself as a pragmatic architect rather than as a theorist or a designer of speculative schemes—he often argued that his designs were based on "common sense," most apparent in his solutions to design problems both on the drawing board and on site. But there are other achievements as well. At the height of his career, he received a series of notable accolades: in 1971, he became the only non-American architect inducted into the American Academy of Arts and Letters; in 1980, he received the Gold Medal of the Royal Australian Institute of Architects; and in 1983, with Denys Lasdun, he was one of two international speakers at China's first national convention of architects in Beijing. In the early 1970s, he was identified by *Japan Architect* as one of 10 major international talents of the decade, and in 1972, he was named by Philip Drew as a leader of the "third generation" of modern architects along with James Stirling, Kiyonori Kikutake, and Robert Venturi. Beginning in 1978, he worked for a decade with the Australia Council, the nation's preeminent arts organization, to promote Australian architecture nationally and internationally. In this time, he served on the juries for two major international architectural competitions: the Australian Parliament House competition of 1979, which effectively culminated the remarkable career of Romaldo Giurgola, and the Hong Kong Peak competition of 1983, which launched the equally remarkable trajectory of Zaha Hadid's. He was not only a builder but also a cultural figure. These accomplishments speak to Andrews's engagement with design culture and its publics that went beyond common sense; they demonstrate that the sensibilities embodied in his work had—and still have—broader application than to just his own buildings. They also suggest that this sensibility was not common at all but remarkable. Uncommon sense.

After 1988, Andrews's fame quickly waned, which no doubt reflected the changes in architectural culture of the period. In the face of postmodernism's rise and the subsequent stylistic eclecticism of architecture, Andrews and his office remained resolutely committed to an essentially modernist approach that considered design capable of redeeming the built world, and of making it better for everyone. The approach was late modernist in that it had a more circumspect view of the realities of building technology than those of first-generation modern architects and demonstrated a concern for the complex relationship between architecture and the urban.

Andrews's diminished popularity also reflected changes in wider society and the economy. The key projects at the peak of his career were nearly all for institutions rather than for commercial clients, and government budget crises of the 1970s and the subsequent rise of neoliberalism in public policy in the 1980s brought the end of institutional commissions. Though Andrews certainly enjoyed some success with commercial projects—hotels, office towers, convention centers (not quite commercial in Australia)—he took no pleasure in how building projects in the 1980s became corporatized and impersonal, particularly with the rise of project managers as intermediaries between designers and decision-makers. Moreover, while Andrews had a healthy ego, unlike many architects he did not see success as an architect as his be-all and end-all. A bruising defamation case in 1979 over newspaper reports critical of the performance of the Cameron Offices—the government project that brought him back to Australia from Canada—resulted in a major win for Andrews but seems to have triggered his spending more time on other pursuits, namely farming and wine-making in the New South Wales countryside and hunting and fishing in New Zealand. But the architecture bug never left him, and in his 80s he still had a drawing board and a roll of yellow tracing paper at hand.

In this book we seek to document and assess Andrews's architecture, taking the view that his body of work is a remarkable achievement that deserves to be better known. Pragmatically, this is necessary to stem the ignorance of, or purposeful disregard, for the importance of his work, which has caused many of his key projects to be destroyed or severely compromised—most notably, the unsympathetic recladding of King George Tower, the successive demolitions of all three of his Australian convention centers, and the destruction of the Miami Seaport Terminal and a major portion of the Cameron Offices. Across Andrews's work, several issues were subject to consistent development: environmental performance, distinctions between architecture and the urban, and design strategy and teamwork among them. These issues will be examined in the various chapters.

Our study of Andrews's career takes other lines of inquiry as well. Following a path from Australia to the United States and Canada and back again, Andrews's career compels us to consider how architectural culture in the 1970s and 1980s started to become internationalized in ways more complex than the earlier modernist flows of ideas and people from center to periphery or metropole to outpost. Adopting the term Drew developed from Sigfried Giedion, the "third generation" of modern architecture was a much more geographically dispersed phenomenon than the first or second generations. But this is not to say that geography does not matter. In both Canada and Australia, the initial local reception of Andrews's first key projects—Scarborough College and the Cameron Offices, respectively—emphasized the particular pertinence of these designs to putatively local architecture despite the international credentials of their architect. In strangely similar terms, these projects were locally endorsed for their relationships to the expansive landscapes of Canada and Australia. In contradistinction to this enthusiasm for Andrews's imagined response to architectural geographies is the perplexity sometimes expressed regarding Andrews's selection for the plum job of Gund Hall—how did an *Australian* architect come to design such a significant building as the Harvard GSD when there were so many other GSD alumni to choose from?

A second line of inquiry that Andrews's architecture raises is the degree to which it shares common themes with that of other architects of the period. Unlike geographical readings of his work, this questioning prompts us think in terms of his generation of architects, the "third generation" of modernism in which Drew included Andrews. How do we relate the work of one architect to other contemporaneous architects according to this generational logic? While the particular configuration of Andrews's oeuvre is unique and indicative of his singular sensibility and sensitivities, there are characteristic forms and patterns across it shared with those of other architects who came to maturity in the 1950s and 1960s. This includes tessellated plan forms, a megastructural tendency to merge urban and architectural form, and a fascination with concrete surfaces and forms that allude to the late work of Le Corbusier. There are also lesser known or less acknowledged aspects of his work and his interests that link him to other architects of his generation: *à la* Rudofsky, an occasional fascination with the anonymous or vernacular (he particularly recalled being impressed by the step wells he encountered in India in 1961); a commitment to environmental performance in line with that of Ian McHarg and Sym Van der Ryn, which he said was simply a matter of common sense and led him to landscape urbanism, green roofs, and passive thermal design strategies that now seem prescient. Andrews's own version of his design approach emphasized that each project is a unique solution to a problem presented by a brief, a site, and the constructional means available: "common sense." Indeed, his very favorite of his own projects—Gund Hall and the Miami Seaport Terminal—are each quite unique in his oeuvre. But, as already suggested, such projects have particular aesthetic qualities that outstrip any common understanding of what Andrews might have meant by "common sense."

Andrews was also always economical in his design approach. While some key projects like Gund Hall and the Miami Seaport Terminal found their solutions in unique building forms, a design idea or a form that served well in one context may well serve a related problem in another project. Lines of design inquiry, often quite formal, appear in one project only to reappear in others, and thus we can see families of projects in his work. Some "problems" reappeared in every project, namely buildability and comfort. Buildability drove a businesslike approach to contractual arrangements, a need for a clear conception for each project, and a clearly articulated and commonly understandable "form idea" that allowed all aspects of a project's design to unfold readily. Physical and psychological comfort also informed the plan strategy of Andrews's buildings, responding to the need of individuals to find an address within the building form and the urban pattern of which the building was a part. This book, then, aims to add to the burgeoning literature reassessing the direction of modern architecture in the postwar years and to demonstrate how one key architect negotiated the advent of postmodernism not by simply ignoring it—as may appear to be the case—but rather by developing approaches within the formal vocabularies of modernism that sought to address some of the issues that postmodern architecture foregrounded, such as identity, history, and place.

This leads to the third line of inquiry, focused on the architect's role in design culture more broadly. Andrews's early success in Canada led to a precocious appointment as professor and chair of architecture at the University of Toronto from 1967 to 1969. While there is no doubt that Andrews always primarily intended to design buildings and build an architectural practice, there is also no doubt that he had a substantial impact on architecture education at Toronto and that this influenced his approach to the design of educational buildings, especially Gund Hall. But beyond this, his Toronto professorship also gave him a certain cachet, certainly enhanced by his personal charisma.

Andrews's return to Australia in 1969 at the peak of his international recognition led him into public-facing roles that drew both on his accomplishments as an architect and his wider influence. While building the Cameron Offices for the National Capital Development Commission, then overseeing the expansion of Canberra, he also advised on the commission's other major projects. In the afterglow of the cultural nationalism brought on by the brief Whitlam Labor government of 1972 to 1975, Andrews served on the jury to select an architect for Australia's New Parliament House. An explicitly nationalist project—the New Parliament House was intended to mark Australia's "bicentenary" of 1988—it nevertheless afforded Andrews opportunities to reestablish his North American connections. This includes with Giurgola, the winner of the competition, who had previously selected Andrews's design in the 1967 competition for the Miami Seaport Terminal, and I. M. Pei, a fellow juror in the New Parliament House competition, Harvard alum, and finalist in the 1958 Toronto City Hall competition. Immediately after the Parliament competition, Andrews took a role in the country's foremost arts body, the Australia Council, in order to promote architecture and design as art forms of economic and community consequence.

Andrews's 10 years with the Australia Council entailed supporting, promoting, and publicizing Australian architecture at home and abroad. During his tenure with the council, its focus on the economic significance of the arts was aligned with the prevailing neoliberalism of Australian politics, which was motivated by the economic uncertainty Australia faced in the late 1970s and 1980s. These years, however, were also times of emerging cultural confidence, as evident in the creation of a pavilion for the Venice Biennale—an Australian stake in a prestigious international cultural event and another architectural project marking the nation's bicentenary. Culminating Andrews's Australia Council commitments, the pavilion was designed by the Sydney architect Philip

Cox, his sometime friend and Australia Council collaborator. There were also achievements that were less high-profile but just as important. For example, following Whitlam's early diplomatic recognition of the People's Republic of China, Andrews used his council position to establish exchanges between design professions in Australia and China. Given the subsequent significance of their Chinese operations to several leading Australian architectural practices and of China generally to the international architectural scene, Andrews's foresight, like his consideration of buildings' environmental performance, is again apparent.

BOOK STRUCTURE

John Andrews: Architect of Uncommon Sense is the product of a collaborative research project undertaken by six scholars located—at least when the project began—at universities in Toronto, Boston, and Australia. Given that Andrews's architecture is scattered across two continents and his archival material is held in several locations in Canada and Australia, it did not seem feasible for one scholar to undertake the project alone. The book was conceived as a collaboration that would produce a multiauthored monograph. In the event, as the careers of the members of our team took their individual trajectories over the term of the project, most of the responsibility to complete the project fell to one author. The book nevertheless aspires to tell a coherent story rather than present a series of individual essays. Some chapters focus on particularly significant projects—Scarborough College, Metro Centre, the Miami Seaport Terminal, Gund Hall, the Cameron Offices, and the Intelsat Headquarters—and some are about groups of projects or building types significant in Andrews's collected works. One positions Andrews as an influential figure in design advocacy and the public realm, and, finally, two chapters, the first and the last, consider aspects of Andrews's biography apart from his role in the realms of architecture and design.

The first chapter, authored by Paul Walker, examines Andrews's education as an architect and his early years in Toronto. Andrews was educated at the University of Sydney and at the Harvard GSD, where he was strongly influenced by architect, city planner, and educator Josep Lluís Sert. While at Harvard, Andrews led a team that entered the Toronto City Hall competition of 1958 and ultimately placed second. Andrews subsequently worked at the John B. Parkin Associates firm in Toronto, where he helped develop the winning design of the City Hall competition by Viljo Revell. He then traveled to Europe and Asia in 1961 in a telling period of architectural tourism. This chapter examines Andrews's early development as an architect in relation to the influential architects of his generation, particularly Le Corbusier and Paul Rudolph. Andrews's Toronto work made him very mindful of climatic exigencies, and his travel to Europe and India affirmed the importance of Le Corbusier to his practice and opened his eyes to vernacular architecture.

In the second chapter, Mary Lou Lobsinger examines Scarborough College, the first built project for which Andrews gained international attention. On his return to Toronto in 1962, Andrews began to teach at the University of Toronto and became engaged with two other young faculty members—planner Michael Hugo-Brunt and landscape architect Michael Hough—to design Scarborough College, a new campus in the eastern suburbs of Toronto. While the project was notable for incorporating television in its pedagogical strategy, this was only partially successful. Expediently completed in 1965, Scarborough College was celebrated immediately for its ambitious urban form and its megastructural aesthetics. In the project, Andrews further developed an environmental sensibility nascent in the Toronto City Hall design and his work at John B. Parkin Associates, and it affirmed for him the importance of teamwork in addressing planning and building issues.

The third chapter, "Open Form and Design Thinking in Andrews's Early Practice, 1964–1967," by Peter Scriver and Antony Moulis, examines the designs of John Andrews Architects for African Place at Expo 67 in Montreal and for the Bellmere Junior Public School. It investigates the emerging practice's philosophy of open design—an original search for open forms of architecture through geometrically ordered plans that could enable greater flexibility in response to change, both technological and social. As well, it considers the original patterns and planning tactics that established formal consistency and distinction in the works to follow, some of which were already in gestation.

The following chapter, on Andrews's educational buildings, is authored by Philip Goad and examines the open design strategy that Andrews continued to develop immediately after African Place in the vast South Residences at the University of Guelph. As at Scarborough, Andrews sought to establish an urban order in the Guelph project, but the South Residences bore the influence of social planning on the architect. The success at both Scarborough College and the University of Guelph led to many further university projects, a mainstay of Andrews's practices both in North America and Australia. As Goad demonstrates, in these projects Andrews continued to explore architecture's potential to make urban propositions, both in greenfield sites and within established urban contexts.

The fifth chapter, on Toronto's Metro Centre, is written by Paolo Scrivano. By far the largest in scale of Andrews's projects, Metro Centre was an urban design proposal for the rehabilitation of the decayed postindustrial railyards south of Toronto's central business district. Building designs were propositional, connected by diagonal circulation routes reminiscent of both the South Residences at the University of Guelph and provocative urban proposals by other architects of the 1960s neo-avant-garde. The failure to realize Metro Centre (and a rival project involving R. Buckminster Fuller) was indicative of political changes in Toronto, which at that time was quickly evolving into Canada's largest and most influential city. The sole built outcome was the CN Tower, which, despite not being constructed to Andrews's preferred design, immediately became one of the city's architectural icons.

The sixth chapter, on the Miami Seaport Terminal, is authored by Paul Walker, who wrote all subsequent chapters except for chapter 10 and the book's coda. Vast in scale—2,000 feet long as built—the Miami project nevertheless solved a straightforward problem: how to disembark passengers from several cruise ships simultaneously and process them comfortably and quickly through customs, immigration, luggage collection, and departure. The outcome was a series of passenger "nodes" with vast open-sided halls covered with canted concrete roofs that were S-shaped in section and aerodynamically designed to minimize lift during hurricanes. While these nodes are quite unlike any other form in Andrews's range of work, the big roof is a recurring feature, from his University of Sydney thesis project and the Toronto City Hall design to that of Gund Hall, the last of which is the focus of chapter 7.

Returning to the Harvard GSD to design Gund Hall, Andrews revisited Sert's teachings about the urban dimension of architecture as well as lessons from Le Corbusier, most obviously through the Carpenter Center at Harvard, which was completed in 1963. But the design of Gund Hall raised issues wider than those relevant to design culture; it coincided with widespread unrest among students on American campuses and was opposed for political reasons by both GSD students and faculty. The architect's difficulties were exacerbated by a meager brief that contained no statement on the GSD's educational goals, and so Andrews drew on his own pedagogical philosophy, which emphasized the centrality of the studio to design education. Upon completion in 1972, the building was praised for its formal bravura, but its reception was muted by concerns that internal tensions within the GSD had not been resolved.

Chapter 8 is on the Cameron Offices project, which enabled Andrews and his family to return to Australia in 1969. Built for the National Capital Development Commission as part of its comprehensive program to expand Australia's capital, Canberra, the Cameron Offices were devised as seven wings of open-plan office space with landscaped courtyards between and landscaped green roofs on top. The offices were linked at one end by a "mall," an elevated walkway intended to integrate the design with a new residential neighborhood and a retail and community center. Andrews's plan was badly compromised when the anticipated retail center was relocated, which coincided with a wider shift in Australian politics that scrapped the commission's grand urban vision of an expanded Canberra for a new commitment to "small government." In this context, the Cameron Offices, despite its exemplary design, was never able to work as envisaged.

Chapter 9 turns to Andrews's role as a public advocate for design in Australia. During the late 1970s and 1980s he actively promoted design work beyond that of his own practice, serving on two key design competition juries and advancing design's cultural and economic significance in leadership roles at the Australia Council. In these undertakings, Andrews looked beyond the rivalries between the period's design ideologies. His approach was strategic rather than partisan. In addition to the engagements with the architectural profession in China and the founding of the Venice Biennale pavilion, Andrews's Australia Council work notably led to two touring exhibitions—one in Europe and the United States and another in Australia. Both exhibitions promoted the whole gamut of Australian architecture and included the late-modern approach Andrews pursued in his own designs and the postmodernism he otherwise disdained. Australian-themed issues of international design journals sponsored by the Australia Council, particularly the July 1985 issue of *Domus*, continued this work.

Authored by Antony Moulis, chapter 10 focuses on projects undertaken by John Andrews International in the Australian state of Queensland that intimate the office's evolving environmental ethos. Mostly for universities and colleges of advanced education, many of these projects were "masterplans" specifying sequenced site development and successive rounds of building over several years, and as such they were vulnerable to change. These Queensland projects also demonstrate the convergence of urban and environmental propositions in many of Andrews's educational designs.

Andrews's designs for office and hotel towers in the 1970s and 1980s, which entailed the architect's sometimes uncomfortable engagement with the world of commercial developers and project managers, are the subject of chapter 11. The first of these buildings was the King George Tower, which was completed in Sydney in 1976 and is the most accomplished of Andrews's triangular-plan towers. In Australia, Andrews also developed an interest in octagons as horizontally dispersed pods and as bundled groups—more closely spaced and much more vertical—extruded into towers. Andrews's commercial office projects culminated in 1988 with an extraordinary design for Sydney's Bond Street that proposed hoisting a 40-story office building 15 floors above late 19th-century mercantile buildings on a huge pier. Andrews's response to postmodern stylistic games, the Bond Street project was not built.

Chapter 12, "Intelsat: A Kind of Culmination," considers Andrews's design for the Intelsat Headquarters in Washington, DC, the commission for which he won in an international competition in 1980. The design included elements developed by Andrews in other projects: the octagonal office pods came from a 1973 project for a Canberra office complex; the exterior transparent screens suspended on triangulated stainless steel tubes first appeared in the King George Tower; and the green roofs he used for the Cameron Offices. But it was Andrews's attention to Intelsat's environmental performance—a design aspect he had honed since his first climate-aware projects in Toronto in the late 1950s—that apparently impressed the jury. Nevertheless, while Intelsat's energy credentials were widely reported, critics were far more interested in how the building looked: a cluster of glittering, high-tech baubles on a beautiful Washington site.

Chapter 13 concerns the three convention centers John Andrews International completed in rapid succession in Adelaide (1987), Sydney (1988), and Melbourne (1990). Each was part of an urban redevelopment project seeking to promote business and a neoliberal service economy through new forms of government intervention. The most prominent of these designs was the Sydney Convention Centre, which was built expediently as part of the Darling Harbour scheme to redevelop a neglected industrial district in central Sydney. The opening of the scheme was timed to celebrate the problematic bicentenary of the founding of

Australia, and Andrews's convention center departed from other Darling Harbour projects—an exhibition center, a maritime museum, a shopping center—in rejecting their architecture of faux festivity. Rather, Andrews responded to the grit of the Sydney Convention Centre site with a tough, concrete monumentality.

The last major project undertaken by the John Andrews International Sydney office was for the veterinary school at the University of Sydney, completed in 1998. Beginning in the late 1970s and through the 1980s, Andrews and his family developed interests in farming and viticulture in inland New South Wales, which increasingly became the architect's focus. Andrews also developed a love of fishing and hunting, and he spent a lot of time on these pursuits in New Zealand. Chapter 14, "Finale," considers these activities alongside Andrews's continued architectural work after the closure of his Sydney practice and the mixed fortunes of his major projects. Andrews's success as a young architect meant that he saw the 50th anniversaries of certain projects come and go and the demolitions or transformations of others. The partial demolition of the Cameron Offices, the recladding of the King George Tower and the reworking of its ground plane, and the demolition since 2014 of all three of Andrews's Australian convention centers figure in this chapter. The book's concluding chapter offers an overview of key themes in Andrews's work: the significance of geography, his place in the "third generation," urbanism, his attitudes to building and sustainability, the importance he gave to teamwork, and Andrews's role in design culture broader than his own practice. The conclusion is followed by a coda, a series of remarkable photographs by visual artist Noritaka Minami of Andrews's remaining buildings in North America and Australia.

This book offers a timely reassessment of John Andrews's architecture and a reclamation of its value. It is ironic and deeply distressing that, despite its prescient environmental and human concerns, Andrews's work can be swept away and replaced by architectural "product" from firms that tout environmental credentials and invent genealogies for their own designs as a kind of reconceived modernism. Andrews was the real thing.

01

early life

by Paul Walker

John Andrews was born in Sydney in 1933. His father came from a family of monumental masons who once had premises on George Street where there is now the preposterously named "World Square," one of central Sydney's tallest buildings. During World War II, monumental masonry was not a permitted occupation, and Andrews's father made ends meet by undertaking small building and carpentry projects, through which Andrews was introduced to the world of construction. He was raised in Gordon on Sydney's North Shore, which at the time was not a particularly affluent suburb, and he attended North Sydney Boys High School. During a period of compulsory military service in the early 1950s, Andrews was accidently shot in the leg, and a lengthy convalescence delayed the completion of his architecture studies at the University of Sydney until 1956.

While Andrews liked some of his teachers—he recalled with fondness the Hungarian architect and cartoonist George Molnar—he was not impressed with the architecture program. Jennifer Towndrow's biography of Philip Cox, who began his studies at the University of Sydney just as Andrews completed his, gives an account of the school of architecture in the late 1950s, then still housed in a remote part of the university's neo-Gothic buildings designed by Edmund Blacket in 1854. The professor of architecture Harry Ingham Ashworth remained aloof from the students, and much of the curriculum was tedious.[1] Ashworth's first-year architectural history subject started with Mesopotamia and dwelt on Egypt before proceeding to Greece and Rome, and the first-year design course included exercises in Beaux-Arts composition and the correct rendering of light and shadow on classical buildings.[2] Students nevertheless revered Le Corbusier and Mies van der Rohe and could count on good jobs when they finished their studies. In this sense, the architecture school at the University of Sydney was like many others in the 1950s. It was steeped in a pragmatic orientation to the exigencies of current professional practice in the local context, and it incorporated the Beaux-Arts classical tradition modeled, in the Commonwealth, on the Liverpool School of Architecture under Charles Reilly in the 1920s and 1930s, but with students attuned to a modernism only hesitantly acknowledged in the curriculum. The 1956 competition for the design of the Sydney Opera House particularly excited architecture students, for whom heroic modern architecture became a prospect in their own city and not simply something in books and journals.

During his studies, Andrews honed his practical skills in architecture by designing and overseeing the construction of three houses in Sydney's burgeoning suburbs. One presented a street-facing glass wall that was Miesian in inspiration but timber in construction. [FIG. 1] Another effectively explored the use of glass gables and split levels on a tight hillside site in Dee Why, in the northern suburbs, offering wide views to the Pacific. [FIG. 2] For his final thesis studio, Andrews designed an airline terminal for the Sydney airport that accommodated the elements required by the brief under a vast roof with a triangulated structure, which in its treatment was the dominant architectural feature. The clarity of the strategy was notable—and prescient. [FIG. 3]

In his last year at architecture school, Andrews met the accomplished American architect Pietro Belluschi. Informed by his Italian heritage and the modesty of his practice's local context of Portland, Oregon, a second-tier American city, Belluschi produced disciplined and nuanced modernist architecture that drew the attention of the Royal Australian Institute of Architects (RAIA), who invited him to give the keynote address at its 1956 conference in Adelaide. While passing through Sydney, Belluschi took the opportunity to meet architecture students at the University of Sydney, and Andrews in turn took the opportunity to ask Belluschi about

---

1   Jennifer Towndrow, *Philip Cox: Portrait of an Australian Architect* (Ringwood, Vic.: Viking, 1991), 77.
2   Ibid., 79–81.

1

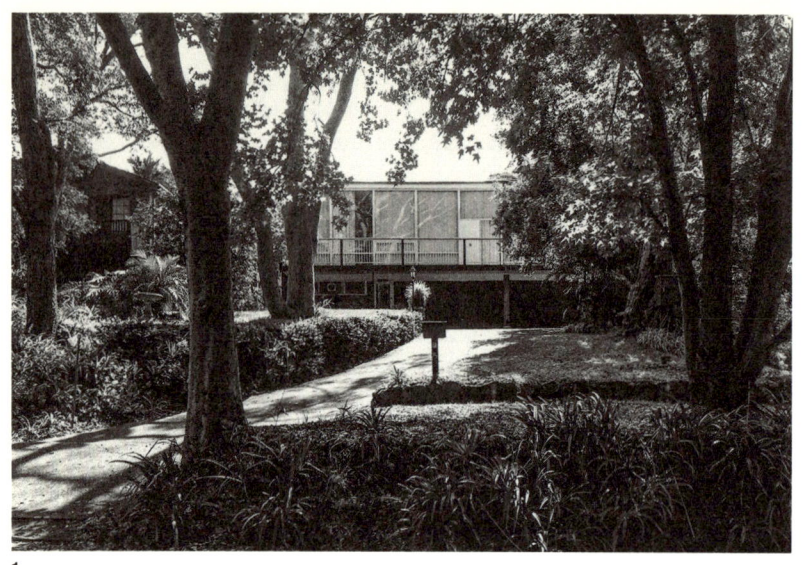

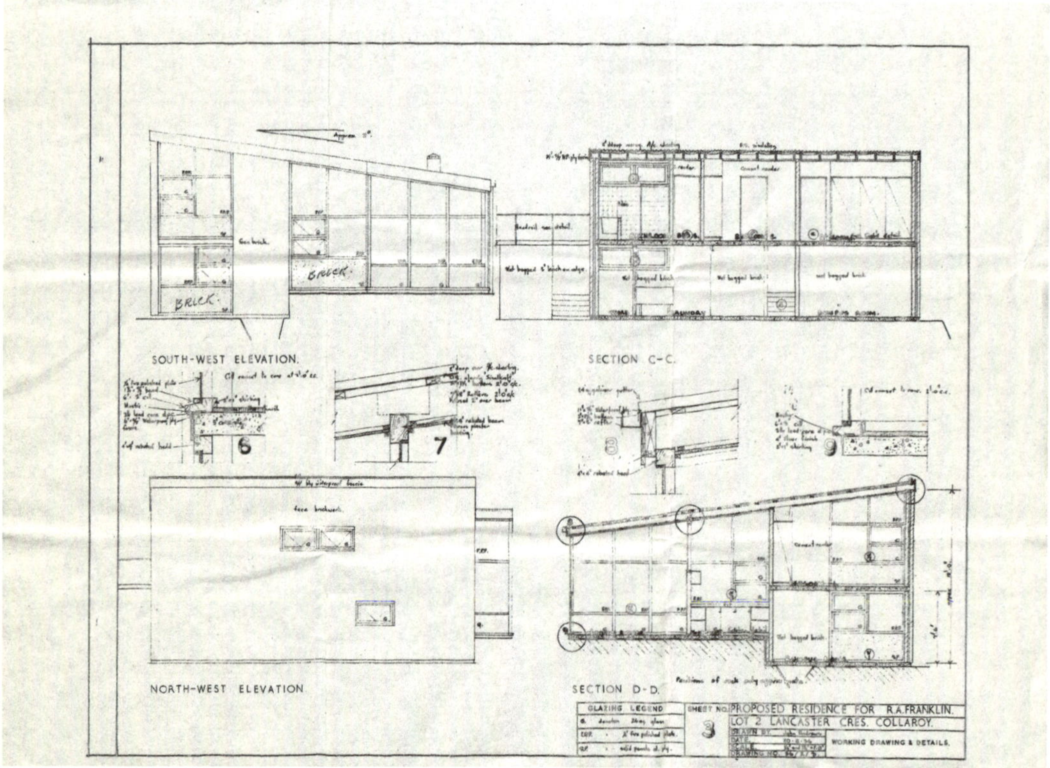
BRICK
BRICK
SOUTH-WEST ELEVATION.
SECTION C-C.
6
7
8
9
NORTH-WEST ELEVATION
SECTION D-D.
GLAZING LEGEND
SHEET NO.
3
PROPOSED RESIDENCE FOR R.A.FRANKLIN.
LOT 2 LANCASTER CRES. COLLAROY.
DRAWN BY
DATE
SCALE
DRAWING NO.
WORKING DRAWING & DETAILS.

2

AN AIRWAY TERMINAL

FIG. 1 House in Gordon, New South Wales, Australia, 1955.
FIG. 2 Plan, house in Collaroy, New South Wales, Australia, 1956.
FIG. 3 Airport design, Sydney, Australia, 1956. Bachelor of Architecture thesis for the University of Sydney.

studying in the United States. Belluschi, then the dean of architecture at the Massachusetts Institute of Technology (MIT), encouraged Andrews's ambition. Why the United States? The increasing American influence in Australian architecture at the time is apparent in Belluschi's invitation by the RAIA and, before him, the invitation to Walter Gropius to attend their 1954 conference.

After graduating, Andrews pursued inquiries with American schools of architecture, worked at the firm Edwards, Madigan and Torzillo, and notably met registration requirements, becoming involved in the firm's design for the Sydney Opera House competition. Andrews recalled a salutary lesson from this experience. Along with Ashworth from the University of Sydney, the jurors for the Opera House competition were English architect Leslie Martin, New South Wales Government Architect Cobden Parkes, and the Finnish American architect Eero Saarinen, a leading member of the "second generation" of modernists. Guessing that he would have a key role in the competition outcome, Andrews looked at Saarinen's work to glean a sense of what might get his attention. In 1957, Saarinen's most recently completed high-profile project was the General Motors Technical Center in Warren, Michigan, a steel-clad dome housing a showroom for new GM cars that was complemented by a careful essay in the disposition of curtain-walled rectangular building volumes. The Edwards, Madigan and Torzillo Opera House competition entry was therefore a composition of glazed boxes. Jørn Utzon's winning design was a revelation, and Andrews learned that expediency was not always the way forward.

The Opera House was not completed until 1974, well after Andrews's return to Sydney in 1969. And while it was a tortured project, perhaps even partially compromised in its realization, the Opera House was also one of the greatest architectural projects of the late 20th century. It was also indicative of a change in Sydney and in Australia as a whole.

HARVARD

Andrews's inquiries into graduate education in the United States led to his acceptance to the Master of Architecture (MArch) program at the Harvard University Graduate School of Design (GSD). To begin his studies in the fall semester of 1957, he traveled by ship to Vancouver, sharing a cabin with three others, and then south to San Francisco, seeing on the way Belluschi's curtain-wall-clad Equitable Building in Portland, which preceded by six years Skidmore, Owings & Merrill's more famous Lever House of 1954 as a paradigm of the glazed curtain-walled office building. [FIG. 4] At the San Francisco Harvard Club, Andrews arranged a shared drive to Boston. Among the few surviving photographs from this trip in early September 1957 are images of the Equitable Building, the San Francisco Civic Center, the California State Capitol in Sacramento, the Assembly Hall in Salt Lake City, the Kansas Statehouse and a hospital in Topeka, the Terminal Hotel in St. Louis, a modern building for the Jones and Laughlin Steel Company in Detroit, and the Jewish Chapel at Brandeis University in Waltham, Massachusetts, which won Max Abramovitz an American Institute of Architects Merit Award in 1956. These offer both a rough itinerary of Andrews's drive across the United States and the sense that he was not only interested in recent buildings.

In 1957, the Harvard GSD was under the leadership of Josep Lluís Sert, who succeeded Walter Gropius as chair of architecture in 1953 and was also appointed dean of the GSD. Sert's agenda at the GSD in some ways continued Gropius's—the architecture curriculum was modernist but hardly radical. There were, however, two innovations in his approach to architectural history and to urban design. Sert reintroduced architectural history into the core MArch program after Gropius had banished it to the status of "elective studies."[3] There were no history survey subjects in Sert's curriculum in the final year of the MArch—during which international students with professional degrees, like Andrews, joined their third-year American peers—but architectural history was important to the program nevertheless. Sigfried Giedion, the Swiss architecture historian long connected with Harvard, was a key critic in Sert's studios and also taught a subject called "The Human Scale." Drawing on themes developed in the postwar discussions of the Congrès Internationaux d'Architecture Moderne (CIAM) while Sert was president (from 1947 until CIAM's dissolution in 1956) and Giedion its secretary, "The Human Scale" examined urban construction and reconstruction projects, such as the rebuilding of Rotterdam, the design of Brasilia, Le Corbusier's Chandigarh, and British and Swedish new towns.[4] Eduard Sekler, an Austrian architecture historian who had studied under Rudolf Wittkower at the Warburg Institute in London, was appointed to the GSD by Sert in 1954 and taught the course alongside Giedion.[5] The urban orientation of this subject was emphasized when it was renamed "The Shaping of Urban Space" and made part of the core curriculum of the Master of Urban Design program, established in 1960 as the first such degree in the United States. The focus on the urban dimensions of architecture in "The Human Scale" reflected the urban character of Sert's GSD.[6]

This related to his broader advocacy for rethinking the relationship between architecture and the city, which he pursued in his writings, in his practice work since he arrived in the United States in 1939, and as president of CIAM.[7] Sert and Giedion, with Fernand Léger, set out their urban agenda for postwar architecture in the 1943 text "Nine Points on Monumentality," in which they wrote, "The people want the buildings that represent their social and community life to give more than functional fulfilment. They want their aspiration for monumentality, joy, pride, and excitement to be satisfied.… The fulfilment of this demand can be accomplished with the new means of expression at hand, though it is no easy task."[8]

Thus, while Sert's 1942 book *Can Our Cities Survive?* essentially presents the functionalist CIAM urbanism of the Athens Charter (which appears in the book's appendix), the monumentality essay sets out a new direction for modern architecture that approaches urbanism compositionally as well as functionally. The view that the built environment should transcend the functional to address the human desire for the symbolic and the aesthetic was repeated by Sert in a text he contributed to *The Heart of the City*, a book that came out of the CIAM 8 conference in 1951, and again in his 1959 GSD lecture, "Architectural Fashions and the People." Sert alluded to "the need for the superfluous" in both. As he commented in the 1959 lecture, "Fortunately, form does not necessarily follow function—though it should not be in conflict with it. We recognize today that there is in man an eternal need for the superfluous, if we call superfluous everything that does not correspond to our material needs. The superfluous appears in the first works of man, in the

3   A detailed history of curriculum developments at the Harvard Graduate School of Design during the Gropius and Sert periods is found in Anthony Alofsin, *The Struggle for Modernism: Architecture, Landscape Architecture, and City Planning at Harvard* (New York: W. W. Norton, 2002). For a critical overview of Gropius's GSD architecture curriculum and his disdain for architectural history, see Klaus Herdeg, *The Decorated Diagram: Harvard Architecture and the Failure of the Bauhaus Legacy* (Cambridge, MA: MIT Press, 1983), 80–82. Herdeg's book includes as an appendix excerpts from the GSD's 1946–1947 bulletin, setting out the courses in architecture offered that academic year. On the controversy surrounding Gropius's introduction of a "Design Fundamentals" course akin to the Bauhaus *Vorkurs*, see Jill Pearlman, "Breaking Common Ground: Joseph Hudnut and the Prehistory of Urban Design" in *Josep Lluís Sert: The Architect of Urban Design, 1953–1969*, eds. Eric Mumford and Hashim Sarkis (New Haven, CT, and Cambridge, MA: Yale University Press and Harvard University Graduate School of Design, 2008), 126.
4   Eric Mumford, *Defining Urban Design: CIAM Architects and the Formation of a Discipline, 1937–69* (New Haven, CT: Yale University Press, 2009), 135.
5   Eduard Sekler, "Sert, CIAM, and the GSD: A Memoir" in *Josep Lluís Sert: The Architect of Urban Design, 1953–1969*, eds. Eric Mumford and Hashim Sarkis (New Haven, CT, and Cambridge, MA: Yale University Press and Harvard University Graduate School of Design, 2008), 16.
6   Ibid., 16.

7   For Sert's career, see Josep M. Rovira, *José Luis Sert 1901–1983*, trans. Leonora Saavedra (Milan: Electa, 2003).
8   Josep Lluís Sert, Fernand Léger, and Sigfried Giedion, "Nine Points on Monumentality," in Joan Ockman, ed., *Architecture Culture 1943–1968*, (New York: Columbia University Graduate School of Architecture, Planning and Preservation and Rizzoli, 1993): 29–30. First published in Sigfried Giedion, *Architektur und Gemeinschaft* (Hamburg: Rowohlt, 1956), 40–42; and in English in Sigfried Giedion, *Architecture, You and Me: The Diary of a Development* (Cambridge, MA.: Harvard University Press, 1958), 48–52.

refinement of shape and ornamentation, in the earliest pottery and objects of everyday use."[9] Sert's 1951 CIAM paper, "Centres of Community Life," repeated other key elements of the 1943 monumentality polemic: it promoted a compositional approach to the design of urban centers, entailing collaboration between architects and contemporary artists, and anticipated the use not only of conventional building means but also of mobile and lightweight elements. Creative artists, Sert wrote, ought to draw inspiration from advertising: "Many of our best artists today still think in terms of murals or monumental sculpture for eternity, but commercial advertising has developed new techniques that could produce wonderful works if used by our most creative artists for non-commercial purposes."[10]

Sert and Giedion's orientation to monumentality put them at odds with other design thinkers trying to move beyond the functional architecture of the 1920s. Lewis Mumford was an outspoken critic of the new monumentality proposed by Sert, Léger, and Giedion, suggesting instead that regional inflections of modernism—exemplified, he found, by the architecture of the San Francisco Bay Area—would make modern architecture more humane and broadly relevant. This regionalist approach was particularly associated with the architecture program at MIT, a principal rival for Sert's GSD. Under the deanship of San Francisco architect William Wurster, from 1944 to 1950, the MIT program became a fulcrum in what Stanford Anderson has characterized as a Bay Area–Scandinavian axis, which brought important architects, such as Finnish architect Alvar Aalto and the Danish architects Steen Eiler Rasmussen and Kay Fisker, to MIT.[11] Just as telling as Mumford's criticism of Sert's position was the emergence of Team 10. As president of CIAM, Sert sought to take a more nuanced position on the city than that of the functionalist Charter of Athens—one of the prime provocations in the young architects tearing CIAM down—by promoting a Charter of Habitat, though this was not assertive enough to counter Team 10's advance.

Sert nevertheless shared much with his putative critics. Sert admired Mumford, and his developing approach to urban issues was influenced by Mumford's promotion of regional planning as well as his criticism that *Can Our Cities Survive?* did not sufficiently acknowledge the "cultural and civic role of cities."[12] Sert's understanding of the details of urban life had much in common with the rather ethnological approach of some Team 10 members. Indeed, during Sert's GSD leadership, Team 10 members Jerzy Soltan and Shadrach Woods were recruited to professional roles at Harvard,[13] and Blanche Lemco van Ginkel, who also had Team 10 associations, was a visitor in 1957.[14] If the drawn out end of CIAM from 1956 to 1959 was a personal defeat for Sert—and for Giedion—he lost no enthusiasm for the issues foregrounded in his agenda. He used his pivotal position at Harvard to continue the debate, though in a less international context, in the series of urban design conferences held at the GSD from 1956 through the 1960s. The Charter for the Human Habitat that he pursued inconclusively through the late meetings of CIAM gained a new lease of life through the Second International Congress of Architects in Persepolis, Iran, in 1974, and was ultimately presented at the United Nations Conference on Human Settlements in Vancouver, Canada, in 1976.[15] A number of key issues subtended all of Sert's urban investigations and discussions:

9 Josep Lluís Sert, "Architectural Fashions and the People," in *The Writings of Josep Lluís Sert*, ed. Eric Mumford (New Haven, CT, and Cambridge MA: Yale University Press and Harvard University Graduate School of Design, 2015), 95. See also Josep Lluís Sert, "Centres of Community Life" in *The Heart of the City: Towards the Humanisation of Urban Life*, eds. Jaqueline Tyrwhitt, Josep Lluís Sert, and Ernesto Nathan Rogers, (London: Lund Humphries, 1952), 13.
10 Sert, "Centres of Community Life," 14.
11 Stanford Anderson, "The 'new empricism - Bay Region axis': Kay Fisker and postwar debates in functionalism, regionalism and monumentality," *Journal of Architectural Education* 50, no.3 (1997): 197–207.
12 Eric Mumford, *The CIAM Discourse on Urbanism, 1928–1960* (Cambridge, MA: MIT Press, 2000), 142.
13 Alofsin, *The Struggle for Modernism*, 256.
14 Mumford, *Defining Urban Design*, 135.
15 See Sert, "Industrialization: An Opportunity for the Design of New communities," in *The Writings of Josep Lluís Sert*, 133–42; and Sert, "Balance in the Human Habitat," in *The Writings of Josep Lluís Sert*, 143–53. Eric Mumford notes the Iranian connections.

the form of the residential neighborhood, and, arising from this, the urban scale required to prioritize pedestrian rather than vehicular movement for local interactions; the need for increased densities; the cultural and symbolic significance of the central core as a place of human interaction; and the relationship of the emerging American megalopolis to local urban formations embedded within it. Sert's leadership of the Harvard GSD during the period of Andrews's MArch, then, was at the very center of the key international debates about how modern architecture should develop and about what architecture's relationship to the contemporary city should or could be.

In his MArch, Andrews took a design studio led by Sert himself and co-taught by Huson Jackson with Alvaro Ortega and Lemco van Ginkel. Jackson would serve as Sert's professional partner in the firm of Sert, Jackson and Gourley from 1958; Ortega, a visiting critic to the GSD, was a Colombian architect who was trained at McGill University in Montreal in the 1940s and then at Harvard; and van Ginkel was also a visiting critic. Harvard's *Official Register* describes the curriculum for this studio as, "Advanced problems dealing with (a) complex buildings of monumental character and (b) civic design. The work is carried on in two studios.… The aim of the course is to develop a broad understanding of the influence of the forces encountered in modern society on the design of buildings and to investigate ways of harnessing the knowledge and techniques of this age in the creation of human environments."

But while Sert's ideas about monumentality were principally developed in relation to the urban core, his 1957 studio focused on the working-class town of Billerica, Massachusetts. [FIG. 5] According to Eric Mumford, the studio "called for rowhouses, walk-up apartments, and tower apartments, a mix that was intended to offer alternatives to both single-family house suburbs and the high-rise housing then being built on cleared sites in central cities. The student projects proposed a density between 80 and 175 people per acre (ppa), considerably more than postwar suburbia (normally about 2–25 ppa) but much less than the

4

5

FIG. 4   Equitable Building, Portland, Oregon, 1944–1948. Architect: Pietro Belluschi. Photo: John Andrews.
FIG. 5   Urban design studio project, Harvard GSD, Cambridge, Massachusetts, 1958. Photo: John Andrews.

Manhattan-type densities of large tower projects (500 or more ppa)."[16]

Andrews seems to have thrived at Harvard. Through it, he built connections with classmates of lasting significance in his professional life, and the GSD experience gave him common ground with fellow student designers and GSD alumni. Andrews recalled that Sert particularly favored the international students and abjured the Americans for their generally privileged backgrounds. Apart from the quality of the teaching, the standing of the teachers, and the fledgling networks, Harvard gave Andrews a glimpse of a world of cultural and financial privilege that contrasted with the material constraints of his upbringing and University of Sydney years and of postwar Australia generally. Sert was a friend of Le Corbusier and Picasso—*Guernica* was painted for Sert's Spanish Pavilion at the 1937 Exposition Universelle in Paris—and at Sert's Cambridge house, Andrews saw artworks by Sert's brother-in-law, Joan Miró. And just a few months after having driven across the United States to get to Harvard—a trip during which he sometimes slept in barns—Andrews found himself sitting in a box at the Metropolitan Opera in New York with Nelson Rockefeller: the mother of one of his American classmates worked for the opera and arranged the visit when Andrews spent his Christmas and New Year's break in New York. During this visit, Andrews also met another Australian through a family connection who was to have an important career as an architect in Sydney, the young Richard Leplastrier, whom Andrews enthusiastically encouraged to take up architecture. The two drove together to New Canaan to see Philip Johnson's Glass House (1949), which was possibly an important design influence on Andrews during his time with the Toronto firm of John B. Parkin Associates from 1958 to 1961.

THE TORONTO CITY HALL COMPETITION

In 1957, the City of Toronto announced an international design competition for a new city hall to be built on a large rectangular city block.[17] The terms of the competition were released in September of that year, just as Andrews began his Harvard studies, and first stage entries were to be submitted the following April, near the end of Andrews's second and final semester at the GSD. Held just one year after the Sydney Opera House competition, it had an equally significant impact on the international scene and shared with that earlier competition a key juror: Eero Saarinen. The other jurors included the distinguished Milanese architect Ernesto Rogers; the English town planner Sir William Holford; another English planner, Gordon Stephenson, then a professor of urban and regional planning at the University of Toronto; and the Vancouver architect Charles ("Ned") Pratt, designer of the widely admired BC Electric Building (1957). Others who had been approached or otherwise considered as jurors included Leslie Martin, who was on the Sydney jury but was unavailable for the Toronto gig; Walter Gropius, who was also unavailable but whose firm The Architects Collaborative (TAC) submitted a design for consideration; Pietro Belluschi; and the Swiss architect Max Bill.

The Toronto competition sought international participation, and Andrews—eligible thanks to his registration as an architect in Australia—entered a design proposal, going against Sert and Jackson's advice that he avoid competing. He and three GSD classmates—Macy DuBois, William ("Bill") Morgan, and William ("Bill") Ireland—worked away from the GSD's architecture studios in Robinson Hall, in the basement of a Cambridge building occupied by TAC. Having learned from his work on Edwards, Madigan and Torzillo's Sydney Opera House design, Andrews focused on analyzing the brief and the site rather than the jury.

Andrews's design for Toronto City Hall, like his airport terminal thesis project, was

---

16 Mumford, *Defining Urban Design*, 135–36.

17 An analysis of the Toronto City Hall competition is found in George Thomas Kapelos, *Competing Modernisms: Toronto's New City Hall and Square* (Halifax: Dalhousie Architectural Press, 2015). Christopher Armstrong has traced the historical genesis of the City Hall project and analyzed its design and realization in *Civic Symbol: Creating Toronto's New City Hall 1952–1966* (Toronto: University of Toronto Press, 2015).

dominated by a massive roof. [FIG. 6] But for Toronto, the rather diagrammatic geometry of his BArch project became more complex, its curvilinear elements supported by branched, monumental concrete structures. The roof shelters a vast space: a public square for winter use. [FIG. 7] Another public square for summer use is in front of the building on the south side of the site. While the roof is the signature element of the design, the building beneath is not merely an undifferentiated "universal" space with the nominal functional subdivisions of Andrews's Sydney airport project. Rather, the roof structure hovers above a range of five-story perimeter buildings that define the edges of the winter space, with a high opening connecting to the summer space. The walls of the offices are canted and designed to be cast in concrete with a complex geometry apparently drawn from stylized maple leaves. As well as echoing Andrews's earlier design from Sydney, the project recalls a significant project by Andrews's Harvard GSD teacher, Sert. In his Presidential Palace project for Havana, developed from 1956 to 1958, Sert organized a presidential residence, offices, and reception halls around a monumental patio, with a parasol roof of repeated concrete shells meant to evoke palm trees.[18] The palace project culminated Sert's investigation of the patio in Latin American urban planning projects of the 1940s and 1950s as a suitable element for pedestrian-oriented residential blocks and monumental complexes in the urban core, which the Presidential Palace epitomized.[19] The importance of this project in Sert's trajectory makes Andrews's citation of it all the more telling. As Sert's roof for the presidential complex in Havana was conceptually abstracted from a grove of royal palms, the great structures of Andrews's Toronto roof were conceived as "tree branches."[20] But instead of responding to Havana's heat and humidity, the roof of Andrews's City Hall offers protection from Toronto's oppressive winter cold, marking the start of an ongoing line of inquiry in Andrews's work into how modern architecture could incorporate responsive climatic strategies, for which Toronto and its environs were Andrews's testing grounds.

Toronto City Hall jurors received approximately 500 entries from architects around the world, including, notably, Kenzo Tange, Kisho Kurokawa, and Kunio Maekawa from Japan, and Balkrishna Doshi from India. One-quarter of the entries were from emerging or established modern architects in the United States, such as Harry Weese, Perkins and Will, TAC, and I. M. Pei. Huson Jackson and the English town planner Jaqueline Tyrwhitt, then, like Jackson, a faculty member at the GSD, also submitted an entry.

In late April 1958, Andrews received the exciting news that his Toronto City Hall design was one of eight selected for the second stage of the competition. The other finalists were the American architects I. M. Pei, Perkins and Will, Frank Mikutowski, and William Hayward, the Canadian architect David Horne, Danish architects Halldor Gunnløgsson and Jørn Nielsen, and the Finnish architect Viljo Revell. Revell, along with his countrymen Alvar Aalto and Aro Ervi, was a leading proponent of moderrnist architecture in Finland in the 1950s.[21] Andrews and his GSD colleagues had beaten not only several prominent modern architects but also their teachers Jackson and Tyrwhitt. With funds from their shortlist prize, they rented a large house on Cape Cod where they finessed their design for the second stage of the competition in September.

The success of Andrews and his colleagues in the first stage of the Toronto City Hall competition profoundly impacted

---

18 Timothy Hyde, "Planos, Planes y Planificación: Josep Lluís Sert and the Idea of Planning," in *Josep Lluís Sert: The Architect of Urban Design, 1953–1969*, eds. Eric Mumford and Hashim Sarkis (New Haven, CT, and Cambridge, MA: Yale University Press and Harvard University Graduate School of Design, 2008), 71.

19 Ibid., 68–72. Hyde points out that Sert's 1952 essay "Centres of Community Life" advocates for the use of urban patios or squares.

20 This is the term used in a report Andrews and his colleagues prepared about their second-stage design in the Toronto City Hall competition.

21 Egon Tempel, *New Finnish Architecture* (New York: Praeger, 1968), 26; Malcolm Quantrill, *Finnish Architecture and the Modernist Tradition* (London: E & F.N. Spon, 1995), 113.

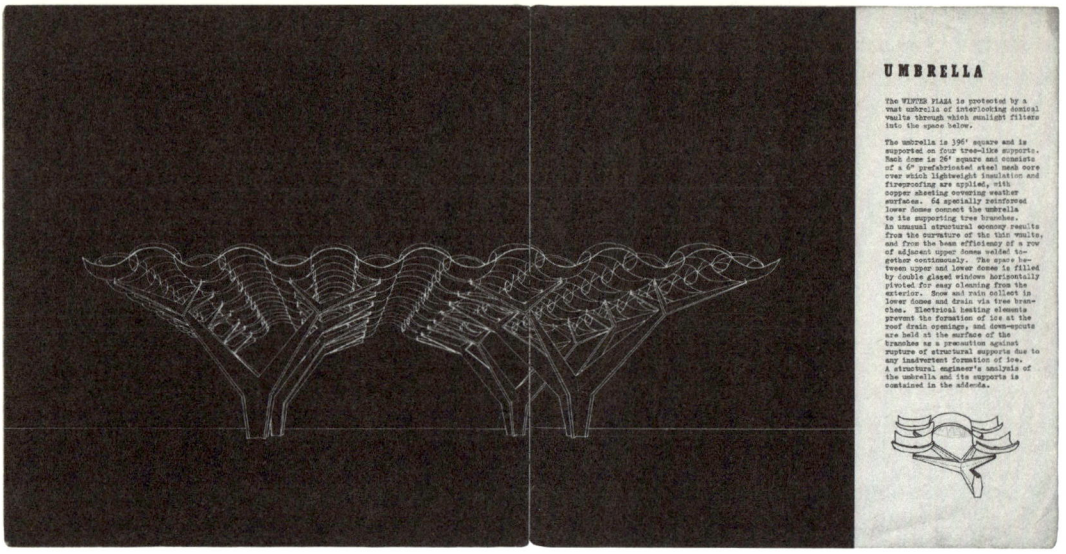

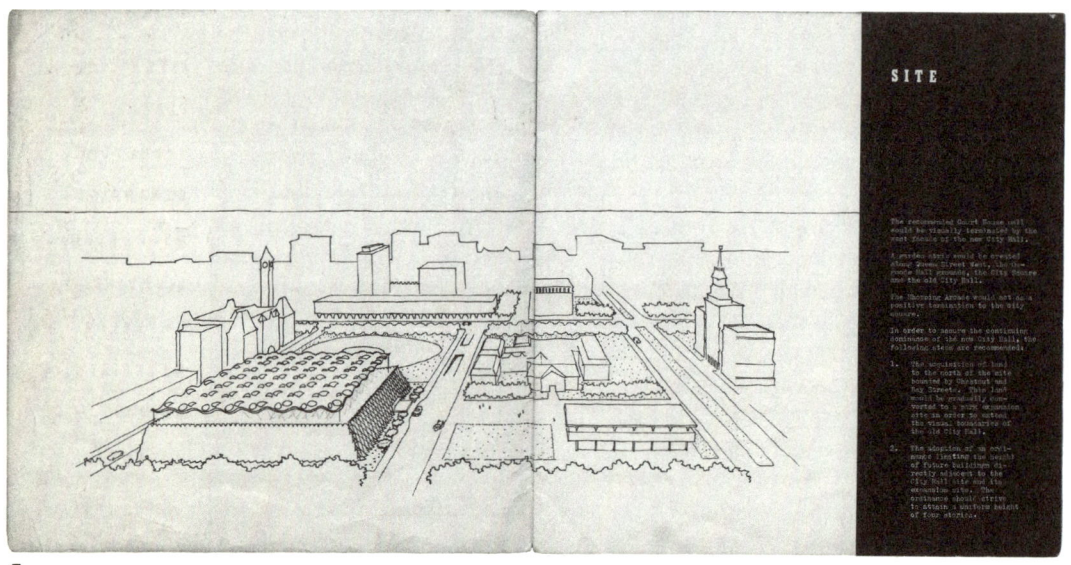

FIG. 6　Entry to Toronto City Hall competition, 1958. Architects: John Andrews, Macy DuBois, William Morgan and William Ireland.

FIG. 7　Brochure, entry to Toronto City Hall competition, 1958.

both Andrews's professional trajectory and his personal circumstances. The money it brought changed his life, and when the second-stage entry was completed, Andrews married. In Sydney, in the months before he left for Harvard, Andrews met Rosemary ("Ro") Randall, an occupational therapist, but the two barely had time to get to know each other. While completing the second-stage design for City Hall, Andrews called Randall in Sydney, asking her to join him on Cape Cod and to marry him.[22] He was sure she was the one for him. Randall left Sydney for New York by air on July 29, 1958, carrying her wedding dress over her arms.[23] John and Ro nearly missed each other at Idlewild Airport: he anticipated meeting her at the international arrivals building, while she disembarked instead at the domestic terminal after layovers in Honolulu and San Francisco. Ro waited for hours in one part of the airport, Andrews in another. They finally found each other as Andrews despondently returned to his car.

Also traveling from Australia for the wedding was architect Peter Courtney, Andrews's best man. Courtney stayed in the United States for some years before returning to Australia and would be greatly important to Andrews's future career. One of Andrews's most trusted colleagues after he too returned to Australia in 1969, Courtney was for some time the site architect on Andrews's first major Australian project, the Cameron Offices, and later he became a partner in the practice of John Andrews International.

Rosemary Randall and John Andrews were married in the new, architecturally innovative Chapel of St. James the Fisherman in Wellfleet, Massachusetts, designed by Finnish architect Olav Hammarstrom. It was the first wedding celebrated in the building, a happy portent in retrospect for what would be a lifelong and supportive partnership.

The principal difference between the first and second stages of Andrews's Toronto City Hall is in the treatment of the council chamber. In the first round, the chamber occupies a position over the entry between the winter and summer plazas, overlooking both. In the second, it sits beneath the threshold between the two spaces and is covered by a glass roof over which pedestrians enter the complex, a symbolic suggestion of the "supremacy of the people over their government."[24] The treatment of the summer plaza is simpler in the second stage, with the unifying elliptical geometry of paving and pool distinct from that of the buildings that defined the winter space.

In the second round of the competition, Andrews's project placed second to Revell's. Revell's design consisted of a striking pair of curved towers of different heights on a raised podium, an elliptical pod housing the council chamber between them, and a curved ramp to the podium level defining the eastern edge of a plaza at the southern half of the site. As in the competition for the Sydney Opera House, Saarinen was instrumental in selecting a Scandinavian architect and a project that avoided rectilinear geometries (with the resultant engineering challenges); and, as for the Sydney competition, Saarinen arrived late for the competition judging and retrieved what was to be the ultimate winner from a pile of projects already discarded by the other judges. Described by the jury as a "tour de force," the Andrews scheme was clearly highly regarded, and their comments on the second-stage design suggest that they anticipated after the first stage that the Andrews team might ultimately produce the winning project: "…the imagination displayed by the team was a certain indication of architects who might well provide the ideal solution at the second stage." However, the jury did not find the council chamber entirely satisfactory and commented that the project had not developed from the first stage.[25]

While Andrews's project was not built, it nevertheless made an impact, not least on his own trajectory. Sigfried Giedion took a great deal of interest in the Toronto City

---

22 "To Marry Architect in America," *Sydney Morning Herald*, May 29, 1958.
23 "Hello! Hello!," *The Sun-Herald* (Sydney), July 20, 1958.
24 Kapelos, *Competing Modernisms*, 54.
25 Ibid., 55. See also Armstrong, *Civic Symbol*, 63.

Hall competition, and wrote in *The Canadian Architect* that it was "the first civic center of this century worthy of the name."[26] Giedion's article discusses the architectural problem posed by the competition in the terms he developed in the early 1940s in relation to a new monumentality and directly comments on and illustrates only the designs by Revell and the Andrews team. Of the latter he writes,

> Among the finalists there is one scheme with which I had an opportunity to become better acquainted, since it was done by a group of students in the Master's Class at Harvard. This is moving in the direction of using the inner court as a huge festival hall. Its architectural treatment may not be adequate to the dimensions involved but the section has great interest. This takes the form of a trapezoid with a series of receding corridors giving onto the interior court. In daily life these would serve normal administrative purposes, but on occasions of public gathering they become inviting galleries for spectators. The entire court has an airy roof covering: not so bad for the Toronto climate![27]

Though he did not win, Andrews's involvement in the Toronto competition led directly to the development of his post-Harvard career there. Initially, this was with the firm John B. Parkin Associates, founded in 1947 by Parkin and his brother, landscape architect Edmund T. Parkin. They were joined by John C. Parkin—no relation to the brothers—as principal design partner. Apparently seeing their shared name as fateful, John B. and John C. had planned for some time to establish a practice together that would only do work in a modern manner, and, following that commitment, the two developed an architecture firm that by the mid-1960s was one of Toronto's largest.[28] While John C. Parkin's own entry to the city hall competition was not successful, he was interested in hiring talent, and approached Andrews on the basis of his competition success. At Harvard, Andrews had contemplated seeking work with Paul Rudolph after graduation, and Jennifer Taylor suggests that Andrews in fact had an offer from Rudolph at hand.[29] In 1958 Rudolph was at the zenith of his professional reputation and had just been made chair of the Department of Architecture at Yale.[30] Andrews sought Rudolph's advice on his Toronto project, and Rudolph apparently suggested that working in the Parkin office would give Andrews wider opportunities than his own practice could offer.[31] Both of Andrews's prospective employers were Harvard GSD alums, Rudolph and John C. Parkin having been classmates under Walter Gropius's tutelage in 1946.[32]

JOHN B. PARKIN ASSOCIATES

As a senior designer at John B. Parkin Associates, Andrews was responsible for several projects the firm took on between 1958 and 1961: the Sault Sainte Marie high school, the Primrose Club, the Federal Equipment administration building, a Simpsons department store at the Yorkdale Shopping Centre, and the control tower at the Toronto International Airport. Each of these was built. An unbuilt

26 Sigfried Giedion, "City Hall and Centre." *Canadian Architect* 4, no. 4 (April 1959): 49–54.
27 Ibid., 52.
28 Christopher Armstrong, *Making Toronto Modern: Architecture and Design 1895–1975* (Montreal: McGill–Queens University Press, 2014), 190. See also Geoffrey Simmons, "John C. Parkin: The Image of a Modern Architect" in Linda Fraser, Michael McMordie, and Geffrey Simmons, *John C. Parkin, Archives, and Photography: Reflections on the Practice and Presentation of Modern Architecture* (Calgary: University of Calgary Press, 2013) 1–11; and "John C. Parkin in Conversation with Michael McMordie," in Fraser, McMordie, and Simmons, *John C. Parkin, Archives, and Photography*, 89–95.
29 Jennifer Taylor and John Andrews, *John Andrews: Architecture, a Performing Art* (Melbourne: Oxford University Press, 1982), 22.
30 Timothy M. Rohan, *The Architecture of Paul Rudolph* (New Haven, CT: Yale University Press, 2014), 56.
31 Kapelos, *Competing Modernisms*, 27; Taylor and Andrews, *John Andrews*, 22. Both Armstrong and Kapelos note that the address for Andrews's entry to the Toronto City Hall competition was altered during the competition process from Harvard GSD to John B. Parkin Associates; however, Andrews did not start working at Parkin until the City Hall competition was over. See Armstrong, *Civic Symbol*, 188n43, and Kapelos, *Competing Modernisms*, 121n17.
32 Armstrong, *Making Toronto Modern*, 189.

project for an airport hotel is also notable for using a staggered section arrangement to mitigate aircraft noise, both because of its innovative design and its use of building form to address environmental factors, which was of continued importance to Andrews. He also worked on the John C. Parkin entry to the Winnipeg City Hall competition of 1958.[33] These designs are significant to understanding Andrews's development insofar as they further demonstrate his sensitivity to climate and environmental exigencies and because they intimate his interest in the work of the prominent architects of the time, namely Eero Saarinen, Paul Rudolph, and Louis Kahn. The statures of these architects were growing at the time, and their work gave material form to the ideas of a new monumentality promulgated by Andrews's Harvard teachers Sert and Giedion. While Andrews's interest in Saarinen and Rudolph did not last, Kahn's influence on him was both more abstract and enduring.

    The first lessons that Andrews adapted from Rudolph, however, were not about monumentality but climate. In an essay titled "The Six Determinants of Architectural Form," published in *Architectural Record* in 1956, Rudolph emphasized contextual factors including the building's environment and materials, the local region and climate, and the psychological needs of inhabitants alongside the standard modernist tenets of function and "the spirit of the times."[34] Environmental and climatic factors were important to Andrews, as is evident in his Toronto City Hall competition design, and they were significant in how he derived architectural form in his work for John B. Parkin Associates. For example, the Malton Hotel project near the Toronto airport was designed both to deflect sound from low-flying aircraft and respond to the location's climate, which in Toronto was always the most important exigency.[35] [FIG. 8]

Here, Andrews appears to have been attentive to Rudolph's designs from the 1950s that were inflected to different climatic conditions than those of Ontario. Before the completion of the Temple Street Parking Garage and the Yale Art and Architecture Building in 1963, Rudolph's reputation was not so connected to the formalist concrete manner of his mid-1960s work as it was to the frame-and-panel construction of his earlier Florida buildings. These projects were widely published in American journals; the February 1959 issue of *Architectural Record*, for instance, featured Rudolph's Riverview High School, one of the most important projects of his Sarasota period.[36] A two-story steel-framed structure, the high school featured pop-up sections in its roof that spanned the width of the building's wings. These accommodated airflow and let daylight into the building's interior. Done in the same year as Rudolph's high school, Andrews's design for the Federal Equipment complex features a section with a similar roof profile, including narrow raised sections spanning the steel-framed roof. But the idea is conceptually transformed. While the sectional arrangement is still justified on practical and environmental grounds, these concerns are very different in the context of Toronto.[37] [FIG. 9] For the Federal Equipment Building, a quickly erected frame was expediently enclosed so that the interior build-out could proceed unimpeded by Ontario's winter weather. When completed, the glazing in the raised sections of roof brought light into the building's deep volumes.[38]

    The strategy of erecting a steel frame and enclosing it to protect interior construction from extreme winter weather was also used for the Primrose Club, a private Jewish men's club

---

33   See "Winnipeg City Hall competition," Canadian Competitions Catalogue, https://www.ccc.umontreal.ca/fiche_concours.php?lang=en&cId=168.

34   Paul Rudolph, "The Six Determinants of Architectural Form," *Architectural Record* 120, no. 4 (October 1956): 183–190. See also Paul Rudolph, "The Changing Philosophy of Architecture." *American Institute of Architects Journal* 22 (1954): 65–70.

35   Taylor and Andrews, *John Andrews*, 25.

36   "Riverview High School," *Architectural Record* 125, no. 2 (February 1959): 217–19.

37   Taylor and Andrews, *John Andrews*, 23.

38   Paul Walker and Antony Moulis, "Before Scarborough: John Andrews in the Office of Parkin Associates 1959–1961," *Proceedings of the Societ of Architectural Historians, Australia and New Zealand*, 34, *What Does History Have in Store for Architecture Today?*, eds. Gevork Hartoonian and John Ting (2017): 778–86. My discussion of Andrews and Rudolph and Kahn here draws on this paper; I would like to acknowledge Antony Moulis's part in formulating these ideas.

8

9

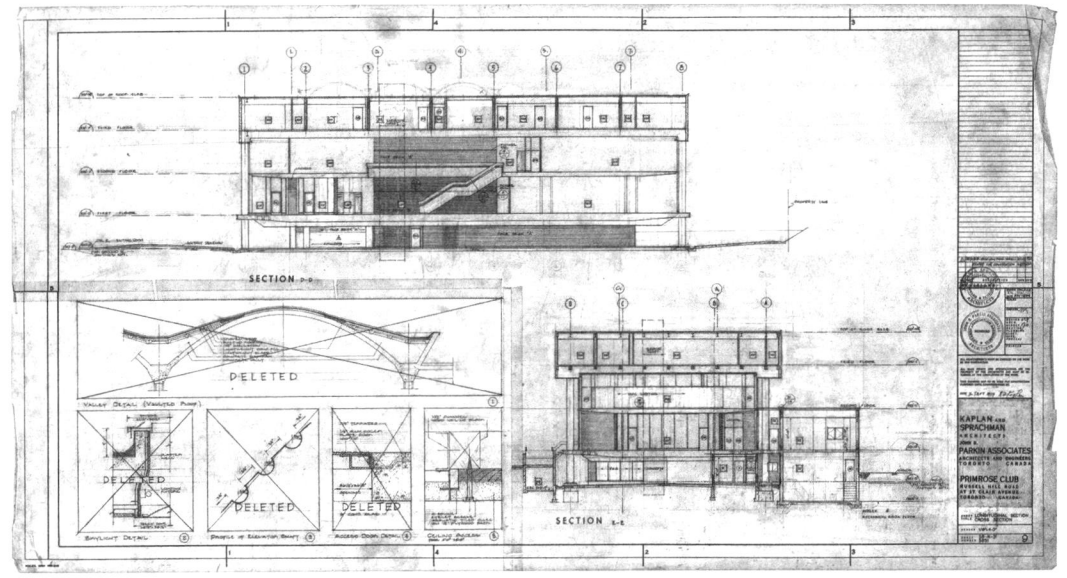

FIG. 8 Malton Hotel, Toronto Airport, Toronto, Canada. Architect: John Andrews at John B. Parkin Associates.
FIG. 9 Federal Equipment Building, Toronto, Canada, 1959. Architect: John Andrews at John B. Parkin Associates.
FIG. 10 Drawings showing late amendments to the Primrose Club design. The Primrose Club, Toronto, Canada. Demolished ca. 1990. Architect: John Andrews at John B. Parkin Associates.
FIG. 11 Original design, the Primrose Club, Toronto, Canada. Architect: John Andrews at John B. Parkin Associates.

in Toronto designed by Andrews for the Parkin office. The Primrose Club shares some similarities with Rudolph's work as well, at least in the design Andrews first envisaged; like the Federal Equipment Building, these coincidences are particularly evident in the roof treatment. But instead of the pop-up clerestories of Riverview High School and the Federal Equipment Building, Andrews's proposal for the Primrose Club featured shallow vaults. [FIG. 11] On the exterior of the Primrose Club design these signaled a two-level void in the heart of the building. Rudolph designs with similar vaults include the Hook House in Florida (1953) and the unbuilt US Embassy in Amman, Jordan (1954–1958), a project contemporaneous with and strikingly similar to Sert's Havana Presidential Palace.[39] Such vaults can also be found in Kahn's early designs for the Yale University Art Gallery.[40] It seems likely that the common source for all of these projects is the work of Le Corbusier, specifically the "Roq et Rob" apartments (1949) and the Maisons Jaoul (1953), the designs of which were published in 1953 in Le Corbusier's *Oeuvre complète 1946–1952*.[41]

The Primrose Club vaults were removed late in the evolution of the design and not built. [FIG. 10] The building's elevations instead returned to an approximation of the Miesian orthodoxy that John C. Parkin made the office norm by the mid-1950s.[42] This Miesian pattern is apparent in a series of Parkin buildings completed between 1955 and 1957: Ortho Pharmaceuticals, the Don Mills Shopping Centre, two bank buildings, and John B. Parkin Associates' own offices, all in Don Mills, and the Ontario Association of Architects offices, in Toronto.[43] In the 1960s, Parkin facilitated a collaboration between his firm, the Toronto practice Bregman + Hamann, and Mies van der Rohe to design the enormous Toronto-Dominion Centre, a steel-and-glass banking pavilion and towers of 54 and 44 floors, all following the precedent of Mies's Chicago Federal Center.[44]

Other last-minute changes to the Primrose Club were the replacement of a circular reading room on the principal floor with an octagonal one and of a cylindrical elevator shaft that cut through the building with one conventionally rectangular in plan. The use of the cylinders in the original Primrose Club plan is perhaps evidence of Louis Kahn's rising influence on American architecture. While it is unlikely that Andrews knew the early vaulted designs for the Yale University Art Gallery, the design as built was certainly known to him. The overall plan-form of the Primrose Club was a rectangle; on the building's principal floor, the locations of two cylindrical volumes implied subdivision of zones for different club activities. The use of cylinders to organize the Primrose Club's interior corresponds with Kahn's much more dramatically articulated Yale University Art Gallery plan and anticipates Andrews's mature architecture, in which concrete cylinders containing vertical circulation elements are a leitmotif. The deployment of cylindrical volumes in the Primrose plan also connects it to another famous postwar project that Andrews had seen, Philip Johnson's Glass House.[45]

Kahn's early influence on Andrews is profound yet evasive. Among the early slides that Andrews kept, there are images of Rudolph's Yale Art and Architecture Building and Temple Street Parking Garage, [FIGS. 12–13] but there are no images of Kahn's projects, though Andrews recalled visiting several Kahn buildings, most likely during his GSD studies, including the Trenton Bath House, the Richards Laboratories, and the Yale University Art Gallery.[46] On Andrews's trip to Europe and India in 1961, he took photographs of postwar *béton brut* buildings by Le Corbusier, and there are slides of the Carpenter Center at Harvard that Andrews made soon after its completion in 1963.

39 Rohan, *The Architecture of Paul Rudolph*, 25–28; 33–40.
40 Sarah Williams Goldhagen, *Louis Kahn's Situated Modernism* (New Haven, CT: Yale University Press, 2001), 56.
41 *Le Corbusier: Oeuvre complète 1946–1952* (Zurich: Editions Girsberger, 1953); Rohan, *The Architecture of Paul Rudolph*, 25.
42 On John C. Parkin's switch of allegiance from Gropius and Breuer to Mies, see Armstrong, *Making Toronto Modern*, 190–91; and "John C. Parkin in Conversation with Michael McMordie," in Fraser, McMordie, and Simmons, *John C. Parkin, Archives, and Photography*, 96.
43 Armstrong, *Making Toronto Modern*, 192–198.
44 Ibid., 282–289.
45 The apparent connection of these designs by Kahn and Johnson is noted in Goldhagen, *Louis Kahn's Situated Modernism*, 55.

12

13

14

FIG. 12 Yale Art and Architecture Building photographed shortly before its completion. Yale University, New Haven, Connecticut, 1963. Architect: Paul Rudolph. Photo: John Andrews.

FIG. 13 Temple Street Parking Garage shortly after its completion. New Haven, Connecticut, 1963. Architect: Paul Rudolph. Photo: John Andrews.

FIG. 14 Model of Sault Sainte Marie high school with model of the Primrose Club displaying vaults on roof in the background. Architect: John Andrews at John B. Parkin Associates.

It is strange then that there are no photographs of Kahn buildings. Moreover, Andrews did not recall ever meeting Kahn or hearing him talk, though he insisted that Kahn was important to him, and Jennifer Taylor, the critic who knew Andrews at the peak of his career better than any other, also averred a strong connection.[47] It seems probable that Andrews first learned of Kahn's work—as he had learned of Rudolph's—through architectural publications, which he could have seen while he was studying in Sydney.

Kahn's work was heavily published in *Perspecta*, the journal of the Yale University School of Architecture that was founded while he was a professor there, but in the 1950s there were also articles on his work in the mainstream American architectural press, namely *Architectural Forum* and *Architectural Record*.[48] The first of the Kahn articles in *Perspecta* was published in the journal's second issue in 1953, and featured Kahn's work in Center City, Philadelphia, including his design for a new city hall building undertaken with Anne Tyng.[49] Details of this design are a likely source for the triangulated stainless steel frames supporting shading screens on Andrews's King George Tower in Sydney, completed in 1976. The second article, in *Perspecta's* third issue in 1955, was on Kahn's Yale University Art Gallery and was extensively illustrated with drawings and photographs, particularly of the building's deep, complex floor structures.[50] It is possible that these drawings helped Andrews develop the roof treatment for his graduation project at the University of Sydney and the roof for his Toronto City Hall design. Circulation cylinders, triangulated secondary structures, deep roofs—themes that are important to Andrews's work—all have precedents in Kahn's.

The influence of one of Kahn's most important conceptions, for served and servant spaces, is most explicit in another project Andrews undertook at John B. Parkin Associates, the Sault Sainte Marie high school. [FIG. 14] The first designs for the school were done in 1955, before Andrews joined the office, and show ranks of classrooms arrayed along corridors on three levels surrounding a central gymnasium. Resolutely axial planning and restrained elevations perhaps intimate the influence of the Hunstanton School, completed by Alison and Peter Smithson in 1954 and widely published thereafter.[51] Rather than design from the whole down to its elements like the first Parkin design for Sault Sainte Marie, Andrews's maintained the overall plan but focused the project's architectural expression on the individual spaces of the classrooms. The construction was concrete, and the ceiling of each room was formed with canted concrete surfaces around its perimeter, behind which were service pipes and ducts—Kahnian servant spaces. Each classroom was architecturally individuated, just as the pyramidal ceilings of Kahn's 1955 Trenton Bath House individualize discrete spaces in that building.[52] [FIGS. 15–16]

---

46 Walker and Moulis, "Before Scarborough," 781. The Andrews images of Rudolph's New Haven buildings were most likely taken in 1963, between the opening of the Temple Street Parking Garage in February of that year and before the completion of the Yale Art and Architecture Building in November. Rohan, *The Architecture of Paul Rudolph*, 69.

47 Taylor and Andrews, *John Andrews*, 17; Jennifer Taylor, "John Andrews, Architecture," *Architecture Australia* 70, no. 2 (May 1981): 30–37.

48 Other early issues of *Perspecta* that featured Kahn's work were *Perspecta* 4 (1957), which included Kahn's prose poem "Architecture is the thoughtful making of spaces" (2–3) and an article by Kahn titled "Order in Architecture" (58–63). Kahn's work is briefly discussed by James Stirling, "'The Functional Tradition' and Expression," *Perspecta* 6 (1960): 88–97; Sybil Moholy-Nagy, "The Future of the Past," *Perspecta* 7 (1961): 65–76; and James Gowan, "Notes on American Architecture," *Perspecta* 7 (1961): 77–82. Other articles on or by Kahn from the period include Walter McQuade. "Architect Louis Kahn and His Strong-Boned Structures," *Architectural Forum* (March 1958): 134–43; "Louis Kahn and the Living City," *Architectural Forum* (March 1958): 114–19; "Logic and Art in Pre-Cast Concrete: Medical Research Laboratory, University of Pennsylvania," *Architectural Record* 126, no. 3 (September 1959): 233–238; and Louis I. Kahn, "Form and Design," *Architectural Design* (April 1961): 145–54.

49 Louis I. Kahn, "Toward a Plan for Midtown Philadelphia," *Perspecta* 2 (1953): 10–27.

50 Louis I. Kahn, "Order and Form," *Perspecta* 3 (1955): 46–58.

51 This was widely published, for example "School at Hunstanton, *Architectural Review* (September 1954) 148–62; and "Secondary School at Hunstanton, Norfolk, Eng.," *Architectural Forum* (May 1955) 142–45.

52 The connection of Andrews's Sault Sainte Marie high school to Kahn's Trenton Bath House is noted by Taylor in Taylor and Andrews, *John Andrews*, 23.

The truncated pyramids at Sault Sainte Marie were also clearly expressed on the building's roof.

In rooms along the building's exterior, the outside wall was diagonally inflected inward from the building's structural frame to coincide with the diagonal plan junction of the ceiling's canted surfaces.[53] Pulling the windows in from the building perimeter had the practical purpose of shading windows from snow glare.[54] Outwardly, the resulting articulation of the elevation is difficult to understand as the building's external composition is subsidiary to its internal organization, an attribute of much of Kahn's architecture.

After he set up a practice of his own, Andrews particularized space using pyramidal roof forms (or variants thereof) in two key projects of the mid-1960s: the Bellmere Junior Public School (1965) and African Place for Expo 67 in Montreal. In both schemes, individual roofs proliferate well beyond the four pyramids of the Trenton Bath House. Trenton, however, was originally envisaged as part of a larger center featuring multiple individually roofed pavilion-like buildings. This larger scheme was published in plan and with a photograph of a part model in *Architectural Forum* in 1957.[55]

The last of the Kahnian themes in Andrews's pre–Scarborough College work is the clear *external* articulation of served and servant spaces, not just in section as at Sault Sainte Marie but expressed overtly in the building's form. This is particularly apparent in two towers on which Andrews worked. One of the most significant projects undertaken by John B. Parkin Associates while Andrews was employed there was the design of Toronto International Airport in Malton, in 1957, with the terminal building opening in 1964. This project was important in establishing the firm's status as a large, multidisciplinary design practice and in establishing its public profile as corporate modernists. Andrews was responsible for the 1960 design of the control tower. Departing from the highly finished surfaces of the airport's terminal and parking buildings, the tower was articulated in off-form concrete with the marks of timber formwork clearly expressed, Andrews's first use of such a finish; three vertically extruded concrete volumes housing services and circulation supported an observation and control room at the top. [FIG. 17] The control tower project won a Massey Medal for Architecture in 1964, then Canada's principal national design award. It also appears to relate to an unbuilt project for a triangle-plan office tower in Toronto that similarly features extruded volumes at its corners. [FIG. 18] (Jennifer Taylor assigned this project to John B. Parkin Associates, but undated drawings held at the Canadian Architectural Archives at the University of Calgary are included in the John Andrews fonds rather than the Parkin fonds.[56]) These projects establish the paradigm of the triangle-plan tower that Andrews would revisit several times in his career. They also relate to the Knights of Columbus Building by Kevin Roche John Dinkeloo and Associates in New Haven, completed in 1969, with four massive, brick-clad cylinders at its corners. Very interestingly, an unrealized design from 1962 for an office tower for Peugeot in Buenos Aires by Viljo Revell—winner of the Toronto City Hall competition—shows a similar plan in which the vertical structure resolves as four massive, tapering piers of concrete at the tower's corners.[57] [FIG. 19]

LEAVING PARKIN

When Viljo Revell arrived in Toronto in 1958 soon after winning the city hall competition, John C. Parkin proposed to him that John B. Parkin Associates collaborate in taking the design and construction of Toronto City Hall forward.[58] [FIG. 20] In due course the joint venture Revell-Parkin was established to do so, and in

---

53 This can be seen clearly in the images of the Sault Sainte Marie high school being demolished. See https://www.flickr.com/photos/68678468@N06/6246466970/in/photostream/.
54 Taylor and Andrews, *John Andrews*, 23.
55 Goldhagen, *Louis Kahn's Situated Modernism*, 103–11.
56 Taylor and Andrews, *John Andrews*, 23.
57 Kyösti Ålander, ed., *Viljo Revell: Works and Projects* (New York: Praeger, 1966) 114–17.
58 Armstrong, *Civic Symbol*, 79.

15

16

17

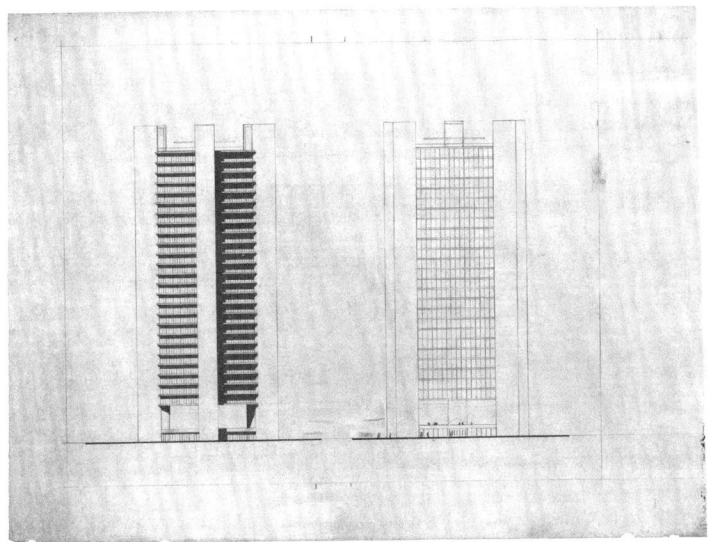

18

FIGS. 15–16 Trenton Jewish Community Center, Trenton, New Jersey. Architect: Louis I. Kahn.
FIG. 17 Tower piers framed by skylight, Toronto airport control tower, Toronto, Canada. Architect: John Andrews at John B. Parkin Associates.
FIG. 18 Triangular office proposal, Toronto, Canada.

19

20

the spring of 1959, Revell relocated to Toronto with his family and three young members of his Helsinki practice: Heikki Castrén, Bengt Lundsten, and Seppo Valjus. The principal challenge in translating the Revell competition project into a resolved design that could proceed to construction lay in the structure of the two towers. Revell envisaged these as having concrete floor slabs cantilevered off the solid back walls of both towers, but engineers consulting on the project deemed that this would not be enough to resist torsion caused by wind forces on the eccentric tower forms, the plan shape of which produced an airfoil action.[59]

According to a 2013 interview Christopher Armstrong conducted with Lundsten, Valjus, and Tuula Revell, Viljo's daughter, the Finnish team was concerned that behind closed doors, Andrews was investigating an alternative structural approach for Revell's design that used steel instead of concrete, "...but the Finns were never allowed to see this proposal (if it really existed)."[60] Andrews recalled, however, that he only became involved in the city hall project after Revell's colleagues returned to Finland and problems became apparent in the resolved design, and that he enjoyed the experience of working with Revell and his Finnish team. Despite the rather gestural qualities of Revell's Toronto design and his connections with Alvar Aalto's office, where he worked as a young architect,[61] in the Finnish context Revell was seen as the rationalist antithesis to the romanticism of Aalto's postwar architecture, interested in industrial materials rather than the timber on which Aalto and other Finnish architects fixated.[62] Revell's approach to architecture, then, was closely akin to Andrews's own emerging design ethos.

Apart from Revell, Andrews found other like-minded colleagues in the Parkin office: the engineer Norbert Seethaler, who consulted on

FIG. 19 Peugeot Tower, Buenos Aires, Argentina, 1962. Architect: Viljo Revell.
FIG. 20 Toronto City Hall, Toronto, Canada, 1965. Architect: Viljo Revell. Photo by John Andrews.

59 "John C. Parkin in Conversation with Michael McMordie," in Fraser, McMordie, and Simmons, *John C. Parkin, Archives, and Photography*: 116–17.
60 Armstrong, *Civic Symbol*, 85.
61 Malcolm Quantrill, *Finnish Architecture and the Modernist Tradition*, (London: E & FN Spon, 1995), 96.
62 Kyösti Ålander, "Viljo Revell and his Studio" in Ålander, *Viljo Revell*, 9.

Andrews's Parkin designs, and the landscape architect Richard ("Dick") Strong, who was also employed by the office and became not only a frequent collaborator of Andrews's but also a lifelong friend. Together with an accountant and the lawyer George Miller, these three formed a group called Integ (short for "integrated professionals"), which planned to take on development projects of its own account.[63] But by 1961, Andrews had tired of the Parkin office. He had come to despise the design partne, John C. Parkin, who drove the firm to adopt a conservative office culture that valued a corporate "look" disdainful of the architecture profession's old bohemianism: beards—and even woolen ties—were not welcome.[64] Andrews recalled a requirement to park his disheveled car away from the entrance to the John B. Parkin Associates offices, a pristine glass box at 1500 Don Mills Road. Andrews's own offices in Toronto and Sydney, in stark contrast, had notably relaxed atmospheres. But more significant than the buttoned-up tone of the Parkin office, John C. Parkin appeared to Andrews to lack architectural principle: he pretended to adhere to a Miesian discipline, but the changes he introduced to the designs for the Federal Equipment Building and the Primrose Club betrayed that as a sham. Parkin insisted on adding extra columns to the end elevations of the Primrose design that had no structural purpose—a series of trusses spanned the entire width of the building, leaving the interior free of structural supports—and did not form part of an integral structural schema like in Mies's pavilions. He also removed the stepped roof section on one of the blocks of the Federal Equipment Building, though he left this arrangement expressed "dishonestly" on the elevations.

With Revell's encouragement and support, Andrews left the Parkin office and set off with his wife and their young son to see the architecture of Europe. Such travel has become a standard part of the early experience of young architects and of young Australians generally. But Andrews's range of experiences were perhaps somewhat different from that of most of his fellow antipodeans carrying out their "overseas experience": he had already ventured—with notable professional success—outside his own familiar context. And though he seems to have enjoyed seeing the sights of Europe, this monthslong tour of European architecture was the only such extended sojourn Andrews ever took. While he did travel extensively across his career, it was mostly for specific purposes and for relatively brief periods. Only a short stopover in Japan in 1965 seems equally to have the observation of architecture as its primary intention.

Andrews and family purchased a Volkswagen Kombi van for the trip, driving from Stuttgart, Germany, to Finland, where they spent six weeks or so, briefly reconnecting with Revell and his colleagues and traveling to see their buildings and the work of the other Finnish moderns, Aalto particularly. Extant slides from the trip show Coca, Spain; the Pyrenees mountain range; Mount Vesuvius, the Dolomites, Alberobello, and Venice, Italy; and Cannes, France. Sert advised Andrews to see the postwar work of Le Corbusier, and so there are images of Ronchamp and the Unité d'Habitation in Marseilles. [FIG. 21] Among the small number of other architectural images that survive from the trip is one of Revell's 1956 kindergarten in Tapiola, Helsinki, and one of Marcel Breuer's UNESCO Headquarters in Paris.

Perhaps less expected are surviving pictures of the Mill Owners' Association Building and the Villa Shodhan in Ahmedabad, India, and of Chandigarh, with Le Corbusier's Palace of Assembly still under construction. [FIG. 22] Anticipating a pattern of travel by adventurous Australians that was more characteristic of the late 1960s and 1970s than 1961 (and that also reflected the multiple layovers of intercontinental air travel at the time), the small Andrews entourage traveled from Europe to Sydney via the Middle East and Asia. There was a diversion to Baghdad to see Sert's US Embassy: Andrews was disappointed. In India, while Andrews went to some effort to see Le Corbusier's work, he later

---

63 Taylor and Andrews, *John Andrews*, 25.
64 Michael J. McMordie, "John B. Parkin Associates and Albert Kahn Inc.: An Industrial View of Architecture," in Fraser, McMordie, and Simmons, *John C. Parkin, Archives, and Photography*, 43–44.

21

22

FIG. 21 Unité d'Habitation, Marseille, France, 1952. Architect: Le Corbusier. Photo: John Andrews.
FIG. 22 Chandigarh Secretariat and the Palace of Assembly, Chandigarh, India. Architect: Le Corbusier. Photo: John Andrews.

recalled the vernacular forms of the step wells of Gujarat impressing him most among the Indian architecture he saw, notable given that he also visited Khajuraho and the Taj Mahal. After a brief period in Burma, Andrews returned to Sydney.

Andrews did not easily settle back into his hometown. He worked with Peter Stephenson of Stephenson and Turner—an Australian firm of corporate modernists—on an entry for the 1962 Johannesburg Civic Centre competition. Their design for this new administrative center consisted of tiered office buildings around colonnaded courtyards.[65] These courtyards and the battered walls of the buildings that define them bear a resemblance to Andrews's Toronto City Hall design, but perhaps the Johannesburg project's quest for conviction is strained given a lack of familiarity with the context. Huge asymmetrical pyramids, which Andrews vaguely recalled were drawn from the shapes of vast mining slag heaps, house unresolved meeting spaces and halls.

With a second child coming, the Andrewses' need for health insurance and the Kombi, which was shipped from Europe to Montreal, Canada, must have seemed very alluring. On returning to Canada, Andrews established his own office in Toronto, starting work on a shopping center that his Integ colleague George Miller brought his way. But in the first year or two, Andrews's main work was on small-scale domestic alterations, and so he also took on teaching at the University of Toronto, leading the final-year design thesis in the architecture program and a specialized master of architecture course devoted to design for Arctic conditions.[66]

---

65 Stephenson studied at Harvard under Gropius, completing the MArch in 1952. See "Architect's Eye on Big Picture," *Sydney Morning Herald*, September 7, 2006.

66 'Toronto to Teach Arctic Building: University Adding Graduate Course in Architecture,' *The New York Times*, August 19 1963: C25; 'Aussie plans city in Arctic, Sydney: *Daily Mirror*, September 26 1963: 32.

07

scar-
borough
college

by   Mary Lou Lobsinger

Vincent Tovell: Is this in some ways a Canadian building?

John Andrews: I think it is. I think it reacts, responds to the very particular conditions that are here on the site, and that's why I think it is Canadian. Canadian in the sense of the way it was built, the type of construction procedure used. Canadian in terms of the site, of what is on the site, in particular indigenous tree growth. Canadian in terms of the academic program, there's [sic] not many places anywhere in the world where a television system or a close circuit television system is as significant as this one is.

— TV interview featured on *The Lively Arts*, Canadian Broadcasting Corporation, 1966.[1]

INTRODUCTION

John Andrews's first major architectural commission, the University of Toronto's Scarborough College, is assuredly one of his most renowned works. Scarborough College gained immediate international recognition upon opening, first amid its construction in 1965 and then more extensively in 1966. The new complex was enthusiastically endorsed by mainstream press, in both local and national Canadian newspapers as well as in international publications. It was also well-received in architectural circles, with coverage in *The Canadian Architect Yearbook*, *World Architecture*, *Canadian Architect*, the *Royal Architecture Institute of Canada Journal (RAIC Journal)*, *Architectural Record*, *Architectural Forum*, *Architectural Review*, and *Architectural Design*, which featured an accompanying essay by Kenneth Frampton. Photographs of Scarborough graced the covers of *L'Architecture d'Aujourd'hui* (December 1966) and *Architecture Forum* (May 1966), dramatically capturing the interplay of light and shadows in the building's overhangs and deep recesses.[2] In *Architectural Forum*, Oscar Newman examined Scarborough College in the context of the global boom in new academic buildings. And, in a 1967 issue of *Harper's Magazine*, architecture historian Edgar Kaufmann insisted on the uniqueness of not only its form, but also its construction process and pedagogical program, as the first college purpose-built for closed-circuit television (CCTV) and multimedia instruction in North America.

In 1965, a committee from the Museum of Modern Art visited Scarborough College, and the campus would later appear in two MoMA exhibitions, *The New City: Architecture and Urban Renewal* (1967) and *Transformations in Modern Architecture* (1979). Both shows featured the same aerial view of the college in the depths of a Canadian winter.[3] [FIG. 1] This image, where the building appears as a stark concrete and dam-like form isolated along the slopes of a ravine, that edged toward the plain below, secured Scarborough College's reputation within the canon of mid-20th century architecture. The repeated publication of the project, the interior photographs of the building's unpopulated pedestrian spaces, three- and four-story interior walkways, and bare concrete surfaces catching light, established an interpretation. [FIG. 2] Its strikingly simple layout and limited palette of materials was easily associated with Brutalism.[4] In 1976, Scarborough

1   Vincent Tovell, "Explorations: Scarborough College, University of Toronto," *The Lively Arts*, Canadian Broadcasting Corporation, 1966, 30 min.

2   "Scarborough College, Ontario," *Canadian Architect Yearbook* (1966): 64–66; "Scarborough College, Toronto," *World Architecture* (1966): 171–77; "Scarborough College, Ontario," *Canadian Architect* (May 1966): 41–62; Oscar Newman, "The New Campus: It Suggests a Changed Scale in Urban Education," *Architectural Forum* (May 1966): 3–41, 52–55. "Close Circuit: College, Toronto University," *Architectural Review* (October 1966): 245–52; "Collège Scarborough, Université de Toronto, Canada," *L'Architecture d'Aujourd'hui* (December 1966): 84–90; Kenneth Frampton, "Scarborough College, Toronto, Ontario," *Architectural Design* (April 1967): 178–87.

3   *The New City: Architecture and Urban Renewal*, January 24–March 13, 1967; *Transformations in Modern Architecture*, February 21–April 24, 1979.

4   In *The Lively Arts* interview, Andrews explained that only four low-maintenance materials were used: glass, concrete, wood, and quarry tile. He considered concrete to be a flexible, natural building material.

FIG. 1 Aerial view of Scarborough College in winter. Scarborough College, University of Toronto, Canada, 1966.

FIG. 2 View of the interior street.

College took on a further characterization with the publication of Reyner Banham's *Megastructure: Urban Futures of the Recent Past*. There Scarborough appears in a chapter on academic building and campus design as an exemplar of the megastructure.[5]

These interpretations came to dominate Scarborough College's place in architectural history. However, overlooked in this reception is the process of the building's construction and importantly, the integration of an innovative pedagogical program for higher education in the humanities and sciences, which informed Andrews's architectural decisions. From its inception Scarborough College was on a shortened time line, and fast-tracked to completion and occupation. On-site construction started while design and engineering decisions were ongoing, which made necessary a highly collaborative building process. It was an astonishingly accomplished debut and a large project for Andrews, still a young 29-year-old architect, who had only recently completed his master's degree in architecture at the Harvard University Graduate School of Design.

Situating Andrews's architectural achievement at Scarborough College and the significance of its form within mid-20th-century architecture requires the balancing of his formal and material concerns with the political, social, and technical transformations that informed its design and construction. What has come to be known as a Brutalist megastructural design is the result of an accelerated first phase in a multistage planning, design, and construction process for a new University of Toronto satellite campus. The project also responded, with other international academic buildings of the era, to the demand to expand higher education campuses in order to meet the increased enrollment numbers. The issue of population growth was often accompanied by rhetoric calling to democratize education and make various types of higher education more widely available, attaching this idealism to expected changes in the job market of the future due to automation. It stands as an attempt to realize a pedagogical initiative that accounts for both synchronized and non-synchronized instruction in undergraduate education. Further, Scarborough College is indicative of changes, not only in education but in the architecture profession as well, that reflect, for example, new strategies in construction management.

This chapter celebrates Andrews's Scarborough College, turning from the well-worn themes regarding its Brutalist style or notions about Canadian architecture's special relationship to landscape and climate, to examine the role of the planning and construction phases in determining the architectural outcome. Many of the issues raised by this chapter, including the pressures on and challenges of building for higher education, the use of multimedia for instruction, and the role of the architect within the construction process, are relevant to our present-day experiences. During the time this chapter was written, university instruction swiftly and radically changed. In a matter of weeks at the onset of the COVID-19 pandemic in March 2020, remote multimedia education became the norm. The pros and cons of the Scarborough College pedagogical program put in place over 50 years ago resonate with this experience as well as with the now common expansion of university buildings to a form that extends beyond the conventional idea of a campus.

COMMITTEE AND TEAMWORK: TOWARD AN INTEGRATED DESIGN PRACTICE

Scarborough College is located 20 miles northeast of Toronto on approximately 200 acres of land purchased by the University of Toronto in 1962. At the time of the purchase, construction, and initial occupation, the site was remote and without essential services, framed by three wide thoroughfares and active farming fields designated for future residential development. [FIG. 3] Once the home of the Indigenous Seneca Nation at Ganatsekwyagon, and later the Mississaugas, the area in the early 19th century was comprised of villages and established by settlers as the township of Scarborough. In the

---

5   Reyner Banham, *Megastructures: Urban Futures of the Recent Past* (London: Thames and Hudson, 1976), 133–35.

FIG. 3 Scarborough College under construction, 1965.
FIG. 4 View toward the central administration area from below the slope.

mid-20th century, the township was incorporated into the Toronto metropolitan region and formally became a borough of Toronto in 1967. More than 15 years later in 1983, Scarborough became a city.

Planning for the University of Toronto's satellite campus in Scarborough began in the early 1960s in response to the 1955 "Sheffield Report" delivered to the annual meeting of the National Conference of Canadian Universities and Colleges (now the Association of Universities and Colleges of Canada). The author of the report, Dr. Edward F. Sheffield, then an employee at the Dominion Bureau of Statistics education division (now Statistics Canada), predicted that college enrollment would double in the following decade.[6] After receiving this information, the Province of Ontario University and Colleges Committee set an agenda for the rapid development and expansion of Ontario colleges and universities. Following the committee's lead, the report also became integral to the University of Toronto's plans for physical expansion and changes to its educational model.

At the time of the report, the University of Toronto's downtown St. George Campus consisted of a collection of historic colleges, and its perimeter was bound by major city streets, as it still is today. In other words, the location had limited potential or purchasable real estate to accommodate an expansion plan, especially one based on the former collegiate model. The university proposed two satellite colleges: Erindale College, located west of Toronto and now known as the University of Toronto at Mississauga (UTM), and Scarborough College, now the University of Toronto Scarborough Campus (UTSC). The university's administrators decided that the satellite colleges would focus on undergraduate education, allowing St. George Campus to dedicate its resources to graduate education and research. This endeavor adhered to Sheffield's predictions, which by the late 1950s were considered conservative and were later amended by additional studies carried out from 1962 to 1964. As evidenced by the creation of these satellite colleges, this major change forced politicians and university administrators to rethink the traditional delivery of and criteria for undergraduate education in order to meet the expected "crisis" facing Canadian universities.

In his book *Test Pattern: Instructional Television at Scarborough College*, a 1971 evaluation of CCTV-facilitated instruction at Scarborough College, author John Lee explains that "in its speed and scale of conception, construction, and commitment to television," the new campus was a hasty response "to the crisis foreseen by the Presidents of Ontario Universities in 1962."[7] Claude Bissell, University of Toronto president from 1958 to 1971, chaired the meetings of the Committee of Presidents of Provincially Assisted Universities and Colleges of Ontario that steered the future of education. In line with the urgency expressed in national reports, Bissell's committee undertook several studies assigned to subcommittees tasked with researching a new higher educational structure to accommodate rapidly changing demographics, new technical environments, and the future of employment. Frequent comparisons were drawn between American and Canadian higher education, including distinctions between public and private institutions and consideration of the Canadian commitment to public universities funded by the government.

The subcommittees produced three reports. The most significant of the reports for Scarborough College investigated the use of television and CCTV for college-level instruction. At the provincial level, Dr. D. Carleton Williams, a University of Toronto psychology professor, chaired the University Television Subcommittee. In 1965, the subcommittee published the "University Television Supplementary Report No. 3" with positive findings. As their report explains: "Two things are happening

---

[6] Martin L. Friedland, *The University of Toronto: A History* (Toronto: University of Toronto Press, 2002), 410–19; "Sheffield, Edward," Senior College Encyclopedia, https://sce.library.utoronto.ca/index.php?title=Sheffield,_Edward.

[7] John Lee, *Test Pattern: Instructional Television at Scarborough College, University of Toronto* (Toronto: University of Toronto Press, 1971), 26.

simultaneously to make universities interested in using television. First, there is the crisis of numbers. Secondly, there is the discovery that many things can be better taught with television than they ever were without it. On two counts, then, one quantitative and the other qualitative, the subject of university television is being explored."[8]

The University Television Subcommittee surveyed primarily American sources, and the authors thanked "American ingenuity and vigor [sic] basic research on the relative efficacy of television," including materials from Stanford University's Institute for Communications Research, the University of California, Berkeley, the Ford Foundation's Fund for the Advancement of Education, and the United Nations.[9] The subcommittee also visited Canadian universities, such as McMaster, McGill, and the economics department at the University of Western Ontario, which experimented with CCTV instruction from 1962 to 1963.[10]

The rationales supporting teaching with CCTV instruction were at times contradictory, ranging from a lack of qualified instructors to those that held that the use of TV presented an economic way to teach without the need of qualified professors. Williams's committee argued that TV instruction had financial benefits. For example, a taped class could be repeatedly viewed and used for up to three years without needing to update its materials. The report also devotes a chapter to the administrative and legal aspects of university television, citing the American Council on Education's approach to clearances and rights in new educational media. These legal and logistical issues, such as the repeated use of instructional materials for which a professor was only compensated once, would haunt the pedagogical imperative at Scarborough College.[11]

The impact of the University Television Subcommittee's report on the planning and design of Scarborough was in any case minimal since its research on the viability of CCTV instruction occurred simultaneously with the design and construction of Scarborough College. The planning consultant's 1963 user report was immediately followed by design development, and, within a year, the initiation of the first phase of construction. By the time the subcomittee's report was published, this initial construction phase was nearly complete, and the university was already looking to admit a cohort of 500 students. However, Williams was a strong advocate for the use of multimedia and television for teaching and heavily invested in its realization at Scarborough.

Prior to chairing the University Television Subcommittee, Williams had been appointed to a new position as director of the extension division at the University of Toronto. Williams eventually acceded to principal of Scarborough College, and by 1964 he became vice president of both Scarborough College and Erindale College, which opened in 1967 in Mississauga. He was not only an agile administrator but was also part of the University of Toronto's professoriate who had experimented with CCTV instruction in the late 1950s. He was even known by his television appearances and was said to have acquired a TV personality for his courses on the psychology and philosophy of modern living, which aired on the show *Live and Learn* on CBLT, a local affiliate of the CBC. In the 1950s Williams had also participated in Marshall McLuhan's Exploration Group seminar on new means of media communication.

As the newly appointed director of extensions, Williams was tasked with assembling

---

8   University Television Subcommittee, "Supplementary Report No. 3 of the Committee of Provincially Assisted Universities and Colleges" (Toronto: University of Toronto Press, 1965), 1.

9   University Television Subcommittee, "Supplementary Report No. 3," 9–11. The studies collected saw research from the 1950s onward on television education. As reported by John W. Meaney in 1962, these courses were not considered experimental by the foundation. Meany, *Televised College Courses: a report about the college faculty released-time program for television instruction* (New York: Fund for the Advancement of Education, 1962).

10   University Television Subcommittee, "Supplementary Report No. 3," 9–11.

11   University Television Subcommittee, "Supplementary Report No. 3," 17. The committee found that the question of rights for the professor lacked "guiding principles." The policies had to do with public television networks and private stations and were not relevant to educational institutions.

the planning committee to oversee the design development and construction of the University of Toronto's two new satellite colleges. He invited professor of zoology William Beckel to join the committee. Like Williams, Beckel was an enthusiastic advocate of televised instruction. He had proudly documented his pivotal role in the restructuring of the Department of Zoology and the department's experimentation with innovative teaching techniques, such as the use of demonstration vidicon cameras and monitors and epidiascope projectors.[12] Beckel had begun using CCTV instruction at the St. George Campus in response to the new teaching challenges presented by the increasing number of university students, who were, in his view, less qualified students in the general education stream.[13] He proposed that small classrooms of 20 students replace the traditional laboratories that held 100 students. In the early 1960s, Beckel fine-tuned this concept of a 20-student classroom to be equipped with CCTV.[14] He claimed to be acquainted with, as he put it, the "vast" literature on the experimental use of television and film for teaching and the "didactic" elements of multimedia disciplines.

After the eventual rejection of CCTV instruction at Scarborough, Beckel left Toronto to become vice president at Lethbridge University in Alberta but remained a stalwart supporter. "I am still convinced that the use of new media, such as television, is an essential part of the development of an improved learning experience," he explained. "To reject it, to hide from it is irresponsible in the face of the need for expansion and improvement in education today."[15] Beckel was instrumental in the development of the pedagogy and program for Scarborough College. He took an assertive role, or, as some viewed, he was relentless in promoting what he saw as pedagogical imperatives. Beckel's administrative presence was a force within the conception and realization of Scarborough College.

In 1962, John Andrews was hired as assistant professor at the University of Toronto's School of Architecture. That same year, he became a member of the planning consultant team for Scarborough College along with his colleagues, landscape architect Michael Hough and planner Michael Hugo-Brunt. Together, they were tasked with preparing a user report for the space allocation and budgeting of the proposed new college.[16] Published in 1963, the planning consultants' report incorporated input from Beckel and Williams, the latter of whom was by then Scarborough's principal designate, to propose a detailed first stage of development. The outline of this stage included not only concept diagrams, which took relationships between program requirements into account, but also schematic design sections that closely resemble the building as completed in 1965. In this early stage, the humanities and science programs were separated into two distinct wings, a decision Andrews later said he regretted. The months following the completion of the user report were devoted to the development of the masterplan followed by a more detailed plan of the humanities and the sciences buildings.

The approach to the site and the proposed building location was determined

---

12   William E. Beckel, "Instructional Television at the University of Toronto: The Zoology Department and Scarborough College: A recollection," typescript (July 1986–November 2000), 2; See also: William E. Beckel, "Scarborough College: Its Beginnings: As Remembered by William E. Beckel," typescript (November 24, 1999), 3. Beckel writes, "The television facility was primitive by later standards, but with a single Vidicon camera viewing a dissecting table, a stereoscopic or compound microscope and the capability of focussing on the lecture/demonstrator, it was possible to project demonstrations of everything we wanted to all students at once, allowing them to see for themselves in a way that was a revelation even to us."

13   The general education stream increased class size to 300, while honors programs or specialized streams hovered at around 25 students per class and lab.

14   Beckel, "Scarborough College," 1.

15   William Beckel, "Appendix 3, In Memoriam, 1970," in John Lee, *Test Pattern: Instructional Television at Scarborough College, University of Toronto* (Toronto: University of Toronto Press, 1971), 118.

16   "Plan for the Scarborough College," facsimile copy, unpaginated, n.d. 67-0006 013 10, University of Toronto Archives and Records Management Services (hereafter U of TA). Published as "A Report from the Planning Consultants. University of Toronto Scarborough College, 1963." The document is appended with photographs of a site and building model, schematic plans, and other sections, along with technical drawings and a climate analysis.

FIG. 5 View of concrete reinforcement in stairwell.
FIG. 6 Plastic scaffolded Science Wing in winter, 1965.

through extensive consultation with climatologist F. B. Watts of the University of Toronto's Department of Geography. The designers also had to adhere to the strict guidelines and regulations of the local authorities, such as the Metropolitan and Regional Conservation Authority. For example, Watts ascertained that the ravine floor was unsuitable for construction. Bisected by Highland Creek, the ravine floor contained significant plants, wildlife, and old-growth trees, and was worthy of conservation. Watts and the planning consultants agreed to prioritize an approach that accounted for both micro- and macroclimate issues, varied weather conditions through harsh seasons, high winds, and desirable sun angles. The climatology report found that the northern edge of the ridge was the best place for the building, and the consulting team recommended that the building descend along the slope, a decision that limited the area available for development to 39 acres. [FIG. 4]

In the user report, the proposed plan organization for the building was explained through conceptual diagrams illustrating ideas for the campus's present and further development. In one such diagram a circle represents the central outdoor area designated as the academic court. On the south side of this area a square represents the administration area from which two rectangles, the future science and humanities wings, extend in east and west directions along the ravine's edge. Dotted outlines to the north and east of the administration block indicate the location of the future library and gym. The planning document included sections with more committed versions of the relationships expressed in the concept diagrams. The report shows the science block developing along a corridor, or an "internal street," that continues through a central, below-grade hub area and from there connecting onward through the humanities block. This would allow for fluid circulation, "without crossing unprotected space," and promote social and visual connections across disciplines, with professors and students moving through the wings in both horizontal and vertical directions.[17]

In analyzing the building concept proposed by the planning consultant team, it is important to note that it was established before Andrews's official appointment as the building's architect and before any of the design team members and construction consultants joined the project. This conveys the ways in which the final building was the realization of a fast-paced, highly collaborative, and continuous design and construction process, which was coordinated among teams of various expertise. After officially being named as architect for Scarborough College, Andrews sought collaborators that were able to adapt to the dynamic decision-making necessary to fast-track building design and construction.

In the summer of 1963, the design group, including Jim Sykes, Ed Galanyk, and I. Stecura from John Andrews Architects, set up shop in three rooms on an abandoned floor of the university's old chemistry building.[18] They had an approximately $6.3-million budget in mind for a first phase that required development of the masterplan, the design, and the construction of a satellite campus that would initially accommodate 1,500 students. The design incorporated enough flexibility to physically expand to accommodate 5,000 students without interfering with ongoing university activities.[19]

The designers and administrators faced an accelerated timeline to realize a building

17 "Plan for Scarborough College," n.d., A67-0006 013 10, U of TA.
18 "University of Toronto Scarborough College: A Report from the Planning Consultants" (Toronto: Elvidge Printing, 1963); Letter from Michael Hugo-Brunt to F. Stone, July 27, 1963 U of TA, A67-0006 013 11. Stone was the University of Toronto's vice president of administration. The letter agrees to a fee for services for planning consultation as part of the design team. See also: letter from Michael Hough to F. J. Hastie, P. Eng. 30 July 1963, U of TA, A67-0006 013 11. The letter itemizes the equipment needed to furnish three rooms listed as a conference room and offices, a model room, and a draughting office. Equipment includes T-squares, drafting boards, stools, and printing materials, with a budget.
19 The budget proposals and final costs vary radically from an initial $1,263,000 for the television studios, leaving as much for the building itself, to $6 million and a university letter citing $11 million in 1966. The statistics on enrollment during the first years of the Scarborough College's operation can be found in John L. Ball, *The First Twenty-Five Years, 1964–1989: Scarborough College, University of Toronto* (Scarborough: University of Toronto, 1989).

program that typically took four years. Of the 25 months allotted to design and construction, the initial six were dedicated to developing the masterplan. In December 1963 the team started working on the design of the building.[20] The deadline for completion was the beginning of the academic year in September 1965, for a building that would be occupied by an initial 500 students. The proposed budget grossly underestimated costs and soon escalated to approximately $8.5 million, which was approved by the Board of Governors in December 1964. In a letter dated February 1965, the University of Toronto's building superintendent demanded that the Scarborough College project manager explain how costs had increased to over $11 million in less than two months.

While continuing to work with Andrews, from the planning-consultant stage through to the masterplan and building design, the university also sought a joint venture with Page and Steele Architects, a well-established Toronto firm. They served as the project managers for the development and implementation of the technical design.[21] Together, the building committee's members now included Williams and Beckel, representing the University of Toronto with Andrews as architect; Robert Anderson, a junior partner at Page and Steele, who oversaw project management; and engineer Frank Hastie, superintendent of the university's Physical Plant Department, coordinating for the university.

The adoption of CCTV technology as the main mode of educational instruction at Scarborough College, an unquestionably unique aspect of the building program, played a decisive role from the initial planning stages through to design development. It determined, for example, wall sections in the auditoriums, classroom dimensions, and the outfitting of classrooms for multimedia presentations. Some of these decisions informed the building's exterior as well, including aspects of the external profile, the lack of natural lighting in the auditoriums, and the skylights in the labs of the science wing. While other North American universities had experimented with television instruction, they often resorted to refurbishing existing rooms and buildings. Scarborough College was the first purpose-built college devoted to televised instruction.

The Scarborough College design committee aimed to make every teaching space and course CCTV-accessible. The program brief called for 200-seat, 100-seat, and 50-seat lecture theaters and 20-person labs.[22] The large lecture theaters were to be equipped with rear projectors and wide screens for frontal viewing, with additional TV monitors located along the side aisles. In the smaller lecture rooms and labs, the TV monitors were located at the front of the classrooms. Beckel's principles for CCTV labs and lecture theaters were translated into design guidelines, which incorporated statistics on space use for academic purposes and would define the nature of the committee's collaborations with external consultants.[23] As a 1966 article in *Architecture Forum* reported, "Typical undergraduate labs were designed to hold 20 students" and were "limited by the preferred distance from a television screen." Further, "each lab is plugged into a closed-circuit television teaching system."[24] The classrooms and labs were connected to the campus television production facilities located at the

20 AND 43A, Box 43-36, John Andrews fonds, Canadian Architectural Archives, University of Calgary (hereafter CAA); Jennifer Taylor and John Andrews, *John Andrews: Architecture, a Performing Art* (Melbourne: Oxford University Press, 1982), 31–32.
21 Taylor and Andrews, *John Andrews*, 38; Anderson, Scarborough College and Project Management, 1 AND 43A, Box 43-36, John Andrews fonds, CAA. In Anderson's account he was first notified in November 1963 by the University of Toronto about a conceptual design completed by a planning team led by architect John Andrews. He was told the first stage of the plan was to open for 500 students in September 1965, in a building designed to accommodate 1,500 with additional stages would take the capacity up to 5,000 students. He explained that there was a very loose association of consultants, including many that were hired prior to the Page and Steele project managers. The building would be ready for occupation in November 1965.

22 Beckel, "Instructional Television at the University of Toronto," 7.
23 Ibid., 7–8; Sasaki, Strong and Associates of Watertown, Massachusetts, letter from Michael Hugo-Brunt to C. Yost, August 21, 1963, A67-0006 013 11, U of TA.
24 Newman, "The New Campus," 37.

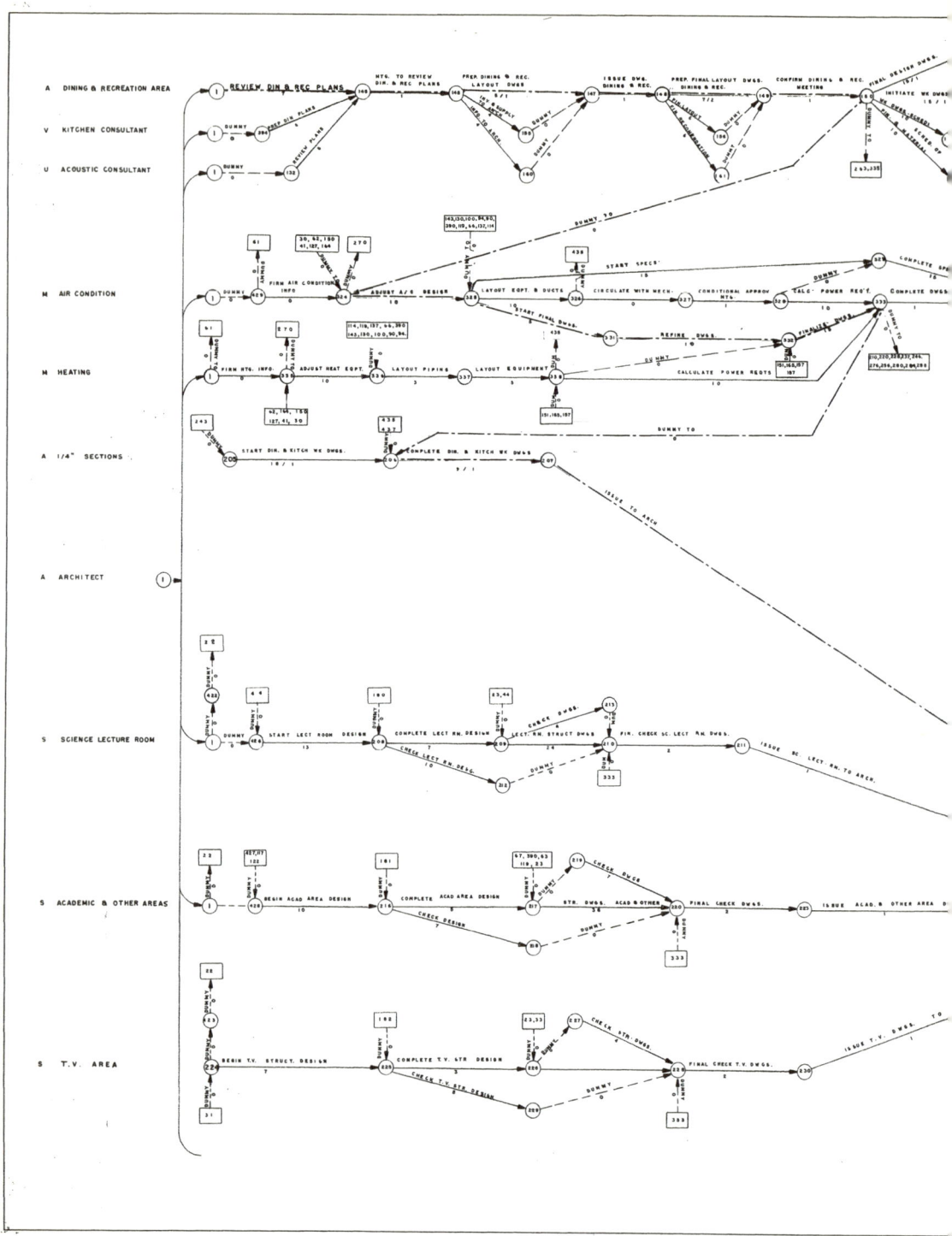

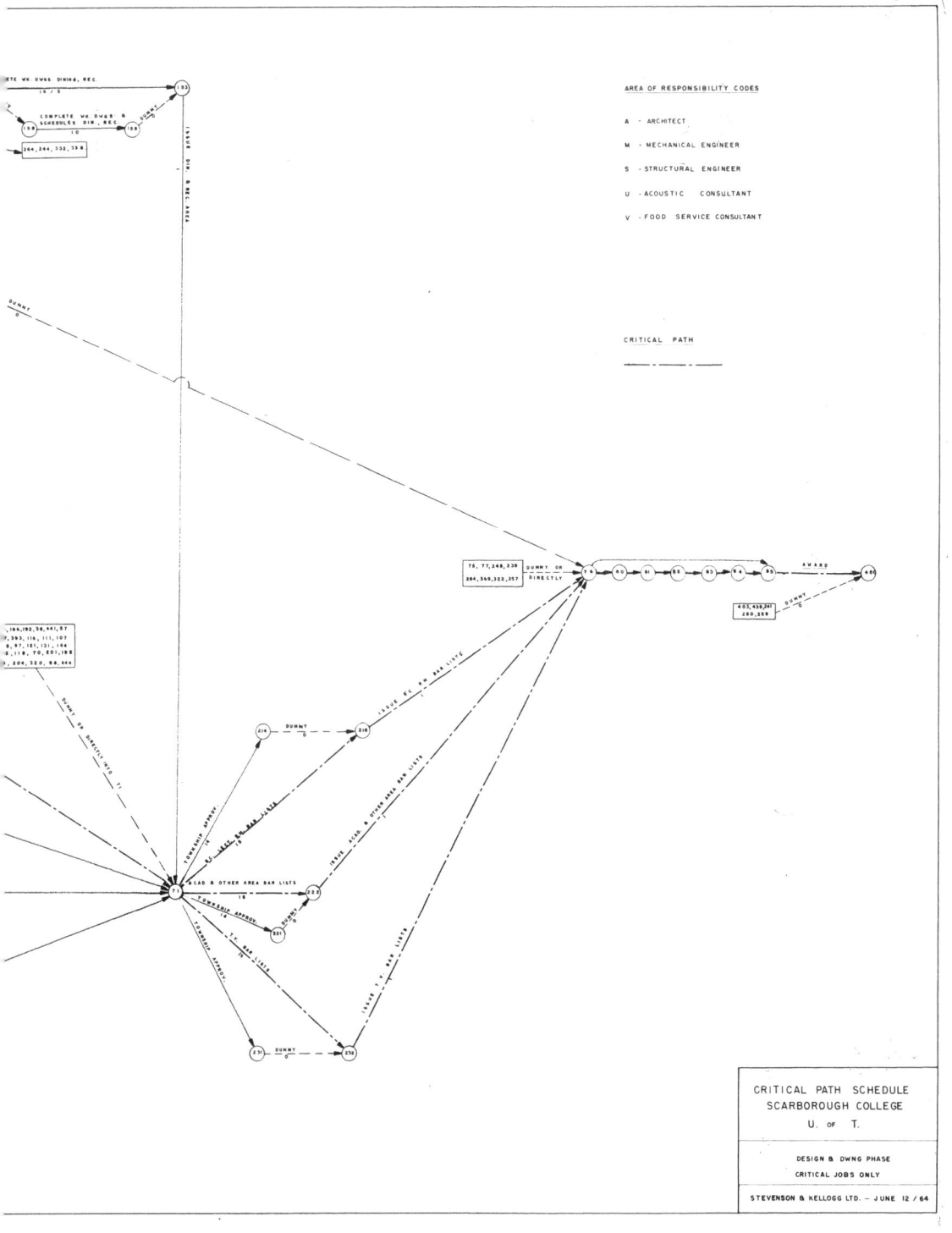

FIG. 7 Critical path system, Scarborough College, Stevenson and Kellogg, Ltd., 1964.

northwest end of the science wing. The facilities included one large and four smaller professionally equipped studios staffed by experienced personnel, who produced informal presentations, seminars, panel discussions, lab talks, and demonstrations. At least half of all the teaching would be delivered by television, and it was expected that all Scarborough College professors engage with multimedia and CCTV instruction.

Among the significant innovations in project management with which the building team engaged, in order to streamline the construction of Scarborough College, was the fast-tracking method called "the critical path system" and the sequential tendering of contracts. The critical path system was at that time unusual in the Canadian construction industry. Given the necessity of beginning construction at the earliest possible date, the team used a "computer monitored critical path network as the integrating and control vehicle," which allowed the building's design and construction to be integrated prior to completion of the design development stage.[25] It projected time-coordinated construction processes for each stage of development. What appears as a flow diagram of sorts is a computer-generated, chronological mapping of time- and material-dependent activities, prepared by Stevenson and Kellogg in 1964. [FIG. 7] The drawing identifies five areas of responsibility, including those for the architect, the mechanical engineer, the structural engineer, the acoustic consultant, and the food service consultant.[26] There are many notable intersections within the construction process marked by frequent overlaps in the required design and construction activities.

The simultaneous design and construction process also required a shift in tendering, from the conventional method of lump-sum tendering to the sequential tendering of contracts as needed. This was a very different approach to financing (perhaps accounting for some of the later cost inflation) and to the organization of construction and site work. For example, in May 1964 the "bulk machine excavation" fell under one specific contract, while the clients invited tenders for other general contractors.[27] The expediency of simultaneous design development and construction meant that accurate quantities and measurements of materials were lacking at times and most importantly for concrete. This presented a significant challenge to many potential contractors.[28]

The adoption of these practices is noteworthy as it connects the design and building of Scarborough College to changes within the architecture profession and building industry in the 1950s and 1960s. The use of computers by quantity surveyors became increasingly important in architecture and construction. The diagrams and network analyses were technical, predictive, and went well beyond the mere representation of ideas. This is of course radically different from metaphorical thinking about technical processes or graphic representations of systems analysis associated with some of the avant-garde practices of modern architecture, and especially of those from the 1950s and 1960s. Scarborough College stands for and represents more than the completed building and its associations to modernism or Brutalism. To be realized, the project required a collaborative effort, a team, and an architect capable of managing a team. As Andrews acknowledges in the book *John Andrews: Architecture, a Performing Art*, the project required teamwork among consultants, and, as team manager, he admits that a unique and perhaps unrepeatable experience enabled the architecture of Scarborough College.[29]

25 Anderson, Scarborough College and Project Management, 2, AND 43A, Box 43-36, CAA.
26 See untitled document, "Reports and Transmittals," 8, 43A, Box 43-36, CAA; "Critical Path Schedule, Scarborough College, U. of T.," June 1964, Drawings: University of Toronto, Scarborough College, Site Planning, AND 67138, CAA.
27 Anderson, Scarborough College and Project Management, 2, AND 43A, Box 43-36, CAA.
28 The Scarborough design committee eventually chose the lowest bidder, which retrospectively seems like a mistake given the number of unknowns within the project prior to and during construction.
29 Taylor and Andrews, *John Andrews*, 47.

8

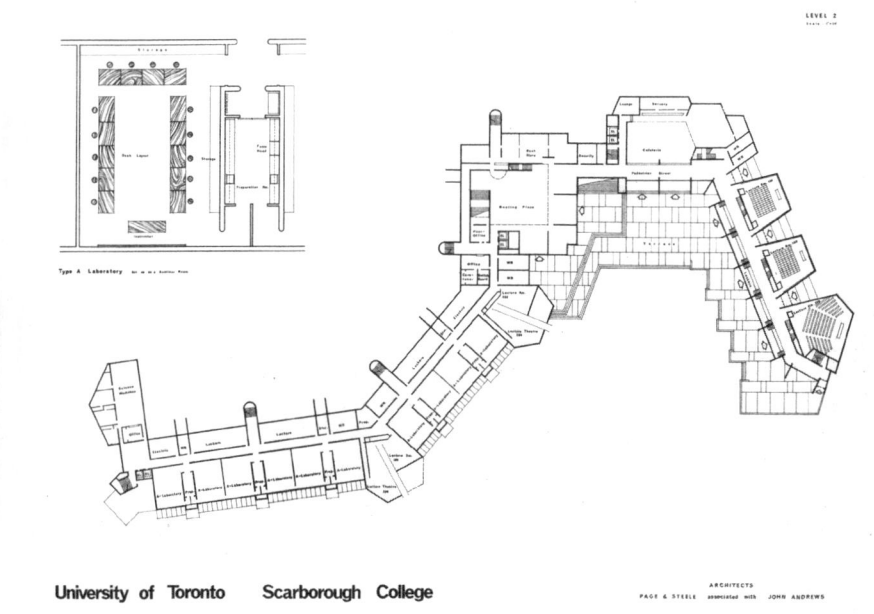

9

FIG. 8 Section, Humanities and Social Science Building. Architects: Page and Steele with John Andrews, ca. 1963.
FIG. 9 Plan phase 1, level 2. Architects: Page and Steele with John Andrews, ca. 1963.

The use of concrete as an adaptable means of construction is recounted in stories of the Scarborough College construction process, often told with heroic overtones.[30] The choice of concrete, however, was more or less based on expediency; the accelerated timeline heavily favored the choice of concrete as the primary building material. [FIG. 5] As Andrews explained, "with concrete, by pouring excessive footings and leaving other margins," it was possible to "move in stages, dealing with each problem as it arose."[31] With the fast-tracked integrated design and construction process, facilitated through computer calculations, construction began before the design was completed. For example, the footings were poured at 10 percent oversize because the engineers had yet to calculate the exact loadings. For the same reason, the buttresses on the south-facing valley side of the science block were added in the middle of construction when, while pouring the concrete for the third floor, the engineers discovered that the beams were not wide enough at the top "to allow for buckling."[32]

Perhaps due to the time constraints to complete the building for partial occupancy, there is a lack of written documentation about the construction process. Nonetheless, from the photographic record, it is possible to approximate the chronology for the first phase of work. In early 1965, the structure was in an advanced stage of realization—an image dated March 1965 shows that the concrete pouring of the science wing was completed up to the second and third floors, with plastic sheets protecting the concrete and scaffolding from the cold and snow.[33] [FIG. 6] In April of the same year, the administration building and the humanities wing appear to be about halfway completed, while the laboratories with their characteristic semicircular windows are still under construction.[34] By June, the humanities wing is still scaffolded, and the administration block and science wing appear completed from the exterior, while on the science wing, the metal covering of the service spines that connect ducts and cables to the rooftop mechanical room have yet to be installed.[35]

Despite the incomplete state of construction, the University of Toronto issued a press packet containing a detailed description of Scarborough College and the arrangements for a press visit on June 17, 1965. Toronto's newspaper *The Telegram* quotes Williams, who remarks, "for years to come the appropriate symbol of the university will not be the traditional ivory tower and ivy-clad halls, but crossed cranes, rampant, on a field of dump trucks, operant."[36] Anderson, the project manager, declared the building ready for occupancy five months later in November 1965, stating that the technical staff was equipping laboratories with glassware and instruments. A photograph from December displays what would become the college's central meeting place being used as a temporary storage area for building materials.[37] Further, visual documentation dated March 1966 indicates that construction on both the science and humanities wings was indeed ongoing. The plume of steam coming from one of the chimneys signals that the building's central power plant, of significant early concern in the planning of a non-serviced site, is active.[38]

FURTHER PLANNING AND DESIGN DEVELOPMENT

The completed Scarborough College that stands today corresponds to stage one of the building plan, or the arrangement accommodating 1,500 students, as proposed in the original consultant's report in 1963.[39] [FIGS. 8–9]

30 William Beckel, interview by Mary Lou Lobsinger, Vancouver, April 10, 2005; John Andrews, interview with Mary Lou Lobsinger, Toronto, December 19, 2005.
31 Taylor and Andrews, *John Andrews*, 40.
32 Ibid., 46.
33 "Scarborough College Presentation Dwgs. and Construction Slides," slide 2048, Box 43-36, CAA.
34 Ibid., slides 2039, 2040, 2047.
35 Ibid., slides 1995, 1999, 2009.
36 "A Cubist Campus For Highland Creek," *The Telegram*, 18 February 1964.
37 "Scarborough College Presentation Dwgs. and Construction Slides," slide 2027, Box 43-36, CAA.
38 Ibid., slides 1634, 1792, 1826.
39 Compare with the plans "Humanities Court Level Plan," "Humanities Lower Level," and "Science Block Lower Plan," n.d., Drawings: University of Toronto, Scarborough College, Site Planning, AND 67138.

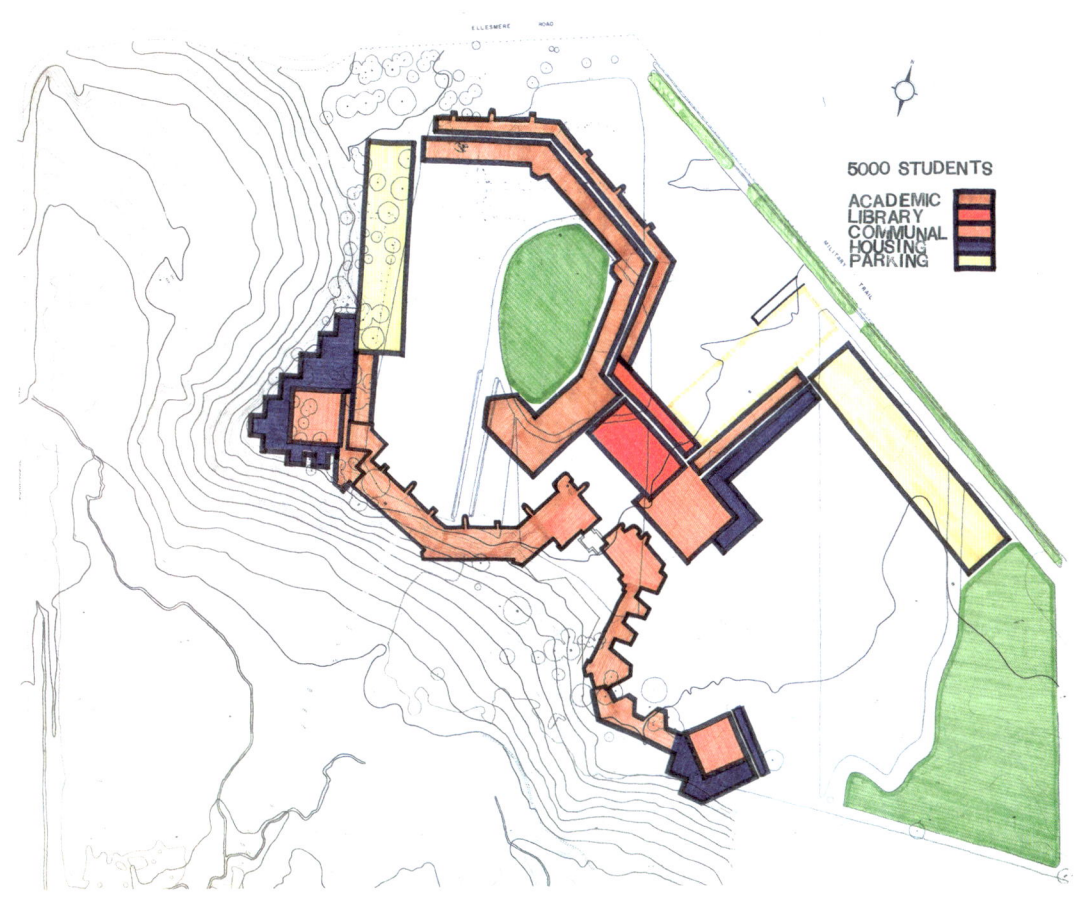

FIG. 10 Interim Master Plan, Scarborough College, February 1968.

A series of labor-related strikes delayed construction for more than three months over the summer of 1965, and the students that enrolled in the academic year beginning that September were initially housed at the downtown St. George Campus.[40] The extensions proposed to the first phase of the science and humanities wings required that the forms curve away from the ravine edge to create semi-enclosures, with student residences and outdoor spaces attached at either end. The February 1968 "Interim Report of the Master Plan" allows for the same extensions, as well as for the construction of a third and fourth wing on the side of the site along the street. The third composite wing accommodated growth to 3,500 students, and the fourth semi-circular wing accommodated the full capacity of 5,000 students.[41] [FIG. 10]

Within this February 1968 plan the proposed new extensions almost mirror the geometries of the humanities and science wings of the first phase, thereby creating two large semi-surrounded outdoor spaces buffered from the roadway.[42] The placement of the gymnasium and library help to define the outdoor space designated as the central courtyard from which the academic wings radiate. The plan also includes much-needed student residences, which were completely missing from the original plan. In this report the university remains committed to CCTV teaching as "an essential element of its teaching programme." The report supports this, stating that it is possible to expand the college's facilities until phase three of construction.[43]

A proposal titled Phase 2A quickly followed. This phase asked for more detail in terms of the location of specific programs, such as offices designated for the earth sciences, anthropology, and botany departments, boiler plant expansion, and the development of gymnasium facilities. Phase 2A also responds to the criticism of the February 1968 plan. For example, the building's north wings were deemed unfeasible from the perspective of servicing of a site initially proposed as car-free. The amendments show a newly created central spine or servicing corridor extending from the central court area to the main access roadway. On either side of the spine, there is conventional space allocation for seminar rooms, offices, a gym, and a library. The "Interim Report Master Plan" dated March 1969, also prepared by John Andrews Architects, shows further development of the program attached to the central spine, with an increase in the depth of the proposed build-out designed to accommodate other academic and servicing needs.

The library, in particular, had moved to various locations over the course of planning. Initially, it occupied the upper floors of the administration building with a proposal to eventually create an independent building. Later, the library appears in the block that is just northwest of the outdoor space, between the science wing and administration building (with setback areas for the stacks above a wide "Main Reading Space").[44] [FIG. 11] In the 1969 planning of Phase 2 the library appears on the southeast humanities side of the complex, which is connected to the north–south circulation spine that services future classrooms and academic offices. In general, the Phase 2 extension is very different from the original conception for the campus. The changes respond to several issues, including different approaches to pedagogy and site access. The final design, now distributed along an interior corridor extending northward from the central meeting area, toward the roadway, echoes only some of the intentions put forth in the earlier stages of the project.

The 1969 "Interim Report Master Plan" proposes changes in the academic curriculum

---

40   *The Globe and Mail*, July 14, 1965. See also Anderson, Scarborough College and Project Management, 2, AND 43A, Box 43-36, CAA.

41   Compare with the plans "Scarborough College" and "5000 students," Drawings: University of Toronto, Scarborough College, Site Planning, AND 67138, CAA.

42   Compare with the plans "Scarborough College 5000 students," "Scarborough College circulation," "Scarborough College services," and "Science block Court Plan," Drawings: University of Toronto, Scarborough College, Site Planning, AND 67138, CAA.

43   John Andrews Architects, "University of Toronto, Scarborough College, Interim Master Plan," February 1968, 3.

44   Compare with "Site Plan," Drawings: University of Toronto, Scarborough College, Site Planning, AND 67138, CAA.

at the college, such as the need to encourage academic overlaps, disciplinary mixing, and the combined use of spaces, rather than, as found in the first phase, the segregation of the humanities and sciences to distinct areas.[45]

By 1969, the curriculum and pedagogical mandates had changed, requiring smaller class sizes and seminar rooms, which were very different in scale from the auditoriums. The document also notes the decline in student interest in the sciences, and the need to accommodate other possible changes in the future with a more flexible approach to academic planning. Still, in the realization of Phase 2, many of the initial planning objectives and architectural forms remain, such as the incremental growth and the climate-controlled interior walkways that are continuous throughout the building complex.

By the time of the 1969 report, instructional television and CCTV teaching were no longer mentioned at this stage of development. Estimated at around $3 million, the expenditure for construction, equipment, and operation of the TV facilities was considered questionable given the low enrollment at Scarborough during these years.[46] The 1967–1968 academic year had 960 students enrolled, and even with the predictions for that figure to double in the coming academic year, these numbers were too low to rationalize the expense. According to John Lee in *Test Pattern*, by 1967 there was growing faculty resentment toward CCTV teaching and actual hostilities between the faculty and technical staff, which made for a difficult working environment and the creation of a new administrative post, the dean of television.[47] In 1967, Williams left the University of Toronto to become vice president and chancellor of the University of Western Ontario. He was succeeded at Scarborough College by Principal A. F. W. Plumptre. In 1968, Beckel resigned as dean of the college to take up the position of vice president at the University of Lethbridge. According to accounts, the departure of these two figures, so central to the realization of Scarborough College, triggered a revolt among faculty and students and brought about the demise of the college's CCTV teaching experiment.

CONCLUSION

The press release prepared in June 1965 for visitors to Scarborough College begins by explaining, in a mode typical of an architectural imagination, that visitors to the college have variously been reminded of:

> the stepped pyramids of Mexico, the sacred mounds of Babylon, a great power dam or the Maginot Line. But, although the massive complex that now dominates Highland Creek boasts characteristics of all these unusual structures, the result represents a completely new architectural approach to the problem of a modern, rapidly expanding university, exposed to a climate that brings extremes of heat and cold.[48]

This description is followed by the building's more prosaic achievements, including the enclosed pedestrian walkway, the amount of concrete poured, the interior climate control, the expected weathering of the concrete exterior, and the rippled surfaces of the concrete interior walls made possible by a fiberglass-reinforced, plastic-ribbed formwork. It also notes the fact that the concrete would remain unpainted along with its other finishes, such as the quarry stone imported by ship from Wales, and, of course, it comments on the "pioneering" use of CCTV.

---

45 John Andrews Architects, "Interim Master Plan 2," March 1969, 1.
46 Lee, *Test Pattern*, 97.
47 Ibid., 30. According to Lee, the dean of television was responsible for acting as a liaison between academic and television production staff and as a "defender of faculty rights."
48 Department of Information, Simcoe Hall, University of Toronto, Press Release, June 14, 1965, AND 43A, Box 43-46, CAA; Draft notes, n.d., AND 43A, Box 43-36, CAA, 1. The draft notes not included in the final version describe the building as a "highly efficient teaching instrument flexible within itself, using the latest technological advances and capable of future adjustment to new disciplines."

FIG. 11　Landscape plan, Scarborough College, 1965. Landscape architect: Michael Hough.

The press release further highlights the extreme rate of construction of Scarborough College, which it says is comparable only to that of Simon Fraser University in British Columbia. The Simon Fraser campus was one of two new Canadian campuses designed by Arthur Erickson and Geoffrey Massey during the same years that Scarborough College was under construction. Historian Georges Teyssot argues that Erickson's work at Simon Fraser (1962–1965), and later at the University of Lethbridge (1967–1971), illustrates a fascination with "technological innovation and scale, shared with progressive thinkers of the time." Teyssot persuasively discusses the development of the building section in relation to scale as a means for breaking down the barriers between academic disciplines.[49] The section and scale of Simon Fraser appear similar to that of Scarborough College, and yet there is more than technological fascination underway at Scarborough, even if these new campuses shared a sprint-like design and construction timeline from planning to occupancy.

Responding to the press release, University of Toronto Physical Plant engineer Frank Hastie challenged the comparison of Scarborough College to Erickson's Simon Fraser, arguing that Simon Fraser's academic program had none of the technical complexity.[50] The relationship between the campus design and academic programming at Simon Fraser may have been integral to its completed form. However, the University of Toronto's investment in CCTV and multimedia teaching systems, along with the ways in which the project timeline was managed, drove the planning and design process at Scarborough. The innovations adopted in design and construction came about as a consequence of the original pedagogical project and its importance, which extended beyond the architect's intentions.

As Andrews acknowledges in *John Andrews: Architecture, a Performing Art*, the building concept was simple and clear. Rather than allowing one aspect of the design to control or dominate the realization of the project, the design, management, and construction process was dynamic and demanded cooperation. For this, Andrews credits Page and Steele architect and project manager Robert Anderson.[51] He also recognizes Frank Hastie for keeping, as Andrews puts it, the "janitocracy" at bay. As he writes, the "dialogue with the contractor during the building and detailed design phases was as important as the dialogue with the academics during the conceptual and design phases."[52] The term "janitocracy" refers to the University of Toronto's administrative bureaucracy and budget keepers who at one point wanted to cancel the project. The project's team dynamic and collaborative approach is crucial to any narrative account of the design and construction of Scarborough College.

The university's press packet cites Andrews's broader intentions for the Scarborough project. He remarks: "The students at Scarborough College… will learn in an environment which responds directly to his educational needs, relates itself to the site and its climatic conditions and, above all, never forgets that *he* is a human being. It represents a giant step by the University of Toronto towards meeting the educational needs of the student in a manner truly related to the technological and sociological achievements of his age."[53] The disjunction between these architectural intentions and the user experience of the campus led to changes in CCTV pedagogy, despite the positive reception of the project in print media within and beyond architecture. The favorable reception of the building was soon countered by those who used it and were strongly

49 Hugh Johnston, *Radical Campus: Making Simon Fraser University* (Vancouver: Douglas and McIntyre, 2005); Georges Teyssot "Western Monoliths: Arthur Erickson's Design for Two Universities," in Nicholas Olsberg and Ricardo L. Castro, *Arthur Erickson: Critical Works* (Vancouver: Douglas & McIntyre and Vancouver Art Gallery; Seattle: University of Washington Press, 2006), 111–23. It is interesting to note that Teyssot cautions against the too-easy identification of Erickson's architecture with the site and landscape and refers to Erickson as a "late modernist of the third or fourth generation."
50 Press release, June 1965, Department of Information, Simcoe Hall, University of Toronto, 5.
51 Taylor and Andrews, *John Andrews*, 40.
52 Ibid., 41.
53 Press release, June, 1965.

opposed to, among other things, the extensive use of unfinished concrete in the interior. Many aspects of the building's design that were thought to encourage social exchange, such as the pedestrian walkway, the overhanging balconies, and the wide open spaces, were instead met with opposition and protest.

In *Test Pattern*, the 1971 published assessment of television instruction at Scarborough, students and faculty alike responded negatively to the CCTV mandate. There was controversy over the distinction between educational content and entertainment; the charismatic lecturer performed rather well while others failed miserably. The mode of delivery led to increased passivity among students, and the need to provoke student curiosity or rouse interest required a professor to be entertaining.[54] Whether due to TV acuity, charisma, or preparation, many scholars were simply inept at TV instruction or considered to be boring presenters. Complaints ranged from "prof looked dead" and "prof read from notes too fast" to a critique of the staging: "same background all the time."[55] The "University Television Subcommittee Report" of 1965 had cautioned that the research into student attitudes toward instructional television was rather incomplete and perfunctory.

The responses of Scarborough College students are unsurprising, ranging from boredom to complaints of tired eyes from staring at a screen for half an hour and the lack of skillful professional delivery by professors. As Lee notes, after all, university students go to the cinema and watch TV. Students also found CCTV instruction alienating. Both students and teachers, though from different perspectives, found or perceived the use of TV technology as increasing the distance between teaching and learning, instructors and students. The instructors complained that preparing professionally recorded lectures increased their workload by at least three times and the time recouped for research through the repeated use of recordings years later did not pan out as administrators had calculated. TV instruction had proved to be infinitely more burdensome than traditional, face-to-face teaching.

This controversy at Scarborough College anticipated current issues of intellectual copyright, media, and sharing rights, which are now written into many course syllabi but were then yet to be tested in terms of legal reach and responsibility. The teaching union raised questions about financial compensation for recorded materials that the university planned to repeatedly use and about the fate of instructional materials after a faculty member departed and was no longer on university payroll.[56] It did not help that the new technologies were often improperly used or unreliable, despite the technical teams, mechanical systems, and architectural planning.[57] Though Beckel had defended TV teaching, by the 1970s he argued for consideration of its long-term operational costs and blamed the failures at Scarborough College on shifting pedagogical and student interests. He also blamed the remote location of the campus, which had little on-site life, and the attitudes of students and faculty, which together, in his view, led to the building not being engaged with in the way it had been imagined.[58]

There have been many attempts to draw comparisons between the experimentation with CCTV at Scarborough College and the ideas of University of Toronto media theorist Marshall McLuhan. In 1966, when McLuhan was nearing the height of his fame, the first part of his two-part essay "The Invisible Environment" was published in an issue of *The Canadian Architect* that featured a review and ample photographs of Scarborough College within the magazine and on the cover. However, McLuhan's essay and the review, though proximate in print, are unrelated. McLuhan retraces aspects of his 1962 book *The Gutenberg Galaxy*, such as its colonial, ethno-psychiatric formulations of oral versus literary cultures and

---

54 Lee, *Test Pattern*, 58.
55 Ibid., 88.
56 Ibid., 25–37.
57 Ibid., 35. As Lee writes, the recorded lectures "were frequently played back in the wrong order, or into the wrong classroom, or not played back at all at the scheduled time."
58 Beckel, "Appendix 3, In Memoriam," 118–21.

the concept of the global village. McLuhan's speculations on the invisible, the sensory, and the relationship between aural and written forms of communication, could not be further from Andrews's pragmatic commitment to the materials and processes that make up the built environment. Beckel also denied any influence of the Canadian media theorist on the pursuit of the pedagogical program of Scarborough College.[59]

And yet, there was a connection between McLuhan and Scarborough College. As previously mentioned, Dr. D. Carleton Williams, Scarborough's first principal and the agile administrator who sat on multiple committees at the University of Toronto in the 1960s, had been an early member of McLuhan's Explorations Group. McLuhan co-founded the Explorations Group and *Explorations* magazine with anthropologist Edward Carpenter in 1953 as an "inter-faculty project investigating the effects of new media of communications."[60] The group and the "Culture and Communications" seminars held at the St. George Campus were funded through a grant from the Behavioral Sciences Division of the Ford Foundation.

Oscar Newman quotes Marshall McLuhan to introduce his essay "The New Campus," published in the 1966 campus-themed issue of *Architectural Forum*: "The very same process of automation that causes a withdrawal of the present workforce from industry causes *learning* itself to become the principal kind of production and consumption. Hence the folly of alarm about unemployment. Paid learning is already becoming both the dominant unemployment and the source of new wealth in our society."[61] The citation comes from the final chapter of McLuhan's 1964 book *Understanding Media*, which addresses education, the electronic age, and changes brought about by automation. McLuhan argues for the positive outcomes, where information is fused with learning, where marketing and consumption become one with learning, and implosion disrupts the stasis of job specialization for continuous processes of transformation. He predicts that the age of automation will see the demise of specialized jobs, and, freed up from "mechanistic" work tasks, he argues, we will require liberal education. The language of pattern, decentralization, diversity, and interdependence used by McLuhan, finds parallels in some aspects of Newman's discussion of new campuses. This includes organizational strategies focusing on circulation; attempts to infuse new campus buildings with urban density; patterns and systems of organization for large-scale buildings; interdepartmental connections; and importantly, flexibility and potential for future growth and change.

In Newman's essay, Scarborough appears favorably when compared with new campuses at Berlin Free University, Forest Park, the University of Marburg, and the University of Illinois at Chicago Circle. In general, these campuses incorporate a clear organizational structure, typically through circulation and delineation of their program around a shared central core, and flexibility in planning for growth and change. And yet, Newman is critical of the very aspects of Scarborough that have remained so significant to contemporary architecture: in his view the building does not maintain a neutral quality; rather its rich and convoluted form, specifically the "mystique of light and towering forms," attracts far too much visual attention. [FIGS. 12–13] What he refers to as the staged, set-like aspects of the building overshadow, in his view, the project's social commitment realized through its programs, specific formal expressions, patterns of circulation, and response to site and climate. For Newman, it would appear the fault lies with the insistence of Scarborough College as architecture, and the building's refusal to disappear or become a form of neutral infrastructure for

---

59 William Beckel, interview by Mary Lou Lobsinger, Vancouver, April 10, 2005.
60 Kevin Plummer, "Historicist: Explorations at the Vanguard of Communications Studies," *Torontoist*, https://torontoist.com/2014/05/historicist-explorations-at-the-vanguard-of-communications-studies/2018-06-26. Planner Jaqueline Tyrwhitt briefly taught planning at University of Toronto in the early 1950s. She was the interlocutor between Sigfried Giedion and McLuhan and was an early member of the Explorations Group. Williams met her through McLuhan.
61 Newman, "The New Campus," 43. Emphasis author's own.

circulation, educational programs, and human agency. This critique signals a critical juncture in architecture characterized by different perspectives on modernist aims and transformation, or what comes after modernism. In fact, this was the main issue associated with the material and formal outcomes of Brutalism.

Returning to Andrews's TV interview with *The Lively Arts*, which introduced this chapter, producer Vincent Tovell's question as to whether Scarborough College is a particularly Canadian building seems, retrospectively, insignificant.[62] The most compelling aspect of Andrews's reply highlights the institutional changes in architecture that extend beyond the building itself and the importance of the team that was required to carry out such a large and complex project. Tovell also asks Andrew for a definition of architecture. He responds, "It's a lot of fun, to attempt to find out what a building wants to be, and not what you want it to be...."[63]

---

62   Tovell, "Explorations: Scarborough College," *The Lively Arts*, 1966.
63   Andrews, quoted in Vincent Tovell, "Explorations: Scarborough College, University of Toronto," *The Lively Arts*, Canadian Broadcasting Corporation, 1966, 30 min.

12

13

FIG. 12 View of the chimney stacks from Central Services.
FIG. 13 View of the Humanities Wing auditoria with chimney stacks.

03

open form and design thinking in andrews's early practice, 1964–1967

by　　　　　　　　　　　　Peter Scriver and Antony Moulis

The critical reception of Scarborough College in the press after the first phase of the campus was built in 1966 made it the most significant and internationally acclaimed architectural project in Canada since the Toronto City Hall competition of 1958. To follow was the design and realization of the 1967 Universal and International Exhibition, or Expo 67 in Montreal, first announced in 1963.[1] However, in early 1965, when John Andrews Architects sealed a contract to design three or potentially four installations for the Montreal fair, the Andrews office was still relatively unknown outside of Toronto. These Expo commissions were therefore a further indication of the young practice's exceptional confidence and ability to seize opportunities for vigorous design inquiry and innovation, while still delivering timely solutions.

African Place (also known as Africa Place), the most substantial and iconic of Andrews's Expo schemes to be realized, was the capstone of a cluster of small early projects, including the design of Bellmere Junior Public School and the planning of an experimental housing system for the Canadian steel company Stelco.[2] These projects defined a formative period of innovation for Andrews. Produced immediately after the initial design of Scarborough College, though without the constraints of a contractual collaboration with architects and consultants from other firms, they also represented Andrews's first truly independent work. In addition to the creation of exhibition facilities, these commissions presented an opportunity to explore the design conventions of other, more everyday building typologies. They clearly engaged in the then-topical idea of open form and other avant-garde architectural concepts, such as those found in the work of Team 10 and the Japanese Metabolist movement. However, these precociously experimental projects were equally informed by a bottom-up approach to architectural problem-solving that was already becoming a hallmark of Andrews's practice, grounded first and foremost in a rigorous rethinking of program. As this chapter will examine, these works were seminal in developing Andrews's own philosophy of open design, which entailed the search for open, geometrically ordered plans that were more flexible and responsive to change, whether technological or social. Further, they established the original motifs and planning tactics that came to define Andrews's larger body of works to come, some of which were already in gestation.

GLOBAL MODERNITY

In the 1960s, Canada was very attractive to young Australian architects seeking work and life experience overseas. Visa privileges, along with the common cultural roots and parallel colonial histories that these privileges presumed, opened the door to Australian professionals and their peers from the United Kingdom and other British Commonwealth countries in southern Africa and the Caribbean. Though postwar immigration programs and the baby boom were stimulating major building activity in both the private and public sectors of these countries, Canada's economy, with its link to the United States, was positively surging by comparison.[3] However, in addition to the

1   The international coverage of Scarborough College, completed in early 1965, was extensive and almost universally positive in both popular and critical press. In-depth documentation and critical analysis in the May 1966 issue of *Architectural Forum*, along with a shorter article the same year in *Time* magazine regarding the integration of architectural and pedagogical innovations at the new college significantly elevated Andrews's emerging international profile. Reyner Banham's later reappraisal of Scarborough College, discussing its pioneering and almost "primitive" realization of widely theorized, early 1960s notions of megastructures, emphasized its particular success as a response to the Canadian system of accountancy for design and construction in an extreme climate. Oscar Newman, "The New Campus," *Architectural Forum* (May 1966): 30–55; "Colleges: A Satellite Built for T.V.," *Time* (January 13, 1967): 46–48; Reyner Banham, *Megastructure: Urban Futures of the Recent Past* (London: Thames and Hudson, 1976), 133–39.
2   Although the project was consistently referred to as "African Place" in all records and references to it by John Andrews Architects, the complex was actually called "Africa Place" in official Expo 67 reports and descriptions and in the press in general.
3   Canada's demographic and economic expansion in the 1960s was dynamic enough to attract the attention of international architecture press. By 1968, with a population of just 20 million, it achieved a respectable merchandise trade surplus of a billion dollars. "City Within a City," *The Architect and Building News* (June 5, 1969): 30–34.

wealth of architectural opportunities arising from this general economic boom, "it was the openness of Canada," as Andrews recalled, that gave young practices like his a break.[4] For Evan Walker, Andrews's Australian colleague who was also working in Toronto at the time, Canada "was ready for pretty much all the things you wanted to do.…There was never the sense which we always had [in Australia] that it wasn't your turn, or you didn't go to the right school."[5]

It was precisely this openness to new talent and ideas that gave Andrews the confidence and encouragement to open his own practice after completing his initial work with John B. Parkin Associates, which included contributing to the realization of Viljo Revell's design for Toronto City Hall. In 1962, John Andrews Architects was established accordingly as a one-man operation, even before the Scarborough College commission was secured the following year. Bolstered by this early success in winning such substantial institutional work, the firm soon began to grow, attracting a range of collaborators of different backgrounds who would collectively expand and test the norms of a conventional architectural practice. Andrews's earliest employees were Frank Final and Jim Sykes, an architecture student and former lake boat captain who would become their chief model maker. In due course, they were joined by others, including Scottish architect John Simpson and South African town planner Roger du Toit, who together contributed to the organic evolution of the practice into an innovative cooperative of 10 partners by the time Andrews relocated to Australia in 1969.

From its start, felicitous collaborations occurred circumstantially with John Andrews Architects and a group of allied professionals who were co-occupants of the same historic sandstone premises located at 47 Colborne Street, next to Toronto's central financial district. The key members of this informal collective (who were mostly also members of Integ) included artist Gerald Gladstone, engineer Norbert Seethaler, landscape architect Dick Strong, lawyer George Miller, and fellow Australian architect Evan Walker, who was practicing independently as a student-housing specialist.[6] Another cotenant who made 47 Colborne Street a creatively vital address was Ron Thom, one of the most critically acclaimed Canadian architects of his generation, who was also questioning relationships between education, community, and contemporary architecture through prestigious commissions for new university campuses. This included working on an entirely new campus, Trent University, designed at the same time Scarborough College was in process at the Andrews office.[7]

While Scarborough College attracted a string of substantial institutional commissions for the office, including ever larger urban design and infrastructure ventures in Toronto and beyond, the Expo 67 projects—designed as Scarborough College was still being constructed—were the culmination of a cluster of smaller projects. Whether built or unbuilt, these smaller projects developed the practice's design thinking and methods in its early years. An examination of their origins and the process of creating these Expo-related designs provides insight into the particular notion of architecture as open structure in which Andrews was invested, along with his contemporaries and other contributors to the 1967 World's Fair in Montreal. For the emerging architect and his growing collective of young expats and internationally experienced collaborators, this ideal seemed to resonate with their transnational sense of agency as third-generation modernists. Together, they would come to operate under the

---

4   John Andrews, interview by Evan Walker, Cape Liptrap, Victoria, April 1, 2003.
5   Ibid.
6   *John Andrews Architects, Colborne Street, Toronto, Ontario, Canada.* (Toronto: John Andrews Architects, n.d., ca. 1970); John Andrews, interview by Evan Walker, Cape Liptrap, Victoria, April 1, 2003.
7   For Thom's Trent University scheme, see: Elsa Lam and Graham Livesey, eds., *Canadian Modern Architecture, 1967 to the Present* (New York: Princeton Architectural Press, 2019), 99–108. Thom's award-winning design of Massey College on the downtown campus of the University of Toronto had only just been completed when Andrews was commissioned to design the satellite Scarborough College campus. See: Lam and Livesey, eds., *Canadian Modern Architecture*, 7, 93–99, 103, 187.

name John Andrews International and realize a coherent body of work on two continents.

Ostensibly representing a third continent, however, the varied reception and interpretations of the Expo 67 commissions underscore the ways in which the universalist assumptions that underpinned the Expo program and design outcome reflected the wishful ethos of the Expo moment. As a whole, the World's Fair tended to overlook the cultural complexities and political ruptures between diverging postindustrial and postcolonial spheres that were emerging in the second half of the 20th century. In the 1960s, the accelerating advance toward global modernity was already beginning to bring these conflicting worldviews into focus in the bourgeoning cosmopolitan metropolises of Canada, as it would in Australia in the following decades.[8]

MONTREAL'S EXPO 67

Montreal's 1967 Universal and International Exhibition, or Expo 67, was marked by exceptional ambition, both conceptual and technical. Not only did its organizers aspire to make it the largest world's fair of the 20th century, but they also intended it to embody a vision of an open, cosmopolitan world of modern technological ingenuity. This vision also entailed a world in which a sense of wonder and optimism might be restored through a renewed focus on the diversity of human values and capital, rather than on the ideological rifts and rhetoric that dominated other global showcases and forums. For bilingual Montreal and for Canada more broadly, which in 1967 also celebrated its centennial as a multicultural democracy, the fair was an opportunity for both civic and national hosts to represent themselves as aspiring microcosms of that same vision.[9]

The earlier Expo 58 in Brussels, Expo 67 in Montreal, and Expo 70 in Osaka were each given a "first-class" rating according to the criteria of the Paris-based Bureau International des Expositions (BIE). But the planners of Expo 67 aimed from the outset to make it the most extraordinary world's fair since the tradition had been established, beginning with the European imperial and international exhibitions held in the second half of the 19th century. In relation to the previous second-class world's fairs held in Seattle (1962) and New York City (1964), Montreal's Expo 67 was intended to be an architectural and urban production of an altogether different scale and message. While the Brussels exhibition privileged the technological power and potential of the ideologically polarized world of the Cold War era, with Europe still on the front line, Expo 67 celebrated a more consciously global world in which technology was the servant of "Man." Its theme and subtitle, "Man and his World/Terre des Hommes," was borrowed from French author and aviator Antoine de Saint-Exupéry, best known for his cosmic children's fable *The Little Prince*. The fair sought to articulate a neo-humanist ideal conceived from the perspective of a modern airborne traveler who saw the universality of humankind and human subjects as the creators and stewards of their respective environments and shared world.[10]

In order to translate this vision into an exhibition format, a series of themed pavilions were proposed in which the various dimensions and modes of man's engagement with his world—Man the Explorer, Man the Creator, Man the Producer, Man the Provider, Man in the Community—were investigated. The overarching theme was further represented and explored through additional structures, such as the audacious experimental housing cluster Habitat 67, designed by Moshe Safdie, which was immediately adjacent to Man in the Community. Further, the extensive transport and media-saturated matrix of the exhibition grounds themselves were literally "man-made" on a pair of artificial islands created in the St. Lawrence River, opposite Montreal's old port.

---

8   Jatinder Mann, *The Search for a New National Identity: The Rise of Multiculturalism in Canada and Australia* (New York: Peter Lang Publishing, 2016).

9   Craig Moyes and Stephen Palmer, eds., *Expo 67 and Its World: Staging Nations in the Crucible of Globalization* (Montreal: McGill–Queen's University Press, 2022).

10 Rhona Richman Kenneally and Johanne Sloan, eds., *Expo 67: Not Just a Souvenir* (Toronto: University of Toronto Press, 2010), 5–9.

1
2

3

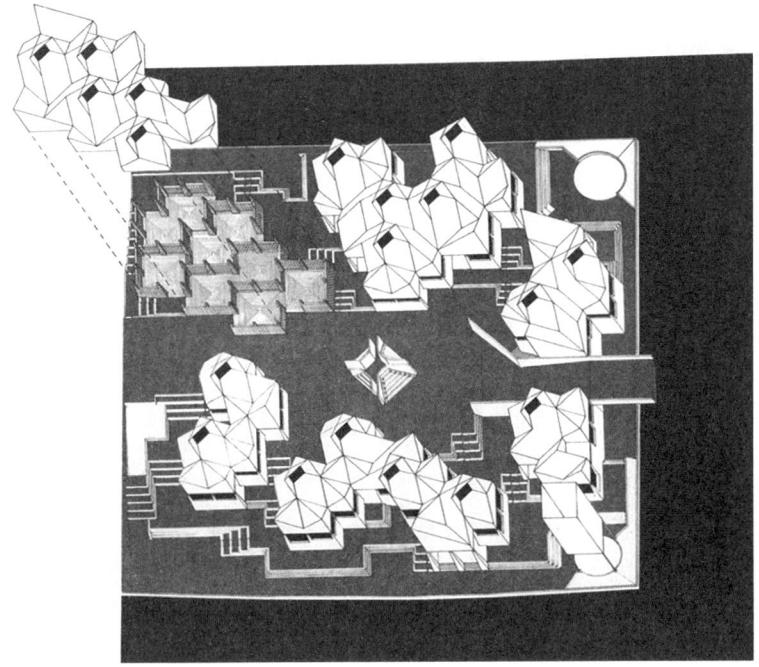

4

FIG. 1 Activity Area F as built, typical kiosk, Montreal Universal and International Exhibition, 1967.
FIG. 2 African Place model, 1965.
FIG. 3 African Place late construction stage, winter 1966. Montreal Universal and International Exhibition, 1967.
FIG. 4 African Place exploded axonometric view.

Exceptional as this conception was, however, the exhibition organizers ultimately declined to realize one of the most radical propositions entertained in the early planning stages. As initially projected, all participating countries were to have collaborated on the design and installation of an even more extensive and holistic array of integrated thematic infrastructure, with no individual national pavilions. The idea had been championed by two members in particular of the initial masterplanning team for the Expo, partners Blanche and H. P. Daniel ("Sandy") van Ginkel. Blanche Lemco van Ginkel was a groundbreaking Canadian architect and city planner who later became the first female dean of the department of architecture at the University of Toronto (now the John H. Daniels Faculty of Architecture, Landscape, and Design), where John Andrews served as chair from 1967 to 1969. Ginkel also served as a critic at the Harvard GSD while Andrews was a student there from 1957 to 1958. Sandy van Ginkel was a Dutch émigré and architect, architectural and urban studies theorist, and professor at McGill University in Montreal. There, he was responsible for advising on the thesis project by Safdie that was realized as Habitat 67 and was arguably the Expo's most iconic architectural legacy. Significantly, in the 1950s, the van Ginkels had also been members of the original Team 10, which produced some of the most influential ideas and forms driving the design thinking of John Andrews Architects at this time.[11] By that route, if not more directly, Andrews's designs for Expo 67 would also resonate with the van Ginkels' "postnational" ideal for the world's fair.

In addition to the themed pavilions and a range of corporate and institutionally sponsored pavilions, a record number of 71 countries exhibited at Expo 67. The majority of these nations designed separate pavilions, including Canada and several of its provinces, not least the host province of Quebec. Indeed, it was relatively inconceivable that the fair's official organizers, The Canadian Corporation for the 1967 World Exhibition (CCWE), could have declined this opportunity for national celebration of Canada's 100th year as a self-governing dominion of the former British Empire. However, in the paradoxical context of the growing nationalist secession movement within predominantly French-speaking Quebec, Expo 67 was also conceived strategically to catalyze further dynamic urban development in Montreal. At the time, Montreal was still Canada's premier metropolis. The fair would counter the separatist cause by upgrading and integrating the city even more thoroughly into the broader transnational economy and infrastructure of North America as a whole.[12]

AFRICAN PLACE

How, then, did the still relatively unknown John Andrews Architects become one of the few Canadian architectural practices not based in Montreal to participate in the design of Expo 67? According to Andrews, there were no invitations forthcoming from "the upper levels of power," including from diplomatic channels.[13] In fact, Australia's rather unremarkable metal and glass box of a pavilion, designed by John McCormick of the Australian Department of Works in Canberra, was built by Andrews's former employer John B. Parkin Associates with no liaison of any sort with John Andrews Architects.[14] A key factor that led to the most progressive work at Expo 67 was what Andrews believed was the exceptional openness of the Canadian architecture scene at that moment

---

11 Ibid., 9. On Blanche Lemco van Ginkel, see Eric Mumford, *Defining Urban Design: CIAM Architects and the Formation of a Discipline, 1937–69* (New Haven, CT: Yale University Press, 2009), 135.

12 For a fuller discussion of design innovation and local urban and cultural development in the context of Expo 67, as well as the design of the Quebec Pavilion in particular, see Peter Scriver, "Innovation and the Prospect of the 'Postnational' in the Architecture of Expo 67," in *Expo 67 and Its World: Staging the Nation in the Crucible of Globalization*, eds. Craig Moyes and Stephen Palmer (Montreal: McGill–Queen's University Press, 2022), 213–36.

13 Recounted by John Andrews in Jennifer Taylor and John Andrews, *John Andrews: Architecture, a Performing Art* (Melbourne: Oxford University Press, 1982), 73.

14 I. Kalin, *Expo '67: Survey of building materials, systems and techniques used at the Universal International Exhibition of 1967* (Ottawa: Queen's Printer, 1969), 134. The pavilion's interior details and furnishings, designed by Robin Boyd, were more notable, such as the "talking chairs" in particular.

FIG. 5   Commonwealth Place model (unbuilt), 1965. Architect: John Andrews Architects.

to emerging practices such as his that were hungry for the challenge. "What an incredible time that was," he later recalled. "They actually decided to give the work to younger architects."[15]

Another equally significant factor involved an acquaintance that the John Andrews team had among the fair's organizers. Recounting the Expo projects in the 1982 monograph *John Andrews: Architecture, a Performing Art*, Andrews conceded, "We knew a fellow working there who was in a position to know what projects could possibly happen."[16] Andrews was characteristically blunt, though possibly a little disingenuous, in adding that their contact "literally manufactured a thing called African Place."[17] Evidently, this contact within the CCWE was responsible for redressing the fact that after the pavilion commissions had begun, it became apparent that many decolonizing nations in Africa, the Middle East, and Asia couldn't afford to build fully fledged pavilions that met the scale and specifications prescribed. Individual pavilions were mandated to be no less than 3,000 square feet to achieve the critical mass and urban qualities envisioned in the master plan for the fair. Participants also had to commit to the cost of demolishing them after the fair was over.

African Place therefore served as the prototype for an additional type of facility in the architecture of the fair, designed as a pavilion-sized complex of smaller, more affordable exhibition spaces that could be shared as common spaces. [FIGS. 2–4] Built by the CCWE and funded by the Canadian government, this addition was crucial, from the perspective of the organizers, to a more equitable and inclusive plan, and helped to ensure that the record number of international participants they were aiming for was in reach.[18] Due to the fact that the CCWE was the effective client, however, John Andrews Architects had no direct designer–client relationship with the individual

FIG. 6 Activity Area F model.
FIG. 7 African Place under construction, Montreal, Canada, summer 1966.

15 John Andrews, interview by Evan Walker, Cape Liptrap, Victoria, April 1, 2003.
16 Taylor and Andrews, *John Andrews*, 73.
17 Ibid.
18 Ibid.

countries exhibiting in these joint facilities, nor with their exhibit designers, though some degree of oversight of space use and fit-out was desired.

African Place was the largest of three such joint pavilion projects that John Andrews Architects was initially commissioned to create by the CCWE in early 1965. Designs for two of these projects were developed, but ultimately only African Place was built. Another joint pavilion, Commonwealth Place, had been envisioned for a site adjacent to African Place and with a similar brief, in this case to represent new nations emerging from colonial rule by the former British Empire in Asia and the Caribbean. [FIG. 5] However, it did not proceed to construction when insufficient commitment was secured from prospective exhibitors. The third potential commission of this sort, a "joint Arab pavilion," was awarded to another small Canadian architecture practice, the Quebec City–based firm C. R. Anderson, before John Andrews Architects developed any substantive ideas for it.[19] Further, one other Expo 67 commission was fully developed and built by John Andrews Architects in collaboration with associate architect Jack Diamond. This was a complex of smaller food service and support buildings referred to as Activity Area F, which comprised part of the architecturally distinctive secondary infrastructure of the fair.[20] [FIGS. 1, 6]

Almost two dozen countries were invited to exhibit in African Place, with 15 ultimately participating: Cameroon, Chad, Democratic Republic of Congo, Gabon, Ghana, Ivory Coast, Kenya, Madagascar, Niger, Nigeria, Rwanda, Senegal, Tanzania, Togo, and Uganda.[21] Together they represented the dominant transnational linguistic communities (anglophone and francophone) to emerge from the recent colonial past in Africa, as well as the extraordinary cultural and geographic diversity that historically differentiated the peoples of sub-Saharan Africa. Nevertheless, representation was not the primary design challenge of this project as Andrews approached it. Where some of the participants would only be able to confirm their commitment to exhibit a few months before the official opening of the fair in April 1967, well after the architecture was already substantially constructed, it was the sheer indeterminacy of the final range and quantities of anticipated multicultural content that posed the essential design "problem" to be addressed. This was an inherently open-ended problem that called for optimal flexibility in the spatial layout of a generic exhibition facility that also had to be as economical to construct and operate as possible.

The "solution" that Andrews and his team arrived at was described in tellingly generic terms in an official retrospective government report on the building materials, systems, and techniques employed at Expo 67. The report explains:

> One of the largest pavilions of the geometrical cellular variety at Expo, Africa Place [sic] was basically realized in terms of the original concept ... Design was based on a natural flow pattern which resulted in a series of interrelated and interdependent spaces arranged within a modular system. A natural ventilation system was devised based upon consistent prevailing winds on this section of the St. Lawrence River.[22]

The formally open design clusters light-colored and eggcrate-like plywood shells floating over

---

19 All three of these prospective projects are listed in the accessions list of drawings and records related to Expo 67, in the John Andrews fonds, Canadian Architectural Archives (hereafter CAA), University of Calgary. However, no actual drawings or documents pertaining to the Joint Arab Pavilion could be found during the April 2013 visit to the CAA by author Peter Scriver. The "pavilion for the Arab Countries" built according to C.R. Anderson's design on a site immediately adjacent to African Place was, in contrast with Andrews's work, a relatively undistinguished response to the design brief in an orientalist manner, harking back to the colonial and empire exhibitions of the previous century. See Kalin, *Expo '67,* 132.

20 A.J. (Jack) Diamond, an expatriate South African architect working in Toronto, was exploring a potential permanent association with John Andrews Architects at the time of this commission. Roger Du Toit, interview by Evan Walker, July 1, 2004.

21 Canadian Corporation for the 1967 World Exhibition, *General Report on the 1967 World Exhibition,* vol. 1 (Ottawa: Queen's Printer, 1969), 391–407.

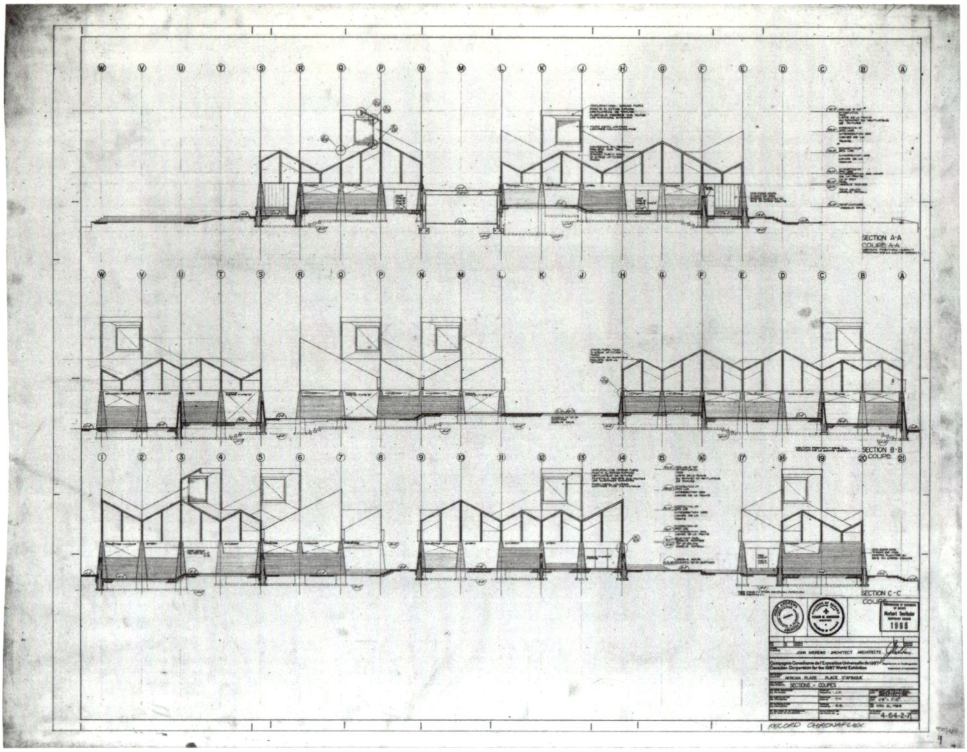

FIG. 8 African Place construction drawings.
FIG. 9 View of African Place looking outward, with Thai Pavilion beyond, Montreal, Canada.

a porous maze of earthy, three-quarter height dividing walls and canted piers constructed of terra-cotta tile.[23] [FIGS. 7–8] The design not only allowed for flexibility in the exhibition planning, but also ensured the flow of air through the passive ventilation system. [FIG. 10] Large and sculptural vertical openings in the plywood roofshells were adapted from wind scoops, a technical device traditionally employed in various building cultures in the desert regions of North Africa and West Asia. However, not merely a picturesque gesture, these elements, which were tested in a wind tunnel at the University of Toronto, were designed by Andrews's engineering collaborator Norbert Seethaler to passively ventilate the complex with evaporatively cooled air drawn off the nearby river and the shallow canals that bounded the site on three sides.[24] Thus, what some promoters and observers of the fair mistook for a "village-like" pastiche made to adhere to the African theme was in fact a highly rational approach to architectural form that could be spatially fluid yet systematic and even energy efficient.[25] [FIG. 9] Moreover, the design was cheap to build, not only due to inexpensive materials but also as a result of its modular structure, which was amenable to prefabrication.

MODULES AND PATTERNS

The use of a modular, pattern-based approach to produce flexible and economical architecture was already a key focus of John Andrews Architects. In order to understand the evolution of Andrews's practice up to this point, it is necessary to explore his designs completed a year prior to the start of the Expo 67 projects. In March 1964, John Andrews signed an agreement with the Steel Company of Canada (now Stelco) to design a building created from steel products for their "Trend" promotional brochure as part of the company's search to see the material used in "interesting and imaginative ways."[26] Andrews proposed using steel for a mid-rise housing complex, arguing that dwelling structures needed to be revolutionized to match the technical advancements made in the fields of communications and travel. [FIGS. 11–13] The hypothetical building consisted of a vertical frame organized like a "filing cabinet," allowing for mobile, prefabricated units that could be altered or replaced at will. The units could be "traded-in" as the needs of its residents changed or more technologically advanced components could be incorporated.

One likely inspiration for Andrews's steel housing scheme stemmed from the contemporary Japanese Metabolist movement, of which architect Kiyoyuki Nishihara, who was then working in Andrews's office, was well aware.[27] In particular, an unbuilt precast concrete housing project by Kisho Kurokawa from 1962 has salient parallels with Andrews's design for Stelco. A key concept expressed in Kurokawa's project is that of material "metabolism," in which cycles of change and obsolescence are accounted for in the components of building, making architecture flexible through the redundancy of its parts.[28] Andrews's design mirrors this idea by adopting a strategy of refit and replacement for the mass-produced components of his Stelco building. There are also strong formal parallels between the two designs. Kurokawa's housing project featured curved and modular elements that are strikingly similar to the arrangement of windows and balconies deployed by Andrews. As Philip Drew has noted, Andrews's sensibility to the approaches of Kurokawa and the Metabolists came from his specific interest in turning

---

22   Kalin, *Expo '67*, 129, 131.
23   Individual clusters bore an uncanny resemblance aesthetically and in sectional principle to Jørn Utzon's design for the Sydney Opera House (still under construction at the time) when viewed across the adjacent canal.
24   "Beyond the Individual Building," *Architectural Record* 140, no. 3 (September 1966): 161–72. "Reaping the Wind: Africa Place, Isle Notre-Dame," *Progressive Architecture* (June 1967): 147.
25   Banque National de Paris, *Montreal Expo 67* (Paris: Banque National de Paris, 1967), 50.
26   John Andrews et al., "The Apartment Building," *Stelco Trend Brochure*, 1965, 127A, Box 1, CAA.
27   Nishihara trained with Kenzo Tange and moved to Toronto in 1963. Information on Nishihara provided by Professor Thomas Daniell, Kyoto University.
28   Philip Drew, *Third Generation: The Changing Meaning of Architecture* (New York: Praeger, 1972), 68.

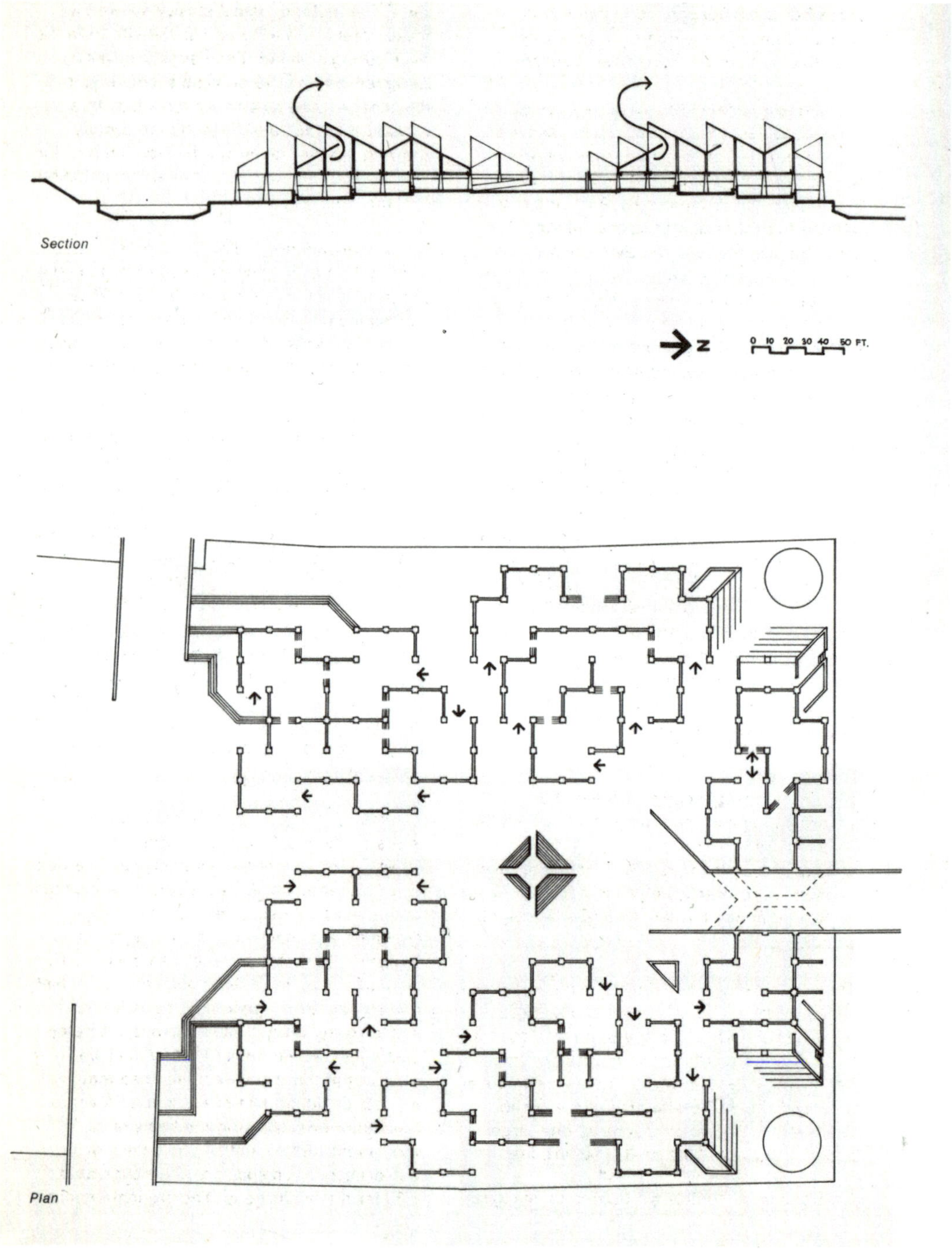

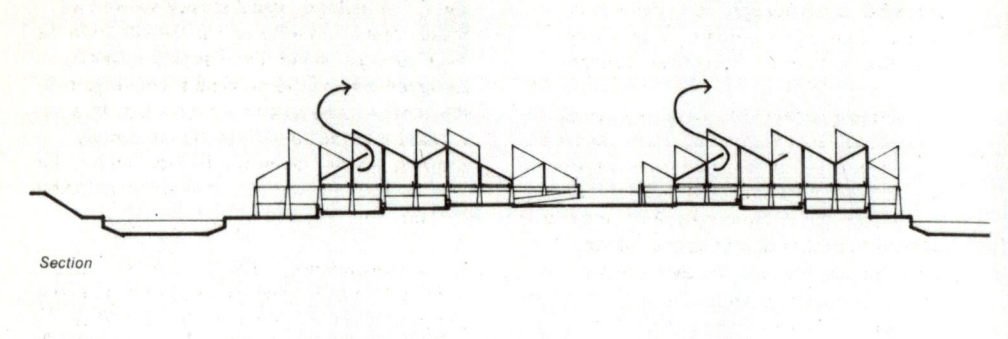

FIG. 10 African Place plan and section.

individual rooms into the key generating element in an orderly hierarchy of spaces. In planning, they form small clusters of rooms which then become the basic nodes of a larger social organization.[29] Andrews's building exhibits this approach through its use of a core, or stem, which allows for vertical circulation and services, with the apartments organized as nodes around it, arranged to form a pinwheel plan.

Andrews's adoption of the pinwheel plan reflects another thread of postwar thinking regarding the expression and organization of flexible planning, which reaches back to Le Corbusier's experiments with spiral and pinwheel forms in the interwar period. Between 1950 and 1963 the pinwheel plan was favored by various members of Team 10 and their circle, who used it in the design of individual buildings as well as in urban planning. As a solution to the problem of creating adaptable open forms, the pinwheel plan was thought to anticipate, through its geometric but loose order, a nuanced response to social needs (both individual and collective) in the context of postwar reconstruction. Andrews's design clearly appropriates the pinwheel plan and its conceptual meaning for Stelco, emphasizing flexibility, growth, and change as key aspects of the building's design.

In the Stelco project, Andrews used the pinwheel plan both practically and symbolically to describe the concepts of flexibility, adaptability, and openness. Logistically, the plan includes four rectilinear axial elements offset from each other and arranged around a central vertical core, which allows for the systematic distribution of people and services around the core. Sketches show circulation passages along the arms of the pinwheel that appear in yellow and provide access to identically sized modular apartments. The pinwheel form accommodates four apartments per floor, each containing a different layout within a large square plan. The long edge of each apartment is located on the perimeter of the building, allowing modules to be replaced at will with the use of an external crane. Other plans display the distribution of services from the core, which extends along the pinwheel arms, and ventilation passages from the exterior that similarly align with the plan's pinwheel pattern. A pinwheel is also represented sculpturally atop the building's lift tower, revealing the form that determines its component structure.[30] Symbolically, the pinwheel plan denotes movement, change, and additive growth, represented by the placement of elements around a central form or nucleus.

BELLMERE SCHOOL

Andrews's design for Stelco was only a staging point for his more studied use of the pinwheel plan and the principles of modular form and construction. In early 1965, shortly before the Expo 67 projects, John Andrews Architects began work on a scheme for Bellmere Junior Public School commissioned by the Scarborough Board of Education in the wake of Andrews's revolutionary design for Scarborough College, then still under construction.[31] [FIG. 17] For Andrews the social aims of the project were the priority: an environment designed to support the emotional and psychological needs of schoolchildren in tandem with learning. However, this brought him into conflict with the commissioning authority. In *John Andrews: Architecture, a Performing Art*, Andrews described his child-centered approach to the design of the school, which sought to create a familiar domestic-scale environment for students and to avoid promoting forms of institutional control thought necessary to surveil students' behavior. [FIG. 14] For example, he did not include long axial corridors that allow for the visual monitoring of space. Instead, Andrews's solution is a one-story complex consisting of clusters of four top-lit classrooms in each corner of a large, central general-purpose space that could be extended over time or linked to other clusters branching across the school campus. As Andrews

29   Ibid.

30   John Andrews, Stelco Modular Apartment sketches, 127A, Box 1, CAA.

31   Taylor and Andrews, *John Andrews*, 50.

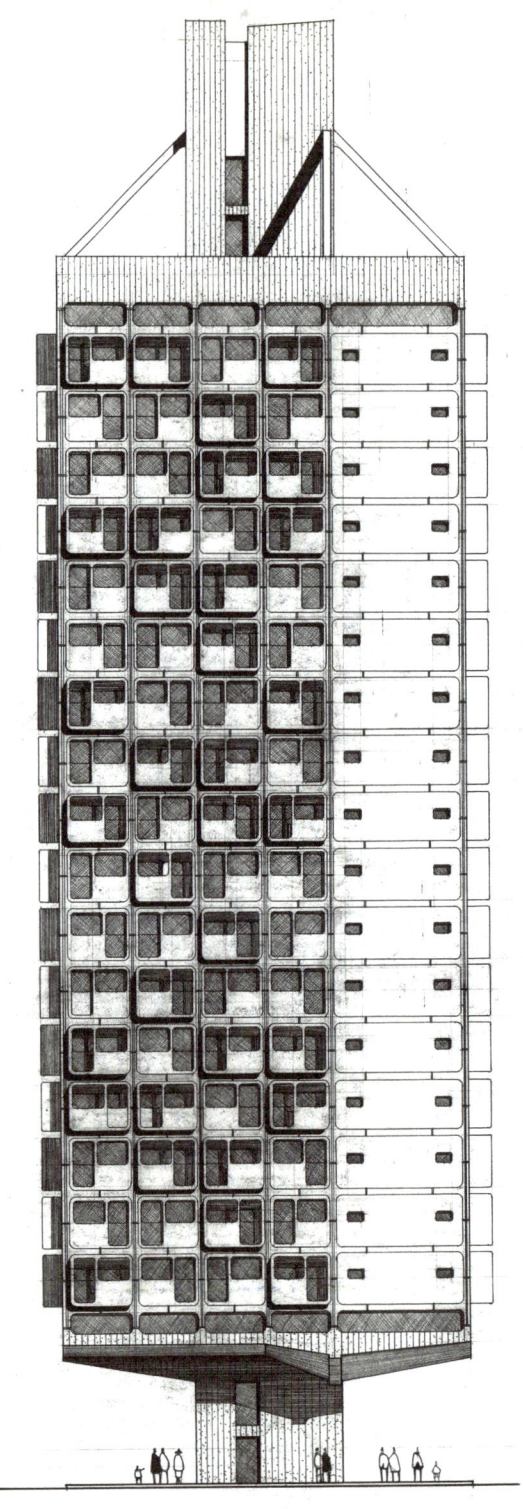

FIG. 11 Stelco elevation, 1965. Architect: John Andrews Architects.

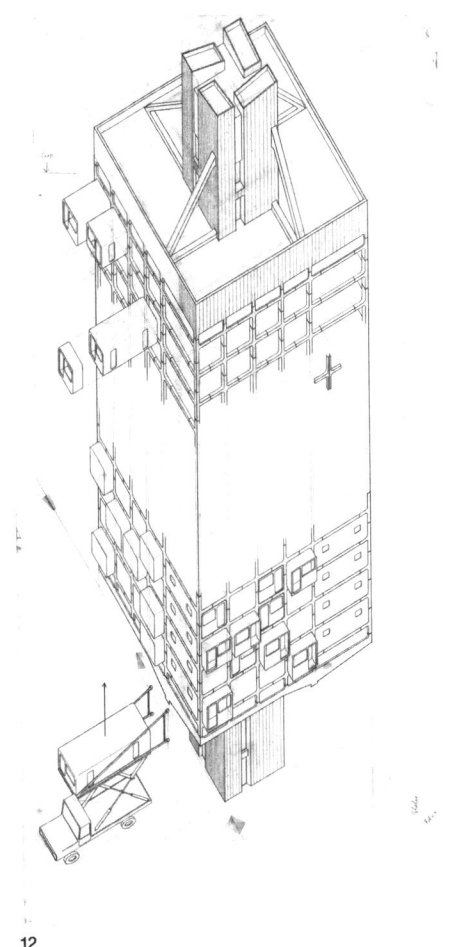

FIG. 12　Stelco tower axonometric view, 1965.
FIG. 13　Stelco towers landscape view, 1965.

explained, his office successfully created a building that "avoided the inefficiencies of the centrally loaded corridor structure and could utilize the concept of selected incremental growth."[32] [FIG. 16]

Schematically, the building's plan features pinwheel forms at two different scales. When viewed as a whole, the pinwheel form is seen in the clusters of classrooms found at the corners of a large gymnasium space at the center of the complex. From the interior, the pinwheel is evident in the ways in which the spaces of the classroom clusters are linked, providing small gathering areas between classrooms. As the corridors connect to other classroom clusters, they create a zigzag passage between the interlinked pinwheels, producing a meandering form. This design intended to recreate a domestic environment for the young students, which would counter the issues of alienation that Andrews saw as a key problem of conventional school building plans. In Andrews's plan for the Bellmere Junior Public School, the pinwheel becomes a vehicle for ameliorating the problems of an entrenched institutional style of architecture that had lost sight of the ways in which architecture can positively engage human behavior. [FIG. 15] Further, this thinking again directly aligns Andrews with the architects of Team 10 and their accompanying professional circle.

The staggered arrangement of classrooms that Andrews envisioned at Bellmere Junior Public School recalls Aldo van Eyck's design for the Amsterdam Orphanage (1960), a seminal project for developing the scale and organization of spaces for children.[33] In both designs, there is an implied diagonal movement, which, broken down to the scale of the building's occupants, is created through stepping forms across the plan. Yet, beyond these formal comparisons are underlying social concerns that Andrews shared with his contemporaries. For Andrews in particular, the attempt to reconcile the individual with the collective by architectural means at Bellmere Junior Public School became key in his later design of student housing for the University of Guelph. More immediately, it influenced the various Expo 67 schemes that John Andrews Architects was developing simultaneously, which involved the creation of collective facilities that could flexibly and respectably accommodate individual exhibits staged by developing nations according to their means.

Despite this committed belief in the pinwheel plan as a means to address new social forms, it had already begun to lose currency by the time Andrews was exploring it in the mid-1960s. Among the Team 10 members, the pinwheel figure was even compared to a swastika, an observation that made its use as a plan uncomfortable by association. Although separate from similar debates occurring in Europe, John Andrews Architects also confronted the limitations of pinwheel planning through their Stelco and Bellmere Junior Public School design experiments. Nevertheless, these projects were critical to the development of the office's own more distinctive design practices, providing a bridge to its subsequent work. In particular, this includes use of grids overlaid by diagonals seen in the realized South Residences of the University of Guelph and the proposed Metro Centre redevelopment of the Toronto railway lands, both of which are examined in the following chapters of this book.

Andrews's reflections on his design for Bellmere Junior Public School in *John Andrews: Architecture, a Performing Art* reveal the greater meaning he attached to the project, which strongly guided the architect's thinking at this formative period of his career. In Andrews's view, the school failed to adequately meet the social aims he initially put forth in the project. As he wrote, "We did not develop the interior-cum-circulation spaces sufficiently in terms of the little people using them. There should have been more places to sit and more things conducive to play."[34] This comment can be seen in part as a reflection on the plan's inability to support variations in spatial

32   Ibid., 52.
33   Francis Strauven, *Aldo van Eyck: The Shape of Relativity* (Amsterdam: Architectura & Natura, 1998), 284-385.
34   Taylor and Andrews, *John Andrews*, 53.

arrangement that would cater to the needs of the students, indicating that the interlocking plans devised were not flexible enough to fully address the project's social aims. Nonetheless, Andrews discusses his work on Bellmere Junior Public School as vital to the realization in his practice that, "all architectural problems are the same, they only vary in dimension."[35] Andrews's use of the pinwheel form on multiple levels in the design of the school, interweaving similar elements at different scales, also proves revelatory for exposing this idea.

The pinwheel plan was also carried forward into the design of African Place for Expo 67, which immediately followed the Bellmere School project. Here Andrews further explored ideas of openness and flexibility, but there is only a vestige of the concern with deeper human behavioral needs explored in the school. Despite the resemblance between the two projects, found in their staggered geometries and modular shell roofs, the Expo 67 scheme clearly deviated from the space-containing character of the pinwheel design for the classrooms and main assembly space in Bellmere Junior Public School. The layout of African Place was still loosely generated through the pinwheel principle, with aggregations of tightly nested and partially overlapping pinwheel patterns determining the structural grid, the interior layouts of its pavilions, and the zigzag circulation routes that led into the site and through the complex. However, the interior spatial boundaries and hierarchies were substantially eliminated in a porous, orthogonally gridded matrix of columns and three-quarter height dividing walls through which it was anticipated that visitors would ambulate back and forth between the different exhibition bays. Despite their evocative shapes and volumes, the cellular modularity of the roof shells also had little bearing on the overall plan. Apart from their primary function as passively activated environmental modulators, the distinctive geometry and materiality of these elements had as much to do with the technical and logistical challenges of getting the project built in time as it did with any intended spatial, behavioral, and/or aesthetic effects.

CONSTRUCTION OF AFRICAN PLACE

In the design of African Place for Expo 67, constructability was one of the most significant factors that dictated the project's final resolution. Indeed, after their whirlwind experience designing and building Scarborough College in a little over two years, the John Andrews Architects team, unlike many of the other consulting architects and designers engaged in Expo 67, was familiar and relatively comfortable with the notion of the "critical path" to project delivery. In the mid-1960s this was a new and fashionable methodology for project management that the CCWE employed with draconian rigor in order to coordinate the myriad architectural and engineering works that had to be built simultaneously to complete the Expo in time.

The executive face of the CCWE and this critical path methodology was Director of the Department of Installations Colonel Edward Churchill. A retired Canadian Army officer and logistics expert from the World War II generation, Churchill was personally responsible for the construction of the entire Expo 67 facilities, beginning with the artificial islands on which the exhibition was to be staged. Andrews respected Churchill's method and sense of command as a decision-maker, regarding him as the client behind a faceless and potentially resistant bureaucracy.[36]

Prompted by the ironclad constraints and logic of Churchill's critical path, Andrews's designs for both African Place and Activity Area F were among a number of other projects at Expo 67 that made innovative use of basic domestic-grade plywood as the principal material. In the context of a superheated local construction market in which all major contractors and material suppliers were already committed to the larger and more sophisticated Expo 67 projects, this humble material

---

35   Ibid., 53.

36   John Andrews in discussion with Peter Scriver, Paul Walker, Philip Goad, and Antony Moulis, Orange, New South Wales, July 2–3, 2012. See also Taylor and Andrews, *John Andrews*, 73–75.

FIG. 14 Bellmere Junior Public School classroom.

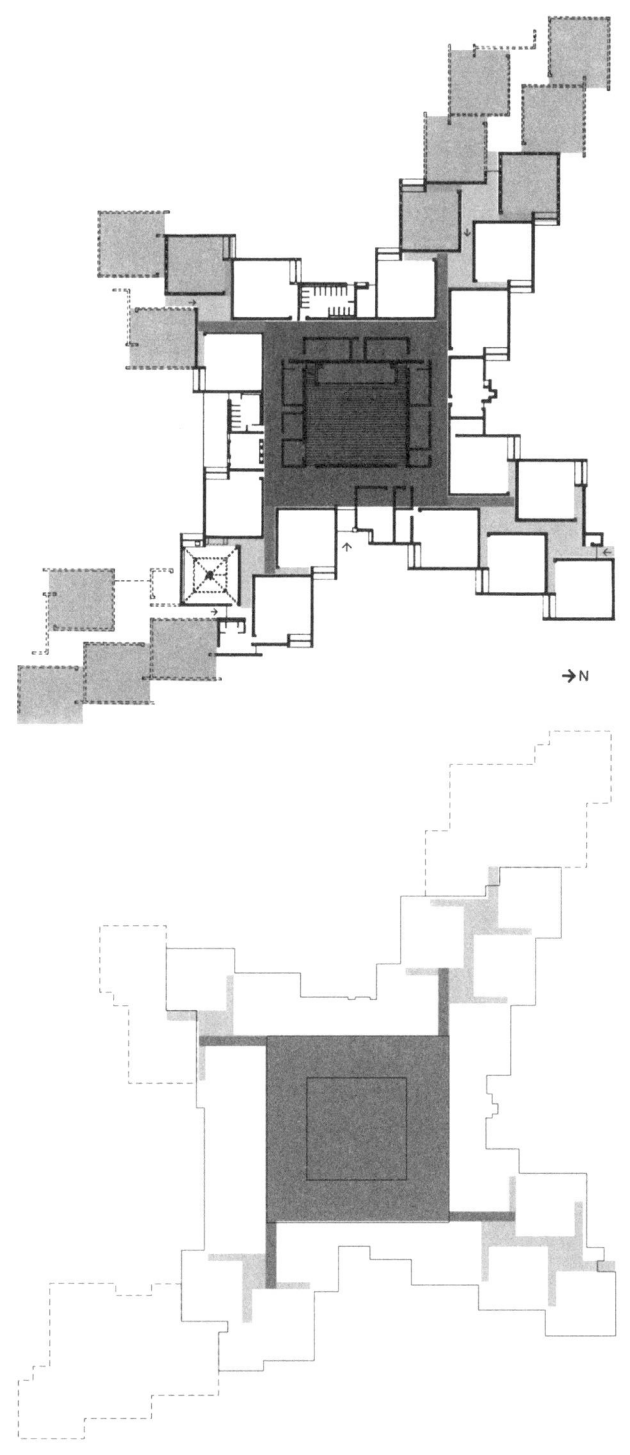

FIG. 15 Bellmere Junior Public School plan.

was relatively inexpensive, widely available off the shelf, and could largely be worked off-site into prefabricated components. This was a particularly significant tactical decision since the only contractors still available to bid on the job were small players with less experienced builders who were only familiar with conventional, domestic-grade construction materials and methods.[37] Andrews relished this challenge and claimed to have been one of only a very select few—including Buckminster Fuller, who completed his colossal geodesic dome for the United States Pavilion—to have fully adhered to Churchill's regime, delivering the results on time and within the required budget.[38]

ARCHITECTURE AND EXHIBITION OUTCOMES

Considering the openness and flexibility of the design for African Place by Andrews and his team, they had little control over how it was actually experienced by visitors and abused, in their view, by the exhibition designers who were independently commissioned to fit out the interior spaces for the African exhibitors.[39] The Andrews team took pains to prepare a report outlining the principles of their design to serve as a guideline for the exhibitors and their designers.[40] But this was either overlooked or intentionally ignored by the Paris-based interior designers hired for Expo 67 who approached the brief as a layout for a conventional trade fair or exhibition in a generic gallery space. Individual exhibits were isolated from each other within a system of additional enclosures that contained standardized lighting and suspended ceilings, which effectively sealed off the volume of the extraordinary roof shells overhead, along with their natural light sources. Moreover, they also missed the opportunity the architecture presented for installing more unique and dramatic displays. Consequently, other key aspects of the design were also seriously compromised as the free-flowing space was partitioned and compartmentalized, simultaneously obstructing airflow and sight lines and thereby impeding the passive ventilation and cooling capacity of the structures.[41]

An official description of African Place in a report of the exhibition, prepared in the immediate afterglow of the fair, overlooked such niggling technical pitfalls in favor of the visual and sensory impressions that its design imparted, together with the diverse cultural content of the pavilion. As the report stated, "in the scope of a distinctive pavilion [...] Africa Place [sic] offers a panorama of modern Africa [...] which will linger in the minds of visitors—together with the haunting beating of the drums welcoming them there."[42] Popular impressions reflected in other nonofficial publications were similarly benign while also patronizing. In a commemorative volume of the fair published by a key corporate sponsor, in which various pavilion designs and fair facilities were previewed, a caption for an image of the model for the African cluster incorrectly explained that "several African nations arranged to pool their individual pavilions in such a way as to give a realistic impression of an African village."[43] Aimed at potential French visitors and preceded by a potted historical account of previous world's fairs since the era of the French colonial empire, this description still ennobled the colonial trope of representing native tradition as a theme against which the technological and cultural advances of other exhibiting nations could be measured. Perhaps because of these misinterpretations, commentary on Andrews's design for African Place from architectural critics was largely muted. A special issue of *Progressive Architecture*, which included a minor technical note about the environmental and structural systems of the complex, gave Ian Morton, a member of Andrews's team, an opportunity to record the

37 John Andrews in discussion with Peter Scriver, Paul Walker, Philip Goad, and Antony Moulis, Orange, New South Wales, July 2–3, 2012.
38 Taylor and Andrews, *John Andrews*, 75.
39 Ibid.
40 John Andrews Architects, "African Place Exhibit Design Co-ordination Report," September 21, 1966, softbound typescript report, Box 43-24, John Andrews fonds, CAA.

41 Kalin, *Expo '67*, 131; John Andrews in discussion with Peter Scriver, Paul Walker, Philip Goad, and Antony Moulis, Orange New South Wales, July 2–3, 2012.
42 *General Report on the 1967 World Exhibition*, vol. 1, 392.
43 Banque National de Paris, *Montreal Expo 67*, 50.

FIG. 16 Model, Bellmere Junior Public School.

team's dismay with the unanticipated sentimentality and misunderstanding in the design's reception. He commented, "It is interesting that the layman finds it necessary to identify with the so-called unusual. The roof and cellular plan has been identified symbolically by news media with African villages. One wonders what the lay description would be if the project were to house a cooperative market in a North American city?"[44]

Expert critical assessment of the architecture of the fair tended to be more equivocal than that of the general viewer. While lay observers in the popular press were mostly wowed by the outcome—a clear measure of success from the perspective of the Expo organizers—writers covering this "Architect's Expo" for professional journals were more discerning. Though few of the architectural ideas and technologies on display were truly novel, the radical propositions in megastructure projects, such as Safdie's Habitat 67, which experimented with prefab modular housing, and Frei Otto's tensile structure for the German Pavilion, were rendered full-scale for the first time. Real progress was imminent. Still, the experience was like a "middle-world of hesitation," as editor of *Progressive Architecture* John C. Rowan expressed it, hovering between the intimate and the monumental, high tech and low tech, and artificially mediated perception versus the atavistic surety of actual physical mass, volume, and space.[45]

The British Pavilion, designed by Sir Basil Spence and located a few paces from African Place, epitomized the latter. As an expressionist ode to monumentality, it was aggressively angular in form and rendered in a Brutalist style through a sprayed-on imitation of roughcast concrete, which at its relatively small scale unintentionally had an almost Disney-like effect. Indeed, with its staggered profile and eroded tower, it could be compared with some of the more iconic features of Andrews's design for Scarborough College. It was a further curiously contextual echo of the Brutalist aesthetics of the moment and competing claims in the international milieu of a world's fair to the particular cultural pedigree and symbolism associated with these aesthetics.

If anything, Andrews's designs for African Place and Activity Area F were encompassed by British critic Reyner Banham's praise for the work of unsung "locals," who, in his opinion, outclassed the more self-conscious and pompous efforts of the better-known and established architects, such as Sir Basil Spence and Buckminster Fuller in their conventional, nation-specific pavilions.[46] Andrews's primary aim, to address the need for an open system that could contend with indeterminate needs and contingencies, resonated, at least in principle, with the potential that Banham also ascribed to the nearby theme pavilion "Man the Producer." Designed by a local Montreal-based architectural partnership, this structure was an important node in the matrix of such megastructure-styled theme pavilions that straddled the Expo 67 site.[47] Banham celebrated the playful situationism that the Expo public experienced spatially and semiotically through their unscripted ramblings within this matrix. As an irascible critic and champion of the avant-garde architectural group Archigram, Banham felt that fairgoers were denied these liberties in the linear experiences that dictated most of the other more conventional Expo 67 pavilions.[48] Built at a smaller scale than the official thematic infrastructure of the fair, though reflecting a similar design ethos, Andrews's Expo 67 schemes were comparable propositions of an open and supportive architecture in which human circulation and connectivity were the driving forces.

Related ideas regarding an interior public "street" and "meeting place" were explored earlier in the Scarborough College scheme

44 "Reaping the Wind: Africa Place, Isle Notre-Dame," 147.
45 John C. Rowan, editorial to special issue on Expo 67, "The Architect's Expo", *Progressive Architecture* (June 1967): 129.
46 Reyner Banham, "Arts in Society: L'Homme a l'Expo," *New Society*, June 1967, 811–13.
47 Affleck, Desbarats, Dimakopoulos, Lebensold, Sise (later incorporated as ARCOP: Architects in Co-Partnership). This award-winning collective simultaneously realized several major urban design and redevelopment projects in Montreal that Banham examined in, *Megastructure: Urban Futures of the Recent Past*.
48 Banham, "Arts in Society: L'Homme a l'Expo," 813.

but those had represented more specific and formally prescriptive design concepts. Through the Bellmere Junior Public School and Expo 67 commissions, circulation became a more open concept related to spatial flow and flux that would continue to drive Andrews's designs of educational buildings and institutions, including student residences, over the next couple of decades.[49]

These design concerns also reflected the currency of such ideas for other North American–trained architects and urban planners of Andrews's generation. For those, like Andrews, who studied under Josep Lluís Sert's widely influential Harvard GSD curriculum, the dual focus on monumental and urban architecture exposed them to the dominating discussions of modernism at the time. This included the increasingly contested discourse on modernist urbanism that circulated in Congrès International d'Architecture Moderne (CIAM) circles throughout the 1950s and the parallel debates both for and against the development a new monumentality in modern architecture that raged simultaneously in the United States and Britain.[50] The tendencies in the Expo 67 projects also aligned Andrews with what Australian architecture commentator Philip Drew defined as the "third generation" of international modernists. This included those that were more attuned to the humanistic dimensions and open-ended flux of social space and more aware of the ecological imperatives of environmental design than their forbearers, who had a narrower, more mechanistic understanding of the functionalism that was upheld by CIAM.[51] Nevertheless, Andrews remained an exponent of an architecture, true to the functionalism of his first- and second-generation modernist mentors, that was still intent on providing "the solution," as he put it, to a given design problem. His solution to the problem of designing freer, less oppressive buildings was to reconceive them as integrated structures of an urban nature and scale in which circulation and communication were the essential issues demanding design thought and innovation.

THE PROBLEM OF MOVEMENT

Andrews's meteoric rise to prominence in his early career was a phenomenon of an era that was already passing. The modernist ideal of internationalism that infused his graduate studies in the postwar United States of the 1950s, and his subsequent experience of Canada in the early 1960s allowed the young Australian architect and his international team to realize bold and untested ideas that were then only "in the air." A key factor determining the team's early success and accomplishments was Andrews's personal capacity to deal directly and decisively with decision-makers who were still accustomed to exercising top-down, technocratic authority. However, such ideals and operative assumptions would fall increasingly out of sync with the evolving ethos and diversity of the multicultural society in which Andrews had made his new home. This discordance was then already manifesting in the rapidly changing national and cultural politics that followed Canada's cosmopolitan "coming out" exercise at Expo 67 and would soon follow Andrews back to a changing Australia.

In the heady moment of Expo 67, Andrews and his team were commissioned to create a space for the exhibiting African nations to show and express themselves on their own terms. What they succeeded in doing was to place the exhibitors in an architecture of the later 20th century that was suitably versatile for the functional requirements and logistical constraints of the client, the Expo's organizing authority. To the extent that the specific cultural content of the pavilion was even acknowledged, it was not thought of as a source to draw formal or conceptual inspiration from but

---

49 Philip Goad, "Open Field, Open Street, Open Choice: John Andrews and the South Residences, University of Guelph (1965–68)," *Proceedings of the Society of Architectural Historians, Australia and New Zealand: 30, Open*, vol. 2, eds. Alexandra Brown and Andrew Leach (2013): 639–50. See also chapter 4 of this book.
50 Paul Walker "Reassessng John Andrews' Architecture: Harvard Connections," *Proceedings of the Society of Architectural Historians, Australia and New Zealand: 30, Open*, vol. 2, eds. Alexandra Brown and Andrew Leach (2013): 611–22. See also the introduction of this book.
51 Drew, *Third Generation*.

was considered another "problem" to address through an architectural "solution."

As the design artifacts of that solution, African Place and its antecedents in the Stelco and Bellmere Junior Public School projects were open, loose, and even unresolved propositions that were never repeated in quite the same way again. They represented the outcome of the team's intentionally open design investigations paired with limited design experience at such an early stage in their career. The lessons learned in the planning of the Bellmere school provided Andrews with a greater understanding of design methods, taking his formal and spatial thinking well beyond the implications of the pinwheel plan. This is reflected in the Expo 67 commissions and in the design of the University of Guelph South Residences to come, which included another key aspect of Andrews's style and approach, a new model based on the deployment of diagonal axes. This would become a distinctive planning technique and hallmark of Andrews's practice. The team's brazen confidence, or even arrogance, as well as forthrightness characterized its next phase of work, which involved the creation of major urban developments, such as Toronto's massive Metro Centre scheme and the Cameron Offices complex in Canberra. The latter commission internationalized the scope of their practice and would take Andrews himself back to Australia. Together these projects provided John Andrews Architects with a new sense of certainty that the future "critical path" of architecture lay in solving, once and for all, the problem of movement.

FIG. 17   Bellmere Junior Public School, 1965.

04

greenfields and urban systems: buildings for education

by Philip Goad

The educational buildings John Andrews and his office completed, often in collaboration with others, from 1965 to 1998 in Canada, the United States, and Australia are key case studies in what ought to be regarded as the global redefinition of the educational campus in the 1960s and 1970s. For over 33 years, Andrews was involved in the design of more than 25 individual buildings and masterplans related to teaching, research, student life, and on-campus living. For Andrews, designing spaces for education had great appeal, in part because his willingness and ability to critique conventional building programs of any type aligned with the educational research of the period that similarly involved experiments with pedagogy and space. In the same way, his designs for student housing recast conventional Oxbridge models. For Andrews and for many of his contemporaries in education, the subject, intellectually and physically, was like a greenfield site, open and ready for redefinition.

Andrews is justifiably well known for Scarborough College and the Harvard GSD's Gund Hall, both of which brought his firm significant international attention. However, these two buildings must be considered within a much larger and arguably little-known collection of buildings for education that formed the backbone of Andrews's practice in Canada and, from 1969, underpinned his Australian practice, culminating with the Veterinary Science Conference Centre at the University of Sydney in 1998. This chapter reveals the design themes of Andrews's work for education, especially his interest in creating or identifying the urban system within which each project was to be located and how the project might consolidate or promote that system. This urban focus, intrinsic to Andrews's thinking, was also directly connected to the global expansion and development of university education in the 1960s.

THE NEW UNIVERSITY

In the May 1966 *Architectural Forum*, Oscar Newman, then coordinator of the master of urban design program at Washington University in St. Louis, captured the optimistic mood and significant currency surrounding campus design around the world: "With the suddenness of a *coup d'etat*, the 'New Campus' has come to occupy the dominant position in current architecture."[1] For Newman, the "New Campus" was "characterized by urban density, stress on circulation and the mixing of disciplines."[2] His review of four new campus projects (Berlin, Forest Park, Marburg, and Chicago Circle) was bracketed in the same issue by his feature on and critical review of Scarborough College. For Newman, Scarborough College was emblematic of a new campus architecture influenced by urban design, a position taken up by other observers. In *Zodiac* 18 (1968), a special issue devoted to contemporary British architecture, Joseph Rykwert, professor of art at the new University of Essex, described universities as the institutional archetypes of the age.[3] Drawing comparisons to the cathedral building of the Middle Ages, Rykwert highlighted the unprecedented design and construction of new universities. What made the British situation remarkable was the creation of 15 universities and their conception, as Rykwert put it, "in a changed urban situation." This includes open sites and often pastoral landscapes that are invariably located near a provincial town and intended to realize a new urban character, though not radically so. Rykwert believed architects and urban planners had failed throughout the 20th century to give coherence and structure to the city and there was now instead the possibility "for finding the paradigm for the city in the university."[4]

Just over 30 years later, historian Stefan Muthesius would reemphasize the importance of these British experiments of the 1960s, giving special attention to the seven new universities of Sussex, York, Essex, East Anglia, Lancaster, Kent, and Warwick, much vaunted by the international architectural press at the time.[5] Yet it

1 Oscar Newman, "The New Campus: It Suggests a Changed Scale in Ubran Architecture," *Architectural Forum* (May 1966): 43.
2 Ibid.
3 Joseph Rykwert, "Universities as Institutional Archetypes of Our Age," *Zodiac* 18 (1968): 61–63.
4 Ibid., 63.

was not only in Great Britain that such developments were taking place. New universities in the United States, Australia, New Zealand, and Europe were also realized.[6] Significantly, both Rykwert and Muthesius made special note of Canada. Muthesius and Peter Dormer noted, "It seems that it was only Canada which produced a New University movement akin to England's."[7]

Canada was indeed comparable: between 1957 and 1967, no fewer than 11 new universities and colleges were established, including Carleton (1957), York (1959, main campus 1964), Laurentian (1960), Simon Fraser (1963), Trent (1964), Guelph (1964), Brock (1964), Calgary (1966), and Lethbridge (1967), as well as Scarborough (1963) and Erindale colleges (1965), both satellites of the University of Toronto. All of these institutions had major building programs invariably designed by architects of note. Professor Thomas Howarth, director of the School of Architecture at the University of Toronto, reported from the 1964 Banff Session devoted to "Campus Architecture" that "almost overnight the Canadian university has become a major patron of the architectural profession.… It is doubtful whether any field of architectural endeavor in Canada has had or will have such a profound effect upon our profession."[8] Echoing Rykwert, Canadian architect Arthur Erickson, a key player in Canada's university-building enterprise as lead architect for Simon Fraser University in Vancouver and the University of Lethbridge in Alberta, went so far as to say that "education is an urban process involving everyone in a total mix as in the city… the needs of the university and the solutions to those needs are the solutions common to any urban situation."[9]

As a consequence of this groundswell in recognition of the city, many architects translated urban intent into their designs of individual and suites of buildings for the new campuses. For example, residential colleges by architects like Eero Saarinen, Louis Kahn, and Giancarlo de Carlo were designed as microcosms of an idealized urban and community setting, a form of redemptive urban residential development that was part monastic, part secular, part utopian, and different from the urgency of rehousing Europe's war-torn cities or the slum reclamation projects typical of most postwar urban centers.[10] In 1963, Michael Brawne highlighted the significance of student living to university planning, suggesting the immediate relevance of the vocabulary of clusters, stem development, and route development documented as the "Team 10 Primer" in the December 1962 *Architectural Design*. As he writes, "Within the total university plan the consideration of student living space is thus crucial both as a planning idea and as an architectural form. Both aspects will be considerably affected by the social organization thought appropriate."[11] Writing in *The Canadian Architect* in 1962, Robert Furneaux-Jordan used the term "social form" to describe the combination of architectural form and social purpose in the university work of English architect Denys Lasdun.[12] In the myriad of examples produced in the postwar decades, many residential colleges could also be described as expressing "social form." Among these, Andrews's South

5   Stefan Muthesius, *The Postwar University: Utopianist Campus and College* (New Haven, CT: Yale University Press, 2000), 94–186.
6   See Paul Venable Turner, *Campus: An American Planning Tradition* (Cambridge, MA: MIT Press, 1984); Philip Goad, "Universities," in Philip Goad and Julie Willis, eds., *The Encyclopedia of Australian Architecture*, (Melbourne: Cambridge University Press, 2012), 723–34; Julia Gatley, ed., *Long Live the Modern: New Zealand's New Architecture, 1904–1984* (Auckland: Auckland University Press, 2008): 169, 177–79, 194, 200, 213.
7   Peter Dormer and Stefan Muthesius, *Concrete and Open Skies: Architecture at the University of East Anglia, 1962–2000* (London: Unicorn Press, 2000), 126–27.
8   Thomas Howarth, "Comments: Banff Session '64," *Journal RAIC/L'IRAC* (July 1964): 48. The Banff Session is a biennial conference held by the Alberta Association of Architects in the Rocky Mountains around Banff, Alberta, Canada. Like the Aspen Design Conference, held in the United States, the Banff Session historically has been attended by architects, interior designers, academics, and students from Canada and the United States.
9   Arthur Erickson, "The University: A New Visual Environment," *Canadian Architect*, January 1968, 35–27.
10 See the theoretical framing of the idea of the postwar university and historical sections on American, Canadian, and European universities in Muthesius, *The Postwar University*.
11 Michael Brawne, "Student Living: Approaches to Residential Planning," *Architectural Review*, October 1963, 290.
12 Robert Furneaux-Jordan, "Denys Lasdun: England," *Canadian Architect* (September 1962): 55–64.

Residences at the University of Guelph (1965) present a significant case study of this redefinition of the student college as a microcosm of broader issues about rethinking the city, housing, and community. Key to this commission was not just its extraordinary scale—housing 1,660 students, it was the largest project of its kind at the time in North America—but also its formal outcomes, which indicate an emergent personal practice of urban-based design solutions derived from programmatic research and critique combined with innovative construction practices determined by local circumstance.

Central to Andrews's developing design approach was Evan Walker, another Australian architect in Toronto, whose graduate research into student housing and briefing document for the South Residences set the groundwork for Andrews to redefine what a contemporary residential college might be. By focusing on community and the individual, Andrews's University of Guelph project confirmed his increasing commitment to a design approach based on repetitive systems; the expression of circulation, structure, and space freed of heroic modernist formalism; and the provision of flexibly planned and flexibly inhabited spaces. Andrews explored these principles in his later buildings for universities and schools, commercial offices, hotels, and convention centers.

THE UNIVERSITY OF GUELPH AND EVAN WALKER

The University of Guelph was formed in 1964 through the merger of three colleges, including Ontario Agricultural College, which had occupied the campus site since 1874. A long-range development plan of the campus was undertaken by Project Planning Associates, led by Macklin L. Hancock of Toronto, and Richard P. Dober, a campus-planning expert from Cambridge, Massachusetts, with Sert Jackson Associates serving as design-review consultants.[13] Hancock was a GSD graduate, having studied under Josep Lluís Sert, and Sert's firm (with Hancock, Little, Calvert Associates) completed the campus's first major new buildings: the MacKinnon Building (1967) and McLaughlin Library (1968).[14] The masterplan proposed inserting new buildings to increase density and create courtyards, with four groups of student housing at the cardinal points on the campus perimeter.

In 1965, the university commissioned Evan Walker to complete a housing study. Son of the progressive Australian educator Charles Walker and a 1959 graduate in architecture from the University of Melbourne, Walker was the first University of Toronto student to complete a master of architecture solely through the completion of a research thesis rather than design studios.[15] Supervised by Tom Howarth, a new professor of architecture, Walker's thesis submitted in April 1962 was a comprehensive survey of contemporary approaches to the design of student residences in Canada, the United States, and Great Britain.[16] The thesis was based on extensive field research as well as Walker's positive experience living in a single room at Wycliffe College in Toronto as opposed to the American tradition of shared bedrooms in college dormitories. When Walker was commissioned to undertake the Guelph study, he was living and working as a don—a resident lecturer in tertiary education of the British Commonwealth—in the recently completed New College (1962) at the University of Toronto, designed by Andrews's GSD classmate Macy DuBois.

Walker concluded that the campus's neighboring city of Guelph could only provide

13 Project Planning Associates Limited and Richard P. Dober, *University of Guelph Long Range Development Plan 1964* (1964). Dober's books include *Campus Planning* (New York: Reinhold, 1963) and *The New Campus in Britain: Ideas of Consequence for the United States* (New York: Educational Facilities Laboratories, 1965).

14 Michael McClelland and Graeme Stewart, eds., *Concrete Toronto: A Guidebook to Concrete Architecture from the Fifties to the Seventies* (Toronto: Coach House Books, 2007), 280–81.

15 Evan Walker, interview by Philip Goad, October 17, 2012. Charles Fitzroy Walker was principal of Box Hill Grammar School, in Melbourne, from 1929 until 1963. See Richard Cotter, "CF Walker and Box Hill Grammar, 1929–1963: An Unconventional Headmaster and His School" (MA thesis, University of Melbourne, 1985) and Richard Cotter, *Farmers, Ringmasters and Builders: A History of Kingswood College* (Box Hill: Kingswood College, 1985).

16 Evan H. Walker, "University Halls of Residence: A Study Relating to Conditions in Canadian Universities," (MArch thesis, University of Toronto, 1962).

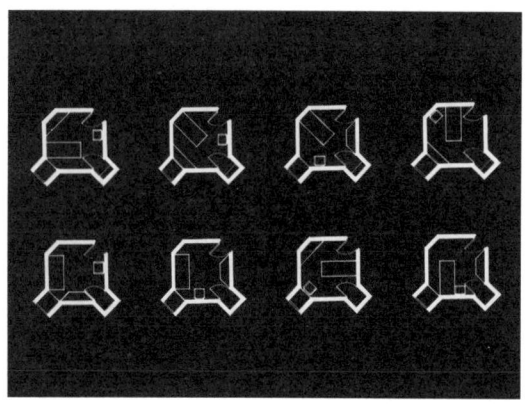

1

2

3,000 new beds, though the university would need 12,000 by 1980. He confirmed the 1964 masterplan location of four undergraduate residence areas, each with 2,300 beds, with the remainder devoted to married-student housing. Walker recommended, as at British colleges, that students should be housed in single rooms with moveable furniture so they could change their spaces to suit different uses and express individuality.[17] He suggested an ideal group of 13 to 16 students share a common sitting room, kitchen, and washroom. Three groups would then form what Walker termed a "house," which would also contain a don's apartment, with 45 students being the maximum number a don could be expected to know. Five houses of 45 students formed a "residence" (another Walker term) with an attached three-bedroom house for a residence head. Hence, 10 "residences" would satisfy the required 2,300-bed undergraduate complex. In a then-progressive move, Walker recommended an equal number of male and female students. Plans stipulated five dining halls for every two residences with a special sixth dining hall for formal events and off-campus students. The communal areas in each complex would also have an infirmary, barber shop, drug store, beauty salon, coffee shop, "tuck shop" (an in-house convenience store), and recreation and music rooms.

The university approved the study and tasked Walker with finding an architect for site B, the South Residences. Walker had an office at 47 Colborne Street in Toronto, the same building as Andrews (on the first floor) and architect Ron Thom (on the second floor), and he intended to approach Thom with the commission due to his precisely detailed and highly regarded design of Massey College (1963), completed for the University of Toronto.[18] On his way upstairs Walker ran into Andrews, whom he'd strangely never met, and, swept away by his charisma, became convinced Andrews

FIG. 1 Room layout studies, South Residences, University of Guelph, Guelph, Ontario, Canada, 1965–1968.

FIG. 2 1:1 student room prototype, South Residences, University of Guelph, constructed in the Andrews office at Colborne Street, Toronto, Canada, c. 1966.

17 Evan Walker, "University of Guelph: Student Housing Study," 50–52. See also John A. Eccles, *The Boarding House: The History of Residences at the University of Guelph* (Guelph, ON: University of Guelph, 1983), 34–35.

18 Evan Walker, interview by Philip Goad, October 17, 2012; Denis Sweetnam, interview by Goad, October 15, 2012.

should do the job.[19] It was the beginning of a lifelong friendship and a professional connection that continued well after Walker finally returned to Australia in 1969.[20]

JOHN ANDREWS AND THE SOUTH RESIDENCES

For Andrews, the commission came at an opportune time. Though Scarborough College (1965) brought him national and international fame almost overnight, his office had no other major commission apart from the small but innovative Bellmere Junior Public School (1965). At Bellmere, Andrews arranged classrooms diagonally off the corners of a central orthogonal volume that housed a multipurpose hall. This meant four "arms" of classrooms could flexibly extend with the addition of more classrooms, with each "arm" a mini-neighborhood and each classroom as its own hip-roofed "home." The diagonal—an intuitive desire line of movement—meeting the corner of a "public" volume at the intersection of internal "streets" that delineated "meeting places" became a key motif of Andrews's buildings for education. This arrangement prioritized legible circulation over significant form. (For further discussion of the Bellmere Junior Public School, see chapter 3.) At the University of Guelph, Andrews applied an urban system to the greenfield site on the campus perimeter.

Walker and Andrews threw themselves into determining a final form for the Guelph project given site and budget constraints. Andrews refined Walker's diagrams, and he appreciated and agreed with Walker's desire for flexibility in furniture arrangement. Though having never visited the Morse and Ezra Stiles colleges at Yale University, Andrews was critical of Eero Saarinen's hundreds of different room shapes, arguing that there was no flexibility at all.[21] Instead, the Andrews office devised a room in which all four walls were left free and the four corners were cut off and replaced with windows and doors, one of which led to a small personal balcony. The furnishings and fixtures were then designed in proportion to the dimensions of the walls and to each other. This allowed each student at least 14 different major furniture-fixture combinations.[22] [FIG. 1]

Using the construction expertise of Jim Sykes, employed by Andrews as a model- and cabinetmaker, a one-to-one model of the polygonal room was built on the top floor of 47 Colborne Street, photographed with a fish-eye lens from above, and tested with various combinations of occupants, furniture arrangements, and scenarios, from private study to a student party.[23] [FIG. 2] This was evidence-based design or a simultaneously sociological and formal study. It was also an early example of Andrews's so-called common sense designs: once a central design problem was identified, it would be interrogated until both the architect and client were satisfied that all options had been explored and flexibility was guaranteed. After further discussions with Walker, Andrews halved the nominally ideal number of 12 students to a group to six based on the idea of six people per floor sharing a washroom and a stair landing, thus forming a smaller, more intimate social unit, much like the average family. As with Oxford and Cambridge colleges, the staircase was the crucial communal connection, with two linked floors forming a group of 12 students. Rooms faced the sun and were laid out like petals fanning around the stair landing, with a shared lounge and kitchenette half a level above and half a level below each group of six. For Andrews, this was a key development: "Implicit in this concept is the theme of choice; the creation of a built form which enhanced rather than discouraged choice. Although our

---

19 Evan Walker, interview by Philip Goad, October 17, 2012.
20 Evan Walker joined architect and fellow university colleague Daryl Jackson in partnership in 1963 in Melbourne but returned to Toronto in 1965, where he specialized in university consulting and masterplanning projects. See Julie Willis, "Evan Walker," in Philip Goad and Julie Willis, eds., *The Encyclopedia of Australian Architecture*, (Melbourne: Cambridge University Press, 2012), 743–44.

21 John Andrews, interview by Philip Goad, July 2, 2012.
22 Jennifer Taylor and John Andrews, *John Andrews: Architecture, a Performing Art* (Melbourne: Oxford University Press, 1982), 60.
23 Series of photographs, Envelope 66189, Box 276, Panda Photography Associates fonds, Canadian Architectural Archives, University of Calgary.

FIG. 3   Meeting place, South Residences, University of Guelph.

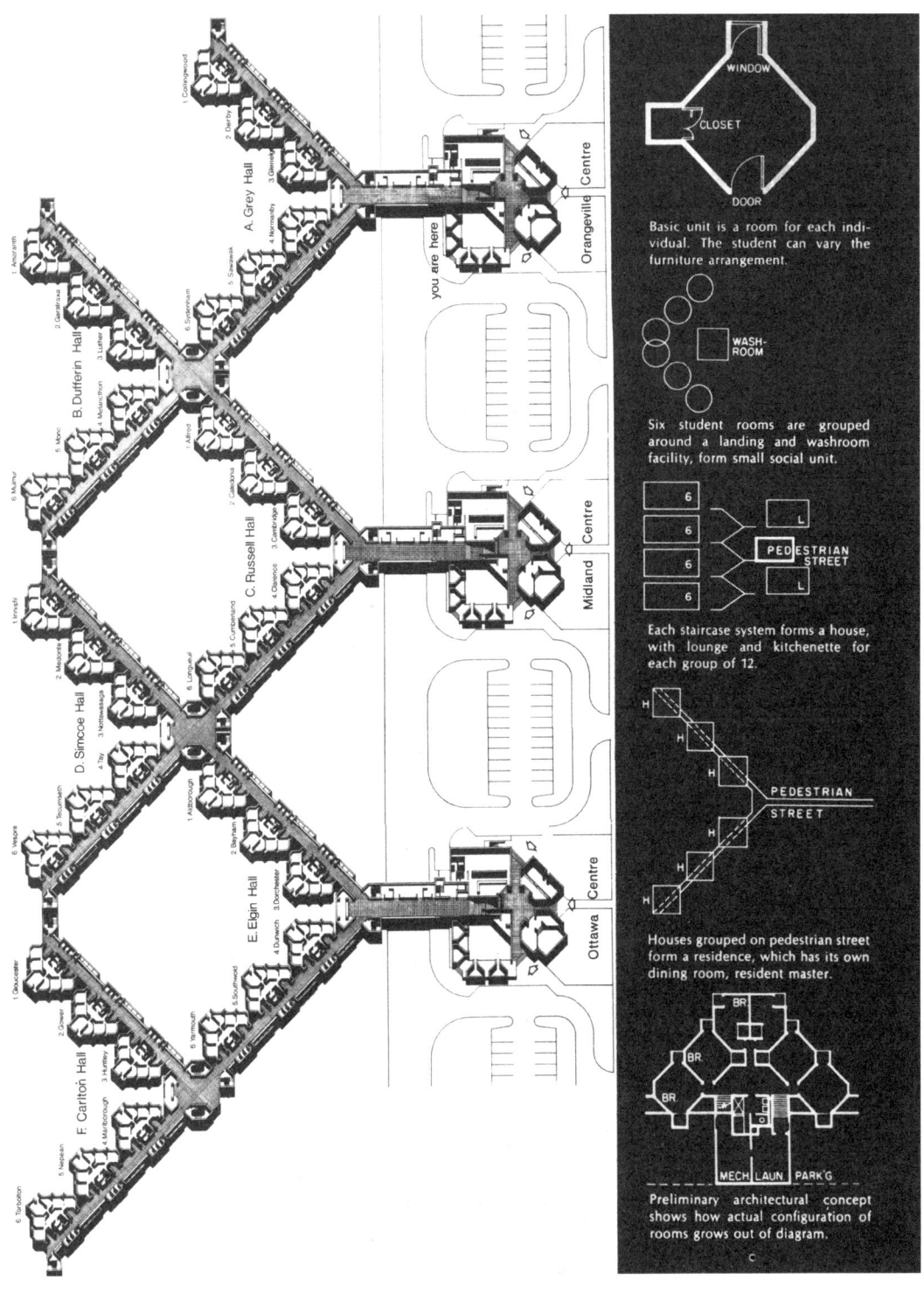

FIG. 4 Plan and design rationale, South Residences, University of Guelph.

thinking was naïve, at the time it represented a substantial advance on the interminable lines of double rooms marching along double-loaded corridors to community washrooms."[24]

Six floors of study-bedrooms built around a staircase with additional accommodation for a don comprised what Andrews described (using Walker's terminology) as a "house." On the second floor, each "house" was connected by an internal pedestrian "street" (Andrews's term, one derived largely from his studies under Giedion and Sert at Harvard).[25] This meant that students could enter their "house" from the "street" and go either up or down to their rooms. To accommodate this diagram, the "streets" were laid out on a diagonal grid, with "meeting places" (another Andrews term) that contained a porter's office, mailboxes, food and drink machines, and fixed lounge seating at their intersections. [FIG. 3] Given the extended scale of the complex, the elevated street was considered necessary to avoid the university ring road that cut through the site. Thus, these streets became bridges (also containing communal laundries) leading to three discrete dining halls, which each served two residences and had attached recreation rooms. The three dining halls also had major "meeting places" at their entrances, each with a generously scaled staircase leading up to the elevated street. The choice to internalize all public spaces made logical sense in terms of Andrews's sophisticated diagram of the functional arrangement and given Ontario's long winter. The building's vast scale lent it a fortress-like appearance and acted almost as a bulwark against the embrace of an outdoor space. [FIGS. 4–6]

Andrews's analogic kit of a street, meeting place, staircase, landing, and the private space of the individual room were paralleled throughout the "Team 10 Primer" (1962). For instance, Jaap Bakema's description of a project by the architectural team Candilis-Josic-Woods could easily be a description of the University of Guelph. As he writes, "The individual flats are here disposed like the leaves of a tree: the trunk (the staircase) enveloped by the leaves (the flats). The individual and the collective, like entities in relation to each other, explain the phenomenon of the total life."[26] However, the circulation themes explored at Guelph derived from Andrews's active and intentional exploration of similar spatial and architectural themes of street, spine, staircase, and meeting place (and their labeling as such) at Scarborough College, which in themselves relate to ideas about urbanism, especially the pedestrian street, promoted by Sert and his colleagues at the Harvard GSD.[27]

At the University of Guelph, Walker's 1965 report provided cutting-edge programmatic data, to which Andrews could respond, work with, and critique, adjusting his spatial and sociometric diagrams to the dictated budgets and local construction conditions.[28] This enabled Andrews to use research as a form of critical invention and subvert the traditional college cloister model and its "high table." At Guelph, the local building industry was incapable of managing a commission of this scale with a single trade, and to meet completion deadlines, in-situ concrete was used for the exterior structure and circulation system, terra-cotta blocks for the "houses," and precast concrete plates for the bedroom floors.[29] In visual terms, this reinforced the appearance and the idea of

24   Taylor and Andrews, *John Andrews*, 63.
25   Paul Walker, "Reassessing John Andrews' Architecture: Harvard Connections," *Proceedings of the Society of Architectural Historians, Australia and New Zealand 30, Open*, no. 2, eds. Alexandra Brown and Andrew Leach (2013): 611–22.
26   Jaap Bakema, excerpt from "Carre Bleu," 1961, reprinted in "Team 10 Primer 1953–62," *Architectural Design* 32, no. 12 (December 1962): 565. The project to which Bakema refers is the apartments at Clos d'Orville (1961), Nimes, France, by Candilis-Josic-Woods.
27   John Andrews, interview by Philip Goad, July 2, 2012. As part of his GSD MArch (Fall 1957–Spring 1958), Andrews took a studio with Sert on housing and density as well as the seminar "The Human Scale" with Sigfried Giedion and Eduard Sekler in spring 1958. The design studio, "The Residential Sector," examined the town of Billerica, Massachusetts, and the Cambridgeport section of Cambridge between Harvard and the Massachusetts Institute of Technology and was taught by Sert, Huson Jackson, Colombian architect Alvaro Ortega, and Blanche Lemco van Ginkel.
28   Spatial/sociometric diagrams, slide collection, AND 5042-5245, John Andrews fonds, Canadian Architectural Archives, University of Calgary.

a pedestrian "spine" or "stem" with attached "clusters" of rooms. The materials palette at Guelph (as at Scarborough College) followed that of Sert: off-form concrete coffered ceilings in the meeting places; floors of terra-cotta quarry tiles; and walls of raw concrete, though, due to budget constraints, without Sert's artistically patterned boarded off-form panels. Instead, Andrews added the warmth of timber-battened ceilings and, for the "houses," walls of rich brown terra-cotta blocks. [FIG. 7] Reviewed positively and comprehensively in the December 1968 issue of *Architectural Forum*, architecture reporter Kenneth Smith gave the South Residences an apposite label: "Dorm City."[30]

UNIVERSITIES AND STUDENTS: A BASIS FOR PRACTICE

Scarborough College and the South Residences at the University of Guelph proved that John Andrews Architects could handle large-scale educational projects, which led to more, increasingly diverse university work for the office. While Scarborough garnered international attention, the briefing and programming experience with Walker at Guelph gave Andrews an edge over other architects. In each subsequent project, the office's work in critical programming and diagramming of client needs, circulation, landscape, site, and urban conditions—in effect, the visualization of data—were key aspects of a design process that not only convinced clients but also became the office's theoretical framework for an open-ended system of design research. With each project, additional aesthetic and tectonic elements were built on a suite of already tried and tested moves, which debuted on a grand scale at Scarborough and Guelph. This was both a practical office strategy and a design ethos that earned Andrews a career-strengthening reputation for straight-shooting, hard-thinking pragmatism.

29 John Andrews, interview by Philip Goad, January 17, 2013; Taylor and Andrews, *John Andrews*, 58.
30 Kenneth B. Smith, "Dorm City," *Architectural Forum* (December 1969): 76–85.

FIG. 5   Approach from the car park, South Residences, University of Guelph.

FIG. 6   Model, South Residences, University of Guelph.

Such expertise was exercised at the time by the completion of masterplans for the University of Toronto for a new satellite college at Erindale (1964) and the university's main St. George campus (1967). This second study involved a staged proposal for a School of Graduate Studies, a Graduate Students' Union, and graduate-student housing, all located in the narrow block bounded by Bloor Street, St. George Street, Hoskin Avenue, and Devonshire Place. Walker worked on the plan with Graham Brawn, a young Sydney-trained architect who had recently completed his postgraduate urban-design studies at the University of Illinois Urbana-Champaign. Titled "The University in the City," their final report recommended the staged development of the site with a projected 1,380 students by 1970 and 1,820 by autumn 1975.[31] It anticipated progressive densification of the inner urban site, so much so that the predicted concentration of functions on a single, centralized site was ultimately rejected in favor of dispersing student facilities across the campus.[32] The report emphasized familiar terms: "Meeting Places"—"paved urban spaces" where major pedestrian systems crossed—were "points of greatest social contact between students and staff and ... [were] associated with facilities having social or symbolic significance."[33] An elevated internal "street" linked all of the functions along the length of the linear block and is alternately covered or open to the sky, sometimes functioning as a bridge overlooking public spaces below.

The 1967 proposal for the Graduate Students' Union was different from the proposal for the University of Toronto's main undergraduate student center, which Andrews had been investigating since 1965. At the time, Andrews had recently completed a competition design (1964) with Ron Thom for a new student union for the University of British

---

31   John Andrews Architects for the Planning Division, University of Toronto, "The School of Graduate Studies: St. George Campus, University of Toronto," briefing document, June 1967, 32.
32   Taylor and Andrews, *John Andrews*, 71.
33   John Andrews Architects, "The School of Graduate Studies," 138.

Columbia in Vancouver. Winning second place, the Andrews/Thom scheme was praised for its "original concept" and as "one of the richest of all submissions."[34] A shopping street on the campus was deployed to link a series of six new conjoined buildings that included a chapel, a theater, and a union building. The intent was clear. Instead of a unitary monumental structure (which was the main feature of the winning entry by Kenneth Snider), Andrews proposed an urban agglomeration, the defining element of which was the public space of the street. Thom's involvement was negligible, explaining Andrews's rancor with him later, and perhaps also the jurors' disappointment in the scheme's second stage, in which they felt the concept was lost.[35]

Since the early 1950s, University of Toronto students had been agitating for a student union. From 1966 to 1967, Andrews produced a design at the students' request based on a programming document completed by his office in November 1965. Planned to be located on the corner of Russell and St. George streets, the design of the student center is massed to harmonize with existing three- and four-story buildings, rising to a six-story L-shaped block for student clubs, the student newspaper, and offices. Major public functions at basement level included a swimming pool and a games area; at street level, an L-shaped internal "street" that opens on one side to a vast meeting place and dining hall and, on the other, to shops along one arm of the L and a bank on the other arm; above this is an auditorium.[36] On the exterior, a series of *piloti*-like blades sit hard on the street like Corbusian fins at Chandigarh, with curving skylights between them. Above and set back from the blades, these skylights shine light over three levels to the internal street below, filtering it across the stepped ceiling of the central meeting place. The building design is densely planned with a complex section, and there are arguably too many functions packed onto a small site. While the project never went ahead, almost all of the design strategies deployed in this unbuilt project reappeared in Andrews's 1968 design for Gund Hall at the Harvard GSD: the L-shaped arm enclosing a series of major functional volumes; the internal street; and the colonnade, though now with actual pilotis instead of the fin-like blades of the Toronto student center.

In May 1971, two years after John Andrews departed for Australia, the idea of a student center for the University of Toronto resurfaced.[37] After four months of work, the team that was appointed to investigate the site recommended that no campus center be built, proposing instead that the entire campus acknowledge its existence as "a territory (or a number of territories) in the fabric of the city." This entailed that the university ought to regard itself as an organism, an intricate and porous network of parts, potentially available to the student 24 hours of the day—much like a real city.[38] Looking back in 1982 on his 1967 proposal for the student center, Andrews conceded that "perhaps fortunately, the scheme was abandoned."[39]

REFINING THE TYPE: STUDENT HOUSING AT BROCK UNIVERSITY

After the University of Guelph project, it was no surprise that the Andrews office was commissioned to design student housing at another recently established university. Brock

---

34 AJ Diamond, "UBC Student Union Competition," *Journal of The Royal Architectural Institute of Canada/Journal de l'Institut Royal d'Architecture du Canada*, 49, no. 2 (September 1965), 60-67. See also "Conditions of Competition: 3—Jury Comment," *Canadian Architect* (August 1969): 37.

35 Ibid.

36 A plan, elevation, and section of Andrews's 1967 design for the University of Toronto Student Union were published in Douglas Engel, "Part I: A Campus Centre for the Campus," *Canadian Architect* (March 1972): 50. A photograph of the model appears in Taylor and Andrews, *John Andrews*, 71.

37 The Students' Administrative Committee commissioned a University of Toronto Department of Architecture team, led by Professor Douglas Engel, in a staff and student project titled "The Campus as the Campus Centre," in which data collection and design studies were undertaken as a way of testing the idea that "the notion of a campus centre or of a student union is a simplistic one. It represents a naive vision of community and of corporate image." See Douglas Engel, "The Campus Centre," *Canadian Architect*, (March 1972): 49.

38 Douglas Engel, "Part II: The Campus as the Campus Centre," *Canadian Architect* (March 1972): 56.

39 Taylor and Andrews, *John Andrews*, 71.

7

8

University in St. Catharines, Ontario, was founded in 1964 and expected to have 8,000 students by 1975.[40] Its campus next to Lake Moodie progressively added buildings from the late 1960s, including the landmark 13-story Arthur Schmon Tower (1968) by Gordon S. Adamson & Associates, which contained the university library and the Thistle Complex (1968), housing a performing arts theater, lecture halls, a bank, shops, and a dining area. The Andrews office, working in association with the local St. Catharines firm Salter Fleming Secord, produced the university's first residence halls, which opened in 1969.

The residences at Brock University are nudged up against one corner of the Thistle Complex to impart an immediate sense of enclosing outdoor space and suggest a future grassy mall. The Andrews design adopted many elements from the University of Guelph project: "internal streets," "meeting places," and a dining hall serving two cruciform residence blocks, which meet at its corner. Similar too were the materials: off-form concrete for the dining hall; dark brown tile blocks for flooring; and deep precast concrete balustrade planks for the residences but with visible sloping roofs of copper. A ground-hugging base of concrete on each residence block's east and south facades indicated the public nature of the internal street within and melded visually with the stairs and hard landscaping of the Thistle Complex.

Key differences between the Guelph design and the residential hall development at Brock included scale—380 students instead of 1,760—and an overall plan form that is conventionally quadrangular rather than comprised of explosive V-shaped wings. [FIG. 8] Gone were the elevated bridge-links to Guelph's three dining rooms; instead, the internal streets, paved in terra-cotta and filled with natural light, are restricted to ground level. Inside, chance meetings on stairs and at corridor intersections continued. On the ground floor, at the intersection of the internal streets and at the center of each Latin-cross-planned block, are "street-knuckle

FIG. 7   Exterior, South Residences, University of Guelph.
FIG. 8   Aerial view, Student Residences (now DeCew Residence), Brock University, St. Catharines, Ontario, Canada, 1969. Architects: John Andrews Architects and Salter Fleming Secord.

40   "Student Residences, Brock University," *Canadian Architect* (November 1970): 31–35.

lounges." On the top level, at these same intersections, are student lounges with the familiar coffered concrete and skylighted ceilings. The student room arrangement differs from Guelph as well. The basic residential unit contains four sleeping units (two double bedrooms and two single bedrooms housing six people) that share a central lounge. To gain further privacy two of the sleeping units (three people) are a half-flight above the central lounge, and two a half-flight below. Each washroom and kitchenette serves 12 residents (two basic units). In this way, the Latin-cross block has its three short arms, each housing 12 students, and its one long arm for 24 students. Andrews and his team created a legible series of mini-communities and a series of spaces that gradually became more public. Altogether, it is arguably a more conventional layout, and the overall scheme feels less hermetic, more internally spacious, and more comprehensible than Guelph's gigantism. A planned expansion, east of two additional conjoined cruciform blocks, and an attached dining room never eventuated.

MAKING THE CAMPUS AN URBAN PLACE: THE D. B. WELDON LIBRARY

Despite the critical success and evident expertise gained in designing student housing at Guelph and Brock, the Andrews office did not receive another commission for student housing in North America after 1969, the year Andrews left for Australia. This was of little immediate concern as the office had already picked up other university commissions for specialized faculty buildings. One of the first of these was the D. B. Weldon Library (1972) at the University of Western Ontario in London, Ontario, designed in association with local architect Ronald E. Murphy. While Jennifer Taylor cited the Weldon Library as the last of Andrews's buildings to have close structural and organizational affinities to Scarborough College, this is not entirely accurate. Weldon should instead be seen as responding to different concerns. First and foremost, the new central library was inserted into an existing campus of Collegiate Gothic buildings dating from the early 1920s: an existing urban system had developed since the university's purchase of the site in 1916. As James Ashby has comprehensively detailed, Murphy designed Collegiate Gothic buildings for the campus into the mid-1960s, effectively acting as a steward for the visual character of the campus, to which Andrews needed to respond.[41] Second, spaces for socializing and individual study, as Oscar Newman noted in 1966, assumed a much more central role in the postwar "New Campus."[42]

Key players from both offices were involved in the project. As Ashby has outlined, in addition to Andrews and Murphy, there was Norbert J. Schuller, a former student of Andrews's at Toronto who formed a partnership with Murphy in 1969, and from the Andrews office, British émigrés Robert (Bob) Anderson and Anthony (Tony) Parsons were closely involved. The Weldon Library's final design was thus distinctly different to that of Scarborough College. [FIG. 9] The concept of the internal street as an underlying plan generator was no longer a feature. Instead, the architects sited the building in line with the existing Gothic-style Somerville House (1955) to form an intersection that, with the additions of new buildings to the north, effectively redirects student life to a new public open space (later known as the "Concrete Beach").

A strong diagonal movement pattern is imparted to the overall parti, a key aspect of Andrews's internal planning that had persisted since the Bellmere School. Especially noteworthy is the diagonal entry from outside the building: students ascended an external landscape of terraces and steps and entered the massive concrete building (later nicknamed "Fort Weldon") at the corner of a conceptual "square" plan to which flexible spaces are attached and imply future growth. They then proceed through to the library's center: a giant lofty volume with a coffered concrete ceiling.

41   James Ashby, "The D.B. Weldon Library by Andrews and Murphy: Modern Experiments in a Collegiate Gothic Campus," *Journal of the Society for the Study of Architecture in Canada/Le Journal de la Société pour l'étude de l'architecture au Canada* 44, no. 2 (2019): 34.
42   Newman, "The New Campus," 45.

More than the "meeting places" at Scarborough and Guelph, the design of Weldon Library boasted a multilevel circulation and meeting hub, complete with Helvetica supergraphics for wayfinding and access to a tunnel that connects with Somerville House. At entry level, undergraduates move off to the left—diagonally—exiting the corner of the "meeting place" into dedicated collections and study spaces planned as two additional squares with coffered concrete eggcrate skylights at their centers and voids to the basement reading and stack areas below. This complex play of volumes and geometry is expressed externally by sloping Kalwall skylights and windowless off-form concrete masses that step down in scale and align with Oxford Avenue. Together with the tall half-round stair towers, this "skirt" of lower-scale concrete and sloping skylight forms establishes a picturesque grouping, sympathetically scaled in material and form to the Collegiate Gothic context.

A key requirement for the study spaces across the library is indirect lighting. The graduate collections and study spaces, positioned above, surrounding, and set off from library's central "meeting place," are two conjoining squares of repetitive book stack floors and half-barrel vault skylighted reading areas. The concrete construction was innovative: for the graduate stack area, economic long spans of 56 feet (17 meters) are achieved through 42 precast, prestressed concrete T-beams spaced at 25 feet (7.6 meters) that support post-tensioned slabs in between. Clearly the intention was to develop a system of parts—all of concrete—as opposed to solely exploring monumental cast-in-place concrete; the Andrews office later explored this idea at a megastructural scale in the long-span concrete construction systems for the Cameron Offices (1976) (see chapter 8).

The Weldon Library earned peer acclaim. It graced the cover of *Canadian Architect* in November 1972, and as Ashby has intimated, the library deserves to be regarded on equal terms alongside other well-known heroic examples such as the McLaughlin Library (University of Guelph, 1968), John P. Roberts Research Library (University of Toronto, 1973), and McLennan Library (McGill University, 1969).[43]

HIGH STAKES: SMITH COLLEGE ART COMPLEX AND GUND HALL

At Smith College in Northampton, Massachusetts, Andrews's plan for a new arts complex (1972) for the prestigious women's liberal arts college was dictated by urban design. The project entailed bringing together two related functions into a single building: the art department (Hillyer Hall), containing offices, library, studio spaces and lecture halls, and the museum of art (Tryon Hall), with its exceptional collections. Working with the Smith College staff, the Cambridge, Massachusetts–based planning firm Dober, Paddock, Upton, and Associates developed the program for the new complex in 1965, but raising funds and appointing the architects took some time. When word of the commission got out, many architects proposed themselves, including Philip Johnson, while Smith College staff members also suggested names for consideration.[44] Many of the staff, including Charles S. Chetham, the college's young art museum director, knew of and had visited Scarborough College: "I believe all of us were overwhelmed by its design."[45] As a consequence and because Andrews promised to finish the job under budget and ahead of schedule (which he did), the firm of John Andrews/Anderson/Baldwin was chosen in 1968. Key members of the design team were Andrews, Brian Hunt, and Ed Galanyk, who was architect-in-charge.

An important educational requirement for the museum was increased exhibition space and storage areas where the entire collection could easily be studied with little distinction

43 "D.B. Weldon Library, University of Western Ontario, London," *Canadian Architect* (November 1972): 26–29.

44 In 1974, Smith College Art Museum Director Charles Chetham wrote in the spring issue of *Art Journal* that the commission came through a faculty member who knew John Andrews in Australia and suggested him for consideration among ten others. Australian expatriate Bernard Boyle, then teaching the history of architecture at Smith College, has stated that this was not the case and that Chetham had misremembered. Boyle had suggested Louis Kahn for the commission. Correspondence with the author, September 25, 2021.

45 Charles Chetham, "The New Smith College Museum of Art," *Art Journal* 33, no. 3 (Spring 1974): 232.

between display and archive. There was to be "no architectural difference between gallery space and storage space, that breadth, length and height be the same though the finish would differ." There were to be no thresholds and all doors, whether in the gallery, storage, or workroom, were 8 feet wide and 10 feet tall, as were all the corridor spaces. The building was intended to be quite literally, as its program and instructions to the architects stated, a "laboratory in the visual arts."

Such an enlightened, active, and object-based learning environment was welcomed by the architects. Assumptions about flexibility, circulation, and a material palette dictated by breaking down hierarchies and deformalizing the program aligned directly with the developing Andrews office design ethos. The Smith College Arts Center was one of the office's first projects in which the client openly accepted the possibility that functional specificity was not germane to the provision of the space, i.e., flexibility of space usage and interchangeable functions were key drivers of the design. This also meant that stronger focus could be given to melding the center into the greater urban pattern of the Smith College campus. A broad internal street, which divided the L-shaped building in two, linked the existing quadrangles of the academic campus with the public, town-facing aspect of Elm Street. It became a key urban link for students moving across campus.

Sitting between the historic red-brick and pale stone dressings of the Gothic Revival–style College Hall (1875) designed by Peabody & Stearns and the gray granite structures and red-tile roofs of the Richardsonian Romanesque-styled St. John's Episcopal Church (1893) by R. W. Gibson, the new arts complex was built and faced in either exposed concrete or the same red-colored concrete block used at Guelph in a deliberate reference to its immediate setting. Underfoot, outside, and in the main entrance was red brick, and from Elm Street, visitors entered between a red-blockwork half-cylindrical stair tower (the third in the broader streetscape with those of College Hall and the church) and a red-block, top-lit bay, while the main structure was faced in sandy-gray concrete.

FIG. 9 Model, proposed "Main Library" (now D. B. Weldon Library), University of Western Ontario, London, Ontario, Canada, c. 1967. Architects: John Andrews Architects and Ronald E. Murphy Architects.

Inside, the internal street, along which the museum, library, and teaching spaces could be accessed, expanded at its center to double as a sculpture gallery featuring Rodin's *The Walking Man* (1907). Overhead, a system of sawtooth gabled skylights (half clear glass, half mirrored) was supported by steel beams clad in stainless steel. At ground level, a wall of one-way mirrors doubled the apparent size of the court. The use of mirrored and clear glass increased the impression of natural light. Chetham was extremely pleased, writing that, "The architects showed unusual alertness and sensitivity in designing their first Museum, a job they approached without prejudgments... there is in our Museum a sense of just proportion and of light which is remarkable."[46]

The completion of the Smith College Arts Center in 1972 coincided with the opening of Gund Hall at Harvard, so in that same year Andrews was involved in producing two buildings for two of North America's most prestigious academic institutions. While the genesis, design lineage, and controversies of Gund Hall are discussed in detail in chapter 7, seen within the context of Andrews's other university buildings, the design elements and even some of the strategic planning decisions of Gund Hall can be seen to have precedent or at least parallel in Andrews's previous buildings for education. As at Smith College, the aim behind the new home for the Harvard GSD was to centralize in one location GSD facilities that had been scattered across several buildings.[47] It was also, like Smith College Arts Center, a building highly attuned to its historical urban context.

PLANS, SYSTEMS, AND LANDSCAPES

While Gund Hall drew public and professional attention to the Andrews office, other university work filled this period. A study undertaken for Prince of Wales College (now Holland College) (1967) in Charlottetown, Prince Edward Island, resulted in a boiler plant, lecture theater, and alterations to an existing building. Perhaps unusually, the Andrews office was prepared for outcomes that did not necessarily result in physical commissions: part of the firm's critical agenda was to question a client's briefing requirements to determine if their stipulations were necessary for and suited to the urban system of the site or campus under consideration. Engaging in the development of a brief as part and parcel of the office's design process, a practice that began early on with Scarborough and continued throughout Andrews's career, was particularly relevant for educational institutions grappling with greenfield sites and the prospect of rapid expansion in the 1960s. This was the case, for example, when the firm was approached to undertake a physical masterplan for the St. Paul campus of the University of Minnesota and instead produced, with David H. Scott Consultants, a "tactical study and an annotated bibliography of information" (1970). It was a strategic framework for future growth and included a "Don't Build" chart noting where not to build and why.[48] Likewise, in exploring options for a new student center at McMaster University in Hamilton, Ontario (1970), it was eventually decided that instead of constructing a new "single student center," Hamilton Hall, a centrally located building at the heart of the campus, could be renovated and better linked urbanistically with existing amenities. The firm's report illustrates the space between Hamilton Hall and University Hall as a busy street under an arched glazed atrium, the whole space conducive to what the report described as "happenings."[49]

In each of these projects, the campus was acknowledged as an urban system that required reinforcement through strategic gestures based in urban design rather than architectural composition. On other occasions, landscape was adopted as a conceptual foil to complement an existing urban condition.

---

46   Chetham, "The New Smith College Museum of Art," 235.
47   "School of Design Requests $2 million in U.S. Funds," *The Harvard Crimson*, October 11, 1965.
48   John Andrews Architect; Architects and David H. Scott Consultants, "Tactical Study: The Development of a Planning Process: University of Minnesota, St. Paul Campus," report, Toronto, 1970. See also Roger Du Toit quoted in "University of Minnesota: St. Paul Campus," *Progressive Architecture* (February 1973): 74.

In a feasibility study undertaken in 1970 by the Andrews office for the hilltop campus of Tufts University in Medford, Massachusetts, the expansion of the behavioral sciences department was designed, as Andrews's partner John Simpson described, so that the "new building actually becomes sort of a very large staircase, and can grow around the brow of the hill without interfering with the spaces between existing buildings."[50] In this way, the Memorial Steps (1929), the handsome monumental entrance to the campus from College Avenue, designed by the Olmsted brothers, would be maintained. A proposed building with skylighted corridors and trafficable roof terraces stepped up the slope and around its contours, leaving the old quadrangles and the heart of the 1852 campus intact. The project, which was never built, earned a Canadian Architect Yearbook Award for architectural excellence in 1971.[51]

The firm's proposals for the Library-Instructional Center at Sarah Lawrence College (1967) in Bronxville, New York, presented a completely different emphasis on the overtly context-driven starting points of these previous schemes, due in part to the interests of the British-trained partners working on the project, Bob Anderson and Tony Parsons, and the college's expressed desire for flexible and physically connected teaching spaces. A liberal arts college for women, the campus was situated in a residential area zoned for single-family dwellings, with a height limit of 35 feet (10.7 meters) above grade and only masonry and glass permitted as external materials. The brief was extensive: a 250,000-volume library, classrooms, laboratories, art studios, and a 175-seat auditorium. A typical plan cell of unpartitioned flexible space of 42 feet 6 inches by 42 feet 6 inches (13 meters by 13 meters) was developed. Andrews's plan for the Library-Instructional Center meanders across the site based on a repetitive unit of three general flexible-space cells linked by service strips (10-feet [3-meters] wide) and a service core located on the inside of the L-shape that is formed by three linked square cells—in effect a tartan grid with service cores attached. Larger specific-use spaces like the auditorium and smaller specific-use spaces like science preparation rooms could be added in the future. The final massing was unassuming, nonhierarchical, and picturesque in form and silhouette. In February 1970, in *Architectural Record*, critic Robert Jensen highlighted the clear difference in this project from other Andrews projects like the Cameron Offices in Belconnen, Metro Centre in Toronto, and Gund Hall at Harvard, and he related it to the work being done contemporaneously by Alfred Newman in Israel and Skidmore, Owings & Merrill's Walter Netsch.[52]

While the Sarah Lawrence College project was ultimately shelved, the Andrews office's creation of its own form of "field theory" through generative geometries was refined in further educational and office projects. Significantly, Tony Parsons, working in association with Ernie Ross of the Cleveland firm Ross Yamane Manggrum, reapplied the notion of an open field of modules in the Andrews office's design for the School of Art at Kent State University (1972) in Kent, Ohio, but in a much more simplified form. The architects worked from a 1968 document, "The Space Problem," prepared by the School of Art, and proposed that a building located next to the existing sawtooth art building be completed in two phases. The first comprised an art gallery, two large lecture halls, a research center, and

---

49   John Andrews Architects, "McMaster University Centre Summary Report," 1970; Mark Osbaldeston, *Unbuilt Hamilton* (Toronto: Dundern Press, 2016), figure 16-8. See also William Bennet, quoted in "McMaster Student Center: A No-Build Decision," *Progressive Architecture*, (February 1973): 64.

50   "Tufts Behavioral Sciences Building: discreet infill," *Progressive Architecture* (February 1973): 65.

51   Stefan Novakovic, "They're 50," *Canadian Architect*, January 2, 2018, https://www.canadianarchitect.com/canadian-architect-awards-50/.

52   Robert Jensen, "Sarah Lawrence Library – Instructional Center," *Architectural Record* 147, no. 2 (February 1970): 143–46. Netsch's "field theory" and his design for the Behavioral Science and Science & Engineering Buildings at the University of Illinois's Chicago Circle campus was reviewed by John Morris Dixon in the same issue of *Architectural Forum* in which Kenneth B. Smith reviewed the South Residences at Guelph. See John Morris Dixon, "Campus City Continued," *Architectural Forum* (December 1968): 28–43.

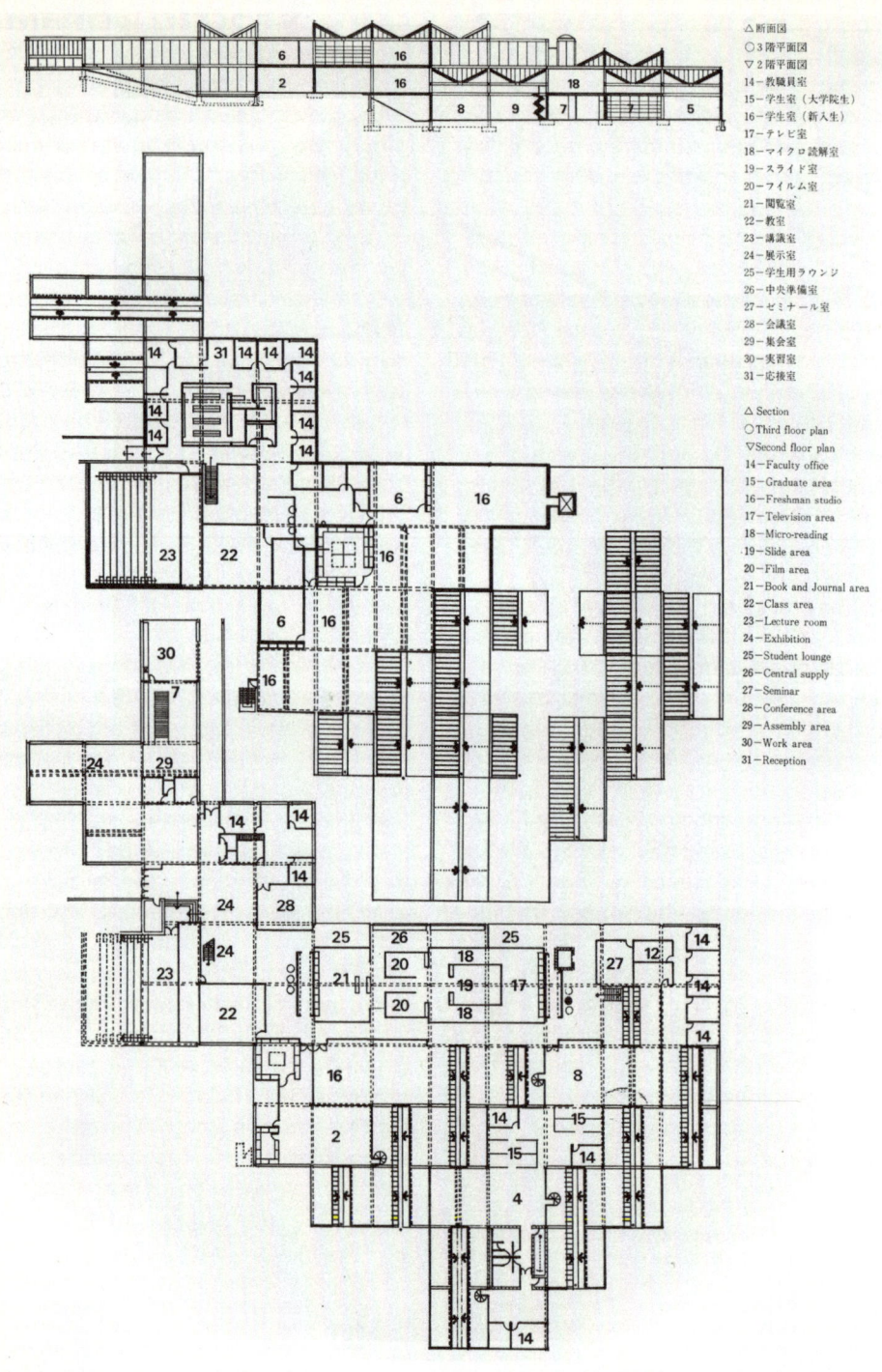

FIG. 10 Plan and section, School of Art, Kent State University, Kent, Ohio, 1970–72. John Andrews Architects in association with Ross Yamane Manggrum.

studio spaces with outdoor sculpture-making courts; a second phase, containing rooms for craft, sculpture, and additional studios, never eventuated. Though the project was approved in February 1968, construction did not begin until spring 1971.[53] With butterfly roofs, a simple post-and-beam frame, and square modules of 25 by 25 feet (7.6 meters by 7.6 meters), the plan could grow in any direction and remained anchored urbanistically by a bridge connection to the upper landscape level of the Kent State campus. [FIG. 10]

Light and ventilation determined the shape of "ideal" modules for making art: naturally lit studios framed in white painted steel, accessed by steel spiral stairs, and clad entirely in standard units of Kalwall insulated translucent cladding spilled across an undulating site.[54] The Andrews office used Kalwall to great effect at Scarborough College and the D. B. Weldon Library. At Kent State, pigmentation and insulation between the prefabricated Kalwall panels varied to achieve different qualities of light and color. The result was a luminous, almost golden warehouse for the teaching of art. [FIG. 11] Sited on the edge of the Commons, the location of the infamous May 4, 1970, student demonstrations against the Vietnam War, and looking toward Taylor Hall, where four students were shot dead and nine others wounded, the School of Art might have marked a new beginning not just for the university but also for university life across the United States. The Kent State Massacre must have seemed to John Andrews a vindication of his decision to leave North America the year before and raise his children in Australia.

BUILDINGS FOR EDUCATION IN AUSTRALIA: TOAD HALL AND "RESSIE 2"

When Andrews left Canada for Australia in 1969, many of the university commissions in North America were still on the drawing board in various stages, and his Canadian partners frequently oversaw the buildings to completion. Andrews trekked back and forth across the Pacific to view the buildings and oversee some, especially Gund Hall, but his focus turned toward Australia, especially for his largest commission to date, the Cameron Offices at Belconnen for the Australian Bureau of Statistics and the National Capital Development Commission. At the same time, Andrews, now based at Palm Beach in Sydney, earned new commissions for educational buildings, first in the Australian Capital Territory and then in other Australian states.

Across Australia in the 1960s, the tertiary education sector experienced unprecedented expansion and accordingly a demand for new campuses and new buildings.[55] Andrews caught the end of this boom, which also coincided with student activism, the embrace of freer lifestyles, and a desire to escape traditional power structures.[56] Students wanted their independence recognized and their voices heard, and that translated into a desire to live on campus as they wished rather than as others thought they should. Thus, when Student Residences B at the Australian National University (ANU) in Canberra (later officially named Toad Hall) opened in April 1974, it numbered among the early examples in Australia of a self-catering university residence hall mainly for postgraduate students. Students Diane Fieldes and Adrian Baddeley wrote in the ANU student newspaper, *Woroni*, in February 1975: "My old Warden (Warder?) wouldn't let me stick up a poster, let alone a towel rail. At Toad you have

---

53 Nicholas Brown, "A New Look on Campus: School of Art to Open New Building," *Daily Kent Stater*, April 13, 1972; "Art Building Dedication Tomorrow," *Daily Kent Stater*, April 9, 1971); Eugenia Robbins, "Art News from Colleges and Elsewhere," *Art Journal* 30, no. 2 (Winter 1970/1971): 206.

54 Kalwall was developed in the United States by inventor and industrialist Robert Keller in 1955. Significant examples of its use included the US Pavilion, World's Fair, Brussels, Belgium (1958) by Edward Durell Stone; New York State Pavilion Skyroof, Flushing Meadow, New York, United States (1964) by Philip Johnson; and St. Louis Abbey, Creve Coeur, Missouri, United States (1962) by Gyo Obata of Hellmuth Obata & Kassabaum (HOK), with the Italian architect and engineer Pier Luigi Nervi serving as consultant.

55 The rise and development of the postwar university in Australia is outlined in Andrew Saniga and Robert Freestone, eds., *Campus: Building Modern Australian Universities* (Nedlands, WA: UWA Publishing, 2022).

56 Andrew Saniga and Hannah Lewi, "*Carte Blanche* on Campus," *Fabrications* 27, no. 3 (2017): 322.

so much more control. That is the whole idea of Toad."⁵⁷

Andrews put forth a similar opinion: "A normal residence still treats students as children whereas society requires that they be adults. Apartment living was what students wanted, but on the open market, could not afford."⁵⁸ The project evolved from early user group meetings that, unusually, included students. A five-level masonry structure with its uppermost level crenellated with balconies open to the sky, Student Residences B was designed to be built in two stages, which together embraced, boomerang-like, Sullivan's Creek.⁵⁹ The Andrews office was trying to make sense of the campus as an urban organism, attempting to physically frame the creek and the sports fields beyond as a giant outdoor room with the student residences forming its southern boundary.

As time went on, the budget shrank and so too did the building program and the ambitious aspirations to embrace the landscape. Instead, the arrangement of student rooms was refined, and Andrews concentrated on a self-contained urbanism within the building itself. The final complex of load-bearing brown brick, on which construction began in 1973, developed externally as a series of serrated tower-like forms set back from the creek with a foreground of mature poplar and willow trees, which encouraged the first residents to adopt the name Toad Hall.⁶⁰ Inside and up close, the building is decidedly urban at ground level, with communal laundries located adjacent to a series of six stair towers, all accessed from the open-air undercroft street and each rising through six conjoined "towers." On the upper floors, two five-person "apartments" share a communal kitchen, bathrooms, and a lounge space (effectively one 10-person community space per tower floor). A narrow corridor connects each tower with its neighbor. What Andrews achieved in this coeducational residence hall was a balance of community and privacy and a level of independence for students. In many respects, it borrows from the Oxbridge "staircase" typology—a collection of four to six rooms grouped around a staircase rather than a corridor and which formed a social unit—but further enables students to form small self-contained communities of 10 students per floor. Students liked it.⁶¹

With the dining halls of Guelph and Brock no longer required, the conceptual idea behind Toad Hall was more akin to that of conjoined affordable urban housing. Another difference is that in the North American examples, invariably for climatic reasons, the major circulation routes are "internal streets." By contrast, in Australia, Andrews made the "street," on the ground floor at least, external and unenclosed: an undercroft space where students could park bicycles, do their washing, and enter the residence hall anywhere along its length.⁶² [FIG. 13]

The success of Toad Hall was such that it was considered soon after its opening an exemplar of the form of affordable student housing that was desperately needed in Canberra.⁶³ The strategy of defining an urban community within a single complex on an open landscape site also informed another Andrews design for student housing, at the campus of the Canberra College of Advanced Education (CCAE, now the University of Canberra), established in 1967 in the satellite suburb of Bruce. Andrews gained this commission in 1973 through Leighton Constructions, the firm then building Toad Hall; the CCAE project was a design-build package in which the architect was assigned to the builder rather than the client, an arrangement that Andrews would later regret. As at Toad Hall, the notion of a shared student "apartment" was adopted. In CCAE Council reports, the German

57 Diane Fieldes and Adrian Baddeley, "Toad Responds," *Woroni*, February 24, 1975.
58 Taylor and Andrews, *John Andrews*, 126.
59 Site Plan, Student Residence and Continuing Education Centre for the Australian National University, John Andrews Architects, 47 Colborne Street, Toronto, Canada, dated March 19, 1971, and initialed A.M.
60 *ANU Reporter* August 23, 1974.
61 Di (surname not provided), "Tales of the Toad," *Woroni*, June 15, 1974.
62 In 1978, the ground floor was enclosed. Toad Hall, Australian National University, Heritage Management Plan, September 2010, 14–16.
63 "New Reid House Plan Put to Ministers," *Canberra Times*, November 25, 1974.

term *Studentenheim* was adopted to describe this form of student living, a concept already successfully explored in the design and construction of CCAE Residential Group 1 (1972) by Hassell, McConnell and Partners, on a site next to Andrews's residence hall.[64]

Hassell, McConnell and Partners planned CCAE in 1967 as a typically modernist campus. It is an academic center with north–south pedestrian spines and a separate residential precinct set amid bushland; the academic center was considered "urban" while the housing was "pastoral." Andrews produced the opposite. For Residence Group 2 (nicknamed "Ressie 2"), he packed a series of 27 six-bedroom self-catering apartments on a sloping site facing north. Completed in 1974, the housing stepped gently down the slope, with groups of apartments separated by narrow pedestrian streets, like a Mediterranean hill town. [FIG. 12]

Differing from the condensed verticality of Toad Hall and Guelph, this form of student housing is more attuned to the openness of its landscape. The whole "Ressie 2" complex is single-story and made a virtue of its constant relationship with the ground. Covered porches at the "front" and "back" doors of each apartment, in conjunction with the stepped streets and multiple landings, provide a truly human aspect to the development.[65] They were described by Andrews, in a telling moment of theoretical candor, as "just some of those little Hertzbergian businesses of stoops and places to stop and gather and meet."[66]

EXPANDING INTERSTATE

By 1974, John Andrews International garnered substantial and diverse commissions in Australia and expanded beyond its main Palm Beach office to branch offices in Canberra and Brisbane.[67] The increasing scale of

11

12

64 Canberra College of Advanced Education, Council, *Report of Council for 1971*, presented June 30, 1972; printed 1973, no. 128, 9.
65 "Student Residence, Canberra College, Canberra," *Canadian Architect* (July 1976): 34–36. Arthur Robb and Bruce James were project architects.
66 Taylor and Andrews, *John Andrews*, 131.

FIG. 11   Exterior, School of Art, Kent State University.
FIG. 12   Aerial view, Student Residences, Canberra College of Advanced Education, Canberra, Australian Capital Territory, Australia, 1973–1974.

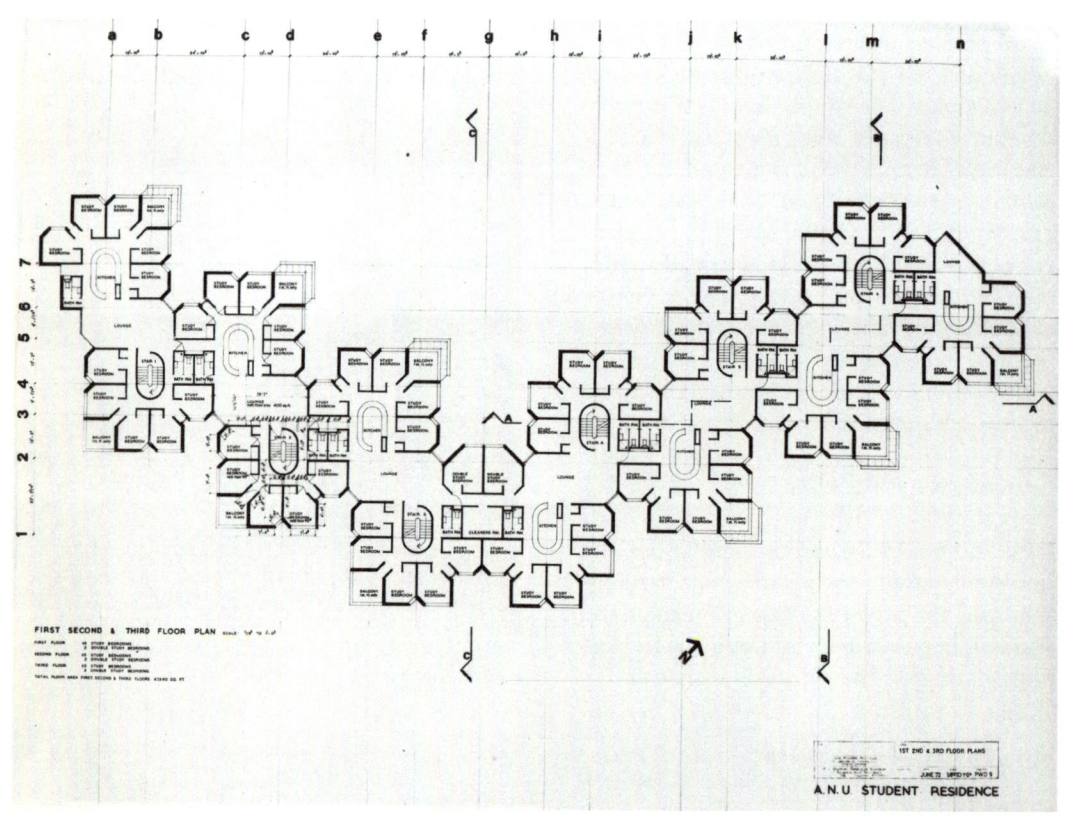

FIG. 13   Plan, Toad Hall, Australian National University, Canberra, Australian Capital Territory, Australia, 1971–1974.

commissions that the office began to acquire in the mid-1970s required various senior staff across a number of states. For example, John Simpson, who was responsible for the second stage of Scarborough College (1969) and, like Andrews, had also relocated to Australia, was put in charge of the Brisbane office. He was with Andrews and Peter Courtney one of three partners in John Andrews International. Simpson soon became largely responsible for all of the office's Queensland work, including masterplans and buildings for the University of Queensland, Griffith University, and colleges of advanced education in Ipswich, Kelvin Grove, Brisbane, and Toowoomba (see chapter 10).

In Western Australia, the Andrews office was commissioned as consulting design architects to design a new high school (1977) at Mandurah, a postwar coastal town 72 kilometers south of Perth. Running the job was the Perth-based office of Neil Loftus and Graham Walker, both former employees of the Andrews office. Like the CCAE student housing, the high school is another single-story "mat" but on a completely flat site. [FIG. 14] Dictating the design was a series of seven covered walkways or "streets" running north–south, each separated by a width of two classrooms. The result was a densely planned modular "city" of classrooms in which natural lighting and ventilation was achieved through south-facing skylights and complemented by a roof-cooling system supplied by bore-water reticulation.[68] Designated at concept stage as a "mall," densely planted courtyards meandered across the school's "urban grid"—a loosely diagonal landscape spine that retained an important copse of trees and connected the school's space-frame entry with its gathering and assembly space. Surrounding this "urban square" were the library, gymnasium, and performing arts center.

The Mandurah high school had a different arrangement from the centralized, contained aspects of Andrews's Sault Sainte Marie and Bellmere School designs in which the gymnasium served as the school's "heart."

A distinguishing aspect of the Mandurah high school design was its focus on passive low-energy design, an issue that the Australian architecture profession began to address in earnest after the 1973 oil crisis. The school's plan, in many respects, was a miniaturized version of the Andrews office's designs for the low-energy satellite town of Monarto (1975), outside Adelaide, which fielded the expert environmental input of other protagonists, such as mechanical engineer Don Thomas.[69] For Monarto, Andrews's scheme comprises an interconnected network of low-rise office buildings with courtyard pools. The pools provide evaporative cooling and are also intended to have a calming psychological effect on the buildings' users. Similarly, at Mandurah, various strategies were put in place to provide localized microclimates to cool the indoor and outdoor spaces of the sprawling campus. Photographs of the model of the developed design show the entire complex surrounded by grassed earth berms for wind protection, while concept drawings indicate shallow, water-carrying, culvert-like concrete roofs supported by a central line of concrete columns that covered the walkways. These water-cooling roofs, interconnected across the campus, spill their contents into ponds, where convective air movement encourages evaporative cooling. Sadly never realized—as with Monarto—the proposal for the Mandurah high school may have been over ambitious, but it was a brilliant and complex solution that encompassed Andrews's career-long interests in climate-responsive design and his long-held beliefs in the urban qualities of his buildings for education.

67   For a description of the office culture of John Andrews, see Philip Goad, "The Translation of Practice: The Offices of John Andrews in Toronto (1962–74) and Palm Beach (1969–90)," *Proceedings of the Society of Architectural Historians, Australia and New Zealand: 31, Translation*, ed. Christoph Schnoor (2014): 691–701.

68   The 1978 planning of the Bateman Catholic Centre, Perth, Western Australia, also unbuilt, followed principles explored at Mandurah high school.

69   Jane Grant, Paul Walker, and David Nichols, "What's It All About, Monarto? John Andrews, Boris Kazanski, and the Centre of South Australia's Unbuilt Second 'New Town,'" *UHPH_14: Landscapes and ecologies of urban and planning history, Proceedings of the 12th Conference of the Australasian Urban History/Planning History Group*, eds. Morten Gjerde and Emina Petrović (2014): 255–69.

Loftus and Walker collaborated again with John Andrews International as consulting design architects on a Catholic center (1978) in Bateman, a suburb south of Perth, following the same urban and climatic design principles explored at Mandurah high school. However, again, the project was not realized. A decade later, a school designed by the collaborative team was finally built in Western Australia. Located in a new suburb in Perth's north, Padbury Senior High School opened in 1987 and was completed in stages until 1990 to cater to its 1,000 students. Padbury works on an urban system that is different from the dense Mandurah "mat." It is configured as a set of four discrete urban clusters, or sub-schools, plus discrete administration buildings, all joined by a cranked street grid of corrugated steel–roofed, barrel-vaulted covered walkways and separated by landscaped courtyards. In its plan and relaxed disposition of buildings, the Padbury school expresses the landscape and climatic intentions of Andrews's earlier works and his persistent beliefs in spaces of community and propinquity, but not through the semiotic references to "suburb" found in contemporaneous school designs in Australia. Andrews remained faithful to his earlier precepts and especially to lessons learned from within his own circle of practice, most importantly, at the time, his embrace of domestic homestead roofs at his own farmhouse at Eugowra (1980).

Faith in seriality and system influenced another 1980s commission for the Andrews office. For some of the first buildings erected on the new campus of the Australian Defence Force Academy (ADFA), a 52-hectare site next to the Royal Military Training College at Duntroon in Canberra, the Andrews office followed a similar planning philosophy to that of Padbury. The construction of the ADFA campus in the early 1980s followed masterplans developed in the late 1970s by the Melbourne firm Yuncken Freeman, and its buildings involved many of Australia's best-known architects, including McConnel Smith & Johnson Architects, Daryl Jackson, and John Andrews International.[70] The 1981 brief to Andrews stipulated two teaching buildings devoted to physics and chemistry and common teaching, with the construction to commence in 1983 and be completed in 1985.[71] The Andrews office designed two separate "cluster" buildings based around cruciform-planned circulation routes with barrel-vaulted roofs to which two- and three-story blocks are attached. At the intersection of these routes are services and vertical circulation and diagonal entry points to "special activities" such as laboratories, while staff offices and smaller teaching spaces are "clipped" as L-shaped blocks onto the circulation routes, thus forming internalized courtyards. As with all of Andrews's Australian buildings for education, the open field of the local landscape lends itself to a relaxed urban system, easily repeated and seamlessly integrated with the simple grid pattern of ADFA's campus masterplan.

The programmatic planning strategies employed at the open sites of Padbury and ADFA were deployed a decade later at Andrews's alma mater, the University of Sydney, but at a reduced scale and in completely different urban circumstances—and, significantly, with a much-changed architectural language. The Veterinary Science Conference Centre (VSCC), designed and documented between 1995 and 1997, was completed in 1998.[72] It was Andrews's last building designed for education and the last completed building of his practice. Located in the northwest precinct of the university's Camperdown campus, the Andrews design completed a courtyard formed by the McMaster Building (1931), Walter Liberty Vernon's J. D. Stewart Building (1913), and the veterinary hospital (1967), and which celebrated, in the courtyard's center, the much-loved polygonal "Round House" (1924)

70 The Australian Defence Force Academy was officially opened on December 11, 1986.
71 File 016: Australian Defence Force Academy (ADFA), Campbell, Australian Capital Territory (1981–1983), PXD 1508, Folders 44-51, John Andrews fonds, State Library of New South Wales.
72 File 114: Veterinary Science Conference Centre, University of Sydney (1995–1997), PXD 1508, Folders 287–289, John Andrews fonds, State Library of New South Wales; "Survey 4: Veterinary Science Conference Centre," *Construction Review*, May 1997, 8.

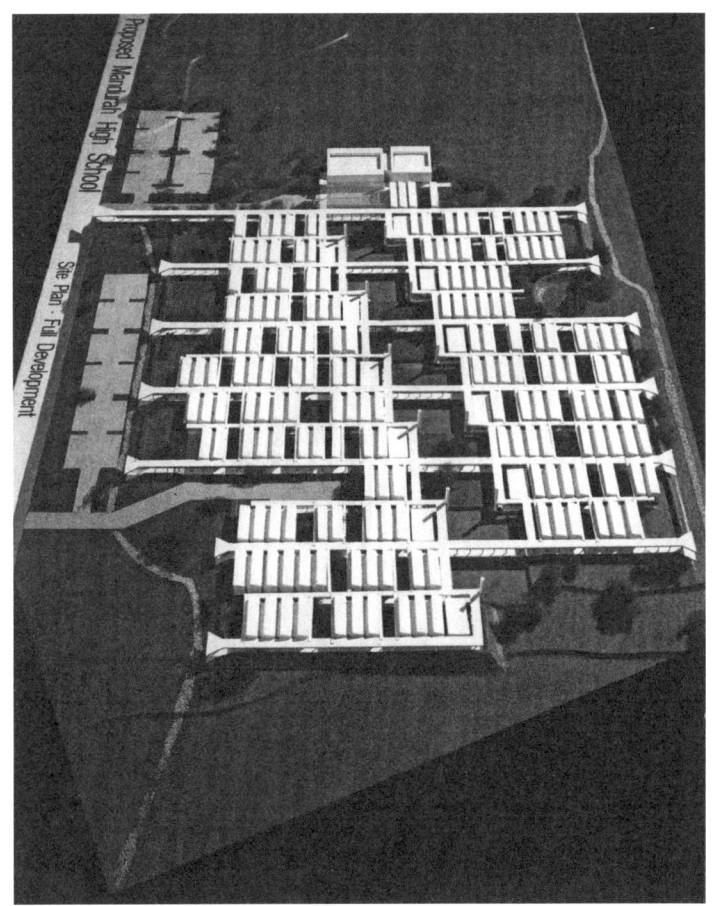

14

15

FIG. 14 Model, Mandurah high school (unbuilt), Mandurah, Perth, Western Australia, Australia, 1977.
FIG. 15 Model of proposed stages 1 and 2, RMIT Library and Student Union, Royal Melbourne Institute of Technology (now RMIT University), Melbourne, Victoria, Australia, 1977–1981.

designed by Leslie Wilkinson. The choice of red brick and golden, sand-colored concrete for lintels, pilotis, and plinth is a direct contextual reference to Vernon's design, but the building's plan and its hovering first floor are signature Andrews. At the building's corner, as was typical of Andrews's planning, is the diagonal main entry, signified now not by off-form concrete but a brick and glass tower form. Inside, a lobby space provides access to elevators, stairs, and a 250-seat lecture theater that was embraced by the L-shaped block. As with all of Andrews's buildings for education, legible wayfinding and context-consolidating gestures strengthened the campus's ability to possess the qualities of scale and texture of a larger urban system. As with the D. B. Weldon Library, Smith College Arts Center, and the Tufts proposal, Andrews recognized and was prepared to defer to an existing urban system.

While the Padbury, ADFA, and VSCC projects went ahead with little fuss, one of Andrews's commissions in Melbourne had faltered some years before. The Royal Melbourne Institute of Technology Library and Student Union (1984) is an important project to close this chapter for several reasons.[73] First, there is the understandably prominent presence accorded to the project in the 1982 monograph on Andrews, in which the architect was arguably the most articulate in print on his design thinking and at the height of his standing within the Australian architecture profession. Second, the project marks the return of Evan Walker, friend and collaborator on the Guelph residence halls. Walker sat on RMIT's council from 1973 to 1983, served as RMIT's president from 1977 to 1979, and was instrumental in awarding Andrews the commission. Third is the design itself, in which Andrews brought together his long-held strategies of urban design with the compositional strategies of an open, flexible system. Fourth is the trajectory of the project in the four decades after its completion, in which the building has survived only as a fragment of its original self, though its urban DNA—at ground level at least—has remained intact.

The brief for the new RMIT Library and Student Union—located in Melbourne's central business district, on a site of greater urban intensity than the University of Toronto Student Union site of 10 years prior—initially entailed renovating two upper-level library floors of the existing Casey Wing (1969), a 13-story late-Brutalist slab block designed by the local Melbourne firm Bates, Smart, McCutcheon, and building student union facilities on the vacant site immediately to the south. In Andrews's words, his team "turned the whole brief around," and in doing so also devised a solution to the existing challenge of a one-and-a-half floor-level change from east to west across the site.[74] They proposed instead an infill building with student union facilities at a half-level below Swanston Street to the west that connects with the floor plates of the Casey Wing and, two levels above, with Bowen Street to the east. Above these student facilities, Andrews then proposed a new library and additional academic spaces on another three floors as well as a penthouse set back from the street, which consists of skylighted teaching and studio spaces.

Connecting the levels diagonally up and across the site is an open-air pedestrian "street" ramp that begins in a laneway-scaled space at the south. Angled at 45 degrees, the broad lane-width ramp doglegs up and underneath an enclosed "bridge" before landing at a forecourt level with Bowen Street. On Bowen Street there are two identifiable entry points, for the new library and the new student lounge and cafeterias.

Integral to that diagonal sweep of pedestrian circulation is the setting of the whole building's column grid at 45 degrees to the street grid. This creates vertical triangular volumes that allow light to penetrate a deep plan, and on Swanston Street it creates a serrated street edge, again maximizing the ability of light to enter the building while not presenting a completely glazed facade to the west. [FIG. 15] It also creates triangular-shaped outdoor

---

73 File 29: Royal Melbourne Institute of Technology, Melbourne (1972, 1975–1984), MLMSS 10302, Boxes 389–407, John Andrews fonds, State Library of New South Wales.

74 Taylor and Andrews, *John Andrews*, 158.

public "rooms" or "places" at ground level, two of which support dramatic, imposing cylindrical concrete stair towers. The architectural language was minimal: an exposed concrete frame articulated at its corners with exposed circular concrete columns was given special emphasis with reverse indentations of clear glass to allow diagonal views of the street from inside the building. And on Swanston Street, full-height glass brick walls between the floor slabs provide acoustic and thermal insulation. Throughout, terra-cotta tiles indicate major circulation areas, and where practical, all internal walls are clear floor-to-ceiling glass. RMIT Library and Student Union was to be an open and transparent hive.

Of key importance to Andrews was the notion of connecting the building to city life—and activating the street and ground level. In describing his intentions for the library and student union in 1982, Andrews could have been describing his entire oeuvre of buildings for education and often what he faced at the beginnings of most of these projects:

> At the moment, there is no apparent organization, no system of movement through the campus. This was an obvious opportunity to pull the whole thing together. It puts the library at the heart of the campus, it puts the major student facilities at the heart of the campus, and it pulls all the ground level pedestrian circulation together into the one system, maximizing the opportunity for convenience and contact. That is an old story for me. It is still what it is all about regardless of whether it is infill or jewel; whether it is in Melbourne or Toronto. It is still the major genesis of any building.[75]

A DIFFERENT HISTORY

In what ought to have been a climactic conclusion to the 1982 monograph, instead only the first stage of the RMIT project was built: the student union facilities and the ramped street from Swanston to Bowen Street. The sawtooth edge of the Andrews building sat two-and-a-half stories high, pancake-like, on the broad Swanston Street site, well below its projected five stories and dwarfed even by historic Storey Hall (1887) to the south. By 1982, architecture culture in Melbourne also irrevocably shifted toward recognizing the historic city, not just in terms of its spatial morphology, but also in terms of its semiotic capacity. In a twist of fate, Andrews's unfinished student union came to be regarded as the antithesis of the future: it "turned its back to the street"—the 45-degree angle seeming not to be "of" the city—and the steps down to its entry points below street level were dubbed "external ashtrays." This, of course, was not an entirely fair assessment, but a new generation of thinkers across Melbourne's architectural culture had moved toward its own version of postmodernism.

In 1994, local architects Edmond and Corrigan succeeded in locating RMIT's Central Library and other academic functions above the union, where Andrews had intended to place them, and added multiple levels above, as Andrews had also intended. However, the architectural language was completely different: a billboard of representation on Swanston Street, complete with a cornice and a three-dimensional flag, while out back a polychrome brick stair tower was attached to a new multistory facade of prefabricated concrete panels punctured by tall rectangular windows. Almost all the glass blocks were removed on the Swanston Street facade and replaced with clear or colored stained glass. Remarkably, the fundamental elements of Andrews's urban gestures remained intact.

The buildings for education designed by the John Andrews office between 1965 and 1998 constitute a significant transnational oeuvre. All bear comparison with contemporary exemplars around the world—some more than others—especially given the global boom in university-building from the early 1950s until the mid-1970s. The South Residences at the University of Guelph, for example, are notable for many aspects, including scale, speed of construction, and urban ambition. In

75   Ibid., 160.

Canada and the United States, there was no real comparison.[76] New research on Andrews may prove emerging affinities between his work and others, but there are dangers in doing so. Differences rather than similarities would be the result.

Recent architectural histories of the postwar decades favor the eloquent polemics of British- and European-based architect–urbanists and underplay the complexity of the theoretical mosaic at the end of the 1950s and into the 1960s.[77] They perpetuate an artificial division between CIAM and Team 10 and accentuate a Eurocentric focus for considering connections between architecture and urbanism. Looking at Andrews's buildings for education, one can see another history at play, one that refutes such a division. This body of work demonstrates the need to acknowledge a parallel trajectory of postwar experiments in architecture and the city in Canada, the United States, and Australia. By doing so, one can discern a history characterized by a special point in time, from the late 1950s to the early 1960s, when there was a global focus on the university—on campus design, buildings for learning, and the residential college. By implication, the utopian aims of the university community realizable at an urban scale revealed common goals and common themes in actual buildings and ambitious projects completed with astonishing rapidity, especially in Canada. Scarborough College was an important moment for the precocious Andrews, but the South Residences represent a pivotal point when Andrews, through collaboration with Evan Walker, brought together social purpose and architectural form to internalize dwelling, privacy, community, the street, and public urban space all within a single building. Over the ensuing decades, his buildings for education continued to negotiate existing urban systems, propose new ones, and to wrestle with the greenfields of the new postwar educational campus with innovation and experimentation. That so many of these ideas were realized is testament not just to John Andrews and his team but also to the commissioning educational institutions, which, in the spirit of the times, were committed to progress, change, and a better, more socially engaging life for their students.

---

76 For example, despite the apparent grandeur of its three-square parti, Louis Kahn's Erdman Hall (1965) at Bryn Mawr College, Pennsylvania, was dainty in size, with accommodation for only 130 female students. An international comparison architecturally and socially was the ziggurat forms of Denys Lasdun's residences (1966) for 684 students at the University of East Anglia. The staircase, as in Andrews's design, was a key linking element, but at East Anglia there was no connection to a generously scaled "internal street" nor "meeting places" as at Guelph. Lasdun's room designs were inflexible, with built-in beds, washbasins, and desks.

77 See for example, Sarah Williams Goldhagen and Rejean Legault, eds., *Anxious Modernisms: Experimentation in Postwar Architectural Culture* (Montreal: Canadian Centre for Architecture; Cambridge, MA: MIT Press, 2000); on Yona Friedman, see María Inés Rodríguez, ed., *Arquitectura con la gente, por la gente, para la gente* [Architecture with the People, by the People, for the People] (Barcelona: Actar, 2011); Tom Avermaete, *Another Modern: The Post-war Architecture and Urbanism of Candilis-Josic-Woods* (Rotterdam: NAi Publishers, 2005); and Tom Avermaete and Janina Gosseye, *Urban Design in the 20th Century: A History* (Zurich: gta Verlag, 2021).

FIG. 16 Student, South Residences, University of Guelph.

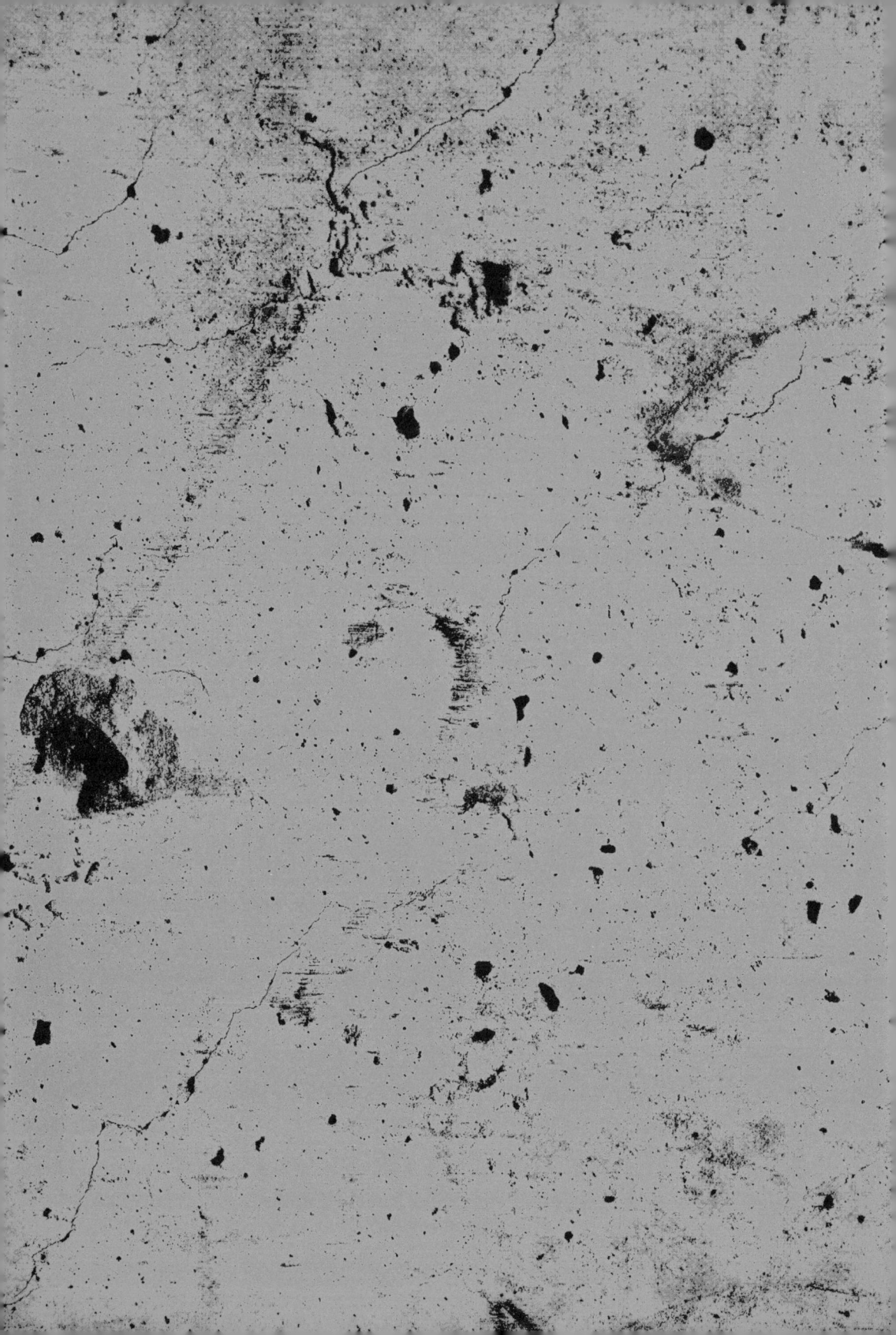

05

metro centre: the "very obvious job" that was never built[1]

by Paolo Scrivano

"Metro Centre was a very obvious job."[2] As one of the largest and most ambitious projects of John Andrews's career, Metro Centre was an imposing yet unaccomplished development plan for Toronto's downtown. Elaborated between 1968 and 1971, the scheme was also one of Andrews's first opportunities to design at urban scale in an already established context, confronting existing street patterns, traffic flows, and pedestrian movements. It was an "obvious" commission, as Andrews put it, since the problem it addressed—a large area of underused railway tracks dividing the city from Lake Ontario—was long overdue for consideration and the proposed scheme offered a straightforward solution. But, in other ways, Metro Centre was not an "obvious job." Its design unveils a complex and fascinating story that intersects with the history of a city experiencing crucial demographic, economic, and cultural transformation and that engages with essential aspects of the postwar debate over architecture and planning both in Canada and internationally.

METRO CENTRE, THE RAILWAYS, AND TORONTO'S WATERFRONT

If Metro Centre has remained somewhat overlooked in the history of architecture, it is definitively not because of its scale. The project was meant to cover a large area of land occupied by tracks serving Canada's two major railway companies and delimited by Front Street at its north, Yonge Street in the east, Bathurst Street in the west, and the Lakeshore Expressway at its south. The railyards were not just a particularly large expanse of land in a central part of the city but also a sizeable barrier between Lake Ontario and downtown Toronto.

The city's separation from the lakeshore dates to Toronto's founding at the beginning of the 19th century, when it was still called York.

Indeed, Toronto's growth was largely due to its access to the network of waterways of the St. Lawrence River basin, which favored the harbor's development into a commercial and industrial zone. The concentration of warehouses and factories in the areas along the lake led to the functional specialization of the waterfront and to a marked division between this part of the city and the residential zones located to the north. The arrival of railroads in the mid-19th century connected Toronto to destinations east and west and expanded industry and storage operations but further separated the lakeshore from downtown. This fracture would never be overcome. During the 1950s, the construction of the Lakeshore Expressway (renamed Gardiner Expressway in 1957), the elevated section of which still runs south of the railway tracks, amplified the disconnect between the city and the lake.[3]

PLANNING TORONTO'S DOWNTOWN IN THE POSTWAR YEARS

After the end of World War II, Toronto dramatically expanded, both demographically and physically. If in 1950 its population amounted to little more than one million, by the beginning of the following decade it doubled to surpass two million. Unlike other large North American metropolises at the time, however, Toronto was not facing inner-city decline, as planning historian Richard White has noted.[4] White writes that "Toronto's suburbs grew but not at the expense of the city," citing the slow adoption of car transportation, the resulting development of expressways, and the presence of a still productive fabric of small industries downtown among the reasons for this.[5] It is therefore not surprising that by the early 1960s an interest in the reorganization of Toronto's

---

1   Paolo Scrivano wishes to thank Noor Mens, Graeme Slaght, and Paul Walker for the help in collecting part of the documentation on which this essay is based.
2   Jennifer Taylor and John Andrews, *John Andrews: Architecture, a Performing Art* (Melbourne: Oxford University Press, 1982), 86.
3   On the Gardiner Expressway and the construction of Toronto's transportation infrastructure, see Richard White, *Urban Infrastructure and Urban Growth in the Toronto Region, 1950s to the 1990s* (Toronto: Neptis Foundation, 2003), 16–17.
4   Richard White, *Planning Toronto: The Planners, The Plans, Their Legacies, 1940–80* (Vancouver: UBC Press, 2016), 147–50.
5   Ibid., 147.

downtown began to take hold among planners and architects. In 1963, for example, the City of Toronto Planning Board published the report "Plan for Downtown Toronto," the result of four years of study.[6] Among other recommendations, the document suggested the formation of "sub-areas" based on functional specialization and indicated possible provisions, such as deeper setbacks for office buildings and lower density standards, to encourage developers to use vacant spaces. It also emphasized the importance of pedestrian paths and routes to revitalize the city center. [FIG. 1]

While the proposals included in the "Plan for Downtown Toronto" had little impact on municipal policies, among the problems the report singled out was the unresolved relationship between the city and its waterfront. The latter, as the document explains, "is another potential asset which for many years has been removed from both sight and contact by the broad swathe of railway trackage."[7] Indicating the entire area between the railroads and Lake Ontario as "The Lower Edge," the report recommended the construction of a transportation terminal integrated into a larger exchange hub. The proposed structure, which in many ways anticipated Metro Centre's scheme, would overcome the barrier formed by the tracks and the Gardiner Expressway "through a series of major connecting projects."[8] Four pedestrian plazas—one north and three south of the expressway—were to be placed on top of multistory garages accessible from the street by escalators and connected by walkways. Several office towers and a hotel completed the scheme.

Crucial to Toronto's transformation were the complex connections between the city's center and its outskirts. The prosperity of downtown lay in the balanced relation it could establish with the residential areas close to the center and the suburbs, a zero-sum game that could only be won through an adequate system of metropolitan communication. It is within this context that the planning board recommended the construction of the integrated transportation terminal to support the expansion of commuter services linking center and periphery. It was within this same context three years later, in 1966, that the Metropolitan Toronto and Region Transportation Study (MTARTS) insisted that commuter transit should focus on linking downtown and the suburbs.[9]

No doubt, interest in downtown was in the air. Almost at the same time as the release of "Plan for Downtown Toronto," a group of young architects and planners—Macy DuBois, Anthony Jackson, Donovan Pinker, Gerald Robinson, and Henry Sears—proposed an unofficial "Plan for Central Toronto."[10] The American-born DuBois had a special connection with Andrews since their days at the Harvard GSD and was part of the group, with Andrews, Bill Ireland, and Bill Morgan, that placed second in the Toronto City Hall competition in 1958.[11] With Andrews, DuBois also worked for one year at John B. Parkin Associates, assisting the firm in developing Viljo Revell's winning design for Toronto City Hall. The "Plan for Central Toronto" by DuBois and his colleagues was first published in *The Canadian Architect* in 1962;[12] shortly after, it appeared in *Ekistics*, the journal founded in 1955 by Constantinos Doxiadis and Jaqueline Tyrwhitt.[13] [FIG. 2]

6   City of Toronto Planning Board, *Plan for Downtown Toronto: A Report by the City of Toronto Planning Board* (Toronto: City of Toronto, 1963). See also White, *Planning Toronto*, 286–89; John Sewell, *Up Against City Hall* (Toronto: Lewis and Samuel, 1972), 183–88.
7   *Plan for Downtown Toronto*, 10.
8   Ibid., 47.
9   *Growth and Travel, Past and Present: A Study of the Basic Components of Growth in the Toronto-centred Region, and their Relationship to Travel Characteristics and Demand* (Toronto: Government of Ontario, 1966). On the Metropolitan Toronto and Region Transportation Study (MTARTS), see White, *Planning Toronto*, 222–32.
10 DuBois, Robinson, and Sears were architects, Pinker a planner, and Jackson an architectural historian.
11 On DuBois, see Paolo Scrivano, Mary Lou Lobsinger, Larry Richards, and E.R.A. Architects, "Macy DuBois: Designing in Toronto, Designing in Concrete: Interview with Macy DuBois," in Michael McClelland and Graeme Stewart, eds., *Concrete Toronto: A Guidebook to Concrete Architecture from the Fifties to the Seventies* (Toronto: Coach House Books, 2007), 88–95.
12 Macy DuBois, Anthony Jackson, Donovan Pinker, Gerald Robinson, and Henry Sears, "A Plan for Central Toronto," *Canadian Architect* (August 1961): 41–72.
13 Macy DuBois, Anthony Jackson, Donovan Pinker, Gerald Robinson, and Henry Sears, "A Plan for Central Toronto," *Ekistics* 15, no. 87 (February 1963): 86–93.

PROJECT FOR CORE OF THE WATERFRONT

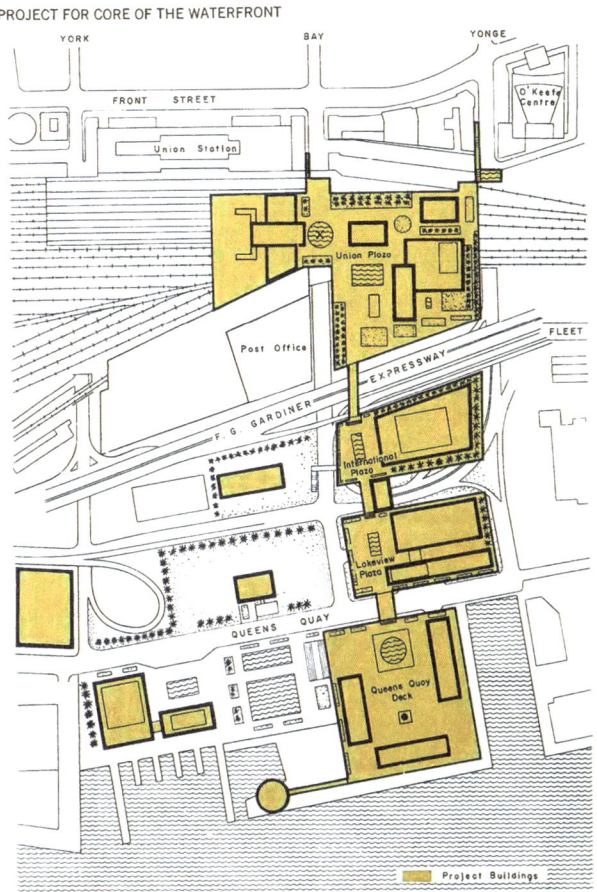

1

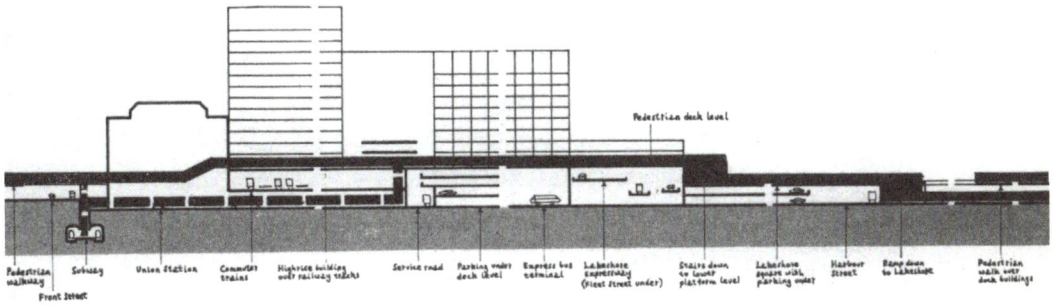

2

FIG. 1 Project for the core of the waterfront, Plan for Downtown Toronto, City of Toronto Planning Board, 1963.

FIG. 2 Cross section of the proposed intervention between Front Street and the lakeshore, Plan for Central Toronto, 1963.

The proposal called for concentrating commercial activities in the city, separating pedestrian and vehicle traffic, and preventing urban industry from leaving downtown. "Recapture the Bayfront" was among the declared aims to be achieved by reestablishing "visual and physical contact with the water" through an "upper-level pedestrian deck" that would unite the waterfront with the residential areas. The envisioned transportation terminal would have been placed under the pedestrian deck, with the Gardiner Expressway running within the structure. It is unclear if this plan had any relation with MTARTS. Presenting their initiative as an opportunity to suggest ideas that would promote change, the proposal's authors claimed that "no public plan exists for Central Toronto—nor is one even prepared."[14] This statement is difficult to believe since the City of Toronto Planning Board's "Plan for Downtown Toronto" was at least likely known by Anthony Jackson, editor of *The Canadian Architect* from 1959 to 1962 and therefore a fixture in the local professional scene.[15] The curious overlaps between the unofficial "Plan for Central Toronto" and the official "Plan for Downtown Toronto" marked a convergence of interests among architects and planners concerned not only with the question of the center but also with the fate of the railyards and the waterfront.

In the two decades before these two competing plans and the Metro Centre initiative itself, urban transformations in Toronto were haphazard, and the events leading to the realization of the Eaton Centre downtown are symptomatic of the dynamics that dominated planning during this period. Initially predicated on the demolition of the late-19th-century city hall by architect Edward J. Lennox, this proposal for a large shopping mall and office complex first ran into popular opposition and then, in 1967, was temporarily halted when the department store Eaton's withdrew from negotiations, apparently following disagreements with the city over the value of the land.[16] A desire to remodel Toronto was evident, yet the time was probably not ripe. As Richard White has noted, Toronto in the 1950s and 1960s was marked by a process of "cautious modernization" since "Toronto's civic leaders simply never 'thought big' as, say, Montreal's did in the 1960s."[17] Metro Centre was definitively a change of gear.

THE METRO CENTRE PROPOSAL

The development of a large-scale project for the downtown railyard was then a "very obvious job" since the problem was, in Andrews's words, "right under everybody's nose."[18] The site was under the noses of two railway companies—one state-controlled and the other privately owned—that had gradually moved freight, maintenance, and technical activities outside the city and that were also becoming increasingly aware of the real estate implications of their land holdings: jointly controlling a prominent piece of land in central Toronto, Canadian National Railway—a Crown corporation—and Canadian Pacific Railway eyed the opportunity to speculatively transform an area that had so far been limited to rail transportation operations. In April 1967 Canadian National and Marathon Realty Company Limited, a real estate subsidiary of Canadian Pacific Investments owned by Canadian Pacific Railway, commissioned the study for the redevelopment project.[19] While presenting the initiative in one of the first released documents as "an opportunity to create a lively and livable core in Metropolitan Toronto," Canadian National and Canadian Pacific betrayed their real goal in declaring their willingness to examine "the full potential

14 Ibid., 88.
15 Years later, DuBois stated that the plan intended to start a "discussion about urban design" by putting together a proposal that could "attract some attention." See Scrivano, Lobsinger, Richards, and E.R.A. Architects, "Macy DuBois: Designing in Toronto, Designing in Concrete," 95.
16 Mathers and Haldenby Architects (Alvan Sherlock Mathers and Eric Wilson Haldenby). See White, *Planning Toronto*, 286–89, and Sewell, *Up Against City Hall*, 97. The Eaton Centre opened in 1977 following a different design by Eberhard Zeidler and Bregman + Hamann Architects.
17 White, *Planning Toronto*, 189.
18 Taylor and Andrews, *John Andrews*, 86.
19 *Metro Centre Development Plan and Programme: A Study for the Development of Canadian National and Canadian Pacific Railway Lands in Central Toronto* (Toronto: Community Development Consultants Limited, May 1968).

of developing some 200 acres—now largely confined to railway uses."[20]

However, the distribution of land ownership represented a significant obstacle. While the railway companies claimed to have the entire site under control, the intricacies of property rights and lease agreements presented a much more complex situation.[21] John Sewell, a politician who—as we shall see—became one of the most vocal opponents of Metro Centre, would use these unresolved ownership questions as a powerful argument. Recounting his tenure as city councilor from 1969 to 1972 in his book *Up Against City Hall*, Sewell points at a number of constraints, the most important being the city and province's titles over crucial pieces of land within the site.[22]

These difficulties did little to deter action, and to support their development aspirations, Canadian National and Canadian Pacific created the joint venture Metro Centre Developments Limited. Stewart M. Andrews, a developer who was involved in the venture through a company called Community Development Consultants Limited, was named its president. John Andrews Architects and Webb Zerafa Menkès Housden were appointed to develop the scheme.[23] The latter firm had been established in 1961 by former associates of Peter Dickinson, a leading modernist architect whose mark on the Canadian scene was attenuated by his untimely death at the age of 35.[24]

The proposal that Metro Centre advanced was of an unprecedented scale, of which its promoters were well aware: "By any standard, Metro Centre promises to be one of the most ambitious and important downtown developments ever undertaken," proclaimed a document released in May 1968. And it was an ambitious one, since, as Richard White notes, Canadian railway companies had a history of "acting independently from governments" regarding land use, in many cases having owned the land "for longer than the Government of Canada had existed."[25]

A key element in the Metro Centre proposal was the outline of a "Transportation Terminal" that integrated existing and new transportation systems. The idea was to move all remaining freight operations to suburban districts, relocate equipment maintenance and train storage, and leave only passenger-handling operations for Canadian National, Canadian Pacific, and GO Transit (the commuter railway company owned by the Government of Ontario). The proposal made reorganizing regional transportation both a practical and symbolic goal, inspiring the Metro Centre logo reproduced on brochures circulated at the time, "a series of concentric rings representing radiation of [Metro Centre's] influence to downtown Toronto, the city proper, the Metro limits, the region beyond, and finally all of Southern Ontario."[26] [FIGS. 3–5]

The scheme, however, also made important provisions for activities other than transportation. The Transportation Terminal would be paired with a "Commercial Core" located between the terminal and the southeast corner of the existing downtown district, to which it would have been connected through pedestrian walkways. This commercial area was specified as "catering to the development of office buildings and retail shopping facilities." The area to the west of Metro Centre was expected to accommodate a residential community—a "city-within-a-city" with a "wide variety of multiple-housing types" ranging from low-density dwellings to small apartments in medium- and high-rise units—as well as schools, shops, and social services.[27] [FIGS. 6–7] Planned to contain some 9,300 units and house around 20,000 inhabitants, the residential area

20 Ibid., 2. The development area totaled 187 acres.
21 Ibid., 9–10.
22 Sewell, *Up Against City Hall*, 97–104.
23 John Andrews Architects and Webb Zerafa Menkès Housden received the commission in June 1967: "Metro Center, Toronto, Canada," *Architectural Record* 147, no. 2 (February 1970): 136.
24 "Webb Zerafa Menkès Housden Partnership," *The Canadian Encyclopedia,* https://www.thecanadianencyclopedia.ca/en/article/webb-zerafa-menkes-housden-partnership.
25 White, *Planning Toronto*, 289.
26 *Metro Centre: Summary of a Study for Development of Lands Owned by Canadian National and Canadian Pacific in Central Toronto* (Toronto: Community Development Consultants Limited, December 1968), 6.
27 *Metro Centre Development Plan and Programme*, 2.

was to encompass high-rise apartment blocks for singles and couples and low-rise housing for families. A strict separation between pedestrians and vehicles would characterize the local traffic.

Given the speculative nature of the investment, particular emphasis was placed on the portion of the estate intended to accommodate commercial and business functions and generate revenue. These included a hotel with 1,600 rooms, a convention and a trade center, areas for shopping, and office towers, all concentrated around Esplanade Street, a new thoroughfare running east–west that revived the old Esplanade Street, taken over by railway operations in the 1850s. Two separate office towers, both 36 stories high, were reserved for Canadian National and Canadian Pacific.[28] [FIGS. 8–9]

The planning document released in May 1968 also stated that a proposal was submitted to the Canadian Broadcasting Corporation (CBC) to establish its headquarters for English language services in a "Communications Area" on the premises of Metro Centre and that this proposal was "under active consideration."[29] Three main elements would characterize this area: an administrative office tower, a television and film production complex, and a transmission tower. Comprised of three reinforced concrete cylindrical shafts containing elevators, stairways, cable ducts, and equipment, the latter was envisaged to reach a height of 1,575 feet with its antennas, twice the height of the next tallest structure in Toronto.[30] An observation gallery and dining and lounge facilities were to be housed in a three-level deck at 1,200 feet. "The tower would give Toronto's skyline a new and exciting focal point," the report emphasized.[31]

The development program indicated five phases of intervention in a planned sequence permitting "the utmost flexibility, so that development timing may react to changing market conditions."[32] The first phase was estimated to last approximately four years, during which work would concentrate on track removal and the demolition of facilities related to freighting as well as on the realization of parts of the passenger station, the hotel complex, the convention center, and two office buildings for Canadian National and Canadian Pacific. The other four phases were planned to last three years each.

Successive studies, supplementary to the May document, were released in June and December 1968.[33] Many elements of the project are better defined in these documents. For example, the extension of University Avenue into Metro Centre stipulated splitting the street into two levels, one rising above the railway tracks and the other descending below to connect to the Gardiner Expressway. The area around Esplanade Street was described as "a transition element between the transportation exchange and the downtown core," while the convention center and trade center were indicated to be part of a large "single-volume flexible space" placed over the commuter station with entrances on University Avenue.[34]

Though these reports clarified that the level of architectural definition remained somewhat unspecific at this early stage and the need to refine future requirements, the six office towers between Front Street and Esplanade Street were designed to adhere to a square footprint with beveled corners. This configuration, which suggested rotating the towers 45 degrees in relation to the street alignment, followed the diagonal arrangement of the pedestrian routes in the shopping areas. The "unique tri-level design" of Esplanade Street was composed of an upper level for pedestrians and vehicles, an intermediate level containing a mall, and a lower level that housed a bus station. The intermediate

28   Ibid., 16–17.
29   Ibid., 19. The possible relocation of Canadian Broadcasting Corporations's main offices and studios is also mentioned in the 1963 Plan for Downtown Toronto. See *Plan for Downtown Toronto*, 46.
30   *Metro Centre Development Plan and Programme*, 19.
31   Ibid.

32   Ibid., 25.
33   *Metro Centre: A Study for the Development of Canadian National and Canadian Pacific Railway Lands in Central Toronto* (Toronto: Community Development Consultants Limited, June 3, 1968); *Metro Centre: Summary* (Toronto: December 1968).
34   *Metro Centre: A Study*, 40–41.

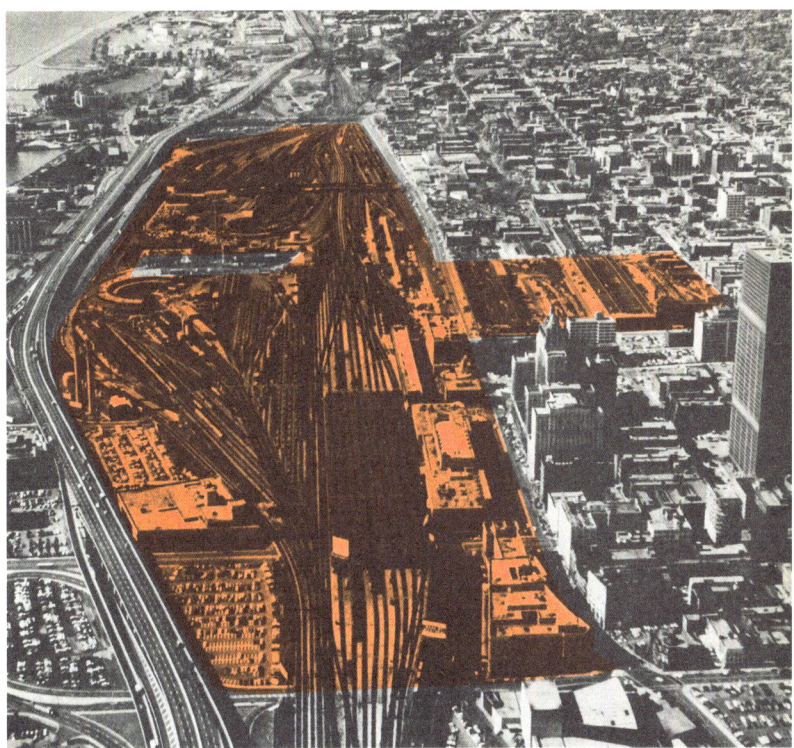

3

4

5

FIG. 3 Aerial view of the area of intervention, Metro Centre, Toronto, Canada, 1968.
FIG. 4 View of the railway station and the prolonged University Avenue, Metro Centre.
FIG. 5 Model with detail of the railway station and communication tower in the background, Metro Centre.

FIG. 6 View of the three levels of Esplanade Street, Metro Centre.

FIG. 7 View of the three levels of Esplanade Street with the subway station beneath, Metro Centre.

FIG. 8 View of the commercial area from Front Street, Metro Centre.

FIG. 9 Model with detail of residential area, Metro Centre.

level was to be lit by large skylights placed at the center of the street above.[35] Together with the residential facilities, the entire undertaking was presented as having a significant chance of success: "Metro Centre has impressive social and economic justification and it can be a major step forward in humanizing the downtown environment of what is potentially one of the world's great urban communities."[36] [FIG. 10]

The release of the last document ended several months of work under the supervision of John Andrews, with Roger du Toit from the Andrews office acting as coordinator of the dedicated design team. Plans for Metro Centre were presented to the public on December 19, 1968, at the Royal York Hotel, a structure that would have faced three of the six office towers planned between Front Street and Esplanade Street had the scheme been realized. For the unveiling, a large model of the project—20 feet long—was exhibited.[37] "It was this super bang of the presentation model that they [Metro Centre opponents] reacted to," Andrews later commented.[38] Now shared with the people of Toronto, the Metro Centre scheme entered a different and problematic phase, that of public communication. [FIGS. 11–12]

METRO CENTRE IN CONTEXT

Despite its timid approach to urban modernization in the 1950s and 1960s, Toronto was emerging from a period of parochialism in its architectural culture at the time of Metro Centre's presentation. The 1958 competition for the new City Hall was, of course, a major starting point. Innovations in the use of building materials and a tendency toward large-scale structures characterized this new wave of architecture in the city. Beginning in the 1950s, Toronto witnessed a widespread diffusion of reinforced concrete technology and concrete aesthetics, which was due in part to the presence of a handful of specialized contractors such as St. Mary Cement and Beer Precast Concrete. The latter contractor was involved in the construction of City Hall after winning the contract for the project's cement works in 1961.[39] This new direction for Toronto's architecture is apparent in the Central Tech Art Centre by Macy DuBois (1962), the Yorkdale Shopping Centre by John Graham Consultants and John B. Parkin Associates, which included the involvement of a young John Andrews (1964), and the Medical Science Building at the University of Toronto by Peter Goering (1969).

Considerable scale linked the Yorkdale Centre and the Medical Science Building to two other projects from the 1960s: Parkin's Aeroquay No. 1 at Malton Airport (now Lester B. Pearson International Airport), inaugurated in 1964, and Mathers and Haldenby's Robarts Library at the University of Toronto, begun in 1968 and opened in 1974.[40] Andrews's design of Scarborough College, in the city's eastern outskirts, also belongs on this list. The Metro Centre project had a clear relationship to Scarborough College, coordinated by Andrews from 1963 and completed in 1965, since Scarborough provided Andrews with the kind of visibility that made him a viable candidate to lead Metro Centre's design team. Besides being a large structure, as Metro Centre would have been if realized, Scarborough put Andrews on "the map" for the stringent conditions within which his design developed.[41]

Of course, Montreal occupies a central place in this Canadian history of large-scale structures realized in concrete for both structural and aesthetic reasons. The completion of complexes such as Place Ville Marie, Place

---

35 *Metro Centre: Summary*, 5.
36 Ibid., 9.
37 Photographs of the presentation are kept in the Clara Thomas Archives and Special Collections, York University, Toronto Telegram Fonds, Accession/Box 1974-002/250; digitalized copies are available at https://digital.library.yorku.ca/yul-f0433/toronto-telegram.
38 Taylor and Andrews, *John Andrews*, 90.
39 Elizabeth Hulse, *The Beers: Canada's First Family in Precast Concrete* (Toronto: Coach House Books, 2002); Elizabeth Hulse, "Beer Precast," in McClelland and Stewart, *Concrete Toronto*, 290–91.
40 May Lou Lobsinger, "John P. Robarts Library," in McClelland and Stewart, *Concrete Toronto*, 164–73.
41 On Scarborough College, see Paolo Scrivano, "Scarborough College's Brutalist Dreams," in McClelland and Stewart, *Concrete Toronto*, 334–39; Paolo Scrivano and Mary Lou Lobsinger, "Experimental Architecture, Progressive Pedagogy: Scarborough College," *Architecture and Ideas* 8: 1 (2009): 4–19.

FIG. 10 Photomontage of model for Metro Centre over an aerial view of the area of intervention, Metro Centre.

FIG. 11 Model detail, Official presentation of Metro Centre at the Royal York Hotel, December 1968.

FIG. 12 Official presentation of Metro Centre at the Royal York Hotel.

des Arts, and Place Bonaventure between the late 1950s and the 1960s left an indelible mark on Montreal's morphology, if not its identity.[42] Place Ville Marie, a real estate venture launched in 1957 by New York developer William Zeckendorf, was often cited in relation to Metro Centre, particularly because of its realization by Donald S. Anderson, who was at one point chairman of the board of directors of Metro Centre Developments.[43] But Place Bonaventure is probably closest, at least conceptually, to the Toronto scheme. Realized between 1964 and 1967 from a design by the firm Affleck, Desbarats, Dimakopoulos, Lebensold, Michaud, Sise, Place Bonaventure integrated, in one structure, a railway terminal and a subway station with offices, a hotel, an exhibition hall, shops, a commercial mall, restaurants, and a swimming pool.

The importance of Montreal's concrete architecture was recognized in 1976 by the British historian and critic Reyner Banham, whose book *Megastructure: Urban Futures of the Recent Past* devoted an entire chapter to it.[44] The diverse examples found in "Megacity Montreal" represented "a comprehensible grouping of architecture united by ambition, ingenuity and the ground on which they stood" and was determined by a variety of factors, including "the mysterious power of the local money establishment to promote major property adventures."[45] Banham's book also suggests why Toronto's waterfront and railway yards prompted such a proliferation of large-scale proposals since the mid-1960s. "Megayear 1964," in Banham's words, marked "the emergence of a kind of canon of large-scale projects that were persistently published,"[46] which,

Banham remarked, was thanks to Japanese architect Fumihiko Maki debuting the word "megastructure" in print that year.[47] If Metro Centre was primarily a masterplan before it was an architectural project, as the accompanying documentation (and later Andrews's recollections) insists, ambition was its most distinct feature.

COMPETING VISIONS FOR DOWNTOWN TORONTO

Considering the cultural climate around architecture in the late 1960s, in Canada and internationally, it is no surprise that a competing project for the area covered by the Metro Centre scheme was unveiled almost at the same time. In June 1968, Buckminster Fuller and Shoji Sadao presented an alternative project commissioned by *The Toronto Telegram* and CFTO-TV in a press conference at the recently opened Toronto-Dominion Centre.[48] According to one reconstruction, Fuller (and his firm Fuller and Sadao/Geometrics) were approached to produce a plan for the site at Expo 67 in Montreal, where he had previously designed the United States Pavilion.[49] [FIG. 13]

Fuller and Sadao's Project Toronto scheme insisted on Toronto's need for a "special image," reflecting the widely held belief that the city lacked distinction and echoing, perhaps unintentionally, the view expressed by architect and educator Eric Arthur in his *Toronto: No Mean City* of 1964.[50] According to the project's proponents, a "specific identity" for modern

---

42   André Lortie, "Montreal 1960: The Singularities of a Metropolitan Archetype," in André Lortie, ed., *The 60s: Montreal Thinks Big* (Montreal: Canadian Centre for Architecture; Vancouver: Douglas & McIntyre, 2004), 75–115.
43   Sewell, *Up Against City Hall*, 98.
44   Reyner Banham, *Megastructure: Urban Futures of the Recent Past* (London: Thames and Hudson, 1976), 104–27.
45   Ibid., 105. The "mysterious power of the local money establishment" was perhaps an allusion to the financial operations that made possible both Place Ville Marie and Tour de la Bourse at Place Victoria.
46   Ibid., 78.
47   Maki used the term "mega-structure" in his *Investigations in Collective Form* (St. Louis: School of Architecture, Washington University, 1964).
48   Mark Osbaldeston, *Unbuilt Toronto: A History of the City that Might Have Been* (Toronto: Dundurn Press, 2008), 40. Photographs of the press conference and the project are kept in Accession/Box 1974-002/357, Toronto Telegram fonds, Clara Thomas Archives and Special Collections, York University; digitalized copies are available at https://digital.library.yorku.ca/yul-f0433/toronto-telegram.
49   Osbaldeston, *Unbuilt Toronto*, 39.
50   For Arthur, an adopted Torontonian, the "admiration and affection [for the city] should not blind [one] … to the all too blatant ugliness of large areas of Toronto." See Eric Arthur, *Toronto: No Mean City* (Toronto: University of Toronto Press, 1964), 225.

13

14

FIG. 13 Richard Buckminster Fuller and Shoji Sadao (Fuller-Sadao/Geometrics), Project Toronto, 1968, photomontage.
FIG. 14 View inside the Galleria, Project Toronto.

Toronto could derive from both precise actions in the realms of culture and knowledge and a highly visible architectural gesture. As a consequence, Project Toronto recommended establishing a third university (after Toronto and York) with a technical and scientific vocation and advanced the then-customary large-scale urban scheme.

Fuller and Sadao proposed a "Galleria," a multifunctional public area stretching 3,000 feet from downtown toward the lake, for "urban social and cultural interchange." The project's highlight was a massive pyramidal hall that was planned to be 800 feet long on each side and 400 feet tall: dubbed "Crystal Pyramid," it was a "solar glass enclosure" meant to accommodate two tall buildings flanking an open space. As in the case of Metro Centre, a "transmitting tower" was included in the scheme. Further, Fuller and Sadao envisaged three "specially designed" islands floating in Toronto's harbor to house their "Pro-To-City," a prototype of urban settlement.[51] [FIG. 14]

The motivations for Project Toronto are unclear, especially because the project involved two high-profile figures such as Fuller and Sadao. It is hard to believe that the designers were given "free reign," as it has been written.[52] Indeed, published documentation alluded to the possible involvement in the project of Canadian National and Canadian Pacific, the sponsors of Metro Centre.[53] In his *John Andrews: Architecture, a Performing Art*, Andrews commented on the "competition" between architects that unfolded around the time of Metro Centre's preparation: "Every architect in Toronto was anxious, and not only those in Toronto."[54] We are left to conjecture whether the urban endeavor involving Canada's two major railway companies was seen at the time as an unrepeatable opportunity.

PUBLIC CRITICISM AND THE FIGHT OVER UNION STATION

The scheme for Metro Centre provoked controversy as soon as it was presented to the public. Among its first objectors were the Architectural Conservancy of Ontario and the Confederation of Resident and Ratepayer Associations (CORRA), two organizations that had successfully campaigned to save the old city hall and to stop the construction of the Spadina Expressway.[55] CORRA, a coalition of more than 30 taxpayer groups, argued that, if realized, Metro Centre would adversely affect the city and those living and working in its proximity.[56]

In city hall, Metro Centre first met opposition through the actions of a handful of councillors, the main protagonist being John Sewell, a young lawyer and freshly elected alderman who entered politics after defending city residents from neighborhood redevelopment and expropriation. Sewell, described as attending council meetings wearing a leather jacket, jeans, and motorcycle boots, tried to delay discussions and decisions by adopting filibustering tactics.[57] Sewell contested the tentative agreement between the city and Canadian National and Canadian Pacific to exchange land needed for Metro Centre for properties owned by the railway companies in other parts of Toronto: pointing at what appeared to him suspicious real estate estimates, he called the deal the "railway swindle."[58] At this stage, however, polemics were still confined to political milieus. When Mayor William Dennison declared that he feared a "rising in arms" if the development were not approved, a journalist from *The Toronto Star* ironically imagined the potential protesters as an "angry rabble of hardhats,

---

51 *Project Toronto: A Study and Proposals for the Future Development of the City and Region of Toronto* (Cambridge, MA: Fuller and Sadao/Geometrics, 1968); Fuller and Sadao/Geometrics, "Project Toronto," *Canadian Architect* (July 1968): 37–44; Richard Buckminster Fuller and Shoji Sadao, "Project Toronto," *Ekistics* 28, no. 165 (August 1969):107–11. The article for *Ekistics* was an abstract from the previous two documents.
52 Osbaldeston, *Unbuilt Toronto*, 39.
53 Fuller and Sadao/Geometrics, "Project Toronto," 42.
54 Taylor and Andrews, *John Andrews*, 87.

55 On the Spadina Expressway and the associated polemics, see White, *Planning Toronto*, 295–302.
56 Sewell, *Up Against City Hall*, 97–98; Osbaldeston, *Unbuilt Toronto*, 48–52.
57 Alexander Ross, "Can They Nail Down Metro Centre before the Public Descends?," *Toronto Star*, December 14, 1971: 73.
58 Sewell, *Up Against City Hall*, 97–116. Sewell was elected mayor in 1978.

stockbrokers, housewives and hippies, carrying rifles and baseball bats."[59] Albeit in principle, the city council approved the Metro Centre scheme in December 1970.

However, a relatively small element of Metro Centre was about to upset the entire decision-making mechanism. It might appear curious that a mammoth proposal such as Metro Centre received its harshest criticism in relation to the suggested demolition of Union Station, a structure occupying a minor portion of the interested area. Built between 1915 and 1927 to replace the precedent station destroyed by the Great Fire of 1904, Union Station was conceived for the Canadian Pacific Railway by a team of architects that included John M. Lyle, Hugh G. Jones, and the Montreal firm George A. Ross and Robert H. McDonald.[60] In Metro Centre's plan, Union Station would be replaced by a group of office towers.

The Union Station Committee formed in June 1971 to protect the station as a historic monument. Mobilizing around 500 concerned citizens, including architects, planners, and university professors, the committee received support from the Toronto chapter of the Architectural Conservancy of Ontario. Its campaigning involved petitions to various administrative bodies and the publication in late 1972 of a volume on the station, *The Open Gate: Toronto Union Station*.[61] The book collected a heterogeneous array of contributions, including an interview with the stationmaster who had worked at the station since 1927 and whose report on the structure's supposedly intact efficiency was read by John Sewell in his city council filibuster.[62]

One of the contributors to *The Open Gate* was Douglas Richardson, a young architecture history professor at the University of Toronto.[63] Richardson argued in favor of Union Station's historical value by portraying it as the example par excellence of North American transportation terminals delineated by Carroll L. V. Meeks in his *The Railroad Station: An Architectural History*.[64] Richardson's most convincing claim was that the station's importance lay in being a symbol of unity, the name "union" embodying the building's role in connecting distant parts of Canada through the railroads.[65] Thanks to this and other actions, Union Station almost unexpectedly emerged as a possible emblem of Toronto's identity. As an article in *The Toronto Star* put it, "People who have thought for years that the Great Hall at Union Station is merely the lobby of a railroad terminal are suddenly craning their necks to gaze at the high-vaulted grandeur of the ancient pile as though it were the Sistine Chapel."[66]

The controversy around the station's planned demolition did not solely erode consensus for the project, it also triggered the chain of events that would eventually stop Metro Centre in its tracks. First, in June 1972, the Ontario Municipal Board, an independent panel on municipal and planning disputes, endorsed the idea of saving the station, increasing the number of apartment units, and doubling the amount of parkland, recommendations initially suggested by CORRA.[67] Then, in 1973, the board demanded the station not be demolished or, at least, that parts of it be retained.[68] In the meantime, the federal government's spending freeze in mid-1969 cooled the Canadian Broadcasting Corporation's

---

59 Ross, "Can They Nail Down Metro Centre."
60 On Union Station, see Patricia McHugh, *Toronto Architecture: A City Guide* (Toronto: Mercury Books, 1985), 103–104; Harold Kalman, *A Concise History of Canadian Architecture* (North York, ON: Oxford University Press, 2000), 330–31.
61 Richard Bébout, ed., *The Open Gate: Toronto Union Station* (Toronto: Peter Martin Associates, 1972).
62 Pierre Berton, "'A Feeling, an Echo…': The Life of Union Station," in Bébout, *The Open Gate*, 1–13; Ross, "Can They Nail Down Metro Centre."
63 Douglas Richardson, "'A Blessed Sense of Civic Excess': The Architecture of Union Station" in Bébout, *The Open Gate*, 67–95.
64 Carroll L. V. Meeks, *The Railroad Station: An Architectural History* (New Haven, CT: Yale University Press, 1956).
65 Richardson, "'A Blessed Sense of Civic Excess,'" 67.
66 Trent Frayne, "Union Station's Grea Hall Is Suddenly Lovely," *Toronto Star*, December 7, 1971.
67 Richard Bébout, "Progress and History: The Future of Union Station," in Bébout, *The Open Gate*, 110; Sewell, *Up Against City Hall*, 116; Osbaldeston, *Unbuilt Toronto*, 50–52.
68 Sewell, *The Shape of the City: Toronto struggles with modern planning* (Toronto & Buffalo: University of Toronto Press, 1993): 148.

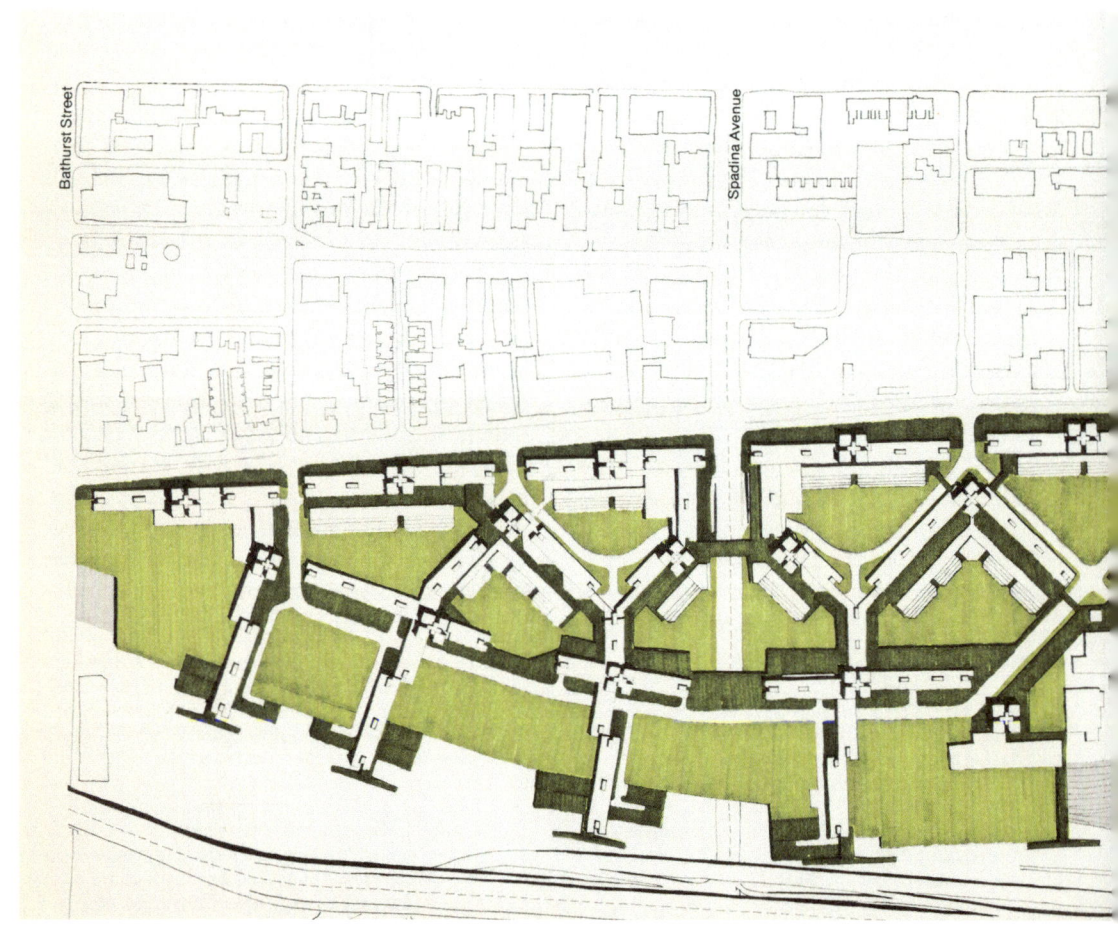

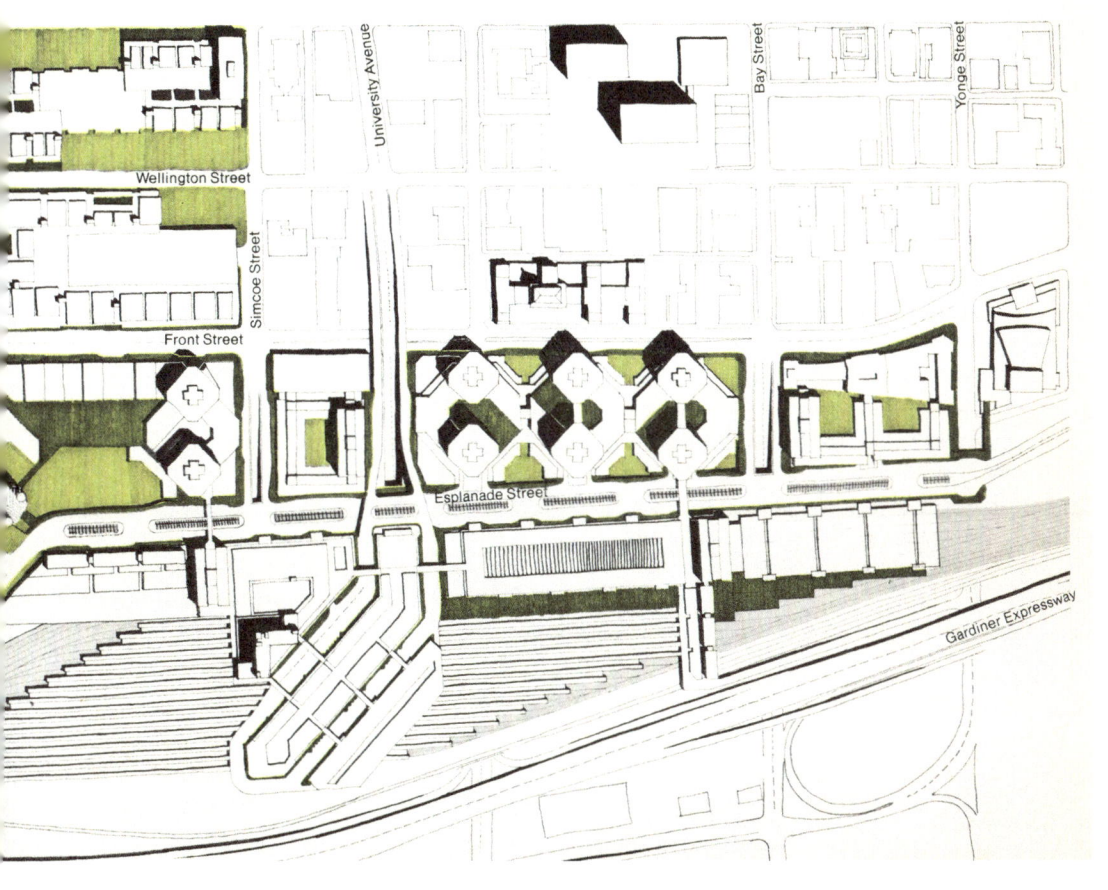

FIG. 15 Masterplan, Metro Centre.

interest in the project.[69] The next blow was the city's decision not to extend the subway loop southward.[70]

In a rescue attempt, Metro Centre Developments accepted the suggestion from architect and planner Anthony Adamson, a member of the Union Station Committee, to preserve the station's Great Hall. As a consequence, in 1974, the design team drafted an alternative project integrating part of Union Station into the overall Metro Centre scheme.[71] Presented in *The Canadian Architect* at the beginning of 1975 and recognizing Roger du Toit's role in the project, the revised plan proposed some possible solutions to retain the hall, making clear that the study was essentially a schematic urban design undertaking.[72] The proposal also tried to address the problem of increasing building densities (implicitly making the investment financially appealing) while avoiding construction over the existing tracks.

By the time the study for the Great Hall appeared in the pages of *The Canadian Architect*, however, Metro Centre's proposal had hit a dead end. In 1975 Canadian National and Canadian Pacific canceled the project. Metro Centre had lost the battle of public opinion: paraphrasing the title of a *Toronto Star* article, the public had ultimately "descended" and prevented "nailing down" the Metro Centre project.[73] Andrews, who had moved to Australia in 1969 to manage the construction of the Cameron Offices in Belconnen, Australian Capital Territory, observed these developments somewhat from the sidelines: his opinion of the scheme's demise was that the "bad handling" of public communication compromised the chance to gain support for the project.

The failure lay in the inability to adequately explain the programmatic nature of Metro Centre, its essential character being an "organization framework capable of many physical interpretations."[74]

THE REMNANT OF METRO CENTRE

In the end, nothing of the grand Metro Centre scheme was built except the communication tower, which came to be known as the CN Tower and is today one of Toronto's major landmarks. In contrast to the original proposal, the tower was erected in a *terrain vague* still occupied by the railway tracks, leading *The Canadian Architect* to call it "an orphan child of the shelved Metro Centre project."[75] Indeed, the CN Tower still has the bearing of an isolated mast in a relatively empty space, despite the densification of the area surrounding it since the end of the 2010s. [FIG. 16]

The project for the communication tower in its new configuration was probably drafted around 1971.[76] The documentation accompanying the revised proposal positioned the structure still within the larger urbanization scheme of Metro Centre, but significantly different was the tower's appearance. No longer formed by three extended cylinders as initially envisioned, the tower instead took on a tapered shape culminating in the rounded volume of the observation deck and topped with a flagpole-like antenna. (Andrews, however, did occasionally continue pursue three-cornered tower design, successfully so for the King George Tower in Sydney, completed in 1976, and an unbuilt communication tower for Singapore, circa 1990.) One aspect of the design remained clear: the project intended to leave a mark, both locally and internationally. The documentation produced by Metro Centre Developments compared the proposed tower

69 Claire Hoy, "Metro Centre Will Start Soon—Or So Officials Say," *Toronto Daily Star*, December 19, 1970.
70 *Metro Centre: A Study*, 19–23; William Bragg, "How Metro Centre Saved $21 Million on Extension of Union Subway Facilities," *Toronto Daily Star*, December 19, 1970.
71 *Metro Centre: Urban Design Guidelines for the Integration of the Great Hall, Transportation and Development* (Toronto: Metro Centre Developments, 1974).
72 "Great Hall Union Station. Architects: John Andrews International–Roger du Toit and Webb Zerafa Menkès Housden Partnership," *Canadian Architect* (March 1975): 26–33.
73 Ross, "Can They Nail Down Metro Centre."
74 Taylor and Andrews, *John Andrews*, 89.
75 "CN Tower, Toronto. Architects: John Andrews International, Roger du Toit; The Webb Zerafa Menkes Housden Partnership," *Canadian Architect* (March 1976): 29.
76 *Metro Centre. Communication Tower* (Toronto: Metro Centre Developments, undated). Some drawings included in this 23-page brochure are dated 1971.

to other buildings in Ontario, such as the Skylon Tower in Niagara Falls and Commerce Court in Toronto; to new and old iconic skyscrapers, such as the Empire State Building and the World Trade Center in New York; and to an epitome of the "race toward the sky," including the Ostankino Tower in Moscow, the supertall rival that the CN Tower more or less explicitly sought to overtake.[77] Perhaps the anxiety of placing the tower in a sort of international contest, unveiled by the documentation of 1971, simply reflected the desperate attempts to keep alive the entire Metro Centre venture.

The CN Tower was completed in three years, starting in 1973 and opening to the public in the summer of 1976. Its construction entailed the use of innovative techniques of concrete forming and testing and employed high-grade concrete. The tower was constructed with poured-in-place, post-tensioned concrete and realized at a quick pace so to provide consistent material quality throughout the building process.[78] At 1,815 feet high, taller than initially planned, the CN Tower was at the time of its completion the tallest freestanding structure in the world, a primacy that lasted until 2007. More significant, however, was the probable impact the tower's construction had on the local building industry in light of the technological challenges it posed to contractors, materials suppliers, and the construction workforce itself—a question that draws an interesting parallel with the Sydney Opera House.[79]

At all events, the CN Tower ended up occupying a marginal part in the history of Metro Centre and of John Andrews's engagement in the latter's design definition. Andrews was ambivalent about claiming the project for the realized tower as his own, even though he was celebrated as its author in the Australian press.[80] Despite this, Metro Centre nonetheless emphasized Andrews's organizational skills in handling a complex design task while managing a variety of competencies, ranging from city transportation planning to urban design, architecture, and engineering. True, the entire Metro Centre scheme remained unrealized, sparing architectural historians from addressing thorny questions about authorship. The CN Tower, however, still epitomized the close relationship between different specializations that Andrews held, which underlies good design work.

"MAYBE, IN A WAY, IT IS A GOOD THING THAT METRO CENTRE NEVER GOT BUILT."

More than a decade after Metro Centre was canceled, Andrews summarized his experience frankly: "Maybe, in a way, it is a good thing that Metro Centre never got built. I do not know. They will argue and fight and have committees and screw around for another 20 years now."[81] Even in the architect's recollections, Metro Centre seemed to have remained in memory for the reactions it provoked rather than for the design characteristics it exhibited.

However, highlighting the polemics and controversies surrounding Metro Centre would yield only a partial reading of the whole venture, since Andrews's plan reveals key aspects of the design philosophy he espoused. In the first place, the project implied an approach for which flexibility was an essential tenet. The design team under Andrews's guidance made this clear from the onset, stating, "This is a masterplan of a different sort. It is not a blueprint for a future edifice, for that would become out of date before the first sod was turned. Its validity is not dependent upon physical form or architectural quality; indeed, it is a framework that will even take bad architecture without losing its identity. It is a flexible network of systems accommodating the ebb and flow of growth

77 Ibid., 5.
78 On Canadian National Tower, see: "Top of the World—Now it's in Toronto," *Architecture Canada News Magazine*, (February, 1973): 1; Franz Knoll, "Structural Design Concepts for the Canadian National Tower: Toronto, Canada," *Canadian Journal of Civil Engineering* 2, no. 2 (June 1975): 123–37; Edward R. Baldwin, "CN Tower," *Canadian Architect*, (March 1976): 30–44.
79 Peter Murray, *The Saga of Sydney Opera House: The Dramatic Story of the Design and Construction of the Icon of Modern Australia* (London: Spon Press, 2004).
80 Taylor and Andrews, *John Andrews*, 90; "Toronto Tower is the World's Highest," *The Australian* (March 14, 1977): 11; "Andrews Towers above His Peers," *The Weekend Australian*, November 17–18, 1990: 4.
81 Taylor and Andrews, *John Andrews*, 90.

and change and acting as a vehicle to ensure the rich mix of our urban experience."[82] In many ways, Andrews's proposal for Metro Centre took the form of an illustration of possibilities rather than a detailed and complete design.

Then the project likely benefited from the vertical rather than horizontal organization of the John Andrews Architects work, granting overall efficiency and productive collaborations between disciplines.[83] Andrews summarized this attitude, both a mode of operation and a theoretical stance, by describing the architect's job as "the assimilation of the information provided by many and various experts, and the synthesis of that into a three-dimensional result."[84] These two aspects might conclusively explain Andrews's involvement in the Metro Centre adventure. His characterization of his firm being selected by the developer Stewart Andrews ascribes to it an almost immediate recognition of affinity and reciprocal understanding, despite some initial "fur flying."[85] In reality, there were deeper motivations behind the hiring. The Andrews office had the capacity to combine different levels of expertise and provide a flexible work template, displayed, for example, in the design and construction supervision of Scarborough College, which rendered Andrews particularly suitable to lead Metro Centre's project.

In the end, both Scarborough College and Metro Centre were anything but "obvious jobs," if the complexity and challenges they entailed are taken into account. On the contrary and for the way Andrews tackled such complex and challenging projects, Scarborough College and Metro Centre revealed a remarkable "design plainness," a rationality and logic of design actions that can be regarded as a veritable trademark of the architect's modus operandi. In this respect, Metro Centre should be given the attention it truly deserves: even if never built, it ought to be viewed as highly emblematic of a historical period, a cultural climate, and, last but not least, a professional career.

82   *Metro Centre: A Study*, 3.
83   Robert Jensen, "Design and Process: Four Projects by the John Andrews Office," *Architectural Record* 147, no. 2 (February 1970): 131, 146.
84   Taylor and Andrews, *John Andrews*, 88.
85   According to John Andrews, the first meeting with Stewart Andrews unfolded this way: "His [Stewart Andrews's] first words were, 'Why the hell should I hire you?' My immediate response was 'I'm not so bloody sure I want to work for you!' [...] It is just that sort of encounter, quick, and with a bit of fur flying that results in a high degree of mutual understanding when the air clears." Ibid., 87. In the text's first draft the exchange of words between the two sounds more colorful: "We sat down in out little boardroom, just he and I and a couple of others from his outfit and from mine, and his first words were 'Alright, what have you got to con me with?' I said, 'Look, if that's your attitude you can (piss off). Just get out. It's not what we're about. If we have got any sort of a reputation at all it's not conning." "The Metro Centre," undated typescript accessed by Paul Walker in the John Andrews archive before its acquisition by the State Library of NSW. It is likely that this typescript came from interviews between Andrews and Earl Berger in Toronto before Andrews returned to Australia. See Taylor and Andrews, 4

FIG. 16 Model, Metro Centre.

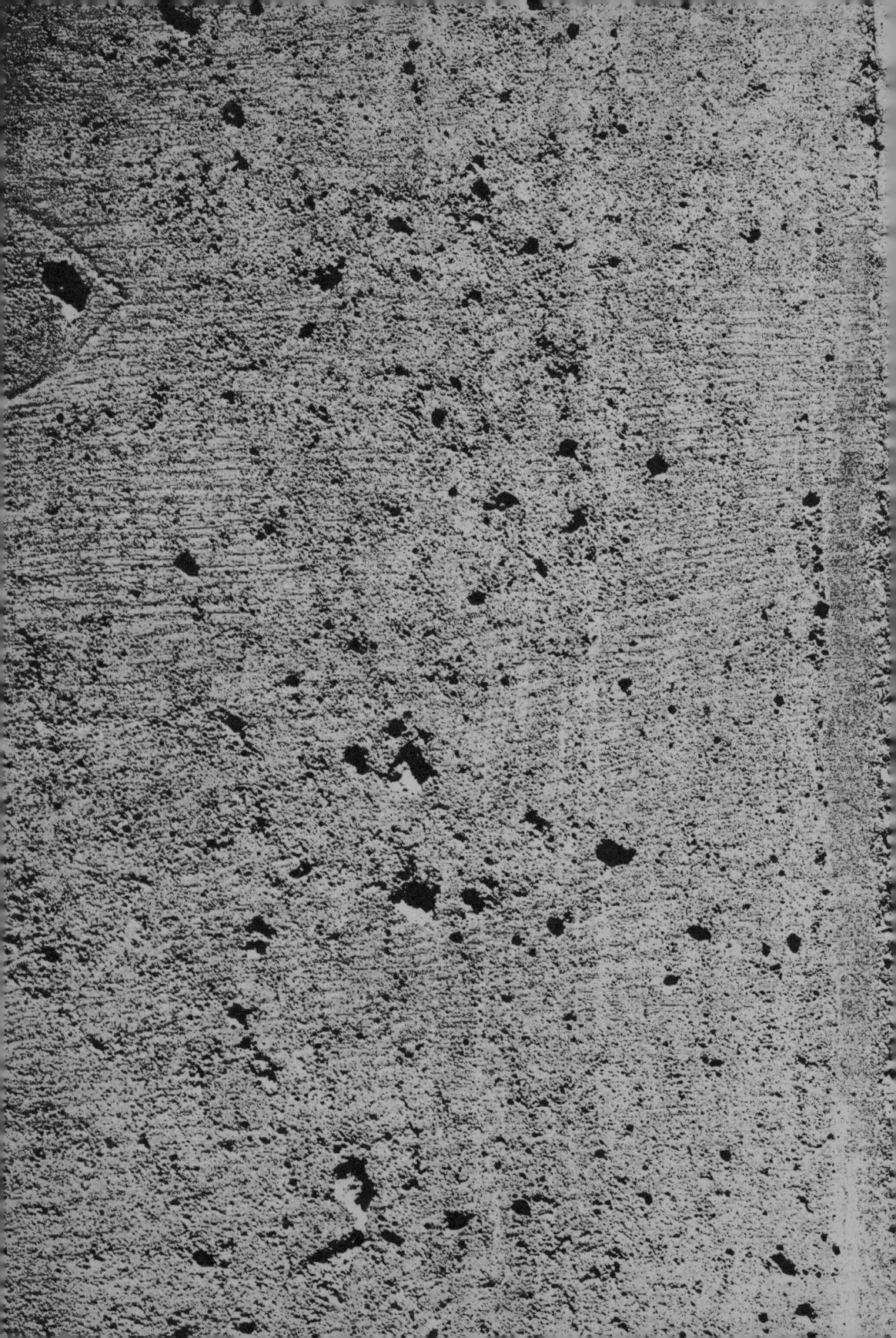

06

miami seaport terminal

by Paul Walker

GETTING THE MIAMI JOB

In 1967, Andrews was commissioned to design a terminal in Miami for Caribbean cruise ships. At first the terminal appears to be unlike anything else that Andrews designed, with its prominent concrete roofs that featured an asymmetrical double curve in section and extruded over 500 feet each. These roofs, designed as four in a row, were the project's signature feature. In no other Andrews project is the roof design as conspicuous as it was at Miami, and in no other Andrews project was the roof as charismatic. Indeed, Miami was a departure from the university commissions that became the mainstay of John Andrews Architects after the success of Scarborough College and the South Residences at the University of Guelph. Andrews maintained that the seaport terminal came the closest to his ethos of architecture as problem-solving. As architectural historian Philip Drew commented, the Scarborough College, University of Guelph, and Miami Seaport Terminal projects "testify to the persistence of John Andrews's alliance with reality."[1]

The Miami Seaport Terminal design departed from university briefs insofar as the requirements that needed to be accommodated were straightforward rather than complex. However, the plan also involved large crowds of people moving through the same space at the same time. In this way, the Miami Seaport Terminal was a typical transportation infrastructure project. It entailed large spaces that needed to be covered overhead, so the primary design condition was to figure out how exactly that covering would occur. This was an opportunity for architectural distinction. The Miami Seaport Terminal, like Scarborough College and the University of Guelph residences, was built at a megastructure scale at a time when architectural culture was fascinated by megastructures. Although in Florida, the seaport terminal can be counted as a Canadian megastructure, which Reyner Banham identified as a particular species of the category, but one that responded to a hot rather than a cold climate.[2] Andrews likely gleaned new climatic lessons from Paul Rudolph's Florida houses, since the project also reversed what he had learned from accommodating Toronto's cold while working in the office of John B. Parkin.

The Miami Seaport Terminal project was part of the effort to relocate the Port of Miami facilities from an area just north of downtown to the artificially constructed Dodge Island in Biscayne Bay, between the old port and Miami Beach. The growth of the port was particularly fueled by the increase in passengers taking cruises, a figure that rose from 115,000 in 1959 to 700,000 in 1971.[3] While four cruise ships were anticipated to use the new terminal when it was completed, this number grew to nine before it opened, and two years later to 11.[4] Miami was quickly emerging as the world's largest center for cruises. Passengers who formerly began their voyages in ports further north on the east coast of the United States, particularly New York City, were now flying to Miami to embark, especially since this obviated several days of sailing in cold weather. In January 1972, the *New York Times* reported that airlines were now also flying directly to Miami from Europe, and that "the development of a large European cruise trade is only a question of time."[5]

---

1   Philip Drew, *Third Generation: The Changing Meaning of Architecture* (New York: Praeger, 1972), 144. Drew also lists the Cameron Offices and Gund Hall as similar testimonials.

2   Reyner Banham, *Megastructure: Urban Histories of the Recent Past* (London: Thames and Hudson, 1976), 133–37. Banham names a "Canadian accountancy megatrend" to refer to the proliferation of megastructures in Canada, the vast interior circulation spaces of which were regarded elsewhere as having an "inherent redundancy that made megastructures economically unconvincing." It is worth noting that this was not a problem when building giant airports.

3   Allan T. Shulman, "Ports and Passenger Terminals: Infrastructure as Spectacle" in *Miami Modern Metropolis: Paradise and Paradox in Midcentury Architecture and Planning*, ed. Allan T. Schulman (Miami: Bass Museum of Art, 2009), 155. See also: Edward C. Burks, "Miami Will Open a Big New Port in May With Eye on Cruise Ships," *New York Times*, February 7, 1965.

4   "New Seaport Passenger Terminal to Open in Miami: Red-Carpet Facility Likely to Cut Time of Clearing Ships," *New York Times,* December 29, 1968; "Miami Enjoys Boom as a Passenger Cruise Port," *New York Times*, January 9, 1972.

5   "Miami Enjoys Boom as a Passenger Cruise Port," *New York Times*, January 9, 1972.

The process through which Andrews was appointed the architect of the Miami Seaport Terminal followed objections from the city's civic leaders to an earlier design by the Port of Miami's consulting engineers David Volkert & Associates. They proposed the design of a vast concrete-vaulted roof that would shelter an upper-level passenger terminal and lower-level cargo areas. It was modeled after an airport terminal, with telescoping walkways connecting a gangway at the building's upper level directly to the cruise ships. It would be able to handle passengers boarding or disembarking from five cruise ships simultaneously. This plan was ultimately viewed by critics as "too prosaic for a seaport in the heart of Biscayne Bay."[6] The location of the terminal, on the north side of Dodge Island, was visible from the MacArthur Causeway, which while connecting the city's downtown to Miami Beach, also serves a chain of artificial islands in Biscayne Bay that feature exclusive residential areas.

The dissatisfaction with the industrial aspects of Volkert's design led Miami-Dade County to hire New York consulting firm Frederic R. Harris to assess the proposal. Harris's analysis included an architectural critique by Italian American architect and Columbia University architecture professor Romaldo Giurgola, who characterized the design as lacking firm conviction. Moreover, the design for Dodge Island had no masterplan and no landscaping. Giurgola regarded the new terminal as a project of civic importance, a quality that was typically neglected in such facilities. As he wrote, "In America, such buildings (seaports) have always been relegated to minor roles in the building of a seaport. I have seen shorelines destroyed by carelessness. Look at New York."[7] He strongly advocated for designing a building of greater civic ambition than Volkert's project offered, as well as one that acknowledged Miami's tropical environment.

Miami-Dade County responded to Giurgola's comments by rejecting Volkert's design and appointing Giurgola to select a new designer, with Volkert remaining on the project as the architect of record. An initial list of 13 candidates was reduced to three: Robert Venturi, Thomas R. Vreeland, and John Andrews. As Allan Shulman has noted, all three architects had limited experience and strong connections to academia, including Venturi to the University of Pennsylvania, Vreeland to the University of New Mexico, and Andrews to the University of Toronto. During this period, Venturi was best known for his 1966 book *Complexity and Contradiction in Architecture*, which featured a small number of theoretically driven but modest built projects: the Vanna Venturi House, built for his mother; Guild House East, an apartment building for the elderly; and the North Penn Visiting Nurses Headquarters, built for the Visiting Nurses Association.[8] Vreeland was the chair of the architecture program at the University of New Mexico and went on to have a distinguished academic career in the United States. Of the three, Andrews was the relative outsider, as Vreeland and Venturi were both connected with the Philadelphia architecture scene in which Giurgola was a key figure. (Vreeland was also the son of fashion columnist and editor, Diana Vreeland.)

Andrews, however, had successfully completed two major buildings, Scarborough College and the South Residences at the University of Guelph, and in the case of Miami, size mattered. As Giurgola explained, "I wanted young men to correspond to the scope of the project, to bring a new spirit and new reputation in Miami as a dynamic place to live and work… in architecture, you have to want to take a chance."[9] Andrews's prior projects, as well as his design for Expo 67's African Place in Montreal, which was still under construction, certainly demonstrated that he was an architect who wanted to take a chance and could design ambitiously scaled buildings.

6 "New Seaport Passenger Terminal to Open in Miami," *New York Times*, December 29, 1968: 54
7 Rich Archbold, "Panel Screens Architects for Dodge Island Terminal," *Miami Herald*, March 27 1967. Quoted in Allan Shulman, "The Concrete Line: Miami's Marine Passenger Terminals," paper presented at the X Seminário DOCOMOMO Brasil, Arquitetura Moderna e Internacional: conexões brutalistas 1955–75 (Curitiba, 2013): 5.
8 Robert Venturi, *Complexity and Contradiction in Architecture* (New York: Museum of Modern Art, 1966).
9 Archbold, "Panel Screens Architects," cited in Shulman, "The Concrete Line," 6.

FIG. 1   Miami Seaport Terminal, Florida, 1970.
FIG. 2   Miami Seaport Terminal, customs and baggage hall.

3

4

In *John Andrews: Architecture, a Performing Art*, Andrews recalled his first meeting with the Port of Miami:

> We were invited to meet with the Port of Miami Authority to discuss a new port terminal. It was necessary to fly to Miami. I hate flying and used to drink my way through flights. By the time we arrived for the interview I was in a state, having had a bad flight and some suspect shrimp for lunch. Standing there in the Port Authority's pseudo-Jacobean boardroom, I suddenly felt queasy. I put my hand over my mouth in time, bolted for the bathroom, came back, and finished the presentation. When you go into a presentation you have to have some means of being remembered.[10]

Whatever the impression of his performance was, in his presentation Andrews emphasized the organization of his firm and its ability to get projects built on time and on budget using the "critical path" method that his team used to great effect in the construction of Scarborough College and the University of Guelph residences. Andrews may have only had a limited number of completed projects to his name, but they included projects of a programmatic complexity and scale that Venturi and Vreeland could not match.

After getting the Miami job, Andrews sent three members of his Toronto team, Ed Galanyk, Ned Baldwin, and Ian Morton, to Miami to familiarize them with the complete cruise experience, from boarding to disembarking. They took a three-day jaunt on a cruise in the Caribbean, and this trip made a key problem apparent: after leaving the cruise, passengers faced a grueling process, including waiting for their baggage to be removed and sorted, struggling through customs with their baggage, and finally fighting to get a taxi. The whole process, Andrews reported, could take up to five hours.

FIGS. 3–4   Miami Seaport Terminal.

10   Jennifer Taylor and John Andrews, *John Andrews: Architecture, a Performing Art* (Melbourne: Oxford University Press, 1982), 79.

While waiting for their baggage, passengers also remained on board the cruise ship, which, without engines running or air-conditioning, was sweltering. To make things worse, drinks were not allowed to be served on the ships once they came within the three-mile territorial limit. It was a mess.

Andrews insisted that his team needed to be in Miami to work on the project. Though technically their client was Volkert, they built a strong informal relationship with Port of Miami director Admiral Irvin J. Stephens, because they worked in the boardroom directly adjacent to his office. Andrews recalled that Stephens "would drop in 10 times a day," having to push beer cans out of the way to get into the room.[11] There, Morton, Galanyk, and Baldwin were joined by Andrews for part of the time to work on the project. Andrews's friend and frequent collaborator, landscape architect Dick Strong, also spent time in Miami, working on the terminal's landscape design. The full design was completed in about a month or so. Norbert Seethaler, another of Andrews's collaborators and former John B. Parkin associate, who, like Strong, was a member of Integ, worked as the project's structural consultant. Further, an 8-foot-long model of the design, which was prefabricated by Jim Sykes in Toronto, was assembled in the Port of Miami workshops.[12]

THE LOGIC OF THE PLAN

The logic of Andrews's plan for the Miami Seaport Terminal was constrained by the linearity of the site, which was located on the straight edge of an artificially engineered island. The design necessarily had to be linear. When the project was completed at the end of 1968, the terminal accommodated berths for five ships. [FIG. 1] The design of five different points to embark and disembark the ships allowed for lounges where passengers could wait for their luggage in the comfort of air-conditioning, with drinks in hand. The waiting lounges were connected to the ships by telescoping walkways, which Volkert's scheme also envisioned. However, unlike Volkert's scheme, the disembarkation points did not link to a general customs and immigration area. Rather, the five nodes were linked by four covered baggage-handling areas in which baggage could be received from the ships through gravity-fed conveyors beneath the gangways. Though the baggage areas were roofed, they were otherwise open to the elements. But, since passengers only moved through these zones when their baggage was ready to collect, any discomfort was minimal. [FIG. 2]

The arrangement of the terminal into four baggage halls required that the customs and immigration staff organize into mobile teams in order to handle each ship individually, but the configuration of the port only allowed ships to dock at 30-minute intervals, so this was not problematic. When the customs and immigration staff was ready for them, passengers moved along elevated walkways that connected the nodes, down to the baggage-holding areas by way of switchback stairways—located between each pair of nodes were six stairways—that were determined by deck number and baggage area. [FIGS. 3-4] On the landward side, these baggage areas remained unimpeded, from the customs and immigration stations to the taxi zones. As Andrews claimed, this arrangement was designed to clear passengers through customs within 50 minutes of docking, and in practice worked to clear them in 40 minutes.[13] This interval meshed well with the 30-minute minimum that individual ships had to dock. This rethinking of the boarding and disembarking process resulted in a truly innovative design. "There is no other terminal like it anywhere,"

13 Admiral Irvin J. Stephens, the Port of Miami director and a retired Coast Guard admiral, suggested that the turnaround time for clearing a ship would be reduced to 30 minutes from about an hour. The five hours that Andrews cited presumably reflected the actual experience of the Andrews staff on the cruise they took. See "New Seaport Passenger Terminal to Open in Miami," *New York Times*, December 29, 1968. The analysis by the Andrews team of the embarking and disembarking processes, baggage handling, and customs and immigration formalities is documented in "Passenger Terminal, Port of Miami," *Canadian Architect* (April 1970): 42–51.

11 Ibid., 80
12 Ibid., 80–81

declared Port of Miami director Admiral Stephens. And, as Peter Blake commented, "The building to which Admiral Stephens points to with pride may reflect some of the most searching reexamination of passenger and baggage movement since somebody invented the gangplank."[14]

Also informing the logic of the project was contemporary airport design. Blake reported that the reexamination of traffic patterns at Miami "curiously enough, owes more to the highly advanced discipline of air terminal design than it does to any studies made in recent years by routine seaport planners."[15] Andrews had previously designed an airport as his culminating project for his undergraduate architecture degree at the University of Sydney. Moreover, while Andrews worked at John B. Parkin Associates, the office undertook the design for Toronto International Airport. In *John Andrews: Architecture, a Performing Art*, Andrews recounted:

> For Miami, we tried to create a human environment in keeping with the activities and atmosphere related to sea travel, and to organize baggage handling, customs and immigration in a way that would sustain the environment. At Toronto International Airport, the baggage is handled beautifully and conveniently, straight off the plane and into the baggage carousels. But the people on international flights are trudging up and down long, dismal lavatory-like corridors, through vast stockyard corrals, and queuing up like a herd of poor, bloody cattle. The principle here seems to be that it costs money to move baggage but people can move themselves. If architects are concerned about people, their concern should be to move the people as directly and comfortably as practical and find some machine to cart the baggage the long way around, if that is the choice.[16]

Andrews's decision to functionally disaggregate the plan for the Miami Seaport Terminal into several discrete passenger nodes and baggage-handling areas meant that neither people nor baggage had far to go. The linearity of the site and scheme also allowed the terminal to be built incrementally, adding extra modules to the building at the north of Dodge Island as passenger and ship numbers grew. When the terminal's first five berths opened in late December 1968 a sixth berth was already planned, and in 1972 a seventh was constructed.[17]

THE BIG ROOF

The nodes of the Miami Seaport Terminal building—originally five of them—were designed with a geometrically diagonal plan that contrasted with the linear character of the baggage halls and their corresponding walkways, which were strictly aligned with the straight edge of the dock. However, the nodes accommodated the movement of passengers, from when they arrived at the terminal with their baggage to when they boarded their cruise ships, and their baggage was delivered to their staterooms. In the terminal's upper-level lounge, the diagonal plan for the nodes facilitated the incorporation of windows oriented to take in the views along the flanks of the cruise ships, which increased the boarding passengers' pleasurable anticipation of their voyage. The lounges featured deep coffered concrete ceilings akin to those in the "meeting place" at Scarborough College and in the Andrews design for the D. B. Weldon Library at the University of Western Ontario. A pattern of reusing ideas developed in other contexts was emerging in his work. The baggage hall staircases in his Miami terminal were

---

14   Peter Blake, "Half-Mile Gangplank," *Architectural Forum*, (March 1970): 54–57. In the Miami Seaport Terminal holdings of the John Andrews fonds at the Canadian Architectural Archives (CAA) are some preliminary drawings for a terminal in New York that apparently incorporated a road in the building section. Although Andrews did not recall this project, it appears that his Miami Seaport Terminal elicited some interest from the New York port authorities.
15   Blake, "Half-Mile Gangplank," 55.
16   Taylor and Andrews, *John Andrews*, 82.
17   "New Seaport Passenger Terminal to Open in Miami," *New York Times*, December 29, 1968; "Miami Enjoys Boom as a Passenger Cruise Port," *New York Times*, January 9, 1972.

5

6

FIGS. 5–6 Miami Seaport Terminal.

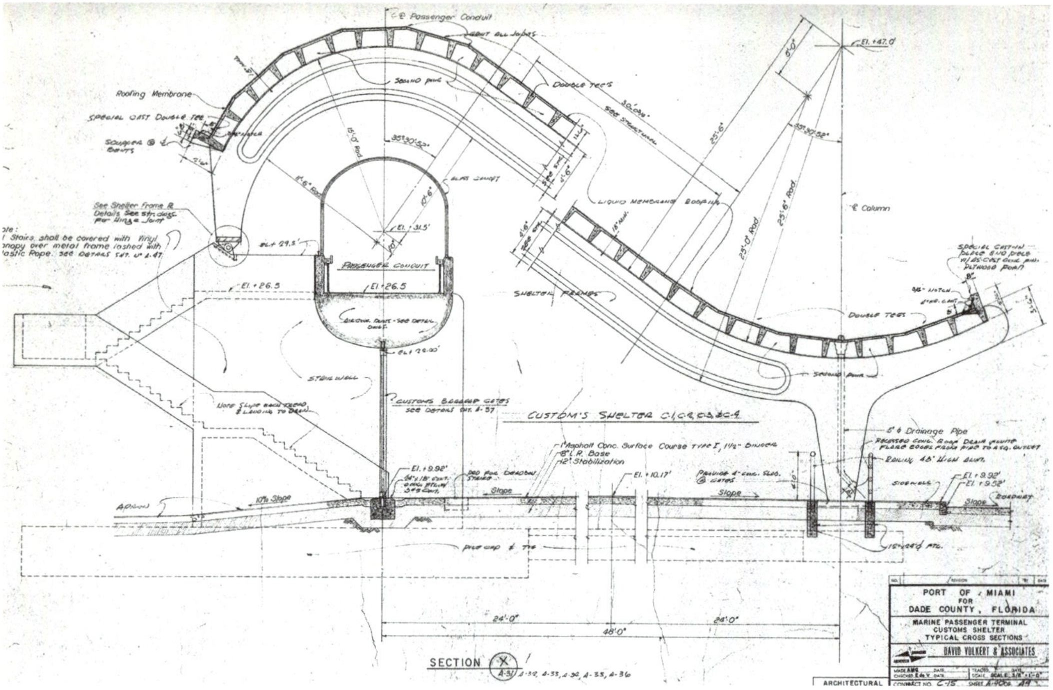

FIG. 7 Section, Miami Seaport Terminal.
FIG. 8 Miami Seaport Terminal, interior of passenger node.
FIG. 9 Miami Seaport Terminal, staircases from elevated passenger walkways to baggage halls.

also similar to open versions of staircases in the science wing of Scarborough College.

The programmatic logic of the Miami Seaport Terminal building was not the only determinant of its form. The nodes also featured vertical concrete cylinders at three of their corners, which corresponded to the location of the transition zones to and from the telescoping gangways and elevated baggage hall walkways. [FIGS. 5–6] These concrete cylinders had an expressive purpose, providing the nodes with a strong external form. They stood as turrets built of smooth-finished, off-form concrete that had a vertical quality, which was emphatically different from the extruded roofs of the baggage halls. The concrete cylinders correspond to many of Andrews's later designs in which vertical concrete cylinders, often containing areas of glass brick fenestration, generally serve as external expressions of internal vertical movement, such as that of stairs or lifts. At the Miami Seaport Terminal, the vertical cylinders did not correspond to the internal movement of people up or down but to a change in the pace of horizontal circulation, from relaxed to purposeful and purposeful to relaxed. Organized in groups of three, they also relate to the reappearance across Andrews's oeuvre of circulation and/or structural cores designed in threes. This was first manifest in the Toronto International Airport control tower he designed while at John B. Parkin Associates, which incorporated three towers made of plank-stamped off-form concrete that supported the control room at their top.[18] The most ambitiously realized design containing this threefold structural-service logic is Andrews's King George Tower, completed in Sydney in 1976.

The roofs of the baggage halls were designed as curved vaults that extruded out over the length of each 500-foot-long hall and were also constructed out of concrete.[19] Structurally, they were made up of vast, asymmetrical supporting elements built of in-situ cast concrete and precast concrete T-sections.

[FIG. 7] On the landward side of the halls, the support structures rested directly on the ground, and on the other side of the halls, they were built with pin joints that connected them to the tops of laterally oriented concrete walls. The switchback stairways were aligned at either side of these walls, which terminated at the height of the walkway balustrade. [FIG. 9] The asymmetrical shape of the vaults over the baggage halls and walkways was designed as an airfoil to mitigate destructive hurricane winds, and their exact shape was determined through wind tunnel tests.[20] The mix of in-situ and precast concrete expedited the construction process, so that the terminal buildings were designed and built in less than 20 months.[21]

The overall form of the complex, then, was the outcome of a combination of pragmatic and aesthetic concerns. Externally, the design of the terminal into passenger nodes and open halls produced a rhythmic disposition along the tremendous length of the dock, which was determined by the scale of the ships. The beautiful asymmetrical vaults of the baggage halls were designed aerodynamically but also in section accommodate the upper-level walkways on the seaward side. These aspects of the Miami Seaport Terminal's design were driven by pragmatic problem-solving; it seems as if the beauty of these vaults was incidental. In contrast to these forms, the diagonally arranged nodes with their vertical concrete cylinders offered visual syncopation. [FIG. 11] Andrews always enjoyed explaining his designs in terms of their pragmatic and social function and perhaps most enjoyed the projects where such functions were very clear. However, the architectural treatment of the nodes at the terminal, which were designed in a manner that contrasts visually with the luggage hall vaults, was not the inevitable outcome of a problem solved. Rather, this treatment appeared to be a

---

18   Shulman relates the pattern of threefold turrets at the Miami terminal to Andrews's unrealized triangular office tower for Toronto. See Shulman, "The Concrete Line," 12n26.

19   Thus, the building was 2000 feet long. "News and Notes from the Field of Travel," *New York Times*, August 13, 1967.

20   Professor Bernard Etkin of the University of Toronto performed the wind analysis; Leslie F. Conover was the consulting meteorologist. John Andrews Architects/David Volkert & Associates, "A Passenger Ship Terminal for the Port of Miami, Florida," report, Miami, Florida, July 1967.

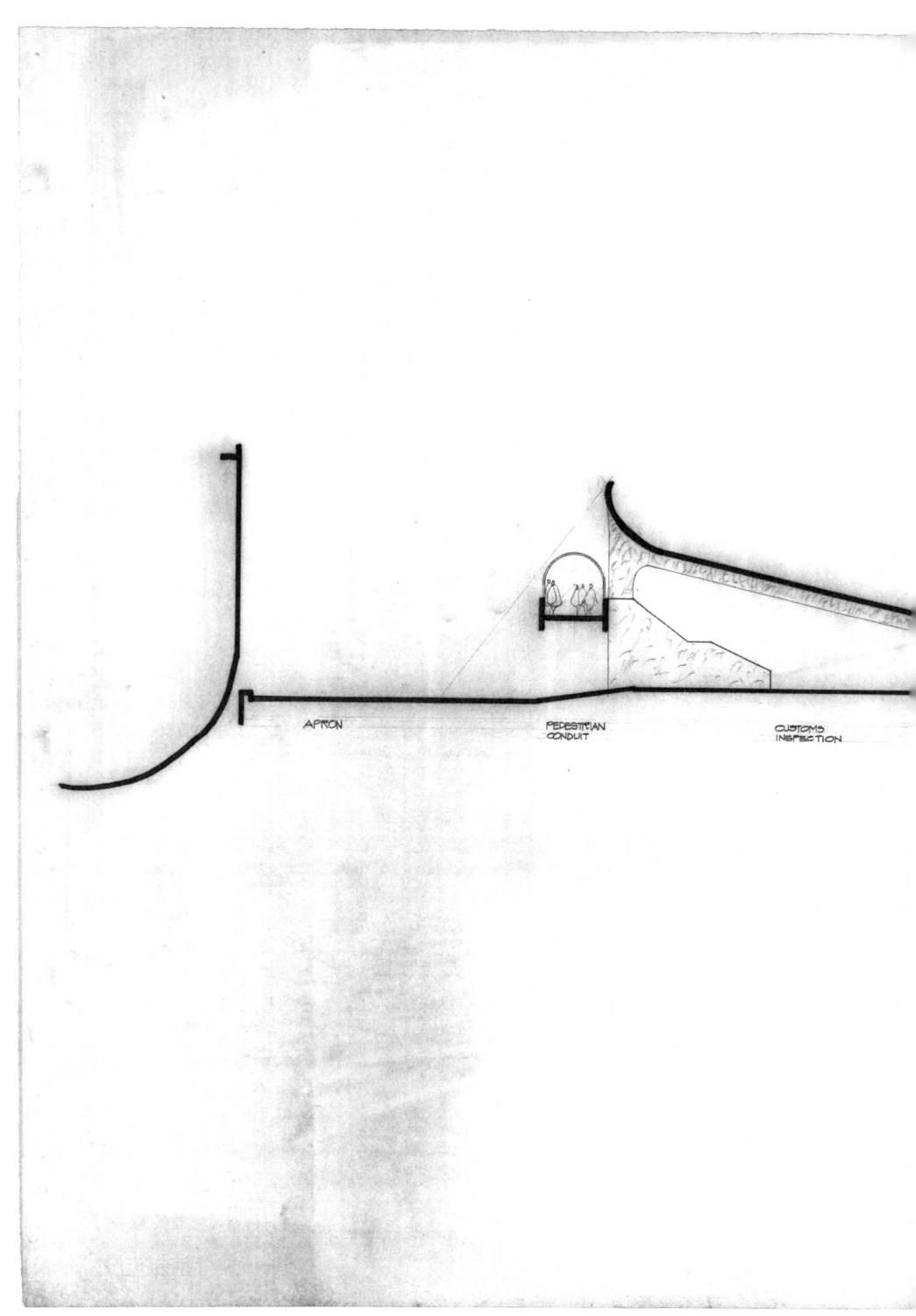

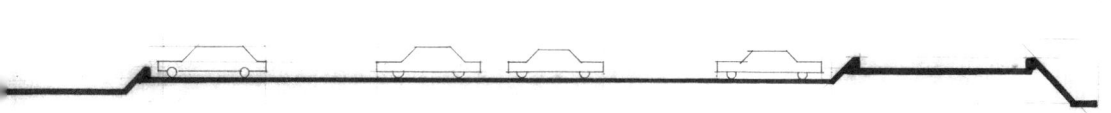

FIG. 10   Preliminary design section of customs area, Miami Seaport Terminal.

FIG. 11 Miami Seaport Terminal.

matter of design choice. Andrews developed a range of design strategies to call on when such choices had to be made. For example, as seen in the Miami terminal, his use of vertical concrete cylinders grouped in threes was one of these repeated strategies.

The composition of the Miami Seaport Terminal, as a series of extruded roofs contrasting with the passenger nodes, gave the building the civic presence that Giurgola initially envisioned. This was especially apparent when looking south toward Dodge Island from the MacArthur Causeway. As Shulman has put it, the architecture of the terminal "conveyed a strong plasticity that tempered Miami's strong light and offered a striking contrast with the sleek metal cruise ships, the blue water, and the green landscape."[22] On the landward side of the terminal, Dick Strong's landscape design supplied the tropicality that Giurgola prescribed. As the *New York Times* reported, "The entire port is to be elaborately landscaped with emphasis on citrus fruits, orchids, palms, and other trees and plants commonly associated with Miami's tropical climate."[23]

The ways in which the plans and forms at the Miami Seaport Terminal were tailored to movement, as Shulman suggests, related the project to the work of Team 10. As he has written, "The successive terminal modules and spine-like connecting bridges of Andrews's terminal seem to approximate the functioning of Stem and Web, the mobility-based conceptual framework develop by Shadrach Woods and Team 10 in the 1960s."[24] Indeed, Andrews's comment, "Transportation structures are our contemporary cathedrals," gives this view some credence.[25] However, the connection to Team 10 is tendentious, though it is often made in discussions of Andrews's work of the 1960s. While the abstract patterns of movement proposed for the Metro Centre have much in

21 Ibid., 8.
22 Shulman, "The Concrete Line," 9.
23 "New Seaport Passenger Terminal to Open in Miami," *New York Times*, December 29, 1968.
24 Shulman, "The Concrete Line," 10; Shulman "Ports and Passenger Terminals: Infrastructure as Spectacle," 157.
25 Taylor and Andrews, *John Andrews*, 83.

common with Team 10 projects, Andrews's focus on movement at the Miami terminal is much more literal, even machine-like.

At the time of the terminal's completion, *The Florida Architect* noted, "The building is a multilevel street with all functions clearly separated yet related as necessary. It becomes a machine in a formal expression of concrete massing while relating successfully to scales of human, autos, and ships."[26] Peter Blake also called the building "a kind of machine, designed to facilitate and express patterns of movement."[27] The original intention to enclose the elevated walkways at the terminal with curved glass—to make them into tubes—would have further underwritten this focus on the expression of patterns of movement.[28]

Shulman also connected the project to Sigfried Giedion's notion of New Monumentality and the designs of the buildings envisioned for Miami's unbuilt Interama, a proposed permanent exposition devoted to Latin America.[29] Considering that both Giedion and Josep Lluís Sert were teachers of great importance to Andrews during his studies at the Harvard GSD, the relationship to the New Monumentality promoted by Giedion, Sert, and others in the postwar years is entirely justified. However, this link to Giedion and Sert must be understood genealogically; by the time Andrews was working on his design for the Miami Seaport Terminal, he had 10 years of design experience since graduating.

While Interama included projects by other architects Andrews admired, such as Sert and Louis Kahn, Shulman has pointed to Paul Rudolph in particular and his International Bazaar proposal for the 1967 Interama as influential in Andrews's design for the Miami terminal.[30] While the section of Andrews's luggage halls resembled the roofs planned to shade large areas in Rudolph's Interama design, it seems unlikely that Andrews would have seen them. Early on, Andrews did have an interest in Rudolph's work, and he may have learned climatic lessons from Rudolph's Florida houses, which he would have been particularly mindful of in Miami. However, the project that likely influenced Andrews's design for the Miami terminal most directly was Rudolph's Temple Street Parking Garage in New Haven, but only in the sense that it demonstrated the ways in which architectural poetry could be generated in a large transportation infrastructure project made of concrete. In fact, Andrews visited and photographed the Temple Street Parking Garage soon after it was completed in 1963.

The drawings for the Miami Seaport Terminal in the John Andrews fonds at the Canadian Architectural Archives (CCA) at the University of Calgary are unusual in that they include many exploratory sketches. Most of the projects represented there by John Andrews Architects are documented with more definitive drawings. The Miami terminal holdings, however, include many undated sketch drawings on yellow trace paper, such as studies for the nodes, the relationship of the walkways to the baggage-area roofs, and especially the roof section and supporting structures. [FIGS. 10, 12–13] These sketches suggest that the overall logic of the design, determining the baggage halls,

26 "Passenger Terminal/New Port of Miami," *The Florida Architect* (March/April 1970): 6–9.
27 Blake, "Half-Mile Gangplank," 5.
28 In the book *John Andrews: Architecture, a Performing Art*, Andrews explained at some length that these circulation tubes were to be enclosed with curved glass so that they also could be air-conditioned. This was abandoned because the tenders from the glass companies to supply the glass were about four times their pre-bid estimates. The cost of the glass would have come in at about a fifth of the overall budget for the terminal building as a whole. Enclosed circulation tubes reappear in Andrews's work in his 1973 project for the Callam Offices in Canberra, where they would have connected the 24 office pods. The Callam Offices were only partly realized, as three pods that make up the the Woden Trade and Further Education (TAFE) building, in 1978. In this project, the walkway glazing was replaced with Perspex (Plexiglas).
29 See Giedion, "The Need for a New Monumentality," in Paul Zucker, ed., *New Architecture and City Planning* (New York: Philosophical Library, 1944). The 1943 text "Nine Points on Monumentality" by Josep Lluís Sert, Fernand Léger, and Sigfried Giedion was first published in Sigfried Giedion, *Arkitektur und Gemeinschft* (Hamburg: Rowohit, 1956), 40–42; English edition: Sigfried Giedion, *Architecture, You and Me* (Cambridge, MA: Harvard University Press, 1958), 48–52.
30 Robert González, "Interama: Visions of a Pan-American City," in *Miami Modern Metropolis: Paradise and Paradox in Midcentury Architecture and Planning*, ed. Allan T. Shulman (Miami: Bass Museum of Art, 2009), 147–51.

iconic roofs, and diagonally oriented nodes, was reached very quickly. Andrews recalled that the only roof plan that was wind-tunnel tested was the roof that was built. Regardless, the range of sketches displays that many design possibilities were considered, from asymmetrically folded roofs to roof folds with curves and to pitched roof plates with upward curves along both edges.

More than any project by Team 10 or other architects that Andrews may have been connected to, the sketches featuring pitched roof plates recall the section of Eero Saarinen's design for Dulles International Airport in Virginia. The scale is similar, but the construction is different. In the sketches by John Andrews Architects, the pitched roof form is straight apart from the outer upward curves, suggesting some kind of linear construction, such as a frame and panel system. From its asymmetrically sculpted and canted pylons, Saarinen's concrete roof drapes in a continuous, sectional curve. But Saarinen's roof, projected to provide a 600-foot-long covering for his terminal building, creating one enormous room, is a clear precedent to Andrews's approach for the Miami Seaport Terminal.

Andrews himself referred to the lessons he learned from the design of the Toronto Airport (also learning what not to do), and perhaps he learned positive lessons from Saarinen's airport design as well. The Dulles Airport plan, featuring departures on the upper level and arrivals on the lower level, which is now standard, was a particularly important innovation. The ways in which Saarinen's design for Dulles Airport anticipated lateral expansion, differentiating it from Saarinen's TWA Flight Center terminal in New York, is also significant.[31] The careful shaping of the massive support structures in Andrew's design for the Miami Seaport Terminal had a strong kinship with the shaping of Saarinen's pylons at Dulles Airport. Not only did the Miami terminal structures form the graceful asymmetrical S-shaped section of the baggage hall roofs but, in their vertical portion, they were subtly tapered. And, along their length, they were sculpted with an attenuated indent, forming shadows that subtly reinforce the curved form. According to Blake, the baggage hall arches were referred to as "sea horses," an affectionate nickname that acknowledges the somewhat zoomorphic character of these massive primary structures.[32]

What survived in Andrews's design for the Miami Seaport Terminal, which may have been influenced by Saarinen's work, was the continuous extrusion of a roof that has an asymmetrical section. Large roofs previously appeared in two of Andrews's major unbuilt projects: the airline terminal he designed as his thesis project at the University of Sydney in 1956 and his design of Toronto City Hall in 1958. His idea for an extruding roof, however, was new. It transformed Saarinen's Dulles Airport precedent through the decision in his design for the Miami terminal to inflect the curve in order to suit climatic exigencies, the patterns of passenger movement, and the building's tremendous length, breaking it up with architecturally distinct nodes. Although the Miami terminal project was unique in Andrews's oeuvre, showcasing its charismatic roof, and unique for having such a singular brief, it in fact developed ideas that the architect had already explored at the University of Guelph and at Scarborough College in particular.[33]

Scarborough College also featured an overall linear parti, which, like the Miami Seaport Terminal, was intended to grow in accordance with that linear pattern.[34] Both Scarborough College and the Miami terminal were developed in section and then extruded along the site. At Scarborough, however, there were two fundamentally different cross sections, one for the sciences and one for the

---

31 Jayne Merkel, *Eero Saarinen* (London: Phaidon, 2005), 219; Susanna Santala, "Airports; Building for the Jet Age," in Eeva-Liisa Pelkonen and Donald Albrecht, *Eero Saarinen: Shaping the Future* (New Haven, CT: Yale University Press, 2006), 300–307. Dulles Airport was expanded laterally in 1996 when a 300-foot addition was added at either end of the building.

32 Blake, "Half-Mile Gangplank," 56.
33 Peter Blake saw the logic of Scarborough College and the Miami terminal being similar. See Blake, "Half-Mile Gangplank," 56.

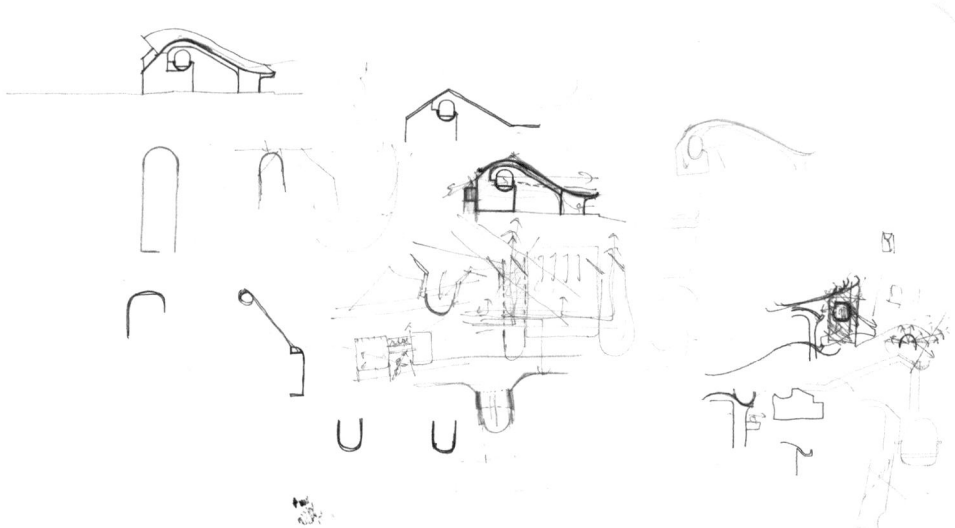

12

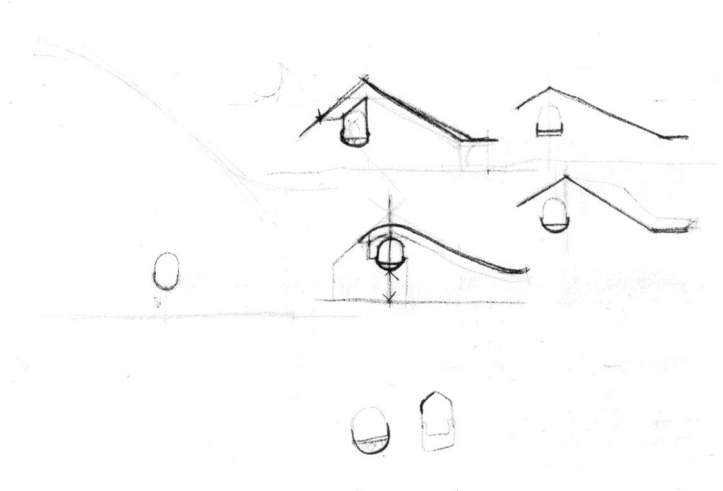

13

FIGS. 12–13   Preliminary sketches, Miami Seaport Terminal.

14

15

FIGS. 14–15   Miami Seaport Terminal.

humanities, while at the Miami terminal, there was only one, since the terminal building facilitated the same activities along its 2,000-foot length. The overall form of the Scarborough College building was determined by the edge of a natural escarpment that was not straight, while the edge at the Miami terminal was an engineered straight line. At both Scarborough College and the Miami terminal, knuckles disrupted the linear form: the "meeting place" and science lecture theaters at the college and the terminal's passenger lounge nodes. And, not unimportantly, both the college and the terminal were alike insofar as they were confident expressions of the off-form, fair-faced concrete aesthetic.

Moreover, Scarborough College and the Miami Seaport Terminal were both outcomes of concentrated design processes that were intensive temporally and spatially. While Scarborough College was developed during an intense summer of activity in an old chemistry classroom at the University of Toronto, the Miami terminal was created through a beer-fueled month or so of hard work in a boardroom at the Port of Miami. In these intensive, focused bursts, Andrews developed a modus operandi of creating design schemes that were both formally compelling and addressed functional needs. This was often also done in ways that were tangential to the conventional terms of a brief: Scarborough College aggregated university facilities that were traditionally divided into separate buildings, and the Miami terminal disaggregated the processing of passengers into separate zones along its full length.

The Miami Seaport Terminal also played an important role in Andrews's work as a crucial project in a line of designs that were developed through the unconventional use of sections. This was true of Scarborough College, but sections as a driving idea first appeared in Andrews's unbuilt Malton Hotel project, which he completed as part of the plan for the Toronto Airport while working in the John B. Parkin office. The use of sections also informed the design of two major projects by Andrews that immediately followed the Miami Seaport Terminal: the Harvard GSD's Gund Hall and the Cameron Offices.

---

34 Reyner Banham noted, however, that Scarborough College did not expand as envisioned: "Alas for stereotyped hopes; the human race at large never waits around for their fulfilment. What happened actually was that the great pedestrian street began to fill up over the next few years with carrells, bookshelves, tables and chairs, until by 1970 parts of it were difficult to perambulate in spite of the fact that Scarborough was supposed by its designers to expand accretively by the repetition of its standard units along extensions of the two wings—accretion which its loosely articulated megaform could absorb without distortion of its aesthetic—that was not what had happened. With barely half of its proposed total volume built, increasing student numbers were accommodated by expanding internally, out of the classrooms and into the welcome gift of unoccupied square-footage presented by the monumental but redundant floor-space if the pedestrian street." Banham, *Megastructure*, 135. New construction, when it happened at Scarborough College, did not extend the existing structure.

07

george gund hall

by   Paul Walker

WHY ANDREWS?

In 1967 the Harvard University Graduate School of Design commissioned John Andrews to design its new building, George Gund Hall, less than a decade after he graduated from the school. Given that the GSD's alumni included some very high-profile architects, exactly why Andrews was selected to design Gund Hall is somewhat unclear. Certainly, his own profile had been boosted by the wide publicity that Scarborough College received in 1966, but other architects with connections to Harvard had more extensive resumes. Andrews himself believed that he was chosen on Josep Lluís Sert's initiative. Sert was appointed to the role of planning consultant by Harvard President Nathan Pusey in 1956.[1] Under Pusey's leadership, beginning in 1953, Harvard's endowments grew substantially. Money was raised to fund new professorships and provide support for students but also to improve buildings both for university teaching programs and for research, which expanded prodigiously during the 1950s and 1960s thanks to growing grant income from government sources. These improvements were mindful of the historic architecture at its heart, since Harvard, before Pusey, favored Georgian Revival architecture. The notable exceptions to this style were several science buildings constructed in the 1940s and Walter Gropius's Harvard Graduate Center completed in 1950.[2]

Pusey, however, favored modern architecture and looked to Sert's expertise to modernize the campus.[3] Sert designed several key buildings in the 1960s: the Center for the Study of World Religions (1960); the Holyoke Center for campus services and administration (1965); the Peabody Terrace housing complex for married students (1964); and the Science Center (1975), a large complex of undergraduate teaching facilities that began construction in 1968. [FIGS. 1–4] The Science Center also features a group of lecture theaters with a curious external radial structure that looks rather like a huge spider.[4] These buildings exemplified Sert's approach, accommodating the demand for facilities from a growing student body, growing faculty numbers, and new research needs. For the most part, these new developments occurred outside of the sensitive context of Harvard Yard, where historic and early 20th-century Georgian-style buildings were generally refurbished rather than replaced.[5] Sert's Holyoke Center and Peabody Terrace were successful exercises in introducing high-rises to Harvard and the broader Cambridge context. This was in line with modern architectural principles and Sert's notion of "the heart of the city," which he promulgated through Congrès International d'Architecture Moderne (CIAM) conferences and through an emphasis on the urban landscape in teaching at the Harvard GSD under his leadership.

Not all of the new buildings constructed at Harvard during this period are as successful as Sert's; take, for example, William James Hall (1963), designed by Minoru Yamasaki, a notably bland 15-story tower for behavioral sciences, located just north of the Harvard GSD site.[6] This collection of Harvard projects is also not as impressive as the catalog of new buildings at Yale, though this is unlikely to have been Sert's doing. According to Morton and Phyllis Keller, historians of Harvard's 20th-century development, Pusey chose the architects of the new buildings on campus.[7] Pusey was mindful of the challenges facing the architectural profession in the 1960s, such as the need to address urban and environmental issues, to develop collaborations with a range of disciplines, and to engage with new research. He aired all these issues in an address he delivered to the 1966 AIA National Annual Conference under the title "The Needed New Man in Architecture." However, there is one

---

1   Morton Keller and Phyllis Keller, *Making Harvard Modern: The Rise of America's University* (New York: Oxford University Press, 2001), 198.
2   Bainbridge Bunting and Margaret Henderson Floyd, *Harvard: An Architectural History*, (Cambridge, MA: Belknap Press for Harvard University Press, 1985), 219–29.
3   Keller and Keller, *Making Harvard Modern*, 198.
4   Josep M. Rovira, *José Luis Sert, 1901–1983*, trans. Leonora Saavedra (Milan: Electa, 2000), 332–41; For a discussion of the four Sert buildings at Harvard, see Ibid., 351–56.
5   Bunting and Floyd, *Harvard*, 232.
6   Ibid., 239–40.
7   Keller and Keller, *Making Harvard Modern*, 268.

1

3

2

4

FIG. 1　Harvard Science Center, Harvard University, Cambridge, Massachusetts, 1968–1975. Architect: Josep Lluís Sert
FIG. 2　Interior, Harvard Science Center.
FIG. 3　Peabody Terrace, Harvard University, Cambridge, Massachusetts, 1962–1964. Architect: Josep Lluís Sert
FIG. 4　Holyoke building, Harvard University, Cambridge, Massachusetts, 1958–1965. Architect: Josep Lluís Sert

highly significant Harvard project where the architect was clearly chosen by Sert and not Pusey: the Carpenter Center for the Visual Arts (1963), Le Corbusier's only North American building. The Carpenter Center was built to house a program that introduced the practice of fine arts to Harvard's undergraduate curriculum under the guidance of Sert's associate, architectural historian Eduard Sekler.

In 1965, the Harvard GSD initiated a fundraising program with an $11.6-million target to fund a new building and new professorships and scholarships.[8] Andrews became involved in garnering contributions from Harvard GSD alumni in Canada as a member of a committee chaired by Macklin Hancock, a prominent Toronto planning consultant and a Harvard GSD alumnus.[9] In a meeting with Pusey that Andrews anticipated to be about the endowment campaign, he was shocked to be offered the commission to design the new Harvard GSD building. The Kellers had suggested that Andrews was Pusey's choice, and Sert wanted the new building to be designed by Gropius.[10] However, the design of the Harvard GSD, like that of the Carpenter Center, was very close to Sert's heart, and whatever internal machinations were involved in the choice, there is good reason to think that both Pusey and Sert welcomed Andrews's appointment. And by 1967, Gropius was already in his mid-80s. When Gund Hall was completed in 1972, architectural critic Peter Blake made it quite clear Andrews's appointment was Sert's initiative: "Sert thought Andrews was exactly right for the GSD, and he persuaded Harvard to hire him."[11]

Andrews himself believed that Sert wanted a graduate of the Harvard GSD from his tenure to design the building rather than a graduate from Gropius's tenure. But this still left a lot of possibilities, including Fumihiko Maki, who was arguably then the most prominent of Sert's former students. The key to the mystery is certainly Scarborough College. Pusey was particularly interested in undergraduate teaching issues, and perhaps the innovations at Scarborough College, including the University of Toronto's attempt to use television as a means of teaching, caught Pusey's attention.[12] Andrews inferred that Pusey had communicated with Scarborough College Principal David Carleton Williams, who was an Andrews supporter. In 1967, when Williams became president of the University of Western Ontario, he promptly commissioned Andrews to design a new library building there. Like the Harvard GSD, the D. B. Weldon Library opened in 1972. Discussions between Pusey and University of Toronto President Claude Bissell also likely took place; for part of the year of 1967, Bissell took leave from his leadership role at the University of Toronto to serve as Harvard's first William Lyon Mackenzie King Professor of Canadian Studies.[13] Like Williams, Bissell was enthusiastic about Andrews's design for Scarborough College and impressed by his initiative in pushing the project forward. In Bissell's memoir of his career at the University of Toronto, he wrote of Andrews's "self-confidence and his unruffled boyish arrogance… his easy grasp of detail and his swift response to practical needs."[14]

Sert was also aware of Scarborough College, and as Peter Blake suggested, perhaps had seen it in person.[15] Further, he had other opportunities to become familiar with Andrews's work in Canada. In 1965, the Andrews office began the design and construction of the vast South Residences at the University of Guelph in western Ontario. The University of Guelph was a new university that grew out of the amalgamation

---

8   Ibid., 268.
9   See "Harvard Fundraising Committee," January 24, 1967, AND 43A/78-33, Box 43-48, John Andrews fonds, Canadian Architectural Archives, University of Calgary (hereafter CAA), which contains a letter from Macklin to Andrews thanking him for agreeing to be a member of this committee.
10 Keller and Keller, *Making Harvard Modern*, 268.
11 Peter Blake, "Harvard's Unhallowed Hall: Why is the School's Architectural Establishment Taking Pot Shots at its New Home?" *Boston Magazine*, December 1972, 26.

12 On the use of television at Scarborough College, see John A. Lee, *Test Pattern: Instructional Television at Scarborough College, University of Toronto* (Toronto: University of Toronto Press, 1971).
13 Claude Bissell, *Halfway Up Parnassus: A Personal Account of the University of Toronto, 1932-1971* (Toronto: University of Toronto Press, 1974), 126–27.
14 Bissell, *Halfway Up Parnassus*, 56. Bissell later contributed a glowing preface to Jennifer Taylor and John Andrews, *John Andrews: Architecture, a Performing Art* (Melbourne: Oxford University Press, 1982).
15 Blake, "Harvard's Unhallowed Hall," 26.

of three existing vocational colleges. As chapter 4 of this book outlines, the University of Guelph hired Macklin Hancock's firm, Project Planning Associates, Ltd., to oversee the plan for the university's development and expansion on the site of the Ontario Agricultural College in 1964. As design consultants, Hancock turned to Richard Dober, a campus-planning expert based in Cambridge, and Sert's firm in Boston.[16] Sert, Jackson & Associates was responsible for Guelph's McLaughlin Library and the MacKinnon Building for humanities and social sciences, designed in a manner akin to Sert's buildings at Harvard and Boston Universities.[17] Sert's projects at the University of Guelph were intended to provide the campus with more intensity, a quality needed there far more than at Harvard. The South Residences were on the periphery of the University of Guelph campus, integrated into the overall campus plan through their location at the southern end of the major north–south pedestrian axis that Project Planning Associates, Ltd., established. Andrews's design at the University of Guelph was mindful of the lessons promoted by Sert about the urban dimensions and potential of architecture.

THE HARVARD GSD IN CRISIS

The brief for the new Harvard GSD building was meager. For example, Andrews recalled that the only concrete requirement for the studio spaces was that each should be provided with a sink. Indeed, the October 1967 document for the GSD "Building Program" specifies this. While it does include more details than Andrews remembered—it outlines that optimal studio size should accommodate 20 students and that each student should be provided with "both a drawing and reference table and some personal storage"—it in fact says very little. The main requirement it calls for is 37,400 square feet of space to accommodate 340 students at 110 square feet per student, which would be divided into three areas accounting for the 20-student studio spaces. The rationale for this arrangement is put forth in a short paragraph, but there is no account of the school's pedagogical strategy or teaching philosophy to flesh out its basic physical needs. The requirements for many other spaces are described much more fully in the "Building Program" document, but invariably these are only lengthier because they have more technical prerequisites. At 24 pages, the most detailed description of requirements by far is for the audiovisual facilities, including a photography studio and processing area, audio recording and editing spaces, and an audiovisual library.

Given the debates that occurred within the Harvard GSD concerning its pedagogical strategies and priorities since the Gropius years, it was perhaps surprising that the brief for the school's new building—and especially for its key studio spaces—was so cryptic and technical. But this was symptomatic of both this particular moment at the GSD and Sert's waning authority in the last years of his deanship. When Sert decided to proceed with a new building in 1965, he certainly considered that bringing the GSD's various departments and programs together under one roof would foster opportunities for the interdisciplinarity he sought during his leadership, which were compromised by the scattering of GSD programs across five locations on campus.[18] However, the building was commissioned and designed during a period that coincided with the peak of college protest movements in the United States, and the GSD was not immune to these movements.

In the spring of 1969, there were protests across the Harvard campus, triggered by the broader political context encompassing the Vietnam War, the American invasion of Cambodia, and the Kent State University

16 "Designing for Growth: The Metamorphosis of a Rural Campus into a University Town," *Architectural Record* 151, no. 5 (May 1972): 89–98.

17 Rovira dates Sert's University of Guelph projects from 1967 to 1968. See Rovira, *José Luis Sert*, 396.

18 Ada Louise Huxtable, "New Harvard Hall: Drama and Questions," *New York Times*, November 8, 1972. Reprinted as "Good Architecture–Bad Vibes," *Canadian Architect* (January 1973): 38.

19 Anthony Alofsin, *The Struggle for Modernism: Architecture, Landscape Architecture, and City Planning at Harvard* (New York: W. W. Norton, 2002), 262; Robert Jensen, "Gund Hall–Harvard's Graduate School of Design under One Roof," *Architectural Record* 152, no. 6 (November 1972): 104.

shootings in Ohio.[19] On April 9, 1969, Harvard students involved in the national protest organization Students for a Democratic Society occupied University Hall, the administrative center for the Faculty of Arts and Sciences. Two days later, as Pusey instigated, state troopers and local police forcibly removed the protestors. The immediate aftermath of this enforced eviction was a student strike, for which design students produced propaganda posters and T-shirts, which were printed on the GSD premises in Robinson Hall.[20] [FIG. 5] While many of Harvard's senior faculty and administrators agreed with Pusey's insistence that the university's normal activities should not be disrupted, there were also leading liberal figures, such as economist John Kenneth Galbraith, who sympathized with the protestors and others who in any case did not think the university's heavy-handed response was appropriate. Having lost the respect of most students and many of his colleagues, Pusey left Harvard in 1971.[21] Sert's departure was more immediate, as he retired right in the middle of the 1969 student revolt.

Within the GSD, the events on campus in the spring of 1969 brought to a head a growing loss of faith in the school's ethos. As Anthony Alofsin has explained,

> Just as massive protests marked a nation in crisis, the strike marked a rupture in the idealistic premise of the GSD that joint efforts and commonality of purpose could ameliorate the conditions under which people live. Now the power of the design arts to change society was being questioned, and that questioning appeared to discourage designers even to attempt to serve society. In its simplest form, the critique of architecture's social efficacy asserted that the political structures in which the design fields operated dominated the efforts of the designer.... Many saw architecture as an indulgence in aesthetics at the expense of political action and social need. The future of architecture appeared to lie

20   Alfosin, *The Struggle for Modernism*, 262.
21   Keller and Keller, *Making Harvard Modern*, 314–36.

FIG. 5   Students had a mass rally in Harvard Stadium on April 14, 1969.

almost solely in its connections to other disciplines—sociology, linguistics, and systems analysis.[22]

The fact that the GSD was in crisis was further signaled in the appointment of Maurice Kilbridge as Sert's successor. An outsider both to the school and the architecture profession, Kilbridge was a professor from the Harvard Business School who had worked with urban planners from the GSD. Kilbridge's position was confirmed in 1970, but he was assailed by both conservatives and reformers within the faculty.[23] The city and regional planning program became a particular hotbed of discontent.[24]

In these circumstances, it was difficult to move forward with the project to design a new building for the GSD. While the leadership of the faculty faltered and changed between 1967 and 1970, the development of the new GSD building's design occurred without a sustained philosophical position on the part of the client. Moreover, reflecting the volatility of campus politics, students and many younger faculty at the GSD took the high-minded view that the money being spent on a new building would be better directed to supporting social and economic development in the underserved communities that were Harvard's neighbors in Cambridge. Design consultation meetings between Andrews and the design team on one side, and the GSD community on the other, were therefore necessarily fraught. Conceding to the importance of engaging with the local neighborhood (or perhaps attempting to co-opt it), at the November 1969 groundbreaking ceremony that marked the start of the construction of Gund Hall, fifth-grade pupils from a local primary school were recruited to turn the sod at the site. Dean Kilbridge grandly stated:

Those who will work and study in George Gund Hall will learn to shape our future buildings, habitats, cities, and landscapes—on all scales for all men. To future generations we pledge this School to the task of creating environmental beauty and preserving what we have. We pledge this so that these children will not be deprived, but will have cities in which life is worth living, will know the glory and the freshness of the earth, and may hear the chant of nature, and not silent springs.[25]

Without a strong and coherent lead from the faculty, or the briefing document, Andrews approached the design of the Harvard GSD from the basis of his developing view of architecture education. Andrews had led architectural design studios at the University of Toronto beginning in 1962, and in 1967, after his success with Scarborough College and his growing reputation as a rising star in the architectural profession, he was made chair of the architecture department at the University of Toronto. Considering the burgeoning success of his architecture practice, he was reluctant to commit fully to this role, and accepted the position on the condition that another senior academic would be appointed to oversee the day-to-day operations of the program. The person assigned to this role was English architect and fellow GSD alum Peter Prangnell.

However, Andrews's academic responsibilities at the University of Toronto did give him time to think about his philosophy of architecture education. In the following two years, before he stepped down as chair of the architecture department at the University of Toronto in 1969, he initiated major changes to the program's teaching while he developed his design for the Harvard GSD. Though often seen as a pragmatic architect, Andrews did not believe that architecture education should be merely about the vocational preparation of students to work in Toronto's architectural offices. For example, he held that prospective students, as was required of him to

22 Alofsin, *The Struggle for Modernism*, 262–63.
23 Jane Holtz Kay, "Design School Trouble Long Time Coming at Harvard," *Boston Globe*, October 3, 1971.
24 Keller and Keller, 269. The Department of Regional Planning was transferred to the John F. Kennedy School of Government in 1980, and a new program focused on the design and physical form of cities was subsequently established within the Harvard GSD. See Alofsin, *The Struggle for Modernism*, 266, 303.

25 "Gund Hall Ground-breaking," *HGDSA News '70/1*, March 1970, 4.

FIG. 6   First sketch, Gund Hall, Harvard University, 1967.

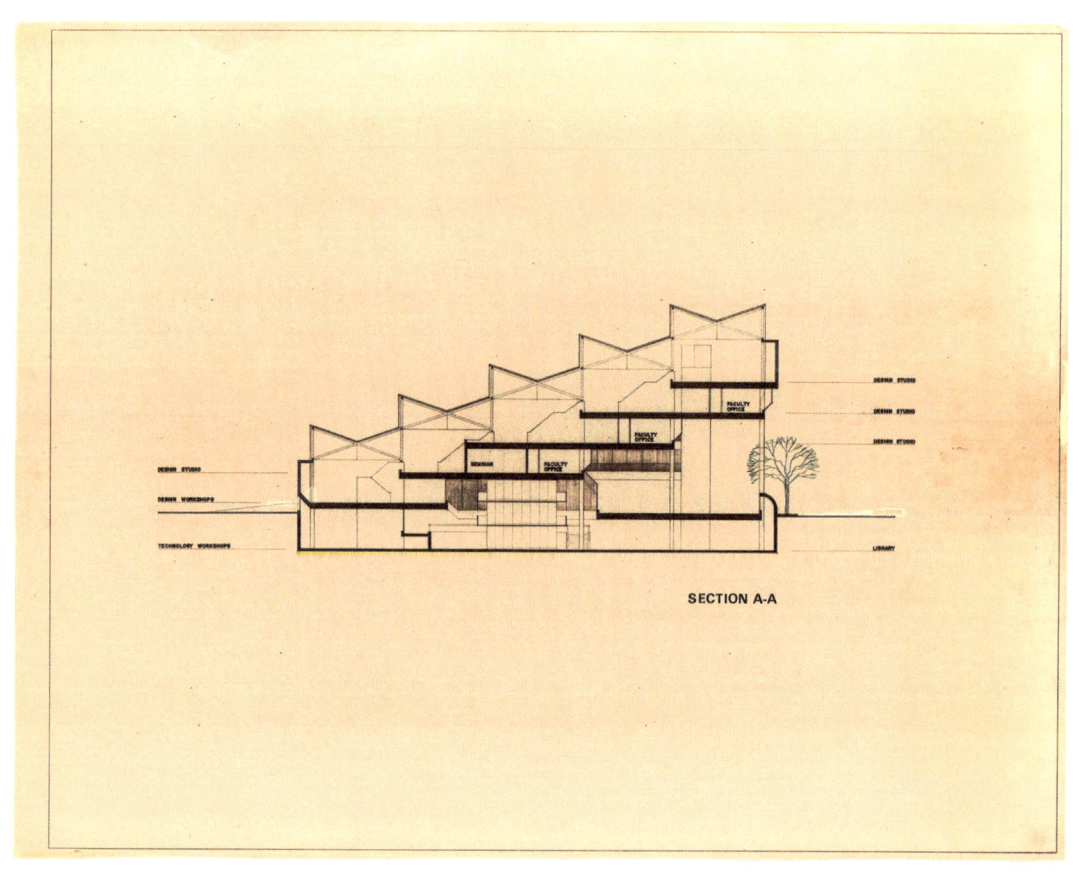

FIG. 7 Section, preliminary scheme, Gund Hall, 1969.

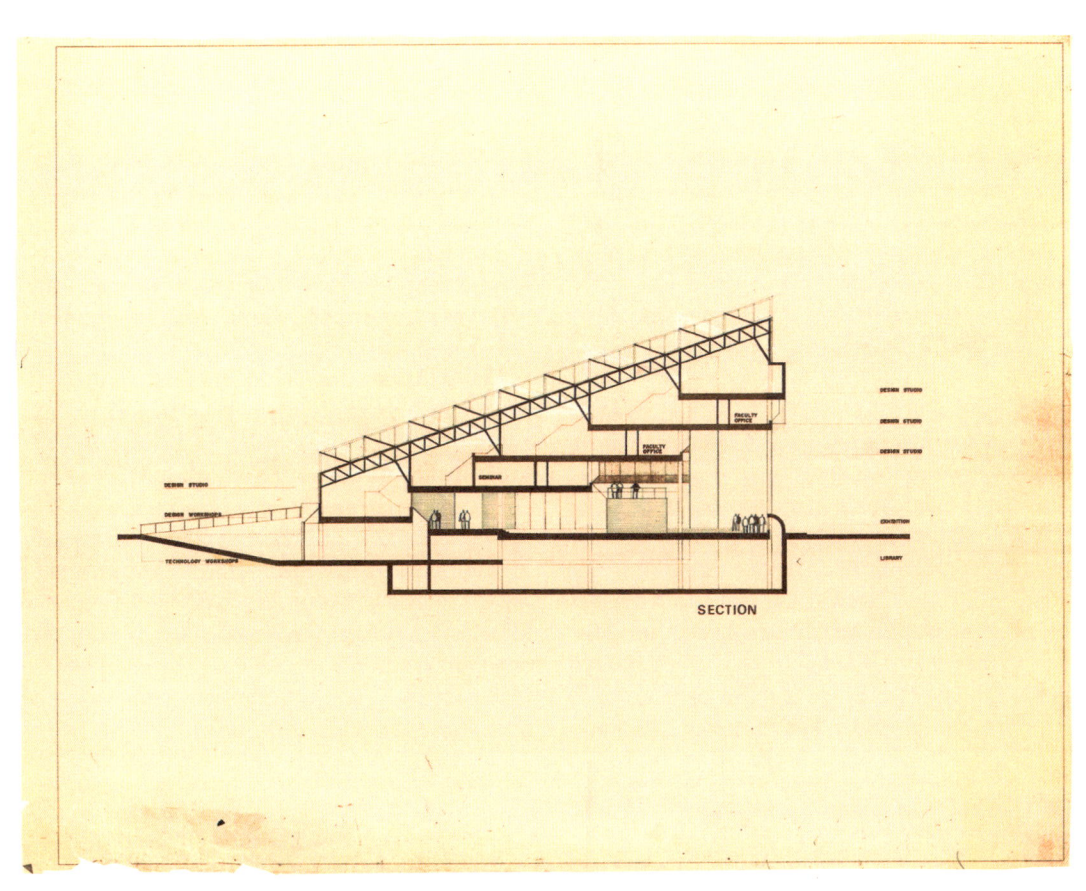

FIG. 8 Section, preliminary scheme, Gund Hall, 1969.

enter the University of Sydney, should complete a course of academic rather than technical education in high school. Once in architecture school, Andrews thought the priority for students should be the studio.

The changes that took effect in the architecture program at the University of Toronto in 1968 and 1969 configured the curriculum of its five-year bachelor of architecture program around a series of "core problems." These included, for example, a "summer place," an "oasis," and a "resort community" that were socially focused but abstract, containing multiple potential design approaches. Building technology and history requirements were reorganized and taught through assignments that were associated with these "core problems."[26] This curriculum restructure was not only intended to expand the conventional approach to design within architecture education, it placed the project-focused pedagogy of the design studio at the center of things. While much of what was achieved at the University of Toronto was actually carried out by the people Andrews hired, notably Prangnell and the young George Baird, the changes reflected Andrews's belief in the importance of design and the need for an overarching educational philosophy.

DESIGN TEACHING

If design was at the core of architecture pedagogy for Andrews, a key issue driving his plan for the GSD was the design of the physical settings in which design teaching would take place. As an admirer of Paul Rudolph's architecture, Andrews was mindful of the central area in Rudolph's 1963 Yale Art and Architecture Building, which featured an exhibition room and a jury pit, emphasizing that both the ceremonial and adversarial atmosphere of the public sphere were at the center of design education.[27] However, Andrews rejected this. He felt that, instead of an area for formal design reviews, studio spaces were the key aspect of an architecture school. Rather than the cut and thrust of the "crit" of a design end point, he prioritized the evolving conversation over the drawing board between student and teacher as the most effective means to an architectural education. When Rudolph's Art and Architecture Building caught on fire, which was widely believed to have been the doing of disaffected students, this event must have surely further sharpened Andrews's thinking as he finalized the GSD design.[28]

The attitude Andrews took to educating architects was also influenced by his professional experience collaborating across design disciplines and more broadly. This collaborative ethos underpinned the establishment of Integ and the relaxed way in which members of the John Andrews Architects office cohabited at Colborne Street with others, such as lawyer George Miller, sculptor Gerry Gladstone, and landscape architect Dick Strong. Gladstone later provided a public sculpture for the Harvard GSD building, while Strong did the landscape design. Reflections on his own experience at Harvard also made an impact; in the 1950s, the studios for various disciplines were spread over several locations, and there was no opportunity for interaction between them. Further, Andrews's educational projects to date, and Scarborough College in particular, indicated his interest in finding points of cooperation between different academic and professional traditions. Scarborough College was not only a singular building project undertaken to ward off the Toronto winters but also an architectural expression signifying the potential of the arts and sciences to come together. Moreover, among Andrews's university work, his designs for student residences foregrounded for him the question of the student experience in educational settings.

---

26 George Baird and Peter Prangnell, "The New Literacy," *Canadian Architect* (February 1969): 32–39. This article was accompanied by two others on the changes in the architecture curriculum at the University of Toronto: Ray Affleck, "A New Structure," 40–42; and Hans Elte, "Noblesse Oblige," 43–44.

27 Timothy M. Rohan, *The Architecture of Paul Rudolph* (New Haven, CT: Yale University Press, 2014), 108.

28 On the burning of the Yale Art and Architecture Building, see ibid., 176. In Peter Blake's discussion of Andrews's design for Gund Hall, he suggests that the Art and Architecture Building was burned because it stood for the Yale Establishment, while if Andrews's Gund Hall should ever be burned, it is because it "is an unmistakable challenge to the Harvard Establishment." See Blake, "Harvard's Unhallowed Hall," 27.

The design studio became the most significant space in Andrews's plan for the GSD. The vast steel truss roof with vertical glazing in the stepped profile of its cladding, with the building's studios arrayed on the floors below, gave form to Andrews's ideal of the design studio as a space that could provide a shared experience across all of the GSD's programs. Further, it allowed for collaboration and interaction between students from different cohorts and programs. Beneath the studios are the building's public spaces, including an auditorium, an exhibition space, and the Loeb Library, while on two sides are the arrayed seminar rooms and offices for professors and administrators.

The design of a prominent roof appeared in Andrews's architecture before Gund Hall, in his design of Toronto City Hall and in his plan of an airport terminal for his University of Sydney thesis project. His design of the GSD evolved at the same time as the development of the Miami Seaport Terminal, which also featured a very pronounced roof. Andrews came up with the idea of using this approach for the GSD while doodling on the back of a letter when the train he was riding to Toronto from Elora, the town he lived in outside the city, was delayed by snow. [FIG. 6] He and his collaborators, Dick Strong and engineer Bill LeMessurier, got together in Elora to brainstorm but to no avail. The drawing on the back of that letter—a typically gestural Andrews sketch in black and red pen—indicates a stronger similarity to his plans for Toronto City Hall than does his final design for the GSD. In the drawing, the triangulated form of the roof trusses is much more amplified than in the final design, and the trusses are supported by canted V-form columns that spring from the edges of each of the studio "trays," which are somewhat reminiscent of the branched tree columns that support the concrete scallops and glazing in the design of the Toronto City Hall roof. [FIGS. 7–8] The supporting columns were removed as the design developed, giving clearer expression to the idea of the studios as a single, shared space.[29] [FIG. 12] The proximity of the trusses, as well as the service pipes they

9

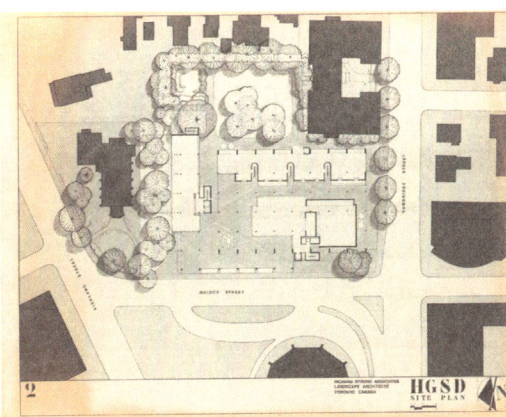

10

FIG. 9 Preliminary scheme, Gund Hall, 1969.
FIG. 10 Plan, preliminary scheme, Gund Hall, 1969. Note that the ground floor is open to pedestrians entering the building.

29 Letter from John Andrews to Josep Lluís Sert, August 2, 1968, AND 43A/78-33, John Andrews fonds, CAA.

FIG. 11   Gund Hall, 1972.

FIG. 12 Gund Hall, 1972.

accommodate, to the studio floors gives the whole space a sense of energetic compression, whereas the loftiness of the roof above the winter "meeting place" in Andrews's Toronto City Hall instead suggests composure.

NEW ARCHITECTURAL ELEMENTS: THE ROUND COLUMN

Another key element in the Harvard GSD design that had previously appeared in Andrews's oeuvre is in the overhanging bands of offices placed along the Quincy Street edge of the site. This form first appears in Andrews's design for the unbuilt Malton Hotel, which he completed while working at John B. Parkin Associates. The first built arrangement of this form is in the administrative and student services building at Scarborough College, which forms the hinge between the humanities and science wings on either side. What we see in the reappearance of such forms is Andrews's growing confidence in his own design investigations and a realization that design ideas, such as the big roof and the inverted stepped profile, can be taken from one project to another, from one context to a new one. Just as Andrews had "repurposed" Rudolph or Kahn in the projects he undertook at John B. Parkin Associates, he now began to repurpose ideas from his own work.

While the inverted, stepped section Andrews designed for the Malton Hotel is intended to mitigate aircraft noise, at Scarborough College it produces a sheltered outdoor courtyard, a kind of clearing on the edge of the forested escarpment on which the college sits. In the urban site of the Harvard GSD, Andrews's stepped arrangement again does something else: it allows the Quincy Street sidewalk to expand onto the GSD site, becoming a wide promenade of a lofty scale. This addresses both the significance of the street in Cambridge's urban pattern and the imposing scale of the university's Gothic Revival Memorial Hall (1878), designed by Ware and van Brunt, on the other side of Quincy Street. The openness of Gund Hall's ground level is more pronounced in some of Andrews's early design explorations. [FIGS. 9–10]

The gestures in the Gund Hall design toward its urban context also demonstrate Andrews's mindfulness, upon returning to Harvard, of Sert's lessons about architecture as an urban enterprise.

Other more specific aspects of the Gund Hall design may have also been influenced by Sert. For example, the massing of Gund Hall's southern facade, which connects Memorial Hall and its huge scale to the two- and three-story houses located to the east along Cambridge Street is akin to the ziggurat forms that Sert used widely in his university work. The demolition of an intervening apartment building east of Gund Hall made this connection that much more apparent. This includes Sert's design of Boston University, Harvard's Peabody Terrace, and Harvard's Science Center, constructed not far north of Gund Hall in 1975. [FIG. 1] The less dramatic stepping on Gund Hall's north side is also informed by a contextual trigger, acknowledging the small, historic Church of New Jerusalem next door.

Andrews's design of Gund Hall also marks his first use of freestanding round concrete columns, and from this point onward, round columns become his preferred form for freestanding structures. Discussing Scarborough College and Gund Hall in a 1975 interview, Andrews commented:

> In fact, if you want to look at Scarborough college, that doesn't have a column in it. Something I was very proud of at that time because I was very hot on the idea that if you're making space out of walls, and they were specific spaces that had no reason to change, then that might as well hold the building up. And then if you go from that extreme to Harvard, for instance, which is incapable of having specific spaces other than something like lecture theaters. That's all bloody columns: a whole language of columns— how you deal with them and how walls should not run into columns that go past them; a column should stand on its own and be recognized; a column should have a head and a bloody foot.[30]

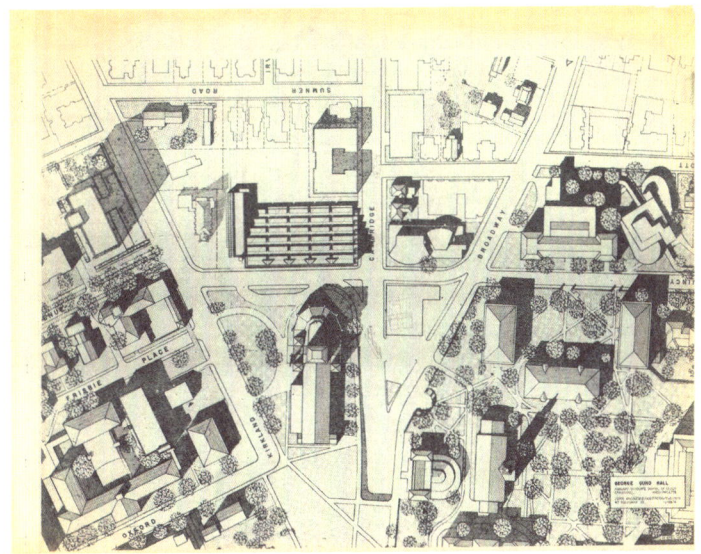

FIG. 13 Gund Hall, with the Carpenter Center at far right, Harvard University, Cambridge, Massachusetts, 1963. Architect: Le Corbusier.
FIGS. 14–15 The Carpenter Center. Photos: John Andrews.

The columns at Gund Hall are the same attenuated concrete cylinders that appear in Sert's work. More directly, they resemble the columns of Le Corbusier's Carpenter Center for the Visual Arts, a block south of Gund Hall on Quincy Street, a building that Andrews visited and photographed soon after its completion in 1963.[31] [FIG. 13] Evidence for this is found in a sequence of nine slides of the building in Andrews's collection, in the same group as his images of Paul Rudolph's Temple Street Parking Garage in New Haven and the nearly completed Yale Art and Architecture Building, also known as Rudolph Hall. Andrews's Carpenter Center photographs show the approach to the building's ramp from Quincy Street and other external views. [FIGS. 14–15]

Some of Andrews's photographs of the Carpenter Center suggest the importance of the columns in its undercroft space. They appear to be a direct precedent for the treatment of Gund Hall's undercroft and the colonnade along Quincy Street. Le Corbusier grouped columns of various diameters, with different spacing between them, and he wanted these columns to be as smooth as possible. This feature was in line with the principles of his postwar work, which was built on the premise that a building's aesthetic qualities were to be achieved by employing local building craft in a manner that transcended its inevitable technical limitations. In Le Corbusier's view, the American building industry had technical capacities that were different and more advanced than those available for his projects in France or India.[32]

Gund Hall's columns are more regular than those of the Carpenter Center, but at the north end of the Gund Hall colonnade, the columns vary in scale in a manner that drew the attention of Macy DuBois, Andrews's old Harvard classmate and collaborator on the Toronto City Hall competition. [FIG. 16] In *The Canadian Architect*, DuBois noted that the Carpenter Center was "definitely an idiosyncratic Gund Hall ancestor." Commenting on the Gund Hall colonnade, he wrote:

> A very amusing trick is used in the tightly spaced group of three different-sized columns to support the three stepped-out floor levels on the north. When I first saw these columns I laughed at their poker-faced directness. The row of trio columns marches over to two rows of columns on the west. The last row seems out of hand with their pompous height. These contribute largely to making the west side too large in scale for the pedestrians it was meant to shelter.[33]

DuBois indulged in a kind of pragmatism that Andrews also regularly entertained. For example, Andrews noted that a round column plan is better than a square column plan for practical reasons: the reinforcing steel within a round column is more evenly and economically covered by the concrete, and a round column in plan lends itself readily to an infinite range of positions for adjacent partitions, compared to one square or rectangular in plan.[34] This is a very selective rationale. Andrews's grouping of columns at Gund Hall that stand adjacent to the building's entrance, an arrangement repeated in many of his subsequent projects, is similar to the irregular grouping of columns supporting the Carpenter Center's ramp and undercroft, which evoke a gathering of people. These columns give the buildings that they structure and dignify the semblance of human presence in built form. They invite us to identify with them.[35]

---

30 John Witzig and John Andrews, "AA Interview: John Andrews," *Architecture Australia* 64, no. 3 (June 1975): 62.
31 The cardboard mounts of these slides are dated May 1963.
32 William Curtis, "History of the Design," in *Le Corbusier at Work: the Genesis of the Carpenter Center for the Visual Arts*, ed. Eduard Sekler (Cambridge, MA: Harvard University Press, 1978), 167.
33 Macy DuBois, "A Protestant Work of Architecture," *Canadian Architect* (January 1973): 40.
34 See Andrews' discussion of the columns in the King George Tower, completed in 1976. Taylor and Andrews, *John Andrews*, 120. See also Paul Walker and Antony Moulis, "Finding Brutalism in the Architecture of John Andrews," *Fabrications* 25, no. 2 (2015): 214–33.
35 Walker and Moulis, "Finding Brutalism."

CRITICAL RECEPTION

The new GSD building opened in October 1972—on Friday the 13th! Its reception was broadly positive, with the exception of a very negative assessment by Wolf Von Eckardt, the architecture critic of the *Washington Post* (who, in contrast, was very positive about Andrews's later Intelsat Headquarters, which opened in Von Eckardt's hometown in 1986). The commentary on Gund Hall's design made two kinds of associations. First, many raised questions about the design's relationship to the profound challenges at universities resulting from the campus protests of the later 1960s and the ways in which these issues had affected GSD students and faculty. Second, critics sought to connect the building's design to broader contemporary themes in architecture, just before the tsunami of postmodernism hit. These parallel lines of critical reflection were summed up in a comment by *New York Times* architecture critic Ada Louise Huxtable, who wrote that the GSD was "a place, paradoxically, of good architecture and bad vibes."[36] Huxtable praised Gund Hall's architectural qualities, writing, "Certainly this is a very powerful building that states its theme and sets its terms with uncompromising clarity." And, commenting on the central significance of the shared, stepped studio space, she asserted, "This is an undeniably exciting and beautiful space, notable for two things—high architectural skill and almost total lack of repose—partly because of its deliberate elimination of privacy, and partly through a subliminal sense of spatial uncertainties due to the tiered open levels." However, she further noted that "a building is as good as its client, and as a client the Graduate School of Design was pretty bad."

As Huxtable highlighted, the placement of the studios of all the built environment disciplines under a single roof reflected the views of Sert and the faculty-student committee he established in 1965 to guide the GSD building project. But Sert's departure and the constant changes to the GSD committee produced

36   Huxtable, "Good Architecture–Bad Vibes," 38.

FIG. 16   Gund Hall, 1972.

"serious ideological disarray," the committee's position "moved from approval to apathy to architect-baiting," and the project "became thoroughly embattled." Further, the appointment of Kilbridge as Sert's successor did not ease things:

> What survives all this trauma is the new building's strong and somewhat questionable concept, the remarkable architectural statement of the studio and a handsome structure that sits well in the street and its surroundings. The architects are understandably bitter. And the school has a long way to go.

Peter Blake also noted Andrews's difficulty working with the GSD after Sert departed. In effect, one client—Sert—was replaced by 30: GSD faculty members who all thought they could do a better job than Andrews. Blake located the project's success in the priority it gave to students and described it as, "a really proletarian act of faith in the future of architecture and those who will practice it, a kind of Hannes Meyer construction (and at Harvard!)." Noting the fate of Paul Rudolph's Art and Architecture Building, Blake also commented, "Rudolph's building, with all its medieval (or Wrightian) grandeur, seemed and probably is very much a stronghold of the Yale Establishment; but John Andrews's GSD is an unmistakable challenge to the Harvard establishment—a challenge of youth, idealism, imagination and general snottiness. If anybody ever does burn *it* down, it will be someone who rightly feels threatened by it."[37]

If Blake gave a positive spin in his veiled allusion to unrest among Harvard's students, Robert Jensen, writing in *Architectural Record*, was much more direct about the difficult period in which the GSD building was designed and constructed and how this affected its reception. The lack of clear direction on behalf of the client was exacerbated by the context of the campus protests. Jensen wrote, "The serious disruptions at Harvard in the spring of 1969 triggered by the invasion of Cambodia and the Kent State shootings are part of it. Earlier, there were local but still university-wide street actions questioning Harvard's role in the community around it…. Some students, and some students within the GSD particularly, believed the university was insensitive to the housing, financial, and job conditions of neighboring people."

Reflecting these conflicts, Andrews's design was subject to scrutiny and criticism during its development in 1969, but Jensen suggests this did little to change it. Regardless of the liberal and inclusive vision of design education that motivated Andrews's design of the GSD building, it came to stand for the values that the students protesting at Harvard rejected. Gund Hall became "the main line," "Cambodia," "a symbol for the corporate state." Jensen linked this viewpoint with emerging problems in late-modern architecture:

> Architectural forms sometimes become associated with social forces we don't mean to strengthen, and the original meanings of forms get lost or mean something else; that is a central problem in modern architecture today. Architects might not believe that new formal metaphors for broad shifts in values are needed but some students and professors at Harvard went through a groping, inarticulate time of trying to establish the existence of the problem through Gund Hall. Moral arguments against important buildings become more common, and they are warning signs of trouble within the style itself.[38]

A decade later, Jensen coauthored *Ornamentalism*, a book promoting postmodernism.[39]

ANDREWS AND THE "THIRD GENERATION"

Another major line of critique that Gund Hall received in the months following its opening

---

37   Blake, "Harvard's Unhallowed Hall," 27.
38   Jensen, "Gund Hall," 104.
39   Robert Jensen and Patricia Conway, *Ornamentalism: The New Decorativeness in Architecture and Design* (New York: Potter, 1983).

concerned the ways in which the building's design related to broader, more recent developments in architecture culture. Wolf Von Eckardt's disparagement of Andrews's design for Gund Hall suggested that Andrews seemed "to have taken his cue from the British 'Brutalist' vogue of some years ago, led by Peter and Alison Smithson, a husband-and-wife team. The Smithsons thought that architecture could be made honest, if you let it all hang out, if you exposed the plumbing and all the other intestines of a building. They thought Mies van der Rohe was hiding too much under his taut glass skins."[40]

This is perhaps the beginning of a line of commentary that has from time to time misrepresented Andrews's architecture as Brutalist, though its evolution did not occur through the anti-CIAM ethos of the Smithsons or the Team 10 challenges to the CIAM line. Andrews was nothing if not a product of the teaching of CIAM's postwar champion, Josep Lluís Sert. While influences attributed to Team 10 can be discerned in Andrews's work, they are more narrowly connected to one of its members, Aldo van Eyck, and to Herman Hertzberger, van Eyck's acolyte. Further, rather than an influence, this relationship is better thought of as a confluence.

In contrast to Von Eckardt's disdain, Huxtable and DuBois both cited a connection between Andrews and another British architect and contemporary of the Smithsons, favorably placing Andrews in the contemporary scene. They related Gund Hall's iconic roof to the work of James Stirling. Presumably referring to Stirling's design for the University of Cambridge's History Faculty Building (1967), Huxtable writes, "the studio building is a spectacular tour de force of steel trusses and reflecting glass. At the moment, the "greenhouse" look of the English work of James Stirling is the profession's great stylistic preoccupation."[41] [FIG. 17] DuBois directly connected Harvard's Gund Hall with Cambridge's

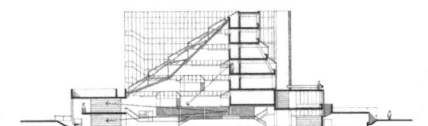

40 Wolf Von Eckardt, "Two Schools at Harvard: Brutal vs. Cheerful Design," *Washington Post*, August 11, 1973.
41 Huxtable, "Good Architecture–Bad Vibes," 38. The connection to Stirling's History Faculty Building is made explicit in a later critique of Gund Hall: Nory Miller, "Evaluation: No One is Neutral about Gund Hall," *AIA Journal* 68, no. 1 (January 1979): 54.

FIG. 17 Section, History Faculty Building, University of Cambridge, Cambridge, England 1963–1967. Architect: James Stirling.

History Faculty Building. His article juxtaposed sectional drawings of the two, suggesting that the History Faculty Building is a progenitor for Gund Hall. However, as DuBois commented, "while the idea and the shape of the space at Cambridge is the same, Andrews's space is clearly more appropriate to the use of the building and far less overpowering than the Stirling building."[42] This comparison between Andrews and Stirling is significant and is worth exploring further. Their careers have distinct parallels: both were educators as well as architects, and both have been identified as sharing a "technological pragmatism." But in the end, their paths diverge substantially, which is clearly demonstrated by the postmodernism of Stirling's design of the Arthur M. Sackler Museum (1985), which is just across the road from Gund Hall.

In 1972, the year that Gund Hall was completed, architecture critic Philip Drew took up Sigfried Giedion's idea that a "third generation" was emerging in modern architecture, in his book *Third Generation: The Changing Meaning of Architecture*. Drew considered 11 architects or architectural partnerships, including both Andrews and Stirling. Drew placed them within a group, which included architects like Kiyonori Kikutake and Kevin Roche, that he labeled as concerned with "technological pragmatism."[43] For Drew, these architects were distinctive in the ways in which they accepted present technological conditions and engaged in a relative primitiveness of construction as their basis for architectural invention.

To explain his thesis Drew evoked the paradigm of "unselfconscious architecture," or the production of forms found in vernacular and primitive building, as critical to understanding the methods of these architects. Drew wrote:

> Unselfconscious architecture—the example of the pueblos, Taxco and Mediterranean villages—contains the promise that an industrial architecture similarly conceived and dedicated to serving human needs could tap the immense productivity of the industrial system and avoid soulless monotony.[44]

Drew's thesis derived from Giedion's original claim of a third generation in which he observed a deepening interest in "the primitive," technology, and collective form, which he thought indicated the way forward in modern architecture's evolution. This aspect of Giedion's thinking is apparent in several texts of the period and most notably in his 1961 book *The Eternal Present: The Beginnings of Art*.[45] It is intriguing to consider whether or not these ideas were presented by Giedion in the Harvard classes he taught with Sekler, such as their seminar "The Human Scale," which Andrews had taken.

Stirling was an architect who, like Andrews, had a tangential relationship with Brutalism, and who, also like Andrews, claimed to have eschewed the "isms" of the 1960s and 1970s (including Brutalism) in pursuit of an architecture of "common sense." He also liked to be called a "humanist," and as Andrews did, Stirling established his name through the design of an exceptional, paradigm-shifting university building, the University of Leicester Engineering Building, completed in 1963.[46] In the same way Andrews's Scarborough College led to a slew of other university commissions, so too did the University of Leicester Engineering Building, which Stirling designed in partnership with James Gowan, and the Cambridge History Faculty Building. The likeness of these buildings is not a matter of the environmental obstacles they share. Stirling's

---

42 DuBois, "Protestant Work of Architecture," 40–42.
43 Philip Drew, *Third Generation: The Changing Meaning of Architecture* (New York: Praeger, 1972), 13.
44 Ibid.
45 Sarah Deyong, "An Architectural Theory of Relations: Sigfried Giedion and Team X," *Journal of the Society of Architectural Historians*, 73, no. 2 (June 2012): 229.
46 Mark Girouard, *Big Jim: The Life and Work of James Stirling* (London: Chatto & Windus, 1998), 148. For Stirling, "humanism" signified a connection to the architectural culture of the Renaissance, as studied by his teacher and early mentor Colin Rowe.
47 Andrews intended the studio space at Gund to have adjustable louvers at the top and bottom to naturally ventilate the space. As it is, it overheats in summer because this feature was omitted by the client. See Taylor and Andrews, *John Andrews*, 107. More criticism on the environmental performance of the building is found in Miller, "Evaluation," 52–61.

take on architectural "common sense" was almost entirely a matter of how buildings were put together in terms of their volumetric relationships and constructional components, while Andrews's experience in Canada only reinforced his sensitivity to environmental performance, as displayed in his design of Toronto City Hall.[47] Nevertheless, it is a notable coincidence that Stirling's completion of Cambridge's History Faculty Building occurred when Andrews began his design of Harvard's Gund Hall, even more so given that Stirling visited Toronto in early 1968, and the two architects likely met.[48]

Andrews and Stirling shared similar views on architecture education. Like Andrews, Stirling was a practicing architect who also held a professorial position, serving as a visiting professor at the Yale School of Architecture from 1966 to 1984. He disdained, as Andrews did, the design of the "crit" space in Paul Rudolph's Yale Art and Architecture Building as the center of an architecture education. Andrews and Stirling both believed that the productive interaction between a student and teacher in the studio, rather than the public confrontation of the crit, was at the core of design teaching. This is a view privileged in both Andrews's design of Gund Hall and in his revision of the architecture curriculum at the University of Toronto.

However, the likenesses between Cambridge's History Faculty Building and Harvard's Gund Hall are also a matter of confluence, as well as coincidence, rather than a matter of influence, as Huxtable and DuBois discerned. Andrews explored the staggered section fundamental to the design of Gund Hall beginning in the early 1960s and explored the use of the big roof even earlier.[49] Andrews's design for the Harvard GSD was followed in 1985 by Stirling's contribution to the Harvard campus, his design for the Arthur M. Sackler Museum, located immediately south of Gund Hall at the intersection of Quincy Street and Cambridge Street. Looking beyond the Sackler Museum's postmodern

18

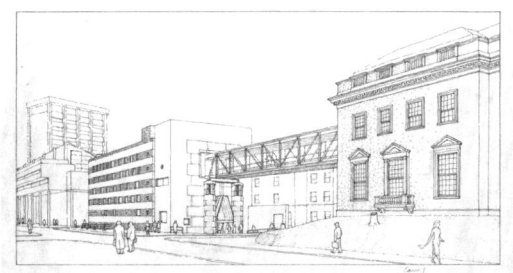

19

48 Girouard, *Big Jim*, 170; John Andrews, interview by Paul Walker, November 14, 2017. As well, John Simpson recalled that Stirling visited Andrews's Toronto office. John Simpson, interview by Paul Walker, December 2, 2015.

49 Taylor and Andrews, *John Andrews*, 25.

FIG. 18 View of interior staircase, Arthur M. Sackler Museum, Harvard University, Cambridge, Massachusetts. Architects: James Stirling, Michael Wilford, and Associates, Perry, Dean, Stahl & Rogers.

FIG. 19 Perspective for bridge, Arthur M. Sackler Museum. Gund Hall at extreme left.

 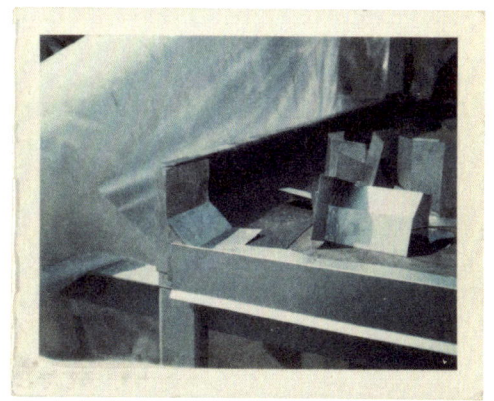

FIG. 20 Color Polaroid photographs of the construction of Gund Hall.

wrappings, if Stirling's design for Cambridge's History Faculty Building can be construed as a precursor to the roof forms of Andrews's Gund Hall, then Gund Hall can be thought of as a precursor to the role of staircases as an organizing form within Stirling's Arthur M. Sackler Museum. [FIGS. 18–19] And, in both architects' designs for Harvard, Le Corbusier's Carpenter Center, just down Quincy Street, is an unavoidable presence, especially since Le Corbusier's work was influential for all members of Drew's "third generation."

There are strong similarities in the careers of Stirling and Andrews that, in retrospect, reaffirm Drew's logic in placing them together. In particular, it is their views of construction technology and its intended use in architecture that perhaps make them most alike. Stirling expressed his views on this issue in the essays he wrote in the 1950s on the work of Le Corbusier.[50] A key difference in the careers of Stirling and Andrews is that, aside from the buildings he designed, Stirling developed and articulated his approach to architecture through writings and commentaries for architectural journals, which, early on in his career, moved beyond reflections on his own designs to those that address work by other architects and importantly, the late work of Le Corbusier. Considered alongside his buildings, these writings raise questions regarding the relationship between the late work of Le Corbusier and Stirling's work specifically and the third generation more generally.[51] They intimate, perhaps, what Harold Bloom called in a literary context, "the anxiety of influence."[52]

Another key difference between Andrews and Stirling is that beginning in the mid-1970s, an abrupt shift occurs in Stirling's work toward overt references to postmodernism that never occurs in Andrews's work. Before this, however, Stirling and Andrews both sought directness and legibility in architecture through the specific expression of building techniques that each project entailed, unconstrained by a commitment to a narrower and predetermined "ethic," "aesthetic," or "style," as the Brutalist label evoked. It is perhaps for this reason that in retrospect, a dialogue can be observed between their various university projects. This includes: the echoing of the Reyner Banhamesque futurist attributes of the Leicester Engineering Building in the boiler house chimneys at Scarborough College; allusions of Scarborough College's landscape-driven megastructure in the dormitory Stirling designed for St. Andrews University; the parti of Gund Hall as an answer to the proposition put forth in Stirling's design for the Cambridge History Faculty Building about the potential of the glass roof as a collective form; and a reflection of the staggered section of Stirling's Florey Building at Queen's College in Oxford and the staircases at the Sackler Museum in Andrews's earlier explorations of these devices. However, this back and forth should not be taken literally. There is no question of influence here. Both Andrews and Stirling were inventive architects whose international work contributed significantly to the late-modern repertoire of forms and to circulation strategies, not least through publications like Drew's *Third Generation*.

While Scarborough College was highly influential when completed in 1965, it could have been construed as a one-off by a talented and precocious architect. The South Residences at the University of Guelph and the Miami Seaport Terminal, which Andrews designed soon after were also highly regarded, individual achievements. The opening of George Gund Hall in 1972, however, demonstrated more than any of these other projects that Andrews was not only a major figure to appear on the international architecture scene, but he had developed a strong and particular design ethos that was visible across an impressive body of work.

---

50   James Stirling, "Garches and Jaoul: Le Corbusier as Domestic Architect in 1927 and 1953," *Architectural Review*, (September 1955): 145–51; James Stirling, "Ronchamp and the Crisis of Rationalism," *Architectural Review* (March 1956): 155–61.

51   On Stirling and Le Corbusier, see Mark Crinson, "L'Architecte Anglais: Stirling and Le Corbusier," in *James Stirling: Early Unpublished Writings on Architecture*, ed. Mark Crinson (London: Routledge, 2010), 108–39.

52   Amanda Reeser Lawrence uses Bloom's analysis of literary influence to explore the complex relationship of Stirling and Le Corbusier. See Amanda Reeser Lawrence, *James Stirling: Revisionary Modernist* (New Haven, CT: Yale University Press, 2012), 15–17.

FIG. 21 Gund Hall, 1972.

08

the cameron offices and the return to australia

by   Paul Walker

The Cameron Offices are among the most important of Andrews's projects. They are significant to his personal history as their commissioning allowed him to return to his home country of Australia, and the project also linked his practices in Canada and Australia: members of the Toronto office, including Ed Galanyk and Roger du Toit, were involved in the Cameron Offices early on, and architects who later became stalwarts of his Sydney firm saw them to completion. The project also involved contributions from two of Andrews's oldest friends and colleagues, landscape architect Richard ("Dick") Strong and public artist Gerald ("Gerry") Gladstone. Further, the Cameron Offices project manifested several of Andrews's most pressing concerns as an architect: establishing a plan pattern in a large building complex that facilitated connections to a wider urban arrangement; using building form to modify environmental performance; and cultivating opportunities for personal address within a large complex. The Cameron Offices project also spanned a period of significant political change in Australia: the cultural expansiveness and confidence of the Labor Whitlam government from 1972 to 1975—anticipated in many ways by the Cameron Offices design—flowered briefly and then was replaced by a polity in which the social and urban ambitions of the Cameron Offices were no longer recognized.

PLANNING THE CAMERON OFFICES

In 1968, the architect responsible for the development of Canberra, Australia's capital, visited the Andrews office in Toronto. John Overall was the Commissioner of the National Capital Development Commission (NCDC), a body established in 1957 to turbocharge the growth and development of Canberra, which had slowed to a virtual halt after the completion of the "temporary" parliament house in 1927, followed by the Great Depression and World War II.[1] In 1958, Canberra's population was only 39,000.[2] The role of the commission was to plan and implement an urban-growth strategy for Canberra, to resolve the urban design of its symbolic heart—Parliamentary Triangle—and to build the key institutional and bureaucratic buildings for Australia's federal government. Overall's advisors on design matters included the University of Western Australia planning professor Gordon Stephenson; in 1958, while working at the University of Toronto, Stephenson served on the jury for the Toronto City Hall design competition, in which Andrews's team of Harvard students placed second.

But Overall's interest in Andrews was almost certainly triggered by the appointment of the Melbourne architect Robin Boyd as an advisor to the NCDC in January 1968.[3] Boyd had a modest yet critically successful practice but was best known in Australia as a "public intellectual"—probably its first—an acerbic and outspoken critic of the country's suburbs and design culture. Abroad, he was known for his books on Kenzo Tange and contemporary Japanese architecture as well as for the essays he contributed to journals, such as *Architectural Review* and *Architectural Forum*. In 1967, Boyd delivered the Boyer Lectures for the Australian Broadcasting Commission, in which he drew attention to Andrews's successes in North America. He strongly condemned Australian architecture's dependency on borrowed ideas and the lack of progressive thought within the country. He regretted the absence of Andrews, whom he claimed was "characteristically Australian by birth, training, attitude, speech, manner, and by his inability to find a satisfying outlet for original talent here at home."[4] Boyd was an enthusiastic supporter of Canberra and the design opportunities afforded by the controlling hand of the NCDC. For a brief period, from the Boyer Lectures in

1   Roger Pegrum, "National Capital Development Commission," in Philip Goad and Julie Willis, eds., *The Encyclopedia of Australian Architecture* (Melbourne: Cambridge University Press, 2012), 487–88.

2   John Overall, *Canberra Yesterday, Today & Tomorrow: A Personal Memoir* (Canberra: Federal Capital Press, 1995), 83.

3   Geoffrey Serle, *Robin Boyd: A Life* (Melbourne: Melbourne University Press, 1995), 298.

4   Jennifer Taylor and John Andrews, *John Andrews: Architecture, a Performing Art* (Melbourne: Oxford University Press, 1982), 173.

1967 until his death in 1971, Boyd was also an enthusiastic supporter of Andrews.

Overall spent some time in the Toronto office, coming to terms with its approach to design and project management:

> Overall called from Washington to say that he wanted to drop in and talk to me in Toronto. By the time he arrived we knew who he was, but not what he had in mind or that, as we later discovered, he ran a very tight ship. He spent two days in Toronto behaving like the perfect potential client. He took the office apart, going through it with a fine toothcomb. He read project reports, looked at drawings, examined Metro Centre very closely, talked to Roger du Toit about it and to Bob Anderson about scheduling and cost control. He spent half a day at Scarborough College looking at it and talking with the Principal and his people about our work. A month later he wrote offering a major project to house thousands of Australian federal bureaucrats which would be an anchor project for a new urban extension of Canberra at Belconnen.[5]

This would be the project that brought Andrews back to Australia and enabled him to build a new practice based in Sydney.

The Belconnen office complex was one project among several envisioned for an expanded Canberra. The NCDC commissioned a transportation plan for the city from American transport specialists Alan M. Voorhees & Associates in 1966. Their scheme was based on a future urban population of 500,000. A broader plan to develop Canberra in a decentralized way followed, accommodating growth in population and jobs through linear extensions of the city to Tuggeranong in the south, Gungahlin in the northeast, and Belconnen in the northwest.[6] This became known as the "Y plan." Each arm of the Y was to have a rapid-bus corridor and its own town center (or, in the long southern arm, multiple centers) with retail, civic functions, and office uses.[7] Growth to the south had already begun with the development of Woden in 1961. Planning work for Belconnen's town center—10 kilometers from the center of Canberra—started in 1966. Belconnen was envisaged to have a population of 80,000 by 1980 and an ultimate population of 120,000 by 2000. Between 1968 and 1972, the NCDC also planned for six major office complexes to house the federal government's expanding bureaucracy: two close to central Canberra, two at Belconnen, one at Woden, and one at Tuggeranong.[8] These latter projects represented a commitment by the NCDC to getting jobs into Canberra's new satellites. The Tuggeranong offices did not proceed and the Woden project was designed in the early 1970s—also by Andrews—but only a small part of it was built. The other office complex at Belconnen was designed by the respected Sydney firm McConnel Smith & Johnson Architects, also with a "mat" plan, and completed just after the Andrews scheme. Though not far from each other, they were not connected.

Andrews recalled that the NCDC's program for the Belconnen complex he was asked to design—known as the Cameron Offices—stipulated "five 15-story towers. There was nothing in the NCDC program or in the specification of spaces required that necessitated a high-rise solution. Two things were clear, however. The NCDC specifically wanted to create an urban downtown environment at Belconnen and, in the minds of the NCDC, urbanity meant towers along the ridge as symbols of the government and the town; the masterplan designated towers in the office complex area reinforcing the ridge."[9] The first work Andrews did involved analyses of the site and its determining factors and the conceptual organization of the bureaucratic work environment. Contextual constraints were minimal—the site was a treeless sheep paddock that was cold in the winter and hot in the summer.

---

5   Ibid., 142.
6   Overall, *Canberra Yesterday, Today & Tomorrow*, 79–81.
7   National Capital Development Commission, *Tomorrow's Canberra: Planning for Growth and Change* (Canberra: Australian National University Press, 1970), 225–29.
8   Overall, *Canberra Yesterday, Today & Tomorrow*, 83.

Among the Belconnen drawings made by the Andrews Toronto office, which are held at the Canadian Architectural Archives at the University of Calgary, are several sketches of rows of multistory buildings—not so much towers as slabs. Some are straight, some contain a diagonal plan form reminiscent of Metro Centre on a smaller scale. [FIGS. 1–2] These are among the earliest architectural drawings of the Belconnen project, appearing in a report dated December 3, 1968.[10] But Andrews's analyses had already moved away from the option of dominant towers or slabs. The site of the Belconnen offices was highly determined, sitting between a projected retail and civic center to the north and designated residential areas to the south and east. To the north of the whole complex was to be an artificial lake (Lake Ginninderra), toward which the site gently sloped. A transit hub was nominally situated between the site for the offices and the retail and civic area. Andrews envisaged a planning strategy that integrated the various elements of the entire Belconnen town center in a horizontal logic. A pedestrian spine, or mall, was proposed to run from the housing in the south to the lake at the north, cutting through the office, retail, and public institutional areas as a single entity and linking them all. A report produced by the office dated October 22, 1968 argued that "a town center of this size can only maintain one strong pedestrian spine if it is to act as a real generator of life and collector of communal activities."[11] This was separate from the vehicular movement pattern, which was linked to the pedestrian spine via a series of parking areas west of the site, with retail on one side

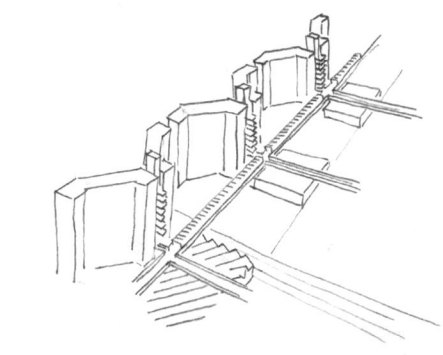

1

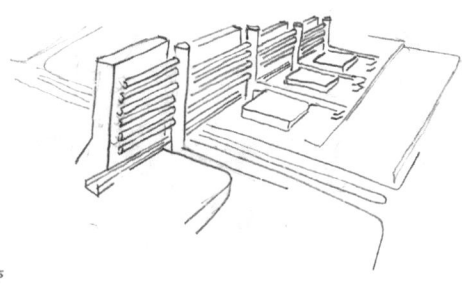

2

9   Taylor and Andrews, *John Andrews*, 146. Descriptions of the urban character the National Capital Development Commission anticipated for Belconnen include "taller office buildings along the ridge," "tall office towers," and "ridge office blocks" as "landmarks." See National Capital Development Commission, *Belconnen Town Centre Master Plan Report* (Canberra, National Capital Development Commission, 1968), paragraphs 205–14.
10 John Andrews Architects, "Government Office Complex Belconnen Town Centre. Addendum to Site Planning Studies," report, Toronto, December 3, 1968.
11 John Andrews Architects, "Government Office Complex Belconnen Town Centre, Site Planning Studies Progress Report: 22 October 1968" report, Toronto, October 22, 1968.

FIGS. 1–2   Early sketches, Belconnen, Canberra, Australia, 1968.

FIG. 3 Schematic model, the Cameron Offices, Canberra, Australia, 1968.

and office buildings on the other, each with an entrance and an address on the mall. In section, this schematic organization showed retail spaces hoisted above covered parking but with uncovered at-grade parking extending further west. It also showed a multistory tower (or towers) rising above large plate office areas on the first two levels, again stacked on top of possible parking. Conceptually, the spine gave the whole of Belconnen a programmatic and experiential clarity and determined that the offices would in one way or another be distributed in relation to it. The primary emphasis on pedestrian movement recalled the Toronto Metro Centre project.

The October 1968 report was incorporated, with two others on site planning, into another John Andrews Architects document dated November 28, 1968. The diagram from October most overtly showing a tower or towers was dropped in this iteration, though some suggestion of elevated offices remained. These survived in the final design, not as towers but as much more visually modest and horizontal forms containing office suites and meeting rooms continuously distributed above the pedestrian mall along the eastern street edge of the Cameron Offices. Beyond the broader issues of the Belconnen town center's layout, the other reports integrated into the November 28 document cover Andrews's consideration for how the Cameron Offices themselves should be organized. Long "fingers" of office space are investigated, crossed by circulation routes; the office wings are variously oriented north–south or east–west (the orientation that prevailed); and schematic massing models show towers remained a possibility. The maximum dimension of each office finger's width was established at 70 feet—allowing a maximum distance of 35 feet from work station to window—which responded to the Australian preference for daylighting offices (the width of the offices is in fact 50 feet, but because floors in section are offset, the total width of an office wing is 70 feet). The length of each finger was not determined. Diagrams suggested 30-foot-wide landscaped courtyards between the office fingers (as built), with car parking underneath the office wings (also as built). Three variations are offered: one provides a maximum of open-office area; another a maximum of "administrative space," with smaller private offices distributed along the cross-circulation elements and expressed as individual pods; and the last a maximum of executive suites, again expressed as pods but "plugged into" vertical service cores rather than horizontal circulation stems. The pod-like expression of these offices evokes the plug-in apartments of the Stelco design of 1965, discussed in chapter 3. A report from November 14, which is also integrated into the November 28 document, explains that the "executive suites" determined the tower form: "Because it could well fit into a tower form, we have used this space type to provide the vertical element desired by the client, and for present purposes have assumed a small floor area to accent the verticality. The number of executive users required will dictate the size and number of towers." Three towers are included in the schematic model illustrating this option. [FIG. 3] In all these options, however, the open-office type dominated. With these plans, the basic logic of the Cameron Offices was established.

THE DESIGN

In December 1968 and January 1969, the final schematic plan emerged. During this period, Andrews and members of his office had a two-week stint in Canberra, just before Christmas.[12] Andrews recalled that there were two major points of contention between him and the NCDC on that occasion; one was about towers and the other parking. On the former, Andrews wrote:

> After going around and around at one meeting, we asked the NCDC what their definition of urbanity was, and where they got it from. A NCDC official replied that if we had read Mumford we would know his definition of urbanity and his description of the urbanity of New York.

We had read Mumford, and know that he believed Amsterdam to be more urban than New York.

> Urbanity can only be realized in the plane a person walks in or drives through. What is stuck up in the air is of no particular consequence in the creation of an urban environment.[13]

The issue of the parking lot was even more intractable: Andrews's conceptual plans envisaged the majority of on-site parking to be covered. The NCDC had to get political approval for any project to proceed to construction; members of Parliament did not have covered parking so civil servants should not have it either.

In the weekend in the middle of the Canberra trip, Andrews went back to the drawing board to produce something very close to the final design. The idea for the project became much clearer. He maintained the horizontal logic of his schematic proposals and got rid of the towers entirely. There were seven east–west oriented office wings, a large volume for a computer center at the south, an elevated mall along the east of the site, with a provision for bridges to residential areas further east, and just two north–south pedestrian connections.

By the beginning of February 1969, the sketch design of the Cameron Offices was basically complete. Drawings dated February 4, 1969, from the Andrews collection at the Canadian Architectural Archives, show a design very close to the built project. Seven wings of office space running east–west are connected at the east by a linear group of elevated executive offices and meeting rooms above a linear circulation route (the mall), and bridges over a road to the east connect to residential areas beyond. The east–west wings are each of three floors, with the upper floors offset in section to shade the lower floors from northern sun. Each wing is comprised of two 150-foot-long modules, with the basic office module being 50 feet wide and 150 feet long. Between these wings are landscaped courtyards. As well as the mall, the office wings

---

12   John Andrews Architects, "A Report on Site Planning Studies for the Government Office Complex, Belconnen Town Centre: November 28, 1968," report, Toronto, November 28, 1968.

13   Taylor and Andrews, *John Andrews*, 147.

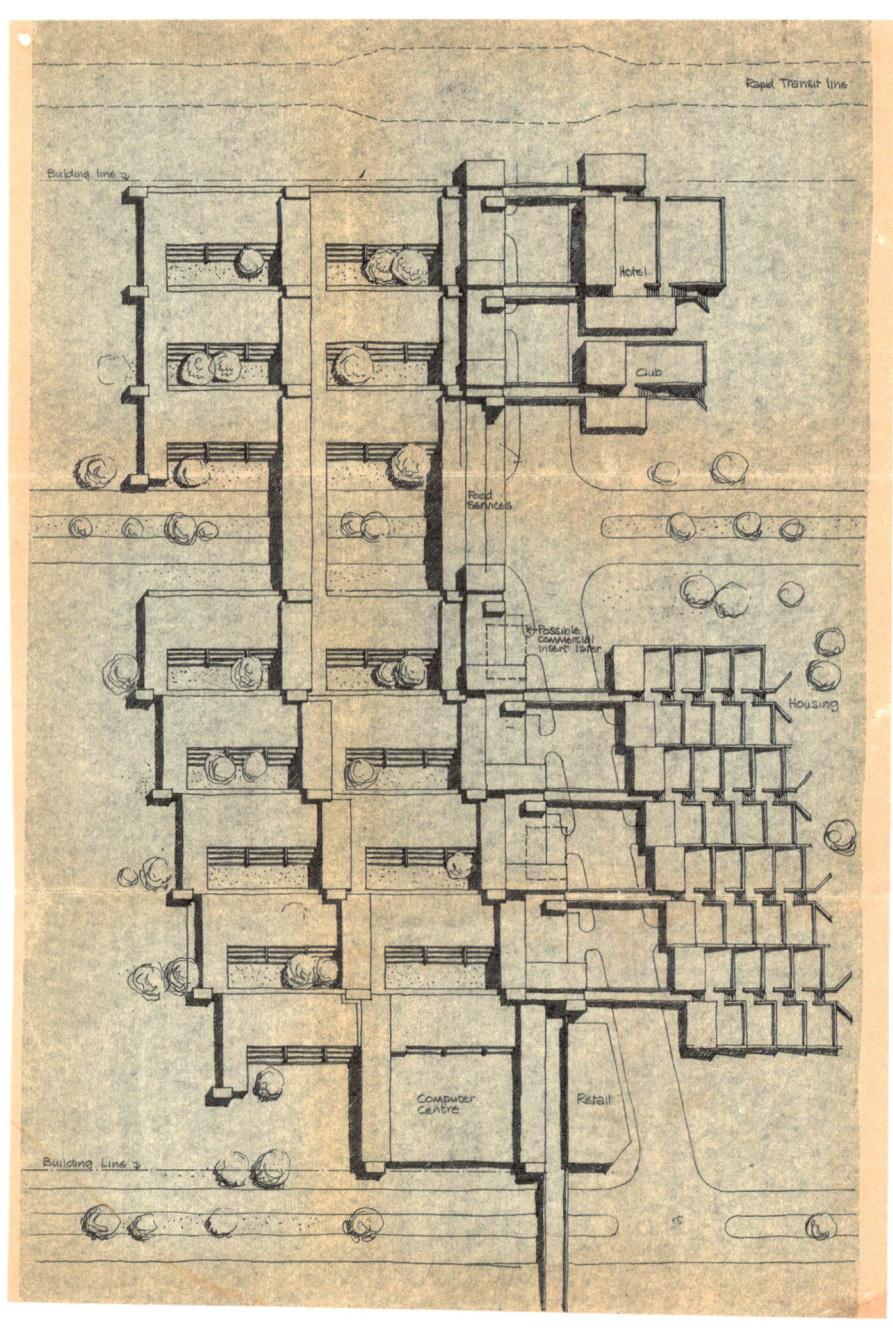

FIG. 4   Sketch, the Cameron Offices, Canberra, February 1969.

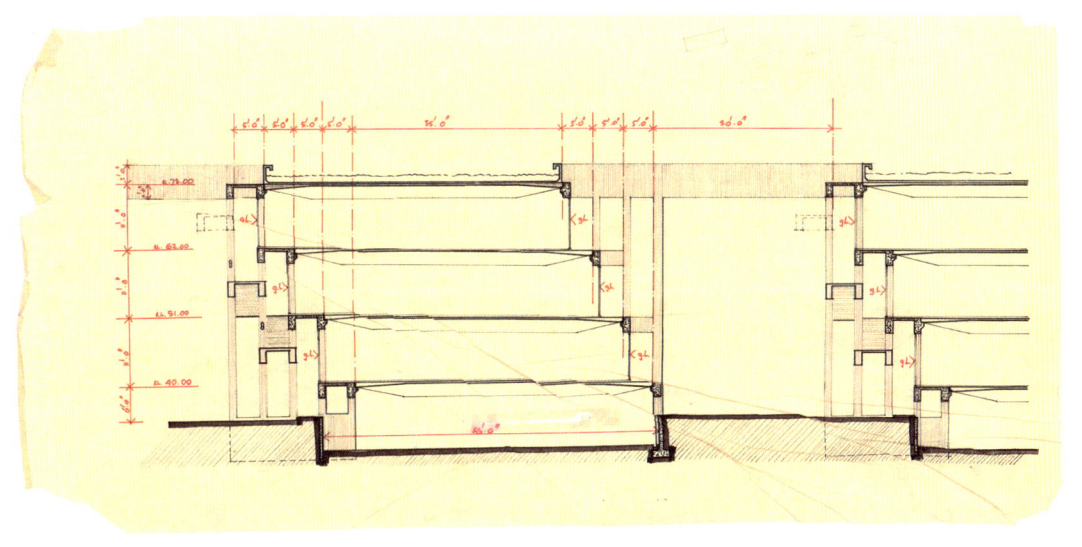

FIG. 5   Sketch, Belconnen (the Cameron Offices), 1969.

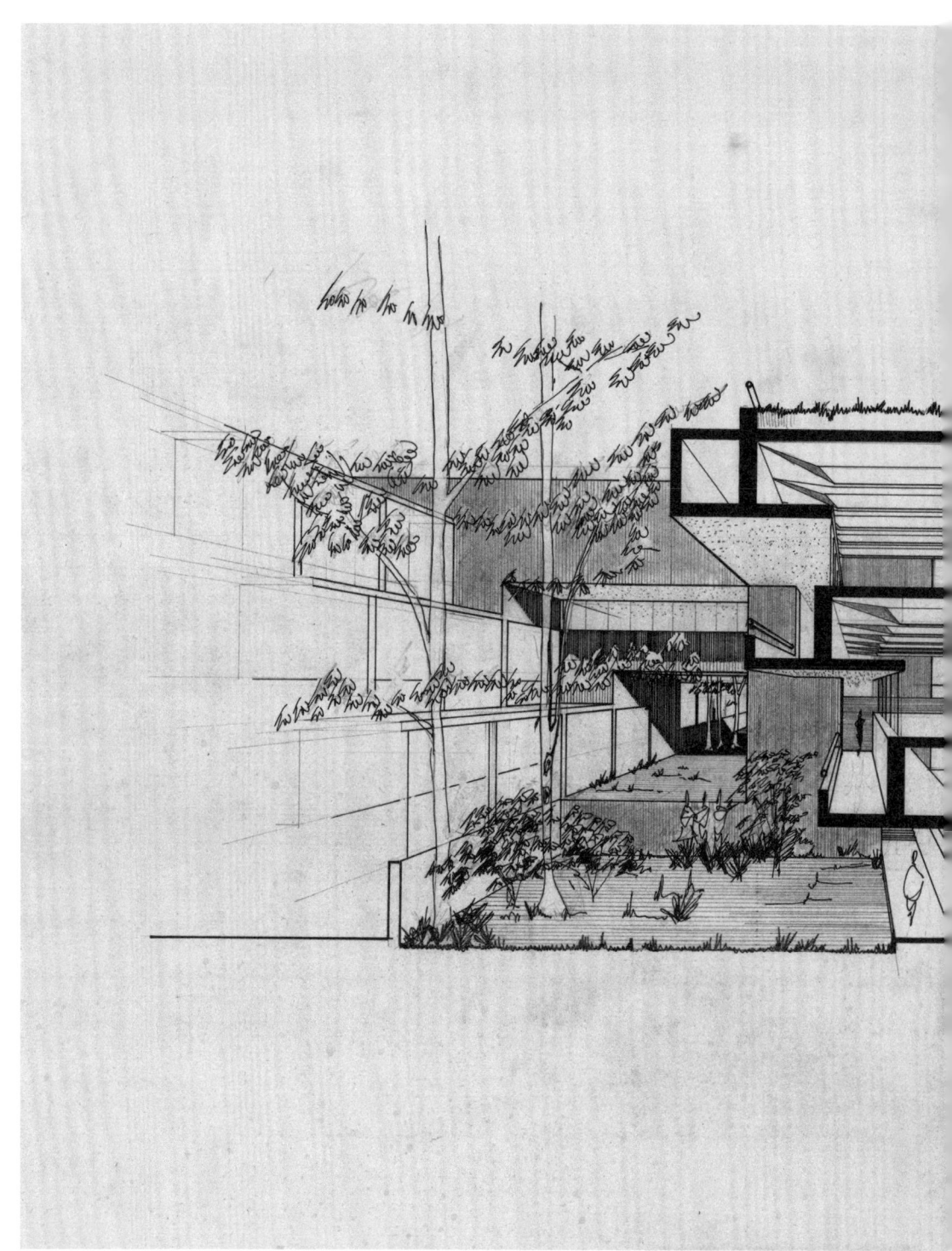

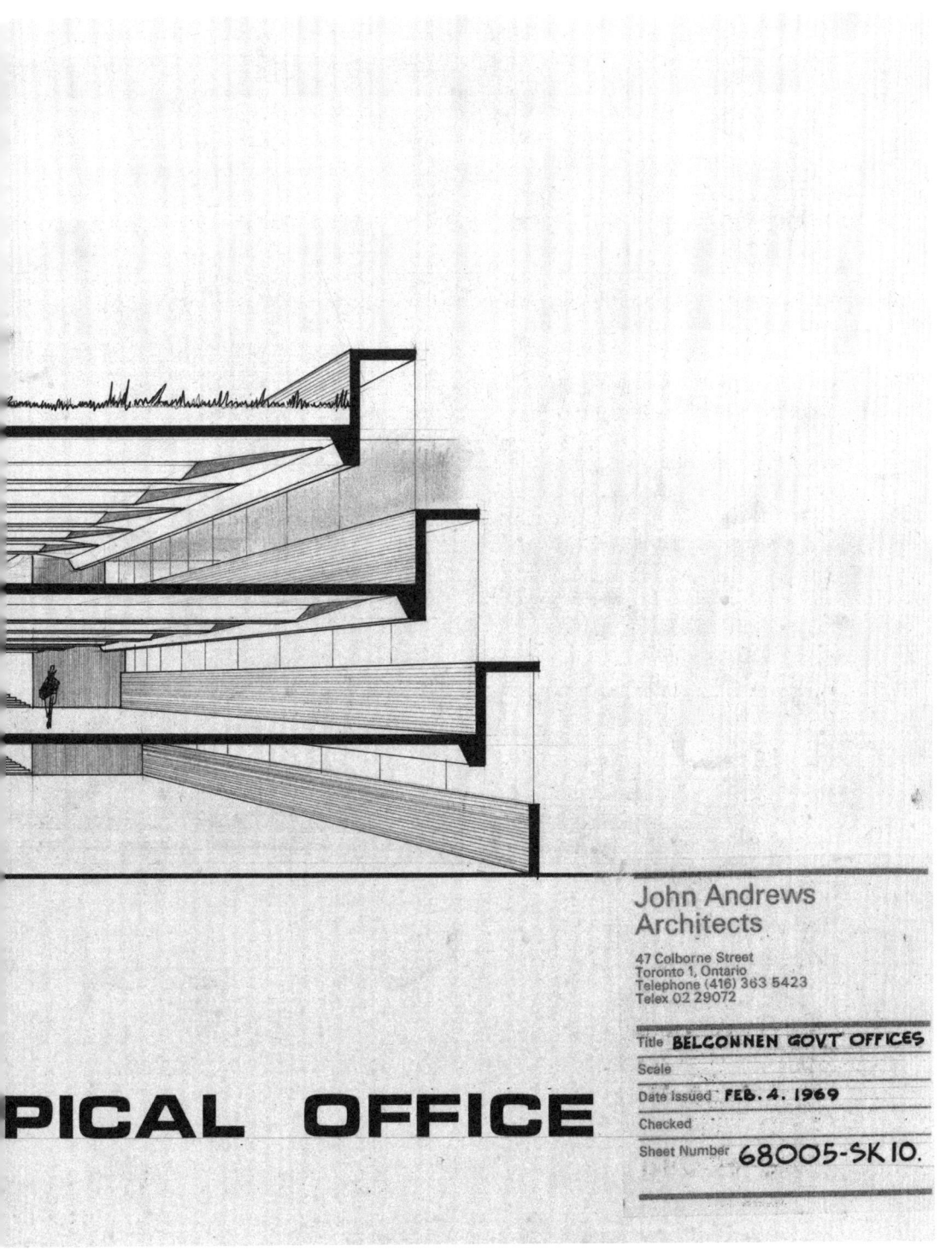

FIG. 6   The Cameron Offices, Canberra, 1969.

are connected by two north–south pedestrian links, internal to the complex rather than publicly accessible. [FIG. 4] The final design differs from earlier iterations in that it contains only one such route. In a drawing of the east elevation of the building, the mall building steps down to the north to a street cutting through the project, as was built. A provision for an east–west transit route below grade is indicated at the northern end of that elevation, with the outline of a tall building beyond—the Belconnen town center. Neither the transit nor the town center eventuated, but an at-grade bus interchange did. The towers, which are still projected in November 1968, are completely gone in February 1969. This omission is explained in a document from the Andrews office, also dated February 4. Under "Site Planning" the document states, "As can be seen, the organization is very similar to taking a conventional tower and laying it down on its side, the mall corresponds to the conventional banks of lifts. However this arrangement allows a much richer mix of land use along the circulation spine—views and interest unknown in a lift—and greater convenience of access and flexibility."[14] A description under the heading "Flexibility" also extols the superiority of Andrews's design approach over towers for the Cameron Offices, explaining that walking distances would be shorter in this arrangement than in the use of towers or slabs. Andrews follows the reflection on towers lying on their sides with one on gardens: "Landscape will play a very strong part in the environmental amenity of the offices. They might well be termed 'offices in a garden.' Everyone will have immediate visual and physical contact with trees and greenery from the time he parks his car and walks through the 'landscape fingers' to his office, to the view from his window.…The roofs, too, will be landscaped, providing terraces and roof-garden access particularly to the top band of administrative offices on the cross-axial grid, which becomes, in effect, penthouse offices." [FIG. 6]

This idea was enthusiastically taken up by the NCDC. In their subsequent revision of the architectural brief for the project—also dated February 1969—they commented, "The 'buildings-within-a garden' concept, evolved during the preliminary sketch plan stage is to be further developed, and consideration should be given to the wide use of advanced planting material during the initial development." The NCDC revision of the architectural brief also reiterates comments about materials contained in Andrews's February 4 document: under "Materials and Finishes," it states, "At present we see the main structure and finish as off-form concrete, vertical components in-situ and horizontal precast of a non-glare light color. Local sands indicate a buff color. Landscaping of the courts and roofs form a major finish. Internally the finishes will be exposed structure and well-designed mechanical systems wherever feasible." The NCDC saw the material and other design choices at the Cameron Offices as extending into the town center. Their revised architectural brief commented that the architect "is to make specific recommendations covering all items which could be carried through into the Town Centre design including such items as structural and facing materials to the buildings; paving; landscaping to courtyard and car parks; lighting (including street lighting, courtyard lighting, car park lighting, security lighting and flood lighting); street furniture and graphics, etc."[15]

While a structural program of precast horizontal members and in-situ vertical ones was decided, the details of the structural system were not yet devised. The drawing of the stepped section of the office wings that accompanied Andrews's February 4, 1969 report indicates no decision about the vertical structure, though the horizontal T-beams would indeed form the final structure of the office floors.

Several sketch drawings in the Andrews fonds at the Canadian Architectural Archives suggest that the final structural design was

---

14   John Andrews Architects, "Report on Architectural Studies for Government Office Complex, Belconnen Preliminary Sketch Plans, February 4, 1969," report, Toronto, February 4, 1969.

15   National Capital Development Commission, "Architectural Brief No 26/68, July 1968, 2nd Revision February 1969: Government Office Complex, Belconnen Town Centre," E1.

derived directly from the stepped section, the T-beams, and a desire to make the Cameron Offices interiors column-free and as flexible as possible in layout. [FIG. 5] The sketch design was finalized during a working session in Toronto with all the consultants included in the project team.[16]

The consultant team was organized in mid-1968. In the first meeting in Australia between the NCDC and Andrews, in September 1968, Andrews was accompanied by his Toronto lawyer George Miller and his good friend, former John B. Parkin Associates colleague, Integ partner, and Colborne Street neighbor, the landscape architect Dick Strong.[17] Strong—who had already designed the landscapes for the Miami Seaport Terminal and Gund Hall—played an important role in devising a landscape strategy for the Cameron Offices. Sculptor Gerry Gladstone, another Colborne Street friend, contributed a large public artwork called *Optical Galaxy* to the project. But who would be engaged for the other consultancy roles? These decisions were important for Andrews, who enjoyed a collaborative approach to design. Also in the John Andrews fonds at Calgary is a copy of a letter dated July 31, 1968, that Robert Anderson of the Andrews Toronto office wrote to Colin Madigan of Edwards Madigan Torzillo and Partners—the architects Andrews worked for in Sydney before going to Harvard—seeking advice on Australian consultants "in the following areas: structural; mechanical; electrical; quantity surveyors," as well as the Royal Australian Institute of Architects' rules, fee scale, and standard forms of contract in Australia.[18] We do not know what Madigan's advice to Andrews was, but the Australian consultants Andrews appointed to work on the Cameron Offices project include Miller, Milston, and Ferris as the structural engineer, D. S. Thomas and Partners the mechanical and services engineer, and McCredie Richmond & Johns Partners as quantity surveyors. Andrews developed productive working relationships with Peter Miller and Don Thomas, working with both on several future projects. In particular, Thomas's approach to a building's environmental performances involved strategies and devices that supported innovation in environmental design and tested the intuitive approach Andrews had developed in his earliest designs—and teaching—in Toronto. At the beginning of the project, Andrews appointed his old friend Peter Courtney as the Australian architect of record. As discussed in chapter 1, Courtney was a member of the small party at Rosemary and John Andrews's wedding on Cape Cod in 1958, and, at the time Andrews received the Cameron Offices commission, was a partner in a Canberra architectural practice. Courtney, Bruce Lincoln, and Geoff Willing variously served as site architects. The Toronto working session of all the consultants on the Cameron Offices project held in early 1969 led to the "Final Sketch Plan Report to the National Capital Development Commission," to which the names of architect, structural and mechanical engineers, landscape architects, and quantity surveyors are attached. Andrews recalled this session lasted a full month![19]

The need for flexible interiors determined that the structure of the east–west office wings be kept to the exterior, which the stepped section made complicated. Deep precast, reinforced concrete beams span each courtyard at the roof level of the higher adjacent wing. On the south side of each wing, columns hang from these "gallows beams," supporting edge beams at each floor level. On the north side, cast in-situ concrete columns support the edge beams. The structure for the office floor decks and the roof consists of precast concrete T-beams supported on the edge beams, with the T's vertical chamfered off at the ends. This allows space for exposed air-conditioning ducts and outlets. Because the office floors are staggered in section, there are multiple rows of columns on both sides of the office wings.

The columns on the north side of each wing also support external walkways at levels

---

16 Taylor and Andrews, *John Andrews*, 142
17 Ibid., 141.
18 Robert Anderson, John Andrews Architects, to Colin Madigan, Edwards Madigan Torzillo and Partners, July 31, 1968, AND 43A/78-33, Box 43-52, John Andrews fonds, Canadian Architectural Archives, University of Calgary.
19 Taylor and Andrews, *John Andrews*, 142.

offset from those of the office floors. The whole arrangement produces a repeating pattern of external concrete elements that shade the complex's glass walls and landscape courtyards. The structure is complicated further in that the two 150-foot-long office units that make up each wing are also offset by half a level in section and slightly in plan. The design was beautifully demonstrated in a sectional model made in Andrews's Toronto office, and an exquisite model of the whole building was also produced. [FIGS. 7–8]

The structure of the north–south oriented mall building at the east of the complex, along what became Chandler Street, is much more straightforward. Columns here are either rectangular piers or cylindrical cast in-situ concrete, with the rough timber shuttering clearly expressed in the imprints left in the concrete. These imprints share a kinship with the fluting of classical columns, and the cylindrical columns, like those at Gund Hall, can be read as an allusive nod to Le Corbusier. South of Cameron Avenue, the east–west street that bisects the complex, the plan and section of the mall building are staggered to accommodate the slope of the site and in plan to align with Chandler Street's slight diagonal shift.

Although the low-rise approach made the complex vast, the sense of the Cameron Offices' scale was made more intimate through each wing claiming an address on the mall and through the outlook available from most of the building interiors to landscaped courtyards. [FIG. 9]

THE BUILD

The Andrews office promoted "cooperative" contracts with contractors. At Cameron Offices, this entailed that "most of the subcontracts are tendered jointly by the client, the architect, and the builder."[20] This reduced the risk to the builder, a strategy that obviated the often adversarial relationship between contractors and clients and architects as principal consultants in traditional building contracts. The Sydney firm TC Whittle was selected to be the contractor in May 1970 and a collaborative selection of subcontractors followed.[21] The go-ahead for construction came late in 1970, with construction starting in earnest in 1971. The project was progressively opened from late in 1974, and an official opening of the Cameron Offices was held on September 24, 1976. While Andrews recalled that his relationship with Tommy Whittle—the owner of TC Whittle—was generally good, there were problems with the Cameron Offices build, namely several industrial disputes, mostly not specific to the project but typical of the Australian industrial scene of the period. More importantly, construction was also slowed by technical problems with the prefabricated concrete elements.

Because the Cameron Offices site was not built up at the time of construction, the plant to produce the prefabricated elements—particularly the gallows beams that spanned the courtyards and the T-beams that formed the roofs and floors of the office wings, but also minor elements like the concrete fins of Gladstone's sculpture—was located on site. [FIGS. 10–11] There were over 1,800 T-beams in the whole project, with several extra of these and other elements being cast to construct "the prototype," an on-site "test facility" comprised of one bay-width of a typical office wing, which was approximately 65 feet by 20 feet in dimension. It was also intended to use the prototype to work out details, such as enclosing elements and interior services and finishes. Construction on the prototype was to start in January 1971, ahead of the main construction phase, and took several months to complete.[22] Through most of 1971 and 1972, the casting of the T-beams did not go well.[23] They visibly cracked, due to

20   Ibid., 144.

21   National Capital Development Commission to TC Whittle, May 1, 1970.

22   P. J. Courtney Architects, "Cameron Offices Belconnen. Report – Prototype Building," report, Canberra, November 29, 1971.

23   This is reflected in the minutes of the special project meetings. The earliest reference to the cracking is in the minutes of the meeting on May 24, 1971. The matter is then reported on regularly until January 16, 1973, when in relation to the "T-beam dispute" it is noted that the contractor withdrew from arbitration and satisfactory T-beam production began. Special Project Meeting Minutes, May 24, 1971; January 16, 1973.

both poor stacking of the completed beams, for which the contractor was responsible, and a progressive deterioration in the beams at the tendon anchorages after casting.[24] It took months for this to be resolved, after specialist engineering advice was sought and some legal toing-and-froing was done by the contractor. The issue turned out to be mostly slight from an engineering perspective, according to Andrews, but nevertheless a solution had to be found because minor but visible cracks in the beams would cause concern among the building's occupants. The final solution was cosmetic: a coat of paint made the cracks less obvious and had the advantage of improving lighting conditions in the offices.[25]

There were also ongoing problems with the landscape design. Strong was involved in the design from the start, and as the sketch design evolved, in late 1968 and early 1969, the landscape became central to the project's concept, expressed in both the roof gardens and the courtyards between the office wings.

A formal agreement for Strong's services on the Cameron Offices was reached on May 9, 1969. To undertake the work, Strong subsequently established the firm Strong Moorhead Sigsby in Toronto and Sydney, with Steven Moorhead and Donald Sigsby. Moorhead had worked with Strong in Toronto since 1963, and Sigsby relocated to Australia to take responsibility for the landscape design of the Cameron Offices. Landscape implementation faced a number of obstacles. Several of the indigenous shrub species specified for the roof gardens were either not readily obtainable or were inappropriate, and this issue was exacerbated when the planned soil depth on the roofs was reduced in late 1971.[26] Contractors sought the advice of Margaret Hendry of the NCDC's landscape division, one of only five women landscape architects in Australia at the time.[27]

7

8

24 P. J. Courtney Architects, architect's weekly report for week ending November 5, 1971.
25 Taylor and Andrews, *John Andrews*, 144.
26 Special project meeting minutes, September 14, 1971; October 27, 1971.
27 "Margaret Hendry, 1930–2001," Australian Women's History Forum, February 29, 2012, https://awhf.wordpress.com/2012/02/29/argaret-hendry-1930-2001/.

FIGS. 7–8   Models, the Cameron Offices, 1969.

FIG. 9   Landscaped courtyard, the Cameron Offices.

Sigsby was apparently not happy. A letter from Strong to Peter Courtney suggests that in late 1972 it was resolved that Sigsby's association with the project should end, but he continued to work on it through most of the following year, until Strong sent Nick Van Vliet, another Canadian landscape architect, to supervise.[28]

The next difficulty with the landscape design came in 1976 when it became apparent that maintenance of the roof gardens on the completed sections of the Cameron Offices was unsatisfactory. This was reported at various special project meetings throughout that year between the project architects, the NCDC, and the government agencies that would occupy the complex. On May 18, John Andrews International architect Geoff Willing "told the meeting that lack of maintenance by City Parks on Rooftops 4–9 had resulted in the planting being dead." The meeting on August 31 found the City Parks' quote of $80,000 for maintaining the Cameron Offices landscaping for the 1976/77 fiscal year excessive. These difficulties were exacerbated under the Department of Administrative Services, which managed the complex after completion, and their poor landscape maintenance practices—particularly under- and overwatering—contributed substantially to leakage problems with the roof of the Cameron Offices. Strong wrote a letter to Willing on June 17, 1980, that offered practical advice on how to remedy the problems caused by neglect of the roof and courtyard gardens and plaintively commented, "The garden courts show a lack of interest by the occupants, and in most cases a commitment to the total Cameron concept, and the maintenance, which one would expect on a project of this importance and magnitude." He ended, "The Cameron Office Complex is of world significance, and we are proud to have been involved in the design and installation of the landscape material. We would hope the owners and occupants will re-instate the building and grounds to the original magnificence."[29]

28 Richard Strong, Strong Moorhead Sigsby, to Peter Courtney, John Andrews International, November 26, 1973.
29 Richard Strong, Strong Moorhead Sigsby, to Geoff Willing, John Andrews International, June 17, 1980.

Leaks in the roof of the Cameron Offices were first observed soon after the first phases of the project were completed.[30] These were minor, associated with heavy rain, and not particularly unusual. Such "teething issues" are normal in the completion of a large building complex. Progress in remedying those at the Cameron Offices was monitored regularly in the special project meetings. Correspondence in the Andrews archive suggests that concerns about leaks became pronounced in 1978, soon after the entire building was completed and occupied; the NCDC forwarded the Andrews office a copy of a letter from the Administrative and Clerical Officers' Association (ACOA), the union representing federal government bureaucrats, to John Howard, the federal treasurer and a formidable conservative politician.[31] The ACOA letter suggested that plastic buckets were widely distributed at the Cameron Offices and that carpets were rotting. It provocatively commented that it was well-known that problems arose at Cameron from "structural faults." As the letter reads, "At the time of construction the building was hailed as a striking example of architectural progress. However, the sorry record of deficiencies subsequently revealed makes one wonder to what extent the architectural innovation had been checked out prior to the contract being awarded." The letter further states that the "plastic membrane covering the roof is not watertight." Willing wrote back to the NCDC, protesting that the comments on the building's structure were unfounded and defamatory. They were also ignorant. Willing outlined the nature of the membrane used—several layers of fiberglass-reinforced, bituminous-saturated roofing felt—and noted that it was only through architectural innovation that the roofing design had been resolved. Such leaks as existed were not due to the membrane but to flashings and joints, and responsibility for these lay not in the design but in the construction work of the roofing subcontractor. Moreover, leaks were systematically solved as they were discovered.

It seems likely that the ACOA's dissatisfaction with the Cameron Offices was behind the articles that appeared in the Australian press in June 1978. On June 15, an article appeared on page 10 of the *Sydney Morning Herald*, the city's leading daily newspaper, under the headline "One Government leak is caught in buckets." An unnamed "senior Government official" is reported as saying that the building "leaks like a sieve." Similar articles appeared in newspapers in Melbourne and Brisbane the following day. Legal action by Andrews and his office followed, and these articles were ultimately deemed by the New South Wales courts to defame the architect.

Nevertheless, the problems with leaks resulting from poor maintenance continued. In 1980, the NCDC sought advice from the architects about alternative landscape options for the roof gardens as the Department of Administrative Services planned to close access to them due to low usage and the ongoing cost of maintenance, an outcome the NCDC wished to avoid. Willing sent a long letter on July 2, 1980, relaying advice that John Andrews International received from Strong on how the roof gardens and the other landscaping at the Cameron Offices also suffering from neglect could be revived and ongoing costs reduced.[32] The problems, however, were not resolved, and in 1986 the *Sydney Morning Herald* again published an article on leaks in the building, reporting that the Minister of Local Government and Territories Tom Uren advised Parliament that the problems with the building would cost $9 million to fix. Under parliamentary privilege, Uren repeated the newspaper's 1978 claim that the building leaked like a sieve and, referring to the 1979 defamation case, noted that he had "no doubt that the publishers John Fairfax and

---

30   Leaks are reported in the special project meeting minutes dated March 2, 1976; April 6, 1976; May 18, 1976; June 22, 1976; July 27, 1976; November 26, 1976; and December 21, 1976. A letter from Geoff Willing, John Andrews International, dated November 22, 1976, lists 14 leaks since June 21, 1976, with seven still unsolved.

31   National Capital Development Commission to Geoff Willing, John Andrews International, April 28, 1978. The letter from the Administrative and Clerical Officers' Association is undated but stamped with a received date of April 13, 1978.

32   Geoff Willing, John Andrews International, to National Capital Development Commission, July 2, 1980.

FIG. 10 Concrete floor structure under construction, the Cameron Offices, 1971.

FIG. 11   Construction, the Cameron Offices, 1971.

FIG. 12 Yorkdale Shopping Centre, Toronto, Canada, 1964, architect: John Graham Consultants. At upper right, Simpson's store, architect: John Andrews at John B. Parkin Associates. At left, photocollaged schematic model for urban intensification through medium-rise office blocks. Architect: John Andrews Architects.

FIG. 13 Bus station to north of the Cameron Offices, February 1976. Architect: John Andrews International.

Sons will take note of that comment."[33] The government was incapable of acknowledging the role of its own departments in the fiasco. The NCDC's early enthusiasm for the "offices in a garden" concept was gone; they certainly had not communicated it to other government agencies.

A LOST VISION

The problems with the maintenance of the Cameron Offices were symptomatic of the loss of the vision that the NCDC, the architects, and the other consultants enthusiastically shared when the project was devised in 1968 and 1969. Andrews envisioned a building that would function primarily as a kind of social infrastructure, a place to work, to be sure, but also a circulation template that could be extended to traverse the entire central Belconnen area. This was implied in the schematic drawings in the design reports from late 1968 that show a single main linear path linking the Cameron Offices in the south to the transit, retail, and civic zones planned to the north, and ultimately to Lake Ginninderra. Connected to this north–south route was a filigree of secondary routes. Inside the building, these routes moved through stairs and half-landings, dispersing in the vast open office areas; outside, they connected the parking areas to the west and, via bridges over the road to the east of the Cameron Offices, to planned residential areas. The project was also intended to accommodate a "district thermal station" to heat and cool water for buildings throughout central Belconnen.

The kind of horizontal, distributive planning found in the Cameron Offices is found in a wide range of the neo-avant-garde work of the 1960s and 1970s, as set out in Alison Smithson's 1974 essay "How to Recognise and Read Mat-Building."[34] But not only neo-avant-garde. In his revisiting of Smithson, Timothy Hyde suggests mat-planning projects of the 1960s and 1970s have as one of their key precedents the shopping centers that appeared in North American suburbs in the 1950s, citing Victor Gruen's Southdale Shopping Center of 1956 as a "building without exterior."[35] Andrews was used to working with building designs with circulation at their heart. This was true of Scarborough College, of Metro Centre, and even more so of the Miami Seaport Terminal. But his experience with retail mall design at Toronto's Yorkdale Shopping Centre might offer the best clue here, not least in his designation of the principal circulation route linking the Cameron Offices' wings with the rest of the town center as "the mall." Andrews first worked at Yorkdale when he designed the Simpsons department store there while at John B. Parkin Associates; work on this project included a stint at Gruen's Los Angeles office, which acted as consultants and interior designers on the Simpsons project.[36] Simpsons was one of the key components of what was at the time of its opening the largest enclosed shopping mall in the world. Later, in his own Toronto office, Andrews worked on projects that sought to increase the urban density of Yorkdale Shopping Centre through modestly scaled office blocks on its periphery—perhaps not unlike those suggested for the Cameron Offices in the first sketches of late 1968—that linked to streets, open-air parking, and a mall. [FIG. 12]

The vision of the Cameron Offices as a project that would establish the infrastructural pattern of pedestrian circulation through the whole of central Belconnen was fatally compromised in 1975 when the NCDC decided to relocate the town center—reduced to a shopping center only—from a site directly north of Cameron Offices to one northwest. This was

33 "Gov't Offices Will Cost Nearly $9m to Repair, Says Uren," *Sydney Morning Herald*, May 9 1986. See also "Leaks in the Cameron Offices: Department Plans to Spend $5.6m," *Canberra Times*, May 7, 1986; "$3.5m for Roof on PS Offices," *Canberra Times*, April 24, 1987.

34 Alison Smithson, "How to Recognise and Read Mat-Building: Mainstream Architecture as It Has Developed towards the Mat-Building" in Hashim Sarkis, ed., *Case: Le Corbusier's Venice Hospital and the Mat Building Revival* (Munich: Prestel, 2001), 90–103.

35 Timothy Hyde, "How to Construct an Architectural Genealogy: Mat-Building... Mat-Buildings... Matted-Buildings," in Hashim Sarkis, ed., *Case: Le Corbusier's Venice Hospital and the Mat Building Revival* (Munich: Prestel, 2001), 107.

36 "Amentia in a Market Place: Yorkdale Shopping Centre Toronto," *Canadian Architect* (June 1964): 47, 50.

completely disconnected from the Cameron Offices. It was also completely contrary to the NCDC's own urban design vision for the development of Belconnen. Overall suggested that this change was motivated by the local community:

> The Commission [NCDC] had wanted to construct Belconnen Mall on the shores of the newly built Lake Ginninderra to avoid a repeat of Lake Burley Griffin, where the city's central water feature was separated by roads and parks from the major buildings, offices, and shops. The Mall was to be the hub of the town's nightlife, with cafes and cinemas spilling along its shore, bringing the town centre's water feature to life. But it was forced to abandon the plan in the face of opposition from the local Ginninderra Community Council which mounted an effective campaign with the backing of the Trades and Labour Council to have the pristine lake shore preserved as parkland. As a result the Mall and Belconnen offices were sited some distance from the lake.[37]

The new site also allowed for a larger shopping center. Rather than community agitation, the *Canberra Times* reported that increased scale motivated the mall's relocation, at the behest of the Canberra Commercial Development Authority, the public agency charged with its development, which wanted to expand its size.[38] Overall retired from the NCDC's leadership in 1972, and by the mid-1970s commercial rather than community interests were primary. Neoliberal economic policies—pursued by both major Australian political parties—focused on market-led development. "After making much of the need to keep Belconnen Mall under public ownership in the 1970s, the Labor government, newly converted to the virtues of lower deficits and privatization, sold the shopping complex in 1986."[39] The NCDC was itself disestablished in 1988, its work developing Canberra into a worthy federal capital supposedly done. The bipartisan consensus on the development of Canberra as a capital that had been maintained since 1957 was over. In this period, government stakeholders agreed not only that the great monuments of the capital—the National Library, National Gallery, High Court, and the New Parliament House—would have an architecture worthy of national dignity but so too would the office buildings that housed the national bureaucracy. The NCDC's highly interventionist style of growing the city and building its infrastructure and workplaces simply fell out of political fashion.

Andrews attacked the decision to relocate the shopping center. "It's ludicrous. And it has all come about because a bunch of amateurs have taken over from the professionals."[40] The NCDC's original vision for Belconnen emerged from the wide range of professional skills represented in the NCDC's institutional apparatus in the 1960s; now that vision was compromised for commercial exigencies alone. As already noted, Andrews had experience with retail mall development and its problems and opportunities. He simply observed that a larger shopping center at Belconnen could be achieved by building two floors on the original site instead of one. He did not prevail. Subsequently, in 1976, the Andrews office was awarded the commission for a bus station immediately north of Cameron Offices—the rapid transit never came. [FIG. 13] Andrews wrote of his disaffection:

> My criticisms would be more of a feeling of intense disappointment and frustration that the NCDC was unable to control the external pressures that changed the planning organization of the town centre, and moved the shopping centre from its place in the overall design system at a time when the Cameron Offices were almost completed. We have been

37 Overall, *Canberra Yesterday, Today & Tomorrow*, 119–20.
38 Bruce Wright, "Architect's Attack: Mall Threatened by 'Amateur' Planners," *Canberra Times*, November 28, 1975.
39 Overall, *Canberra Yesterday, Today & Tomorrow*, 123.
40 Wright, "Architect's Attack."

14

15

16

FIGS. 14–16   The Cameron Offices, 1976.

FIG. 17   Potted plants in interior, the Cameron Offices, 1976.

able to remedy this situation partially by connecting the mall to the bus station, and thence in a very tenuous way to the new location of the shopping centre. It is impossible to assess to what extent this replanning will affect the fundamental premise of the organization of the Cameron Offices.[41]

ARCHITECTURE/INFRASTRUCTURE

The architecture of the Cameron Offices has often been described as "Brutalist" for its extensive use of unadorned concrete. For example, Jaquelin T. Robertson referred to the "Brutalist color and material palette" of the Cameron Offices.[42] Jennifer Taylor wrote that the complex has "roots in Brutalism and ultimately in Corbusier's concrete architecture."[43] [FIG. 14] The Le Corbusier connection is apt—Scarborough College has stairs akin to Le Corbusier's in the Chandigarh Secretariat; Gund Hall has columns from the Carpenter Center, and so on. But Andrews was disdainful of the term "Brutalism," and saw his work rather as "humanist." A later assessment by Taylor echoes this notion: "The Cameron Offices (1976) further exhibited his humanitarian concerns and the development of planning principles to provide for self-identity, to open possibilities for social contact, and to serve as a generator of a vital urban order."[44] The success of the Cameron Offices in offering both a coherent, systematic approach to the design of a big building and making something comfortable to inhabit was identified by Robertson: "It is an assemblage of rationally conceived additive parts which gives paramount importance to

41   Taylor and Andrews, *John Andrews*, 153.
42   Jaquelin T. Robertson, "Architecture as Urban Precinct: An Office Block by John Andrews which Eloquently Reaches the High Planning Standards of Walter Burley Griffin's Canberra," *Architectural Record* 167, no. 5 (October 1980): 78–85
43   Jennifer Taylor, *Australian Architecture Since 1960* (Sydney: Law Book Company, 1986), 79. See also Paul Walker and Antony Moulis, "Finding Brutalism in the Architecture of John Andrews," *Fabrications* 25, no. 2 (2015): 214–33.
44   Jennifer Taylor, "John Andrews," in Philip Goad and Julie Willis, eds., *The Encyclopedia of Australian Architecture* (Melbourne: Cambridge University Press, 2012), 23–24.

light and nature and human scale at its core and enhances the circulation system so the building is appreciated through its use." Robertson argued that the Cameron Offices were a new type of office building, as Frank Lloyd Wright's Larkin and Johnson Wax Buildings and Herman Hertzberger's Centraal Beheer had been previously.[45] He also suggested that in his design for the Cameron Offices, Andrews was a worthy successor to Walter Burley Griffin and Marion Mahony Griffin's conception for Canberra in producing a building so responsive to its landscape setting. [FIG. 15]

It is in the concern for the experience of wayfinding and inhabitation within such a large complex that the claim for a humane quality in the Cameron Offices is justified. In this—as already noted—the design relates to the "mat-planning" approach that arose in the work of the Team 10 architects in the 1960s, including Aldo van Eyck and Candilis-Josic-Woods. Andrews had the opportunity to become familiar with van Eyck's work. The mall at Cameron and the subsidiary routes off it are very close to the "stem" planning logic of Shadrach Woods; the mall also has kinship with the elevated "streets" Alison and Peter Smithson explored in their entry to the Golden Lane Estate competition of 1952. However, while Andrews knew of van Eyck's work (and Hertzberger's), the conceptual framework adopted in designing the Cameron Offices came first from the ethos promulgated in his studies at the Harvard GSD of seeing architecture as an urban endeavor and second from the megastructural approach he used in his first major projects in independent practice, namely Scarborough College (1965), the South Residences at the University of Guelph (1967), and the Miami Seaport Terminal (1970). Taylor overtly connects the Cameron Offices to the megastructure movement. Her critique of the project in the *Architectural Review* begins: "Reyner Banham informs us that the megastructure has met its demise. He does so without noting the recent erection of one of the largest and most consistent examples—John Andrews's Cameron Offices. This is excusable perhaps as Cameron is located outside Canberra in the back blocks of Australia—a place where no one, not even Banham, would think to look! If the megastructure is indeed dead then it is fitting that the architect of the first major constructed example, Scarborough College (complete in concept, organization, and imagery), should also be the designer of one of the last."[46] [FIG. 16]

The challenge of the megastructure or the mat is to find and own a location within it. Such buildings also raise the question of how their exteriors can cohere—they are by nature, as Hyde says, buildings without exteriors. At the Cameron Offices, the location issue was to be solved through the connection of each office finger to the mall and each government department within the vast complex having its own mall "street address." The mall was also a street insofar as it supported small-scale retail and had street lighting, furniture, and quarry-tile paving, which was intended to continue into the town center. Stainless steel strip ceilings added a lively glitter to the mall's public space. Individuality for the offices was also to be achieved through the landscaped courtyards: each was to have cited a different kind of Australian landscape—from desert to rain forest—with this diversity producing an identity for the office wings that looked out onto it. The computer center and the architecturally undifferentiated office spaces of the seven office wings (three floors each; two plan modules of 50 by 150 feet on each level of each wing; the total housing 4,000 workstations) were fitted out by Gordon Andrews, John Andrews's older cousin and an accomplished graphic and furniture designer. These interiors were informed by *Bürolandschaft* principles, then of considerable interest to the NCDC as it simultaneously developed several large-scale office projects. Different dominant colors differentiated the interior treatment of the different wings.[47] Carpets, screens, furniture, and signage were all designed, and Andrews even scrutinized

---

45   Robertson, "Architecture as Urban Precinct," 81.

46   Jennifer Taylor, "Civil Service City," *Architectural Review* (March 1978): 136–46.

47   Gordon Andrews, *A Designer's Life* (Sydney: University of New South Wales Press, 1993), 158–59.

18

19

FIGS. 18–19 The Cameron Offices, 1976.

potted plants. [FIG. 17] Landscape was also key to endowing the Cameron Offices with a coherent exterior form. The staggering of the finger blocks of offices up the low ridge of the site, the stepping of the plan-form, and the elevation of the mall produced a sense of changeful mass that, from a distance, made the fundamental landform of the site visible, especially in the building's roofline.

Despite his general enthusiasm for the project, Robertson was skeptical of some aspects of the architecture of the Cameron Offices. As he writes, "too many level changes and entry options, and the by now familiar drabness of 'Brutalist'-designed exposed concrete...."[48] In his critique of the building that appeared in *Architecture Australia*, the architectural historian David Saunders expressed similar views: "I am inclined not to include plain graey cement-rich concrete among the family of materials fit to be brought close to people. There are many ways of modifying it or distancing it that can be used. Here, concrete which was poured in plywood forms is to be found all around with the usual hardness, blemishes, and stains. Where that's a background to plants it's one thing, where it confronts you personally it's another and less pleasant thing."[49]

Saunders was also puzzled by some of the fundamental decisions at the Cameron Offices. For example, the bravura structural system of gallows beams across the courtyard gardens with columns hanging off them on one side and anchored by the columns on the other was an ingenious response to a problem that was of the design's own making: the floors stepping in section to obviate solar gain would have been unnecessary if the simple device of shading the glass with hoods had been adopted. Hoods, however, would not have yielded the architectural excitement equivalent to the amazing forest of Cameron's concrete elements as built. [FIG. 18] The Saunders essay on the Cameron Offices also included a critique of Harry Seidler's Trade Group Offices, one of the other large NCDC office projects of the period. While admiring the precision and clarity of Seidler's building, and taking into account the eccentricities and concrete of the Cameron Offices, Saunders tellingly preferred Andrews's project:

> While Seidler's Trade arrives at an impressive simplicity by choosing to deal superbly with selected aspects, Andrews's Cameron is complex to the point of being, in some respects, baffling.
>
> A refusal to simplify seems apparent in Cameron but this becomes an endearing quality because it goes with the emphasis upon occupation, circulation and facilities like gardens. Pointers to people possessing the place, not just occupying it, and compatible with a life-like complexity.
>
> In such a building aspects which may feel under-solved, such as materials, can more readily be balanced against virtues, because the whole thing seems more a matter of Life than Art....[50]

More a matter of life than art. Or, we could say, of infrastructure than architecture. At the end of her *Architectural Review* article on the building, published well after the disastrous decision to remove the shopping center from its initial location immediately north of the Cameron Offices, Taylor remained optimistic: "While the building itself remains unaffected, it has been deprived of the opportunity to fully function as the architect and initial town planners intended. But the statement of Cameron is a strong one that cannot be overlooked for long. I suspect that with this building Australia once again bought far more than she bargained for."[51] [FIG. 19] This optimism turned out to be misplaced. Australia, or at least its federal government, would not forgive the Cameron Offices for its social, technical, and aesthetic ambition.

---

48 Robertson, "Architecture as Urban Precinct," 83.
49 David Saunders, "Homes for the Bureaucrats," *Architecture Australia* 65, no. 3 (June/July 1976): 68.
50 Saunders, "Homes for the Bureaucrats," 68.
51 Taylor, "Civil Service City," 146.

09

andrews as a public advocate for design

by   Paul Walker

During the late 1970s, John Andrews was increasingly called upon to take up public responsibilities in Australia alongside his professional activities, his public profile having peaked after the completion of the King George Tower and the Cameron Offices in 1976. But in 1978, Andrews's name was in the press for another reason: reporting by three Australian newspapers on problems alleged to be widespread at the Cameron Offices and attributed to the complex's design prompted Andrews to sue for defamation. While the defamation case led to some anxiety on Andrews's part regarding his reputation, this concern was not shared by his fellow architects. If anything, the architectural profession rallied behind him. In 1980, in recognition of his considerable achievements as an architect, Andrews received the Australian architectural profession's highest accolade, the Gold Medal of the Royal Australian Institute of Architects (RAIA). In connection with the award, Andrews delivered the A. S. Hook Memorial Address to members of the institute the following year. Rather than comment on his own design work, however Andrews reflected on what architecture in Australia should strive to achieve, and this lecture remained his only lengthy public prognostication on the country's design future.

Coinciding with the defamation case and the RAIA Gold Medal, Andrews took on two public-facing roles in which he reveled. The first was the role of a juror in the design competition for the new Australian Parliament House in Canberra, and the second was with the country's preeminent arts body, the Australia Council. There, Andrews fostered an interest and investment in design first as a member of the council's Visual Arts Board and then as chair of its newly established Design Arts Board. This work involved Andrews in a decade of effort until 1988. While he did not cultivate his own profile through his work with the Australia Council—perhaps due to his reticence in the aftermath of the defamation case—he was nevertheless an effective advocate for design within the institution, and its decade-long engagement with Australian design and architecture can be attributed to his bluff leadership style and charisma.

DEFAMATION

On June 15, 1978, an article appeared on page 10 of the *Sydney Morning Herald* under the headline "One Government Leak is Caught in Buckets." It claimed that federal government officials in Canberra were concerned with security issues associated with the design of the recently opened Cameron Offices complex in Belconnen and with leaks in the building's roof. As the article explains, "A senior government official says that, not only does the building have 240 doors which have to be locked and unlocked daily, but it leaks like a sieve." The article goes on to attribute the following comments to this unnamed bureaucrat: "They're not your usual leaks of information. These are leaks caused by water seeping through the ceilings. Some of the public servants working in the complex have to bring plastic buckets to work to catch the dripping water. Every time they plug one leak another opens up. It's like maintaining the Sydney Harbour Bridge—an endless process."[1] Other articles based on this one appeared the following day in the Brisbane *Telegraph* and the Melbourne *Herald*.[2]

Andrews and his firm John Andrews International sued the *Sydney Morning Herald*'s proprietors and those of the other two newspapers for defamation. The case went to court in August 1979, and over the two weeks of proceedings, it was widely reported on in the Australian media. Press outlets aired matters such as Andrews's high international standing, the lack of commissions John Andrews International had received since the first newspaper report, and technical issues related to the roof construction of the Cameron Offices.[3] Andrews and his firm were awarded damages of $480,000, reportedly the highest award in an Australian defamation case to that date.[4]

1 "One Government Leak Is Caught in Buckets," *Sydney Morning Herald*, June 15, 1978.
2 "Wet Leaks Upset the P.S.," *The Telegraph* (Brisbane), June 16, 1978; Angela Long, "Public Service 'leak' gets a bucket," *The Herald* (Melbourne), June 16, 1978.
3 "'Cruel attack' on architect," *The Australian*, August 14, 1978; "Three Publishers Sued over Article," *Sydney Morning Herald*, August 14, 1978; "Only 3 Leaks at Cameron Offices, Architect Says," *Canberra Times*, August 23, 1979.

The three newspapers appealed. The New South Wales Court of Appeal upheld the damages awarded to John Andrews International ($180,000). However, they determined that a new hearing reconsider not the finding of defamation itself but the damages awarded to Andrews personally. These matters dragged on through 1980, and Andrews and the newspapers reached an out-of-court settlement in March 1981.[5] It was during this final phase of legal proceedings that RAIA would deliberate on awarding Andrews the Gold Medal and that the texts celebrating the award in *Architecture Australia* were written.[6] Andrews's Gold Medal win was announced in May 1981.

The design of the Cameron Offices was acclaimed in the profession and published in journals, including *Architecture + Urbanism*, *Canadian Architect*, and *The Architectural Review*. A 1980 *Architectural Record* article by Jaquelin T. Robertson described the complex as "eloquently reach[ing] the high planning standards of Walter Burley Griffin's Canberra."[7] Andrews received widespread support for taking legal action. The distinguished American urban planner Edmund Bacon sent Andrews a letter about the Cameron Offices, dated the same day as the *Sydney Morning Herald*'s article. As Bacon wrote, "[Cameron Offices] is one of the most interesting building complexes I have seen anywhere in the world because it relates to the larger city of which it is a part in a valid and original way.... I think Australia has shown the world new possibilities of providing the government office worker with a personal and humanistic kind of environment in which he or she is given personal recognition, yet which functions as a whole and which is not an isolated kind of institution but is clearly a part of a larger, vital functioning community."[8]

That the Cameron Offices were so widely admired in the profession made the attack on the integrity of its design particularly galling. Andrews's friend and occasional collaborator, Sydney architect Philip Cox, encouraged him to sue, and so too did the Royal Australian Institute of Architects.[9] RAIA President John H. Davidson wrote to Andrews:

> Few would doubt that the Cameron Offices will be recorded in history as a significant contribution to the advancement of architecture, not only nationally but internationally.
>
> As this is one of the foremost aims of our Institute, I am seriously concerned lest obviously ill-informed and unsubstantiated criticism of this kind will reflect adversely not only on you as the architect but also on the architectural profession as a whole.
>
> I presume you intend to take some action to correct the record, and in doing so, providing it is within our mandate, I would like to offer the support of RAIA following any reasonable request you might make.[10]

In light of this offer of support from the institute, we might surmise that the timing of the award of the Gold Medal to Andrews was influenced by the defamation case. Andrews's reputation is linked to that of the architectural profession more broadly, and therefore the profession has an investment to defend its members. Perhaps it was mere coincidence, but the phraseology around "the advancement of architecture" in Davidson's letter of support to Andrews echoed that of the terms of the

---

4   "Jury Awards $480,000 Damages for Defamation," *Sydney Morning Herald*, August 31, 1979.
5   "Defamation Actions by John Andrews," *Sydney Morning Herald*, March 28, 1981.
6   This was announced in *Architecture Australia* in May 1981; presumably, this matter had been discussed within the Royal Australian Institute of Architects in late 1980 and early 1981.
7   "Cameron Offices," *Architecture + Urbanism* (May 1974): 55–64; "Five projects by John Andrews International," *Canadian Architect* (July 1976): 18–39. Jennifer Taylor, "Government Offices, Canberra," *Architectural Review* (March 1978): 136–146; Jaquelin T. Robertson, "Architecture as urban precinct: An office block by John Andrews," *Architectural Record* 168, no. 5 (October 1980): 78–85.

8   Edmond Bacon to John Andrews, June 15, 1978. John Andrews archive.
9   Philip Cox to John Andrews, June 23, 1978. John Andrews archive.
10 John H. Davidson to John Andrews, June 26, 1978. John Andrews archive.

Gold Medal: "to recognize Architects who have given distinguished service by designing or executing buildings of high merit or who have produced work of great distinction resulting in the advancement of architecture or who have endowed the profession of Architecture in such a distinguished manner as to merit the receipt of the award."

GOLD, AND GRAY AND WHITE

The protracted defamation proceedings were personally grueling for Andrews and, despite his winning the case, detrimental to his professional reputation. Yet in his own comments on receiving the RAIA Gold Medal, Andrews was neither defensive nor introspective but rather philosophical and projective. In his A. S. Hook Memorial Address delivered to mark the award of the Gold Medal, Andrews confidently set out an agenda for an Australian architecture as part of an emergent national design sensibility. He alluded to the personal draw his homeland had in his decision to return to Sydney, despite the great success of his career in Canada and the United States. An honor bestowed by his colleagues and peers, Andrew said that the Gold Medal "is the most important award that one, as an architect, could ever hope to achieve and is something that will outlive any other form of accolade I could receive... [It] is of special significance to me, having spent many years overseas, establishing a practice and seeing how the other half lives. But finally I came to the realization that Australia was my *home*. This is where I wanted to work and above all be *recognized* as an architect."[11] [FIGS. 1–2]

Continuing his address, Andrews described the attraction Australia held for him in terms familiar in much Australian architectural discourse, noting the country's open spaces, the quality of its light, and its landscapes. In addition to these rather romantic ideas, Andrews also characterized Australia in more novel terms, namely "its urbanity and its incredible solitude." But it was not merely

1

2

FIG. 1 Celebration of Andrews's win of the RAIA Gold Medal, *Architecture Australia* 70, no. 2 (May 1981).

FIG. 2 John Andrews International staff celebrating Andrews's win of the RAIA Gold Medal, *Architecture Australia* 70, no. 2 (May 1981).

11 John Andrews, "A. S. Hook 1981," *Architecture Australia* 70, no. 5 (November 1981): 70. Emphasis in the original.

nostalgia for Australia that called Andrews back. He was also driven by a sense that the degree of affluence in North America made anything in architecture possible but nothing a challenge. As he remarked in his speech, "Technology was at a level where anything an architect conceived could be built. Wealth was enormous. There was no need to think. No need to ask *Why?* Only the need to dream. Preferably a different dream every time."[12]

Australian architecture was not conditioned by such excess. Reflecting on this, Andrews turned again to common tropes, such as the practical exigencies of climate and limited resources that led European settlers in Australia to produce "an architecture totally suited to this land." Andrews suggested that his contemporaries were not sufficiently mindful of this, but by looking at the achievements of the early builders and carefully cultivating resources—as required by the energy crisis—Australian architecture could again find a way forward. And in these concerns, Andrews believed Australia had an advantage: "We must now look at ourselves as having a *head start*. We don't need the catchphrases from New York. We don't need grays and the whites or the *-isms*. What we need to do is our own architecture and believe in ourselves."

Here, "grays and the whites" refers of course to the dispute in the early 1970s between the New York Five (Peter Eisenman, John Hejduk, Richard Meier, Charles Gwathmey, and Michael Graves)—the Whites—and Romaldo Giurgola, Robert A. M. Stern, Allan Greenberg, Jaquelin T. Robertson, and Charles Moore—the Grays.[13] While the Whites undertook design as an inquiry into architecture's autonomous compositional and syntactic strategies, the Grays insisted that architectural designs should respond to their socioeconomic settings. It would be too easy to assume that Andrews's disdain for such arcane disputes came from an anti-intellectualism. This is not an easy matter to untangle. While Andrews believed that architecture should be driven by a philosophy of "common sense" (an expression he used frequently, including in his Hook address) and often presented himself as a pragmatist, his own ideological position was more complex. Jennifer Taylor alluded to this in her Gold Medal essay on Andrews: "Words... rather than buildings, make the strongest impressions on his thinking, and he acknowledges this debt to the sensitive writings of Kahn, Hertzberger, and van Eyck."[14] But there is no evidence that Andrews himself read the literary works of such figures; he likely mostly absorbed knowledge of the broader architectural culture through direct interactions with other architects. While these included key figures whom he met both in North America and Australia—Herman Hertzberger and Aldo van Eyck were both visitors to Toronto, for example, when Andrews was the University of Toronto's chair of architecture—they were also the architects employed in his own practice. Just as architectural history has recently adopted more nuanced ideas of architectural authorship to apprehend the collective and culturally situated nature of architectural work, so too must it understand that the broader agency of the architect is not conditioned merely by their own intellectual and professional development but also by the context of the design ideals and ideologies through which that development proceeds.[15]

Andrews further suggested in his Hook address that Australian architecture and the country's wider design culture needed nurturing like other art forms. One aspect of Australia's "colonial mentality" was an inferiority complex that could only be overcome through education. Design education, Andrews advised, must start early. Moreover, the development of a national design sensibility must be promoted institutionally through such activities as the Australia Council's support for design, which Andrews advocated ought to be elevated to the

12 Ibid.
13 *Five Architects: Eisenman, Graves, Gwathmey, Hejduk, Meier* (New York: Wittenborn, 1972); Romaldo Giurgola, Allan Greenberg, Charles Moore, Jaquelin T. Robertson, and Robert A. M. Stern, "Five on Five," *Architectural Forum*, (May 1973): 46–57.

14 Jennifer Taylor, "John Andrews, Architect," *Architecture Australia* 70, no. 2 (May 1981): 32.
15 Tim Antsey, Katja Grillner, and Rolf Hughes, eds., *Architecture and Authorship* (London: Black Dog, 2007).

same status as the council's boards for literature, theater, and visual arts. He explained:

> I believe this is essential so that Australia can be seen both nationally and internationally as a country publicly concerned about design. It is essential if architecture and design are to develop a national attitude and identity. It will enable the design professions to take advantage of all the resources of other countries with sympathetic attitudes, and make the rest of the world aware that Australians know what they are doing and allow us to become part of the world community of design. We must leave behind the parochial, insular attitude that has restricted international appreciation of the most resourceful country in the world.[16]

THE PARLIAMENT COMPETITION

In the 1970s and 1980s, the clearest evidence that Australia had left behind parochial attitudes in architecture was in the construction of the New Parliament House designed by the Italian American architect Romaldo Giurgola, one of the original Grays. (Jaquelin T. Robertson, the author of the article on the Cameron Offices that appeared in *Architectural Record* was another core Gray.) One of Andrews's highest-profile roles in the late 1970s was as a member of the jury that selected the Giurgola design.

The origins of the New Parliament House competition begin in 1913, when an international competition for the design of Parliament House for a site identified in Walter Burley Griffin and Marion Mahony Griffin's Canberra plan was announced. This competition was deferred and then canceled due to World War I. Following that, a provisional Parliament House was built in 1927. After several decades of occupation, this building was overcrowded and clearly insufficient, and in 1965 a Joint Select Committee of Parliament was appointed to consider the need for a new building for Parliament. In 1970, the committee recommended that the project should proceed and that the Joint Standing Committee on the New and Permanent Parliament House be established as the client body. In its first report to Parliament in March 1977, the committee recommended that the new building should be completed in 1988, the bicentenary of the British settlement of Australia.[17] There was bipartisan support for the project, both from Prime Minister Malcom Fraser's Liberal government and the Labor opposition, and connecting it with the bicentenary was key to cultivating public support.[18] A two-stage competition was agreed upon after two years of consultations with parliamentary officers and the National Capital Development Commission, and in November 1977 the government announced that the project would proceed. In early 1979, a panel of six assessors was appointed to adjudicate on both phases of the competition and to select the winner.

The panel of assessors consisted of Senator Gareth Evans (Labor), Member of Parliament Barry Simon (Liberal), professor of civil engineering Len Stevens, and architects John Andrews and I. M. Pei, with John Overall serving as chair in his role as a board member of the Parliament House Construction Authority.[19] Overall assembled the jury, inviting Andrews to participate at least a year before the competition was announced and the brief released. Overall first met Andrews at his office in Toronto in 1968 when he was chair of the National Capital Development Commission, which led to Andrews's commission for the Cameron Offices. Overall traveled to New York to ask Giurgola to serve on the jury, but

---

16 Andrews, "A. S. Hook 1981," 73.

17 Parliament House Construction Authority, "Australia's Parliament House 1988… The Competition Process," (Canberra: Australian Government Publishing Service, 1980), unpaginated.

18 John Overall, *Canberra Yesterday, Today & Tomorrow: A Personal Memoir* (Canberra: Federal Capital Press, 1995), 104.

19 Andrew Hutson, "'…A Design That Is at Once Natural and Monumental': The Political Conception of New Parliament House, Canberra," *Proceedings of the Society of Architectural Historians, Australia and New Zealand: 21, Limits*, no. 2, eds. Harriet Edquist and Hélène Frichot (2004): 240–45.

Giurgola declined as he preferred to participate in the competition. Overall then spoke to I. M. Pei, on Andrews's recommendation.[20] Andrews was acquainted with Giurgola from the limited competition that he won for the Miami Seaport Terminal building in 1967, for which Giurgola was a professional advisor. He also knew of Pei—a fellow Harvard GSD graduate—from when they were both finalists for the Toronto City Hall competition in 1958.

On April 7, 1979, the two-part competition for the design of the New Parliament House was announced. Open to Australian-accredited architects or associations including even one Australian architect, 961 architects from 28 countries registered to compete. On August 31, 1979, at the close of first-stage submissions 329 entries were received.[21]

Beginning October 1, 1979, the assessors spent eight days reviewing the first-stage entries. Overall recounted the process: "For the next eight days we lived together, ate together and judged together. We slept in Canberra's Lakeside Hotel and spent the days poring over the plans which filled five floors of a Belconnen office block… The judging process was brisk and robust as you would expect with politicians and professionals working together. John Andrews lost his block on several occasions, and some thought their dignity was assaulted when wheelchairs were organized to aid us in getting around the five floors of designs."[22] Jurors awarded 10 designs prizes of $20,000 each, and selected five of these to advance to the next stage, with an honorarium of $80,000 to defray the costs of producing the drawings and models. These five designs were by Bickerdike Allen Simovic (United Kingdom); Denton Corker Marshall (Australia); Parson and Waite (Canada); Edwards Madigan Torzillo and Briggs (Australia); and Mitchell/Giurgola and Thorpe (United States).[23] The second stage closed on May 23, 1980. Assessment took place over eight days at the Australian Academy of Science (the modernist copper-domed building known in Canberra as the Martian Embassy), with the assessor team being assisted by technical and construction advisors. On June 26, the announcement was made before an invited audience and press that entry 177 was chosen as the winner; a sealed envelope was opened to reveal that this winning design was by Mitchell/Giurgola and Thorpe.[24] [FIG. 3]

Richard Thorpe was an Australian architect who had worked with Mitchell/Giurgola in New York since 1971. The Parliament House design was carried out by him and Giurgola. It was distinct from the other finalists in hunkering down into the site of Capital Hill, with the profile of the hill maintained between two vast, curved walls that formed the backdrop of the Senate and the House of Representatives, with their respective offices. The design was surmounted by a green, turfed roof on which members of the public could wander and a huge 82-meter-high flagpole, a Pop-ish gesture that intimated Giurgola's credentials as a Gray. Early sketches included with the design report for an entry from Robert Venturi's office with Australian architect Jerry Wayne Carroll also indicated a giant flagpole akin to that in Venturi's Thousand Oaks Civic Center design competition entry of 1969, but this did not appear in the final design. The Venturi team entry was among the 10 premiated first-stage designs, though it was not included in the five selected for the second design stage.[25]

Andrew Hutson has suggested that the panel of assessors and the political context of the competition for the New Parliament House "imparted a conservative tone and that may

---

20   Andrew Hutson, "Spots Before My Eyes: Assessor's Deliberations for the New Parliament House Competition," *Proceedings of the Society of Architectural Historians, Australia and New Zealand: 22, Celebration*, eds. Andrew Leach and Gill Matthewson (2005): 179–84. In Overall's account, Pei was asked first. However, Andrews's familiarity with both Giurgola and Pei perhaps gives more credence to his account. See Overall, *Canberra: Yesterday, Today & Tomorrow*, 109.
21   Parliament House Construction Authority, "Australia's Parliament House 1988."
22   Overall, *Canberra: Yesterday, Today & Tomorrow*, 110.
23   Hutson, "'…A Design….'" 5.
24   Overall, *Canberra: Yesterday, Today & Tomorrow*, 110
25   Andrew Hutson, "The Influence of the Architectural Avant-garde on the Entries for the New Parliament House Competition," *Proceedings of the Society of Architectural Historians, Australia and New Zealand: 23, Contested Terrains*, eds. Terrence McMinn, John Stephens, and Steve Basson (2006): 251–57.

FIG. 3　The jury for the competition for the New Parliament House, Canberra, Australia, 1978–1979. On left: I. M. Pei; on right: John Andrews.

have impacted on the submissions. But it is not clear whether the submissions in the main reflected a conservative approach."[26] The details of the Giurgola design were, however, more postmodern than Andrews's general taste. While the overall parti of the Giurgola design convincingly met the competition criteria around symbolism and dignity, the flagpole indicated that Andrews was more open to architectural inflections of postmodernism—at least when they were found in the otherwise convincing architecture of accomplished designers—than the rejection of "isms" in his Hook address would suggest. Andrews was particularly mindful of the problem of finding a design for Parliament that would respond to the brief in a dignified manner but without monumental bombast. Andrews was almost certainly the source of the brief statement regarding "symbolism" that appeared in the conditions for the New Parliament House competition, which were otherwise concerned principally with the building's utility and security. As the statement outlines:[27]

> Parliament House must be more than a functional building. It should become a major national symbol, in the way that the spires of Westminster or Washington's Capitol dome have become known to people all over the world.... Competitors should consciously evaluate these factors during the design process. They should question whether it is appropriate that a building of the late 20th century use the language of bygone eras. What would be the connotations—in the mind of a visitor—of a building with a monumental scale, sited on a hill? Does significance necessarily mean bigness? Should the functional aspects of the building be molded into an abstraction of checks and balances (Brasilia)? Does the nature of the requirements imply an acknowledgement of the forces of growth and change?[28]

In response to this brief, Hutson writes that its comments "entreating entrants not to dabble in monumentality, to be wary of symmetry and to avoid the language of past eras painted a picture that angled toward modernism..." But, he notes, the premiated designs, including the schemes by Venturi, Denton Corker Marshall, and Giurgola, "extended into the broad church of postmodernism."[29]

The Mitchell/Giurgola and Thorpe design for the New Parliament House was widely welcomed in Australia, both in design press and mainstream newspapers. In Andrews's Hook address, he noted the affirmative words of Edmund Bacon in the American journal *Progressive Architecture* on the Giurgola design for the Australian Parliament: "The Australians have seen the design of their Capital as an international issue, in which their national pride can best be served by the finest design the world can produce. That, I think, they have."[30] Australia might have been developing its own design sensibility, but it did so not only with international appreciation but also with international input.

THE DESIGN ARTS BOARD

Cultivating Australian design culture and representing Australian architectural achievements to the world were major concerns of Andrews's other key foray into public life, his role between 1977 and 1988 with the Australia Council, the country's peak arts body. Established in 1968, the Australia Council became a statutory authority under Australian

---

26 Ibid., 251.
27 Hutson, "Spots Before My Eyes," 180; Paul Walker and Karen Burns, "Architecture and the Australia Council in the 1980s," *Proceedings of the Society of Architectural Historians, Australia and New Zealand: 32, Architecture, Institutions, and Change*, eds. Paul Hogben and Judy O'Callaghan (2015): 692.
28 Parliament House Construction Authority, "Parliament House Canberra: Conditions for a Two-Stage Competition" (Canberra: Parliament House Construction Authority, 1979), 15.
29 Hutson, "Spots Before My Eyes," 182.
30 Edmund Bacon, "Commentary," *Progressive Architecture*, (March 1981): 95.

federal legislation in 1975. Organized as a series of boards that were responsible for funding programs and for policy in particular fields—such as visual arts, music, literature, theater, and Aboriginal arts—in its first years of operation and particularly under historian Geoffrey Blainey's chairmanship until 1981, the Australia Council mostly coordinated the activities of its various constituent boards, which otherwise were left to their own devices. Other initiatives of the Whitlam and Fraser governments, however, bore on the council, particularly to promote three foci across the activities of all its boards. One focus was to consider the economic value and impact of the arts construed as industries; the second entailed an emphasis on community access and increased participation in the arts; and the third was to align arts policy more specifically with the policies of federal government, especially in regard to multiculturalism and cultural identity.[31] It was in the context of these developing themes that architecture and design were included in the Australia Council's agenda.

Andrews was invited to join the Australia Council's Visual Arts Board in 1977, succeeding the Melbourne architect Neil Clerehan. Andrews immediately championed design and architecture, and in 1980, an Architecture and Design Panel was established within the Australia Council on his initiative. Just a year later in 1981, this panel became a committee responsible directly to the Australia Council's board rather than through the Visual Arts Board.[32] Andrews chaired the panel with three other members, including Sydney architect and Andrews's erstwhile friend Philip Cox.[33] In 1984, the panel expanded to become the Design Arts Board. Andrews was instrumental in promoting design in the Australia Council's operations to become equivalent in importance to its more conventional concerns. In 1986, the government proposed reconfiguring the Australia Council into five boards, with the Design Board (as it was then styled) being one of those selected to continue.[34] However, Donald Horne, chair of the Australia Council since 1985, attempted to stave off the full extent of the government's plan by proposing four boards of a different configuration. The Design Board was disestablished. Support of design within the Australia Council was returned to a committee of the council, which was dissolved two years later.[35] Andrews remained on board throughout this rocky institutional ride, and Cox remained for most of it.

The trajectory of the Australia Council's interest in matters of architecture and design corresponded exactly with a particularly reflective moment in Australian architecture and in cultural activities more broadly. This moment was bracketed by the groundbreaking of the New Parliament House in 1979 and its opening in 1988, a period in which the government and its agencies were occupied intermittently with the meaning of the forthcoming bicentennial. The federal government established a Bicentennial Authority in 1979,[36] with which the Australia Council anticipated collaborating to produce a bicentenary arts program for 1988.[37] The prospect of national jubilation was, however, mixed with a sense of anxiety about the country's economic prospects and about what might in retrospect be understood as its postcolonial condition.

Under Andrews's leadership, the Design Arts Board and its precursors within the Australia Council promoted architecture in several ways, with its most significant undertakings corresponding to the three themes of industry, community, and identity, emergent across the Australia Council's activities in the 1980s. Andrews's approach, however, was not ideological: it did not favor only his own attitude toward design but rather facilitated engagement with a wide range of design enterprises and activities. In support of design professions, the board arranged visits to Australia

---

31 Katya Johanson, "The Role of Australia's Cultural Council 1945–1995" (PhD diss., University of Melbourne, 2000), 149.
32 "Australia Council Annual Report, 1981–82," 22.
33 The other two original members were the engineer Peter Miller and the industrial designer David Terry. Ibid., 9.
34 John Gardiner-Garden, *Commonwealth Arts Policy and Administration* (Canberra: Australian Parliamentary Library, 2009), 20.
35 "Australia Council Annual Report, 1987–88," 4.
36 "Australia Council Annual Report, 1979–80," 11.
37 "Australia Council Annual Report, 1980–81," 13.

4

5

6

FIG. 4 Drawing of winning entry to the competition for The Peak, Hong Kong, 1983. Architect: Zaha Hadid.
FIG. 5 Forbidden City, Beijing, China, 1983. Photo: John Andrews.
FIG. 6 Fragrant Hills Hotel, Beijing, China, 1983. Architect: I. M. Pei. Photo: John Andrews.

by the contrarian historian of modernism Reyner Banham and American landscape architect Lawrence Halprin and sponsored other international visitors through the Royal Australian Institute of Architects' International Architecture speaker series, including Zaha Hadid and James Wines. Anticipating China's future significance for Australian architectural practices, a pathbreaking delegation of Chinese architects visited Australia in June 1983, sponsored by the Australia-China Council and the Design Arts Committee. An ongoing collaboration was subsequently established with China's Ministry of Urban Construction and Environmental Protection, with exchanges of Chinese and Australian designers across engineering, architecture, interior design, and industrial design established in 1984.[38] This connection with China followed Andrews's role in early 1983 chairing the jury for The Peak architectural competition in Hong Kong, which included Japanese architect Arata Isozaki. The winner they picked was Hadid, and the project made her reputation.[39] [FIG. 4] Andrews subsequently visited China in an official capacity.[40] With Denys Lasdun, Andrews was keynote speaker at the first Chinese architectural congress in Beijing, and he used the opportunity to see the Forbidden City and Suzhou as well as to visit Pei's Fragrant Hills Hotel. [FIGS. 5–6]

The board's community involvement primarily entailed developing audiences for design and architecture within Australia. To this end, in 1981, a national seminar was staged in Melbourne titled "Design Education in Secondary Schools."[41] Follow-up conferences were held in Adelaide the following year, and in Canberra in 1984, when a national organization called the Design in Education Council Australia was formed.[42] Soon after its establishment, grants were made available to place designers and architects in schools, which continued at least until the 1988–1989 academic year.[43]

Finally, in regard to identity, the Australia Council's design programs were strongly motivated to articulate a national design profile for Australia, a demonstration of the bipartisan—albeit diffident—commitment of Australian governments to multiculturalism. This was a time before the "culture wars" of the 2000s and the ensuing political stigmatization of cultural difference. The national design profile that the Australia Council's programs promoted was inclusive of postmodernism. This was apparent in the two architectural exhibitions the council staged. The first of these was *Old Continent, New Building: Contemporary Australian Architecture*, which traveled to six European cities and five in the United States, where it coincided with the 1984 Summer Olympics in Los Angeles.[44] The second was *Australian Built: Responding to the Place*, which was shown in 25 locations in Australia between 1985 and 1988.[45] [FIGS. 7, 9] It was also apparent in the two publications that came from these exhibitions and in the issues of international architectural journals on Australia that the council supported. These include an issue of *UIA International Architect* from 1984 and the editions of *Domus* and *Architectural Review* published in July and December 1985, respectively. [FIG. 8] They presented a consistent cross section of Australian architecture of the mid-1980s, including design work from the explicit postmodernists Edmond and Corrigan and Norman Day—both

38 "Australia Council Annual Report, 1984–85," 80; Australia Council Annual Report, 1986–87, 39.
39 "The Peak Architectural Competition," *Architectural Record* 171, no. 11 (July 1983): 54–59
40 See the Chinese publication *Architectural Journal* 7 (1983). This journal issue has an article on Andrews's architecture, including illustrations of the Eugowra house, the King George Tower, Callam Offices, and Intelsat Headquarters. My thanks to Jianfei Zhu for alerting me to this. On a delegation of Chinese architects who undertook a corresponding tour of Australia, see Michael Foster, "Chinese Architects admire Canberra," *Canberra Times*, June 22, 1983.
41 "Australia Council Annual Report, 1981–82," 22.
42 "Australia Council Annual Report, 1984–85," 81.
43 "Australia Council Annual Report, 1985–86," 36; "Australia Council Annual Report, 1988–89," 16.
44 The European cities were Paris, London, Geneva, Ghent, Bonn, and Milan. "Australia Council Annual Report 1983–84," 60. The American cities were Washington, DC, San Francisco, Los Angeles, and Memphis—and "Tennessee," so perhaps four. "Australia Council Annual Report 1984–85," 80.
45 *Australian Built* opened at the Art Gallery of New South Wales in September 1985. "Australia Council Annual Report, 1985–86," 35. See also "Australia Council Annual Report, 1987–88," 22.

7

9

8

FIG. 7 Cover, *Old Continent New Building*, 1983.
FIG. 8 Cover, *Domus*, July 1985.
FIG. 9 Cover, *Australian Built*, 1985.

represented in all five publications—and the "late modernism" of Glenn Murcutt and Philip Cox, who were also covered in all publications.

A retrospective review of these publications and the projects they present makes two things apparent. First, while there were clear distinctions to be drawn between late modernism and postmodernism in the Australian architecture of the 1980s, it is nevertheless possible to see confluences as well. Second, while postmodernism has been widely seen internationally as an architecture of the enterprise culture unleashed by the end of the welfare state and "big government," in Australia postmodern architecture enjoyed patronage from public agencies and was directly associated with the issues of community and identity that concerned the Australian government during the period. The international connection between neoliberal markets and architecture was explored most famously by Fredric Jameson in his 1984 essay "Postmodernism, or, the Cultural Logic of Late Capitalism" and more skeptically by Mary McLeod in her 1989 essay "Architecture and Politics in the Reagan Era: From Postmodernism to Deconstructivism."[46] But looking at the volumes on architecture sponsored by the Australia Council we find multiple examples of government-funded projects in an explicitly postmodern manner, from the small-scale public housing projects of the reformed Victorian Housing Commission, including the work of Edmond and Corrigan and Day, to the work-in-progress of the Mitchell/Giurgola and Thorpe design for the New Parliament House.

Beyond the similarities between their documented projects, the five publications otherwise vary; the journals particularly use a common range of projects to make distinctive propositions in line with their respective editorial stances. Notably, *Domus* used its Australian issue to further its promotion of a radically critical architectural approach. Titled "Ciao Australia: Coast to Coast; the last wave," it featured sections on architecture, design, art, and fashion. The architecture section was visually inclusive—featuring postmodern Melbourne infill housing by Edmond and Corrigan and Norman Day alongside the late modernism of Seidler's Hannes House, Murcutt's Kempsey Museum, and Cox's Yulara Tourist Village. Textually, however, postmodernism prevailed. The only lengthy piece by an Australian architectural commentator was Peter Corrigan's "Learning from Suburbia."

In contrast to the editorial hand apparent in each of the journals, the two exhibition publications are explicitly committed to inclusivity in their texts as well as in their selection of projects. *Old Continent, New Building* demonstrates this through the different voices of its four writers: Philip Cox, Leon Paroissien, Conrad Hamann, and Jennifer Taylor.[47] The *Australian Built* publication features only a single author, Craig McGregor, but he argues for multiplicity. Under the title "Responding to the Place," an essay by McGregor follows Jencks's pop semiotics line that the buildings in the exhibition are "not just shelters, though they are that, but communication systems as well." He continues, writing, "And in the conflicts which exist between these signal systems—between the modern and the postmodern movements, between the regional and the international, the vernacular and the theoretical reflected the tensions and conflicts which exist within Australian society… There is no mainstream; current Australian architecture is nothing if not pluralist."[48] *Australian Built* and *Old Continent, New Building* proposed a collective

---

46 Fredric Jameson, "Postmodernism, or, the Cultural Logic of Late Capitalism," *New Left Review* 146 (July/August 1984): 53–92; Mary McLeod, "Architecture and Politics in the Reagan Era: From Postmodernism to Deconstructivism," *Assemblage* 8 (1989): 22–59.

47 Philip Cox, "An Architecture in an Australian Landscape," in *Old Continent, New Building: Contemporary Australian Architecture*, eds. Leon Paroissien and Michael Griggs (Sydney: David Ell Press, 1983), 13–16; Leon Paroissien, "The Urbanisation of Terra Australis," in *Old Continent, New Building*, 19–31; Conrad Hamann, "The Return to the City," in *Old Continent, New Building*, 33–42; Jennifer Taylor, "History and Place in Recent Australian Architecture," in *Old Continent, New Building*, 45–54.

48 Craig McGregor, "Responding to the Place," in Michael Griggs and Craig McGregor, eds., *Australian Built: Responding to the Place, A Photographic Exhibition of Recent Australian Architecture* (Sydney: Design Arts Board of the Australia Council, 1985), 8.

representation of Australian architecture that was varied and inclusive. Nevertheless, unlike the *UIA International Architect*, *Domus*, and *Architectural Review* special issues, these Australian publications also featured a single dominant image—John Andrews's Eugowra farmhouse of 1980. [FIGS. 10–11]

The Eugowra house, a steel-framed and steel- and glass-clad pavilion, is the cover image for the *Old Continent, New Building* publication and appears twice within its pages. [FIGS. 12–13] It features as the first of a small number of images in color in *Australian Built*, and twice more in black and white. Eugowra does not appear in the Australian issues of the international journals at all. A cynical reading of this might suggest that the Australian writers and curators the Design Arts Board patronized felt obliged to acknowledge Andrews, their man on the Australia Council, the guy who got them the gig. There were, however, many Andrews projects to choose from, and the explanation for the Eugowra house's prominence lies in the high regard with which this project was held. It was and is a complex project not in its program—a house for Andrews and his family—but in its symbolism and in its hint that post- and late-modern lines could be linked, as alluded to earlier. The Eugowra house can be read as a project driven by its use of construction and environmental technologies appropriate for its isolated situation. Indeed, the same descriptive text on the house that appears in both *Old Continent, New Building*, and *Australian Built* describes it in just these terms. But the house can also be read in terms of symbolic projection and historical allusion. Taylor, the critic who knew Andrews's work best, describes it in her essay in *Old Continent, New Building*, as follows: "The time-honored homestead is revived, transformed, and imbued with a new and startling imagery. With its water tanks, spreading roof, and energy tower, the building tells of the stringent conditions of the area. This gleaming house of corrugated iron shimmers in the stark landscape and highlights the sun's strength and intensity. Like Murcutt's houses it is a classical pavilion, but the Andrews house reaches back into history through the colonial period and Georgian England rather than through continental classicism."[49]

Eugowra is the small house precursor to the big house of the New Parliament; the questions formulated in 1979 for the entrants in the Parliament House design competition about the contemporary significance of symbolism, siting, and symmetry could just as well be directed at Andrews's Eugowra. Eugowra's "energy tower" and its spreading, hipped roofs might have impeccable pragmatic sense, but they also made an iconic representation of what Australian architecture apparently wanted to aspire to in its postmodern moment.

AN AUSTRALIAN PAVILION FOR THE VENICE BIENNALE

Eugowra's power as an architectural icon was overshadowed by the New Parliament House when it was completed in 1988. The Giurgola design also put into the shade the Australia Council's major architectural achievement of that year and the final outcome of its engagement with design and architecture, the Philip Cox–designed Australian Pavilion in the Giardini della Biennale in Venice. [FIG. 14]

The Visual Arts Board first discussed an Australian Pavilion in 1973, but 15 years passed before the building was realized.[50] After a 20-year hiatus and without its own pavilion, Australia returned to exhibiting at the Venice Biennale in 1978, and the Sydney businessman Franco Belgiorno-Nettis began to champion the idea of an Australian national pavilion. Belgiorno-Nettis lobbied the Venetian authorities for a site in the Giardini and—apparently independently of the Australia Council—commissioned a design from the Melbourne architects Edmond and Corrigan, which was ready by 1983.[51] Two years later, the Visual Arts Board reclaimed the initiative. Its 1985–1986 Annual Report includes the information that the board "committed itself to supporting the establishment of an Australian Pavilion

---

49   Taylor, "History and Place in Recent Australian Architecture," 54.
50   "Australia Council Annual Report, 1986–87," 55.

10

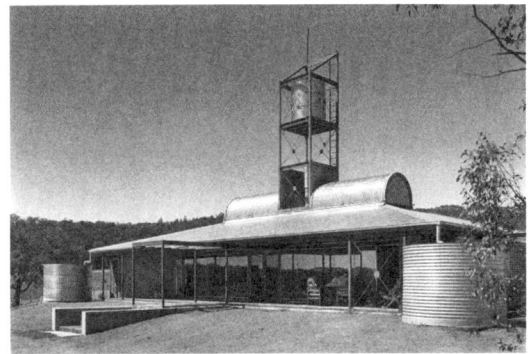

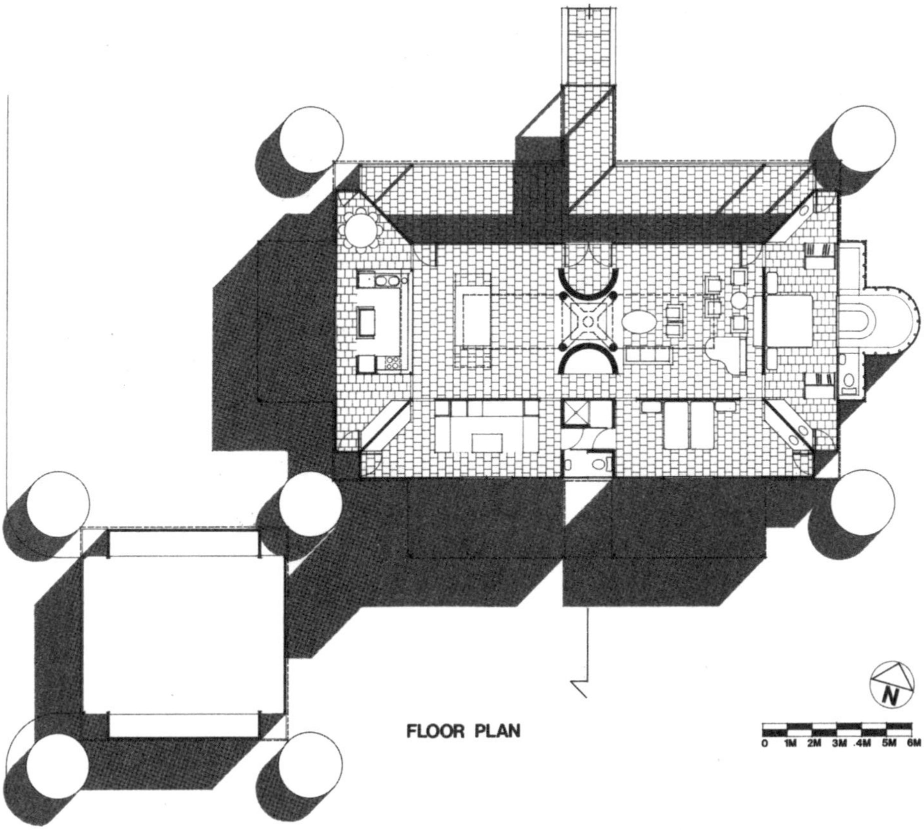

11

FIG. 10 Farmhouse at Eugowra, Eugowra, New South Wales, Australia, ca. 1980.

FIG. 11 Plan, farmhouse at Eugowra.

FIGS. 12–13 Page spreads, Farmhouse at Eugowra in *Old Continent New Building*.

in Venice."[52] By 1987, this project became connected to the Australian bicentenary of 1988 and thus assumed an urgency that it had previously lacked. Urgency led to an expedient decision that the architect members of the Design Arts Board—Cox and Andrews—undertake the design themselves.[53]

Sketch drawings of the pavilion in the Andrews collection suggest the two explored a range of design possibilities. Most of these have a similar, stepped triangular footprint, with staggered roof forms. [FIGS. 15–19] But the design of the pavilion that opened in June 1988 was simplified, and its authorship was attributed to Cox alone. It was in an idiom of an expressed steel frame and claddings that had become the dominant manner of Cox's large public projects, such the Exhibition Centre, the Aquarium, and the National Maritime Museum buildings at Sydney's Darling Harbour.[54] The rural vernacular inspiration for the pavilion is stated explicitly by Cox. Echoing Andrews's words about Australian settler architecture in his Hook address, Cox wrote in 1988, "The architecture was sincere in its belief that it was a 'bare bones' architecture displaying its complete skeletal anatomy. It related fully to the cathedrals of the Australian bush, the woolsheds, incredibly beautiful buildings where structure delights and inspires."[55]

The pavilion's Australian rural connotation was underlined by the Australia Council's general manager: "It's a house on stumps. Our own shearing shed in Venice."[56] This allusion to a heritage of farm buildings from which the pavilion ostensibly drew was also picked up in the Italian architectural press. In an article in *Casabella* that attributes the design to both Cox and Andrews, the pavilion is characterized in terms of both pragmatics (modular construction, the fit of its design to the contours of its site) and the "identifiability" it claimed through its reference to a putative Australian vernacular.[57]

Unfortunately, construction of the pavilion did not proceed smoothly, and at the opening of the 43rd Venice Biennale in June 1988, the building was not complete. Regardless, the Australian exhibition—eight large paintings by the venerated artist Arthur Boyd—went ahead in the unfinished building. According to Nicholas Baume, writing in the critical Melbourne architecture journal *Transition*, it was a debacle. Baume blamed the Australia Council. He contended that at the time that Belgiorno-Nettis commissioned the Edmond and Corrigan design there had been an agreement with the Venetian authorities that a site would be made available. When the Australia Council asked if this offer was still open several years later, it was given an ultimatum to complete the pavilion quickly. As Baume writes, "That it took such a threat from the Biennale for us to accept the long-standing invitation is a serious failure of our public arts administration." Baume suggests that the ensuing haste led to the decision that members of the Design Arts Board would design the pavilion "in-house": "Perhaps the circumventing of normal procedures for developing a brief, awarding a commission, and reviewing the design could be excused had the project been a brilliant success."[58] But without Andrews's and Cox's initiative to quickly produce a pavilion design that the Australia Council bureaucrats would commit to, it seems unlikely that a pavilion would have happened at all.

Retrospectively, the forms of the pavilion design can be seen to align with other

51 On the chronology of the pavilion designs, see Paul Walker and Karen Burns, "'Ciao Australia': Postmodern Australian and Italian Exchanges, 1983–1988," 290n10. Conrad Hamann dates the Edmond and Corrigan scheme to 1982. See Conrad Hamann, *Cities of Hope: Australian Architecture and Design by Edmond and Corrigan 1962–92* (Melbourne: Oxford University Press, 1993), 110.
52 "Australia Council Annual Report, 1985–86," 50.
53 Kevin Childs, "Australian Art in Venice, Encased in a Pavilion of BHP Steel," *The Age*, June 9, 1987, 2.
54 "Australian Pavilion Venice Biennale, Italy," in *Australian Architects: Philip Cox, Richardson, Taylor and Partners* (Canberra: Royal Australian Institute of Architects Education Division, 1988), 100.
55 Philip Cox, "Statement by the Architect," in *Australian Architects: Philip Cox, Richardson, Taylor and Partners*, 7.
56 Kevin Childs, "Australia Builds a 'Shearing Shed' in Ancient Venice," *The Age*, June 3, 1988, 11.
57 Paolo Tombesi and Riccardo Vannucci, "Effetto leggerezza: Il Padiglione Australiano alla Biennale di Venezia," *Casabella* 52, no. 547 (June 1988): 34–35
58 Nicholas Baume, "Guests in Venice: Australia's Biennale Pavilion," *Transition* 29 (Winter 1989): 65.

late-modern projects, with an Australianness that was, while widely claimed, at best evasive. On one hand, the Cox design appears to rehearse aspects of Murcutt's Kempsey Museum, one of Australia's most internationally admired projects of the time, which includes a barrel-vaulted pavilion with an offset plan, clerestory glazing, and corrugated steel cladding. Like Cox's work, the museum was widely seen to draw on an Australian rural vernacular. On the other hand, Kempsey's vaults and elongated plan modules appear to have a significant precedent in Louis Kahn's Kimbell Art Museum (1972). As realized in Cox's final design, the profile of the pavilion roof has a strong affiliation with a widely admired Andrews design, that of the Miami Seaport Terminal (1970). This may be a coincidence, but it is also readable as Cox's acknowledgment of Andrews, a nod to his colleague's contribution to the design process and role in shepherding the pavilion project through the Australia Council bureaucracy. Rather than in relation to an ostensible Australian tradition, all of this in retrospect places the realized Australian Pavilion design in line with Alessandro Mendini's comments in the 1985 *Domus* special issue on Australia that "eclecticism and adhocism" are ingrained within the "history and tradition of Australian thinking" about architecture. This deflects straightforward claims that architecture can represent or perform identity.[59]

By 1990, when the second Biennale exhibition was installed in the Australian Pavilion, the Australia Council was ascribing its design not to the Design Board but rather to Philip Cox personally.[60] The Australia Council's commitment to design as one of its responsibilities was finished. Andrews and Donald Horne—the Australia Council's chair from 1985—did not get along, and Andrews's commitment had strongly underwritten the Australia Council's engagement with design issues and culture. But more broadly, the economic rationalism that subtended the council's interest in "design arts" in the 1980s receded in its influence on arts policy in Australia—at least temporarily—as a more traditional, elite view of the arts began again to prevail. This bureaucratic dead end, however, does not diminish the achievements of Andrews's public role in the late 1970s and 1980s. He was instrumental in the Australia Council's promotion of Australian architecture locally and internationally, and this in turn sponsored inquiries into Australian architecture's contemporary condition. Some of these inquiries were sympathetic to Andrews's own thoughts on Australian architecture, as expressed in his Hook address and as apparent in his own buildings, and some were not. Some were notably postmodern in their orientation. As well, Andrews played key roles in two competitions that had a broad effect in their outcomes on architectural discourse internationally. The Mitchell/Giurgola and Thorpe design for the New Parliament House featured a postmodernism that for Andrews was secondary to its compelling answer to the competition brief. The selection of Zaha Hadid as winner of The Peak is not so easy to explain. The report on the outcome of The Peak design competition in *Architectural Record* notes that the jurors faulted Hadid's design for a "certain lack of resolution in details" but praised it for promising "to extend the imagination and symbolize the essence of a new building type in a unique location."[61] Andrews's common sense apparently had room for some very unconventional projects.

---

59 Paul Walker and Karen Burns, "Constructing Australian Architecture for International Audiences: Regionalism, Postmodernism, and the Design Arts Board, 1980–1988," *Fabrications* 28, no. 1 (2018): 41–43.
60 "Australia Council Annual Report, 1989–90," 20.
61 "The Peak Architectural Competition," *Architectural Record* 171, no. 7 (July 1983): 54–59.

14

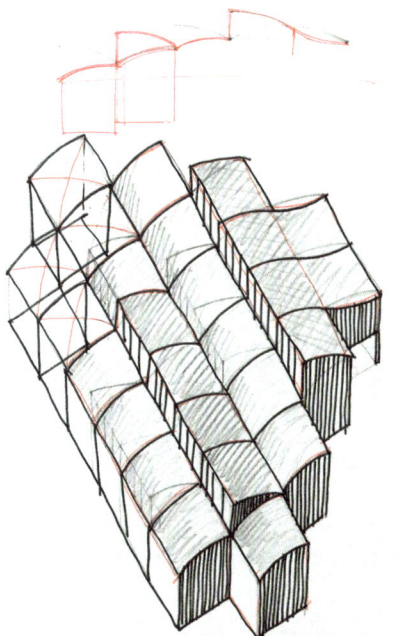
15

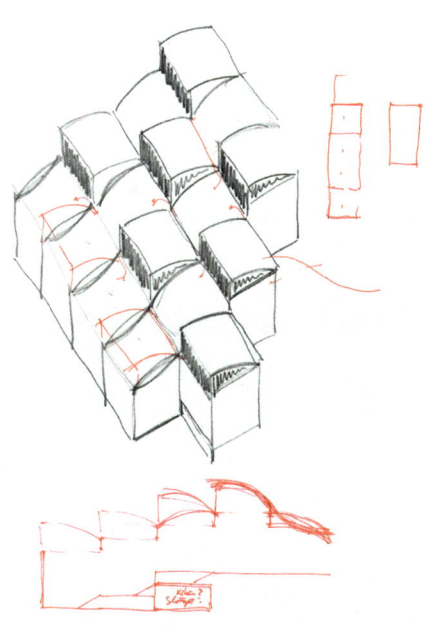
16

FIG. 14   Australian Pavilion, Venice Biennale, 1988. Architect: Philip Cox.
FIGS. 15–16   Drawings, Australian Pavilion, Venice Biennale, August–September 1987.

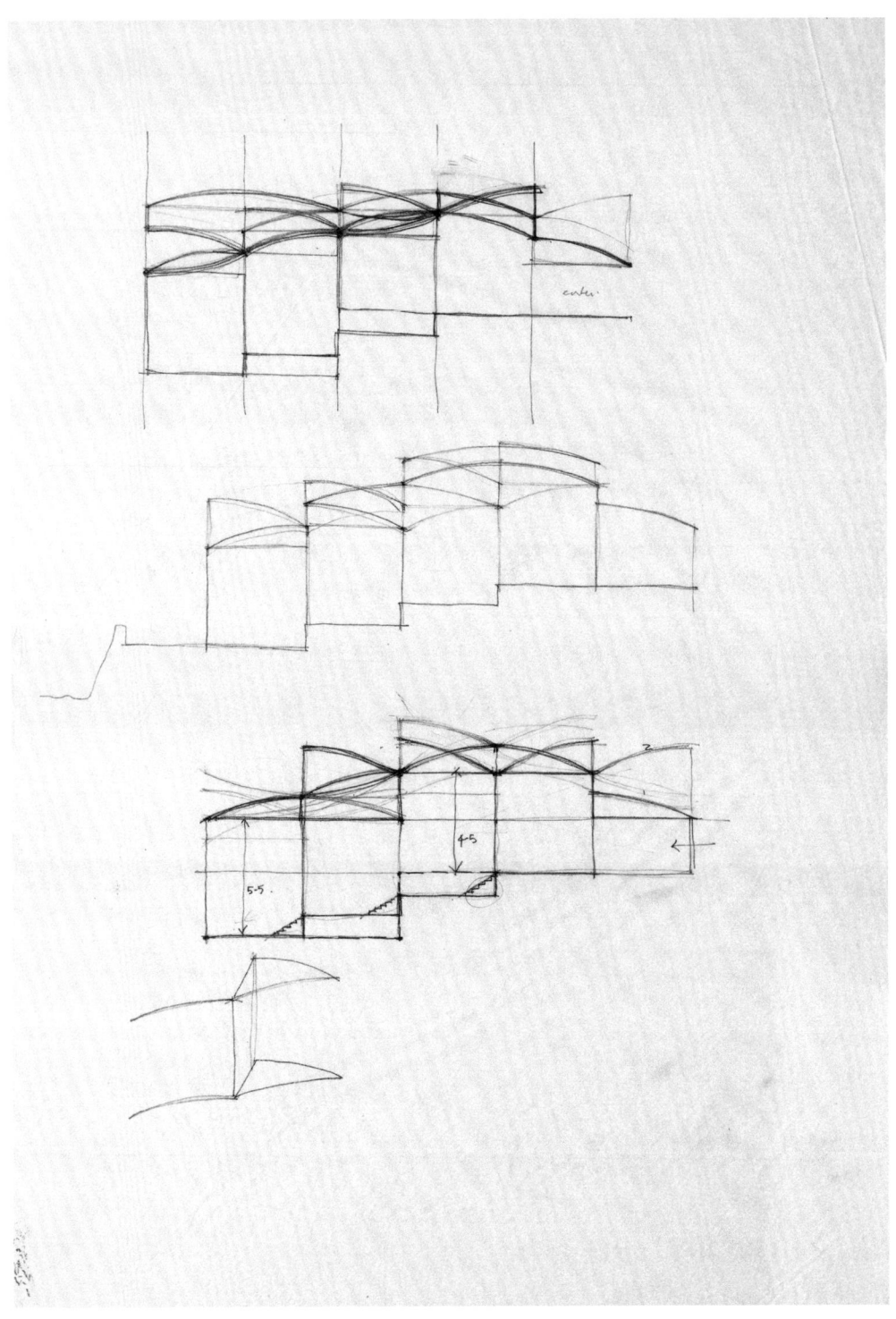

FIG. 17 Drawing, Australian Pavilion, Venice Biennale, August–September 1987.

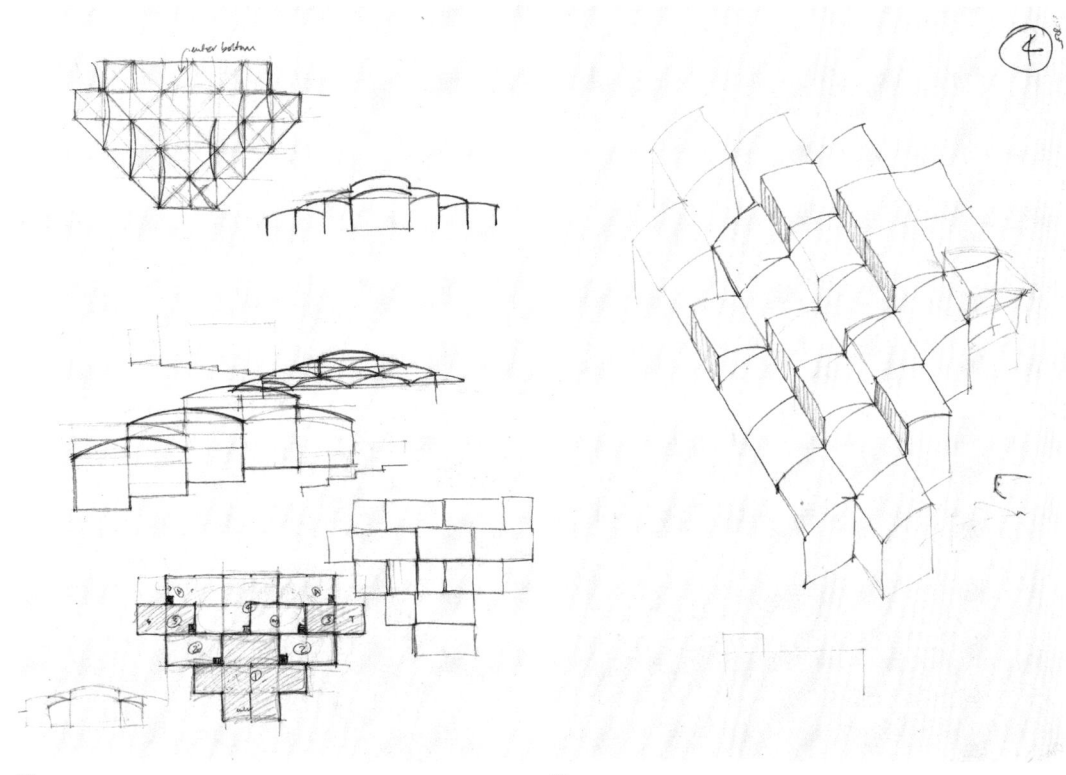

FIGS. 18–19 Drawings, Australian Pavilion, Venice Biennale, August–September 1987.

10

environment- alism and the queensland projects

by Antony Moulis

THE SCHOOL OF AUSTRALIAN ENVIRONMENTAL STUDIES, GRIFFITH UNIVERSITY

A 1978 article in the *Queensland Master Builder* begins, "If environmentalists were given just what they wanted in a building, what would it be like?"[1] One answer is John Andrews's design for the School of Australian Environmental Studies (AES), which had just opened that year on Griffith University's Nathan Campus, an expanse of bushland located 12 kilometers outside of central Brisbane, Queensland. At a latitude of 27° 28´ south, Brisbane has a subtropical climate and developed architectural traditions such as, for example, its veranda-lined timber houses that self-consciously respond to this environment. Within the Queensland context and despite its modest scale, the School of Australian Environmental Studies is a concise and welcome statement of Andrews's environmental approach that is linked to over a decade of architectural thought and practice. [FIGS. 1–2]

The building's form is organized around several small courtyards that diagonally step down tree-covered terrain. The top of the building's site connects to the main circulation spine of the Nathan Campus, which features a large, sheltered colonnade that offers a dynamic contrast between the urban setting and nature. Within the complex, a pedestrian walkway, which is occasionally skylit and laid with earth-colored tiles, acts as a street or a wandering passage through the building. [FIG. 3] This street is open laterally to the courtyards and the surrounding bush and provides internal access to research and teaching spaces. The site's terraces, set at different heights, provide vistas of the building's exterior landscape and interior volumes. Throughout the plan, architectural edges are created through smooth off-form concrete walls that step and fold and are set at highly controlled elevations. They are also solid yet porous where necessary, maximizing the natural light and ventilation to the staff offices, circulation areas, and occasional study spaces without overexposing them to the Queensland sun.

Rooms requiring air-conditioning, such as laboratories and technical service areas, are grouped around service cores that house and distribute the building's mechanical services. This allows for a clear zonal strategy to accommodate spaces that are passively and actively controlled.

The Australian Environmental Studies building was deemed "state of the art" in terms of its environmental strategies. Perceived as compact for the facilities it accommodated, as it cleverly merged with its surroundings at a sympathetic scale within the enveloping bush, the building was lauded for avoiding the destruction of significant trees on the site. Griffith University was founded in 1971, Queensland's second university, and began teaching in 1975. The original choice for the university's new Nathan Campus was linked to excitement over the presence of significant flora and fauna, and the Griffith University Interim Council enacted a committed policy of preservation. Rare trees including *Eucalyptus baileyana* and *Eucalyptus planchoniana*, as well as *Xanthorrhoea* (grass tree), proliferated on the site.[2] These environmental concerns were also linked to financial concerns. The new building included an on-budget plan that would mitigate long-term maintenance costs through its durable concrete forms, a tactical approach to the provision of natural light and ventilation, and open-air spaces used for informal teaching. Together, these attributes made it seem as if nothing in this building was being wasted—not even the rooftops, which were used to house solar power units.[3]

The design's environmental credentials echoed the agenda-setting ideals put forward by the university and particularly those of its environmental studies program. Calvin Rose, founding chairman of the School of Australian Environmental Studies, led the development of the school, which pioneered environmental science as a new field of study nationally. Its program was based on four essential concepts, including, "a systems approach to

---

1   "The School of Australian Environmental Studies at Griffith University," *Queensland Master Builder* (April 1978): 13.

2   Noel Quirke, *Preparing for the Future: A History of Griffith University 1971–1996* (Nathan, QLD: Boolarong Press, 1996), 90.

3   "School of Australian Environmental Studies," 15.

FIGS. 1–2 School of Australian Environmental Studies, Griffith University, Nathan, Queensland, 1975–1978, exterior views.

environmental concerns; an evidentiary base for the study of environmental problems; a strong database involving field work, analysis, and statistics; and a strong interdisciplinary linkage between the social and the natural sciences."[4] Rose had previously held a position at the Commonwealth Scientific and Industrial Research Organisation (CSIRO) in Canberra, Australia's main governmental center for innovation in environmental research, and had prior academic experience in North America working as a visiting professor at the University of Guelph and the University of California, Berkeley, from 1969 to 1970. From the outset, Rose and his academic colleagues were welcomed into design discussions for the new Australian Environmental Studies building as representatives of the AES "User Group."

The program's emphasis on interdisciplinary connections resonated with Andrews and architect John Simpson, partner-in-charge of the John Andrews International Queensland office, who led the building's project team. Simpson later recalled how the building's circulation pattern was critical for producing the urbanity that would facilitate open academic exchange, composing various formal points of address as well as casual meeting spaces both indoors and out.[5] At the same time, interdisciplinary connections were incorporated in John Andrews's design practice through the inclusion of a range of expertise in the project team. Mechanical and electrical engineer Don Thomas, who worked on a range of Andrews's projects, made key contributions to the environmental and technical strategies of the AES building from its initial design stage. Rose brought the latest developments in environmental research to Queensland and beyond through the AES program, while Andrews and his team engaged, through the building's design, in an environmentally conscious approach rendered through architectural form, organization, and materiality.

It might be assumed that the approach to the environment that Andrews brought to Queensland stemmed from his immersion in the environmental consciousness that had taken hold in North America in the 1960s, which is also reflected in the ambitions of Griffith University and the AES building. However, this relationship needs some unpacking to first acknowledge the thread of thinking that Andrews brought with him to North America as a young architect and, second, to understand how Andrews's inventory of projects and design preoccupations intersect with the environmental movement he encountered.

ANDREWS'S ENVIRONMENTALISM

Andrews's environmental approach was embedded in his understanding of "total architecture," the belief that a building and its context operate in synergy with one another, beginning with the building's design and organization and through to its construction, final occupation, and use. For Andrews, architecture was not simply passive but an active contributor to a place. As he explained, architecture was about "a building doing something to make its environment."[6] One starting point for Andrews's thinking on the nexus of architecture and the environment emerged from his education at the University of Sydney School of Architecture, where he discovered relationships between landscape and building through art in particular. Two of Andrews's key professors were prominent landscape artists, including Lloyd Rees from Queensland and Roland Wakelin from New Zealand, who instructed students in the painting of landscapes within the university's courtyards.[7] Early experiences on work sites in Australia and training in architectural drafting also gave Andrews a keen practical sense, stressing the importance of the economy of building and the ways in which adjusting architecture to its context was an important way to produce such an economy.[8] The value of these

---

4   Quirke, *Preparing for the Future*, 20.
5   John Simpson, interview by Antony Moulis, September 7, 2016.
6   John Andrews, interview by Antony Moulis, September 2014.
7   Ibid.
8   Jennifer Taylor and John Andrews, *John Andrews: Architecture, a Performing Art* (Melbourne: Oxford University Press, 1982), 20.

Australian beginnings was strongly felt by Andrews when he arrived at Harvard University, where he discovered that his "on-the-ground" knowledge of construction and site planning far outstripped that of his colleagues, allowing him to take full advantage of the new design lessons on offer.[9]

In both Australia and in his early experience in North America, one of Andrews's chief preoccupations included designing the ambient environment of built spaces. This was first apparent in his thesis project at the University of Sydney, in the design of articulated roof structures over the interior plaza of a new Sydney airport terminal (1956), and later in his submission to the Toronto City Hall design competition, undertaken with his Harvard colleagues, which contained a parasol-sheltered "winter court" (1958). In 1959, in two schemes Andrews executed while working in the office of John B. Parkin Associates, his interest in the moderated environment continued. For example, the design scheme for the Malton Hotel at the Toronto International Airport used canted sectional forms to deflect the noise of air and vehicular traffic from courtyard spaces. The design of the Federal Equipment Complex, a steel-framed structure featuring alternative pop-up sections, was justified on practical and environmental grounds by creating an arrangement that efficiently gathered light into the building's deep volumes (see chapter 1).

Andrews's 1961 architectural tour of Europe and Asia, taken just before he established his own practice in Toronto, included visits to canonical works but also to those that directly reflected his thinking on the relationship of architecture to the environment. The Adalaj Stepwell in Gujarat, India, impressed the young architect for what he called its "inescapable logic." This entails a staircase structure cut into the earth in order to provide naturally cool spaces as well as access to fresh groundwater.[10] [FIG. 4] In Europe, on the advice of Harvard GSD dean Josep Lluís Sert, Andrews visited Antoni Gaudí's work in Barcelona. One of Gaudí's projects proved to be a revelation. In an interview, Andrews later recalled:

> [Gaudí's] Parc Guell was impressive.... [it] made me think about the question "how do you make a landscape into a building?"—that was most significant. I was thinking of it while designing Scarborough College. I wanted the building to be a bit like it, a wandering edge in a landscape.[11]

Andrews's fascination with works from outside the architectural canon, such as the Adalaj Stepwell, directed him to another source he considered vital. Bernard Rudofsky's 1964 MoMA exhibition and book *Architecture Without Architects: A Short Introduction to Non-Pedigreed Architecture* was a confirmation of his thinking, mirroring his beliefs about architectural design method. Presenting a catalog of vernacular buildings and structures produced by local populations across different cultural and historical circumstances, *Architecture Without Architects* became emblematic of Andrews's broader search for new ideas concerning the connections between human habitation, building, and landscape through architecture. Andrews felt particularly driven by what he saw in its pages because, as he remarked, "it was about buildings emerging from their environment—having the purpose and look of the building come from that—from reason without applied meaning."[12] Through this view, Andrews revealed a constant within his architectural thinking, that environmental and social concerns provide answers to the technical and spatial issues of a building. The "proof" was the work of architecture, which was adequate to "explain its own forms [and] the attitudes that went into its design."[13]

---

9   John Andrews, interview by Antony Moulis, September 2014.
10 Taylor and Andrews, *John Andrews*, 25.
11 John Andrews, interview by Antony Moulis, September 2014.
12 Ibid.
13 Taylor and Andrews, *John Andrews*, 47.

ECOLOGICAL PLANNING AND ACTIVISM

With a resolutely pragmatic stance, Andrews felt already committed to a design approach that valued the environment before he moved to North America. Nonetheless, his arrival coincided with the emergence of ecology as a social ethic, and through his education and early practice, he found himself part of a network of ambitious colleagues—landscape architects, artists, and other professionals—who pursued ecological ideas and values both personally and professionally. At a disciplinary level, this moment was catalyzed by the influential work of landscape architect Ian McHarg, whose practice, teaching, and writing recast the fields of landscape architecture and regional planning to involve the interrelation of natural and human systems. Andrews, too, placed great store in the address of architecture to the environment, and as such, he did not experience McHarg's views on design and ecology, relayed through the North American scene, as a eureka moment. Though Andrews acknowledged McHarg as an important contemporary, he did not claim to have followed his work closely.[14] Indeed, Andrews's experiences in education, professional practice, and teaching can be seen as parallel with those of McHarg.

McHarg attended the Harvard GSD from 1946 to 1949, earning a degree in landscape architecture and city planning, which included multidisciplinary courses and teams that fostered a mode of collaboration he would take to the holistic address of environmental concerns.[15] In 1956, four years after joining the faculty of the University of Pennsylvania, he established the Department of Landscape Architecture, setting out to advance thinking about the environment in the field of landscape architecture as a totality, enlisting a diverse range of scientific specialists, including biologists, meteorologists, and anthropologists, to

3

4

14 John Andrews, interview by Paul Walker, April 2013.
15 Anne Spirin, "Ian McHarg, Landscape Architecture, and Environmentalism: Ideas and Methods in Context," in *Environmentalism in Landscape Architecture*, ed. Michel Conan (Washington, DC: Dumbarton Oaks Research Library and Collection, 2000), 97–114.

FIG. 3 Interior view, street passageway, the School of Australian Environmental Studies, Griffith University.
FIG. 4 Adalaj Stepwell, Gujarat, India.

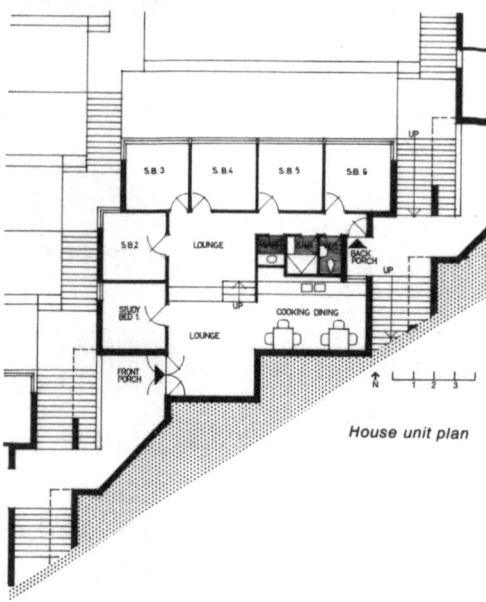

FIG. 5 House unit plan, Canberra College of Advanced Education student residence, Canberra, Australia.

interact with his students.[16] In 1962, along with his university role, McHarg also established the firm Wallace McHarg Roberts & Todd, with the aim of instrumentalizing his teaching methods in practice. Coining the term "ecological planning," McHarg promoted the idea of "nature as process."[17] He believed that places, as the outcome of processes, could be understood through design by incorporating concepts of adaptation and best fit.

Andrews, who attended Harvard from 1957 to 1958, almost a decade after McHarg, also used his experiences there to advance his design practice. Working on projects in cross-disciplinary teams and learning the importance of integrating architecture, structure, and landscape were particularly eye opening for Andrews within a period in which, he recalled, "the penny really dropped" on how to pursue a holistic approach to design. In 1962, when establishing John Andrews Architects in Toronto, the design he completed for Scarborough College was strongly driven by environmental determinants. Key to the building's siting and design were the local microclimatic conditions in Scarborough. Andrews's experiences pursuing environmental concerns through collaboration, and those of McHarg, crossed over. Joining the Scarborough College team was expert meteorologist and professor B. F. Watts and landscape architect Michael Hough, who was taught by McHarg at the University of Pennsylvania and served as an instrumental collaborator, having been fully immersed in an environmentally led approach.[18]

Key environmental parameters of the Scarborough College design cited by Andrews include the microclimatic conditions of wind, snow, and rain, the maintenance of marshlands at the base of the ravine that crossed the Scarborough site, and the location of established trees closer to the hilltops.[19] These seemingly minor features became architectural determinants, controlling the building's position in its context, its cranked linear arrangement,

16   Ibid., 98.
17   Ibid., 103.
18   Taylor and Andrews, *John Andrews*, 31–32.
19   Ibid., 33.

and the concentration of form on the site. Andrews also had the opportunity to take his ideas on architecture and the environment to his work reshaping architecture education. In 1967, he was appointed chair of the University of Toronto Department of Architecture, leading the faculty to implement sweeping changes to the curriculum. He hired English architect Peter Prangnell, who graduated from the Harvard GSD a year after Andrews, to assist him. Together, they proceeded to institute educational strategies at the University of Toronto founded on the multidisciplinary experiences and collaborations they had absorbed at Harvard.

Throughout the late 1960s, McHarg's approach became a touchstone for the discipline of landscape architecture, as well as for architecture and planning in general. In 1971, McHarg's invitation to Sydney to address the Royal Australian Institute of Architects Centenary Convention, "The Environmental Crisis," was an acknowledgment of his international standing and the reach of his ecological message. However, Andrews had encountered McHarg's work indirectly in the 1960s. Though, rarely citing McHarg, direct uptake of his ideas appeared in a 1975 environmental planning report for Palm Beach, New South Wales, in which Andrews quoted McHarg's 1969 book *Design With Nature*.[20] Parallels in McHarg's and Andrews's early careers underwrite the connections between their ideas on ecology rather than the influence of the former on the latter.[21] Both architects operated as independent points in a broader network, pursuing environmental values that were promoted in their educations at the Harvard GSD, which significantly informed their disciplinary practices and influenced those who moved through their professional circles.

Alongside conventional disciplinary practice, the issue of ecology was also pursued through environmental activism. Three of Andrews's close associates at the time—members of Integ from the office at Colborne Street—took up ecological causes as part of political advocacy and protest actions in Canada: lawyer George Miller, landscape architect Richard Strong, and artist and sculptor Gerald Gladstone. For all of them, ecology was a broad societal issue that could be pursued through collaboration and diverse disciplinary perspectives.[22] They sought to create a greater impact through their advocacy as a group, achieving more than they might have individually.[23] For example, while practicing and working at Colborne Street, they made a self-financed documentary film on Gros Morne National Park in Newfoundland, a wilderness area threatened by commercial logging, as a means to pressure the Canadian government to declare the area a national reserve, which it eventually did in 1973.

Gladstone also took to the expression of ecological themes in his art practice. He specifically described his works as concerned with the fate of cities and of nature whose relationship he understood as one of mutual interdependence and deep synergy.[24] Andrews developed a close friendship with Gladstone, whose studio was in the basement at Colborne Street, and he owned several of Gladstone's smaller works. He included Gladstone as an occasional collaborator, organizing commissions for him to produce sculptural installations for high-profile projects, including George Gund Hall at Harvard and the Cameron Offices in Canberra. In 1973, Gladstone's art installation at Gund Hall was inaugurated as part of the building's dedication ceremony, attended by both Andrews and the artist. At the Cameron Offices, Gladstone produced *Optical Galaxy*, a large-scale outdoor sculpture featuring metal assemblages cast in acrylic that represent an amalgam of machine images and organic forms atop a set of concrete fins. Yet Andrews's

20   See Paul Walker, Jane Grant, and David Nichols, "Monarto's Contested Landscape," *Landscape Review: A Southern Hemisphere Journal of Landscape Architecture* 16, no. 1 (2015): 25.
21   John Andrews, interview by Paul Walker, April 2013.
22   See Antony Moulis, "The Mechanical Organic: On the Discourse of Ecology in the Architecture of John Andrews," *Proceedings of the Society of Architectural Historians, Australia and New Zealand: 31, Translation*, ed. Christoph Schnoor (2014): 545–54.
23   Gerald Gladstone, interview by Evan Walker, June 2004.
24   Moulis, "The Mechanical Organic," 551.

interest in collaboration with Gladstone emerged from his interdisciplinary views rather than his direct espousal of ecological concerns. When privately pressed by Sert on his inclusion of Gladstone as a collaborator for Gund Hall, Andrews defended his position, reminding Sert of his own collaboration with Spanish modern artist Joan Miró and advocating for the relationship struck between architects and artists in the creation of buildings as a time-honored practice.[25]

Andrews's unique place in the architecture discourse was reinforced by his appearance in the 1966 American Institute of Architects and the Association of Collegiate Schools of Architecture (AIA/ACSA) Teacher Seminar at the Cranbrook Academy of Art, in which he was included alongside leading architects such as Aldo van Eyck, Sim Van der Ryn, and Donlyn Lyndon. While the seminar focused on how architects were restructuring problems in both humanist and rational terms, Andrews's design for Scarborough College, in light of environmental concerns, was greeted as an "intuitive" work, a description seemingly at odds with the approaches taken to the design work of others.[26] Critic Gordon Heck offered him a "special award" for "Most Appropriate Use of the English Language," a tongue-in-cheek reference to his direct and sometimes colorful expressions.[27] Not for the first time, Andrews took up a position in his milieu that demonstrated an independent stance and thinking. He pursued an architecture that addressed environmental concerns in a time of ecological activism, and though he didn't necessarily identify as an activist, he was happy to support those in his circle who did. While Andrews's North American experiences were not the only ones to inform his practice as an environmentally conscious architect, they gave him the means to flourish as one.

DEPLOYING ENVIRONMENTAL ARCHITECTURE

A clear set of strategies emerged as Andrews pursued an environmental line. The specific shaping of plan and section as a means to passive climate control became a tried-and-true approach. In particular, the manipulation of building edges and spatial volumes that were developed in sections became critical to environmental fit. With the design of the Malton Hotel's canted walls as an early experiment, shaping the section came into its own with projects like Scarborough College, Gund Hall, and the Miami Seaport Terminal. In each of these projects, strong sectional articulation commanded local conditions to produce environmental outcomes, such as the capture of natural light, solar access, the deflection of wind, patterns of air circulation, and the glancing of sound through angling, stepping, and curving, which could all be expressed diagrammatically. Andrews's belief was that the section's role in creating ambient conditions made it architecture's new design "generator."[28]

However, Andrews did not abandon Le Corbusier's edict on the architectural plan, he merely updated it. The plan remained the primary means to determine a building's social organization—the facilitator of community—and Andrews's architecture favored two urban spatial types: the courtyard and the street. Both were places of gathering and interaction that he returned to time and again, separately and in combination. With each use, the material envelope of the spatial type became an environmental filter, acclimatizing space for inhabitation in different climate contexts. For example, Andrews's speculative projects for a Sydney airport terminal and Toronto City Hall were early versions of the courtyard type in which the use of an articulated roof plane served as a climate modifier. The seminal version of the street type was the interior circulation spine at Scarborough College. Skylit along its length, it was protected from the harsh Canadian

---

25 John Andrews, interview by Antony Moulis, September 2014.
26 Gordon Heck, "1966: Architects Restructure Problems," *Journal of Architectural Education* 21, no. 4 (1967): 3–8.
27 Ibid., 8.

28 John Andrews, interview by Antony Moulis, September 2014.

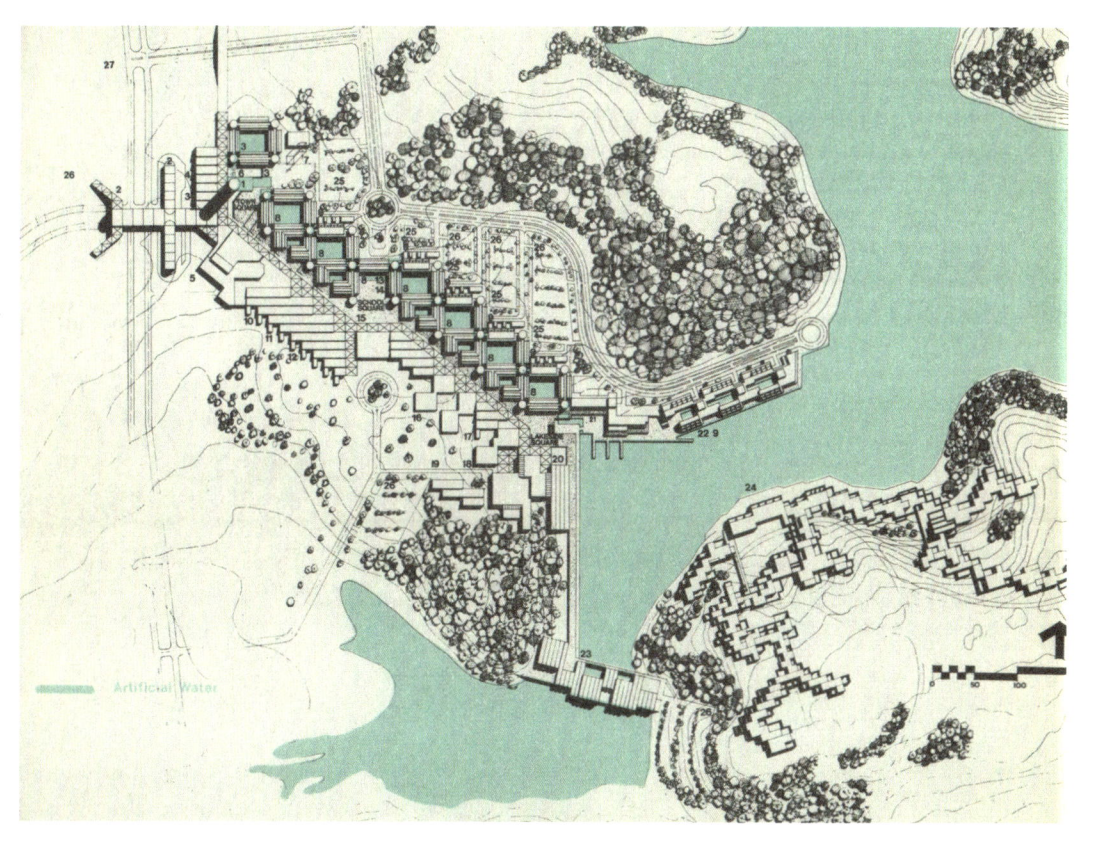

FIG. 6 Site plan, Monarto, South Australia.

conditions by tiers of offices and teaching spaces that enclosed its edges.

Once back in Australia, Andrews applied these spatial types tested in North America, modifying them to new environmental conditions. For the Cameron Offices in Canberra, the main circulation spine became an elevated street that was sheltered but otherwise open to the warmer Australian climate.[29] The large courtyard spaces between the office wings, designed in collaboration with landscape architect Richard Strong, became outdoor gardens rather than indoor gathering spaces, as was often the case in North America. Not roofed, but framed from above by large-span concrete beams, the Cameron Offices courtyards are further defined by Australian landscapes. In his 1973 design of the Canberra College of Advanced Education (CCAE) Student Residence Group 2, located in Belconnen, miniature open-air "streets" that traverse the site's north-facing slope are organized to limit exposure to cold winter winds. Their design and orientation are also justified with reference to topographic studies produced by aerodynamic consultants.[30] Sectional diagrams in the project's Design Report show how built form and organization emerged directly from the site's particular environmental characteristics. [FIGS. 5, 7]

The connection between the urban landscape and the environment was central to the 1975 Urban Design Study for the Monarto Town Centre, South Australia. Monarto formed around the idea that tertiary industries could act as the driver of city planning, alongside a focus on environmentally sensitive design.[31] Monarto was planned by the South Australian government as a new city 80 kilometers east of Adelaide. Intended for an environmentally

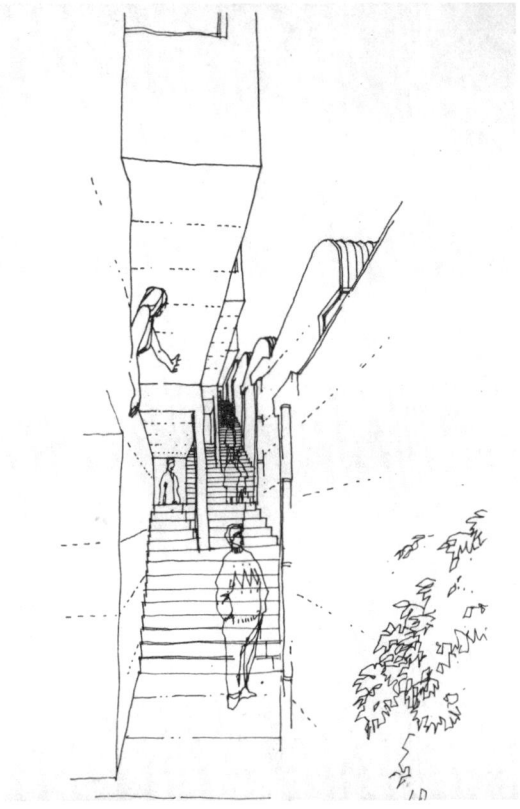

7

8

29 Taylor and Andrews, *John Andrews*, 138.
30 John Andrews International, "Canberra College of Advanced Education (CCAE) Residence Group 2," 1973.
31 See Jane Grant, Paul Walker, and David Nichols, "What's It All About, Monarto? John Andrews, Boris Kazanski, and the Centre of South Australia's Unbuilt Second 'New Town,'" *UHPH_14: Landscapes and ecologies of urban and planning history, Proceedings of the 12th Conference of the Australasian Urban History/Planning History Group*, eds. Morten Gjerde and Emina Petrović (2014): 255–69.

FIG. 7 CCAE Student Residence Group 2, pedestrian street.
FIG. 8 View of Roma Street precinct, Brisbane, Queensland, Australia, 1972.

challenging site with very high summer temperatures and low winter temperatures, Andrews's design for the Monarto town center addressed these environmental expectations with a range of design elements. Some of the elements were fanciful, such as an "energy tower" that would harvest wind and solar energy in unexplained ways. Others were more straightforward.

For example, Andrews envisioned most of the central Monarto buildings as a sequence of three-story bars arranged to form square courtyards between them that were placed on an orthogonal grid and cut across by a diagonal pedestrian route. The grid arrangement creates large courtyards with circular access towers at cruciform intersections. [FIG. 6] The whole urban layout is then draped over the landscape, responding to the fall across the site. The Urban Design Study for Monarto speaks to those issues directly, outlining how the scheme is fundamentally people-oriented, structuring relationships between individuals and their surroundings. In particular, as the study states, "From an urban design point of view it is essential that the connections and interdependencies of the design elements are reinforced and displayed to users so that they may orientate themselves and feel part of the environment."[32] This proposed that urban spatial types, like the street and the court, were only useful in so far as they respond to environmental conditions.

Another aspect of Andrews's environmental approach was technology driven, a specific focus on strategies that reduced a building's energy load. In his design of the King George Tower in Sydney, Andrews debuted an externally mounted, fine steel-framed structure containing polycarbonate sun shields. This outer screen was designed to mitigate the glare and heat gain through the glazing, a deliberate move away from modeling a building's concrete surface with steps and folds as a method to produce shade.[33] This was a new direction for Andrews in tackling environmental issues in the economy of large-scale office buildings. Later projects such as the Callam Offices in Canberra, the Intelsat Headquarters in Washington, DC, and the Octagon in Parramatta were similarly designed with flat, glazed facades mounted with external screens. The result was the invention of a generic architectural form that could be tailored to various contexts through applied treatments, moving beyond the highly articulated and figural forms that generated climatic responsiveness in Andrews's designs for Scarborough College and the Miami Seaport Terminal. Plant-covered rooftops were also put forward as an environmental strategy. Thought to insulate and cool buildings, the "green roof" approach was also justified for its re-creation of landscape space consumed in the process of construction.[34] The concept was implemented at the Cameron Offices, but the landscaping did not survive. However, it resurfaced successfully in later projects including the Garden Island Parking Structure in Sydney (1980) and the Intelsat Headquarters (1988).

John Andrews Architects' close work with consultants on environmental issues that began in North America continued in Australia. For the design of the Callam Offices, adjacent to the Woden Town Centre, consulting engineers Ove Arup & Partners were employed as hydraulic consultants, analyzing how the site's periodic flooding would affect the design. This prompted the decision to suspend the building over the topography, a solution recalling Le Corbusier's famous scheme for Venice Hospital over the lagoon in Venice.[35] The office also benefited from the input of mechanical and electrical engineer Don Thomas. Working on the idea of zonal air-conditioning strategies for the Cameron Offices and the School of Australian Environmental Studies building at Griffith University, Thomas was also hired to join the design team for the Intelsat Headquarters. There he contributed to strategies for environmental control, blending passive and active

---

32   John Andrews International, "Monarto City Centre, Stage One, Design Proposal," 1975.
33   Taylor and Andrews, *John Andrews*, 122.
34   Ibid., 151.
35   John Andrews International, "Woden East, Government Offices, Report 1," 1974.

approaches, including using ornamental ponds in the building's atrium spaces for the natural cooling of outside air. These had a precedent in the pools proposed by Andrews—again with Thomas's input—for the courtyards of the Monarto town center. The increasing use of active environmental systems in Andrews's work, achieved in collaboration with Thomas, can be seen from the Callam Offices proposal in 1973 through to the design of the Octagon in 1990.

Andrews also considered the needs of users from an environmental perspective. For example, in the "Master Plan Report" for the Callam Offices there is reference to a comprehensive set of "environmental principles" described under the heading, "The building as environment."[36] Chief among them is a recognition of what are called the "metabolic needs" of workers, which include access to "light, air, sounds [and] the relationship to nature."[37] In relating the design to a set of essential human needs, Andrews asserted the idea that architecture is not simply about the making of a building. The project of architecture is the creation of an integrated whole, encompassing user experience and the adaptation of context to make conditions right, which in Andrews's terms meant nothing less than a necessary response to the evident problems that lay before the architect.

As far as environmental strategies went, Queensland was an important testing ground. Indeed, it offered a setting ripe for Andrews's ideas on architecture and the environment. As Australia's second-largest state, it has a land area three times the size of France, yet it was populated by fewer than one million people in 1970. Its climatic zones stretch from the subtropics to the tropics, places where passive design strategies were sensible. At the same time, the state had ambitions for developing new civic and institutional infrastructure on building budgets that were comparatively meager. This scenario provided the type of challenges and opportunities for practical design thinking on which the Andrews office thrived.

ESTABLISHING THE QUEENSLAND OFFICE

In 1972, John Andrews International established a branch in Brisbane, Queensland, as a satellite of the main office located in Palm Beach, north of Sydney. It proved to be a significant generator of projects for Andrews after the 1973 closure of his Toronto office and through the economic downturn of the oil crisis, when work out of Queensland briefly served as the office's mainstay. It was also Andrews's most substantial office presence outside of Sydney, continuing to operate until 1983. The Brisbane enterprise was headed by Scottish architect John Simpson, who trained in architecture at the Glasgow School of Art, graduating with a silver medal in 1958, and had joined Andrews's Toronto office in 1963. Prior to his arrival in Canada, Simpson worked with Alex Strang Associates in Stirling, Scotland, from 1958 to 1960, and with Sir Basil Spence in London from 1961 to 1963, where he was involved in the design of the Hampstead Civic Centre (1964).[38]

After entering Andrews's office, Simpson found himself immediately involved in the design for Scarborough College, then African Place at Expo 67, and the South Residences at the University of Guelph. From 1966 to 1967, Simpson briefly left the office to earn his Master of Architecture degree at the Harvard GSD. Arriving at the GSD in the last years of Sert's tenure as dean, Simpson recalled the teaching of Joseph Zalewski, an associate of Sert's office, and Albert Szabo, who headed Harvard's Department of Architectural Sciences.[39] In 1968, only a year after completing his degree, Simpson found himself back in Boston working alongside Andrews as partner-in-charge of the project for Gund Hall (1972). Thereafter, Simpson also made his way to Australia with Andrews to work on a major commercial project in Sydney, the King George Tower (1976), and began setting up the Queensland office simultaneously.

36   Ibid.
37   Ibid.
38   Andrew Wilson, "John Simpson," in Philip Goad and Julie Willis, eds., *The Encyclopedia of Australian Architecture* (Melbourne: Cambridge University Press, 2012), 628.
39   John Simpson, interview by Antony Moulis, September 2016.

FIGS. 9–10 Model, Roma Street.

Simpson's connection to Brisbane also grew out of circumstance. He met his spouse, Lorri Simpson, who was from Brisbane, while traveling by ship from Scotland to Toronto in 1963. She had initially connected Simpson with Andrews, whom she already knew. Simpson first visited Brisbane in 1967 and found it to be a modest town in terms of its architecture and cultural scene.[40] Fronting the office in Queensland would be an opportunity for him to assist John Andrews International in transferring knowledge from a heady period of practice in North America to a distant city with a sense of remoteness beyond that of other Australian cities, including Canberra, Sydney, and Melbourne. Notwithstanding, Andrews's office in Brisbane proved a success with Simpson as its lead. In time, Simpson experienced it as a type of homecoming.

The office's projects in Queensland were mainly related to the expansion and updating of university campuses as the state government reinvigorated its tertiary education facilities supported by national funding programs. Andrews's decade-long experience in the education sector in North America meant that the office was well positioned to provide its expertise. Yet, the path for the practice to flourish in Queensland was not as straightforward as expected since the office faced very different conditions to those present elsewhere in Australia, including new physical, institutional, and commercial conditions.

The initial catalyst for Andrews's work in Brisbane was a major city redevelopment project for the Roma Street precinct. [FIG. 8] The opportunity came through Keith Campbell, managing director of the Australian development company LJ Hooker. Campbell had visited the Colborne Street office in Toronto and witnessed John Andrews's work on the urban masterplan for Toronto's Metro Centre. Impressed by it, he was drawn to the idea that a similar planning scenario could work in Brisbane. The city had been seeking a strategic direction in its urban development since the mid-1960s. Initially, Roma Street was actively considered as the site for a new university campus for Griffith University, which eventually became the Nathan Campus, where Andrews built the AES building.[41] While the office was producing the King George Tower for LJ Hooker in Sydney, it began work on a masterplan for the Roma Street precinct, and Andrews's bold design methods and approach, which had evolved in North America, found some application in the scheme.

The urban planning intentions evident in Andrews's design for Toronto's Metro Centre are also taken up in Brisbane, albeit at a far-reduced scale. The creation of a major mixed-use commercial and residential development at the neglected fringe of the city again offered the chance to develop "people-orientated" strategies in public space. Roma Street's location between the gridded city center and a major train station to the west provided the occasion to forge new pedestrian streets serving as links across the site through a tight but staggered arrangement of towers. [FIGS. 9–10] The proposal was intent upon changing the city's urban dynamic by shaping the public space between buildings and introducing a new urban scenography for inhabitants, which extended beyond that of the conventional vehicle-dominated city grid. The form of the towers themselves recalled Andrews's prior North American work, resembling a 1965 building designed for Canadian steel company Stelco, in which modular units, arranged on a pinwheel plan, were cantilevered off a central core. In Andrews's design, the expression was simple and environmental considerations were also apparent. The towers were oriented to the northern aspect, favorable in the southern hemisphere, instead of by default to the existing city grid. Though the Roma Street development failed to materialize, the presence of John Andrews International in Queensland was established.

QUEENSLAND EDUCATION MASTER PLANS

After the design for Roma Street, John Andrews International obtained work for education

---

40   Ibid.
41   Quirke, *Preparing for the Future*, 4.

projects, largely on "brownfield" sites, where existing facilities required adaptation to fresh agendas. The 1964 Federal Martin Committee of Enquiry into the Future of Education focused on the development of new educational models. It called for greater diversity in the educational programs offered and the national establishment of institutions with a strong technological and practical focus.[42] It sought more integration between disciplines and wider campus communities, with a renewed approach to institutional planning. Andrews's office led "corrective" strategies of infill planning to address moribund building stock and poorly organized sites.[43] It continued its emphasis on urban planning through strategies of access, communication, and circulation, advocating for the direction of human movement as critical to creating the best conditions for learning on campus.[44]

In Queensland, Andrews's work to produce an urban experience also led to addressing environmental conditions. In 1973, his first Queensland institutional planning project was the masterplan for the Kelvin Grove campus of Queensland University of Technology (QUT) in Brisbane that was being updated from a former teaching college to the Brisbane College of Advanced Education.[45] Following this were Andrews's proposals in 1974 for the Darling Downs Institute of Advanced Education and Ithaca Technical College, and in 1975 for the Ipswich College of Technical and Further Education. After completing these initial masterplans, the office received architectural commissions for projects on three of the campuses, including libraries at both QUT Kelvin Grove and Ipswich College and a general-purpose building at the Darling Downs Institute.[46] Each of the masterplans presented a case for responding to site-specific constraints of topography, climate, and access, with an emphasis on environmental fit and future growth.

The 1974 "Master Plan Report" by John Andrews International for the Darling Downs Institute identifies a conflict between the existing built form and the new aspirations for education. As the report states, "the campus does not express to outsiders the fundamental concern with the application of knowledge."[47] They propose a "Spine Concept," which would extend across the site to relate old and new facilities. [FIG. 11] It is conceptualized as "a system of articulating in-place and between-place activities rather than as buildings strung along an axis."[48] The idea was to foster meaningful connections along a circulation route that is open and flexible to both formal and informal uses, yet "protected from wind, rain, and sun."[49] The spine is referred to as a "main street" supported by "back streets" and is also weather protected. Landscaping was also proposed to achieve environmental benefits at the street level. This includes the thickening of an existing belt of eucalyptus and acacia trees to provide a "heat sink effect," absorbing the energy produced by nearby buildings.

In a follow-up to the initial plan, the 1976 "Developed Plan Report," the mutual relationship between the environment and the building form is further developed. In this report, parallel to the circulation spine, a "natural spine" of dense trees is proposed "to give desired climatic effects such as reduction in wind velocity and summer heat intensity."[50] Clumps of trees

---

42   John A. Bowden and John Anwyl, "Some Characteristics and Attitudes of Academics in Australian Universities and Colleges of Advanced Education," *Higher Education Research and Development* 2, no. 1 (1983): 39–61.
43   See Antony Moulis and Georgina Russell, "Design as Remedial Practice: John Andrews International Education Projects in Queensland," *Proceedings of the Society of Architectural Historians, Australia and New Zealand: 32, Architecture, Institutions and Change*, eds. Paul Hogben and Judith O'Callaghan (2015): 425–34.
44   See Mary Lou Lobsinger and Paolo Scrivano, "Experimental Architecture and Progressive Pedagogy: Scarborough College," *Architecture and Ideas* 8 (2009): 4–19.
45   Noeline Kyle, Catherine Manathunga, and Joanne Scott, *A Class of Its Own: A History of Queensland University of Technology* (Alexandria, NSW: Hale & Iremonger in association with Queensland University of Technology, 1999).
46   Other architectural commissions were executed by the Andrews Office for other Queensland campuses. These include the Chemical Engineering Building at the University of Queensland St. Lucia Campus in 1973–75 and the School of Australian Environmental Studies at the Griffith University Nathan Campus in 1975–78.
47   John Andrews International, "Darling Downs Institute of Advanced Education Development Plan," 1974.
48   Ibid., 19.
49   Ibid.
50   Ibid.

FIG. 11 Site view along proposed spine route, Darling Downs Institute, Queensland, Australia.

FIG. 12 Kelvin Grove Education Resource Centre, Brisbane, Queensland, Australia.

3 : 3.1 THE SPINE CONCEPT

The Master Plan Brief suggests that the Schools of the new College should be grouped around a central resource, teaching and amenity core. It envisages each School as a separate entity.

The relative narrowness of the site does not favour such a solution. Furthermore, an organisational system such as this tends to confine students of a particular school to their own school area, giving little opportunity for them to become aware of the work, interests and concerns of students of other schools.

Instead, an organisational system which promotes maximum interaction between full and part time students and staff, as well as lending itself to the configuration of the site, is proposed.

It is a system which concentrates the pedestrian movement of the College on a major street or spine, and organises the core facilities and schools of the College around it.

The nature of the site suggests that the pedestrian spine should follow a mid-level contour around the slopes of Station Hill, with the noisy workshop areas of the School of Technology located on the lower, flatter slopes adjacent to the industrial area east of Byrne Street and the laboratory and classroom areas of the Schools of General and Business Studies and Applied Science on the slopes above the spine.

Core facilities such as the Resource Materials Centre, shared classrooms and laboratories, administration and staff and student amenities can also be located along the quiet side of the spine, and be designed in such a way as to also open out onto the retained hilltop.

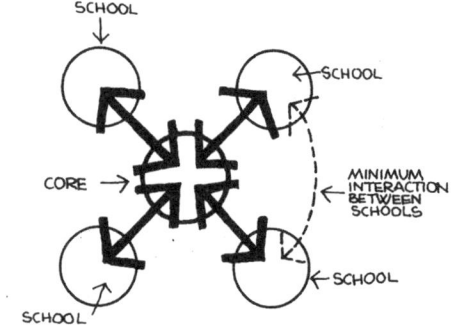

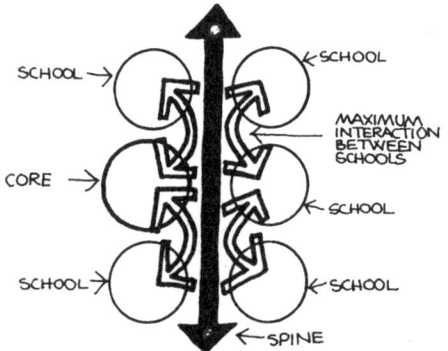

FIG. 13 Comparative diagrams, Ipswich Technical and Further Education, Queensland, Australia.

along the street are designed to create "localized wind effects,"moderating the prevailing east breeze while also guaranteeing natural air circulation.[51]

In the 1976 Ipswich College of Technical and Further Education Master Plan, the educational benefits of the circulation spine put forth in the organizational diagram are clearly articulated. [FIG. 13] The urban character of "the street" is intended to encourage maximum human interaction. However, it is also a means to harness the environment for human habitation. This includes accounting for the fall of the land across the site, the encouragement of natural ventilation, and the attenuation of the space, allowing for vistas and connections to the natural landscape. Together, these features make "the street" an open but protected space that fits with its environment.

MAKING "STREETS" FOR QUEENSLAND CAMPUSES

Alongside its masterplanning, the Queensland office commenced building work for other projects. The first project to be realized was the University of Queensland Chemical Engineering Building located on the St. Lucia Campus in Brisbane (1973–75). The university's architect, James McCormick, engaged John Andrews International to take on the project. McCormick had been the architect of the Australian Pavilion at Expo 70 in Osaka and at Expo 67 in Montreal, where Andrews carried out his design for African Place. McCormick was fascinated by the presence of Andrews's office in Brisbane. Further, there was another stroke of luck. John Simpson, principal architect for John Andrews International, happened to be McCormick's neighbor. The budget for the Chemical Engineering Building was small for its time, under $1 million, a figure that the office initially believed represented the architecture fee.[52] Despite its budget, the project offered an early test of the pedestrian street concept in the Brisbane local context.

The University of Queensland's St. Lucia Campus, originally planned in 1936, is located on a reach of the Brisbane River. The Andrews project took the place of the old plan, constructing a new engineering precinct. Housing staff offices, teaching spaces, and specialist laboratories, the Chemical Engineering Building was designed on modular geometric grids based on previous plans from the office's North American projects. [FIG. 14] The project's site was predicated on the removal of an existing university roadway and the planned reinstatement of the link with a pedestrian walkway. The complex was thus divided at its central "knuckle" by a void that pierced the building, creating a route designed to connect residents of the university's riverside colleges to the hilltop of the main campus. [FIG. 15] This new pathway involved students passing by a three-story skylit atrium that contained experimental equipment just inside the building where researchers could be seen at work. Despite the building's modest scale, its larger intention was clear: it aimed to rethink the campus's circulation as a pattern of protected interactive streets linking academic activities, inside and out.

The project for the Kelvin Grove Education Resource Centre was completed by the office in 1976. [FIG. 12] The building's scheme created a new spatial hub at the top of the existing campus, located in a courtyard loosely formed by extant buildings. It was merely a fragment of the original concept for the office's masterplan produced in 1973, which proposed a mat-like expanse of built spaces closely following the site's topography. The plan takes its cue from the unrealized design for the expansion of the Behavioral Sciences Department of Tufts University (1970), which proposed a terraced infill development around existing hilltop buildings.[53] In both designs, spaces are nestled into the hillside in such a way that the buildings resemble the form of the landscape, extending it rather than reacting in contrast to it. The synergistic relationship conjured between the built form and the landscape also recalls Rudofsky's

---

51 Ibid.
52 John Simpson, interview by Antony Moulis, September 2016.

53 Taylor and Andrews, *John Andrews*, 174.

14

15

FIG. 14 Exterior view, Chemical Engineering Building, the University of Queensland, Brisbane, Queensland, Australia.
FIG. 15 Pedestrian "street," Chemical Engineering Building, the University of Queensland.

Architecture Without Architects and the idea of large-scale collective structures set within the natural environment. At the same time, the choice of a dense urban arrangement cut by open-circulation streets that traverse the site's topography reflects the design of the student residence created for the Canberra College of Advanced Education (CCAE) in Belconnen, which the office was working on in parallel.

In 1978 Andrews's Queensland office completed the Australian Environmental Studies building on the new Griffith University Nathan Campus, with John Simpson as partner-in-charge. Its design was also based on the idea of pedestrian "streets" that were linked to nature and put environmental concerns at the forefront. The concept of the street was already present in architect Roger Johnson's 1972 university masterplan for the Nathan Campus, which proposed a main circulation spine linking the buildings that were sited sensitively in the bush and interspersed with natural courtyards. Johnson's report to the Griffith Interim Committee concluded that this arrangement would create a memorable image for the campus.[54] However, the idea was not Johnson's alone. In his previous role as the first assistant commissioner for architecture of the National Capital Development Commission, which he held from 1968 to 1971, Johnson had already encountered Andrews's work through the Cameron Offices project. In the design of the Cameron Offices, the concept of the attenuated circulation street, reseeded by Johnson for the Nathan Campus, was foundational, creating a place for human interaction and connecting planted courtyards, office accommodations, housing, and a town center within a greater landscape context. For Andrews, however, its lineage went back further, to Scarborough College, where the internal pedestrian "street" was piloted in very different environmental conditions. If the Cameron Offices signaled the relevance of this urban type in the Australian climate, with its sheltering form, then in Andrews's designs for the Queensland's

54 See Susan Holden and Jared Bird, "Bush Civics," *Architecture Australia* 104, no. 4 (July/August 2015): 68–70.

subtropics this exploration continued. In Queensland, the "street" was purposefully rethought through environmental designs that spanned an array of masterplans and buildings. In effect, Andrews was able to loosen public space from the conventions of interiority and strategize new forms of openness.

A QUEENSLAND LEGACY

As a manifestation of one of Andrews's open-air but protected streets, the void passage at the University of Queensland's Chemical Engineering Building was a small beginning, though it spoke to a larger concept initiated by John Andrews International for the projects and plans it undertook in Queensland. The idea would grow beyond Andrews's presence in Brisbane. Its direct legacy can be seen in the construction of the Hawken Engineering Building on the University of Queensland campus over a decade later. The design of the Hawken Engineering Building was also led by John Simpson, but this time for his own practice, John Simpson & Associates, which he established in 1983. Featuring covered walkways resembling arcades and lanes laid out as large voids between bars of accommodation, the project consciously and literally expands on the connective urban strategy and public openness of the Chemical Engineering Building, which occupies an adjacent site. In Simpson's design, a set of parallel bowstring-truss roofs protects the outdoor "streets" from the weather, with long atria entirely open at their ends that provide natural air ventilation to account for Brisbane's seasonal heat and humidity.

Other examples can be found in designs from the 1970s up until the early 2000s, reinforcing the idea that the open-air street expressed a developing regional sensibility. Local architect Robin Gibson produced a set of major projects containing the form for Brisbane in the 1970s and 1980s. This includes the Griffith University Library and Humanities Building (1975), with its airy and cavernous concourse laid out in accordance with Johnson's masterplan for the Nathan Campus, which was linked to Andrews's ideas. Another example is Gibson's magnum opus, the Queensland Cultural Centre (1988), a set piece of late-modernism and Brutalism comprising the Queensland Art Gallery, Museum, Library, and Performing Arts Centre, which has as its main public circulation armature an elevated mall space. This space is vast and covered but otherwise open to the elements, creating connections across the entire complex. Even in the more recent past, in 2006, the type has continued to be used in the refurbishment and expansion of Gibson's design for the State Library of Queensland by Brisbane-based firms Donovan Hill and Peddle Thorp Architects. Their plan again includes open-air public space through the design of a four-story atrium that creates a passage known as the Knowledge Walk. Locally in Brisbane, such places are celebrated for exhibiting a vernacular architecture style in public space. However, their form can be traced to the precedent of Andrews's internationally inspired Queensland works of the 1970s.

The environmental approach that Andrews brought to Queensland was not a one-way transfer of ideas from "elsewhere," or the arrival of a discourse on ecology that had already emerged in North America. Nor could it be described as simply local and "regionalist," a response to Australian environmental conditions and the Queensland vernacular. Rather, it began circuitously. Andrews, an architect trained in Sydney and then at Harvard, subsequently transferred his knowledge and experiences from North America back home to Australia, while having developed, in the space between the two hemispheres, a suite of techniques for managing the environment that could be counted on to produce the "correct fit." Shared among members of his office and local architects that were influenced by Andrews's designs were techniques for making architecture only what it needed be, a practical and effective response to the environment, in whatever natural setting it might be found.

11

towers

by   Paul Walker

KING GEORGE TOWER

The King George Tower is a major office building in central Sydney, completed in 1976. It is also widely known by the corporate name it held for 20 years: the American Express Building. In 1965 Keith Campbell, managing director of LJ Hooker, the large Australian real estate company that commissioned the King George Tower, visited John Andrews in his office in Toronto, offering his contact should Andrews be in Sydney. Campbell's secretary was also one of Andrews's relatives. In 1968, during one of his trips to Australia in connection with the Cameron Offices project, Andrews had lunch with Campbell, and an invitation to design an office tower at Milsons Point on Sydney's North Shore soon followed. Andrews declined, as he was still busy working on the Cameron Offices. However, after Andrews's final move to Sydney, Campbell proposed another project, initiating the King George Tower.[1] It is an important building in the architect's oeuvre and the most prominent building he designed in his hometown of Sydney. Even after unsympathetic alterations, it is still one of the city's signature buildings. Moreover, the King George Tower is critical in Andrews's explorations of architectural responses to the climate exigencies that buildings face, and it is a key exemplar of his curious interest in three-cornered towers.

Precursors in Andrews's work to the King George Tower stretch as far back as to a project he undertook while working in the office of John B. Parkin Associates, the design of the Toronto International Airport control tower, which won the Massey Medal in 1964. This tower consisted of three separate piers of plank-stamped, cast-in-place concrete, which contained services and vertical circulation that held the control room aloft. A design for a triangular office tower has also been attributed to Andrews by Jennifer Taylor, also from his time at John B. Parkin Associates, though it is included in the John Andrews fonds rather than the John B. Parkin fonds at the Canadian Architectural Archives.[2]

Other tripartite tower projects by Andrews and examples of elements in his work that are clustered into threes are touched upon in later sections of this chapter.

At the King George Tower, the triangular plan form works well with its site configuration. The building sits on the northeast corner of the intersection of two of Sydney's principal commercial streets, King Street and George Street. The site is irregular in shape, which the first five levels of the building incorporate, including two basement parking levels. The tower itself is hoisted above these parking, lobby, and shopping levels, and in plan is fundamentally a right triangle, with the right angle located at the northeast. The tower consists of 32 levels and rises to a height of 127 meters. The lower pedestrian level is below grade, permitting a visually open plaza to be the end point for various underground pedestrian routes for which the King George Tower was intended to be an important node. [FIG. 1] The two sharp angles of the triangle are chamfered off. The plan form of the tower means that it pulls back from the street corner. On one hand, this allows the morning sun to reach the outer parts of the pedestrian area, and on the other, it also allows for sun to reach the main face of the building. A tower up against the street edges of the site would have meant that one of its main facades would face south, and if it were triangular in footprint, one of its main facades would also face northwest, the most problematic orientation in Sydney for afternoon solar heat gain. [FIG. 2]

The tower is supported by a grid of columns, but externally three vertical off-form concrete extrusions appear to visually anchor the building. These are its poetic structural components. Two of these elements contain fire stairways and vertical ducts. The third, located at the right angle of the triangle, is much larger than the other two and contains the elevator core of the building. Further, in another semicircular extrusion off the back of the elevator bank, it also contains bathrooms. Until alterations in the 1990s, the weighty mass of the extruding concrete corner elements contrasted with the glazed walls of the tower, which were visually characterized by a fine filigree of triangulated stainless steel tubes supporting polycarbonate

---

1   Jennifer Taylor and John Andrews, *John Andrews: Architecture, a Performing Art* (Melbourne: Oxford University Press, 1982), 114.

2   Taylor and Andrews, *John Andrews*, 24.

1

2

3

4

FIG. 1   Model, King George Tower, Sydney, Australia, 1970.
FIG. 2   Photocollage, King George Tower, 1970.
FIG. 3   Model, King George Tower, 1970.
FIG. 4   Design for the City Hall Building, Philadelphia, Pennsylvania. *Perspecta* 2, 1953. Architects: Louis I. Kahn and Anne Tyng.

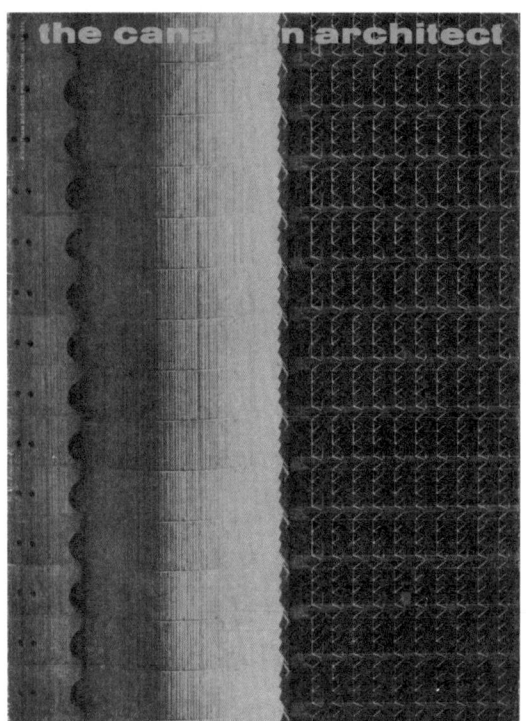

FIG. 5 King George Tower on the cover of *Canadian Architect*.

shading panels and maintenance walkways. Cleaning gantries were done away with. Behind this filigree, the glazing at the King George Tower was installed at the full heights of the office walls. The appearance of the building, then, was a composition of superscale elements—such as the concrete extrusions—and very fine elements. The stainless steel tubes produced a repeated, abstracting veil over the glazing and the exposed floor edges, so that the building had a peculiarly scaleless visual quality. Nevertheless, the floors of the building were inscribed in the breaks in the planking marks of the off-form concrete used on the corner elements.

The services engineer for the King George Tower was Don Thomas, who previously worked with Andrews on the Cameron Offices project. The use of a secondary frame and supporting shading elements as a strategy at the King George Tower to stop solar gain on glazed walls, particularly those exposed to sunlight in the north and the west, was notably different than the strategy used in the design of the Cameron Offices. At Cameron, the section of the office wings was organized into offset steps, as Andrews had favored since his design of the Malton Hotel for John B. Parkin Associates, with the effect of one floor shading another. The King George Tower, however, featured a pattern that introduced shade using lightweight secondary elements, which became an important precedent for later Andrews projects. In the King George Tower, then, we find Andrews's evolving response to environmental issues, and Thomas was to play an ongoing role in these developments. The design for the King George Tower was followed in 1973 by the design of the Callam Offices, which also featured triangulated stainless steel–tube shading structures. Further, the Callam design included solar water-heating and heat recovery from the air-conditioning system. Subsequent Andrews designs that Thomas worked on, such as the Intelsat headquarters and the Octagon office building, became increasingly technically sophisticated in their environmental systems, both active and passive (see chapters 10 and 12).

The shading elements used at the King George Tower departed not only from Andrews's previous practice but also the common pattern in Sydney in the 1960s of using heavy concrete hoods to shade windows. Nevertheless, the shading screens used in the design of the King George Tower were among the most expressive sunscreening devices used in Australian architecture up to that time. As Jennifer Taylor and Susan Stewart explained:

> So the story of the tall office building in Australia has been conditioned by the battle to deal with the sun and control the heat, and at the same time keep the modern appearance and the outlook. For this battle the Australian tall building donned various sun-screening guises, giving it a distinct appearance amongst the world's office towers. This concern eventually reached its most expressive statement in the space-frame grills of the American Express Tower, Sydney, of 1976, by John Andrews.[3]

Many of the design decisions at the King George Tower are the outcome of the architect's response to local conditions and circumstances, including the incidence of sun on facades and the ground plane to be sure, but also the particulars of the site topography, the contingencies of developments realized and planned on adjacent sites, and Sydney's regulation of development intensity. The scale of the King George Tower is determined by the mean setback from each street and is maximized by the introduction of the diagonally-oriented main facade.[4] The idea of a three-sided tower with expressed corner elements was also clearly important to Andrews across his career, first appearing in his earlier Toronto projects already touched on. However, in its response to the particularities of its site, the King George Tower is a much more nuanced work than the Toronto International Airport control tower or the Toronto triangular office project speculatively designed by Andrews.[5] It is also a more nuanced work than Viljo Revell's Peugeot Building designed in Buenos Aires in 1962, with its four massive corner piers (see chapter 1).[6]

The other major visual element used in the design of the King George Tower, the triangulated stainless steel–tube screens, provides a clue to one of the generators of the triangle tower scheme. [FIG. 3] One of the published drawings of Revell's design for the Peugeot Building shows its cladding resolved as triangular elements. But there is also another, more distant precursor to consider. In 1953, in the second issue of *Perspecta*, Louis Kahn published the article "Toward a Plan for Midtown Philadelphia." It included commentary on the triangulated structure proposal of City Tower, designed for Philadelphia City Hall by Louis Kahn with Anne Tyng. The design is documented over five pages, and though somewhat diagrammatic, it displays a building with a floor plan that consists of three conjoined hexagons. A triangulated truss is the primary structure, proposed to be constructed of precast concrete struts. Cylindrical shafts house vertical services, with horizontal services to be housed in the interstices of tetrahedral concrete-floor structures, which are akin to those in Kahn's design of the Yale University Art Gallery. The drawings of the design show it as clad with a secondary triangulated structure, but the text does not describe this element. The final page of the article includes two plans and an elevation study of an earlier design for City Tower, which also contains a trussed structure, though as part of an overall triangular plan that again features a fine-grain triangulated cladding element.[7] [FIG. 4]

3   Susan Stewart and Jennifer Taylor, "The Building and the Sun" in Jennifer Taylor, *Tall Buildings: Australian Business Going Up: 1945-1970* (Sydney: Craftsman House, 2001), 113.

4   "King George Tower, Sydney," *Canadian Architect* (July 1976): 29.

5   Taylor attributes this triangle tower for downtown Toronto to Andrews's period at John B. Parkin Associates. See Taylor and Andrews, *John Andrews*, 23–24. Drawings of it at the Canadian Architectural Archives at the University of Calgary are held in the John Andrews Architects fonds, which otherwise doesn't contain any work he completed at Parkin. These drawings do not include title blocks or dates, which is also the case for most of the John Andrews Architects design drawings.

6   Kÿosti Ålander, ed., *Viljo Revell: Works and Projects* (New York: Praeger, 1966), 114–17.

7   Louis I. Kahn, "Toward a Plan for Midtown Philadelphia," *Perspecta* 2 (1953): 10–27. For comments on the final version of City Tower, see *Louis Kahn to Anne Tyng: The Rome Letters 1953–1954*, ed. Anne Griswold Tyng (New York: Rizzoli, 1997), 54–59.

6

7

8

FIG. 6   Photocollage of preliminary tower scheme, Metro Centre, Toronto, Canada.
FIG. 7   Control Tower, Toronto International Airport, Toronto, 1964. Demolished 2004. Architect: John Andrews at John B. Parkin Associates.
FIG. 8   Preliminary tower scheme, Metro Centre.

Clearly there are differences between Kahn and Tyng's schemes and Andrews's design for the King George Tower. Andrews's tower was designed for a real site in the commercial center of the city, with the tight constraints and topographic contingencies of such a location, whereas City Tower was designed for an idealized, flat, and unencumbered site. On one hand, the Andrews tower is structurally more conventional than the plan for City Tower, but on the other, the muscular expression of the vertical corner shafts emphasizes the differences between the service and inhabited areas of the building externally, which itself is a somewhat Kahnian theme. The first of Kahn and Tyng's designs dissolves the form of the building entirely in the fuzz of its triangulated cladding, while later versions of the building, as a tower in schematic models, instead emphasize the radical primary structure.

Despite these differences, the things in common between the Sydney building and the Philadelphia projects are striking. It is perhaps unreasonable to see continuities between Andrews's tower completed in 1976 and a project that Andrews most likely saw in the mid-1950s as an undergraduate in Sydney perusing the pages of *Perspecta*, if he saw it at all. However, there is a history of Andrews designing triangle-plan towers that goes back to at least 1960, not so long after this possible undergraduate perusing. Furthermore, there are continuities in his work that can be traced to the scheme he completed for his thesis project at the University of Sydney, such as the big roof with three-dimensional structuring, that may itself have been influenced by Kahn's tetrahedral floor structures for the Yale University Art Gallery. Andrews recalled that he did know of Kahn's work before he left Sydney. Somewhere, it seems, Andrews must have seen Kahn's designs and apprehended his words. Journals could have been that place.

The influence of Kahn on the King George Tower seems much more likely than another, more synchronous possible source of influence, the Knights of Columbus building in New Haven, designed by Kevin Roche and John Dinkerloo between 1967 and 1969. At first glance, this building has a strong likeness to the King George Tower, which Andrews began the design for in 1970.

At 23 stories, the Knights of Columbus Building has a square plan with cylindrical shafts at its corners. But the similarities are limited. The Knights of Columbus Building contains stairs and bathrooms in the corner shafts, but the lifts are located in a concrete structure at the center of the square floorplates. The building's structure is a hybrid of steel beams supporting floorplates, spanning between the structural concrete of the corner shafts, which are faced with dark brown bricks. The wish for a symmetrical, homogeneous appearance for the Knights of Columbus Building drives the design. The brick gives the building a scaleless appearance, which, along with the corten steel spandrels and dark glass, tends to make it look like an abstracted brown monolith. The King George Tower by comparison is attuned to its site, with fine scale elements at the pedestrian level and semicircular openings in the concrete shafts that allow for outlook points from the service areas, signaling a human-scale design from the exterior despite its monumental overall appearance.

Images of the King George Tower were widely published in architecture press, as well as in specialized construction journals. The building appeared on the covers of *Architecture Australia* and *Canadian Architect* and in model on the cover of *Architecture+Urbanism*. [FIG. 5] It was also featured in a 1973 profile of Andrews in *Progressive Architecture* and in an Australian-themed issue of *Architectural Review* in 1978.[8] Two Australian construction journals, *NSW Builder* and *Construction Review*, published the building on their covers, and it was the subject of a lengthy technical study in *L'Industria Italiana del Cemento*.[9] The geographic spread of these

8 The *Architecture Australia* cover was in acknowledgement of the interview with Andrews in the issue: John Witzig and John Andrews, "AA Interview: John Andrews," *Architecture Australia* 64, no. 3 (June 1975): 58–67. The *Canadian Architect* cover was for an issue with several designs by Andrews: "Projects by John Andrews International," *Canadian Architect* (July 1976): 18–39. The *Architecture + Urbanism* issue was devoted to Andrews: *Architecture + Urbanism* (May 1974). See also *Architectural Review* (September 1978): 140–41.

9 "King George Tower, Sydney," *Construction Review* (August 1976): 11–19; "King George Tower," *Builder NSW* (February 1977): 4–15; F. Irace, "La King George Tower a Sydney," *L'Industria Italiana del Cemento* 6 (1980): 408–22.

publications—including Australia, Canada, the United Kingdom, the United States, Japan, and Italy—is an intimation of Andrews's international standing at the time of the King George Tower's conception and construction.

Through the prosaic style of many of the technical journals, we can detect a deep admiration for how the building was built. These journals in particular focus on the ingenuity of the construction of the concrete shafts, which dominate the external expression of the building. The decision to build the King George Tower with a concrete structure was a logistical one, with the structure of shafts, the 7.6-meter column grid, and the floors built entirely of in-situ concrete.[10] Externally, Andrews's design revels in the contrast of the concrete with the techy-looking screens. This contrast is heightened by the external formwork board marks on the concrete shafts. The shafts were formed by pouring the concrete into a gang form that was lined on the external side with rough, bandsaw-cut vertical boarding. The static forms were then stripped four days after the concrete pour and raised to the next floor level.

The internal formwork of the King George Tower shafts was steel, to produce a smooth finish. (In the event, internal concrete surfaces were rendered because of imperfections.) This also applied to the rationale of the interior surfaces at Scarborough College—board-marked in areas away from human contact and smooth where they could be touched. A rigid overhead platform with jacks was used to manage the internal formwork: the external formwork served as a support for the platform, and in turn, was fixed to the concrete below by soldiers bolted to the form ties. Afterward, reinforcements, the facing timber, and the internal form, supported by chains from the platform, were put in place and the concrete was poured. When the concrete was set, the platform was jacked up a level and the process repeated. This obviated the need to use the site crane for lifting formwork.

In comparison with the enthusiasm in construction journals, the statements about the King George Tower that appear in architecture journals are rather tentative, certainly in relation to the dramatic images of the building, under construction and completed, that illustrate them. The texts describe the main elements of the architecture, using Andrews's own words, or come close enough. Perhaps this critical reticence was a measure of the postmodern critical doubt creeping into architectural culture at that time; in the interview with Andrews in the issue of *Architecture Australia*, which featured the King George Tower under construction on its cover, his interlocutor commented: "Charles Jencks has drawn a distinction between 'architecture for architects' and 'architecture for people,' and yet sees no reason why the demands of both shouldn't be satisfied." When asked if he agrees, Andrews responded in regard to Jencks, "Who's he?"

Previously in the interview, however, commenting on the King George Tower, he explained that making decent environments for people to work in is a matter of the architect's conscience and previous education. Somewhat poetically, Andrews later discussed the verandas on a farmhouse he was renovating: "And you can go beyond the verandas and shade the veranda with the pergola which is another classic thing… with wisteria or grapes or some damn thing where the leaves fall so it's not shaded in the winter.… The Hooker building [King George Tower] is just like leaves on a tree, but it's an evergreen tree."[11] [FIG. 9] Jencks might not have been known to Andrews, but Andrews was nevertheless able to occasionally break into Jencksian-sounding metaphor.

The tree metaphor was one that Andrews returned to when describing the King George Tower in his 1982 book coauthored with Jennifer Taylor, *John Andrews: Architecture, a Performing Art*. In it Andrews first described the shading system of the building in pragmatic terms. He explained that it provides a sense of security for areas of the building interior that are adjacent to the full-height glazing, and the gangways that integrated with the sunshades provide access for window cleaners. Further, the stainless steel tube and polycarbonate panels were very light for the site construction crane to lift into position,

---

10   Taylor and Andrews, *John Andrews*, 119.

11   Witzig and Andrews, "AA Interview: John Andrews," 67.

especially compared to the heavy concrete brise soleil often used on Sydney buildings at that time. What follows is another rare moment of poetry: "It is more like a tree with leaves—it does not eliminate all of the sun. The corners of the polycarbonate and the stainless steel do not merge completely so you get little shafts of sunlight through. That gives a fantastic sort of pattern inside." However, he then immediately returned to the pragmatic: "Australia has more sun than some places, but I do not see this as a regional solution. The air-conditioning costs are less than half the normal amount because heat is not building up in the office spaces."[12]

There is a single exception to the descriptive tone of the architectural critiques of the King George Tower. A short, anonymous piece in *The Architectural Review*, no more than 250 words long, begins with a startling declaration: "This is arguably the most imaginative speculative office building in the world. You may not think it beautiful, but it is very clever."[13]

ANDREWS'S HIGH-RISE TYPES

In 1976 Andrews was interviewed by *Canadian Architect*. When first asked about how the economic situation was affecting Australian architects, he replied:

> Two months ago, you would have got a marvellous story on a firm of three partners and twenty people building the biggest building that the country has ever produced. That's the Belconnen offices in Canberra, which are nearly finished. We were about to embark on another one similar to that, not similar in design, but of a similar size [the Callam Offices]. We had five university projects in Brisbane, one in Melbourne, and a redevelopment in the centre of Sydney which is also nearly finished [King George Tower].
> But all of a sudden, by a government budgetary decision in the face of

FIG. 9 King George Tower. Office interior with glazing shaded by sun screens.

12 Taylor and Andrews, *John Andrews*, 122.
13 "King George Tower, Sydney," *Architectural Review* (September 1978): 140.

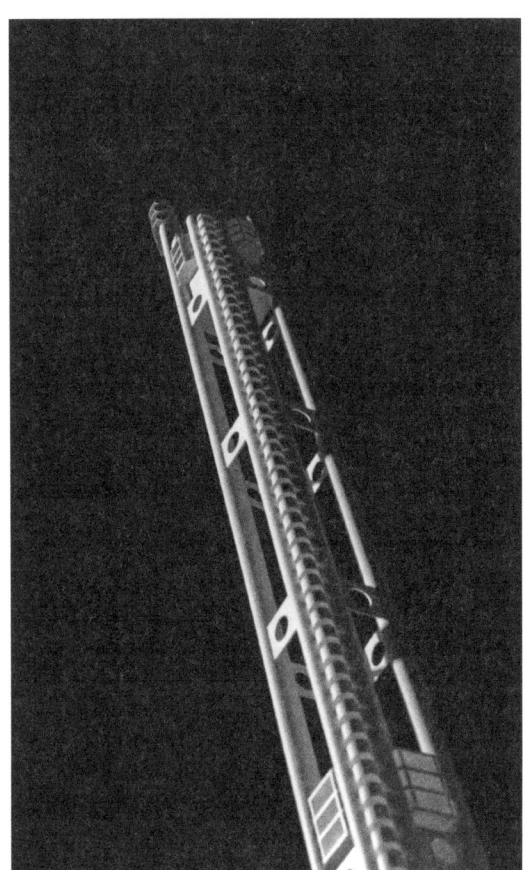

FIG. 10   Model, Telecommunications Tower, Singapore Telecom, Singapore.

inflation, all of this work disappeared and today you'll find that something in excess of eighty percent of the architects in Australia are unemployed. A lot of them are driving cabs, a lot of them working on construction sites. Just today, I had a meeting with my lawyer who told me the biggest architectural firm in Australia let fifty per cent of its staff go last week. And I think that's symptomatic of all the architectural firms.[14]

Until the 1980s, the King George Tower was unique in Andrews's work for being the only major commercial project realized in his offices. Virtually everything else he took on in his early years back in Sydney was an institutional or government project. His office had done work on another office project on Roma Street in Brisbane for LJ Hooker, but this did not proceed to construction (see chapter 10). However, in the mid-1970s, Australia suffered an economic recession, and when things recovered in the 1980s, both the center-left and center-right parties that dominated Australian politics adopted variants of neoliberal policies that constrained spending on public projects. In the 1980s, the John Andrews International firm sought private commercial work, instead of publicly funded work. This was not entirely to Andrews's taste. But nevertheless, the firm developed strategies for carrying out commercial high-rises, which, in contrast to the design of King George Tower, veered toward the generic.

In general, tall buildings designed by John Andrews fall into two main groups. The first clear type are towers based on a triangle plan, with extruded concrete forms at each corner. These provide the building with a strong external expression as a thing of mass, in contrast to the typical office tower, which is resolved visually, usually as a system of surfaces that serve as expressions of enclosure. The most significant realized example of the triangle type is the King George Tower in Sydney. As previously

14   "Notes from Down Under: An Informal Discussion with John Andrews," *Canadian Architect* (June 1976): 38.

mentioned, its precursors included the Toronto International Airport control tower designed by Andrews while working in the office of John B. Parkin, and the design for a triangular office tower that may or may not have been designed by Andrews at Parkin. An outlier to this approach is the bundle of three large, attenuated concrete columns that Andrews proposed in one design for the CN Tower in Toronto, which is quite different from the final design featuring tapered concrete buttresses. The bundle scheme was Andrews's preferred approach to this gigantic building. [FIGS. 6, 8] A last such tower design that Andrews completed was for a telecommunications tower for Singapore Telecom, which was done circa 1990 in a limited competition and did not proceed to a commission. The final version of this design features four tubes, but the initial sketch designs show that its origins began with the three-tube bundle. [FIG. 10]

This group of designs is driven by the structural and expressive potential of the concrete tube as a dominant form, defining the overall visual profile of the building. These tubes are related to the cylindrical circulation volumes that Andrews used, for example, at the Sydney Convention Centre and the Intelsat Headquarters building, both completed in 1988. But in these buildings, the tubes are external subsidiary forms composed into complex assemblages of building volumes and shapes. Along with the glazing and the triangulated steel tube screens that Andrews deployed on several of his buildings—and notably so at the King George Tower—the tubes, when used as primary structural and visual elements, recall Kahn's architecture. The expressive quality of these vertical concrete structures grouped in threes veers toward monumentality.

A second group of high-rises by Andrews have a different and more modest architectural logic. They show that in his commercial work, mostly completed the 1980s, Andrews was working to find a language that was less heroic than his designs for the institutional buildings that were a mainstay of his design work of the 1960s and 1970s and less heroic than the King George Tower. This generic approach was appropriate for the lesser status of these buildings that represented a new commercial vernacular of hotels and speculative office buildings. These were buildings that might incidentally become notable because of a unique topographic position within their urban settings but were, based on their programmatic character, relatively anonymous. They also did not warrant ongoing architectural invention once the programmatic problem was solved. The buildings designed by John Andrews in this group include the Merlin Hotel in Perth; the Hyatt Regency Hotel in Adelaide; the Adelaide Station and Environs Redevelopment (ASER) project offices; and the Octagon in Parramatta (confusingly, the Octagon actually refers to a cluster of octagonal plan office modules). Together, these designs seem to be driven not so much by the expressive potential of structural and environmental systems as by a desire to realize the social space—the work unit or the temporary habitation of a hotel room—as an irreducible programmatic element. The social space is a fundamental part of the plan and extrudes upwards as much as needed, with chamfered corners and stepbacks that externally express the scale of the inhabited internal unit. [FIGS. 11–13] Further, in the office buildings that Andrews designed, these units are invariably octagons.

The two last such designs in this group are Andrews's design for the World Bank (1990) and office buildings of the enormous Park Place project in Los Angeles in the late 1980s.[15] The World Bank design was created for a competition won by Kohn Pedersen Fox, and although Andrews was the winner in a limited competition to design Park Place, the project was also never built.[16] [FIGS. 14–15] It seems as if Andrews's

15 The architects competing in the World Bank competition were John Andrews International; Arthur Erickson Architects (Canada) with HTB/DMJM (United States); Cannon Corp (United States) with Moriyama & Teshima Architects (Canada) and Dissing+Weitling (Denmark); Edward Larabee Barnes/John M.Y. Lee and Partners (United States); Hellmuth, Obata+Kassabaum (United States) with Kajima Corporation (Japan); Kohn Pedersen Fox Associates with KressCox Associates (United States) and Naegle, Hofmann & Tiedemann (Federal Republic of Germany); Norconsult with Platou Architects and Lund & Slaatto Architects (Norway); and Skidmore Owings & Merrill with Nihon Sekkei (Japan) and Charles Correa (India) as design consultant. Alan Drattell, "The New Main Complex: 'An Exciting, Memorable Place,'" *The Bank's World*, 9, no.5 (May 1990): 7–8.

16 "Kohn Pedersen Fox Wins World Bank," *Progressive Architecture*, (July 1990): 23–24.

designs for these projects and for those that were actually built, such as the Octagon, are all fragments of the extensive, repeated "mat" plans of Andrews's office designs for the Callam Offices or Intelsat Headquarters, fragments that are then developed vertically and tightened horizontally. Their exterior treatments tend toward the generic rather than the monumental and include a sense of anonymity appropriate for the ubiquitous, utilitarian quality of the contemporary office building.

There are also occasional variations on and departures from these two outlined tower species. First, there is Andrews's design for a modular apartment building sponsored by the Canadian steel company Stelco in 1965.[17] This is akin to some projects by the Japanese Metabolists, notably Kisho Kurokawa's Nagakin Capsule Tower of 1970.[18] The connection between the two projects is likely due to the presence in Andrews's office at this time of architect Kiyoyuki Nishihara, who moved from Tokyo—where he studied under Kenzo Tange—to Toronto in 1963. (Nishihara later returned to Japan and worked on the 1974 special issue of *A+U* on Andrews.)[19] The building Andrews designed for Stelco is a tower with a central structural and services core, with a steel frame hanging off it (see chapter 3). Habitable units complete with built-in plumbing and furniture are hoisted and plugged into the frame according to demand, and the units are based on the construction of standard Canadian railcars. Andrews argued that in essence the building was not a tower design, insofar as the primary element is the capsule, and these could be assembled in many kinds of configurations.

A second important variant, of the extruded hotel, is perhaps a fully independent high-rise type in the Andrews oeuvre. It entails a building with an overall semicircular plan form. Such a form was realized in Andrews's Crowne Plaza Hotel (formerly Eden on the Yarra Hotel) for the Melbourne World Congress Centre in 1990 (see figures 4–7 in chapter 13). Here, the 10 stories of hotel rooms are designed so those on the outer perimeter of the semicircle are splayed to maximize views of the Yarra River, with the room units clearly articulated in the external expression of the building. A monumental, cylindrical circulation core of cast in-situ concrete is at the center of the curved outer surface of the building, and a colonnade of concrete columns suspends the hotel floors above the vehicle areas and services at ground level. Through its bold projection toward the river, the building announces itself as a significant departure from the urban grid. This is a case where a privileged site in the city warranted the turning of a modest type of building—the anonymous commercial hotel—into a landmark. The parti of this building was repeated in the hotel component of Andrews's Darling Harbour casino designs, carried out in 1986 and 1991, and in Park Place. In these designs, we see Andrews recycling the ideas tried out at the Melbourne World Congress Centre, where the semicircular hotel was similarly part of an urban ensemble of various building forms. The Darling Harbour Casino in Sydney, like the Park Place complex in Los Angeles, was not built. Andrews did not regret this as neither were very compelling projects for him.

There is also one other significant tower variant among Andrews's projects. This includes the schematic design prepared in the early 1970s for the Roma Street Railway Station site in Brisbane, commissioned by LJ Hooker, which displays a cluster of repeated tower forms, each with floors cantilevered from a structural core. Like the towers for Andrews's much larger Toronto Metro Centre design, these cores worked to reduce the ground-level footprint of the building to a minimum in order to accommodate railway tracks. They are also akin to the central core used in the design of the Stelco building. The design for Roma Street is perhaps also related to a design by John Andrews Architects in Toronto for the urban intensification

---

17 Antony Moulis, "Searching for Open Form: The Pinwheel Plan in the Work of John Andrews," *Proceedings of the Society of Architectural Historians, Australia and New Zealand: 30, Open*, no. 2, eds. Alexandra Brown and Andrew Leach (2013): 651–60.
18 Philip Drew connects Andrews's design approach at Scarborough College to Kurokawa's concept of "fibre form" and the South Residences at Guelph University to Kurokawa's "porous space." See Philip Drew, *Third Generation: The Changing Meaning of Architecture* (New York: Praeger Publishers, 1972), 145.
19 My thanks to Professor Thomas Daniell of Kyoto University for this information.

of Yorkdale Shopping Centre, beginning in the late 1960s, which entailed a series of repeated, mid-rise office buildings built along one edge of the suburban Toronto complex (see figure 12 in chapter 8).

THE OCTAGON OFFICES AND RELATED PROJECTS

The Octagon in Parramatta, New South Wales, a secondary business district in Greater Western Sydney is paradigmatic of the second major type of Andrews high-rise. [FIG. 12] Here, the plan is formulated by clustering octagonal elements, each of which houses a group of office workers that make up a social unit. The design strategy is generic since the approach involves a commercial vernacular, which, though it can be attuned to local circumstances, can be replicated from site to site as office work is largely similar from place to place. It is also a strategy that eschews an overall monumental form that would not be appropriate in the case of most office buildings.

The Octagon consists of eight octagonal-plan office towers, built to five or six stories, that are arrayed in two groups of four, with an atrium at the center of each group. [FIGS. 16–17] Between the two groups is a generously landscaped courtyard. Two of the octagonal towers are connected by a 20-meter-wide wing along the side of the courtyard, allowing a maximum tenancy area per floor of 3,300 square meters. Completed in 1990, the Octagon is the culmination of a line of inquiry in the Andrews office that began with the Callam Offices project in 1973. That design envisioned 24 octagonal units at three stories high with an entry signaled by symmetrically situated 10-story octagonal towers. In its array of widely dispersed pods, the Callam Offices project was also an important precursor to the Intelsat Headquarters in Washington, DC (1988). However, the Callam Offices had other progeny: Andrews's series of tower buildings conceived as tight clusters of extruded octagonal volumes. These include not only the Octagon but also the ASER offices in Adelaide, the office buildings for Park Place, and the design for the World Bank competition, all undertaken in the

11

12

FIG. 11 Adelaide Station and Environs Redevelopment (ASER), Adelaide, Australia.
FIG. 12 The Octagon, Parramatta, Sydney, Australia, 1990.

aftermath of the success of his design for the Intelsat Headquarters.[20] These closely related designs all date from the late 1980s, though the Callam Offices proposal was designed more than a decade earlier. These projects are also conceptually linked to two hotels that Andrews worked on at the same time, the Merlin Hotel in Perth and the Hyatt Regency in Adelaide, insofar as the external expression of these buildings derived substantially from the extrusion of the articulated hotel rooms.

This pattern of expressing inhabited volumes on the building exterior stretches back to Andrews's work for the treatment of the student dorm rooms in his design for the University of Guelph South Residences. This pattern can also be found in other student accommodations that the Andrews office carried out, including Toad Hall at the Australian National University and the University of Canberra Student Residences (designed for the university's predecessor, the Canberra College of Advanced Education (CCAE)). In these schemes however, the horizontal extension of the buildings dominates how they appear, and the buildings are massed like landscapes. And, indeed at CCAE the repetition of the units is formulated in relation to the hillside on which the building sits.

By contrast, in Andrews's hotels and office buildings of the 1980s, the stacking of the inhabited units and the vertiginous atria they contain give the buildings a sense of verticality even when their overall dimensions are wider than they are tall.

Unlike the King George Tower, in these octagonal-plan office projects structure is generally not expressed overtly on the building exterior. At the Octagon, structural articulation is absent since the structure is discreetly positioned within the octagon plan, though the projected office towers for Park Place included externally expressed braced frames. But even these elements, though they would likely have been visually powerful, are depicted in drawings of this scheme as subsidiary to the building's external volumetric expression. Thus, they are unlike the concrete corner towers at the King George Tower, which register as more powerful than the walls that enclose the habitable parts of the building. These octagonal schemes do feature circulation elements, expressed as lift and stair cores in the atria between the octagons or as stairways in concrete and glass-block cylinders. The expression of these circulation devices, however, is for the most part crisp and not particularly aggressive. While the King George Tower is monumental and assertive, the Octagon is polished but somewhat reticent; it does not visually privilege one aspect of the building over another.

Another element of this reticence is that the Octagon has a modest presence in its urban setting. Of Andrews's octagonal-plan buildings, only the ASER offices in Adelaide stands out in its context through its relative scale. This building is a 12-story block made up of four octagonal towers that contain an atrium in between them and a lift core at their center, which is connected to the office areas by radiating walkways. Completed in 1988, it is a relatively anonymous building, though with the adjacent 22-story Hyatt Regency and the Adelaide Convention Centre, both designed by Andrews, it was the subject of some controversy as a "tall and dense development and with commercial use where only public and institutional existed before."[21]

In relation to ASER, the size of the Octagon is rather self-effacing. At the time of the Octagon's construction in Parramatta, the buildings immediately adjacent to it on George Street were taller and bulkier. Though the Octagon yielded large floor areas per level in comparison with its neighbors, its highly articulated volumes and design elements were relatively intimate in scale. Since the Octagon was built, Parramatta's business district has grown dramatically in intensity and building height, underscoring this attribute of the building. While the geometrical forms of the Octagon do not lend themselves to aligning with an urbane street edge—a big ask in 1980s Parramatta—the inclusion of a courtyard in the design created a pleasantly scaled public

---

20 David Saunders, "The Best Address in Adelaide," *The Adelaide Review*, October 1984, 3.

21 Noni Boyd, "A.L. and G. McCredie," in *The Encyclopedia of Australian Architecture*, eds. Philip Goad and Julie Willis (Melbourne: Cambridge University Press, 2012), 438–39.

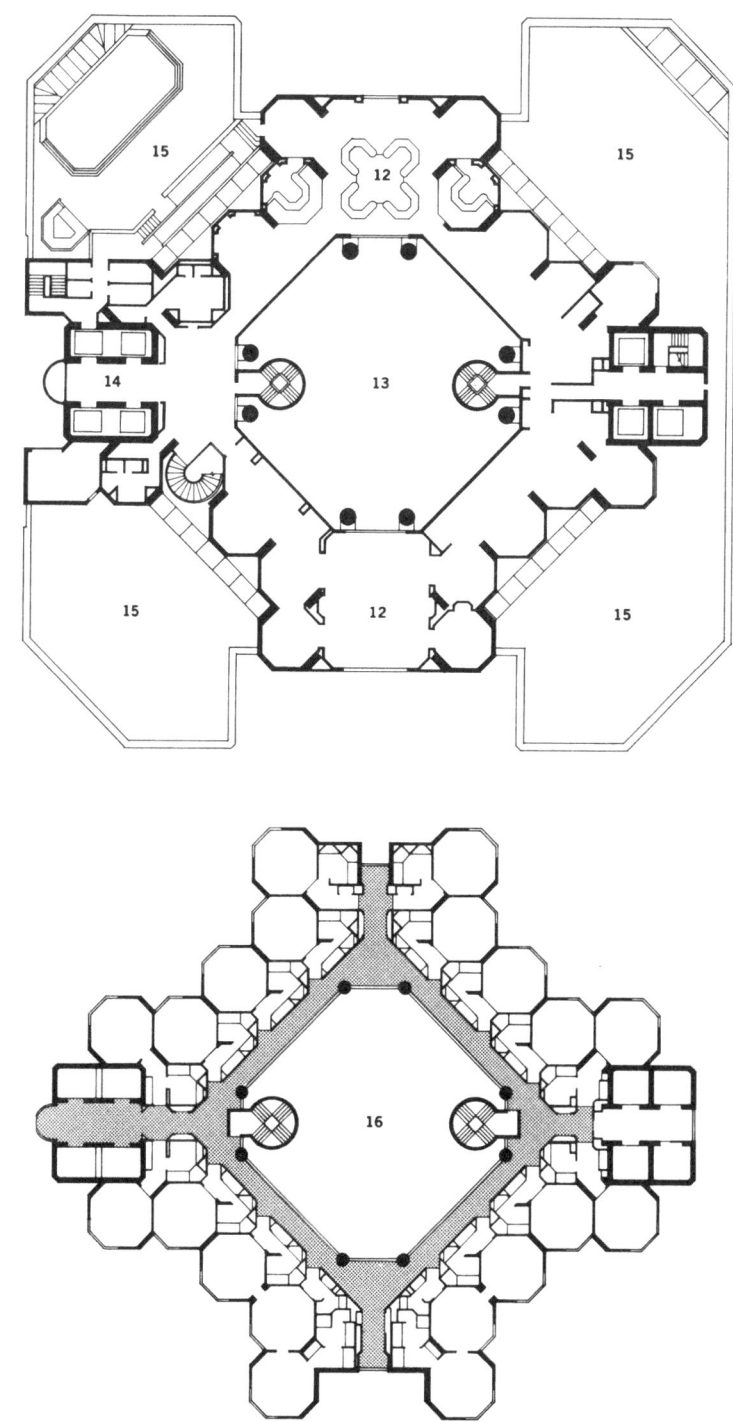

FIG. 13　Hyatt Regency Hotel, Adelaide, Australia.

14

15

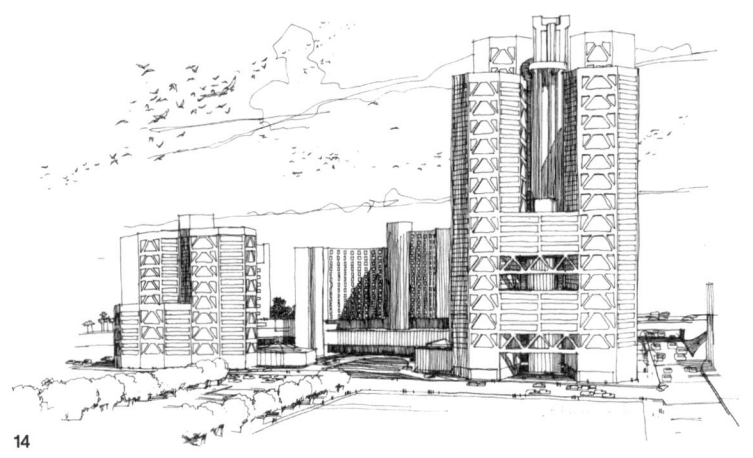

FIGS. 14–15 Park Place, Los Angeles, CA, ca. 1988.

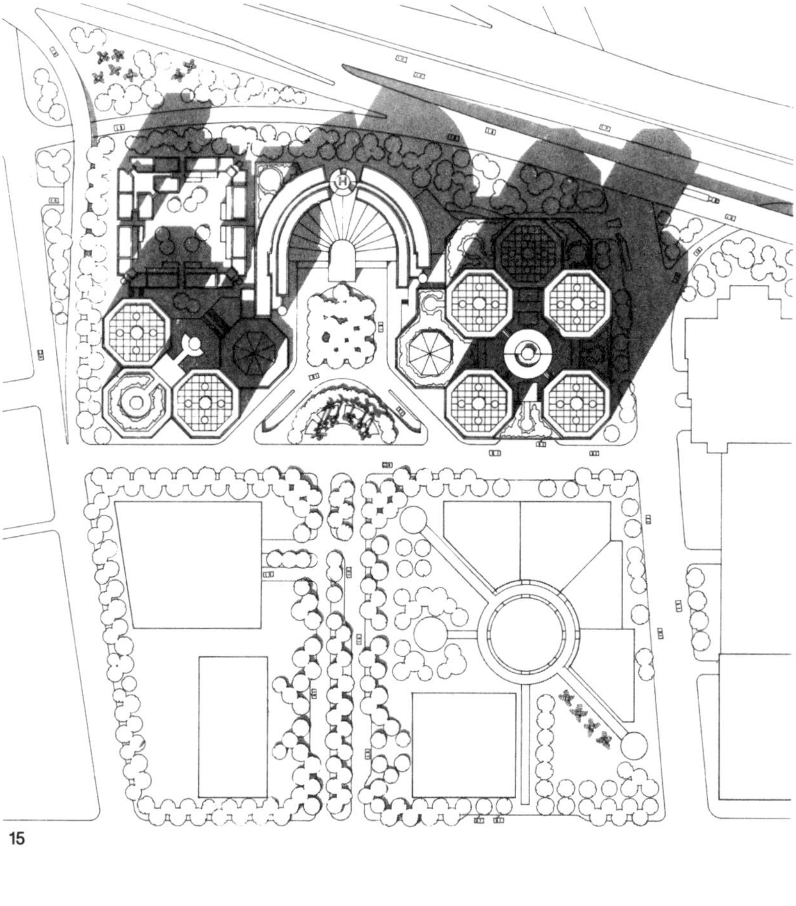

space in the interior of the site. This sense of situational modesty is also apparent in the design for the Park Place complex, though its site on the periphery of downtown Los Angeles was very different in scale and visual drama from that of Parramatta. Consequently, the design of the Park Place complex adheres to this visual drama.

The Park Place complex was initially envisioned to include towers of up to 36 stories, and its octagonal floor plans were over 30 meters wide; the Octagon, by comparison, is six stories high with octagonal floor plans that are 20 meters across. However, the Park Place towers were intended to be scaled to provide a transition between the low-rise neighborhood to the south of the site and the tall skyscrapers at the center of downtown Los Angeles. Andrews's design for the World Bank also responded to its context in central Washington. The scheme included 12 octagonal-plan towers at around 12 stories, and on their exterior, the octagons were fused (in the same way two of the towers of the Octagon are fused by the connecting wing on the east side of the complex), giving the whole building an institutional, horizontal expression, attuned to the Washington environment. On the interior, the World Bank design nevertheless maintained the use of vertical atria between its towers.

The disaggregation of the plans for buildings like the Octagon into equal volumes distributed around atria and courtyards expands the perimeter office areas and provides external exposure, as Andrews's design of the octagonal pods and atria did at the Intelsat Headquarters. Also, like Intelsat, the atria at the Octagon are part of the project's passive-energy design, which was developed with the assistance of Don Thomas. Evaporatively cooled air passes into the atria, reducing the difference in heat between the interior air-conditioned spaces and the outdoor ambient environment. During the summer, the Octagon is cooled in part from ice thermal energy stores that are chilled overnight using off-peak electricity. Further, the Octagon, like the Intelsat Headquarters and the Callam Offices, has external glazing shielded by transparent screens that are suspended externally with a filigree of stainless steel tubes. Also used in the design of the King George building, this became a signature element in the second half of Andrews's architecture career.

2 BOND STREET

The King George Tower and the Octagon exemplify two opposite impulses in Andrews's high-rise buildings: one is a monumental icon for a prominent corner site in Sydney's busiest pedestrian location, and the other is a refined design for a generic office building in a generic context. However, neither is an obvious precursor to the last major high-rise that Andrews designed. 2 Bond Street was commissioned, as the Octagon was, by the developer Bill McNamara in the late 1980s. Like the King George Tower, its site was at a key location in central Sydney. 2 Bond Street is important to consider in detail as it demonstrates a spirited response by Andrews to the postmodernism that was becoming endemic in the design of tall office towers at the time. Further, it is also a rare case of Andrews having to deal with heritage buildings on a tight urban site.

The site of the 2 Bond Street building is in a neighborhood containing 19th-century mercantile buildings fronting on George Street, Sydney's main retail and commercial strip. Immediately to the north of the site, on Bridge Street, is the very accomplished American Romanesque building, the Burns Philp Building (1901), designed by architects Arthur and George McCredie.[22] Immediately to the south of the site is Australia Square (1967), which is the earliest of architect Harry Seidler's suite of central Sydney freestanding high-rises, including a 50-story circular office tower in a plaza, and forming its eastern boundary, a low-rise building elevated on canted columns.[23]

Unlike Seidler's designs at Australia Square, Andrews did not have the option of completely clearing his site, which featured

22 Neville Quarry, "Australia Square, Sydney," in Jennifer Taylor, *Tall Buildings: Australian Business Going Up: 1945–1970* (Sydney: Craftsman House, 2001), 250–59.
23 "Former 'George Patterson House' Including Interiors," Heritage Places and Items, New South Wales Office of Environment and Heritage, https://www.environment.nsw.gov.au/heritageapp/ViewHeritageItemDetails.aspx?ID=2423866.

16

17

another important heritage building designed by the McCredie brothers, the seven-story Holdsworth Macpherson Building (1895), and the Metropolitan Hotel, a listed pub built in the first decade of the 20th century.[24] Stylistically, the Holdsworth Macpherson Building is late 19th-century commercial eclectic, and it was once the headquarters for the *Bulletin*, the venerable Australian literary and news magazine. It is also a long building, with a narrow tower at the center of its long north face. The 20-year interval between the commissioning of Australia Square and that of 2 Bond Street saw Sydney's burgeoning interest in its heritage. As a result, there was an imperative at 2 Bond Street to retain the two historically significant buildings on the site. Despite the developer having obtained permission for the demolition of the Holdsworth Macpherson Building, Andrews argued for its retention, gaining him development bonuses along the way.

Andrews's design response was brave. As Taylor noted, "Andrews broke from the modular, geometric approach of his earlier work and splintered the composition...."[25] While the upper half of 2 Bond Street looks like a conventional, late-modern downtown high-rise, at the ground level, aside from its cylindrical core, the building pulls itself up with immense triangulated structures. At the south end of the tower, the diagonal piers holding the tower respond in scale to the similar elements supporting the eastern building at Australia Square. However, on the opposite side of the complex, the office tower is suspended 15 stories up. This allows the George Street side of the Holdsworth Macpherson Building to be sheltered beneath the hovering north half of 2 Bond Street. Further, a giant pier holds the end of the office tower up, developing into a triangulated structure at its upper levels that appears as a kind of gigantic skeletal capital receiving the load of the building above. [FIG. 18]

In Andrews's design of 2 Bond Street, the new building has been massively eroded at its

24   Jennifer Taylor, *Australian Architecture Since 1960*, 2nd ed. (Canberra: RAIA National Education Division, 1990), 226.
25   Ada Louise Huxtable, *The Tall Building Artistically Reconsidered: The Search for a Skyscraper Style* (New York: Pantheon Books, 1984), 94.

FIGS. 16–17   The Octagon, Parramatta, 1990.

lower levels to make way for the old. All the effort that went into making the complex sculpted crowns and spires of so many 1980s commercial buildings, in central business districts all over the world, was instead directed in this building to designing that triangulated capital. It is a crest or a spire oriented upside down. One of postmodernism's favorite devices—the iconic building crown—is inverted. As Ada Louise Huxtable wrote in 1984, "the newest skyscrapers… are considered incomplete without party hats, regal crowns, or ambitious 'fioritura.'"[26] Another postmodern device, the capital, is deconstructed and massively inflated in 2 Bond Street's design.[27]

Most of the Holdsworth Macpherson Building was retained and rehabilitated for retail, restaurants, offices, and apartments. The Metropolitan Hotel was fully conserved. Between these two heritage structures, a low-rise retail building was planned. And below street level, the complex was intended to link to Australia Square in the south and Westpac Plaza on the other side of George Street through underground pedestrian connections. Access to 2 Bond Street was through a circular core, away from the site's heritage fabric, that was exposed on the west side to about two-thirds of the height of the tower. The 38-story tower became more abstract the higher it got, with the upper part appearing similar to the prismatic, crystalline office blocks of a generation earlier.

Several versions of the 2 Bond Street tower were designed, with different treatments of its external fabric. For example, the initial version, in 1988, differentiates the skin of tower on the north from that of the south, so the tower appears as two conjoined buildings. In a version of the design from October 1988, the western elevation fragments the tower at the southern end into three pieces, and the top-most fragment is merged with the portion of the tower suspended above the Holdsworth Macpherson Building. In a 1989 version, this elevational composition is simplified, doing away with the canted columns at the south.[28] However, in each of these versions, the building does not offer much of a long-distance urban view, and its top is blank or generic. Rather than being concerned with its place in the urban panorama, the 2 Bond Street design is always concerned with the street view at ground level and accommodating the fine grain of the remnant 19th-century mercantile neighborhood into which it is assertively but carefully situated. In each version, the new building is also more intricate at street level than at the upper levels of the tower.

If at first glance 2 Bond Street looks entirely unprecedented, it should be understood not only as a bravura response to a unique set of urban circumstances, but also in relation to other lines of development in the architect's oeuvre. In the reticence of the tower's upper parts, the building is akin to Andrews's octagonal-plan buildings. Its cylindrical core, assertively expressed at the lower levels, is genealogically connected to the King George Tower, and it similarly displays a sense of confidence that a big building on a key urban site can afford to be exciting.

In her book, *The Tall Building Artistically Reconsidered*, Huxtable wrote of American skyscrapers that were truly innovative:

> When an unconventional appearance grows out of a painstaking and creative analysis of the uses and synthesis of the sources being explored, usually done experimentally and as a part of systematic and developing search for new solutions, a kind of work is produced that continues to stimulate reactions to the theories proposed and the way in which they are carried out. This stimulation, which can be troubling or pleasing with equal legitimacy, draws one into a deeper understanding of how appearance relates to all of the factors of reference and utility of which a building's

26 See Paul Walker, "No. 2 Bond Street," in *Augmented Australia: Regenerating Lost Architecture 1914–2014*, Australian Pavilion, 14th International Architecture Exhibition, La Biennale di Venezia, ed. Philip Goad (Canberra: Australian Institute of Architects, 2014), 70–73.

27 Jennifer Taylor's, *Australian Architecture Since 1960* illustrates two versions of 2 Bond Street, with the second dated 1989. The project book from the John Andrews International office, dated October 1988, illustrates a third version.

28 Huxtable, *The Tall Building Artistically Reconsidered*, 72–73.

FIG. 18   2 Bond Street, Sydney, Australia, 1988.

vocabulary is constructed. Such integration is not easy; it is the only conclusive test of an architectural vision and the only real route to style.[29]

While Andrews rejected the term "style," these words come close to describing the excitement and innovation found in his 2 Bond Street design. The building's design demonstrated a relational attitude to the existing urban fabric, a trait that Andrews had no other opportunities to exercise. In integrating new and old architectural forms and using the new to frame and enhance the existing urban fabric, it stepped past the relational understanding of site expressed in his design for the King George Tower.

2 Bond Street should also be seen as in dialogue with the buildings designed by Harry Seidler nearby. As already noted, the diagonal columns located on the south end of the building in most versions of Andrews's design for 2 Bond Street answer to the similar columns of the mid-rise block on Pitt Street at Australia Square. Further, the lofty urban volume established by 2 Bond Street's enormous pier, with the northern end of the tower suspended above, seems mindful of Seidler's design for the Capita Centre located to the east of the 2 Bond Street site, on Castlereagh Street. Seidler's interest in structural bravura is driven by a compositional logic confined to each site—each of his big projects in the Sydney central business district is an attempt at a *hortus conclusus* in the city's chaotic urban jungle. However, the monumental design of Andrews's largest towers achieves wider urban ends. This is certainly so in the opportunities that his approach to building towers sets up for complex, cross-site circulation systems, partly achieved at the King George Tower and proposed at 2 Bond Street. Andrews's design for 2 Bond Street is also an inversion of the visual language of the postmodern office building, but this inversion is performed not to reassert tabula rasa modernism. At Bond Street, it is as if the huge investment in making a commercial tower and hoisting its structure high enough to register in the urban skyline is used in order to find unanticipated opportunities at ground level. This includes not only opportunities for human movement and habitation but also for an engagement with the city's past. This form of engagement is modern in being neither nostalgic nor morbid.

The plan for 2 Bond Street did not go ahead. At a talk he gave at the University of New South Wales in May 1988, Andrews said of Bill McNamara, his client for 2 Bond Street, "He is certainly in my mind probably the last great client because we go to a meeting, he goes and I go, we talk to each other, I haven't got to talk to his managing director or his lieutenant or some smart arse who is trying to work his way up a ladder. I actually talk to the guy who has the money and has the site and wants to make a building."[29] This turned out not to be quite so. The Japanese financiers funding the project appear to have been frightened by the design's bravura. Having gone through several iterations of the design, Andrews felt this blow acutely. He did not enjoy the world of speculative commercial development and saw little reason to continue engaging with it. It might be surmised that Andrews's work did not suit the postmodern times, but, though he expressed disdain for the postmodernism that by the mid-1980s was commercial orthodoxy in architecture, 2 Bond Street demonstrated that he was able to address one of postmodernism's ostensible drivers—response to context—without adopting its stylistic mannerisms. And he could do so while having a considerable amount of fun. Andrews's departure from developer-driven commercial architecture was brought about not by changes in the culture of architectural design, but by changes in the commercial context in which property development took place.

---

29   John Andrews, "Fair Dinkum Architecture," typescript (lecture, University of New South Wales, May 31, 1988).

intelsat:
a kind of
culmination

by   Paul Walker

The Intelsat Headquarters design has an important place in Andrews's oeuvre. John Andrews International completed several significant projects after Intelsat (1988), including facilities for the University of Sydney School of Veterinary Sciences (1998), and after the office closed, Andrews independently completed the Age of Fishes Museum at Canowindra, New South Wales (2001). There are also interesting unbuilt projects that are contemporaneous with Intelsat, such as a schematic design from 1982 for another intergovernmental satellite organization, Arabsat, to have been built in Riyadh; an office and hotel complex for Los Angeles called Park Place; and an office tower for Bond Street in the Sydney central business district (see chapter 11).[1] But like the Sydney Convention Centre, also completed in 1988, the Intelsat Headquarters was the last of Andrews's projects to be widely published. It was also the last project Andrews completed outside Australia and his only realized North American project fully designed from the Sydney office.

THE INTELSAT COMPETITION

The Intelsat Headquarters building sits among tall oak trees on a sloping site on Connecticut Avenue, one of Washington, DC's main thoroughfares, in the northern reaches of the city proper, about five kilometers northwest of the White House and downtown. [FIGS. 1–3] It is part of a group of government and official buildings known as the International Center, which also includes an enclave of embassies and chanceries to its west. Intelsat was an intergovernmental agency that promoted international collaboration by expanding global satellite communications networks, ensuring the participation of both developing and economically advanced nations, predominantly Western or Non-Aligned. The agency was responsible for establishing international protocols and policy, as well as managing the launch and deployment of communications satellites and coordinating the construction of an international network of earth stations in member countries. Intelsat, therefore, was simultaneously a major bureaucracy and a technological enterprise that required both a lot of office space and accommodations for other, exciting things, such as a "spacecraft control center" with an adjacent public viewing area as well as simulation and testing facilities. Intelsat was also an international agency whose headquarters involved the full architectural paraphernalia of international diplomacy: a vast boardroom for representatives from its member nations, along with facilities for simultaneous translation; lavish offices for the organization's director and governors; and reception spaces for hosting glittering social occasions.

Intelsat's ability to command a highly significant site owned by the US government in a diplomatic neighborhood is a measure of the prestige it enjoyed in the 1970s and 1980s.[2] However, in the face of growing competition from private providers of satellite communications services—exacerbated by changes in relevant US policy and legislation—Intelsat was privatized in 2001. In 2014, it moved its operations to an anonymous office block in Tysons Corner, Virginia.[3] Its former headquarters became occupied by other tenants including embassies and the University of the District of Columbia, and it is now the premises of the Whittle School.[4]

The John Andrews International design was selected through an international competition. Given Intelsat's intergovernmental nature, the competition was open to architects from all member countries, with the Royal Australian Institute of Architects (RAIA) suggesting potential architects from Australia. From these recommendations, the American architect

---

1   Paul Walker, "No. 2 Bond Street," in *Augmented Australia: Regenerating Lost Architecture, 1914–2014*, Australian Pavilion, 14th International Architecture Exhibition, La Biennale di Venezia, ed. Philip Goad (Canberra: Australian Institute of Architects, 2014), 70–73.

2   On the site ownership, see Wolf Von Eckardt, "Pods and Pools," *Washington Post*, April 19, 1980.

3   Steven Overly, "Intelsat moves into new Tysons office, part of a wave of tenants wooed by Silver Line," *Washington Post*, July 27, 2014.

4   See "Our Home in Washington, DC," Whittle School & Studios, https://www.whittleschool.org/en/architecture/dc. The school website notes that the building is being renovated by Renzo Piano Building Workshop.

Paul Spreiregen—an Intelsat advisor—and two architects nominated by the International Union of Architects (UIA), the Australian Ronald Gilling and the Frenchman Pierre Devinoy, drafted a long list. Intelsat's director general Santiago Astrain then determined the short list of architects who would be invited to submit designs in a competitive process in 1979.[5] The six participating firms were Arthur Erickson Architects (Canada); Raila and Reima Pietilä (rendered Pietilae in the Intelsat documents) (Finland); Hentrich, Petschnigg und Partner (West Germany); Holabird and Root (United States); Hellmuth, Obata + Kassabaum (United States); and John Andrews International (Australia). Their design submissions were assessed in Washington in January 1980 by a panel of assessors, chaired by Intelsat's then-deputy director Andrew Caruso, which included senior Intelsat executives and three architects: Michael Austin-Smith from the United Kingdom, Marco Zanuso from Italy, and Pietro Belluschi, originally from Italy but practicing in the United States since the early 1920s.

Belluschi was selected to serve on the Intelsat design competition assessment panel because he had a long and distinguished career, including serving as dean of architecture and planning at the Massachusetts Institute of Technology from 1952 to 1965 and as a juror on many design panels. Most significantly, Belluschi was also a key advisor for the Foreign Buildings Operation of the United States Department of State, which guided the US embassy building program of the 1950s and 1960s toward a ceremonious and somewhat monumental modernism.[6] Coincidentally, Belluschi had played a role in Andrews's decision to go to the United States to complete a master's degree. When Belluschi visited Australia in 1956 as a speaker at the RAIA National Convention in Adelaide that year, he met with Andrews's graduating bachelor of architecture class at the University of Sydney,

FIG. 1 Main entrance from Van Ness Avenue, Intelsat Headquarters, Washington, DC, 1980–1988.

5   Paul D. Spreiregen, "The Anatomy of a Design Competition: Intelsat Headquarters in Washington, DC," *Architecture Australia* 77, no. 1 (January 1988): 44–49.

6   Timothy M. Rohan, *The Architecture of Paul Rudolph* (New Haven, CT: Yale University Press, 2014), 33–34.

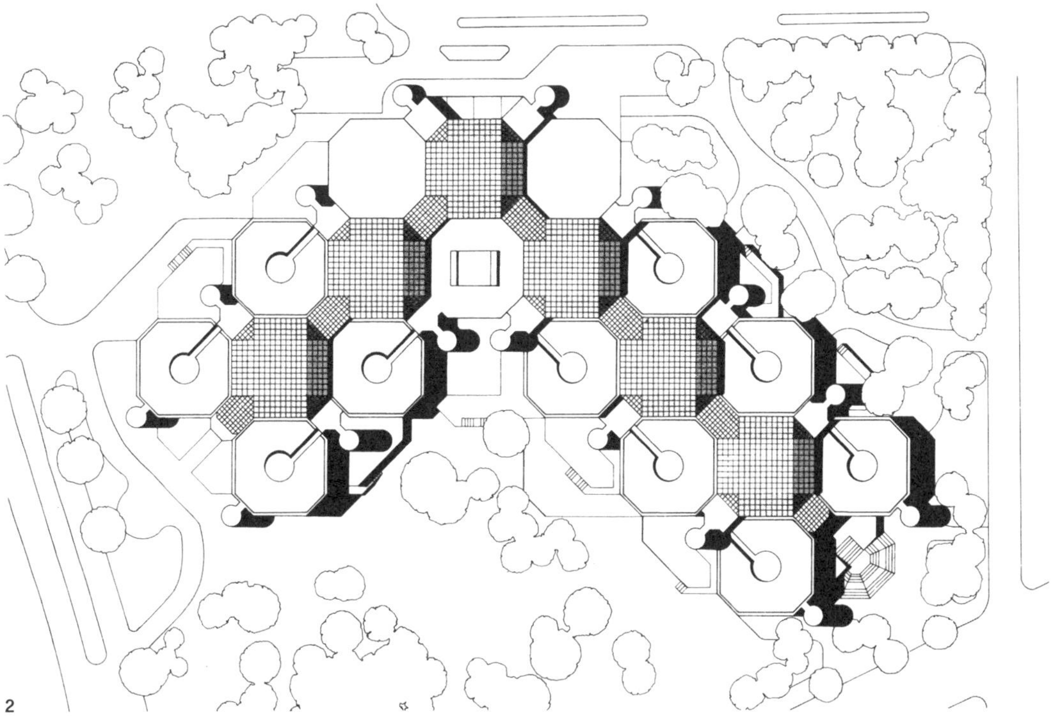

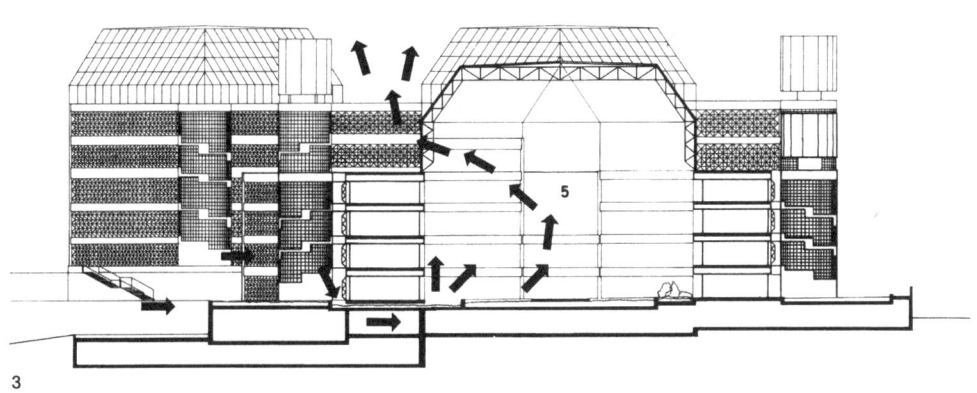

FIG. 2   Plan, Intelsat Headquarters.
FIG. 3   Section showing air movement through atrium, Intelsat Headquarters.

FIG. 4 Glazed roofs above office pods, Intelsat Headquarters.

FIG. 5

FIG. 6

and Andrews consulted him on his future plans. Austin-Smith and Zanuso were not as senior in the profession as Belluschi, but both were well-regarded architects and had held important institutional appointments. Austin-Smith had served as president of the Architectural Association and vice president of the Royal Institute of British Architects (RIBA) and Zanuso had served as director of the Milan Architecture and Design Triennale. Both had also designed buildings or fit-outs for "high-tech" clients, with Austin-Smith completing a project for IBM and Zanuso completing projects for IBM and Olivetti.[7]

The assessment panel provided a lengthy report on the Andrews design in relation to three sets of requirements, including "Design Considerations," "Accommodation of INTELSAT's Use Requirements," and "Implementation and Costs." A note on the report indicates that the comments on "Design Considerations" were prepared by the "Architect-Assessors" alone, though presumably the other elements of the report reflected not only their views but also those of the Intelsat executives on the jury for expertise in legal, procurement, and engineering matters. There were six design considerations: "Distinction, excellence and quality of architectural design"; "Fulfillment of the space program requirements in a functional, appropriate and imaginative design"; "Satisfaction of the image requirements and goals of Intelsat"; "Satisfaction of the urban design requirements of Washington, DC"; "Sensitivity to the environment and energy efficient"; and "Practicality of the facility, both in terms of a reasonable cost of construction as well as long term maintenance and operating costs." The expectations that the Intelsat design had to meet were thus wide-ranging, from qualitative criteria, indicated by words such as "distinction," "excellence," and "image," to technical issues, alluded to in terms like "energy efficient," "practicality," and "operating costs." Across these criteria, architecture's relation to science was at stake. Science mattered both

FIG. 5 Intelsat Headquarters, vertical circulation node in atrium.
FIG. 6 Intelsat Headquarters, external circulation cylinder.

7   "Who We Are," Austin-Smith:Lord, https://www.austin-smithlord.com/about-us/.

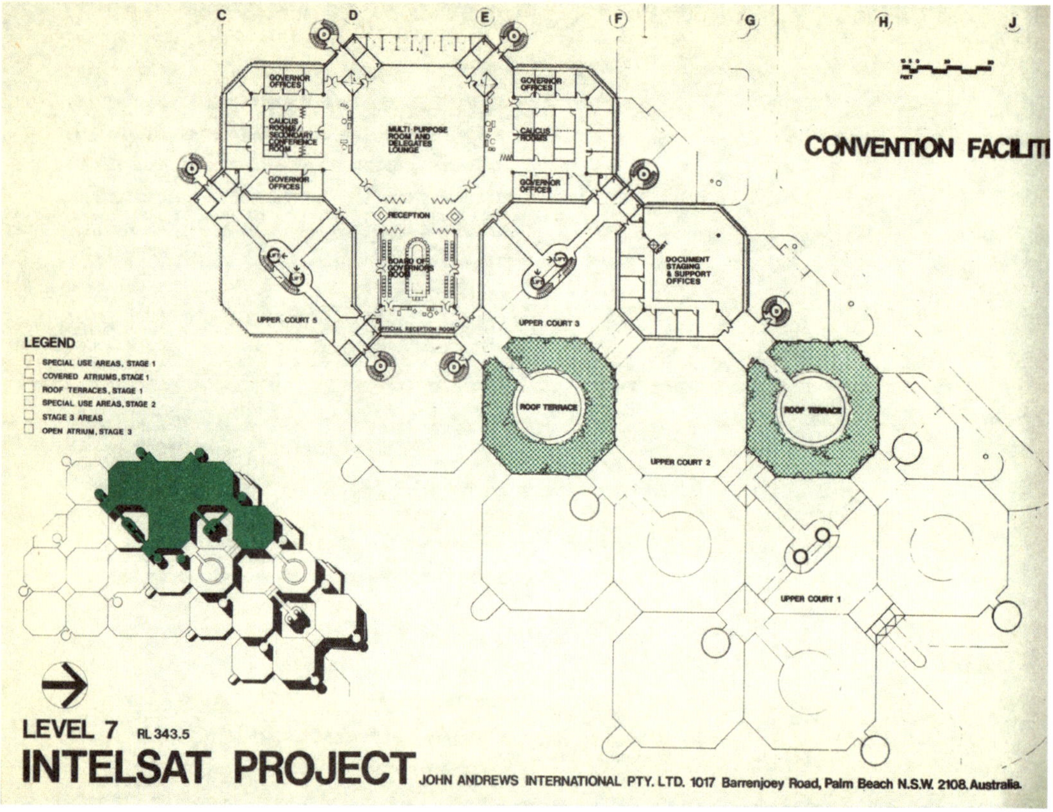

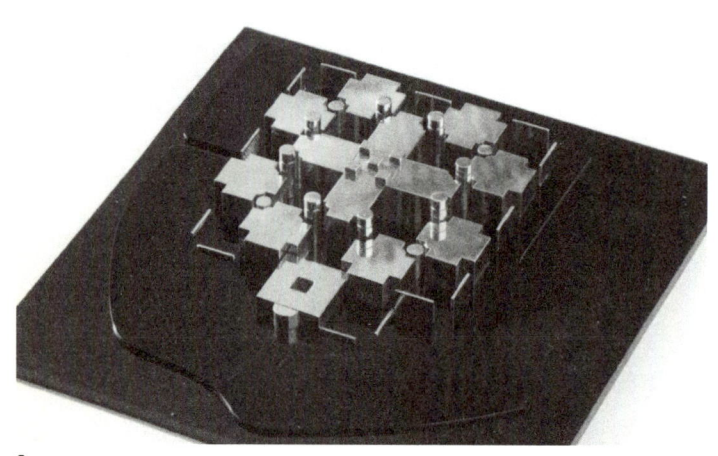

FIG. 7   Plan, stage 1, Intelsat Headquarters.
FIG. 8   Schematic design, Arabsat, Riyadh, Saudi Arabia, 1982.

qualitatively and technologically, imaginatively, and functionally.

The Andrews project was resolved as a series of octagonal office "pods," each based on an 85-foot square with chamfered corners and varying from four to six stories tall. Between the pods are courtyards with pools and, in most cases, extensive planting designed by Andrews's friend and frequent collaborator, Canadian landscape architect Richard Strong, which are enclosed by glazed roofs that "pop-up" between the office pods to create atria. [FIGS. 4–5] Strong also designed roof gardens for most of the office pods. The glazed courtyards are traversed at the upper levels by open walkways, and some feature vertical circulation cores at their centers. Circular towers of concrete and mirrored glass blocks on the exterior of the building between the office pods house staircases. [FIG. 6] On the west end of the complex, a ceremonious entrance to the building, the lower levels of two pods, and what would otherwise be a courtyard between them are subsumed into a sequence of public and quasi-public spaces, the courtyard being realized only at upper levels in the form of a conservatory-like space called "the moon garden." Parking is accommodated in the building's basement.

The modular design approach facilitated the staging of Intelsat's construction, with the first stage of nine office pods, three courtyards, and public entrances at the west and northeast completed in 1986. [FIG. 7] The second stage of four pods and two courtyards was completed two years later. A third stage was also envisaged, which would have added more office pods at the southern end of the site. Various configurations for this stage were explored but it did not proceed to construction.

INTELSAT'S DESIGN LOGIC

The design of the Intelsat building is connected to a number of other projects from the Andrews office, notably the 1973 design for the Callam Offices in the Canberra suburb of Woden. Of the 24 office pods specified in that design, three were built in 1978 to house the Woden Technical and Further Education College (TAFE). [FIGS. 9 & 11] The office's interest in realizing building designs as distributed systems of building nodes dispersed across spatial fields—with interstices realized as courtyards between them—can also be seen in the speculative design by John Andrews International from 1975 for the central city of Monarto, a new town projected for South Australia. In 1977, the office also produced a diagrammatic sketch of a plan for a new National Museum of Australia in Canberra, in which a plan concept for the museum is realized as a tessellated pattern of exhibition pavilions with diagonally distributed courtyards between them. (Reflecting the recommendations of the Australian federal government's Committee of Inquiry on Museums and National Collections, convened from 1974 to 1975, the pavilions problematically housed "Aboriginal" Australia at one end and "European" Australia at the other, with spaces for the natural environment linking the two.)[8] A schematic design for Arabsat of 1982, with a program much like Intelsat's, also belongs to this group. [FIG. 8]

This group of projects can also be linked more abstractly to the low-rise, distributed pattern of the Cameron Offices and to the clustering of octagonal plans that appear in several mid-rise towers for hotels and offices designed by John Andrews International in the 1980s. The diagonally distributed plan had also been used in the work of Andrews's Toronto office, in the circulation system and overall organization of building volumes for the South Residences at the University of Guelph and in the building slabs proposed for the unbuilt Metro Centre project, which briefly reappeared (and were quickly discarded) in early investigations for the Cameron Offices. The diagonal dispersal of classrooms in the Bellmere Junior Public School also works with the same planning logic, but at a much smaller scale.

---

8   Ann-Marie Condé, "'The Orphans of Government': The Committee of Inquiry on Museums and National Collections (the Pigott Report), 1974–75," in Des Griffin and Leon Paroissien, eds., *Understanding Museums: Australian Museums and Museology* (Canberra: National Museum of Australia, 2011), published online at nma.gov.au/research/understanding-museums/AMConde_2011.html/.

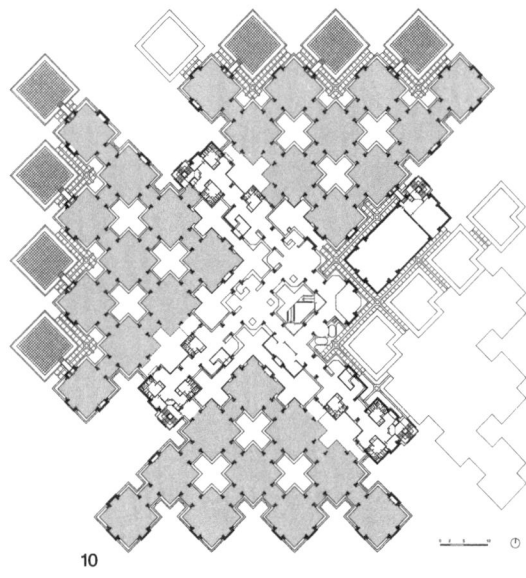

FIG. 9 Photocollage, proposal, the Callam Offices, Canberra, Australia, 1973.
FIG. 10 Plan, Centraal Beheer, Apeldoorn, Netherlands. Architect: Herman Hertzberger.

Andrews's interest in horizontally distributed buildings, beginning at least with the Cameron Offices, is linked to the wider interest in "mat-plan" buildings in the 1960s and 1970s. In this, Andrews's work does link to that of Team 10, but more specifically to the work of Aldo van Eyck and his student Herman Hertzberger. Timothy Hyde has identified Hertzberger's Centraal Beheer office building in Apeldoorn (1972) as a key mat-building exemplar.[9] [FIG. 10] The Andrews projects of the 1970s and 1980s—Callam Offices, Woden TAFE, and Intelsat, specifically—have a close kinship with the tight clustering of diagonally distributed spaces found in Hertzberger's work, especially the Centraal Beheer and the Ministry of Social Welfare and Employment in The Hague (1990). Indeed, the recent description by Kenneth Frampton of the design rationale entailed in these two projects by Hertzberger could equally apply to projects by Andrews, including the Cameron Offices, Woden TAFE, and Intelsat Headquarters. As Frampton writes:

> an interstitial cellular workplace, interwoven with structure, services and circulation—and capable, through the manipulation of furniture, of constituting a varied pattern of decentralized work areas. This pattern, interspersed with relaxation corners equipped with coffee machines and so forth, was Hertzberger's "counter-panoptic" principle. While it furthered the idea of creative teamwork it was seemingly antithetical to bureaucratic efficiency, and in this regard, designed in 1968 in the spirit [of] the European student revolt, it was inherently sympathetic to the anarchic spirit of *les évènements du mai* which took place in Paris that year under the hedonistic slogan "*Sur le pave, la plage*."[10]

While Andrews was probably little effected by the events in Paris of May 1968, whatever his motivations were, his design philosophy for workplaces and the buildings that housed them was entirely in line with that of Hertzberger. Centraal Beheer was completed in 1972, the year before the Andrews office began the Woden scheme, and although it is possible that there was some influence, Andrews, as previously noted, was already working with diagonally arranged circulation systems, linking projects of considerable horizontal extent. Instead, Hertzberger and Andrews's convergence in design direction predates the coincidence of Centraal Beheer's completion and the start of the Callam Offices. In her 1982 book written with the architect, *John Andrews: Architecture, A Performing Art*, Jennifer Taylor connects Andrews with Hertzberger and with his mentor Aldo van Eyck:

> Perhaps more than those from any other designer today, his buildings show the development and the realization of the planning theories that emerged following the dissolution of CIAM after the Otterlo Congress of 1959. Scarborough College, completed in 1965, was immediately recognized as the first built major statement of the concept of an open-ended lineal structure, organizing and relating functional units. The Bellmere Primary School of 1965 followed the centralizing yet expandable cellular matrix seen in Aldo van Eyck's Children's Home, Amsterdam, and Louis Kahn's Trenton Bath House. Future projects, with few exceptions, adapt one or other of these organizational patterns, with communication through circulation as the uniting theme.
>
> Where possible the buildings are kept low and spread within a controlling geometrical structure to allow for diversity without disintegration. Particularly clear examples of this can be seen in the diagonal grid pattern of the Woden Offices Project and the lineal arrangement of the Cameron Offices.

---

9 Timothy Hyde, "How to Construct an Architectural Genealogy: Mat-Building… Mat-Buildings… Matted-Buildings," in Hashim Sarkis, ed., *CASE: Le Corbusier's Venice Hospital and the Mat Building Revival* (Munich: Prestel, 2001), 107.

10 Kenneth Frampton, foreword to *Herman Hertzberger*, by Robert McCarter (Rotterdam: nai010 publishers, 2015), 6.

Andrews's architecture is strongly conditioned by an intuitive response to human need, and his interpretation of suitable spaces and relationships to further personal and social well-being. In this respect his most challenging problems have arisen in attempting to provide identity for individuals in large-scale single-purpose schemes, such as the student residences for Guelph University and the offices for the Australian Government at Belconnen. Contact with Aldo van Eyck and Herman Hertzberger is reflected in his attitude to design. The influence of their ideas of place and occasion, and of the universality of the fundamental human problems of design is evident in his words and his buildings.[11]

In 1975, in answering a question about his philosophy in architecture, Andrews said, "I really don't know a great deal about [what] is going on in all the current movements. I know something about the things I want to know about, the van Eycks or the Hertzbergers or people who are saying or have said things that appeal to me. I'm just not too interested in things like… that bloke in Philadelphia with the eyebrows…."[12]

Taylor also identified a conceptual connection from Andrews to Hertzberger and van Eyck in her essay on Andrews written on the occasion of his RAIA Gold Medal award in 1980: "Words… rather than buildings, make the strongest impressions on his thinking, and he acknowledges this debt to the sensitive writings of Kahn, Hertzberger and van Eyck."[13]

While there is no direct evidence that Andrews himself read the writings of these figures, he had opportunities to meet both Hertzberger and van Eyck. He and van Eyck were both speakers at a June 1966 event at the Cranbrook Academy in Bloomfield Hills, Michigan, the 11th Annual American Institute of Architects–Association of Collegiate Schools of Architecture Teacher's Seminar (referred to in chapter 10). Andrews was invited because of the great impact of his recently completed Scarborough College, and van Eyck was invited presumably because of the considerable notoriety of his attacks on the modern movement. The reporting on the event that appeared in the *Journal of Architectural Education* the following year noted that the "Evening with Aldo van Eyck" at the seminar was a five-hour marathon.[14] The text of this Cranbrook talk is not extant in van Eyck's publications, but his contributions to a discussion between the speakers at the seminar touched on themes that appeared in his writings of the time.[15]

Andrews most likely met Hertzberger in Toronto after he had engaged Peter Prangnell to teach at the University of Toronto School of Architecture in 1967. Prangnell was an

---

11 Jennifer Taylor and John Andrews, *John Andrews: Architecture, a Performing Art* (Melbourne: Oxford University Press, 1982), 18–19.
12 John Witzig and John Andrews, "AA Interview: John Andrews," *Architecture Australia* 64, no. 3 (June 1975): 61. The "bloke with the eyebrows" was presumably Robert Venturi.
13 Jennifer Taylor, "John Andrews, Architect," *Architecture Australia* 70, no. 2 (May 1981): 30. See also Paul Walker, "John Andrews's RAIA Gold Medal: Green and Gold + Grey and White," *Proceedings of the Society of Architectural Historians, Australia and New Zealand: 33, Gold*, eds. AnnMarie Brennan and Philip Goad (2016): 696.
14 Gordon Heck, "1966: Architects Restructure Problems," *Journal of Architectural Education* 21, no. 4 (July 1967): 3.
15 See "The Interior of Time," *Forum* (July 1967). Republished in Aldo van Eyck, *Collected Articles and Other Writings, 1947–1998*, Vincent Ligtelijn and Francis Strauven, eds. (Amsterdam: Sum Publishers, 2008) 474–75.
16 Peter Prangnell, *Arch. Ed.* (Toronto: the author, 2009), vii. See also George Baird, *Writings on Architecture and the City* (London: Artifice Books, 2015), 51n2, where Baird notes that he, Hertzberger, and Prangnell were critics for a studio on the design of a "summer place" that led to Baird's article "The Dining Position: A Question of Langue and Parole," first published in 1976 in *Dutch Forum*, a journal then edited by Hertzberger. The "summer place" studio was one of Prangnell's introductions when he revised the University of Toronto architecture curriculum under Andrews as chair of architecture. A possible source of Hertzberger's influence on the Andrews Toronto office late in its life—but not on Andrews himself—is through Ken Greenberg. Greenberg was an architecture student at Columbia University in 1968 when Hertzberger was a guest professor there. Hertzberger subsequently invited Greenberg to go to the Netherlands to work in his office, which he did. In October 1968 Greenberg relocated to Toronto, where he enrolled in the School of Architecture and landed a part-time job in Andrews's office. Ken Greenberg, *Walking Home: The Life and Lessons of a City Builder* (Toronto: Random House Canada, 2011), 53–55.

enthusiast for both van Eyck and Hertzberger, and his self-published account of his teaching records that both van Eyck and Hertzberger were among the visitors he brought to Toronto as part of his transformation of the design education programs there.[16] Hertzberger's visits to Toronto would have coincided with the start of the design for the Centraal Beheer building. They would also have coincided with Andrews's start on his design for the Cameron Offices.

ENVIRONMENTAL DRIVERS

The Intelsat Headquarters is also conceptually important in Andrews's work as its design entailed the final point of development for a career-long line of inquiry into the environmental performance of buildings. Since his design, which placed second, for the Toronto City Hall design competition of 1958, Andrews had been interested in using building form to address climate issues. This interest developed further in the period from 1958 to 1969 when he lived in Toronto and confronted the challenge of designing for its cold winter climate, both while he was employed in the office of John B. Parkin Associates until 1961, and then in his own office. He had also investigated designs for the extreme climate of the Canadian Arctic in his teaching in the architecture program at the University of Toronto.[17]

Andrews's interest in the environmental implications of building form became more technical through his collaborations with the Sydney-based mechanical engineer Don Thomas, with whom he first worked on the Cameron Offices project in 1968. This concern sharpened with the energy crisis from 1972 to 1973 and with the general environmental ethos that emerged across that decade. Thomas also consulted on the Callam Offices and on the Monarto city center, both important forebears of the environmental systems approach developed in the Intelsat design. He continued his association with Andrews working on the Octagon office project. As suggested in

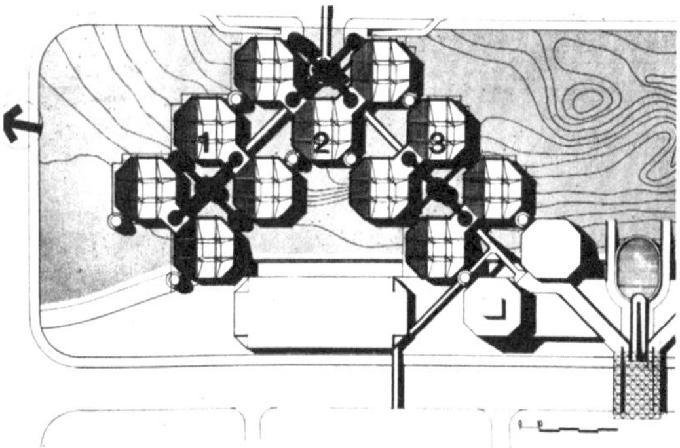

FIG. 11   Part-plan, the Callam Offices, 1973.

17   "Architect Looks North for Man's Next Home," *Globe and Mail*, July 23, 1963.

12

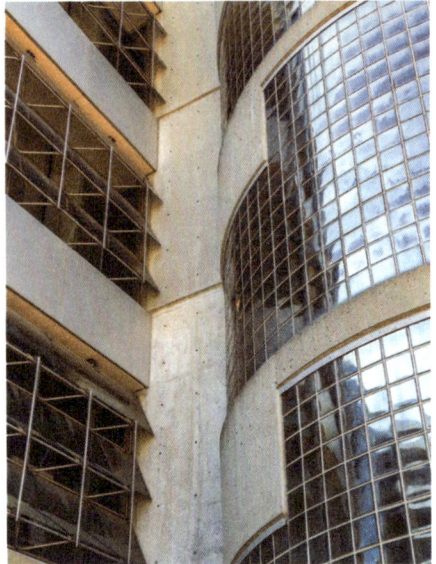

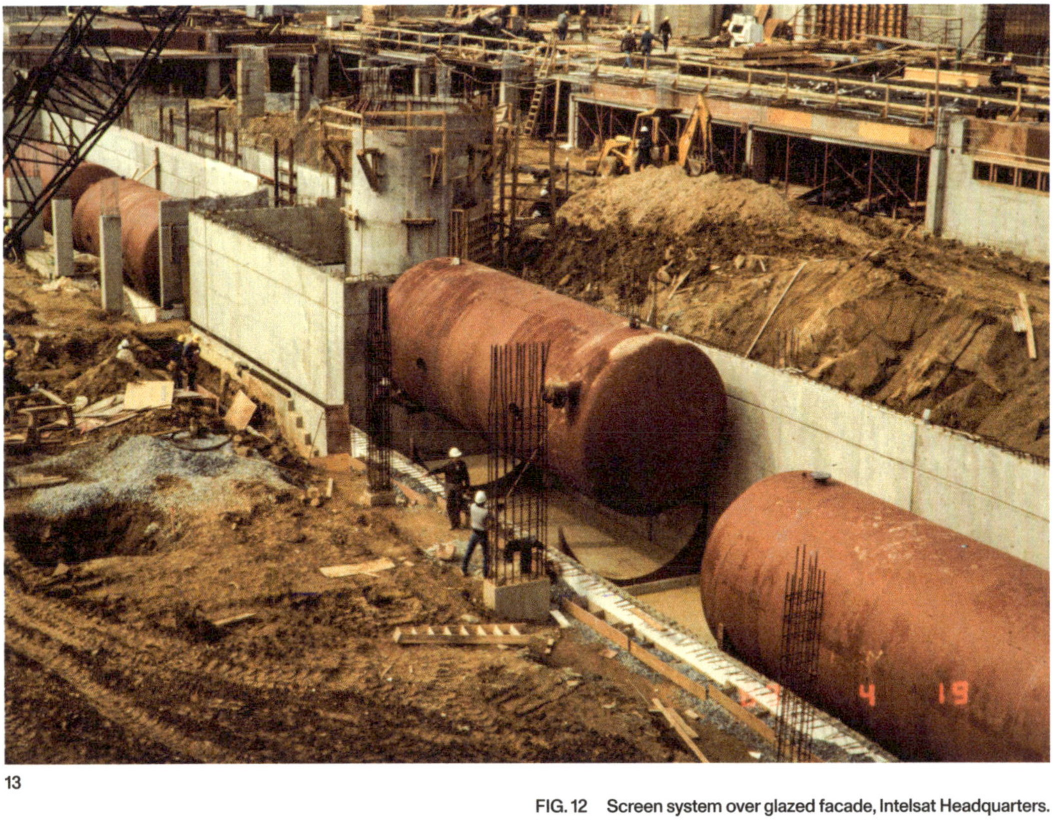

13

FIG. 12 Screen system over glazed facade, Intelsat Headquarters.

FIG. 13 Heat recovery system being installed, Intelsat Headquarters.

chapters 10 and 11, through these projects Andrews's approach to environmental performance became increasingly sophisticated and technological rather than architectonic.

Commissioned in 1973, the Callam Offices were anticipated to accommodate some 6,000 Australian federal government civil servants. The Callam Offices pods were each based on a 30-meter square with chamfered corners, virtually of the same scale and geometry as Intelsat's corresponding pods, and similarly dispersed across a regular grid and connected by circulation towers and walkways. [FIG. 11] The major difference between them is that at Intelsat, the spaces between the office pavilions are roofed with glazed space-frames, creating a necklace of atria through the building, while at Callam, the spaces between pods are open and connected by elevated walkways suspended above the floodplain on which the complex was sited. Moreover, each of the Callam pods hangs structurally from four centrally grouped columns, while the Intelsat pods have conventional steel frames.

As we have seen, the plan approach adopted by Andrews at both Intelsat and Callam lent itself to incremental expansion. This, however, also permits subtraction. As a government office project, the Callam Offices was canceled in 1975 and subsequently realized only in part—three pods total—as Woden TAFE.[18]

The Intelsat Headquarters design can be considered to be directly derived from the Callam plan. Andrews regularly explored architectural ideas across multiple projects, but in this case the translation from one project to the other is very straightforward, possibly indicating a certain frustration that Callam was extremely compromised in its realization at a much-diminished scale. Yet, the plan pursued a line of architectural investigation that was too good to discard so easily. It possibly also suggests that Andrews was not willing to invest too much in preliminary design work for a competition, so recycling an already-developed idea was a good compromise.

Despite the reduced scale of Woden TAFE, Thomas honed his environmental approach there. As Taylor writes, "Three modified modules of the Woden scheme, for use as a technical college (with expected future additions for other uses), were constructed in 1979. In this scheme, heat is recovered from the refrigeration plant, laboratory discharges, and general space use, for storage in large water tanks adequate to accommodate all winter loading fluctuations. The tanks will also store heat from solar collectors (integral parts of the original design) once (if) they are installed."[19]

A similar system of heat recovery was included in the sophisticated Intelsat environmental systems. [FIG. 13] Intelsat's design also used the same screening system over its glazed facades as implemented at Woden TAFE. [FIG. 12] This system both reduces direct solar gain and encourages vertical airflow, which in the summer draws warm air away from the glazing. Together with the articulation of the hanging structure, walkways, and vertical circulation nodes, Woden TAFE exhibits a high-tech look, which was repeated at Intelsat.

The modular plan approach found at Woden TAFE and at Intelsat is also found in Andrews's 1975 design for the Monarto town center. In section, the buildings grouped around courtyards at Monarto stagger down a gentle incline, producing in profile the look of a contemporary hill town. The staggered building volumes of the Cameron Offices had a similar distant appearance. The confluence of urban and environmental performance concerns that emerged in the Queensland campus projects (see chapter 10) is also apparent here. Pools were to be constructed within the Monarto courtyards to produce both physiological and psychological cooling.[20] [FIG. 15] These relate to the atrium pools at Intelsat, which helped humidify air drawn through the atria via the stack effect.

---

18   Taylor and Andrews, *John Andrews*, 133–35.
19   Ibid., 156.
20   Paul Walker, Jane Grant, and David Nichols, "Monarto's Contested Landscape," *Landscape Review* 16, no. 1 (2015): 20–35.

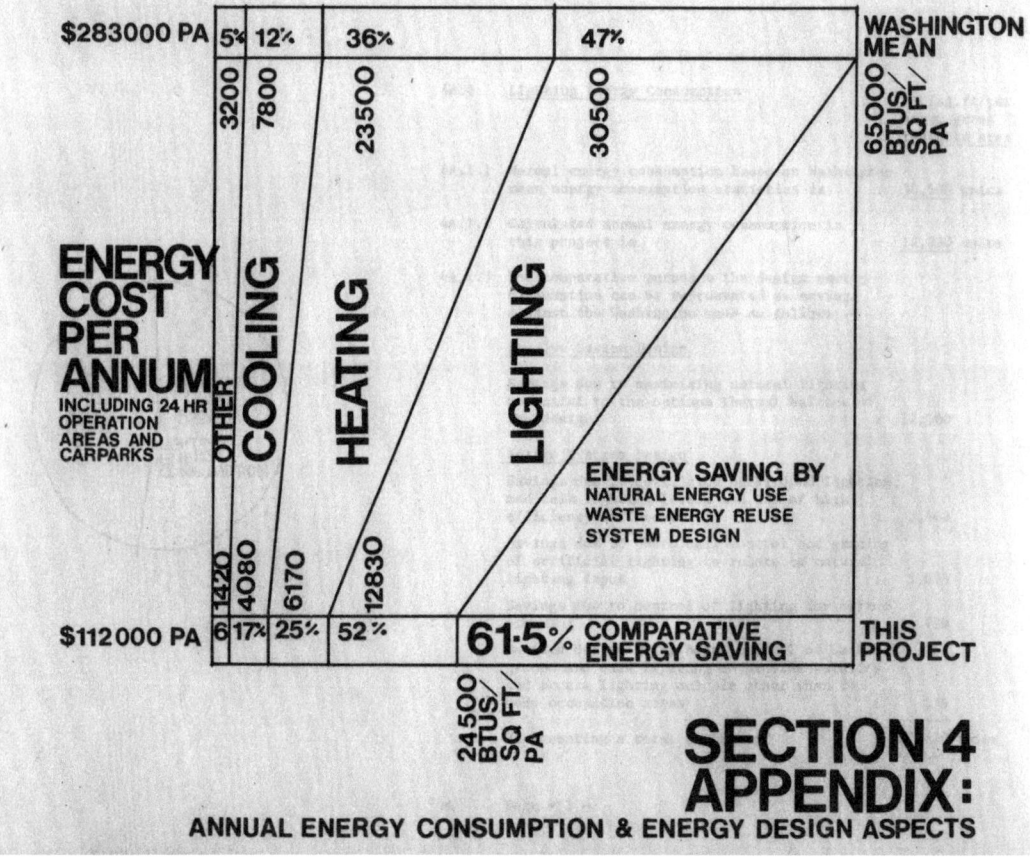

FIG. 14　Diagram from Andrews's Intelsat Headquarters design competition report showing annual energy consumption and energy design aspects.

FRAUD

The staging of Intelsat's construction created unexpected problems for the Andrews team. Between the first stage of construction and the signing of the second-stage contract, Intelsat's leadership changed. Despite their satisfactory performance, Richard Colino, the new director general of Intelsat, would not allow Gilbane, the first-phase contractor, to bid for the second stage. The bid selected by Colino was from William P. Lipscomb, a company that was unable to raise a "bid bond," a financial guarantee of a firm's ability to deliver a building project.[21] Geoff Willing, the Andrews representative in Washington, was the first to surmise something was wrong. Willing wrote to Intelsat in December 1984 to protest Lipscomb's appointment, but to no end. Before work started on the construction of stage two in 1985, Willing was asked to authorize a $1.2 million payment up front to the contractor to allow them to start work. His understanding was that this sum would cover early progress payments, but when the first claims for these payments were lodged in August of that year, Willing's recommendation that they be substantially less than the sums requisitioned was ignored. Willing also questioned the need for three contracts for preliminary site-preparation work to be added to the general contract. These contracts coincidentally also had a total value of $1.2 million.

Intelsat's project manager for the second-stage commission, Arthur Gelven, supported the Andrews office's view of the first of Lipscomb's applications, but he was subsequently removed from the role. Claims 4, 5, and 6 were not referred by Intelsat to John Andrews International but rather to Lehrer McGovern, an independent firm of project managers, though its services were also dismissed by Intelsat. Claims 7 and 8 were referred to Andrews, up to the end of April 1986, and again drew adverse criticism and recommendations that considerable percentages of the invoiced sums not be paid. Willing's advice was again ignored by Intelsat, who paid Lipscomb the full amount that they charged. Intelsat then directed the Andrews office not "concern itself with a review and recommendation role" regarding payment applications by Lipscomb, even though such a role was included in the agreement on architectural services between John Andrews International and Intelsat.[22]

In May 1986, Notter Finegold + Alexander—the American architects in association with John Andrews International for the Intelsat job—indicated to Andrews that his firm's services were to be terminated on June 17. Intelsat wrote to Andrews that the architectural services agreement for the second stage was to be null effective by June 30.

By this time, Willing's suspicions that someone had their hand in the till were compelling. In Australia, Andrews approached the Overseas Telecommunications Agency, the government body responsible for the country's representation on Intelsat.[23] He recalled: "I'm an Australian, I thought. Earlier, an Australian, the late Randy Payne, had been chairman of the board of Intelsat. Australia was one of the 10 original signatories to the whole Intelsat set-up. I wasn't going to put up with what was happening."[24] The Australians talked at the next Intelsat board meeting to the British and American representatives, and an audit was ordered.

Due to improprieties discovered by the auditors Peat Marwick, Colino and his deputy José Alegrett were placed on administrative leave on November 24, 1986.[25] These

---

21   "The Great Intelsat Scandal," *The Weekend Australian Magazine*, January 16–17, 1988, 3.
22   "International Telecommunications and Satellite Organization: Washington, DC, Headquarters Facility Phase II Project: Background Paper Dealing with Architect's Involvement and Payments to General Contractor," John Andrews International, Sydney, August 20, 1986, 7.
23   Andrews made a submission to the Overseas Telecommunications Agency that set out the firm's concerns about the Intelsat Stage II contract and the various communications the firm had with Intelsat from December 1984 expressing those concerns. See "International Telecommunications and Satellite Organization."
24   "The Great Intelsat Scandal."
25   "2 Intelsat Officers Are Put on Leave," *New York Times*, November 25, 1986. Memorandum from Robert P. Davis of Anderson, Hibey, Nauheim & Blair, John Andrews International's Washington lawyers, to Walter J. Raine of Westgarth Baldick, John Andrews International's Sydney lawyers, November 24, 1986.

improprieties extended further than the problems with the Intelsat building contract: the report in the *New York Times* on Colino's and Alegrett's suspensions focused on their approval of an improper commission payment of $1.3 million to the brokers behind the bank deal financing the new building. In December, the Intelsat board fired them. Willing, in the meantime, was back in Washington cooperating with the Federal Bureau of Investigation in assembling evidence against Colino and Alegrett. A series of break-ins happened at his Washington house, and a recreational vehicle was broken into as well; Willing became concerned for his family's safety.

The following May, *The Wall Street Journal* reported that Intelsat had sued Colino, alleging he had taken kickbacks from the Intelsat Stage II construction company, loan brokers, and consulting firms:

> For example, in the spring of 1984, Mr. Colino and unnamed associates conspired with Lipscomb to get a kickback of $2.4 million, the suit alleged. Mr. Colino told Lipscomb how much to bid for construction work on the company's headquarters, the suit alleged, so it could underbid a competitor by $25,000.
>
> When Lipscomb hadn't enough cash to pay the kickback, he directed the company to submit false vouchers to Intelsat to raise $1.2 million, the suit said. Then $1 million of that sum was sent to the Swiss bank account of a Panamanian company that Mr. Colino controlled.[26]

A criminal case followed, and on September 22, 1987, Colino was handed a six-year sentence "for leading a bid-rigging and kickback scheme that defrauded the agency of $4.8 million."[27]

It took considerable effort for John Andrews International to get a financial settlement for their work on the administration of the second-stage contracts.[28] And though fully vindicated, they were not reinstated as the project architects, but, nevertheless, stage two was completed following the Andrews working drawings with adherence to every detail.

ASSESSING INTELSAT'S ENVIRONMENTAL PERFORMANCE

The overall form, plan, and section arrangements of the Intelsat Headquarters design were described by the architects as the outcomes of their analysis of the organization's needs, its preferences for cellular rather than open-plan offices (the pod and atrium design maximized the number of perimeter offices), and its request for efficiency in its combination of passive-energy principles and active systems. This is apparent in the report the Andrews office supplied as part of their competition entry, which set out all the measures that would achieve major energy savings, including the atria and the facade screens.[29]

As already mentioned, the assessment criteria for the Intelsat design competition were threefold: "Design Considerations," "Accommodation of INTELSAT's Use Requirements," and "Implementation and Costs." The competition jury produced an extensive assessment of the Andrews design in relation to these criteria.[30] The first of the six design considerations—"distinction, excellence and quality"—emphasized the integration and coherence of the entire design, and on this point, Belluschi, Austin-Smith, and Zanuso

---

26   *The Wall Street Journal*, May 21, 1987.
27   "Ex-Intelsat Head Sentenced," *New York Times*, September 23, 1987.
28   Anderson, Hibey, Nauheim & Blair to William W. Goodrich of Arent, Fox, Kintner, Plotkin & Kahn, December 16, 1986, states that John Andrews International's claim against Intelsat in connection with the termination of the architectural services agreement would be settled by the payment of a lump sum of $472,000. Letters and correspondence come from the John Andrews archive. The John Andrews archive collection has been transferred from Andrews to the State Library of New South Wales. Access by the author was to the archive when it was still in the possession of the Andrews family.
29   John Andrews International, "Intelsat Project, Washington DC," report, January 1980.
30   "Report of the Assessment Panel for the Limited Invited Architectural Design Competition for the New INTELSAT Headquarters, 5 February 1980."

believed that the Andrews design excelled: "It is this test which the recommended design has met in a much more brilliant manner than any of the other entries."[31] Of the other design criteria, three were essentially technical in nature and two were aesthetic. But even in considering the Andrews design against such technical matters as space requirements and environmental performance, the jurors for Intelsat consistently fell back to the question of what the design would look like and how it would be experienced. In relation to the design criterion of construction and running costs, they had nothing to say at all, deferring instead to the full jury's report, which in turn deferred to Andrews's design report.

Under the design criterion of "Fulfilment of the Space Program Requirements in a Functional, Appropriate and Imaginative Manner," the architect jurors commented that the winning design's "checkerboard" of office modules and interior courtyards facilitated flexibility, expansion, and service requirements. They praised the plan to link courtyards at their corners for creating "a flowing pattern" of movement. While the jury touched on pragmatic issues, such as entry points, car access, the disposition of services and plant rooms, and the integration of "low energy principles," it offered little on the technical details of these matters, focusing instead on how the elements used in the Andrews design to address environmental performance drove the building's aesthetics: "The overall appearance of the building is largely determined by the energy saving requirements."[32]

Further, under the consideration of "Sensitivity to the environment and energy efficient," it is again the aesthetic outcome of the design's environmental and energy-saving strategies that is endorsed rather than their technological resolution. As the jurors write, "Even the tri-dimensional screens, placed as a protection of the exterior walls, become important architectural elements when we think of the richness of effect which can be derived from the very complex casting of shadows by the elements of the screens themselves and of the light-weight structures which support them."[33] The design's focus on energy issues is "not expressed in reduced or punitive terms but is optimistically suggested as a development of explicit and expressive volumes, which especially at night when lighted will communicate the image of appositive technology rich in imagination, both vital and essential."[34]

Perhaps it is not surprising that the architects serving on the Intelsat design competition jury did not undertake any technical analysis of the design. But the full jury, including Intelsat's director of engineering, also made no technical assessments, instead deferring to Andrews's claims about technical performance of his design. This is especially apparent in the jury's analysis of the Andrews design in relation to energy use. Under the heading "Accommodation of INTELSAT's Use Requirements," they noted that the Andrews design involved much lower lighting costs than were usual in Washington: "In a typical Washington office building with an annual energy consumption of 65,000 BTUs per square foot, some 30,500 BTUs are associated with lighting. In the Andrews design, by providing much exterior exposure, a photocell automatic turnoff system and the use of a space-frame to give insulation without blocking wanted light, a projected light energy budget for INTELSAT headquarters is estimated to be only 12,830 BTUs."[35] This was transcribed directly from information supplied by the Andrews office: the figures of 65,000, 30,500, and 12,830 BTUs all appear in a clear diagram included in Andrews's Intelsat design report. [FIG. 14] The report also included a figure of 24,500 BTUs per square foot per year for total annual energy consumption and a calculated energy savings of 61.5 percent compared to Washington norms.[36]

31 "Report of the Assessment Panel," 2.
32 Ibid., 8.
33 Ibid., 13.
34 Ibid.
35 Ibid., 10.
36 John Andrews International, "Section 4 Appendix: Annual Energy Consumption & Energy Design Aspects," in "Intelsat Project, Washington DC," report, January 1980.

FIG. 15 Detail: Monarto city center, 1975.

These figures, or near variations, were then widely reported in the architecture press. Writing in April 1980 on the selection of the Andrews design, the architecture critic of the *Washington Post*, Wolf Von Eckardt noted, "While the average Washington office building consumes 65,000 Btu's [sic] (British thermal units) per square foot per year, the Intelsat building is estimated to require only 24,000 per square foot per year."[37] After the first stage of the Intelsat Headquarters was completed, BTU consumption—both Intelsat's and the Washington norm—went up (though it is unclear if actual performance or estimates thereof increased). Nevertheless, architecture press continued to riff on the Andrews statement of a "61.5 percent comparative energy saving" in the Intelsat design. *Architectural Record* suggested that Intelsat's energy use was "less than 40 percent of the norm for comparable Washington buildings" and Peter Buchanan in *Architectural Review* noted, "energy consumption is less than 40 percent of the norm for comparable buildings in Washington." Reporting the same BTU figures that appeared in *Architectural Record*, the writer "N. R. G." at least acknowledged in *Architecture*, the journal of the American Institute of Architects, that such figures were estimates only.[38] Data on the building's actual energy performance has not been located.

"A HIGH-TECH CASTLE ON A WOODED HILL"

Of the six design considerations on which the Intelsat jury deliberated, two were more overtly based on appearance than the others. These visual criteria were about Intelsat's "image," choosing a design that would "satisfy the image requirements and goals of INTELSAT" and to respond to the local context by providing "satisfaction of the urban design requirements of Washington, DC."

37 Von Eckardt, "Pods and Pools."
38 Margaret Gaskie, "Uncommon Sense," *Architectural Record* 173, no. 10 (October 1985): 138–47; Peter Buchanan, "Intelsat Interlock," *Architectural Review* (October 1986): 103–8. N.R.G., "High-Tech Castle on a Wooded Hill," *Architecture* 74, no. 11 (November 1985): 68–75.

Belluschi, Austin-Smith, and Zanuso wrote in their assessors' report that Intelsat's "image goals" were such that the selected design "must reflect an optimistic view of mankind, a belief in its ability to grow in awareness, to be inspired and to create new relationships and new environments." The jury deemed that the Andrews design accomplished this: "innovative in appearance, yet solidly related to the past in general character" and respectful of the hillside topography and the trees, "which are such an ornament to the site." The urban-design requirement was also deemed to have been successfully addressed through the building's organization on the site, with green space, parking, and vehicular movement all suitably handled, as well as its connection to Connecticut Avenue. This includes an entry point specified to be close to the location of a new Metro station and the design's potential to be a suitable landmark on a key city thoroughfare.

Technology was not relevant to the Intelsat Headquarters merely in relation to its services and environmental performance. It was also central to its look. While the particular attention paid to the shading treatment of the building's fenestration produced a glitter of stainless steel and glass that lent its surfaces a techy appearance, the fragmented, office-pod, stair-capsule, and space-frame look of the place took this much further than was required for only technical purposes.

While the criminal fraud that tainted the second stage of the Intelsat project was widely reported in American press, architectural critics who wrote about the building were oblivious to these problems. Indeed, critiques of the design as built in the *Washington Post* and in international architecture press were published at the completion of only the first stage. Playing on Intelsat's "off-planet" responsibilities, architectural critics writing on the building could not help themselves in making sci-fi connections. In their assessments of the building's aesthetics they were ready to be inventive and speculative, contrasting with the ways in which they merely reported on the architect's energy-saving plans. Nor did they concede Andrews's claims of "common sense" as they did his claims about energy efficiency. For Von Eckardt, the Intelsat Headquarters was precisely "Architecture for Year 2001."[39] Writing in *The Architectural Review* soon after the first phase of the building opened in 1986, Peter Buchanan claimed that Intelsat's staff affectionately called the building "Starship Enterprise."[40] Meanwhile, under the title "Uncommon sense," *Architectural Record*'s Margaret Gaskie wrote, "insisting all the while that 'architecture is simply common sense,' John Andrews continues to confute his own thesis with a stream of buildings not common in any sense.... Perhaps through subliminal confusion of the building with the client, the headquarters has since it first began to rise on Connecticut Avenue near Embassy Row evoked the space-city imagery of *Star Wars*, and indeed its shimmering many-faceted pavilions seem rather to float than to march up the thickly wooded hill on which they rest...."[41] And under the headline "High-Tech Castle on a Wooded Hill," "N. R. G." wrote in *Architecture* that the building was "futuristic" and a "tour de force," suggesting that one of the atria was reminiscent of both Russian Constructivism (the central stair tower) and Luis Barragán (the pools), "with a little Darth Vader thrown in."[42] Darth Vader was as "noir" as the sci-fi references went—no one mentioned the contemporaneous *Alien* or *Blade Runner*. However, the space references were not entirely without critical allusion. This is perhaps most overt in an article by *Washington Post* staff writer and architecture critic Benjamin Forgey titled "Intelsat: The Space-Age Stunner," which makes the point that many architects were disdainful of the Intelsat building because it is a "suburban building in an urban setting."[43]

At stake in Forgey's comment is the problem of the building's relationship to its context. Visually arresting and intriguing, the

---

39 Von Eckardt, "Pods and Pools."
40 Buchanan, "Intelsat Interlock," 104.
41 Gaskie, "Uncommon Sense."
42 N.R.G., "High-Tech Castle on a Wooded Hill," 72.
43 Benjamin Forgey, "Intelsat: The Space-Age Stunner," *Washington Post* (January 5, 1985).

Intelsat building sits on a major arterial road in a well-heeled part of Washington. But in its beautiful park, the building floats at a visual and conceptual distance from its surroundings. While its immediate neighbors are the embassies to its west, the broader neighborhood of Cleveland Park is a late 19th-century residential district, inhabited now by professionals and politicians.[44] It is a neighborhood that successfully organized to stop a freeway being run through it in the 1960s and organized to subsequently attract one of the first trunk lines of the Washington Metro, which started construction in 1969. The Metro station at the corner of Connecticut Avenue and Van Ness Street, just north of the Intelsat site, opened in 1981. The stretch of Connecticut Avenue through Cleveland Park and as far north as Van Ness is described by Forgey as "the city's most urbane residential boulevard, lined with fine masonry apartment buildings," a pattern that was reinforced by developments that followed on from the building of the Metro. But for the most part, these buildings are banal. Commenting on the contextualism with which most Washington architecture complied at the time Andrews designed Intelsat, Von Eckardt, Forgey's colleague at the *Washington Post*, wrote that the buildings then being constructed close to the Intelsat site by the University of the District of Columbia exemplified "the current Washington vogue of making institutional buildings as gravely monumental, ponderous, heavy and pharaonic as possible. They are thin architectural concepts set in thick concrete, as though the architects felt their idea might otherwise too readily blow away."[45]

Forgey, however, did not find the Intelsat Headquarters entirely alien:

> The issue of the building's style is not an easy one to decipher. I watched it go up with increasing fascination. It just got busier and busier, until the notion of high-tech, space-age imagery almost disappeared and I found, to my great surprise, that the building began to assume a highly romantic, somewhat 19th-century character. What building in Washington, excepting the Smithsonian Castle, has a more active, picturesque profile? What Queen Anne house has more handsome turrets or bays than Intelsat's cylindrical, nearly free-standing stairwells? What rambling Victorian-era mansion has a more interesting set of gables than the many-sided glass roofs of Intelsat's atria? And those delicate ribbon sun screens and reflective glass blocks—are they not very like the lively mix of textures we so admire in buildings of the Shingle style?[46]

Importantly, the Intelsat design also offers a clear ceremonial entry and an equally clear pedestrian entry at the corner of Van Ness Street and Connecticut Avenue. A key difference between Andrews's horizontally distributed designs and most "mat-plan" projects is that the Andrews projects deal with the problem of having a street address. This is very clear at the Cameron Offices, where an elevated, stepped "mall" along the length of the building edge creates a series of porticoes that serve as entry points to the seven fingers of office accommodation. Address was to be achieved at the Callam Offices by an entry point marked by two towers—extrusions of the individual pod plan—with parking structures on either side. At a much smaller scale, the ceremonial, western entry to Intelsat is similar: two of the office pods are linked spatially to produce a generous entry space between them, connecting to a series of semi-public interior spaces. An external entry canopy stretches between the pods, unifying them into a portal.

Compared to new commercial and institutional buildings being erected at the same time in Cleveland Park—and indeed, throughout most of Washington and much of the rest of the Western world—Intelsat eschewed postmodern

---

[44] Zachary M. Schrag, *The Great Society Subway: A History of the Washington Metro* (Baltimore: Johns Hopkins University Press, 2006), 41.

[45] Von Eckardt, "Pods and Pools."

[46] Forgey, "Intelsat: The Space-Age Stunner."

contextualism. Instead, it adopted an approach that foregrounded the building's energy performance on the one hand and the physiological and psychological comfort of its inhabitants on the other. These matters focused design on the building interior. Maintaining the park-like aspect of the site, this approach therefore turned away from the signs of urban intensification that were otherwise appearing in its neighborhood. It gave the building a kinship with mid-century American suburban corporate complexes and the government complexes of Canberra's 1960s and 1970s expansion to which the Andrews office had already applied considerable thought.

But this is too simple. While the Andrews design for the Intelsat Headquarters was legitimated substantially in relation to building science and environmental measures, the jury that selected the design consistently subordinated the question of the design's environmental performance to the question of its appearance. Science was subordinated to science's look. For the architect members of the jury, this might not be remarkable, but it seems that the technical members also acquiesced to this move. As we have seen, this was then repeated in critiques of the Intelsat design that appeared in the *Washington Post* and in the international architecture press.

This is not to say that the Intelsat building did not perform in the way its designers' analyses demonstrated it would. Moreover, Intelsat concluded a line of inquiry into environmental design concerns in Andrews's work that started with his intuitive responses to the climate of Toronto and became increasingly sophisticated and technical in his collaboration with Don Thomas from the Cameron Offices onward. Rather, this aspect of the Intelsat design's success still did not matter enough in architectural culture to be scrutinized. Or, more likely, those who critiqued the building—for the most part positively—lacked the skills to assess its technical performance. Intelsat's beguiling appearance, as a techy-looking complex glittering among the trees, could be reclaimed for imaginative speculation so to be construed as an updated Victorian pile or cinematic spaceship.

FIGS. 16–17   Interior, Intelsat Headquarters.

13

convention centers

by Paul Walker

During the 1980s, commissions from the public and quasi-public institutions that were Andrews's major Australian clients in the 1970s mostly disappeared. One kind of government commission, however, became significantly important to him and his practice during this period: convention centers. Between 1986 and 1990 he completed convention centers in Adelaide, Sydney, and Melbourne, each involving extensive state government initiative and intervention. Despite this government involvement, the development of each was driven by commercial exigencies rather than any sense of the immediate public good, a reflection of the focus of federal and local governments on commercial matters in decisions about public investment during the period. The prevailing view held by both center-left and center-right governments in Australia at the time was that economic growth had to be prioritized; public good would follow, funded by taxes generated from expanded business activity. Or so the fantasy went. The Australian government's version of neoliberalism did not so much reduce government intervention in the economy as it redirected resources away from supporting manufacturing and the working class to stimulating investment in the postindustrial economy of finance, tourism, festivals, and sporting events.

The convention centers designed by Andrews were projects in which Australian state and city agencies sought to participate in an increasingly globalized market for meetings and congresses. Each of the convention centers Andrews designed was built on a brownfield site, such as built-over railyards in Adelaide's case and underutilized port and warehousing sites in Sydney and Melbourne. Through their adjacency to areas that could have been used for recreation (parklands, a harbor, and a river), the location of each of the convention centers was of potential public sensitivity. This was particularly true in Adelaide, where, despite the railyard and station having disrupted the connection between the central city and the Adelaide Park Lands to its north for decades, public controversy surrounded the location and scale of the whole convention center and associated development scheme.

The three convention centers designed by Andrews were all parts of larger tourism and commercial developments. The Adelaide project involved a large hotel and an office block designed by Andrews, as well as the conversion of the historic main Adelaide railway station into a casino, not designed by Andrews. The Sydney Convention Centre was part of the redevelopment of Darling Harbour by the New South Wales government to celebrate Australia's bicentenary in 1988 and was apparently influenced by projects in the United States, such as the redevelopment of Baltimore's Inner Harbor. Andrews provided designs for two casinos projected for the same site at Darling Harbour, neither of which proceeded to construction. In Melbourne, the grandly named World Congress Centre was developed by state agencies alongside the earlier World Trade Centre and partially integrated with it. When the Victoria state government decided in 1992 to promote the development of a casino in Melbourne, temporary casino facilities opened in the World Trade Centre while permanent premises for the casino were built on the other side of the Yarra River.

Andrews relished the challenges of designing convention centers; they entailed problems of scale and the movement of crowds that had so engaged him in the Miami Seaport Terminal project 20 years earlier. The Sydney Convention Centre held special significance for him as a prominent public—or almost public—building in his hometown. He did not relish the casino designs he undertook for Darling Harbour and was glad they weren't built.

ADELAIDE STATION AND ENVIRONS REDEVELOPMENT

The Adelaide Station and Environs Redevelopment (ASER) is akin to Toronto's Metro Centre but at a greatly diminished scale. As Metro Centre evolved to include as one of its key elements a restored and redeveloped heritage railway station, the retention of a grand station (though certainly not as impressive as Toronto's Union Station) also became a key part of the ASER project. The preservation of the historic Adelaide Station entailed finding an

FIG. 1 Adelaide Station and Environs Redevelopment (ASER), Adelaide, Australia, 1987–1988. Hotel at center, convention center at left, and office building at right.

FIG. 2 Convention Centre auditorium, Adelaide Station and Environs Redevelopment (ASER).

entirely new use for the building—an imposing, classical structure from 1928 designed by the local firm Garlick & Jackman—as terminus operations for interstate rail routes moved in early 1984 to a new station west of Adelaide's central city.[1] While suburban commuter services continued to use the platforms at Adelaide Station, except for a concourse connecting these platforms to the street, the station building itself was no longer needed.

The Adelaide railway station slated for repurposing in the ASER plan is located on the north side of the city's North Terrace, one of the streets demarcating the city's retail and business district. Originally, parkland started immediately north of the Terrace, as designated in Colonel William Light's plan for the city devised on its foundation in 1836. This land was later repurposed for rail lines, and so too were neighboring sites for other purposes, in particular a series of institutions including South Australia's State Parliament, governor's residence, library, art gallery, museum, and the University of Adelaide. Arrayed along the north side of North Terrace, these institutions still give the street an air of civic decorum. They also quite conclusively separate the street from the parks further to the north. The City of Adelaide Plan for the period of 1981 to 1986 anticipated that new development on the rail site would occur but envisaged such development between North Terrace and the River Torrens (Lake Torrens where it is locally dammed) to be both modest and sedate. As the plan outlines, "New development should be sympathetic with, and contribute to, the sober and grand architectural styles in the Precinct. The intensity and height of development should drop markedly on the north side of North Terrace and progressively diminish between the Terrace and the river."[2] Presumably, the Adelaide Festival Hall built in 1973 just northeast of the railway station was the sort of project the planners had in mind—a building with late-modern geometry but not too

much exuberance. However, departing from the city's intentions for the area, in 1982 the government of South Australia called for submissions for the redevelopment of the railway station and the air space over the platforms.[3] Under the Liberal Premier David Tonkin, the local developer Pak Poy & Kneebone was appointed to redevelop the site in partnership with the Japanese construction firm Kumagai Gumi and the South Australian Superannuation Fund Investment Trust. Tonkin lost government in an election in November 1982, but the new Labor government under John Bannon proceeded with the Pak Poy & Kneebone scheme, with John Andrews International appointed as architects in 1983.

The scheme that was soon announced was very different in scale and ambience from what the city council anticipated. Alongside the railway station, now recuperated as a casino, was a convention center, an office building, and a hotel.[4] Both Liberal and Labor representatives construed that the casino and other commercial elements of the project were necessary to fund the convention center; the casino gained support in the State Parliament shortly after Bannon's election as it would exclude poker machines.[5] The local firm Woodhead Hall McDonald Shaw was responsible for the design of the casino, and Andrews was responsible for the design of the rest of the buildings on the site. In early 1984, the government of South Australia passed legislation that gave it planning control over the land occupied by the historic station and associated platforms and tracks.

The City of Adelaide opposed the ASER development on the basis that its concentrated commercial use was inappropriate and out of scale with the neighborhood. An April 1984 report by John Andrews International and the

1   Philip Goad, "Railway Stations," in Philip Goad and Julie Willis, eds., *The Encyclopedia of Australian Architecture* (Melbourne: Cambridge University Press, 2012), 581–83.
2   Cited in Judith Brine, "The Plan of Adelaide and the ASER Scheme," *Australian Planner* 22, no. 5 (December 1984): 9.
3   "Hyatt Hotel and Convention Centre," *Construction Review* (May 1989): 19.
4   The project was announced in October 1983. See Rick Burnett, "Station Casino Project Rises to $20m," *The Advertiser* (Adelaide), August 17, 1984; and Stephen Middleton, "It's Go for $160m Station Complex," *The News* (Adelaide), August 17, 1984.
5   Jan McMillen, "Risky Business: Political Economy of Australian Casino Development" (PhD diss., University of Queensland, 1993), 226.

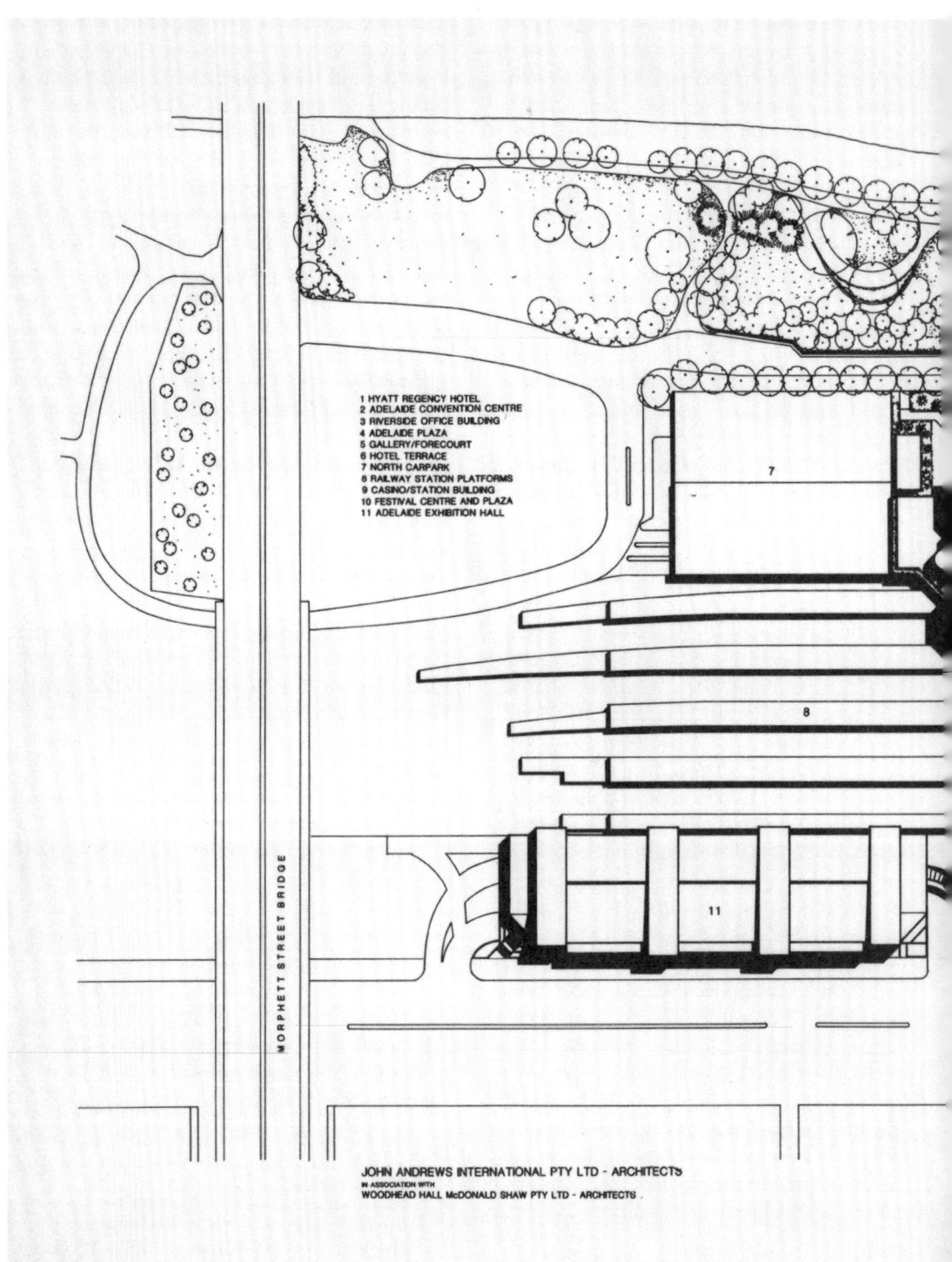

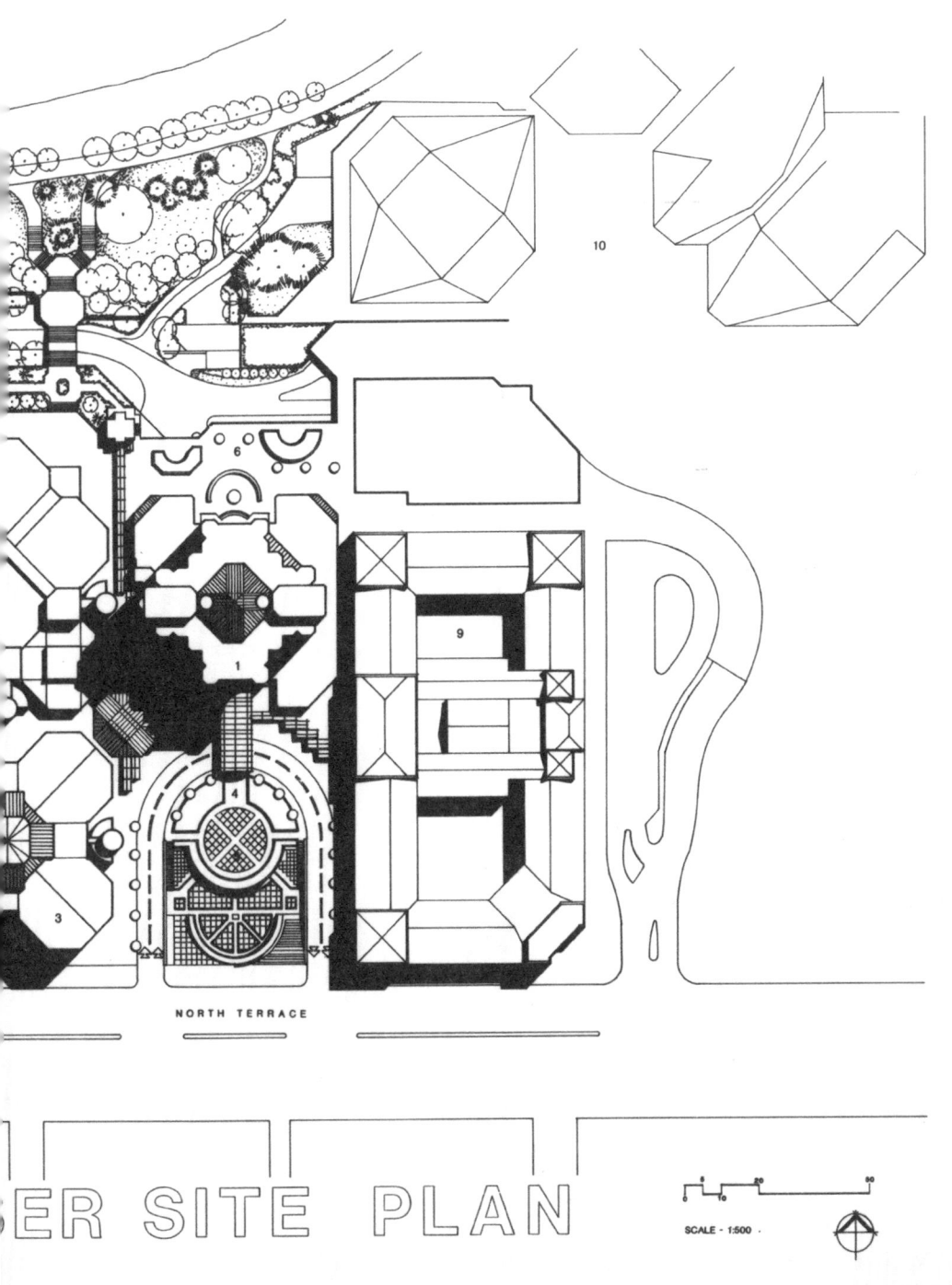

FIG. 3 Plan, Adelaide Station and Environs Redevelopment (ASER).

other consultants to ASER advised that Hyatt's appointment to manage the hotel resulted in that building's height being reconsidered from the 13 stories briefed in 1983 to 14, 22, or 26 floors depending on the plan configuration. Conversely, the height of the office building was halved from its original 22 stories. The project also drew criticism that it would permanently alienate the land on which it was built from its historical parkland use and would impede movement between North Terrace and the Torrens. But didn't all those older institutional buildings and the Festival Hall built just a decade earlier do exactly this? And while Andrews's design for the Hyatt—in the event the 22-floor option was selected—was quite different in scale and form from the other buildings on North Terrace, it was no larger than the largest office buildings in the business area of Adelaide just two blocks south. University of Adelaide architectural historians David Saunders and Judith Brine were part of the vanguard of the criticism. Brine wrote:

> It is clearly time for planning principles and policies to be reestablished for this area. In my view the policies should be based on two principles. First, that the number of new buildings should be few and that they should be sited so that the relatively scattered nature of the buildings in the parklands is maintained. Secondly, that the only buildings that should be encouraged are those of formal government or the culture of the State or those directly associated with the function of parklands as parkland.
>
> By these means this area will still be seen to be part of the parklands and be visually differentiated from the city itself. Further, the original purpose of the parklands as an area for health, welfare, and recreation of the people of Adelaide would be maintained. The purpose of the principles is to ensure that the heritage value of Light's plan for the City of Adelaide, arguably South Australia's most important man-made item of heritage, be conserved in both its form and its concept.[6]

Such historical delicacy, however, was far from the mind of the South Australian government. Successive Liberal and Labor governments had been unable to achieve political and community support for a casino in Adelaide, but Bannon accomplished this soon after becoming premier. The plans for a casino and a convention center were part of an economic strategy to develop tourism; commercial investment in the hotel and office building on the ASER site would offset the cost of building the convention center and the preservation of the historic Adelaide Station building. As Jan McMillen writes, "From the government's point of view, the main benefits would be that casino revenues would reduce the budget deficit and allow development of capital works such as a much-needed convention center. Developers argued that an adequate return for investment in a convention center would only be possible if a casino was part of the complex."[7] While the city council remained adamantly opposed to the development, views in the Adelaide community were divided. *The News*—one of two daily newspapers then published in Adelaide—was a strong advocate. As they put forth in a 1984 editorial, "Almost a year ago, when it was first announced from Tokyo, *The News* hailed the $180 million Adelaide Railway Station redevelopment as bold and impressive.... Adelaide needs such symbols and ASER will provide one spectacularly. The plan does not entail a major loss of Park Lands. It puts already alienated space to exciting new use. The council frets about tradition. But Adelaide is what it is today because, instead of thinking back, its founders thought ahead and thought big."[8]

At the time, the state government shook off most of the criticism. *The Advertiser*, the city's other daily, reported that state regulations permitting ASER to proceed were published in the previous week's *SA Government Gazette*. However, this excluded the office building, which the report said was "being redesigned after Government acceptance of some of the

6 Brine, "The Plan of Adelaide and the ASER Scheme," 10.
7 McMillen, "Risky Business," 221.
8 "A Bold Symbol of Adelaide," editorial, *The News*, Adelaide, September 11, 1984.

criticism of the plans."[9] The most vocal criticism was, in fact, on the height of the hotel. Saunders wrote in *The Adelaide Review*:

> Hotels do most often adopt a simple tower form, but the world holds many other proven possibilities, and this is no routine site. There are designs using a cluster of more stubby towers; one of those was completed only this year in Perth, designed by the very same design consultant, John Andrews International. The Merlin Hotel in Perth uses a cluster of four blocks around a cruciform atrium. There are also many variations upon a slab form rather than a tower.... It is not too late. Even though plans of the hotel and conference centre were gazetted on October 15th, the ASER Act makes it quite simple to change those plans at any time.[10]

Site work started in late 1984. Changes to the office building design were unveiled in May 1985, apparently emphasizing its form as a group of octagonal volumes to visually break the bulk of the building.[11] *The Advertiser* criticized these changes as "cosmetic," and the newspaper appealed to the premier to accede to criticisms that now were apparently focused on this building, not the hotel.[12] The hotel construction contract was awarded in June 1985 and the construction contract for the convention center was awarded in August. The casino opened on December 12, 1985, the Adelaide Convention Centre opened in June 1987, and the Hyatt in 1988. Further controversy then emerged in relation to the office building when it became apparent that it was not clad with the same warm-toned concrete as the hotel and the convention center but rather with a gray metallic material. [FIG. 1] An exhibition building on North Terrace was subsequently added to the ASER group.[13]

Throughout the extended period of construction—made longer still by various industrial disputes between unions and builders—Andrews commented only occasionally on the controversies that bedeviled ASER. However, a 1986 newspaper article titled "Stop knocking ASER, says project designer," quotes Andrews as follows: "'I'm surprised at the attitude of Adelaide people,' he said. 'They have taken every opportunity to knock the greatest thing that has happened since Colonel Light designed the city....'"[14] And just before the opening of the hotel, in a newspaper article titled "I'm hurt, says ASER designer," Andrews commented that he was appointed to the ASER commission not because of his convention center expertise but because of his experience with hotels, particularly the Merlin in Perth. That article also reveals that the exhibition center—the last piece of the ASER puzzle—was to start construction at the end of the year, with completion planned for the end of 1989.[15]

Andrews's buildings for the Adelaide Station and Environs Redevelopment are more or less discrete projects sitting on the lid constructed over the railway platforms, the scheme's most basic gesture, which entailed relaying the tracks underneath. [FIG. 3] The broad strategies for the ASER office building and the hotel have already been described in chapter 11: octagon plan forms are conceptually bundled and extruded upwards. In the case of the office building, the scale of the octagons corresponds to the idea of an optimal work unit, and in that of the hotel, to the size of a hotel room. In both, the octagons are arrayed around an atrium. In the case of the office building, an elevator core occupies the center of the atrium and stairs are pulled into independent towers on the east and west sides of the building's perimeter. Here, the atrium becomes energetically compressed and vertiginous. In the hotel, however, the atrium—in fact, three stacked atria, two of

9   Chris Russell, "Green Light for Station Plan," *The Advertiser* (Adelaide), October 15, 1984.
10 David Saunders, "The best address in Adelaide," *The Adelaide Review* 7 (October 1984): 2.
11 Nick Hopton, "Adelaide Grows Up," *The News* (Adelaide), May 6, 1985.
12 "The ASER outlook," editorial, *The Advertiser* (Adelaide), June 7, 1985.
13 *The Advertiser* (Adelaide), July 19, 1986.
14 *The Advertiser* (Adelaide), September 22, 1986.
15 Mary Palazzo, "I'm Hurt, Says ASER Designer," *The Sunday Mail* (Adelaide), May 15, 1988.

eight floors and one of four—is more spacious and sedate, with the elevators confined to two concrete towers on the outer perimeter of the plan.[16] Stairs are housed in concrete tubes on the edges of the atrium. The formal strategy of extruding the inhabited units—office volumes and hotel rooms—along with separately articulated volumes for stairs and elevators, emphasizes the verticality of these buildings. The hotel's appearance is made loftier still as it sits at the top of a plaza ramped up from North Terrace to accommodate the railway platforms underneath. Meant as a public space, the ramp is more like a forecourt to the buildings arrayed around it, particularly the hotel. While the material treatment and finishes of the office building are muted, by contrast, those of the hotel are lush and luxurious (in fact, this was also a contrast with everything Andrews had done before). Not surprising for a hotel intended to serve, in part, a casino. The precast concrete cladding for the hotel exterior, many interior walls, and the balustrades around the atria is a warm apricot, sand-blasted matte. Board-marked off-form gray concrete used for the lift towers recalls Andrews's earlier buildings. The warm-toned exterior often appears quite orange in the harsh Adelaide sunlight. Polished dark red granite floors in the public areas, lighting, and fashionable furnishings gave the hotel a warm, deluxe feel. The apricot concrete and the luxe quality extended to the convention center itself. On the one hand, it appears that a diagonal grid organized the site, and on the other, the siting of the convention center with an octagonal office building to its south and an octagonal hotel to its east implied that octagons should also form its plan geometry.

Foregrounding Andrews's problem-solving skills, the internal arrangement of the Adelaide Convention Centre is ingenious. [FIG. 2] Five meeting auditoria with seating capacities ranging from 450 to 1,200 seats are arrayed so that operable walls connect them to form a large hall with 2,000 square meters for exhibition space or for 2,000-seat banquets. Banks of tiered seating that retract into the ceiling plenum allow the combined hall to serve as a 3,500-seat convention or performance space; the timber-veneered soffits of the seating platforms incorporate air-conditioning, lighting, and sound systems that service the interior when it is configured into the smaller rooms.[17] These smaller rooms can also be arranged with flat floors or tiered seating. Doors allow direct access for vehicles to the main hall to load and unload exhibition materials. The exterior of the convention center articulates the forms of the octagonal geometry of the five auditoria plus a lobby, with vertical concrete cylinders housing ducts and stairs.

Writing about the Adelaide Convention Centre in a building-type study on convention centers, including another by Andrews at Sydney and two contemporaneous ones in San Jose, California, and Miami Beach, Florida, *Architectural Record* critic Margaret Gaskie praised the Adelaide design for something its detractors said it would make impossible. As Gaskie writes, "The flexible multi-use center joins a hotel, office building, and connecting entry plaza (also designed by John Andrews) in a complex that spans the tracks of a historic, now-rejuvenated railroad station next door. In addition to recapturing a lakefront which the tracks had split off from the city's core, the scheme reaches out to such complementary near neighbors as an exhibition hall and an arts center."[18]

MELBOURNE WORLD CONGRESS CENTRE

The second of the convention centers that Andrews worked on was the grandly named World Congress Centre, adjacent to the equally grandly named World Trade Centre in Melbourne. Andrews was commissioned in December 1983, but Melbourne was the last of the Andrews convention centers to open, not being completed until 1990.[19] It was delayed not by public controversy as was the case in

---

16   Brian Walters, "Track Star," *Building Design*, June 10, 1988, 17.

17   "Hyatt Hotel and Convention Centre," 26; Walters, "Track Star," 16.

18   Margaret Gaskie, "Specializing in Ready Versatility: A Multi-Use Center Offers Two Facilities in One," *Architectural Record* 178, no. 3 (March 1990): 108.

4

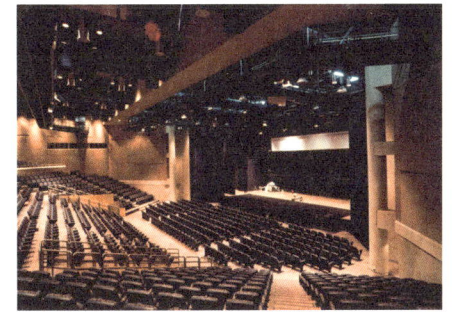

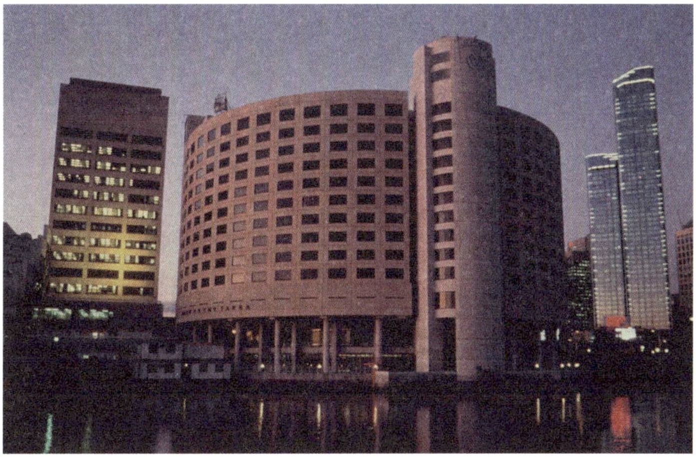

5

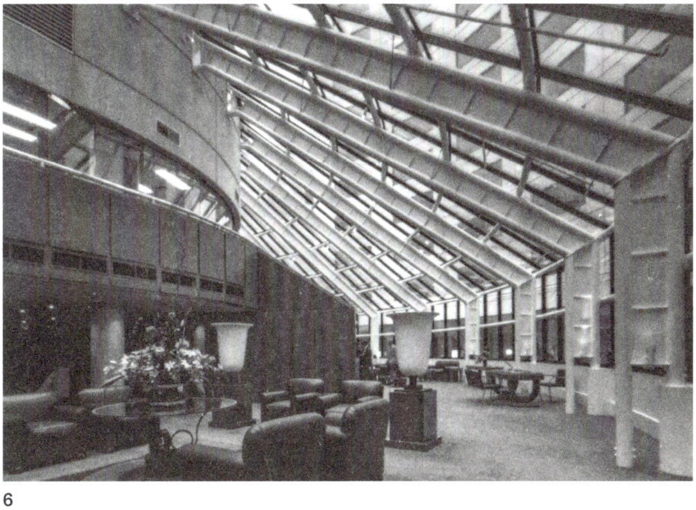

6

FIG. 4 World Congress Centre, Melbourne, Australia, 1990.
FIGS. 5–6 Hotel, World Congress Centre.

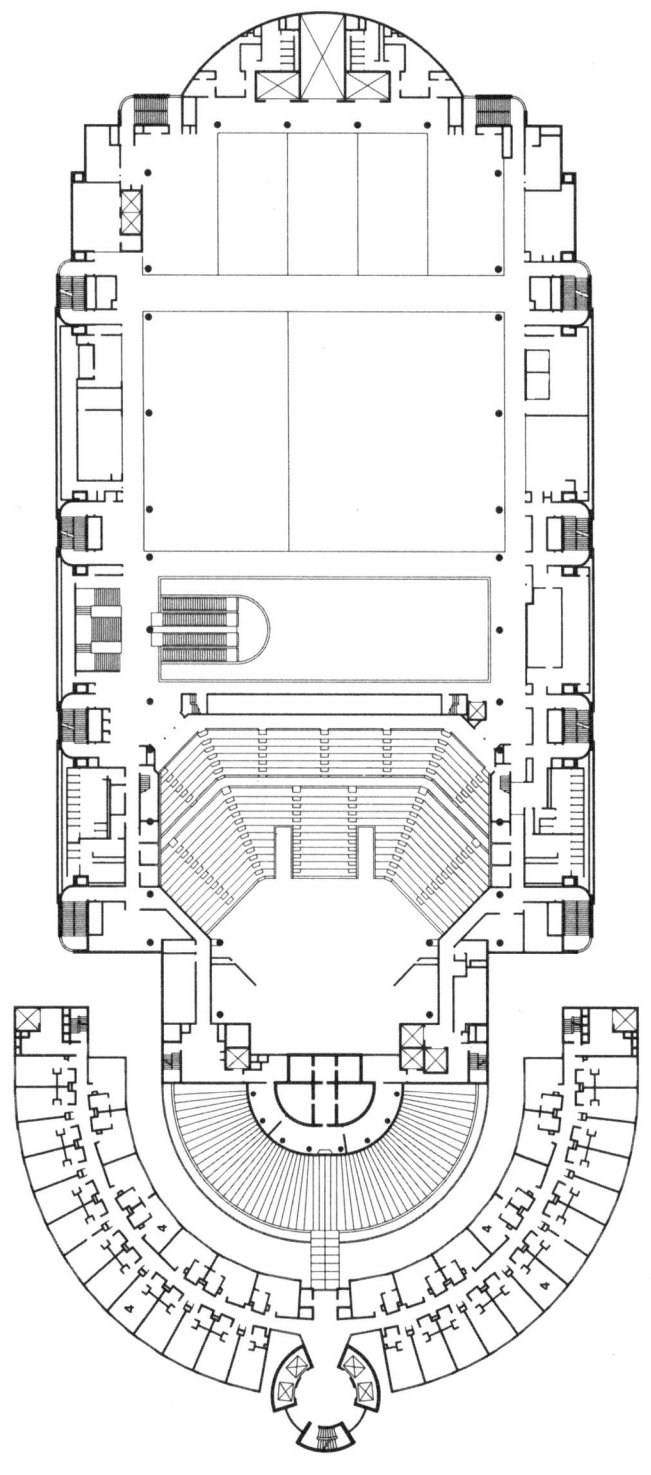

FIG. 7   Plan, World Congress Centre, Melbourne.

Adelaide, but rather through state political machinations, which also involved the question of a casino.

Opened in 1983, the World Trade Centre (WTC) was built on the north bank of the Yarra River by the Port of Melbourne Authority as one of the earliest projects in Melbourne to develop underused port land. Its architects were Grahame Shaw & Partners.[20] The 1978 planning permit for the WTC included a convention center and a hotel, but these did not proceed with the rest of the project.[21] The question of a convention center for Melbourne, however, was soon revisited. Preceding the state elections in 1982—in which Labor leader John Cain became the Premier of Victoria—the Victorian Tourism Commission and the Melbourne Tourism Authority had lobbied strongly for a casino to finance a large 4,000-seat convention center on the site of the new World Trade Centre.[22] Cain, like John Bannon, his Labor colleague in South Australia, looked to improve the ailing state economy through growth in tourism, and a casino figured into his thinking, but the inquiry that he established to examine the question of casinos recommended against their introduction in Victoria.[23]

In December 1983, the Victoria state government resolved to build a convention center next to the WTC, with an integral hotel. But without the subsidy of a casino's income, the convention center would have to be more modest in scale. The Port of Melbourne Authority appointed a project team that included Andrews and prepared a costed schematic proposal with input from convention and exhibition professionals.[24] However, two years later, nothing had happened. An environmental effects statement prepared by the Port of Melbourne Authority in November 1985 specified the accommodations that the convention center would provide, including convention space hosting a maximum of 2,500 persons; a minimum exhibition area of 10,000 square meters; functional and visual links to the WTC; and a 400-room hotel separate from the convention facilities and under different ownership.[25] Three options for the location of the hotel were considered—at the north, center, and south of the site. South was identified as best, with the hotel situated on the north bank of the Yarra River. Hotel bedroom floors were to be elevated to allow light and winter sun to reach the riverbank promenade. The statement also elaborated on the visual relationship that the convention center was projected to maintain with the WTC, namely that window and external material treatments would be the same and "tall elements" in the conference center would complement those in the WTC: "the visual effect is that of an incremental addition to an existing structure, not the intrusion of a new structure on the landscape."[26]

The environmental effects statement commented not just on the convention center brief and architecture but also on matters of urban strategy and competition. It noted that the City of Melbourne's 1985 Strategy Plan acknowledged the development of central Melbourne as of direct concern to the state government. The development of the WTC and the convention center notably were not matters of dispute between city and state governments as ASER was in Adelaide.[27] Nevertheless, amid its economic rust-belt malaise and competition with other Australian capitals, Melbourne had fallen behind in regard to convention center planning. As the environmental effects statement noted, since the state government's decision to proceed with a convention center, "actual proposals have been approved in Adelaide, Sydney, Canberra, Perth and Brisbane and construction has commenced

---

19   Port of Melbourne Authority, "Melbourne Convention Centre & Hotel Project: Environment Effects Statement," November 1985, 11.
20   Amy Zurrer, *Wharves to the World: The Development of Melbourne's World Trade Centre* (Melbourne: Melbourne Books, 2011), 83.
21   Port of Melbourne Authority, "Environment Effects Statement," 14.
22   McMillen, "Risky Business," 295.
23   Ibid., 297–98.
24   Port of Melbourne Authority, "Environment Effects Statement," 3.
25   Ibid., 4.
26   Ibid., 7.
27   Ibid., 16.

in Sydney and Canberra and is well advanced in Adelaide. All of these centers are targeting for completion before 1988."[28] Construction, however, did not begin for another 20 months, until August 1987. The hotel was completed in November 1989; the convention center in March 1990.

To undertake the project, John Andrews International partnered with the Melbourne firm Eggleston, MacDonald & Secomb, which was known for its modestly Brutalist portfolio of buildings, many for Monash University and the University of Melbourne.[29] The design was constrained by a relatively tight site, with the busy Spencer and Flinders streets to the east and north, the WTC to the west, and the Yarra River to the south, as well as by the requirement to accommodate an existing access road, Siddeley Street, which ran east–west through the site. Vehicular access ramped up from Siddeley Street southward to drop-off points for the hotel and the convention center and then looped back down to the street. On the north side of Siddeley was truck access to the center, with truck lifts bringing exhibition material up from ground level. At ground level, below the hotel lobby and main convention center floors, were restaurants and kitchens; at basement level was a parking garage for hotel patrons. The project was essentially zoned for the exhibition center at the north, the main convention hall in the middle, and the hotel at the south. The lobby level connected to an existing exhibition area within the WTC to the west through a "galleria." The next floor up accommodated a flat-floored exhibition hall, the lower level of the main convention hall—an elongated octagonal room with a fan of tiered seating for 2,500 people—and a hotel reception area, lounge, and the lowest floor of hotel rooms. [FIG. 6] This level also had a lateral link to the WTC. The next level accommodated the upper part of the convention hall, meeting rooms, and a 700-person banquet hall.

Except for the hotel component, the project was very inward-looking, with the plushly furnished main exhibition, banqueting, and convention rooms separated from the exterior by circulation, kitchen, and storage spaces. These were developed as strongly introverted spaces.[30] With elevated rail tracks directly north and the WTC immediately west, there was no potential for outlook in either of those directions. The strong sense of symmetry in plan, around a central north–south axis, obviated the possibility of outlook to the east, which could have been possible over Batman Park (named for one of Melbourne's 19th-century founders) on the opposite side of Spencer Street. [FIG. 7]

The hotel is decidedly not inward-looking and is the only built example of several hotels Andrews designed that takes a semicircle as its basic plan form. The 10 floors of guest rooms on the outer arc of the semicircle splay to city, river, and port views. [FIGS. 5–6] The external cladding of the rooms is done in warm-colored, smooth precast concrete panels. At the lower levels of the hotel building, the central hotel and vehicular functions are pulled back from the river behind a colonnade of cast-in situ concrete columns with a brut finish; at the middle of the arc, a brut concrete cylinder contains elevators and a staircase. The exterior of the convention and exhibition area of the complex was divided into four bays, also clad in gray off-form concrete. With vertical ribs, this concrete to some degree recalls the ribbed concrete of the Weldon Library at the University of Western Ontario, but it was produced with a remarkable degree of finesse more akin to Japanese construction than North American or Australian. Andrews's exteriors, therefore, departed from the intention that they should conform to those of the WTC, in which windows and smooth white spandrels horizontally band the building exterior. Only a utilitarian 10-level parking garage built at the same time as the convention center, but on the western side of the WTC, nearly matched the WTC's appearance.

28   Ibid., 13.
29   Philip Goad, "Eggleston MacDonald & Secomb" in Philip Goad and Julie Willis, eds., *The Encyclopedia of Australian Architecture* (Melbourne: Cambridge University Press, 2012), 227–28.
30   Port of Melbourne Authority, "Environment Effects Statement," 25.

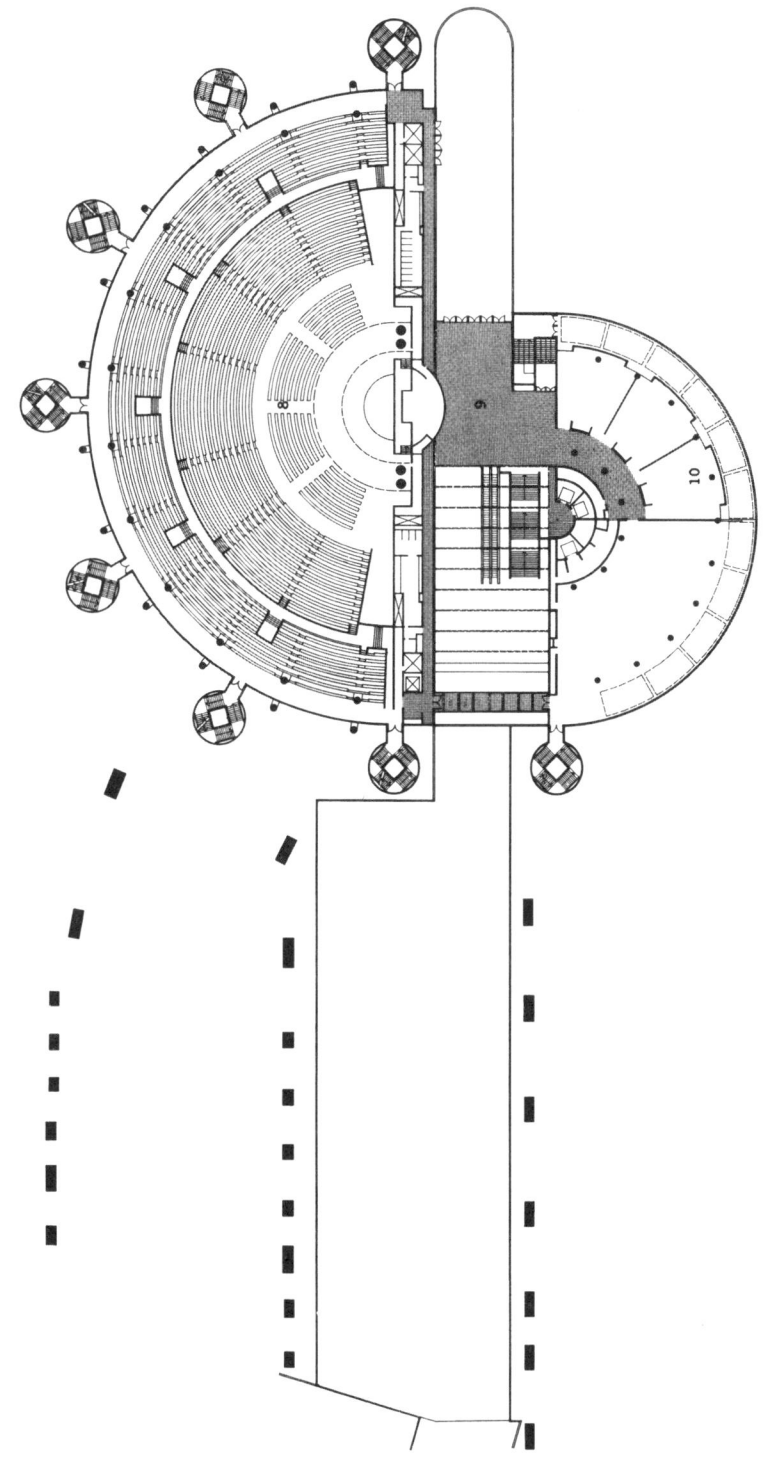

FIG. 8 Plan, Sydney Convention Centre, Sydney, Australia, 1988.

9

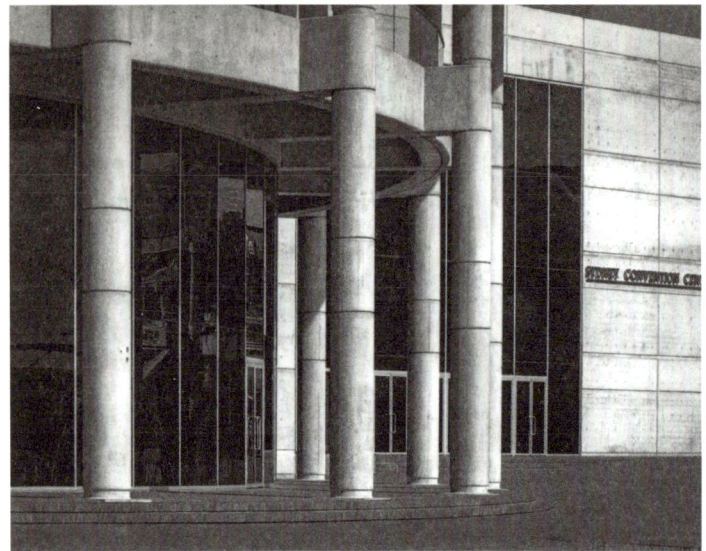

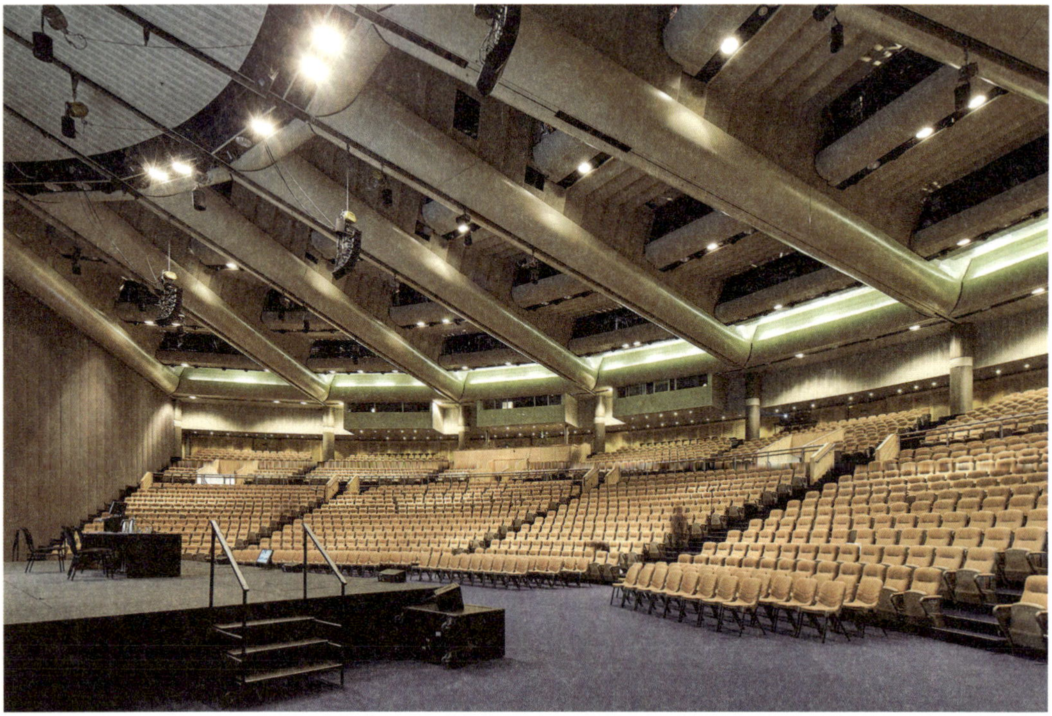

10

FIG. 9 Sydney Convention Centre, 1988.
FIG. 10 Auditorium, Sydney Convention Centre, 1988.

Built without the casino envisaged in 1983, the fortunes of the Melbourne World Congress Centre nevertheless came to be associated with another—this time successful—casino proposal for Melbourne. In 1990, against the background of further economic crisis, Cain resigned as premier and was replaced by Joan Kirner. Seeing taxes from the expansion of legal gambling as a means of addressing the government's budget problems, Kirner overturned previous prohibitive policies.[31] The government identified Docklands—an area of underused port land west of the WTC—as the location for a large casino. When expressions of interest were called early in 1992, however, potential casino sites were not restricted to Docklands.

In elections in October 1992, Kirner and Labor lost, and the pugnacious and strongly pro-development Jeff Kennett became premier. In September 1993, Crown Resorts was announced as the winner of a 12-year casino license.[32] In the event, Crown did not build at Docklands but rather at Southbank, across the Yarra River from the World Trade Centre and the World Congress Centre, where a huge and elaborate pleasure palace designed by Bates Smart, Perrott Lyon Mathieson, and Daryl Jackson opened in 1997. This was preceded by a temporary casino that operated for three years at the WTC. Designed by Denton Corker, a massive exhibition center—colloquially and ironically known as "Jeff's Shed"—had already been built at Southbank in 1996. The critical mass of activity that the casino and exhibition center attracted was removed from the World Congress Centre; it was thus doomed to be superseded less than 20 years after it opened by a much bigger convention center matching the large-scaled Crown Melbourne and Jeff's Shed on the other side of the Yarra.

SYDNEY CONVENTION CENTRE

As in Adelaide and Melbourne, the development of a convention center in Sydney was closely entangled with the changing relationship between state and city urban development policies. As in Adelaide and Melbourne, casinos factored into the Sydney development scheme. This was complicated in Sydney's case by the plans for a casino, convention center, exhibition center, and entertainment center—to name only its major components—being parts of a major urban renewal plan for Darling Harbour to the immediate west of the central business district. With this, the state of New South Wales intended to celebrate the 1988 bicentennial of the founding of Australia (in fact, the bicentenary of British colonization of New South Wales). This plan was implemented hastily, with complications following for the Darling Harbour building projects. As well, controversies over Australia's identity and its treatment of its Indigenous people came to cloud how Darling Harbour and other bicentennial celebrations were critically received. This was particularly so of the Darling Harbour projects—notably designed by the architect Philip Cox—which adopted a self-conscious Australian identity in their references to maritime forms that evoked, perhaps unconsciously, colonial themes. Concerned with other architectural issues, Andrews's Sydney Convention Centre avoided this. But only one architectural critic, Elizabeth Farrelly, really understood how different the convention center's architecture was from that of its neighbors.

The construction of Darling Harbour and New South Wales's Australian bicentennial celebrations were integral to the reinvention of Sydney as a "global" city in the new international order of neoliberal politics and economic policy. It was one of several projects of urban transformation within central Sydney promoted by Neville Wran, the long-serving Labor premier of New South Wales. These projects included the remaking of Macquarie Street, the site of important institutional and historic buildings on the eastern side of the central business district, such as the New South Wales State Parliament, and the reconstruction of the public spaces of Circular Quay, the central city harbor-front promenade that extends from the Sydney Opera House to the historical and

---

31 McMillen, "Risky Business," 301–302.
32 Ibid., 306.

tourist-saturated area of The Rocks.[33] This was the first time that Australian state government systematically promoted such urban-design interventions as part of urban policy, which previously focused not on qualitative aspects of the city experience but quantitative planning issues around demographics and activity. These state government interventions in the central city coincided with the preparation of a metropolitan strategy for Greater Sydney, driven for the first time primarily by New South Wales rather than local Sydney concerns. The economic objectives of the strategy sought to proactively "augment Sydney's role as a major international financial, technological, tourist and industrial centre," while social development objectives included "acknowledgement and enhancement of the multicultural nature of Sydney's population and ensuring services and facilities are accessible to different ethnic communities." Key to meeting the latter objective was consultation with "user groups and disadvantaged groups (e.g., Aborigines, and the unemployed)."[34]

Such consultation, however, was excluded from the implementation of Darling Harbour's redevelopment of 54 hectares of run-down and often derelict warehouses, railyards, and dockside facilities into a collection of large-scale public facilities. This included a 12,000-seat entertainment center, convention and exhibition centers, an aquarium and a maritime museum, a vast "colonial-style" shopping center, and a casino, all stitched together with a patchwork of landscaping and public promenades.[35] Industrial facilities were replaced by those of the service economy. The New South Wales government decided only in 1984 that the rebuilding of Darling Harbour would be its major project celebrating the 1988 bicentenary. To meet a deadline of January 1988 (January 26 being Australia Day, the day on which the "first fleet" of British settlement brought the first convicts to New South Wales in 1788, also known as Invasion Day), legislation was passed to exempt the site from normal planning procedures and controls.[36]

Andrews's design for the Sydney convention center is unlike those for Adelaide and Melbourne. In contrast, the Sydney Convention Centre would be seen from many viewpoints and by a lot of passing pedestrians. Like shopping centers and casinos, convention centers are buildings without exteriors, or to be more precise, their exteriors barely matter to their internal logic. In Melbourne, except for its hotel, the World Congress Centre was only visible externally on its eastern facade; in Adelaide, the convention center was veiled from North Terrace by the ASER office building and then by the Exhibition Centre built immediately upon the convention center's completion. The Sydney Convention Centre's external form mattered visually. Few site boundary constraints permitted both interior planning that was more relaxed and an exterior form that was more elaborated. The basic form at Sydney Convention Centre is two semicircular plan forms disposed on either side of a linear element that projects south, past the semicircles. [FIG. 8] The bigger of the semicircles on the west flank contains the main convention hall with 3,500 seats at the upper levels and a banquet hall at ground. [FIG. 10] Meeting rooms are placed between, under the upper levels of the main hall. The smaller semicircle to the east has a restaurant and bar at the lower levels, glazed toward the public pedestrian areas of Darling Harbour beyond. [FIG. 9] The projecting upper levels of this form contain more meeting rooms, with precast concrete as the dominant exterior cladding. The linear form between the two semicircles hosts the main circulation spaces and lobbies. At the main entrance, at the north of the building, the entrance area is especially lofty, and while various patterns of movement

---

33 Jennifer Taylor, *Australian Architecture Since 1960*, 2nd ed. (Canberra: Royal Australian Institute of Architects National Education Division, 1990), 231.

34 David Wilmoth, "Sydney's Metropolitan Strategy" (working paper, Australian National University Research School of Social Sciences Urban Research Unit, 1988), 8, 18. See also Richard Hu, "Shaping a Global Sydney: The City of Sydney's Planning Transformation in the 1980s and 1990s," *Planning Perspectives* 27, no. 3 (July 2007): 347–68.

35 For the colonial reference, see The Darling Harbour Authority, "Sydney's New Dimension: Darling Harbour," 1986, 12.

36 Taylor, *Australian Architecture Since 1960*, 232, 254n26.

are accommodated, the location of the main stairs and escalators emphasizes movement up toward the meeting rooms and the main plenary hall.

The arrangement of the building's forms produces a mostly blank exterior to the west—the walls of the main plenary hall volume. This elevation is, however, enlivened with dramatic concrete and glass-block cylinders containing stairs that connect the upper levels of the plenary hall with the lower levels of the building and fire exits. These repeated concrete and reflective glass-block cylinders were previously used by Andrews at the Intelsat Headquarters and later reappear at the Octagon. While the placement of vertical circulation in expressed concrete tubes was a constant theme in Andrews's work, these later tubes with stepped panels of reflective glass block are especially lively visually. [FIG. 13]

While the circulation cylinders at the convention center are the most obvious element that repeats Andrews's previous designs, there are other, more subtle connections to the architect's earlier work. The Sydney Convention Centre is especially mindful of the design of Gund Hall. Halfway along the north–south pedestrian spine of the convention center, the upper levels discontinue; the space is lowered with sections of stepped roof supported on trusses of tubular steel with glazed vertical panels between them. This section is of course a quotation of the roof over the studios at Gund Hall. [FIG. 14] More allusively, the concatenation of "round" concrete columns on the exterior of the convention center, supporting lofty concrete volumes at the entry and the pedestrian-oriented eastern elevation of the building, seem very much like Andrews's treatment of the Quincy Street facade of Gund Hall (and thus of Le Corbusier's at the Carpenter Center). This emphasis on a play of heavy concrete elements and glass gives the Sydney Convention Centre an especially robust quality, apparent also in the broad use of concrete surfaces in the interior. [FIG. 15] The entry to the Adelaide Convention Centre, by comparison, was a visually lightweight volume of glazed steel, postmodern-ish in its glazed barrel-vault top.

11

12

FIG. 11 Photo collage of model, Darling Harbour Casino, Darling Harbour, Sydney, Australia, 1986.
FIG. 12 Model, Darling Harbour Casino, with Sydney Convention Centre in the foreground, Darling Harbour, Sydney, Australia, 1992.

13

14

FIG. 13 Main entrance, Sydney Convention Centre, 1988.
FIG. 14 Sydney Convention Centre, 1988.

As already mentioned, a casino was included in the Darling Harbour proposals but did not eventuate, though the casino was announced by the government of New South Wales in November 1985. The American casino company Harrah's was first selected as the operator, but shortly after the announcement, Harrah's was placed "under investigation" in New Jersey, and the license was revoked. New tenders were called, and an elimination process led to the Malaysian firm Genting Berhad, partners in the operation of the Adelaide Casino.[37] Their architect for the Sydney casino was John Andrews International, which prepared designs for a site on the eastern edge of Darling Harbour, on the other side of the newly repurposed district from the convention center. Genting Berhad proposed that its casino and bars would open on January 26, 1988—the very day of the bicentenary—with the rest of the complex scheduled to open in July of that year. It seems likely that by the time it had emerged as the favored casino operator, it was too late to meet this deadline.[38] As it was, the Genting Berhad bid was ultimately rejected, Labor lost the state election early in 1988, and the question of a casino was put to rest for several years. It was resuscitated in 1991, partly through the belief that a casino could generate government income to fund Sydney's hosting of the 2000 Summer Olympics.[39] While the Liberal-National government of the time favored a casino site at Pyrmont, west of Darling Harbour, they accepted proposals for other sites as well. Andrews was the architect for one of these, for the same site as his Genting Berhad design, but this time for the American casino mogul Steve Wynn, who walked away when the New South Wales government confirmed in September 1992 that the casino would be built in Pyrmont.[40]

Prominently featuring semicircular plan forms, Andrews's Darling Harbour casino designs are formally aligned with his Sydney Convention Centre project. The Genting Berhad proposal was to be "the World's Largest Casino." Accommodating 300 gaming tables, it was "aesthetically designed over two levels," with a 200-suite hotel, which would "not compete with existing hotels as it will be a class above them;" an 800-room convention hotel, which would be "the largest hotel in Australia;" and a "1000-seat cabaret."[41] The plan forms of the two hotels in the project also relate to the contemporaneous hotel for the Melbourne World Congress Centre; one of the hotels fronts the Darling Harbour foreshore as the Melbourne hotel fronts the Yarra River but with lower floors flared outward. On the side of the casino facing the central business district, the design of the larger of the hotels—over 30 floors high—featured a wing with a stepped profile. [FIG. 11]

The other Andrews casino design is configured quite differently. There is apparently just one hotel building and low-rise buildings at approximately five stories tall with extensive areas of glazing to the north. The hotel building follows the pattern of the hotel at the Melbourne World Congress Centre very closely: a semicircular overall plan, with hotel rooms on the outer arc oriented toward harbor views to the north and west and city views to the south. A concrete cylinder at the middle of the outer arc apparently contains vertical circulation. In general, the hotel in the second casino design is larger than its Melbourne predecessor, with a step down in the height of the hotel at its southern end at the central circulation volume.[42] [FIG. 12]

Reception of all the built Darling Harbour projects became mixed up with the ambivalent views of the bicentennial. But while this was a problematic moment in Australian history, intentionally or otherwise, the bicentennial led

---

37   McMillen, "Risky Business," 264.
38   Civil & Civic/Genting International, "Darling Harbour Resort & Casino Management Proposal," ca. 1986, 42.
39   McMillen, "Risky Business," 285.
40   McMillen, "Risky Business," 288; Bridget Carter, "Wynn Founder's Exit Clears Way For $10bn Crown Tilt," *The Australian*, April 10, 2019.
41   Civil & Civic/Genting International, "Management Proposal," 44.
42   The renders of this project done for John Andrews International have the British Telecom Tower (1 Market Street) in the background; this building was started in 1989 and completed in 1991, placing this drawing at least in an approximate range of dates. See "British Telecom Tower," SkyscraperPage, https://skyscraperpage.com/cities/?buildingID=7733.

at least some communities to reflect on the country's multiculturalism and its pre-British history.[43] While such a reflective frame of mind could not be claimed of the making of Darling Harbour, the construction of the convention center and the Darling Harbour precinct was nevertheless an opening in the commercial city of a space where—no matter how contested—architectural, urban, and community ideals were projected. Perhaps perversely, places like exhibition centers, entertainment centers, and convention centers underwrite the urban opportunity for face-to-face interaction. This collective gathering—not of the community (such a singular thing no longer exists) but of a community in adjacency with multiple other communities—is opposed to a competing contemporary version of city life that insists that such face-to-face gathering is unnecessary. Darling Harbour opened just seven years before the publication of the book City of Bits by William Mitchell, another Australian architect who made it big abroad. Mitchell's book apocalyptically predicts the end of the physical city in the face of the onslaught of the virtual; this observation has taken on new urgency during the COVID-19 pandemic.

There was a kind of untimeliness in Andrews's design of the Sydney Convention Centre, apparent in the weight and mass of the building's concrete that contrasted so markedly with the lightweight construction and rather desperate festivity of much of the rest of Darling Harbour: steel structures, sheet claddings, tensile canopies. The convention center's architecture did not, that is, participate in the place's "mobilization of the spectacle"; it was not an architecture given over to consumption and consumability. Nor was it architecture-as-image (not in the Reyner Banham Brutalist sense but rather in the sense of an assertive but transient impression, or what Terry Smith has called the "iconomy").[44] The more theorized criticisms of Darling Harbour at the time of its completion employed Jean Baudrillard's discourse on simulacra to comprehend its logic.[45] But the heft in the fabric of the convention center, its sheer materiality, seems resistant to this. "It was built to last 500 years, not 50," as one commentator noted.[46] This quality was the inheritance in Andrews's work of Sert, particularly of Sert's finding in Le Corbusier's late work the apotheosis of the new monumentality.[47]

What can be referred to as the untimeliness of Andrews's Sydney Convention Centre—the manner in which its modern monumentality reaches back to unresolved paradoxes in the program of mid-century modernism—is perhaps indicated in how critical opinion received the design when it was new. The convention center was not reviewed with the other major projects in the September 1988 Darling Harbour issue of Architecture Australia. In her critique of Darling Harbour's buildings in Transition, Australia's main attempt at a theorized journal of architecture, Karen Burns also focuses only on the Philip Cox buildings, querying the problematic, nationalist attempts to legitimate their forms in reference to the maritime technologies of the settlement period and ultimately contesting that perhaps they had no local particularity at all. While two other critics—Elizabeth Farrelly and Jennifer Taylor—each gave Andrews and Cox about the same amount of attention, both analyzed the work of the two architects separately and on different terms. As Taylor noted, "The Darling Harbour Convention Centre is a

---

43 Peter Spearritt, "Celebration of a Nation: The Triumph of Spectacle," Australian Historical Studies 23, no. 91 (1988): 3–20.

44 Margo Huxley and Kate Kerkin, "What Price the Bicentennial? A Political Economy of Darling Harbour," Transition 26 (Spring 1988): 63; Terry Smith, The Architecture of Aftermath (Chicago: University of Chicago Press, 2006).

45 For example, Martin Thomas, "Making the State Grate: The Pretensions of Darling Harbour" Art & Text 29 (June–August 1988): 64–75. This article is cited by Karen Burns, "Seeing the Sites: Sydney's Darling Harbour," Transition 26 (Spring 1988): 65–68. Huxley and Kerkin depend heavily on the postmodern geography of David Harvey in their account of Darling Harbour.

46 Frank Lowe, "Critique: John Andrews," The Architecture Show, Summer 1989, 5–6.

47 Josep Lluís Sert, Fernand Léger, and Sigfried Giedion, "Nine Points on Monumentality," in Joan Ockman, ed., Architecture Culture 1943–1968: A Documentary Anthology (New York: Columbia University Graduate School of Architecture, Planning & Preservation and Rizzoli, 1993), 99.

monumental building both in its outward presence and internal spaces. With its roots in the imagery and dictates of modernism it clearly demonstrates Andrews's continuing faith in that position."[48] But her tone was almost apologetic, as if Andrews's "continuing faith" were slightly embarrassing compared to the forward-looking Cox. Farrelly, in comparison, was unequivocal, writing about the Sydney Convention Centre in the *Architectural Review*, "Amid all the frivolity of Sydney's Darling Harbour, serious architecture is a welcome rarity. And John Andrews's Convention Centre, unperturbed and uncompromised by the permanent cocktail party surrounding it, is nothing if not serious."[49]

15

16

[48] Taylor, *Australian Architecture Since 1960*, 234.
[49] Elizabeth Farrelly, "Serious in Sydney," *Architectural Review* (June 1989): 50–57. See also Elizabeth Farrelly, "Out of the Swing of the Sea, Darling." *Architectural Review* (April 1989): 63–66. Elizabeth Farrelly, "Amid the Frivolity, a Serious Interloper," *Sydney Morning Herald*, March 25, 1989; and Jennifer Taylor, "Philip Cox's Bicentennial Buildings for Sydney," *Architectural Review* (October 1988): 67–72.

FIGS. 15–16 Sydney Convention Centre, 1988.

14

finale

by Paul Walker

During the 1980s, Andrews was increasingly involved in activities outside architecture, including farming and viticulture as commercial enterprises, but also in personal pastimes, such as fishing and hunting. These activities often involved the members of his immediate family, and they often took him to New Zealand. In the 1990s, John Andrews International was winding down, while Andrews nevertheless continued to be involved with design projects to which he had a personal connection. Because the ethos of Andrews's architecture was not in line with the times, changes were proposed to projects he completed 20 or 30 years prior, and he was either disregarded or he resisted being involved in these alterations that he considered egregious. While architecture from the 1960s to the 1980s has been subject to recent popular and critical reassessment, as part of the general rethinking of the modernist tradition, Andrews's work has continued to be subject to thoughtless demolitions and reconfigurations. Even though Andrews had a wider set of interests than most architects at his level of professional achievement, this process of change was not easy for him to witness. It is particularly tragic and ironic that although the times have become much more attuned to the environmental values that Andrews espoused, his work nevertheless continues to be destroyed.

LATE WORK

In 1989, an article by the Sydney architect and critic Frank Lowe on Andrews and his practice appeared in the small Sydney architectural magazine *The Architecture Show*. At the start of the piece, Lowe commented, "It's a real shock to catch up with the enfant terrible designer of Scarborough College and have him tell you that his latest project may be his last, and that he intends to go trout fishing."[1] The piece was accompanied by an interview with Andrews and two long-standing members of his firm, Arthur Robb and Doug McKay, in which Andrews aired his enthusiasm for fishing:

Frank Lowe: What's the fascination with trout fishing?

John Andrews: Well, first of all it gets me the hell out of the office, which is a good idea. Secondly, I think there is an art to it. You need to practice. But most of all it doesn't matter whether you catch anything—you get outside, you get outdoors. That's its appeal to me—to be outside and on a river where the water's not polluted. It's fresh. There's nobody else. It just appeals to me. And if you catch a fish—that's terrific.

FL: Is it anything to do with architecture at all?

JA: Yeah, probably, I think the values are fairly similar. I think an appreciation of something like that, has really got a lot to do with what you think about architecture. I think it is just a ridiculous sort of phase we are going through. I don't think there is any truth in it. I don't think there is any value in it.

Now I suppose I could say the same thing about fishing with a worm as opposed to fly fishing. It's all too easy and the other guy hasn't got a chance. But with fly fishing, it's a fairly equal battle.

FL: I couldn't quite get the connection between postmodernism and worm fishing.

JA: Well, I think there is a very good connection. The worm's on the other end and postmodernism....[2]

Andrews did not finish the sentence; the connection between postmodernism and fishing with live bait remained unresolved. But Andrews's passion for fishing was clear, as was his disdain for postmodernism. Later in the interview, Andrews also revisited his disdain for the managerialism that took over the property development industry, and several times he alluded to the prospect of finishing his architecture career. He commented that his design of the 2 Bond Street building would be a good end point.

---

1   Frank Lowe, "Critique: John Andrews, *The Architecture Show* (Summer 1989): 5–6.

2   "Trout, Trade Unions and Architecture: Frank Lowe speaks with John Andrews, Arthur Robb and Doug McKay," *The Architecture Show* (Summer 1989): 2.

Andrews had a wide range of interests outside architecture. In 1973 he purchased a farm at Eugowra in the Central West region of New South Wales, rehabilitated an early colonial house on the property, and built a steel-framed, prefabricated pavilion house for himself and his wife, Ro Andrews. He later developed a herd of farmed deer on the property, which became a particular passion for him. He also became an avid trout fisherman, often traveling to New Zealand in serious pursuit of this pastime. His interest in deer also took him to New Zealand, where deer farming was more extensively and successfully developed than in Australia. Near Eugowra, just outside Canowindra, another town in the Central West region, Andrews also had a vineyard that produced highly sought-after wines under the label "Hamiltons Bluff." The name "Hamilton" was his middle name and the middle name of his son Jamie, who worked closely with him on the vineyard project.[3]

Andrews's quip about going trout fishing, then, was meant seriously. After 1990 Andrews began to wind his Sydney practice down, perhaps unconsciously. He did not intend to repeat the experience of leaving his Toronto practice, for which he developed a succession plan that ultimately left it in the hands of his Canadian partners, all of whom Andrews had worked with in the Colborne Street office.[4] He was disappointed when that plan did not work out. While Roger du Toit and Ned Baldwin left to start their own firms that became independently successful (including Baldwin's overseeing of the construction of the CN Tower), those who remained did not secure ongoing commissions that compared in scale and complexity to the work that the office had become accustomed to before Andrews returned to Australia.

The last project to be built by John Andrews International in Sydney was an academic building for the University of Sydney, the

FIG. 1   University of Sydney Veterinary Science Conference Centre, Sydney, Australia, 1988.

3   Halliday Wine Companion, "Hamiltons Bluff, New South Wales, Cowra," See https://www.winecompanion.com.au/wineries/new-south-wales/cowra/hamiltons-bluff.

4   John Andrews's partners were Edward (Ed) Galanyk, John Simpson, Anthony (Tony) Parsons, Edward (Ned) Baldwin, Roger du Toit, Robert (Bob) Anderson, William Bennet, Lawrence Diamond, Frank Carter.

Veterinary Science Conference Centre (VSCC), which opened in 1998. It had office spaces for doctoral students and a 250-seat lecture theater.[5] [FIG. 1] This project was carried out with the assistance of Warwick Werner, a stalwart in the John Andrews International office—the last man standing, so to speak. The office had recently moved, in 1994, from Palm Beach in the far north of Sydney's urban area, to an office at Milsons Point, which while a more conventional location in lower North Shore Sydney for an architectural practice, was, like the Palm Beach office, in a boat shed.[6] The other members of the firm had left by the time the office moved. In an article on the University of Sydney project, *Construction Review* reported, "The focal building for the rehabilitation of the veterinary science precinct provides a conference facility for the Faculty of Veterinary Science and office accommodation for the Post Graduate Foundation in Veterinary Science. Surrounded by 19th- and 20th-century buildings of varying and disparate architectural styles, the new Centre has been designed to complement and link the surrounding buildings through sympathetic scale, detailing and materials, and to define the external spaces, creating the new Veterinary Science Courtyard."[7]

Andrews's design for the Veterinary Science Conference Centre was modest but refined. At the ground level, a concrete frame was expressed by the external envelope of the building being pulled inward to create a colonnade. On the third floor, the concrete columns were also revealed in front of recessed fenestration. The cladding of the second floor was done with red brick panels to allude to the materials of the Victorian and early 20th-century buildings around it. With a low-pitched roof, carefully proportioned fenestration, and material references to its immediate surroundings, this building could be seen as a polite, contextual postmodernism that is at odds with the general run of Andrews's work. However, this was because he had few opportunities to work in circumstances that were so informed by the context of the site. In many ways, the project connected to his smaller, more situated projects from the late 1960s for American colleges, such as Smith College, or Tufts University (see chapter 4).[8] Programmatically it was a fitting finale given the significance of university work to Andrews's design career, in both North America and Australia. While relatively small, it was a project that Andrews particularly valued, not least because it was for his alma mater. He had built projects for other universities with which he had a close personal connection as well, Harvard University and the University of Toronto, and for this reason, he was pleased to design a building for the University of Sydney. It closed off another loop in his personal trajectory.

Beginning in the late 1980s and continuing into the 1990s, Andrews took on a range of large-scale speculative projects for international locations, including plans for the Hong Kong University of Science and Technology (1987); a competition in Warsaw; a competition for a massive scheme for Hong Kong's Kowloon Point (1992) in conjunction with the new transportation infrastructure being developed by Norman Foster to service the new Hong Kong International Airport; [FIG. 2] and preliminary drawings for a casino in Haiphong, Vietnam. But these projects did not progress very far and apparently were not personally important to Andrews.

There were other small projects as well that were important to Andrews. He did not often design houses, but in 1994, he built two. One was a house Andrews designed for Stan and Margaret Edwards in Northbridge, on Sydney's North Shore. Stan Edwards was a successful builder who had worked

---

5   Bruce Williams, *Liberal Education and Useful Knowledge: A Brief History of the University of Sydney 1850-2000* (Sydney: Chancellor's Committee, University of Sydney, 2002), 40.

6   This happened when Andrews sold the Palm Beach marina where his office had been located. See "Sydney Marinas on the Market," *Sydney Morning Herald*, March 15, 1994.

7   "Survey 4: Veterinary Science Conference Centre," *Construction Review* (May 1997): 8.

8   The projects for Tufts University and Smith College are documented in "Conversations with the John Andrews Architects," *Progressive Architecture* (February 1973): 62–75, and in the Andrews special issue of *Architecture + Urbanism* (May 1974): 46–47, 69–73.

on projects with Andrews. Notably, the construction company Edwards took over from his father, A. W. Edwards, was involved in the Callam Offices project, and later, Edwards was involved with Andrews in the Steve Wynn bid for a Sydney casino. The house built for the Edwardses is on a vertiginous site overlooking a sheltered cove of Sydney Harbour. At over three stories, with generous rooms, it is a comfortable and well-appointed house for affluent clients.

Previously, the Edwardses owned a house in Palm Beach that Andrews renovated for them. He also renovated a house in Palm Beach for his own family, and in 1976, he designed two houses there for himself and for his mother, which were never built.[9] It was primarily for a circle of friends and acquaintances connected to Palm Beach for which Andrews undertook house designs. In 1994, another house he built was located at Whale Beach, just south of Palm Beach. Designed in collaboration with Tina Curtis, an architect who worked in his office and who is his son Dal's personal partner, this property is a series of comfortable pavilions overlooking the ocean.[10] Limited in number, the houses Andrews designed clearly demonstrate a sensibility that valued ease, comfort, and generosity in domestic settings, rather than architectural fireworks.

In the 1990s Andrews also worked on projects that were not handled through the John Andrews International office. A key project of this type was a design for a small museum at Canowindra, which Andrews carried out on a pro bono basis for the local community with which he had long-standing connections, particularly through his vineyard. This design was for the Age of Fishes Museum, which houses thousands of 360-million-year-old fish fossils that are globally rare and were unearthed in Canowindra.[11] The museum opened in 2001, and the building takes the form of a corrugated iron shed, with a simple rectangular plan and a shallow barrel-vault roof. [FIG. 3] Some complexity is apparent in the high fenestration and the treatment of the eaves that extend over the walls, shading the elevations.

On one hand, Andrews's design for the museum appears to be mindful of the work of Glenn Murcutt, an Australian architect whose work he admired. On the other, the simple form and its materials connect it to the vernacular sheds typical of rural Australia, with several graceful examples found along a rail line that passes near the museum. [FIG. 4] Warwick Werner worked on the construction drawings, paid for on an hourly basis, but unlike Andrews's other work, the Canowindra museum was designed to be built by contractors without close supervision. Up close, this is more telling than Andrews wished, and the building has been subject to crude changes. (Upon visiting the museum with Andrews, he declined to get out of the car when we arrived.) Other local projects in the vicinity that he designed include a winery and a veterinary hospital in the small city of Orange. The winery Andrews designed for Cumulus Vineyards is a stark assemblage of industrial stainless steel that sits on a concrete plinth and is without an iota of vineyard romanticism. Trucks delivering grapes grown on various properties in the district drive onto the concrete platform to dump their loads of fruit into the frankly expressed machine.

If these late, independent projects suggested Andrews's retiring to an occasional small-scale practice in the locality in which he lived, other late work suggests something else. During the 1990s, Andrews was invited by his old friend, Canadian landscape architect Dick Strong, to collaborate on a project to expand and develop the campus of the University of Lethbridge in Alberta. In 1977, Strong moved from Toronto to Calgary, not long after the completion of his firm's contribution to the landscaping of the Cameron Offices.[12] He also served on Lethbridge's Board of Governors Design Review Panel. The University of Lethbridge was famously designed by

9   Jennifer Taylor and John Andrews, *John Andrews: Architecture, A Performing Art* (Melbourne: Oxford University Press, 1982), 175.
10   Melissa Walker-Smith, "Natural Manner," *Belle* (December 1994/January 1995): 68–73.
11   See "Devonian Billabong our Jurassic Park," *Sydney Morning Herald*, June 23, 1994, and "New-age Home for the Fossils," *Sydney Morning Herald*, January 22, 1995.
12   On Strong, see the obituary in *Ground* (Fall 2019): 33.

Canadian architect Arthur Erickson, whose earlier design of Simon Fraser University was completed in 1965, at the same time as Andrews's Scarborough College and to just as rapturous a reception. (Andrews had also undertaken designs for the Simon Fraser University competition.) Completed in 1968, the design of the University of Lethbridge shared much in common with Simon Fraser.[13]

The University of Lethbridge's basic parti was the building of two horizontal bars to accommodate academic functions that bridged north and south across two ravines in the foothills of the Rocky Mountains. The site sloped down to the Oldman River to the east. A crescent of student housing was envisioned to embrace the top of the southern ravine. Erickson's design for University Hall was only partly built, and one bar bridged only one ravine. Student housing was built where Erickson planned, but it was designed as a series of four discrete buildings. Other academic and service buildings were constructed scattered over the western plateau of the university campus. In 1993, Andrews proposed to the University of Lethbridge ways in which the university could grow without utilizing the part of its grounds that Erickson planned as the site of the second bar. There were major problems with the foundations of Erickson's building being in unstable ground.[14] Andrews proposed a plan for the development of the campus, concentrating core campus accommodations such as the library in a spine west of University Hall. Further specialist facilities would be located to the north and south of this spine. Andrews further elaborated on this, with an expanded campus plan he devised in 2000.[15]

However, proposing a project that ameliorated problems with an iconic design by one of Canada's most famous architects was not appreciated by Erickson's fans. In 2006,

2

3

13 Arthur Erickson, *The Architecture of Arthur Erickson* (London: Thames and Hudson, 1988), 62
14 John Andrews International, *The University of Lethbridge Campus Development Plan Review* (Lethbridge, AB: University of Lethbridge, 1993), 8.
15 Moriyama and Teshima/Gibbs Gage Architects/Education Consulting Services, University of Lethbridge Master Plan, n.d., 28.

FIG. 2 Kowloon Point Competition, Hong Kong, ca. 1992.
FIG. 3 Age of Fishes Museum, Canowindra, Australia, 2001.

FIG. 4   Shed, Canowindra, Australia.

FIG. 5 John and Ro Andrews, Kiembah, Eugowra, New South Wales, Australia, ca. 1980.

ignoring University Hall's structural problems, Ricardo L. Castro and David Theodore wrote, "Recent unsympathetic additions and renovations add complexity to the intricate task of comprehending Erickson's original intention to erect a single powerful structure."[16] Nevertheless, Andrews's plans guided the development of the University of Lethbridge for 18 years, though he designed none of its new buildings.[17]

FAMILY, FARMING, FISHING

John and Ro Andrews had a family of four sons, Dal, Lee, Craig, and James ("Jamie"), who were all born in Canada. Andrews's return to Australia was in part motivated by a desire for his sons to enjoy a typical Australian upbringing of swimming at the beach rather than Canadian ice hockey. Living and working in Palm Beach, in Sydney's Upper Northern Beaches, enabled this. However, Andrews was drawn into weekly trips between Palm Beach and meetings in Canberra over the Cameron Offices and other projects. The 3,000-acre farm at Eugowra, called Kiembah, which was a three-hour drive north of Canberra, was a good escape that relieved the commute to Sydney's far north. [FIG. 5] It also became an important part of his family life, a place where his four sons could develop their work ethic, carrying out farm work on the property during their school breaks, and where they could learn to drive, and so on. Three of Andrews's four children became designers, including Dal Andrews as an architect, Lee Andrews as a landscape architect, and Craig Andrews as an industrial designer. They followed in their father's footsteps, studying at master's level in the United States at Harvard University, the University of Pennsylvania, and the Cranbrook Academy. However, Dal Andrews had no interest in designing public-scale buildings. Jamie Andrews studied at the University of British Columbia and completed an arts degree at the Australian National University in Canberra. Though not formally qualified as a designer, he is an accomplished amateur maker of bricolage sculpture.

The Kiembah farm was used to run livestock. Beginning in 1985, Andrews developed an interest in farming deer on the property, ultimately having a herd of 1,000 animals. Andrews traveled to New Zealand for this particular passion since commercial deer farming in New Zealand developed ahead of that in Australia, its bloodlines of deer stock were improved by importing superior animals from Europe, and the stock-handling procedures and gear for deer farming were more advanced. Andrews used his design skills to finesse equipment he imported from New Zealand. As one New Zealand supplier wrote:

> … we found it was a whole new ball game working with a leading Australian architect who had designed the tallest building in the world. This caught me on the hop as we had made his unit especially to new specifications for him and we hadn't had time to put it all down on paper. Some of our ideas and concepts in deer handling were quickly accepted or discarded as suited Australian conditions and John soon disappeared to his office to emerge later with a complete interior plan for Arnie the builder to follow. As could be expected measurements were down to the last centimeter.[18]

Andrews's own deer-breeding activities "greatly improved the genetics of the Australian red deer herd" through the importation of frozen embryos, first from New Zealand and then from Germany and Yugoslavia. He formed a particular friendship with Graham Carr, the owner of the Peel Forest Estate and a leader in the New Zealand deer industry. Andrews also contributed to organizations in the trade,

---

16 Ricardo L. Castro and David Theodore, "The University of Lethbridge, Alberta," in Nicholas Olsberg and Ricardo L. Castro, *Arthur Erickson: Critical Works* (Vancouver: Douglas & McIntyre & Vancouver Art Gallery, 2006), 94.
17 The Andrews fonds at the State Library of New South Wales includes drawings for a neuroscience building at the University of Lethbridge (1999–2000), but this did not proceed.
18 John R. Dennis, "Australian Deer Farming Today—A View," *Australian Deer Farming* (October 1991): 27–28.

serving first as the president of the New South Wales Deer Farmers Association and then as president of the Deer Farmers Federation of Australia from 1995 to 1997. There, he carried out many reforms, reconstituting the federation as the Deer Industry Association of Australia, setting up a five-year plan for the development of deer farming, and building connections to the Rural Industries Research and Development Corporation (RIRDC), which enabled the establishment of research staff positions for the association.[19]

Owned by Andrews for 30 years, the Kiembah property was sold in 2003 and the deer herd dispersed.[20] Andrews first moved to a smaller farm, without deer, in Lidster, closer to the regional city of Orange, in order to facilitate Ro Andrews's volunteer work at the Orange Botanic Gardens and access medical services. John and Ro Andrews then moved to Orange in 2007.

On his visits to New Zealand, Andrews was also introduced to fly-fishing for trout. This became an enthusiasm he shared with Ro Andrews—both of them were hooked. Together, they were briefly owners of a lodge at Lake Rotoroa, a pristine mountain lake, in the north of the South Island, and built a small house there. They later sold the lodge to Graham Carr. Andrews gained registration as an architect in New Zealand and designed a hotel with octagonal-plan rooms in Nelson, the closest city to his fishing retreat.[21] But this was never built, and Andrews did not build anything else there. His most high-profile professional activities in New Zealand included serving on the jury of a design award in Auckland in 1984 and participating as a speaker at the annual conference of the New Zealand Institute of Architects in Christchurch in 1987. While New Zealand was mostly a relaxing break for Andrews from the routine of an architectural practice, these engagements turned out to be problematic for different reasons.

The jury that Andrews served on in 1984 for the Auckland Architecture Association Monier Design Awards, an annual competition for unbuilt design work, including by students, distributed a single award to a competent postmodern design to extend an urban courthouse. This did not attract any comment, but one of the other notable projects did. This project was a "celebration of renewal" by Jeanette Budgett, a speculative design for an installation on Auckland's Maungawhau Mount Eden, which contained forms with "male–female symbolism," to quote the jury citation. When presenting the jury decisions, Andrews called on the other judges to comment, making it apparent that they had been divided on Budgett's scheme and another overtly feminist project that was not recognized by the jury.[22] An article that appeared in the New Zealand Institute of Architects journal *New Zealand Architect* implied that these projects were unpalatable for Andrews simply for their feminist stance. But whatever his reservations, they were not about the gender of the designers of these projects; after all, he was chair of the jury that selected Zaha Hadid as the winner of the competition for the Peak Leisure Club in Hong Kong just a year before.

Andrews participated in the 1987 New Zealand Institute of Architects conference with the theme "A Pacific Response." As *New Zealand Architect* noted, Andrews brought "topline experience from both sides of the Pacific together in one career spanning 25 years…."[23] Another Australian speaker at that conference was Andrews's colleague from the Design Arts Board, Philip Cox. Andrews anticipated that after the conference they would go to his property at Lake Rotoroa to work together on the design for the Venice Biennale's Australian Pavilion, which was due for completion the following year. But this did not happen, and their collaboration, on this project and otherwise, was over from this point forward. Again, this was a disappointing outcome.

---

19   See John Andrews, "President's Report," *Australian Deer Farming* (April 1996): 2; (August 1996): 2; (July 1997): 2.
20   Andrew Hansen, "John Andrews AO," *Australian Deer Farming* (June 2003): 18–19.
21   This is almost certainly the project listed as "Golden Bay Lodge, 1993" in the John Andrews fonds at the State Library of New South Wales.
22   Pete Bossley, Rewi Thompson, Chris Johns, Andy Anderson and Chris Sage, "Inescapable Ennui: The 1984 AAA/Monier Design Awards," *New Zealand Architect* 6 (1984): 37–42.
23   Russell Devlin, "John Andrews," *New Zealand Architect* 4 (1987): 31.

DEMOLITION AND ALTERATION

The breakdown of the collaboration Andrews sought with Cox over the Venice Biennale Australian Pavilion and the minor controversy at the 1984 Monier Awards were annoyances. However, they were slight in comparison to the disappointment Andrews felt over the changing fortunes of his buildings in Australia. Even before John Andrews International closed, his designs began to suffer egregious changes. And the worst was to come: demolitions. While for the past 20 years, there has been growing scholarly, professional, and enthusiast interest in modern architecture designed from the 1950s to the 1980s, this has not yet moderated ravenous redevelopment of it by governments and corporations. In 1989, Frank Lowe commented that Andrews's Sydney Convention Centre "was built to last 500 years, not 50."[24] But in fact, it was demolished just 25 years after its completion. The World Congress Centre in Melbourne was abandoned after only 15 years.

The first indignity carried out on an Andrews building was not a demolition but rather the completion of Building 8 at the Royal Melbourne Institute of Technology (RMIT) as a postmodern design. [FIG. 6] Andrews's design of this building in 1976 included plans to house the university's library and student facilities. In 1977, this design was first revised as a project staged to house the student union and then to include four levels of library, with further levels above the library to house other academic facilities to be built later.[25] Due to lack of money, only four stories of the ten envisioned were built (see chapter 4). In 1990 the project was reactivated with new architects, the Melbourne firm Edmond and Corrigan. Peter Corrigan was an outspoken critic of Australian architecture, and his design work was theatrically postmodern. He was a teacher in RMIT's architecture program and studied at the Yale School of Architecture in the late 1960s when Charles Moore was the dean.[26] Corrigan was also an important contributor to the July 1985 issue of *Domus* that focused on Australian architecture and design culture, which was sponsored by the Australia Council's Design Arts Board under Andrews's leadership.[27] While Evan Walker's championing of Andrews for the RMIT job was pivotal, as a Yale alum, Corrigan was mindful enough of the Kahnian qualities of Andrews's work to also advocate for Andrews to be appointed as the architect for the RMIT student union and library building in the mid-1970s.[28]

However, by 1990, Andrews seemed to have become anathema to Corrigan. The Andrews project for RMIT entailed entrances to the building a half-level down from Swanston Street, one of central Melbourne's main thoroughfares, with a striking zigzag facade above made of glass blocks in a concrete frame. Its exaggerated modeling appeared to have been a response to the vigorous Victorian facades typical of central Melbourne, which experienced a commercial property boom in the 1880s. In the 1990s, Edmond and Corrigan superimposed on this a very colorful, graphic, flat facade, with jewel-like projections of blue reflective glass, a very different reading of the Victorian and Edwardian context. In their alteration, two piers supported this facade, with exaggerated diagonal beams placed in front of Andrews's design, visually burying it.[29] Postmodernism's revenge.

The next indignity carried out, in 1998, was the recladding of the King George Tower in Sydney and the reworking of the pedestrian levels at the base of the building by architects Kevin Rice and John Daubney. This entailed the creation of several "sky gardens," which involved the cutting back of the tower's floor plates to create five atria, each extending over four floors. It also

---

24 Frank Lowe, "Critique: John Andrews," *The Architecture Show* (Summer 1989): 5–6.
25 Taylor and Andrews, *John Andrews*, 175.
26 Conrad Hamann, *Cities of Hope: Australian Architecture and Design by Edmond and Corrigan, 1962-92* (Melbourne: Oxford University Press, 1993), 139.
27 Peter Corrigan, "Learning from Suburbia," *Domus*, 663 (July/August 1985): 6–7; Paul Walker and Karen Burns, "Constructing Australian Architecture for International Audiences: Regionalism, Postmodernism, and the Design Arts Board, 1980-1988," *Fabrications* 28, no. 1 (March 2018): 25–46.
28 Hamann, *Cities of Hope*, 139. See also chapter 4 in which Philip Goad makes the case that the RMIT commission was awarded to Andrews through Evan Walker.
29 Hamann, *Cities of Hope*, 139–47.

involved the recladding of the glazed facades and the removing of the access platforms and polycarbonate sunshields, which were replaced with "high-performance glazing systems." [FIG. 7] While the polycarbonate sunshields had not aged as well as first envisioned in the mid-1970s, this change reduced the sense of contrast between the concrete corner elements and the glazed facades by introducing more complexity and diminishing the visual effect of the fine structure in front of the glazed walls.[30]

The redesign of the pedestrian levels attempted to address the fact that the underground connections anticipated in the original Andrews design had not been realized. However, the changes introduced did not improve pedestrian flow. In fact, the introduction of a building element diagonally across the Andrews plaza, as well as more ground-level shops, impeded movement. The first proposals for this reworking had been even more radical and would have hidden the building's concrete frame behind smooth glass. Peter Mould, a senior architect in the New South Wales Government Architect's office, noted:

> As an alternate member of the Central Sydney Planning Committee, I was part of the vote that rejected the original DA [development application] and was subsequently a member of a subcommittee established to negotiate changes to the application. These changes included maintaining the concrete frame rather than cladding it, and developing a more detailed facade treatment in an attempt to recapture the original interplay between the lightness of the textured shade panels and the solidity of the Brutalist frame.... The smooth glass skin of the building's envelope was enlivened by the development of an external bracing system to interpret the filigree of the original sunshade by adding texture and detail to the facade. This has been only partially successful. The

FIG. 6 RMIT Building 8, Melbourne, Australia. Architects: John Andrews International, 1976–1984; Edmond and Corrigan, 1990.

30 Peter Mould, "Corporate Overhaul," *Architecture Australia* 88, no. 4 (July/August 1999): 68–73.

FIG. 7 King George Tower after interventions, 1998. Architect: Rice Daubney.

detailed modelling is apparent up close and especially when seen at an angle, but face on, it is too delicate to recreate the texture of the original. The facade is now ordered by horizontal spandrels and the sky gardens, with their ceilings overly dominant when seen from the street.[31]

The changes that Rice Daubney introduced to the plaza levels of the King George Tower were themselves soon outdated and replaced by another design, which involved even more building in what had been in Andrews's design an open, multilevel public setting. This new work, designed by Francis-Jones Morehen Thorp (fjmt) in 2015, introduced a five-story building of shops and restaurants that entirely replaced the plaza. The architects wrote that Andrews's tower "was from an era in architecture that is now being increasingly valued and placed in historical/cultural perspective. Any new work needs to be respectful of the quality and geometry of this significant John Andrews project."[32] However, it is hard to construe how fjmt's project, entailing the complete obliteration of the plaza and a sinuous—almost Art Deco—horizontal composition of glass and sandstone, did any such thing.

The next piece to fall was the Cameron Offices. The ongoing neglect of the Cameron Offices by its public custodians continued until 1997 when the Australian government announced that it would divest 70,000 square meters of office space in Canberra that it held due to cuts in the federal public service and in order to rejuvenate the commercial property market.[33] Proposals to demolish or partly demolish the Cameron Offices were considered as part of this program. In 2000, the building was sold to developers Bovis Lend Lease. Through this deal, they constructed a new headquarters for the main government agency occupying the complex, the Australian Bureau of Statistics (ABS), which was designed by architecture studio Woods Bagot, to the immediate west of the three northernmost fingers of Cameron Offices.

Completed in 2002, the Woods Bagot building is a large, slick, corporate box of six stories, built around a featureless atrium. Philip Drew, a one-time advocate for Andrews's importance as a leading light of the "third generation," commented on the ABS building, "In 2002, the brutal Atlantic Wall appearance of the Cameron blocks can seem dated and out of touch with today's slick corporate styling." He also repeated the story about 250 insecure doors at the Cameron Offices, one of the points of contention in the notorious defamation case. Ironically, Woods Bagot designer Earle Arney, was identified as having "studied in John Andrews's Harvard GSD building and is a staunch defender of the Cameron Offices."[34] Inevitably, once its primary occupant was committed to move, pressure mounted to demolish the Cameron Offices. However, in 2001, John Andrews was asked to investigate redevelopment strategies that retained the most significant elements of the Cameron Offices while partitioning the wings for redevelopment as apartments or small-scale commercial tenancies.[35]

The fate of the Cameron Offices did motivate Australia's building conservation lobby and the Royal Australian Institute of Architects (RAIA) to take action to recognize the building's heritage value. In 2001, in an unsuccessful attempt to influence the consideration of the building's heritage status at a federal level, RAIA nominated the Cameron Offices to the International Union of Architects (UIA) World Register of Significant Twentieth Century Architecture.[36] In 2004, when the proposals for partial demolition were well advanced, the

---

31 Ibid.
32 "FJMT Designs Addition to John Andrews's Sulman Medal-winning Sydney Tower," *ArchitectureAU*, June 1, 2018, https://architectureau.com/articles/fjmt-designs-addition-to-john-andrewss-sulman-medal-winning-sydney-tower/.
33 See "Cameron Offices (Wings 3, 4, and 5, and Bridge), Chandler St, Belconnen, ACT, Australia," Australian Heritage Database, Department of Climate Change, Energy, the Environment and Water, Government of Australia.
34 Philip Drew, "Binary Blockbuster," *Indesign* (February 2003): 142.
35 "Cameron Offices," Australian Heritage Database.
36 See "ACT Notable Buildings," Australian Institute of Architects, https://www.architecture.com.au/explore/notable-buildings/act.

building was indeed nominated for inclusion on the Australian Commonwealth Heritage List. The Australian Heritage Council judged that it did not meet the conditions to be listed as National Heritage but should be accorded the lesser recognition of Commonwealth Heritage. Phew! However, the Minister for the Environment and Heritage determined that this would exclude the parts of the building already identified for demolition.[37] In 2006, as the building was entered into the Docomomo Australia Buildings Register (one of only two projects on that list from Canberra), four wings of the building, two at its northern end and two at the southern end plus the old computer center at the southernmost part of the complex, were destroyed.[38] The remaining wings have been partially converted into student accommodations for the University of Canberra. The land cleared in the south is now occupied by banal apartment buildings and the land cleared in the north is a parking lot.

The demolition of all of Andrews's convention centers was the next blow. The World Congress Centre in Melbourne was in operation for only 15 years when, in 2005, the Victoria state government called for proposals from three short-listed consortia for a new convention center on the other side of the Yarra River. The signature feature of the new center was an auditorium that could accommodate 5,000 people and was twice as large as the plenary hall in the World Congress Centre.[39] The new center was expected to achieve a Six-Star Green Star rating, the first convention center in the world to achieve such a distinction.[40] In his book on the new building, *The Private Life of Public Architecture*, Andrew McKenzie frequently refers to its sustainability credentials, writing, for example, that "all the primary drivers of a sustainable building were on the design agenda from the beginning" and "exceeding the brief's green aspirations and creating an audaciously large plenary hall were just some of the major construction challenges inherent in this project." McKenzie also writes, "Between the new convention center and existing exhibition center is a linear garden planted with natural grasses in keeping with the Green Star rating of the project." Lastly, the architects Woods Bagot comment in the book that, "Woods Bagot made a commitment to embedding sustainable design practices into our culture. Since December 2006, our practice has been 100 percent climate neutral."[41] However, not once does this book mention that the new convention center project entailed the abandonment of a building less than 20 years old that was left unused until its demolition to make way for an also unused pocket park; nor does McKenzie mention the energy and water consumed in making the abandoned building, let alone the refinement of its immaculate concrete work. Presumably, these do not figure into the new convention center's Six-Star Green Rating. Still, look at those natural grasses!

The first major extension of the Convention Centre and Exhibition Centre in Adelaide was completed in 2001 and also designed by Woods Bagot, with Larry Oltmanns of Skidmore, Owings & Merrill as design consultant.[42] The extension included a new entrance at North Terrace that led to a promenade with an extensive glass wall to the north of Andrews's original building, which completely blocked it from view. Further expansion was announced in 2011, again by Woods Bagot with Oltmanns (but now Oltmanns was with the firm Vx3 Architects). This newest extension occurred in two phases. The first phase involved the building of the West Building, completed in 2015, which was "inspired by the dramatic layered geology and color of South Australia's Flinders Ranges." The second phase, the building of the East Building, completed in 2017, was alternatively inspired by "the great

---

37 "Cameron Offices," Australian Heritage Database.
38 See "Docomomo Australia Fiches by State," Docomomo Australia, https://docomomoaustralia.com.au/international-fiches/power-and-modernism/.
39 Andrew McKenzie, ed., *The Private Life of Public Architecture* (Melbourne: URO Media, 2009), 68.
40 Ibid., 27, 89.
41 Ibid., 31, 97, 122, 210.
42 Scott Drake and Rachel Hurst, "Radar: Adelaide Convention Centre Extension," *Architecture Australia* 91, no. 2 (March 2002): 32.

FIG. 8　Sydney Convention Centre being demolished, Sydney, Australia, 2014.

granite boulders of the Remarkable Rocks on Kangaroo Island."[43] Far from geological, the buildings are in fact merely large, irregularly shaped glass volumes. The East Building was built on the site of Andrews's original Adelaide Convention Centre, now not just hidden but completely obliterated.

The most egregious of the convention center demolitions was that of the Sydney Convention Centre in 2014, which was knocked over to be replaced by a convention center that was larger but did not match the architectural attributes of what was Andrews's major public building in his own city. The apparent need for a larger plenary hall (the new one accommodates 8,000 people, compared to the old one that accommodated 3,500) could easily have been met with the existing facilities in Darling Harbour if the Sydney Convention Centre and the Sydney Entertainment Centre, with a seating capacity of 12,000, were jointly managed. Barry O'Farrell, the premier of New South Wales who made the decision to demolish the Sydney Convention Centre and the Philip Cox–designed Exhibition Centre, seems to have been motivated, not only by the parochial need to outdo facilities in Melbourne and Adelaide, but also by the desire to create construction jobs, sustainability be damned.

The outcome of this rebuilding exercise is competence but architectural banality. Designed by a consortium of Hassell and Populous (OMA was also originally a partner but withdrew), the new International Convention Centre (ICC) in Sydney combines the functions of a convention center with those of an exhibition center, wrapping them in glass and metal surfaces that are perpendicular *and* canted, just to make sure we understand it's architecture, with a few patches of timber also fashionably on display. But at least we are not told that the building volumes share a kinship with some rocks. In his review of the new building in *Architecture Australia*, Michael Keniger focused on the project's intricate disposition of facilities and services.[44] While admiring the building's planning, however, he also evinced some disdain for the process that produced it. As he wrote, "The loss of the original convention and exhibition buildings will continue to be recalled and regretted by many and should serve to ensure that we continue to press for the wider community's appreciation of the signature buildings of its city, including those that have so recently been completed."[45] Indeed.

Finally, in this gallery of horrors, Griffith University in Brisbane is currently proposing the demolition of Andrews's Australian Environmental Studies building, ironically so, given the university's touting of its environmental credentials. Its current "vision statement" includes the following: "We have a long-standing commitment to environmental sustainability and guardianship of our unique campus ecosystems."[46] However, in some good news, the Octagon building in Paramatta, which was recently threatened with demolition, has apparently been saved—at least temporarily—through the uncertainty of the office space market in Sydney.[47] Paramatta, like many concentrations of high-rise office and apartment buildings in Australian cities, went through a recent real estate and building boom that has now slowed due to the Covid-19 pandemic.

Of course, buildings can outlive their usefulness, and then something must be done about them. This accords with Andrews's view of architecture as "common sense" and problem-solving. The Miami Seaport Terminal long survived only as unused spaces and in remnants incorporated into larger, more complex terminals. The last remaining pieces of it have recently been demolished. In this case, the terminal became obsolete because new cruise ships quickly outgrew the vessels for

43 "A Centre Transformed: Adelaide Convention Centre Celebrates Completion of $397 Million Redevelopment," Adelaide Convention Centre, https://www.adelaidecc.com.au/a-centre-transformed-adelaide-convention-centre-celebrates-completion-of-397-million-redevelopment/.
44 Michael Keniger, "ICC Sydney," *Architecture Australia* 106, no. 3 (May/June 2017): 50–56.
45 Ibid., 56.
46 Office of the Vice Chancellor, "Vision and Mission, Strategic Plan 2020–2025," Griffith University, https://www.griffith.edu.au/office-vice-chancellor/strategic-plan/vision-and-mission/.
47 Personal communication with Sydney conservation architect Noni Boyd, January 19, 2022.

which Andrews's Miami terminal was built. But changes to the Australian projects previously outlined in this chapter have not been carried out in response to changes in human use and technology so profound that the buildings could not be modified to accommodate them. Rather, it seems that John Andrews suffered from being a prophet in his own land and the wider purport of his projects has either not been fully grasped or has otherwise been rejected. In Australia there is a fetishization of the immediately new—new materials, new equipment, new spaces, new slogans—that has blinded building owners and governments to the wider social and environmental innovations proposed in Andrews's buildings. While some of Andrews's North American projects have faced threats, the architectural quality of the best of these buildings has underwritten their survival. This remains true even when, as in the case of the Intelsat Headquarters, the original uses and users are gone. In at least one case, Andrews's hand in his buildings has been celebrated, in the designation by the University of Toronto of the original Scarborough College edifice as the Andrews Building.

conclusion

by Paul Walker

GEOGRAPHY

John Andrews's career followed a unique geographical trajectory. Few Australian architects had studied in the United States, and none had made major careers in North America when he did. And no Australian architect that made it abroad, as Andrews did, chose to return to Australia at the peak of their careers. Andrews belonged to a generation of architects whose leading lights were more geographically dispersed than was the case previously. While the "third generation" that Philip Drew identified, after Sigfried Giedion, was still all male, the greater geographic spread from the first and second generations indicated how the profession had become more diverse. Of the 11 individuals and firms that Drew singled out as leaders of the third generation, three were Japanese, including Kisho Kurokawa, Kiyonori Kikutake, and Arata Isozaki. The movement of ideas and influences had increasingly become more various than a one-way flow from the center to the periphery.

However, this is a complex matter. Andrews's career paralleled the increasing engagement after World War II of Australian culture with that of the United States rather than that of the United Kingdom. One influential center replaced another. In 1960, in his locally notorious book *The Australian Ugliness*, architect Robin Boyd noted that there were Australians "who do not picture Australia ultimately connected with Britain, but who would sign her up tomorrow to economic junior partnership with the United States in a ceremony tumultuously applauded by a million jiving teenagers."[1] England meant nothing to Andrews, and except for Le Corbusier's buildings and the vernacular architecture he saw on his 1961 tour, Europe too meant very little.

But Andrews's encounter with the United States was primarily experienced through Josep Lluís Sert. For Sert, modern architecture had an ethical dimension that, as is often said, was excised in the uptake of modernism in the United States. From the 1950s to the 1970s, North America became more affluent, and this ethical engagement, where it survived, became even harder for architecture to maintain. While living in Canada, Andrews enjoyed the country's developing sense of cultural confidence and cosmopolitanism, which he particularly felt in Montreal while he worked on his Expo 67 commissions. He perhaps enjoyed Toronto less, but the provincial city he arrived to in 1958 was a burgeoning metropolis by the time he left in 1969. However, the experience of working in the United States gave Andrews pause to think. In the A. S. Hook Memorial address that he delivered in 1981 upon receiving the Gold Medal of the Royal Australian Institute of Architects, Andrews lamented that architecture in the United States had lost its sense of connection to real problems—anything was possible. For him, it had lost its ethical dimension.

In the Hook Address, Andrews countered an American "anything goes" attitude with Australian architectural principles that evolved from an engagement with landscape and maintained a "problem-solving" ethos. In North America, as Andrews explained,

> Architecture had become a fantasy and an art form only. Irresponsibility had reached its peak with the division between

1 Robin Boyd, *The Australian Ugliness*, 2nd ed. (Harmondsworth, UK: Penguin, 1963), 71; 1st ed. (Melbourne: F. W. Cheshire, 1960). See also Philip Goad, "Importing Expertise: Australian–US Architects and the Large-scale, 1945–1990," *Fabrications* 26, no. 3 (2016): 357–91.

drawing and building becoming wider every day. Today... this direction has manifested itself in a collection of 'isms' that have nothing whatsoever to do with the betterment of our environment and serve only to extend the ego and drafting prowess of architectural dilettantes who have little desire, and certainly not the courage, to venture further off the drawing board than stage settings for the elite.

In contrast, Australia was characterized "by open space, the magical quality of light, its geographical combination of land and sea, its urbanity and its incredible solitude, its marvelous twisted landscape."[2] He provided a very positive view of Australia. Did he really believe it? It was certainly at odds with how angry he must have felt with the Australian government over their treatment of the Cameron Offices. But only occasionally did Andrews regret that he left North America.

Andrews's return to Australia, then, was complicated. Certainly, he did not confine himself to Australian projects. The success of the Intelsat Headquarters in Washington, DC, his work at the University of Lethbridge in Alberta, and his pursuit of the Los Angeles Park Place project are indicative of this. And, in the later years of John Andrews International—the name speaks to its geographical ambition—there were several speculative projects in Asia. This serves as a precursor for how practices now, both large and small, have found ways to work globally.

With few exceptions, Andrews's Australian projects are Australian only by virtue of their response to the contextual exigencies of their physical locations, including climate and topography. With its use of corrugated steel—a material that by the 1980s was seen as an icon of Australian architecture—only the Eugowra house seems to play with signature Australian imagery in the way that, say, Glenn Murcutt's architecture does. In general, Andrews's approach to architectural design in Australia was no different than his approach in Canada. It is notable that his first major projects as an independent practitioner in both countries, Scarborough College and the Cameron Offices, were understood by critics in relation to their broader geographical settings. Paolo Scrivano and Mary Lou Lobsinger have pointed to such readings of Scarborough College, but it is important to note that Andrews's Australian nationality and American training problematize any nationalist reading of his work.[3] Rather, they suggest that Scarborough College was symptomatic of the openness in the 1960s of Canadian architecture—and Canadian culture as a whole—to international influence.

Nevertheless, the Canadian discourse on architecture in relation to national attributes, which occurred in the 1960s and 1970s, anticipates a similar discourse in Australia slightly later. Jennifer Taylor wrote of the Cameron Offices in 1988, it was "the first building constructed in this country to give architectural expression to the expansive essence of the land itself.... The Cameron Offices is a raw but intellectual building with a vigor and life that seem in phase with this country."[4] But in concluding the book in which she made these comments, Taylor was critical of Australian cultural insularity, writing, "Geographically [Australia] is a part of Asia and the South Pacific, culturally it is part of Europe. It is isolated yet it is inexorably united with the rest of the world. The slouch hat alone will be far too limiting, and someone else's hat will not do at all."[5]

2 John Andrews, "A. S. Hook 1981," *Architecture Australia* 70, no. 5 (November 1981): 70.
3 Paolo Scrivano and Mary Lou Lobsinger, "Experimental Architecture, Progressive Pedagogy: Scarborough College," *Architecture and Ideas* 8 (2009): 4–19.
4 Jennifer Taylor, *Australian Architecture Since 1960*, 2nd ed. (Canberra: Royal Australian Institute of Architects National Education Division, 1990): 108–9.
5 Ibid., 246.

The Canadian writers on Scarborough College, which Scrivano and Lobsinger point to, and Australian writers on the Cameron Offices, such as Taylor, used tropes of landscape and place to characterize architectural identity. This accorded with international expectations applied to locations outside the metropolitan centers of the United States and Western Europe. The "third generation" of architects may have begun to increase the geographical diversity of the profession's leading designers, but architectural ideology and discourse still have a long way to go to catch up. In Australia, it is the house in particular that bears the external expectation of how architecture should perform its relationship to its locality in a designerly way. This is apparent in the global reception of Murcutt, who is probably Australia's most internationally celebrated architect of the present moment. Most of Murcutt's work consists of private houses that few can visit; few Murcutt projects have any public dimension. Published photographs of them can therefore project a perfect fantasy.

It is telling that Andrews was not particularly engaged in the design of houses, even though they are generally so important to Australian architects. Houses that John Andrews International designed were mostly created for a circle of contacts connected to Palm Beach, the location of Andrews's office and residence north of Sydney. They were not central to the office's work. Andrews was the architect of but one iconic house design, his farm property in Eugowra. As noted in chapter 9, that house, with its symmetrical form, its roofs that shelter its glazed walls from the harsh local sun, its frank steel structure and corrugated steel walls, and its rainwater tanks and energy-conscious design, may be an architectural problem straightforwardly solved, but its forms also allude to the history of the Australian farmhouse in a manner that is almost postmodern. In other houses he designed, Andrews opted not to produce this strong Australian imagery; rather, these other houses focused on comfort and domestic amenity. In his farmhouse in Eugowra, architectural pragmatics and architectural imagery coincide. Is this intentional? It is not clear.

THE THIRD GENERATION

As well as thinking about the geography of Andrews's career, we can productively think of it in relation to his generation of architects and the ways in which this generation reacted to the concerns of those who came earlier. How does Andrews's work relate to the work of other architects of the same generation and of architects slightly older? How does Andrews's architecture relate to that of his teachers? I believe it is historiographically important to ask these questions. Architects do not develop their careers and their design strategies in isolation. This is complicated in the case of the architects of Andrews's generation, who were architecturally acculturated when an ethos of individual creativity still prevailed but also when the belief in an all-prevailing zeitgeist that could explain the commonalities across different architects' work was no longer credible.

Early in his career, the influence of two American architects who had emerging reputations in the 1950s figured strongly in Andrews's work: Paul Rudolph and Louis Kahn. This is particularly evident in the work that

Andrews did at John B. Parkin Associates from 1958 to 1961, including Federal Equipment Building, the Primrose Club, and the Sault Sainte Marie high school, all of which display attributes that reference one or both these architects. Some drawings for Scarborough College adopt Rudolph's favored representational technique of rendering perspectival sections with careful vertical hatching, but Andrews soon left this behind. Kahn's shadow was more lasting. The evolution across Andrews's work of vertical concrete tubes that contain stairs and lifts probably started with him encountering similar elements in Kahn's, the iconic stairs at the Yale University Art Gallery for example.

However, in Andrews's work these attributes become independent architectural features that come to leave their traces of Kahn behind, in an exuberant and expressive wake. They have their own independent life and line of development. The triangulated secondary structures of stainless steel tubes supporting sun-shading elements, appear throughout Andrews's projects, from the King George Tower (1976) to the Callam Offices (1973), Woden College of Technical and Further Education (1978), Intelsat Headquarters (1988), and the Octagon (1990). In scale and visual effect, the King George Tower appears to be akin to the drawings of City Tower in Philadelphia that Kahn did in collaboration with Anne Tyng and that were published in *Perspecta* in 1953.[6] But Kahn realized no such feature in any of his built projects, and again, Andrews made this element expressively his own.

In opposition to the apparent early influence of Rudolph and Kahn, we need to also recall how accomplished the Andrews-led design for Toronto City Hall was, which in 1958, right at the beginning of his career, placed second in an international competition. He did not need to borrow. Perhaps his employment of Kahn and Rudolph while he was at John B. Parkin Associates was an attempt to modify the influence of Mies van der Rohe on that office.

After leaving Rudolph and Kahn behind, we can locate encounters with other architects in Andrews's work. The relationship of his work to that of Team 10, Aldo van Eyck, and Herman Hertzberger, for example, is one of convergence rather than influence. Andrews's design for the Bellmere Junior Public School contained a diagonally distributed plan that is akin to that of the Amsterdam orphanage designed by van Eyck, and the planning of African Place for Expo 67 is based on a similar logic. However, it is doubtful that Andrews was familiar with van Eyck's work when he designed African Place or the Bellmere Junior Public School.

Most of Andrews's large office projects from the Cameron Offices onward utilize a plan strategy akin to the mat plans explored by many architects internationally in the 1960s and 1970s. This particularly includes the architects associated with Team 10, but formally there is little in common between Team 10 and Andrews. Certainly, Andrews did not share Team 10's disdain for the postwar leadership of the Congrès Internationaux d'Architecture Moderne (CIAM). What Andrews and Team 10 shared was the philosophy of differentiating a hierarchy of circulation spaces from those for inhabitation according to a system that could articulate the potential for individual experience and address within a large building. When the Cameron Offices were designed, Andrews was aware of both van Eyck and

6   Louis Kahn, "Toward a Plan for Midtown Philadelphia," *Perspecta* 2 (1953): 10–27.

his acolyte Herman Hertzberger. He admired Hertzberger, whose work became a cipher for Andrews to refer to a broad design strategy that they had in common.

More speculatively, there is a possible relationship between Andrews and James Stirling. The grounds on which a connection can be made between them are slimmer. While Andrews referred a number of times to Hertzberger in his coauthored book, and in the occasional lectures he gave, he did not mention Stirling. Nevertheless, a likeness in the roofs of the Harvard GSD's Gund Hall and the University of Cambridge's History Faculty Building, designed by Stirling, was thought by Ada Louise Huxtable and Macy DuBois to suggest a relationship. Further, this relationship is surely requited in Stirling's Arthur M. Sackler Museum, just across Cambridge Street from Gund Hall, which is built around an internal staircase configured as a single run-up of four floors. Can it really be a coincidence that Stirling used such a device in a building he designed adjacent to Gund Hall, with its external stairway of the same scale placed at its Cambridge Street facade?

URBANISM

The late modernisms of Hertzberger and Andrews have different genealogies. While Hertzberger was a product of Aldo van Eyck's take on Team 10 revisionism, with its rejection of the CIAM, Andrews's intellectual roots are with Sert and precisely a continuation of CIAM. But both emphasized a relationship between architecture and urbanism. Through Sert, this relationship was emphasized at the GSD while Andrews was a student there. Not only did the design problems that Sert set in his master of architecture studios have a strong urban dimension, but so too did the theoretical studies that Giedion and Eduard Sekler taught. This exposure to Sert's urban orientation continued after Andrews completed his MArch through his attendance of the urban design conferences that Sert hosted at Harvard from 1956 to 1970.[7] These conferences were successors to the CIAM meetings, which under Sert's postwar leadership investigated urbanism in its cultural dimensions, rather than the functionalism of the Athens Charter.

Andrews's view of architecture as an urban issue is most apparent in his megastructure designs for Scarborough College, the South Residences at the University of Guelph, and the Cameron Offices. These are buildings as cities. They are monumental in scale and expression. Sert's thoughts about architecture at the urban scale are connected in the 1940s and 1950s to the views he expressed, with Giedion, on the aesthetic of modern monuments. Sert, Giedion, and Fernand Léger's famous 1943 text on this issue makes it clear that the modern monument is—or is part of—an urban ensemble.[8]

At Scarborough College, Guelph, and the Cameron Offices, Andrews used an architectural commission to invent an urban order for an unencumbered site that was intended to become intensely inhabited. In each, a circulation system, made apparent in overall form, was created in anticipation of connecting the scheme to a larger pattern that would determine future building and development. Andrews's design for Toronto's Metro Centre went further: the circulation system was the primary focus and the buildings were only nominal proposals. Andrews's urban imagination

[7] See Richard Marshall, "Josep Lluís Sert's Urban Design Legacy," in *Josep Lluís Sert: The Architect of Urban Design, 1953–1969*, eds. Eric Mumford and Hashim Sarkis, with Neyran Turan (New Haven, CT: Yale University Press; Cambridge, MA: Harvard University Graduate School of Design, 2008) 130–43. Andrews was on the alumni planning committee for the Harvard GSD's 1967 Urban Design Conference. See letter of thanks, Jaqueline Tyrwhitt to John Andrews, May 8, 1967, "Harvard Fund Raising Committee," file in AND 43A/78-33, Box 43-48, John Andrews fonds, Canadian Architectural Archives, University of Calgary.

[8] Josep Lluís Sert, Fernand Léger, and Sigfried Giedion, "Nine Points on Monumentality," in Joan Ockman, ed., *Architecture Culture 1943–1968* (New York: Columbia University Graduate School of Architecture, Planning and Preservation and Rizzoli, 1993), 29–30.

was also apparent in more modest projects which enhanced or set up an urban order. For example, his designs for Smith College and Tufts University both entailed building insertions in existing contexts, such that the newly reinforced connections and movement patterns enabled inhabitants and visitors to realize local urban orders.

The work done a decade later on campuses in the Australian state of Queensland uses new interventions to give coherence to dispersed patterns of building. In these projects, the "urban" pattern organizes buildings that are otherwise fairly anonymous and does so to address environmental performance as well as planning issues. Other Australian university projects—Toad Hall and the residences for the Canberra College of Advanced Education—set up a more local urban order in which street-like spaces produce opportunities for social interaction. This is true also of Andrews's school projects from Bellmere Junior Public School (1965), with its pinwheel plan, to Padbury Senior High School (1987).

Even when Andrews produced projects that were very singular architectural proposals, an urban imagination was at play. The D. B. Weldon Library at the University of Western Ontario and George Gund Hall at Harvard University are both projects of this kind. Both are iconic and very assertive architectural objects that seem to exist as singular entities. But in both cases, their designs are inflected to enhance an existing urban order beyond themselves. At the Weldon Library, the building establishes paths of movement that reinforce an emerging urban pattern. At Gund Hall, the building is configured along Quincy Street so that the sidewalk is widened and intrudes into the building's footprint and a lofty colonnade adds an elevated sense of dignity to the ordinary urban experience of moving along the street.

Andrews's unrealized intention at Gund Hall to offer pedestrians routes through the building, though without entering it—as in Le Corbusier's design of the Carpenter Center for the Visual Arts—would have further developed its urban proposition. The King George Tower and the unbuilt tower at 2 Bond Street have similar intentions, but in the context of the much more intensely developed downtown of central Sydney. Both these Sydney projects are again iconic architectural objects, but are placed on their sites to develop opportunities for passing pedestrians to occupy the ground plane and the levels immediately above and below it. For 2 Bond Street, this also accommodates the preservation of heritage buildings but with a sense of urban drama that is usually missing from such earnest exercises.

In his design for the Toronto Metro Centre and the Cameron Offices, Andrews's urban ordering is systematic. As already mentioned, this is coincidental in relation to his exposure to the structuralism of Aldo van Eyck and Herman Hertzberger, however this occurred. At Metro Centre, the circulation system he proposed is at the level of broad urban strategy. In more developed projects, a pattern emerges of repeated circulation elements that are distinct architecturally from repeated elements of inhabitation. Horizontally, these circulation routes may be covered or, if incorporated into larger interior spaces, uncovered. Vertically, they nearly always take the form of concrete or concrete and glass-block cylinders. This approach is most developed in Andrews's oeuvre in his design for the Callam Offices

(1973) and the closely related design for the Intelsat Headquarters (1980–1988), in which circulation systems are rendered with high architectural drama and connect the octagonal pods of the office facilities. The logic of these horizontally expansive schemes, which differentiate an architectural language of circulation from one of inhabitation, is also taken up in Andrews's 1980s designs for hotels and office buildings. However, in these buildings, the lateral expansion of the Callam Offices and Intelsat becomes vertical extrusion. Movement and stasis are the fundamental themes of this work, with the element of movement providing an opportunity for unanticipated, incidental human interaction and the attribute of stasis providing an opportunity for work or withdrawal.

In the 1980s, Andrews's urban imagination, apparent in both his large-scale projects and those of a more conventional building size, comes up against a different idea of the city. This encounter is not resolved in his work and remains a problem in contemporary urban architecture. On one hand, this idea of the city involves speculative development. The Cameron Offices are in some part a victim of this. On the other, it involves the city becoming a spectacle. Neither speculation nor spectacle construe buildings as permanent. While the Australian federal government condemned the Cameron Offices to support the property industry, in their own jurisdictions Australia's states attempted to address the country's faltering economy of the 1980s by promoting tourism, gambling, and entertainment events. In this political view, the city, particularly the inner city, is not so much a system of human relations and interaction, as Andrews viewed it, as it is a series of spectacles.

The central cities of the state's capitals—in Australia, these are invariably also their largest cities—become the theaters for these spectacles. The infrastructural dimension of much of Andrews's architectural work is repudiated in such a dispensation: rather than buildings setting down patterns of connection that should survive the comings and goings of particular uses, they are stage sets that can be regularly changed. Indeed, they need to be regularly changed to keep the spectacle's impact alive. This is why the monumentality and sheer materiality of the Sydney Convention Centre contrasted so strongly with the faux festivity of Darling Harbour. It is as if the Darling Harbour site was created to stage but one event, its opening on January 26, 1988, by Queen Elizabeth II. The Sydney Convention Centre, by comparison, looked as if it had been built to last half a millennium. With its calamitously early demolition, spectacle prevailed. But as sustainability issues intensify, will this view of the city prevail?

BUILDING

Behind both Team 10 and CIAM, even as they unfolded toward their ends, there stands the figure of Le Corbusier. The "third generation" of modern architects were more strongly influenced by Le Corbusier than any other architect of the first generation. It was the late Le Corbusier, the auteur of *béton brut*, who counted. To Andrews, his encounters with Le Corbusier's buildings at Ronchamp, Marseilles, and Chandigarh were likely the most consequential aspect of his 1961 European and Asian tour. This is not the

Le Corbusier of the 1920s who wanted to make buildings machines and who, being unable to do so, signaled his commitment to this idea by making them look machined or machine-like. Rather, the Le Corbusier of the 1950s sought to find a poetry in the means of ordinary building construction, often exaggeratedly so, as a complement to his extraordinary formal inventions.

After his encounters with Le Corbusier, concrete was always Andrews's preferred construction material. In the control tower he designed for the Toronto International Airport, carried out while in the office of John B. Parkin Associates, Andrews had already taken up the use of raw concrete, cast in-situ into timber board formwork, to produce a look that became known as "Brutalism." This is Brutalism, not in the narrow sense of the "New Brutalism," originally termed by Alison and Peter Smithson and Reyner Banham in a fruitless attempt to confine it to a limited number of projects, notably by the Smithsons themselves. Rather, this indicated Brutalism in the wider, generalized sense of an architectural aesthetic of concrete surfaces that became common in the 1960s.

Brutalism is a term that Andrews disliked applying to his buildings. In his perspective, in their concern for human interaction and repose, they were, rather, "humanist." This humanism he shared with the late Le Corbusier. Upon Andrews's return to Harvard University to design Gund Hall, he became particularly mindful of the Carpenter Center for the Visual Arts, located just a block away on Quincy Street. Andrews's intention in his design of Gund Hall for people to pass through the building at ground level without ever entering seems related to the similar strategy used at the Carpenter Center. However, it is the taking up of the round concrete column as the basic structural element of much of his subsequent architecture that is, I believe, a consequence of his encounter with the Carpenter Center. Those columns of Le Corbusier's are transcriptions of the anthropomorphic columns of classical architecture, rendered in a modern medium to invite human identification. This is the source of their humanism. They are repeated by Andrews regularly thereafter and particularly in honorific locations, such as in the Quincy Street colonnade at Gund Hall, along the mall at the Cameron Offices, in the lobby of the King George Tower, and in the public areas of the Sydney Convention Centre.

Another aspect of Le Corbusier's late work that is relevant to Andrews's is that it seeks to locate an architectural aesthetic in the real, craft means of construction that pertain to each site where the architect builds. In Le Corbusier's case, this is somewhat overstated, hence the use of rough concrete in Chandigarh or smooth concrete in Boston since Boston had more sophisticated construction capabilities.[9] Andrews also followed the strategy of making the building aesthetic out of the frank means of construction. Sometimes, this meant hybrid construction systems, such as at the South Residences at the University of Guelph and the Cameron Offices: chosen to expedite the building process through a mix of different means, this is then made evident in the building structure and envelope. For Andrews, this also meant repeating elements and materials regularly. This applies both to overall design strategies and relatively modest things, including quarry-tile floors in circulation areas; reflective metal ceilings that add a sense of flickering life to spaces in the Cameron Offices mall, the King

9   On this, see William Curtis, "History of the Design," in Eduard Sekler, *Le Corbusier at Work: The Genesis of the Carpenter Center for the Visual Arts* (Cambridge, MA: Harvard University Press, 1978): 206–8.

George Tower, and the circulation areas of the Sydney Convention Centre; triangulated metal tube frameworks that support sun-shades; round columns; and vertical circulation cylinders of concrete and glass block.

Among Andrews's repeated overall strategies, we have already considered his tessellated plans of linear circulation elements and octagonal pods of inhabitation. Before those, there were the big, sheltering roofs of his design for the Toronto City Hall competition, the Miami Seaport Terminal, and Gund Hall. He first used this strategy in the airport terminal he designed as his thesis project at the University of Sydney in 1956. And there is the repetition of stepped and inverted stepped sections, appearing first at the unbuilt Malton Hotel designed at John B. Parkin Associates. Another, somewhat mysterious case is the repetition in Andrews's work of the three-cornered tower, which is found in his designs from the Toronto International Airport control tower to his preferred design for what became the CN Tower, his design for King George Tower (the most accomplished of these projects in that it takes the geometric ideal and massages it into a particular place), and his first design for the Singapore telecommunications tower competition of 1990. Realized low-rise versions of his trinity-of-cylinders strategy are found in the nodes of the Miami Seaport Terminal. The "why" of these threefold tubes is still elusive.

Andrews often alluded to his architecture practice as common sense or problem-solving. But problem-solving here is not so much related to the invention of new building forms to produce a close indication of the "functional" problem, as might be construed by this appeal to common sense, as it is related to the selection of forms and elements from a developing repertoire in a combination that will work. It is a kind of bricolage. The key to this strategy is that the "fit" of form and activity is loose enough so that the ongoing invention of the very particular is not needed. It is through this looseness that unexpected, unprogrammed human intervention and imagination can occur.

ENVIRONMENT AND SUSTAINABILITY

Another aspect of Andrews's buildings that developed across his work is the commitment to energy conservation and other environmental matters, now subsumed under the label of sustainability. Beginning with Andrews's first design for a Canadian site, Toronto City Hall, he was mindful of buildings as climatic modifiers. The impacts of climate on construction practices and sequencing became further apparent to him through his projects while at John B. Parkin Associates. The unbuilt design for the Malton Hotel, in which the stepped section of the building and its courtyard layout were to mitigate the noise of low-flying aircraft, was another step in apprehending building form as an environmental modifier. At Scarborough College, this environmental sensibility ceased being a matter of design intuition when Michael Hough, the landscape architect who worked with him on the design, brought in a climatologist to analyze the site and advise on the best location to build.

At least from the design of the King George Tower, Andrews became acutely aware of the energy use of buildings and the ways in which design features can reduce this consumption. This aspect of Andrews's design ethos developed alongside his connection with the Sydney services engineer Don Thomas. In their first collaboration, on the Cameron Offices, Andrews again used the primary form of the building to achieve a climate response: in the office wings, upper-level floors step out to shelter the floors below from sun. The next collaboration between Andrews and Thomas, on the design of the King George Tower, was the first to introduce a secondary element to shade the building's glazed walls. Further, the triangulated, stainless steel frames, bearing transparent sunshades made of polycarbonate or glass, became a constant feature of Andrews's work that was always devised with Thomas's input. From the design of the Callam Offices in 1973 to the Octagon in 1990, the passive strategies of manipulating building form and adding lightweight shading elements to address solar exposure were increasingly complemented by the introduction of active systems, engineered by Thomas, that modulated environmental performance.

As Andrews noted in his A. S. Hook Memorial Address, "energy conservation is the operative word in architecture."[10] However, the design of the King George Tower was envisioned three years before the energy crisis of 1973. Andrews was prescient. At some point his interest in climate and energy conservation grew into a more inclusive environmental awareness, akin to the thinking of Ian McHarg, most famously expressed in his 1969 book *Design With Nature*. Most likely, Andrews was first introduced to McHarg by Hough. Andrews's son Lee would later study landscape architecture with McHarg at the University of Pennsylvania. While Andrews's long and deep friendship with the landscape architect Dick Strong is also crucial, North American landscape architecture was broadly influenced by McHarg's ideas.

TEAMWORK

Andrews's professional relationship with Don Thomas was one of several long-term collaborations that he maintained. Another, which also dated back to the Cameron Offices project, was his collaboration with the structural engineer Peter Miller of the Sydney firm Miller, Milston, and Ferris.[11] The longest of Andrews's collaborations was with Strong, whom he met when they were both employed at John B. Parkin Associates in Toronto in the late 1950s. Their association developed into a personal friendship that was the most important of Andrews's life. They worked together on many key projects: the Miami Seaport Terminal, George Gund Hall, the Cameron Offices, and the Intelsat Headquarters. The integration of landscape strategies into major Andrews buildings, such as the inclusion of green roofs in the Cameron Offices and the Intelsat Headquarters, was the outcome of this friendship. Around the time Andrews closed his Sydney office, Strong invited Andrews to advise on development at the University of Lethbridge, taking him back to Canada late in his life.

While long-term or serial collaborations like those with Thomas, Miller, and Strong were no doubt motivated by Andrews's preference for informality and personal connections, there is more to them than this. Andrews's commitment to the *idea* of collaboration is apparent in the formation of Integ (Integrated Professionals) before he departed on his

10 Andrews, "A. S. Hook 1981," 71.
11 Andrews met Miller while he was in the office of Edwards, Madigan and Torzillo. John Andrews, interview by Paul Walker, December 2, 2015.

1961 journey to Europe and Asia. Integ was a collective of an accountant, engineer Norbert Seethaler, lawyer George Miller, and landscape architect Strong, along with Andrews, who together planned to undertake project developments. This did not pan out, but Andrews still had ongoing professional relationships with George Miller and Norbert Seethaler, as well as Strong. As with Strong, Andrews met Seethaler while working at John B. Parkin Associates, and he had offices at 47 Colborne Street, in the same premises as Andrews, which Integ purchased in 1962 and Andrews renovated. Later, Seethaler became the structural engineer for the Miami Seaport Terminal. Sculptor Gerry Gladstone, who later provided public art works both for Gund Hall and the Cameron Offices, was also based at Colborne Street, as was Evan Walker, the Australian architect whose research on student housing strongly informed Andrews's design for the South Residences at the University of Guelph and subsequent student-accommodation projects.[12]

What we can discern here is a pattern of engagement by Andrews with known expertise that is akin to his employment across his career of known design strategies and building forms. A frequent tactic for resolving a design early in its development was to call the team of architects and consultants together to work on the project without distraction, secluded away from other demands. This led to a common understanding of what the design was attempting to do and the techniques to be employed in achieving it. Andrews first used this approach in his earliest major scheme as an independent architect, Scarborough College, when he convened the design team to work intensively on the project on an abandoned floor of the University of Toronto's old chemistry building in the summer of 1963 (see chapter 2). When possible, Andrews extended this collaborative approach to include builders. Andrews often then established temporary offices to oversee projects with somewhat more design authority than a usual site office.

Through collaboration, Andrews's designs were placed in the care of experienced colleagues who understood Andrews's design ethos. In the case of John Andrews Architects in Toronto, nine of these trusted colleagues were made partners with Andrews in the firm, before his final departure for Australia in 1969: Ed Galanyk, John Simpson, Tony Parsons, Ned Baldwin, Roger du Toit, Bob Anderson, William Bennet, Lawrence Diamond, and Frank Carter.[13] Andrews chose to keep his Sydney office, John Andrews International, much closer. Only Peter Courtney and John Simpson, when he came to Australia, were ever partners in the firm. Courtney, badly stressed by the legal actions over the Cameron Offices defamation case, left in 1983 to live and work in Tasmania, and at the same time, Simpson departed to start his own firm in Brisbane. After this, Andrews was the sole proprietor of John Andrews International. However, a group of highly trusted senior staff members cohered around the office: Doug McKay, Bruce Lincoln, Geoff Willing, Arthur Robb, Terry Edmondson, Warwick Werner, Ole Saeverud, and Bruce James.[14] Andrews preferred to keep staff numbers to around 15 to avoid hierarchy and encourage collaboration.[15] Tina Curtis was also an important member of the office in its later years.[16]

12 Philip Goad, "The Translation of Practice: The Offices of John Andrews in Toronto and Palm Beach," *Proceedings of the Society of Architectural Historians, Australia and New Zealand: 31, Translation*, ed. Christoph Schnoor (2014): 691–701.

13 Carter appears to have left the partnership to take up a teaching role at the School of Architecture at Carleton University in 1973. See Janine Debanné, "Frank Carter, the Thumbnail Sketch, and the Joy of Architecture," Azrieli School of Architecture & Urbanism, Carleton University, February 28, 2022, https://architecture.carleton.ca/archives/21500.

14 "The Firm," *Architecture Australia* 70, no. 2 (May 1981): 38.

15 Jennifer Taylor and John Andrews, *John Andrews: Architecture, a Performing Art* (Melbourne: Oxford University Press, 1982), 15

16 Some other Andrews employees who later went on to prominence in the Australian architectural profession are Andrew Metcalf, Tim Shannon, Diane Jones, Stephen Neille, and Graham Brawn.

CULTURAL AGENCY

The later period of Andrews's career coincided with the phenomenon of postmodernism. Andrews was and continued to be a modernist insofar as he believed in the ability of design to redeem the built world. In the 1980s, in the office of John Andrews International, there was a joke that they were not postmodernists, but most-podernists. Postmodernism as a style only touches Andrews's practice tangentially. For example, an almost postmodern style characterizes the allusive historical references found in the design of his farmhouse in Eugowra and a knowing play with the stylistic conventions of postmodern office towers is incorporated into his design of 2 Bond Street. In these projects, Andrews responded to the advent of postmodernism by addressing identity, history, and place—issues that postmodern architecture foregrounded—but by trying to do so within the formal vocabularies of modernism. This strategy and these examples are in line with the proposition put forth by Mark Crinson and Claire Zimmerman in their book *Neo-avant-garde and Postmodern*, which finds that the distinction between the rethought modernism of the 1950s and 1960s and postmodernism is not as clear-cut as it once seemed to be. As they write, modernism and postmodernism are "practices that were themselves perhaps only provisionally opposed."[17]

The complex interface between modern and postmodern architecture particularly played out in Andrews's role as a public figure or cultural agent advocating for design. The Australian architectural competitions he judged, for the New Parliament House and, less famously, for the Australian National Archives, both resulted in the selection of postmodern designs. While the National Archives project did not proceed to building, the design by Mitchell/Giurgola and Thorpe Architects for the New Parliament House is one of the most accomplished of postmodern building complexes.[18] Andrews's view of the parliament competition was that the winning design met the requirements of the brief better than any other, no matter its style. Chosen by a team of judges that included not only Andrews but also I. M. Pei, the selected design met the functional criteria of the parliament brief, but the architects also adhered to the expectations that it have an appropriate expressive character. The design's expressive qualities could be read as aligned with the modern monumentality that Andrews pursued in his designs for Scarborough College, the University of Guelph, and the Cameron Offices. But its classical symmetry, the use in its interior of marble revetments in a manner consistent with postmodern quotations of Renaissance architecture, and the giant sign of the flagstaff surmounting the building, veer its expressive qualities into a different territory. It is both a modern monument and a postmodern reference to monumentality. If we see in Australia's New Parliament House a propensity for the architectural sign to be a monument, perhaps the reverse is also true. Perhaps Andrews's building-as-city projects—Scarborough College, the South Residences at the University of Guelph, and the Cameron Offices—can also be thought of as *representations* of urbanity.

In Andrews's advocacy for design and architecture as part of his role at the Australia Council from 1978 to 1988, we also see the modern architect

17   Mark Crinson and Claire Zimmerman, *Neo-avant-garde and Postmodern: Postwar Architecture in Britain and Beyond* (New Haven, CT: Yale University Press, 2010), 7.

18   "Announcement of competition for the Australian Archives National Headquarters Building," *Sydney Morning Herald*, December 9, 1978; Hilary Golder, *Documenting a Nation: Australian Archives—The First Fifty Years* (Canberra: Australian Archives and AGPS Press, 1994), 40–41. Another juror was the architect Col Madigan.

promoting postmodern architecture. This is evident in the obvious sense, through the exhibitions and publications that the Australia Council's Design Arts Board sponsored under Andrews's leadership, which featured both the late-modernism that was dominant in Australian architecture in the early 1980s and the vigorously postmodern work of the emerging generation. However, it is also the case that the Australia Council's policies were driven by an ideology that could be considered postmodern in its intention to undo socioeconomic hierarchies that are traditional in the arts. It wanted to build new audiences for art. Further, it aimed to integrate art into the economy—the new audiences were to be consumers.

While these agendas at the Australia Council did not last, Andrews used his period with the Australia Council to pursue initiatives that would have ongoing cultural and commercial consequences for Australian architecture. This is particularly apparent in the connections established with the Chinese architectural profession under Andrews's leadership of the Design Arts Board. Given the subsequent significance of China to the international architectural scene, and the relationship of Chinese operations to several leading Australian architectural practices, in retrospect, Andrews's interest in engaging with China looks, like his interest in sustainability, prescient. Ironically, however, two now highly globalized Australian architectural practices who could be seen as beneficiaries of the relationship with China fostered by Andrews—Woods Bagot and Hassell, both with "studios" in Shanghai—have also been the architects of projects that replaced key buildings by Andrews. This includes Hassell as designer of the new convention center in Sydney and Woods Bagot as codesigner of both the current Adelaide and Melbourne convention centers and the Australian Bureau of Statistics Building, which was constructed when the Cameron Offices were abandoned.

Andrews often stated that architecture is common sense. In this book we have unpacked this notion in order to consider how the architect operated in the contexts in which he worked from the 1950s to the 1990s, including in Canada, the United States, and Australia, on projects with a range of scales, from a farmhouse for Andrews's family to a bureaucratic mini-city for 4,000 workers at the Cameron Offices. We have considered how his work developed from the architectural milieu to which he was introduced at the Harvard GSD under Josep Lluís Sert, and sometimes in relation to the work of other key architects, to an independent and coherent repertoire of design strategies, elements, and materials. Andrews employed a language of architecture that generously accommodates human habitation in many dimensions. His strategies may find their rationale in pragmatic concerns, but they are linked to produce complexities that evade reductivism. Late in his career, Andrews's work came up against different views that either saw architecture as an autonomous art form or a commercial commodity and expendable spectacle. His response was to go fishing, literally and figuratively. Andrews also adopted the role of advocate for architecture and design beyond just his own. Common sense it may have seemed to him, but Andrews built his way through these various paths of his career with an individual sensibility and energy. Uncommon sense.

coda

by   Noritaka Minami

WHAT REMAINS

It is a common practice to document a building upon its completion to create formal records of that work by the architect. Carefully composed photographs are selected to promote the new structure. In that instance, the camera captures the building in what will likely be the most pristine state of its existence. Weathering and stains that inevitably arise over time are not present on the building's surfaces. The structure has yet to encounter circumstances beyond the anticipation or control of the architect. These photographs that depict a building at the start of its life, before it begins to accumulate history, can even become its definitive representations in the media for decades.

A practice that is not as established is documenting what becomes of a building after the years have passed. Yet, how a building ultimately performs as a work of architecture can only be determined after it exists in the world and is used by people over a period of time. This photographic project is based on revisiting John Andrews's works that remain to this day. The camera explores the current conditions of buildings that were completed primarily during the most prolific period of his career.

The various states his works have come to enter after standing for a half-century or less reflect the precariousness of Andrews's legacy as an architect today despite his importance to late modernism. Scarborough College and the Callam Offices largely maintain their original forms and continue to be used for their intended purposes. But there are also projects—including the South Residences at the University of Guelph and the former Intelsat Headquarters—where extensive alterations to introduce current architectural sensibilities have rendered Andrews's distinct design features unrecognizable. Only after this photographic project began did it become clear that it was no longer possible to photograph the Miami Seaport Terminal and the School of Art at Kent State University, as these sites were recently demolished without fanfare.

The erratic treatment of Andrews's architecture in recent years is most strongly represented in the Cameron Offices, a structure that was simultaneously destroyed and preserved. Despite being a landmark work that signaled the architect's return to Australia, the majority of the massive concrete complex was demolished after only three decades of operation. The office structures, courtyards, and pedestrian bridges that formed the north and south ends of this structure were cleared to make way for conventional apartment buildings and parking spaces. Three of the seven office wings that initially comprised the Cameron Offices were maintained as a gesture of historical preservation. However, this complex exists today in a significantly compromised state as Andrews's design was contingent on the numerous components that stretched across the landscape to form the megastructure. What remains of the Cameron Offices shows subtle but visible signs of sections that used to be part of the structure but that were severed in the demolition.

The photographs in this project capture how Andrews's unique approach to design reflected the social and architectural values that were considered viable in the era in which these buildings were conceived. With many of his buildings demolished in recent years or facing uncertain futures, there is an added urgency in reexamining the relevance of his career in retrospect. Moreover, one must consider the implications behind the gradual disappearance of Andrews's works to understand the directions society and architecture have taken since his most prolific period as an architect. These photographs are documents of the current state of Andrews's buildings and the values that brought them into existence.

Scarborough College

Scarborough College

Scarborough College

Scarborough College

Scarborough College

Scarborough College

Scarborough College

Bellmere Junior Public School

University of Guelph Residences

University of Guelph Residences

D. B. Weldon Library

D. B. Weldon Library

D. B. Weldon Library

D. B. Weldon Library

George Gund Hall

George Gund Hall

George Gund Hall

George Gund Hall

George Gund Hall

George Gund Hall

George Gund Hall

Cameron Offices

Cameron Offices

Cameron Offices

King George Tower

Callam Offices

Callam Offices

Callam Offices

Callam Offices

Eugowra House

Eugowra House

Eugowra House

Eugowra House

Garden Island Parking Structure

Intelsat Headquarters

Intelsat Headquarters

Intelsat Headquarters

The Octagon

The Octagon

MAJOR PROJECTS

The following list of major projects is compiled from two main sources. For the period between 1962 and 1980, it is based on the information in *John Andrews: Architecture, a Performing Art*, by Jennifer Taylor and John Andrews (Melbourne: Oxford University Press, 1982), with additions and amendments that have come to light in the research for this book, particularly through the drawings held at the Canadian Architectural Archives at the University of Calgary. For the period after 1980, it has been compiled from the lists of Andrews drawings held in the State Library of New South Wales.

The firm John Andrews Architects operated from its base in Toronto from 1962 to 1973. John Andrews International was established in Sydney in 1969 and closed in 1998, but Andrews continued to work on projects intermittently after its closure. Work undertaken by Andrews before 1962 in his own name or in the firms he worked for (Edwards, Madigan and Torzillo; John B. Parkin Associates; Stephenson and Turner) is documented in chapter 1 and not reflected in this list. Minor house alterations are not included in this list. Completed projects are italicized.

1962
Scarborough College Masterplan, Scarborough, Ontario.
1963–1966
Scarborough College, phase 1, Scarborough, Ontario. With Page and Steele Architects.
1963
Simon Fraser University, Vancouver; competition.
1964–1967
47 Colborne Street alterations, Toronto.
1964
University of British Columbia Student Union, Vancouver; placed second in competition. With Ron Thom.
1964
Erindale College Masterplan, Erindale, Ontario.
1964
Streetsville Public Library, Mississauga, Ontario.
1964–1966
Bellmere Junior Public School, Scarborough, Ontario.
1965–1968
Student Housing Complex B (South Residences), University of Guelph, Ontario.
1965
Stelco housing complex study.
1965
Red Coach Inn, Mandeville, Jamaica.
1965
Goddard Library, Clark University, Worcester, Massachusetts.
1965–1967
African Place, Expo 67, Montreal; demolished.
1965–1967
Activity Area F, Expo 67, Montreal; demolished.
1965
Commonwealth Place, Expo 67, Montreal.
1966–1967
University of Toronto St. George Campus masterplan, Toronto.
1967
Prince of Wales College, Charlottetown, Prince Edward Island.
1967–1972
D. B. Weldon Library, University of Western Ontario, London, Ontario. With Ronald E. Murphy.
1967–1971
Metro Centre, Toronto; not built except *CN Tower, completed 1976.*
1966–1967
Student Center, University of Toronto.
1967–1970
Miami Seaport Terminal, Miami; extended 1972; demolished.
1967
City of Hamilton Civic Square study, Hamilton, Ontario.
1967–1970
Yorkdale Shopping Centre development and offices, Toronto.
1967–1969
Student residence, Brock University, St. Catharines, Ontario. With Salter Fleming Secord.
1967
Sarah Lawrence College Library Instructional Center, Bronxville, New York.
1968–1972
George Gund Hall, Harvard University, Cambridge, Massachusetts.
1968–1977
Cameron Offices, Belconnen, Australian Capital Territory; partially demolished.
1968–1972
Smith College Arts Center, Northampton, Massachusetts.
1969–1972
Scarborough College, phase 2, Scarborough, Ontario.
1969–1972
David Mirvish Gallery, Toronto.
1970–1972
School of Art, Kent State University, Kent, Ohio; demolished.
1970
University of Minnesota, St. Paul campus; masterplan study.
1970
McMaster University Student Centre, Hamilton, Ontario.
1970
Behavioral Sciences Department, Tufts University, Medford, Massachusetts.
1970–1976
King George Tower, Sydney; substantially altered.
1971–1974
Student residences B (Toad Hall), Australian National University, Canberra.

1972
Roma Street development, Brisbane.
1972–1976
Belconnen Town Centre retail study.
1973
Callam Offices, Woden, Australian Capital Territory; not built but *realized on a much-reduced scale as the Woden College of Technical and Further Education, 1977.*
1973–1974
Student residence, Canberra College of Advanced Education, Belconnen, Australian Capital Territory.
1973–1975
Chemical Engineering Building, University of Queensland, St. Lucia, Queensland; much altered.
1973
Kelvin Grove College of Advanced Education masterplan, Kelvin Grove, Queensland.
1974
Darling Downs Institute of Advanced Education development plan, Toowoomba, Queensland.
1974
Ithaca Technical College development plan, Ithaca, Queensland.
1974
Transportation interchange and sporting/commercial development, Canberra.
1974–1988
Palm Beach Marine Services alterations, Palm Beach, New South Wales.
1975–1978
School of Australian Environmental Studies, Griffith University, Nathan, Queensland, demolition planned.
1975–1981
Little Bay public housing, Little Bay, New South Wales.
1975
Palm Beach environmental study, Palm Beach, New South Wales.
1975
Monarto town center urban design study, Monarto, South Australia.
1975
Ipswich College of Technical and Further Education masterplan, Ipswich, Queensland.
1975
Gordon Andrews house, Lovett Bay, New South Wales.
1975, 1980
Woolloomooloo housing scheme, Woolloomooloo, New South Wales.
1976
Andrews houses, Palm Beach, New South Wales.
1976
Education Resource Centre, Kelvin Grove College of Advanced Education, Kelvin Grove, Queensland.
1977–79
Belconnen Bus Terminal, Belconnen, Australian Capital Territory.
1976–1984
Royal Melbourne Institute of Technology Library and Student Union, Melbourne; partially built and then substantially altered.
1977
Museum of Australia study, Canberra.
1977–1978
Sydney Central Station development.
1977
Lecture theater and staff offices, Darling Downs Institute of Advanced Education, Queensland.
1977
Mandurah High School, Mandurah, Western Australia.
1977
M. Andrews house alterations, Palm Beach, New South Wales.
1978
Resource Material Centre, Ipswich College of Technical and Further Education, Ipswich, Queensland.
1978
Housing village, Griffith University, Nathan, Queensland.
1978–1980
Andrews farmhouse, Eugowra, New South Wales.
1978
Bateman Catholic Centre, Perth.
1979
Glebe cluster housing project, Glebe, New South Wales.
1984–1985
McNamara office building proposals, Parramatta, New South Wales.
1980–1988
Intelsat Headquarters, Washington, DC; placed first in competition, commission followed. With Notter Finegold + Alexander.
1980
Garden Island parking structure, Woolloomooloo, New South Wales.
1981–1983
Australian Defence Force Academy, Canberra.
1981–1984
Merlin Hotel, Perth.
1982–1988
Adelaide Station and Environs Redevelopment (ASER). Adelaide Convention Centre (demolished), office building, hotel, and exhibition center.
1982
R. Andrews house, Palm Beach, New South Wales.
1982
Arabsat Headquarters, Riyadh.
1983
Hotel, Perth.
1983–1990
Melbourne World Congress Centre, convention center (demolished), hotel, and parking structure, Melbourne. With Eggleston, MacDonald & Secomb.
1984
Mackay Cultural Centre, Mackay, Queensland.
1984
West Forum Sporting and Leisure Centre, Harris Park, New South Wales.
1984–86
Commonwealth Centre, Parramatta, New South Wales.
1984–1988
Sydney Convention Centre, Sydney; demolished.
1985
Burswood Casino, Burswood, Western Australia.
1985–1990
Octagon, Parramatta, New South Wales; demolition planned.
1986
Barton Telephone Exchange, Barton, Australian Capital Territory.
1986
Sydney Casino at Darling Harbour, first scheme, Sydney.
ca. 1987
Hong Kong University of Science and Technology masterplan.
1987
Australian Pavilion for the Venice Biennale, Venice.
1987
Canberra International Hotel and Casino, Canberra.
1987–1988
Edwards house, Palm Beach, New South Wales.
1987–1990
Padbury Senior High School, Padbury, Western Australia.
1987–1990
2 Bond Street, Sydney.
1987–1990
Kirra Beach Resort, Gold Coast, Queensland.
1988
Flinders Street Station redevelopment, Melbourne.
1988
Park Place development, Los Angeles.
1988–1989
Canberra planning study, Canberra.
1988–1990
Rivercentre, Parramatta, New South Wales.
1988–1998
North Shore Medical Research Centre, St. Leonards, New South Wales.
1989–1990
World Bank Headquarters, Washington, DC; competition.
1990
South Melbourne housing, South Melbourne, Victoria; competition.
ca. 1990
Perth Foreshore, Perth; competition.
ca. 1990–1992
Brisbane Convention and Exhibition Centre, Brisbane.
1991
Andrews house alterations, Mackerel Beach, New South Wales.
1991–1992
Sydney Casino at Darling Harbour, second scheme, Sydney.
1991–1992
Fort Canning Telecom Tower, Singapore; competition.
ca. 1992
Kowloon Point development, Hong Kong; competition.
ca. 1992
Whitlam house, Whale Beach, New South Wales.

ca. 1993
Golden Bay Lodge, Nelson, New Zealand.

1993–2000
University of Lethbridge site report and campus plan, Alberta, Canada.

1993–1994
Edwards house, Northbridge, New South Wales.

1994
House at Whale Beach, Whale Beach, New South Wales.

1995–2001
Age of Fishes Museum, Canowindra, New South Wales.

1995–1998
University of Sydney Veterinary Science Conference Centre, Sydney.

1997
Veterinary hospital, Orange, New South Wales.

1999
Quandong Winery, New South Wales.

1999–2000
University of Lethbridge Neuroscience Building, Lethbridge, Alberta.

INDEX

A

A. S. Hook Memorial Address (Hook address), 241, 243–45, 381–82, 390
Aalto, Alvar, 26, 29, 42–43
activism, ecological, 271
Activity Area F (Expo 67), 84–85, 93, 98
Adalaj Stepwell, 268–69
Adelaide Festival Hall, 339
Adelaide Station and Environs Redevelopment (ASER)
  alterations to, 374, 376
  casino, 339, 342–43
  construction, 343
  convention center, 342–44, 374, 376
  design strategies, 340–41, 343–44
  entry, 353
  exterior, 352
  generic high-rise approach, 299, 301
  hotel, 299, 302–3, 342–44
  internal arrangement, 344
  office buildings, 299, 302, 342–44
  opposition to, 339, 342–43
  overview, 337–39
ADFA (Australian Defence Force Academy) campus, 128
Administrative and Clerical Officers' Association (ACOA), 227
Aeroquay No. 1, Toronto International Airport, 147
AES (Australian Environmental Studies) building, 265–67, 269, 284, 376
aesthetic, making out of means of construction, 388–89
Affleck, Desbarats, Dimakopoulos, Lebensold, Michaud, Sise (firm), 152
African Place
  architecture and exhibition outcomes, 96, 98
  construction, 93, 96
  design, 80–81, 84, 85–88
  influences on design, 384
  overview, 77, 82, 84–85
  pinwheel plan, 93
  and problem of movement, 100
  pyramidal roof forms, 39
Age of Fishes Museum, 364–66
airport design. *See also* Toronto International Airport
  and design of Miami Seaport Terminal, 170, 178
  Dulles International Airport, 178
  Sydney terminal thesis project,
21, 23, 28–29, 268, 274, 389
Alegrett, José, 327–28
Alofsin, Anthony, 189–90
ambient environment of built spaces, design of, 268, 272
American Express Building. *See* King George Tower
American Institute of Architects and the Association of Collegiate Schools of Architecture (AIA/ACSA) Teacher Seminar, 272, 322
Amsterdam Orphanage, 92, 321, 384
Anderson, Robert, 59, 117, 121, 223, 391
Andrews, Craig, 368
Andrews, Dal, 368
Andrews, Gordon, 235
Andrews, Jamie, 368
Andrews, John. *See also* collaborative ethos; common sense approach to architecture; public advocacy for design; *specific architectural projects*; *specific building types*
  A. S. Hook Memorial Address, 241, 243–45, 381–82, 390
  achievements, 9
  architectural tour (1961), 43, 268
  book structure, 13–17
  construction techniques, 387–89
  cultural agency, 392–93
  defamation case, 241–43
  demolition and alteration of projects, 370–77
  departure from Parkin firm, 39, 42–43
  diminished popularity of, 9–10
  documenting buildings over time, 397
  early life, 21
  economical design approach, 11–12
  education, 13, 21–28
  family, 368
  geographical trajectory, 381–83
  Gold Medal win, 241, 242–43
  independent projects, 364–65
  interests outside of architecture, 361–62, 368–70
  at John B. Parkin Associates, 13, 32–39
  later career, 17, 361–68
  lines of inquiry related to, 10–13
move back to Australia, 123, 382
  at University of Toronto, 12, 45, 190, 194, 271
Andrews, Lee, 368
Andrews, Rosemary, 29, 31, 367–69
Andrews, Stewart, 141, 160
ANU (Australian National University), 123–25, 302
Arabsat, 313, 318
Architectural Conservancy of Ontario, 154–55
"Architectural Fashions and the People" (Sert), 25
Architectural Review, 251, 253
architecture. *See also* common sense approach to architecture; *specific architectural projects*; *specific building types*
  Andrews's Hook address on Australian, 243–45, 381–82
  architectural history, 21, 24–25
  documenting buildings over time, 397
  ethical dimension of, 381–82
  geography and, 10–11, 381–83
  internationalized architectural culture, 10–11
  at University of Sydney, 21
  unselfconscious, 204
  and urbanism, 385–87
Architecture and Design Panel, 249
"Architecture and Politics in the Reagan Era" (McLeod), 253
Architecture Without Architects (Rudofsky), 268
Arney, Earle, 373
Art and Architecture Building (Yale), 36–37, 194, 202
Arthur, Eric, 152
Arthur M. Sackler Museum, 205, 385
ASER. *See* Adelaide Station and Environs Redevelopment
Ashby, James, 117–18
Ashworth, Harry Ingham, 21
Auckland Architecture Association Monier Design Awards, 369
Austin-Smith, Michael, 314, 317, 328–29, 330–31
Australia. *See also* John Andrews International; *specific Australian architectural projects*
  Andrews's Hook address on architecture of, 243–45, 381–82

Andrews's move back to, 123, 382
bicentennial celebrations, 249, 351–52, 355
educational buildings in, 123–31
Australia Council
　Australian Pavilion for Venice Biennale, 254, 257–61
　Design Arts Board, 248–54
　and interface between modernism and postmodernism, 392–93
　overview, 12–13, 15–16, 241, 248–49
Australia pavilion (Expo 67), 82
Australia Square, 305–6
Australian Built exhibition and publication, 251–54, 256
Australian Defence Force Academy (ADFA) campus, 128
Australian design culture. *See* public advocacy for design
Australian Environmental Studies (AES) building, 265–67, 269, 284, 376
Australian National University (ANU), 123–25, 302
Australian Parliament House, 241, 245–48, 258, 392
Australian Pavilion for Venice Biennale, 254, 257–61
Australian Ugliness, The (Boyd), 381

B
Bacon, Edmund, 242, 248
Baddeley, Adrian, 124
Baird, George, 194
Bakema, Jaap, 112
Baldwin, Ned, 168–69, 362, 391
Banham, Reyner, 98, 152, 165, 235, 251
Bateman Catholic Centre, 128
Baudrillard, Jean, 356
Baume, Nicholas, 257
Beckel, William, 55–56, 59, 67, 71
Behavioral Sciences Building (Tufts University), 121, 283–84, 386
Belconnen, Australia, 214–16, 232. *See also* Cameron Offices
Belgiorno-Nettis, Franco, 254
Bellmere School (Bellmere Junior Public School)
　connection to Intelsat Headquarters, 319
　current conditions of, 412–13
　design strategies, 89, 92–95, 97, 101
　diagonal in, 92, 109

influences on design, 384
lessons learned in planning, 100
overview, 77
roof design, 39
urbanism, 386
Belluschi, Pietro
　as encouraging Andrews's ambition, 21, 24
　Equitable Building, 24, 27
　Intelsat design competition, 314, 317, 328–29, 330–31
Berlin Free University, 72
bicentennial celebrations, Australian, 351–52, 355
Bissell, Claude, 54, 187
Blake, Peter, 170, 177–78, 187, 202
Bloom, Harold, 208
Bond Street project. *See* 2 Bond Street project
Bovis Lend Lease (developers), 373
Boyd, Robin, 213–14, 381
Brawn, Graham, 114
Brawne, Michael, 106
Brine, Judith, 342
Brisbane city redevelopment project, Australia, 274, 277–78
British Pavilion (Expo 67), 98
British universities, 105–6
Brock University residences, 115–17
Brussels World's Fair of 1958, 79
Brutalism. *See also* Scarborough College
　British Pavilion at Expo 67, 98
　misrepresentation of Andrews's architecture as, 202–3, 234
　overview, 388
Buchanan, Peter, 330, 331
Budgett, Jeanette, 369
buildability, 11–12
buildings, documenting state of over time, 397. *See also specific buildings*
Burns, Karen, 356
Burns Philp Building, 305

C
Cain, John, 347, 351
Callam Offices, 384
　address at, 332
　connection to Intelsat Headquarters, 319–20, 325
　current conditions of, 397, 464–71
　environmental design, 275–76, 292, 323, 325
　kinship with Hertzberger's work, 321
　octagonal plan in, 301–2

urbanism, 387
Cambridge University History Faculty Building, 203–5, 385
Cameron Offices
　alterations to, 373–74, 397
　architecture/infrastructure of, 234–37
　and broader geographical setting, 382
　bus station north of, 230, 232, 234
　circulation, 215–16, 231–32
　collaborative ethos in, 223
　construction, 224–31
　current conditions of, 397, 444–55
　defamation case, 241–43
　design strategies, 217–24, 332
　environmental design, 390
　heritage status, 374
　interiors, 234, 235, 237
　kinship with Hertzberger's work, 321
　landscape plan, 220–22, 224–27, 231, 235, 274
　local reception, 10–11
　loss of vision for, 231–34
　maintenance problems, 226–27, 231
　making aesthetic out of means of construction, 388–89
　overview, 15, 213
　planning for, 213–17
　shading elements in, 292
　spatial types in, 274, 284
　urbanism in, 217, 231–32, 235, 237, 385–86, 387
Campbell, Keith, 278, 289
campus design, 105–7. *See also* educational buildings
Can Our Cities Survive? (Sert), 25
Canada. *See also* John Andrews Architects; *specific architectural projects*
　Andrews's encounter with, 381–32
　attractiveness in 1960s, 77–78
　New University movement in, 106
Canadian Corporation for the 1967 World Exhibition (CCWE), 82, 84–85, 93
Canadian National Railway, 140–42, 154, 158
Canadian Pacific Railway, 140–42, 154, 158
Canberra College of Advanced Education (CCAE) "Ressie 2," 124–25, 274, 302, 386, 456–61
Canberra development plan,

Australia, 213–214, 232. *See also* Cameron Offices
Candilis-Josic-Woods (firm), 112, 235
Carpenter Center for the Visual Arts, 187, 199–200, 205, 388
Carroll, Jerry Wayne, 246
casinos
　in Adelaide Station and Environs Redevelopment, 339, 342–43
　Darling Harbour designs, 300, 337, 351, 353, 355–56
　in Melbourne, 347, 348, 351
Castro, Ricardo L., 368
Catholic Centre, 128
CCTV (closed-circuit television) in instruction, 54–56, 59, 66–67, 70–71
Center for the Study of World Religions, 185
Centraal Beheer office building, 320, 321
Central Tech Art Centre, 147
"Centres of Community Life" (Sert), 25–26
Chandigarh Secretariat and Assembly Buildings, 43, 44
Chapel of Saint James the Fisherman, 31
Charter of Habitat, 26
Chemical Engineering Building (University of Queensland), 283–85
Chetham, Charles S., 118, 120
China, connection with Australia Council, 250–51, 393
Churchill, Edward, 93, 96
CIAM (Congrès internationaux d'architecture moderne), 25–26, 203, 385
circulation
　Australian Defence Force Academy campus, 128
　Australian Environmental Studies building, 265–67
　Bellmere School, 109
　Cameron Offices, 215–16, 231–32
　D. B. Weldon Library, 118
　Expo 67, 93, 99
　Miami Seaport Terminal, 173
　in octagonal plan, 302
　in Queensland educational buildings, 279, 283
　RMIT Library and Student Union, 130–31
　Scarborough College, 58, 72, 112
　South Residences, 112
　Stelco housing complex, 89
　Sydney Convention Centre, 353

495

Toad Hall, 124
and urbanism, 386–87
City of Bits (Mitchell), 356
City Tower, 291, 293, 295, 384
climate issues, 29, 33, 323, 389–90. *See also* environmental design
closed-circuit television (CCTV) in instruction, 54–56, 59, 66–67, 70–71
CN Tower, 14, 158–59, 161, 299
Colino, Richard, 327–28
collaborative ethos
　Australian Environmental Studies building, 267
　Cameron Offices, 223–24
　and ecological activism, 271–72
　in environmental design, 275–76
　John Andrews Architects, 78, 160, 391
　John Andrews International, 391
　overview, 390–91
　Scarborough College, 52, 56–64, 194, 391
colleges, expansion of in 1960s, 54. *See also* educational buildings; *specific colleges*
columns
　Cameron Offices, 223–24, 237
　Carpenter Center for the Visual Arts, 199, 200, 388
　Gund Hall, 198, 200–201, 388
　humanism and, 388
comfort, role in design, 11–12
"Commercial Core" (Metro Centre), 141, 146
commercial projects. *See also* convention centers; King George Tower; Octagon
　high-rise types created by Andrews, 294, 299–301
　octagonal plan, 299–300, 301–2, 305
　overview, 16
　reasons for seeking, 297–99
　2 Bond Street project, 16, 305–09, 386, 392
common sense approach to architecture
　Intelsat Headquarters, 331
　of James Stirling, 204
　looseness of, 389
　Metro Centre, 160
　overview, 9, 11, 393
　South Residences, 109
Commonwealth Place (Expo 67), 83, 85
"Communications Area" (Metro Centre), 142
community theme, Design Arts Board, 249, 251

Complexity and Contradiction in Architecture (Venturi), 166
Confederation of Resident and Ratepayer Associations (CORRA), 154
Congrès internationaux d'architecture moderne (CIAM), 25, 26, 203, 385
conservation. *See* environmental design
construction techniques, 387–89
contextualism, 331–32, 363
convention centers. *See also* Adelaide Station and Environs Redevelopment; Sydney Convention Centre; World Congress Centre
　demolition of, 374
　overview, 16–17, 337
"cooperative" contracts, Cameron Offices, 224
Corrigan, Peter, 253, 370
Courtney, Peter, 31, 223, 391
courtyards
　Cameron Offices, 226
　in environmental architecture, 272, 274–75
　in Intelsat Headquarters, 319
　Mandurah high school, 127
Cox, Philip
　and Andrews's defamation case, 242
　Architecture and Design Panel, 249
　architecture of, 253
　Australian Pavilion for Venice Biennale, 254, 257–61
　Darling Harbour, 351, 356–57
　end of collaboration with Andrews, 369–30
　Old Continent, New Building, 253
Crinson, Mark, 392
critical path system, 60–62, 93
Crown Melbourne, 351
Crowne Plaza Hotel (World Congress Centre), 300, 345, 347–48
cruises, Miami as center for, 165. *See also* Miami Seaport Terminal
Cumulus Vineyards winery, 364
curtain-walled office buildings, 24, 27
Curtis, Tina, 364, 391

D

D. B. Weldon Library, 119, 187
　current conditions, 422–29
　urbanism, 117–18, 386
D. S. Thomas and Partners (firm), 223
Darling Downs Institute of

Advanced Education, 279, 280, 283
Darling Harbour
　casino designs, 300, 337, 353, 355–57
　and city as spectacle, 387
　urban renewal plan for, 351–52
Daubney, John, 371–73
David Volkert & Associates (firm), 166, 169
Davidson, John H., 242
Day, Norman, 253
de Carlo, Giancarlo, 106
deer farming, 362, 368–69
defamation case, 241–43
demolition of projects by Andrews, 370–77
Denton Corker Marshall (firm), 246, 248, 351
design advocacy. *See* public advocacy for design
Design Arts Board, 248–54, 393
design culture, architect's role in, 12–13
design teaching, in plan for Gund Hall, 194–98
diagonal
　Bellmere School, 109
　D. B. Weldon Library, 117–18
　Intelsat Headquarters, 319
　Miami Seaport Terminal, 170, 173, 176
　overview, 100
　South Residences, 112
　and work of van Eyck and Hertzberger, 321
Diamond, Jack, 85
Dickinson, Peter, 141
Dinkerloo, John, 295
Domus, 251–53
Donovan Hill and Peddle Thorp Architects (firm), 285
Dormer, Peter, 106
Drew, Philip, 87, 99, 165, 204, 208, 373, 381
du Toit, Roger, 78, 147, 158, 213, 362, 391
DuBois, Macy, 28–32, 138, 147, 200, 203, 385
Dulles International Airport, 178

E

Eaton Centre, 140
ecological planning and activism, 269–72
economical design approach, 11–12
Edmond & Corrigan (firm), 131, 253, 370–71
educational buildings. *See also* Gund Hall; Scarborough College; South Residences
　in architectural histories, 131–32

Australian Defence Force Academy campus, 128
basis for practice, 113–15
Brock University residences, 115–17
D. B. Weldon Library, 117–19, 187, 386, 422–29
environmental design in, 278–85
Mandurah high school, 127–29
New University movement, 105–7
overview, 14, 105
Padbury Senior High School, 128, 386
plans, systems, and landscapes, 120–23
"Ressie 2" complex, 124–25, 274, 302, 386
RMIT Building 8, 370–71
RMIT Library and Student Union, 129, 130–31
Smith College Arts Center, 118–20, 386
Toad Hall, 123–26, 302, 386
University of Guelph housing study, 107–9
University of Lethbridge, 364–65, 368
　and urbanism, 385–86
Veterinary Science Conference Centre, 128, 130, 362–63
Edwards, Madigan and Torzillo (firm), 24
Edwards, Stan, 363–64
Eggleston, MacDonald & Secomb (firm), 348
energy use, 127, 329–30, 390
Engineering Building (University of Leicester), 204
environmental design
　Andrews's approach to, 267–68
　in Andrews's work for Parkin office, 33
　Callam Offices, 275, 276, 292, 323, 325
　Cameron Offices, 390
　collaborative ethos in, 275–76
　and demolition of World Congress Centre, 374
　Don Thomas's approach to, 223
　ecological planning and activism, 269–72
　education masterplans, 278–83
　establishment of Queensland branch John Andrews International, 276–78

496

increasing technical sophistication of, 292–293
Intelsat Headquarters, 27–76, 323–25, 329–30, 333
King George Tower, 275, 292–93, 390
legacy of, 285
Mandurah high school, 127–28
overview, 16, 389–90
Rudolph's influence on Andrews related to, 33
Scarborough College, 56, 58, 270–72, 389
School of Australian Environmental Studies, 265–67, 269
"streets" for Queensland campuses, 283–85
and urbanism, 386
Equitable Building, 24, 27
Erickson, Arthur, 67, 70, 106, 365, 368
Erindale College, 54, 55
Esplanade Street (Metro Centre), 142, 144–45, 147
ethical dimension of architecture, 381–82
Eugowra, 362, 368
 Andrews's response to postmodernism in, 392
 and broader geographical setting, 383
 current conditions, 472–77
 design strategies, 254, 255–56
Explorations Group, 71–72
Expo 67 (Universal and International Exhibition). *See also* African Place
 Activity Area F, 84–85, 93, 98
 architecture and exhibition outcomes, 96, 98
 Australia pavilion, 82
 British Pavilion, 98
 Commonwealth Place, 83, 85
 German Pavilion, 98
 Habitat 67, 79, 82, 98
 Joint Arab Pavilion, 85
 Man the Producer pavilion, 98
 overview, 77, 78–79
 and problem of movement, 99–100

F
Farrelly, Elizabeth, 351, 356, 357
Federal Equipment Building, 33, 34, 43, 268, 384
Federal Martin Committee of Enquiry into the Future of Education, 279
field theory, 121–22
Fieldes, Diane, 124
flexible design. *See* open design

Florida houses, 165, 177
Forbidden City, China, 250
Forest Park, 72
Forgey, Benjamin, 331–32
Fragrant Hills Hotel, China, 250–51
Frampton, Kenneth, 321
Francis-Jones Morehen Thorp (fjmt) (firm), 373
Frederic R. Harris (firm), 166
Fuller, Richard Buckminster, 96, 98, 152–54
Fuller and Sadao/Geometrics (firm), 152–54
functionalism, 25
Furneaux-Jordan, Robert, 106

G
Galanyk, Ed, 118, 168–69, 213, 391
Garden Island Parking Structure, 275, 478–79
Gaskie, Margaret, 331, 344
Gaudí, Antoni, 268
General Motors Technical Center, 24
generic high-rises, 299–300
Genting Berhad (firm), 355
geography and architecture, 10–11, 381–83
George Gund Hall. *See* Gund Hall
German Pavilion (Expo 67), 98
Gibson, Robin, 285
Giedion, Sigfried, 24–25, 31–32, 177, 204, 385
Giurgola, Romaldo, 12, 166, 244–46, 248
Gladstone, Gerald, 194, 213, 223, 270–72, 391
Glass House, 28, 36
Goering, Peter, 147
Graduate School of Design (GSD). *See* Gund Hall; Harvard University Graduate School of Design
Grays, the, 244
"green roof" approach, 275
Griffith University
 Library and Humanities Building, 285
 Nathan Campus, 284
 School of Australian Environmental Studies, 265–27, 269, 284, 376
Gropius, Walter, 24, 185, 187
Gruen, Victor, 230
GSD. *See* Gund Hall; Harvard University Graduate School of Design
Gund Hall (Harvard GSD)
 Andrews and "third generation," 202–9, 385
 Andrews's view of

architectural education, 190, 194
 choice of Andrews as architect, 185–88
 columns in, 198, 200–201, 388
 connection to Sydney Convention Centre, 353
 construction techniques, 388
 and crisis in Harvard GSD, 188–90
 critical reception, 200–202
 current conditions, 430–43
 design strategies, 115
 design teaching in plan for, 194–98
 Gladstone's art installation at, 270–72
 and internationalized architectural culture, 11
 new architectural elements in, 195, 197, 198–200
 overview, 15
 roof design, 191, 192–93, 195–96
 sections in environmental fit, 272
 and Smith College Arts Center, 120
 urbanism, 198, 386
Gutenberg Galaxy, The (McLuhan), 71

H
Habitat 67, 79, 82, 98
Hadid, Zaha, 250–51, 258
Hancock, Macklin, 107, 188
Harvard Science Center, 185–86
Harvard University Graduate School of Design (GSD). *See also* Gund Hall
 Andrews's education at, 24–28
 crisis in, 188–190, 201–2
 selection of Andrews as architect by, 185–88
 urbanism, 385
Harvard Yard, 185
Hassell (firm), 376, 393
Hassell, McConnell and Partners (firm), 125
Hastie, Frank, 59, 70
Hawken Engineering Building (University of Queensland), 285
Heart of the City, The (Sert), 25
Heck, Gordon, 272
Hendry, Margaret, 225–26
Herald, The, 241–43
Hertzberger, Herman, 203, 244, 321–23, 384–85
high-rises. *See also* King George Tower; Octagon

octagonal plan, 299–300, 301–2, 305
 overview, 16
 reasons for seeking commercial work, 297–99
 2 Bond Street project, 16, 305–9, 386, 392
 types created by Andrews, 294, 299–301
History Faculty Building (University of Cambridge), 203–5, 385
Holdsworth Macpherson Building, 306–7
Holyoke Center (Harvard), 185–86
Hook address (A. S. Hook Memorial Address), 241, 243–45, 381–82, 390
horizontally distributed buildings, 319, 321–23, 332
Horne, Donald, 249, 258
hotels. *See also* Malton Hotel project
 in Darling Harbour casino designs, 355
 Fragrant Hills Hotel, 250, 251
 Hyatt Regency Hotel, Adelaide, 299, 302–3, 342–44
 Merlin Hotel, 299, 302, 343
 Metropolitan Hotel, 306–7
 in World Congress Centre, 300, 345, 347–48
Hough, Michael, 56, 270, 389
house designs, 363–64, 383. *See also* Eugowra
Howarth, Thomas, 106
Hugo-Brunt, Michael, 14, 56
"Human Scale, The" course (Harvard GSD), 24–25
humanism, 99, 204, 234–35, 388
Hutson, Andrew, 248
Huxtable, Ada Louise, 201, 203, 307, 309, 385
Hyatt Regency Hotel, Adelaide, 299, 302–3, 342–344
Hyde, Timothy, 231, 235

I
ICC (International Convention Centre), 376
identity theme, Design Arts Board, 249, 251–53
industry theme, Design Arts Board, 249, 251
Integ, 43, 194, 271, 391
Intelsat Headquarters, 377, 384
 assessment for design competition, 328–29, 330–31
 concrete tubes in, 299
 critical reception, 331–33
 current conditions of, 397, 480–87

497

design logic, 319–23
energy use, 329–30
environmental design, 275–76, 323–25, 329–30, 333
fraud during construction of, 325, 327–28
international competition, 313–19
landscape plan, 319
overview, 16, 313
urbanism, 331, 387
Interama, 177
International Convention Centre (ICC), 376
internationalized architectural culture, 10–11
"Invisible Environment, The" (McLuhan), 71
Ipswich College of Technical and Further Education, 279, 282–83
Ireland, William, 28–32

J
Jackson, Anthony, 138, 140
Jackson, Huson, 27
Jameson, Fredric, 253
Jeff's Shed, 351
Jencks, Charles, 296
Jensen, Robert, 121, 202
Johannesburg Civic Centre competition, 43, 45
John Andrews: Architecture, a Performing Art (Taylor and Andrews)
   Bellmere School, 89, 92–93
   connection of Andrews with Hertzberger and van Eyck, 321–22
   Expo 67, 84
   King George Tower, 297
   Metro Centre, 154
   Miami Seaport Terminal, 168, 170
   Scarborough College, 62, 70
John Andrews Architects (Toronto). See also environmental design; *specific architectural projects*
   Andrews's departure from, 362
   basis for practice, 113–15
   collaborative ethos at, 78, 160, 391
   connection to Intelsat Headquarters, 319
   educational buildings by, 105, 120–23
   and global modernity, 77–79
   overview, 14, 77
   problem of movement, 99–100
John Andrews International (Sydney). See also commercial projects; convention centers; environmental design; *specific architectural projects*
   Andrews's winding down of, 362–63
   collaborative ethos at, 391
   defamation case, 241–43
   educational buildings by, 105, 123–31, 278–85
   establishment of Queensland branch, 276–78
   geographical ambition of, 382
   projects contemporaneous with Intelsat, 313
John B. Parkin Associates (firm)
   Andrews's departure from, 32, 42–43
   Andrews's work at, 32–39, 40–41, 268, 384
   precursors to King George Tower, 289
   Yorkdale Shopping Centre, 147, 230, 231, 301
John Simpson & Associates (firm), 285
Johnson, Philip, 28, 36
Johnson, Roger, 284
Joint Arab Pavilion (Expo 67), 85

K
Kahn, Louis, 106, 258
   City Tower, 291, 293, 295
   influence on Andrews's work, 33, 36, 38–39, 299, 384
Keller, Morton, 185, 187
Keller, Phyllis, 185, 187
Kelvin Grove campus (Queensland University of Technology), 279, 281
Kelvin Grove Education Resource Centre, 281, 283–84
Kempsey Museum, 258
Keniger, Michael, 376
Kent State Massacre, 123
Kent State University School of Art, 121–23, 125, 397
Kiembah farm, 367, 368–69
Kilbridge, Maurice, 190, 201
Kimbell Art Museum, 258
King George Tower, 305, 384
   alterations to, 371–73
   construction, 296
   critical reception, 295–97
   current conditions, 463
   design strategies, 289–93
   environmental design, 275, 292–93, 390
   making aesthetic out of means of construction, 389
   versus octagonal plan, 302
   overview, 16, 289
   precursors in Andrews's work to, 289
   shading elements, 292–93, 297
   tree metaphor to describe, 296–97
   triangle-plan towers, 158, 173, 293, 295
   urbanism, 386
Kirner, Joan, 351
Knights of Columbus Building, 39, 295
Kowloon Point, 363, 365
Kurokawa, Kisho, 87, 89, 300

L
landscape plan
   Cameron Offices, 220–2122, 224, 225–27, 231, 235, 274
   ecological planning in, 269–70, 271
   for educational settings, 121
   "green roof" approach, 275
   Intelsat Headquarters, 319
   Miami Seaport Terminal, 176
Lasdun, Denys, 106, 251
late modernism, 253–54, 385
Le Corbusier
   Carpenter Center for the Visual Arts, 187, 199–200, 205
   connection to Cameron Offices, 234
   influence on Andrews's designs, 36, 43–44, 387–88
   pinwheel plan, 89
   Stirling's writings on, 208
Lee, John A., 54, 67, 70
Léger, Fernand, 25, 385
Leighton Construction, 124–25
Leplastrier, Richard, 28
Library and Humanities Building (Griffith University), 285
Library and Student Union (RMIT), 129, 130–31
Library-Instructional Center (Sarah Lawrence College), 121
Little Bay Housing, 462
LJ Hooker (firm), 289
Lobsinger, Mary Lou, 382
Loftus, Neil, 127, 128
Lowe, Frank, 361, 370

M
MacKinnon Building, 188
Madigan, Colin, 223
Maki, Fumihiko, 152, 187
Malton Hotel project
   architectural elements, 181, 198
   environmental design, 33–34, 268, 272, 389
Man the Producer pavilion (Expo 67), 98
Mandurah high school, 127–28, 129
Marathon Realty Company Limited, 140–42
Massachusetts Institute of Technology (MIT), 26
Master of Architecture (MArch) program, Harvard GSD, 24–25, 27
Mathers and Haldenby Architects (firm), 147
"mat-planning" approach
   Andrews's convergence with Team 10, 384
   and Andrews's horizontally distributed designs, 319, 321–23, 332
   Cameron Offices, 231–32, 235, 237
   in generic high-rises, 300
McConnel Smith & Johnson Architects (firm), 214
McCormick, James, 283
McCormick, John, 82
McCredie, Arthur, 305–6
McCredie, George, 305–6
McGregor, Craig, 253
McHarg, Ian, 269–71, 390
McKenzie, Andrew, 374
McLaughlin Library, 188
McLeod, Mary, 253
McLuhan, Marshall, 55, 71–72
McMaster University, 120
McNamara, Bill, 309
Medical Science Building (University of Toronto), 147
Megastructure: Urban Futures of the Recent Past (Banham), 152
megastructure design, 52, 98, 235, 237. See also Miami Seaport Terminal; Scarborough College; South Residences
Melbourne World Congress Centre. See World Congress Centre
Mendini, Alessandro, 258
Merlin Hotel, 299, 302, 343
Metabolist movement, 87, 89, 300
Metro Centre
   CN Tower as remnant of, 158–59
   "Commercial Core," 141, 146
   "Communications Area," 142
   competing visions for downtown Toronto, 152–54
   connection to Intelsat Headquarters, 319
   in context, 147, 152
   Esplanade Street, 142, 144–45, 147
   general discussion, 159–60
   kinship to Adelaide Station and Environs

Redevelopment, 337
overview, 14, 137
presentation to public, 147, 149–51
proposal, 140–47, 148
public criticism and fight over Union Station, 154–58
residential area, 141–42, 146
"Transportation Terminal," 141, 143
triangle-plan tower concept in, 294, 299
urbanism, 386
Metro Centre Developments Limited, 141, 158, 159
Metropolitan Hotel, 306–7
Miami Seaport Terminal
airport design and, 170
baggage areas, 167–69
boarding and disembarking process, 169–70
customs and immigration, 169
demolition of, 397
design strategies, 170–81
landscape plan, 176
logic of plan for, 169–70
nodes of, 170, 173, 176
obsolescence of, 377
overview, 15
process of appointing Andrews as architect, 165–69
roof design, 165, 172–75, 178–79
sections in environmental fit, 272
vertical concrete cylinders, 171, 173
Mies van der Rohe, Ludwig, 36, 43
Miller, George, 42–43, 271, 391
Miller, Peter, 223, 390
Ministry of Social Welfare and Employment, The Hague, 321
MIT (Massachusetts Institute of Technology), 26
Mitchell, William, 356
Mitchell/Giurgola and Thorpe (firm), 246, 248, 258, 392
modernism
Andrews's approach to, 9–10
in Australian architecture, 253–54
discussions on in 1950s, 99
and Harvard GSD, 25–27
and postmodernism, 392
"third generation," 10–12, 99, 202–9, 381, 383–85
modular designs
African Place, 85, 87
Bellmere School, 89, 92–93
Callam Offices, 325
environmental design, 325

Intelsat Headquarters, 319
Miami Seaport Terminal, 170
School of Art at Kent State University, 121–23
Stelco housing complex, 87–89, 300
Monarto town center, Australia, 319
environmental design, 323, 325, 326
overview, 273, 274–75
passive low-energy design, 127
Monier Design Awards, 369
Montreal, Canada, 82, 147, 152. See also Expo 67
monumentality, 33
Australian Parliament House, 392
debates for and against, 99
new monumentality, 25–26, 177, 385
Sydney Convention Centre, 356
of triangle-plan towers, 299
Moorhead, Steven, 225
Morgan, William, 28–32
Morton, Ian, 98, 168–69
Mould, Peter, 371, 373
multimedia instruction, college-level, 54–56, 59, 66–67, 70–71
Mumford, Eric, 27
Mumford, Lewis, 26
Murcutt, Glenn, 253, 258, 364, 383
Murphy, Ronald E., 117
Muthesius, Stefan, 105–6

N
Nakagin Capsule tower, 300
Nathan Campus (Griffith University), 265–67, 284
National Capital Development Commission (NCDC), 12, 213–14, 216, 222, 227, 231–32
National Museum of Australia, 319
Neo-avant-garde and Postmodern (Crinson & Zimmerman), 392
neoliberalism, 232, 253, 298, 337
"New Campus, The" (Newman), 72
new monumentality, 25–26, 177, 385
New University movement, 105–7
New York Five, 244
New Zealand Institute of Architects, 369
Newman, Oscar, 72–73, 105, 117
"Nine Points on Monumentality" (Sert, Léger, Giedion), 25
Nishihara, Kiyoyuki, 87, 300

O
Octagon, 384
current conditions, 488–93
design strategies, 301–2, 305
as example of generic high-rise type, 299
threat of demolition, 376
octagonal plan
in architectural projects, 301–2, 305, 319, 343–44
overview, 299–300
O'Farrell, Barry, 376
Old Continent, New Building
exhibition and publication, 251–54, 256
Oltmanns, Larry, 374, 376
Ontario Municipal Board, 155
open design
African Place, 80–81, 82, 84–87, 88, 93, 96, 98, 100
basis for practice, 113–115
Bellmere School, 89, 92–95, 97, 100–101, 109
in educational buildings, 107
educational plans, systems, and landscapes, 120–23
Expo 67 architecture and exhibition outcomes, 96, 98–99
Expo 67 overview, 79–82
and global modernity, 77–79
modules and patterns in, 87–89
overview, 14, 77
problem of movement, 99–100
RMIT Library and Student Union, 130–31
South Residences, 108–113, 114, 116
Stelco housing complex, 87, 89, 90–91, 92
Open Gate, The (Bébout, ed.), 155
Optical Galaxy (Gladstone), 272
Ortega, Alvaro, 27
Ostankino Tower, 159
Otto, Frei, 98
Ove Arup & Partners (firm), 275
Overall, John, 213–14, 232, 245–46
Overseas Telecommunications Agency, 327

P
Padbury Senior High School, 128, 386
Page and Steele Architects, 59, 70
Pak Poy & Kneebone (developer), 339
Park Place, 299–300, 302, 304–5
Parkin, Edmund T., 32

Parkin, John B., 32
Parkin, John C., 32, 43
Parliament House, Australian, 241, 245–48, 258, 392
Parsons, Anthony, 117, 121, 123, 391
pattern-based approach, 87–89
Peabody Terrace (Harvard), 185–86
Peak Leisure Club, 250–51, 258
Pei, I. M., 12, 245–47, 250–51
Perspecta, 38
Peugeot Building, 39, 42, 293
Philadelphia City Hall, 291, 293, 295
photography, role in documenting buildings, 397
Pinker, Donovan, 138
pinwheel plan
African Place, 93
background, 89
Bellmere School, 92, 95
Stelco housing complex, 89
Place Bonaventure, 152
Place Ville Marie, 152
"Plan for Central Toronto" (1963), 138–40
"Plan for Downtown Toronto" (1963), 138–40
Populous (firm), 376
Port of Melbourne Authority, 347
Port of Miami, 165. See also Miami Seaport Terminal
postmodernism, 131
Andrews's disdain for, 361
Andrews's response to, 12, 305–9, 392
in Australian architecture, 253–54
Australian Parliament House, 248
Royal Melbourne Institute of Technology Building 8, 370–71
Veterinary Science Conference Centre, 363
"Postmodernism, or, the Cultural Logic of Late Capitalism" (Jameson), 253
Prangnell, Peter, 190, 194, 271, 322–23
Presidential Palace project, Havana, 29
Primrose Club, 33–37, 43, 384
Prince of Wales College, 120
private commercial work. See commercial projects
Private Life of Public Architecture, The (McKenzie), 374
problem-solving. See common sense approach to architecture

499

Project Planning Associates, 107, 188
Project Toronto, 152–54
public advocacy for design
  A. S. Hook Memorial Address, 241, 243–25
  Australian Parliament House competition, 241, 245–48
  Australian Pavilion for Venice Biennale, 254, 257–61
  defamation case, 241–43
  Design Arts Board, 248–54
  and interface between modernism and postmodernism, 392–93
  overview, 15–16, 241
  as public advocate for design in Australia, 241
Pusey, Nathan, 185, 187, 189

Q
Queensland, environmental design projects in
  Andrews's environmental approach, 267–68
  deploying environmental architecture, 272–76
  ecological planning and activism, 269–72
  education master plans, 278–83
  establishment of Queensland branch, 276–78
  legacy of, 285
  making "streets" for campuses, 283–85
  School of Australian Environmental Studies, 265–67, 269
  and urbanism, 386
Queensland Cultural Centre, 285
Queensland University of Technology (QUT) Kelvin Grove campus, 279, 281

R
RAIA (Royal Australian Institute of Architects), 241, 242–45, 374
Rees, Lloyd, 267
regional inflections of modernism, 26
repetition, in Andrews's work, 388–89
residential area (Metro Centre), 141–42, 146
residential colleges, 106–7. *See also* educational buildings; specific colleges
"Responding to the Place" (McGregor), 253
responsive climatic strategies, 29
"Ressie 2" (CCAE Student Residence Group 2), 124–25,
274, 302, 386, 456–61
Revell, Viljo, 29, 31, 39, 42, 43, 293
Revell-Parkin (firm), 39, 42
Rice Daubney (firm), 371–73
Richardson, Douglas, 155
Riverview High School, 33
Robarts Library, 147
Robertson, Jaquelin T., 234–35, 237, 242, 244–45
Robinson, Gerald, 138
Roche, Kevin, 39, 204, 295
Roma Street precinct, Brisbane, 274, 277–78, 300–301
Rose, Calvin, 265, 267
Ross, Ernie, 121, 123
Rowan, John C., 98
Royal Australian Institute of Architects (RAIA), 241–45, 374
Royal Melbourne Institute of Technology (RMIT), 129–31, 370–71
Rudofsky, Bernard, 268
Rudolph, Paul
  Art and Architecture building at Yale, 36–37, 194, 202
  Florida houses, 165, 177
  influence on Andrews's work, 33, 36, 37, 165, 177, 384
  Interama design, 177
  Riverview High School, 33
  suggestion to Andrews to work with Parkin firm, 32
  Temple Street Parking Garage, 36, 37, 177
Rykwert, Joseph, 105–6

S
Saarinen, Eero, 24, 31, 33, 106, 109, 178
Sadao, Shoji, 152–54
Safdie, Moshe, 82, 98
Saint George Campus (University of Toronto), 54, 114–15
Saint Lucia Campus (University of Queensland), 283
Sarah Lawrence College, 121
Sault Sainte Marie high school, 37, 38–39, 384
Saunders, David, 237, 342–43
Scarborough College, 377, 384
  assessment of television instruction, 70–71
  background, 52–56
  and broader geographical setting, 382
  circulation, 58, 72, 112
  collaborative ethos in, 52, 56–64, 194, 391
  construction, 52, 55, 58, 62, 64, 67
in context of Metro Centre, 147, 160
critical reception, 77
current conditions, 397, 398–411
environmental design, 56, 58, 270–72, 389
further planning and design development, 64–67
Interim Report Master Plan of 1968, 64–66
Interim Report Master Plan of 1969, 66–67
interview with John Andrews regarding, 49, 72
inverted stepped profile, 198
landscape plan, 68
local reception, 10–11
and Marshall McLuhan, 71–72
and Miami Seaport Terminal, 178, 181
and New University movement, 105
Oscar Newman's critique of, 72–73
overview, 14, 49–52
Phase 2A, 66
press release of 1965, 67, 70
and selection of Andrews for Gund Hall, 187
street type in, 274, 284–85
urbanism in, 112, 385–86
School of Art at Kent State University, 121–23, 125, 397
School of Australian Environmental Studies (Griffith University), 265–67, 269, 284, 376
Science Center (Harvard), 185–86
Scrivano, Paolo, 14, 382–83
Sears, Henry, 138
Seethaler, Norbert, 42–43, 87, 169, 391
Seidler, Harry, 237, 305–6, 309
Sekler, Eduard, 25, 204
semicircle plan, 300, 345, 348, 349, 352, 355
Sert, Jackson & Associates (firm), 107, 188
Sert, Josep Lluís, 99, 272
  and Andrews's education at Harvard, 24–27
  and Andrews's encounter with United States, 381
  departure from Harvard, 189, 201
  Harvard buildings by, 185–86
  influence on Andrews's work, 28, 113, 177, 198, 356
  interdisciplinarity sought by, 188
  Presidential Palace project, 29
  selection of Andrews for
Gund Hall, 185, 187
University of Guelph buildings by, 107, 188
urbanism, 385
served and servant spaces, 38–39
Sewell, John, 141, 154
"Shaping of Urban Space, The" course (Harvard GSD), 25
Sheffield Report (1955), 52
shopping centers, 230–32, 234
Shulman, Allan, 166, 176–77
Sigsby, Donald, 225–26
Simon Fraser University, 67, 69–70, 365
Simpson, John
  Australian Environmental Studies building, 267
  Chemical Engineering Building, 283
  collaboration with Andrews, 391
  Hawken Engineering Building, 285
  at John Andrews Architects, 78
  in Queensland office, 127, 276, 278
  Tufts University Behavioral Sciences Building, 121
Simpsons department store, 230–31
Singapore Telecommunications Tower, 298–99
"Six Determinants of Architectural Form, The" (Rudolph), 33
Smith, Kenneth, 113
Smith, Terry, 356
Smith College Arts Center, 386
Smithson, Alison, 202–3, 231, 235
Smithson, Peter, 202–3, 235
social form, 106–7
South Residences (University of Guelph), 133
  in architectural histories, 132
  connection to Intelsat Headquarters, 319
  current conditions, 397, 414–21
  design strategies, 108–14, 116
  expressing inhabited volumes on exterior, 302
  as expressing social form, 107
  making aesthetic out of means of construction, 388
  overview, 14
  and selection of Andrews for Gund Hall, 187, 188
  urbanism, 112, 385–86
Spence, Basil, 98, 276
spatial types, in environmental architecture, 272, 274

spine concept, 279–83
State Library of Queensland, 285
Stelco housing complex
  modules and patterns in, 87, 89–92, 278
  overview, 77
  as variation from typical tower design, 300
Stephenson, Gordon, 28, 213
Stephenson, Peter, 43, 45
stepped profile, 198
Stevens, Irvin J., 169, 170
Stewart, Susan, 293
Stirling, James, 203–5, 208, 385
streets. *See also* urbanism
  in Brock University residences, 116–17
  in environmental architecture, 272, 274–75
  legacy of Andrews, 285
  in Queensland educational buildings, 279, 283–85
  in "Ressie 2," 125
  in South Residences, 109, 112
  in Toad Hall, 124
Strong, Richard
  Cameron Offices, 213, 223, 225–27
  collaboration with Andrews, 194, 390–91
  ecological activism, 271
  Intelsat Headquarters, 319
  Miami Seaport Terminal, 169, 176
  at Parkin firm, 42–43
  University of Lethbridge, 364–65
Strong Moorhead Sigsby (firm), 225–26
student center (University of Toronto), 115
student living, 106–107. *See also* educational buildings
student protests at Harvard, 188–89, 201–2
sustainability, 389–90. *See also* environmental design
Sydney airport terminal design, 21, 23, 28–29, 268, 274, 389
Sydney Convention Centre
  and city as spectacle, 387
  concrete tubes in, 299
  critical reception, 356–57
  Darling Harbour casino designs, 300, 337, 351, 353, 355–56
  demolition, 370, 375–76
  design strategies, 349–50, 352–54
  exterior, 352–354
  making aesthetic out of means of construction, 389
  overview, 16–17, 337, 351–52
  untimeliness of, 356–57
Sydney Morning Herald, 241–43
Sydney Opera House competition, 21, 24
Sydney urban transformation projects, Australia, 351–52
Sykes, Jim, 109, 169

T
Tall Building Artistically Reconsidered, The (Huxtable), 307, 309
Taylor, Jennifer. *See also John Andrews: Architecture, a Performing Art* (Taylor and Andrews)
  Andrews's ideological position, 244
  Australian cultural insularity, 382–83
  Cameron Offices, 234–35, 237, 382
  connection of Andrews with Hertzberger and van Eyck, 322
  D. B. Weldon Library, 117
  King George Tower, 293
  Old Continent, New Building, 253–54
  Sydney Convention Centre, 356–57
  triangle-plan tower concept, 289
  2 Bond Street project, 306
TC Whittle (firm), 224
Team 10, 82, 132
  Andrews's convergence with, 112, 176–77, 203, 384–85
  emergence of, 26
  "mat-planning" approach, 235
  pinwheel plan, 89, 92
teamwork. *See* collaborative ethos
Telegraph, The, 241–43
television, in college-level instruction, 54–56, 59, 66–67, 70–71
Temple Street Parking Garage, 36, 37, 177
Test Pattern (Lee), 54, 67, 70
Teyssot, Georges, 67
Theodore, David, 368
Third Generation (Drew), 204
"third generation" of modernism, 10–12, 99, 202–9, 381, 383–85
Thom, Ron, 78, 108–9, 115
Thomas, Don
  Australian Environmental Studies building, 267
  Callam Offices, 275–76
  Cameron Offices, 223
  climate and energy conservation, 390
  Octagon, 305
  technical environmental systems, 292–93, 323
  Woden TAFE, 325
Thorpe, Richard, 246, 248
three-cornered tower design. *See* triangle-plan towers
Toad Hall, 123–26, 302, 386
Toronto. *See also* Metro Centre
  architectural culture in 1960s, 147
  competing visions for downtown, 152–54
  railways and waterfront in, 137
  reorganization of downtown, 137–40
Toronto (Arthur), 152
Toronto City Hall (building), 39, 42, 195, 198, 384
Toronto City Hall competition, 28–32, 147, 268, 272, 274
Toronto International Airport control tower, 39, 41, 173, 289, 294, 299, 388
  and design of Miami Seaport Terminal, 170
  role of John B. Parkin Associates, 39
Toronto Metro Centre. *See* Metro Centre
Toronto-Dominion Centre, 36
total architecture, 267
Tovell, Vincent, 49, 72
towers. *See* high-rises; *specific buildings*
Trade Group Offices, 237
"Transportation Terminal" (Metro Centre), 141, 143
Trenton Bath House, 38–40
triangle-plan towers. *See also* King George Tower
  CN Tower, 158
  generators of scheme, 293–95
  importance to Andrews across career, 293
  and Miami Seaport Terminal, 173
  overview, 39, 41, 299, 389
  precursors to King George Tower, 289
Tufts University Behavioral Sciences Building, 121, 283–84, 386
2 Bond Street project
  Andrews's response to postmodernism in, 392
  design strategies, 305–9
  overview, 16
  urbanism, 386
Tyng, Anne, 291, 293, 295, 384

U
UIA International Architect, 251, 253
Understanding Media (McLuhan), 72
Union Station, fight over, 155, 158. *See also* Metro Centre
Unité d'Habitation, 43–44
United States, Andrews's encounter with, 381–82
Universal and International Exhibition. *See* African Place; Expo 67
university education, expansion and development of, 105–7. *See also* educational buildings
University of British Columbia, 115
University of Canberra. *See* Canberra College of Advanced Education "Ressie 2"
University of Guelph, 14, 107–9, 187–88. *See also* South Residences
University of Illinois at Chicago Circle, 72
University of Leicester Engineering Building, 204
University of Lethbridge, 364–65, 368
University of Marburg, 72
University of Minnesota, 120
University of Queensland, 283, 284–85
University of Sydney
  Andrews's education at, 21, 23, 267
  Veterinary Science Conference Centre, 128, 130, 362–63
University of Toronto. *See also* Scarborough College
  Andrews as chair of architecture at, 12, 190, 194, 271
  designs by Andrews for, 114–15
  expansion in 1960s, 52, 54–59
  Medical Science Building, 147
  Robarts Library, 147
University of Western Ontario, 117–19, 187. *See also* D. B. Weldon Library
University Television Subcommittee, 54–55
unselfconscious architecture, 204
Up Against City Hall (Sewell), 141
Urban Design Studio Project (Harvard GSD), 27

501

urbanism. *See also* high-rises; Metro Centre
    Australian Defence Force Academy campus, 128
    Australian Environmental Studies building, 265, 267
    Cameron Offices, 217, 231–32, 235, 237, 385–87
    D. B. Weldon Library, 117–18, 386
    development of Canberra, 213–14
    discussions on in 1950s, 99
    and educational building design, 105–6, 279, 283–85
    educational plans, systems, and landscapes, 120–23
    environmental design, 272–75
    Gund Hall, 198, 386
    at Harvard GSD, 25–27
    Intelsat Headquarters, 331, 387
    Mandurah high school, 127–28
    Monarto town center, 273–75
    overview, 385–87
    Padbury Senior High School, 128, 386
    "Ressie 2" complex, 124–25
    RMIT Library and Student Union, 130–31
    Roma Street precinct, 278
    Scarborough College, 112, 385–86
    Smith College Arts Center, 118–19
    South Residences, 112, 385–86
    Sydney urban design, 351–52
    Toad Hall, 123–26
    University of Toronto projects, 114–15
Uren, Tom, 231
user experience, in environmental design, 276

V
van Eyck, Aldo
    Amsterdam Orphanage, 92, 321, 384
    Andrews's convergence with, 203, 235, 244, 321–22, 384–85
van Ginkel, Blanche Lemco, 26–27, 82
van Ginkel, H. P. Daniel, 82
Van Vliet, Nick, 226
Venice Biennale, Australian Pavilion for, 254, 257–61
Venturi, Robert, 166, 246
Veterinary Science Conference Centre (VSCC), 128, 130, 362–63

Visual Arts Board, 249, 254, 257
Volkert, David, 166, 169
von Eckardt, Wolf, 200–201, 202–3, 330–32
Vreeland, Thomas R., 166

W
Wakelin, Roland, 267
Walker, Evan, 78, 107–9, 130, 391
Walker, Graham, 127, 128
Watts, F. B., 56, 58, 270
Webb Zerafa Menkès Housden (firm), 141
Weldon Library. *See* D. B. Weldon Library
Werner, Warwick, 363, 364
White, Richard, 137, 140–41
Whites, the, 244
William James Hall (Harvard), 185
William P. Lipscomb (company), 327
Williams, D. Carleton, 54–56, 59, 64, 67, 71, 187
Willing, Geoff, 223, 226–27, 327–28
Woden Technical and Further Education College (Woden TAFE), 321, 325, 384
Woods, Shadrach, 26, 176, 235
Woods Bagot (firm), 373, 374, 376, 393
World Bank competition, 299–300, 302, 305
World Congress Centre
    delay in construction of, 344, 347–48
    demolition of, 370, 374
    design strategies, 345–46, 348, 351
    exterior of, 352
    hotel design, 300, 345, 347, 348
    overview, 337
World Trade Centre (WTC), Melbourne, 347–48
World's Fair, 79. *See also* Expo 67

Y
Yale Art and Architecture Building, 36–37, 194, 202
Yale University Art Gallery, 36, 38
Yamasaki, Minoru, 185
Yorkdale Shopping Centre, 147, 230–31, 301

Z
Zanuso, Marco, 314, 317, 328–29, 330–31
Zeckendorf, William, 152
Zimmerman, Claire, 392

IMAGE CREDITS

01: EARLY LIFE
Fig. 1: Photo: Lee Andrews, 2015. Figs. 2–3: John Andrews. Figs. 4–5, 12–13, 20–22: Photos: John Andrews, 1957 (4), 1958 (5), 1963 (12–13), 1965 (20), 1961 (21–22). Figs. 6–7: Andrews Toronto City Hall competition booklet, 1958. Figs. 8, 11: Andrews Parkin office portfolio. Figs. 9, 14: Photos: PANDA Associates, courtesy of the Canadian Architectural Archives, Archives and Special Collections, University of Calgary. Figs. 10, 17–18: Courtesy of the Canadian Architectural Archives. Figs. 15–16: Louis I. Kahn Collection, University of Pennsylvania and Pennsylvania Historical and Museum Commission. Fig. 19: Photo: Pertti Ingervo, Museum of Finnish Architecture.

02: SCARBOROUGH COLLEGE
Figs. 1–5, 8–9, 11, 14: Photos: PANDA Associates. Courtesy of the Canadian Architectural Archives. Fig. 6: Scarborough College Presentation Drawings and Construction Slides (Box 43-36, slide 2048), Canadian Architectural Archives. Fig. 7: Scarborough College (43A, Box 43-36, Reports and Transmittals, 8), Canadian Architectural Archives. Figs. 10, 12: Courtesy of the Canadian Architectural Archives. Fig. 13: John Andrews Architects, photographer unknown.

03: OPEN FORM AND DESIGN THINKING IN ANDREWS'S EARLY PRACTICE, 1964–1967
Figs. 1–9, 11–13: Courtesy of the Canadian Architectural Archives. Fig. 10: Jennifer Taylor and John Andrews, *John Andrews: Architecture, a Performing Art* (Melbourne: Oxford University Press, 1982), 74. Figs. 14, 16–17: John Andrews Architects, photographer unknown. Fig. 15: Antony Moulis, based on Taylor and Andrews, 49.

04: GREENFIELDS AND URBAN SYSTEMS: BUILDINGS FOR EDUCATION

Figs. 1–2, 4, 6–8, 16: Courtesy of the Canadian Architectural Archives. Fig. 3: Photo: Ken Barton; RE1 UOG A1884, Regional and Campus History Collection, Archival and Special Collections, University of Guelph Library. Fig. 5: Photographer unknown. Fig. 9: Courtesy of the Western Archives and Special Collections, Western University. Fig. 10: *A+U* 5 (1974), 53. Fig. 11: "Art Building," Kent State University Libraries. Special Collections and Archives, https://omeka.library.kent.edu/special-collections/items/show/320. Fig. 12: Powerhouse Museum (Museum of Applied Arts and Sciences [MAAS]), Sydney; photo: David Moore. Fig. 13: John Andrews International. Fig. 14: Photo: Fritz Kos; Fritz Kos Collection of Photographs, State Library of Western Australia, BA1595/A241-1-9 224186PD. Fig. 15: John Andrews International, photographer unknown.

05: METRO CENTRE: THE "VERY OBVIOUS JOB" THAT WAS NEVER BUILT

Fig. 1: "Plan for Downtown Toronto: A Report by the City of Toronto Planning Board" (Toronto: City of Toronto, 1963), 48. Fig. 2: Macy DuBois, Anthony Jackson, Donovan Pinker, Gerald Robinson, and Henry Sears, "A Plan for Central Toronto," *Ekistics* 15: 87 (February 1963), 93. Figs. 3–10, 15: "Metro Centre Development Plan and Programme: A Study for the Development of Canadian National and Canadian Pacific Railway Lands in Central Toronto," Community Development Consultants, May 1968. Figs. 11–13: York University Libraries, Clara Thomas Archives and Special Collections, Toronto Telegram fonds, ASC [04394]. Fig. 14: R. Buckminster Fuller and Shoji Sadao, "Project Toronto," *Ekistics* 28: 165 (August 1969), 109. Fig. 16: Photo: PANDA Associates, courtesy of the Canadian Architectural Archives.

06: MIAMI SEAPORT TERMINAL

Figs. 1, 3–4: Photos: David Moore. Figs. 2, 5–6, 8–9, 11, 14–15: Photos: Marc Treib. Figs. 7, 10, 12–13: Courtesy of the Canadian Architectural Archives.

07: GEORGE GUND HALL

Figs. 1–2: Kidder Smith Collection, Rotch Visual Collections, MIT. Figs. 3–4: Photos: Paul Walker, 2012. Fig. 5: Leonard McCombe/The LIFE Picture Collection/Shutterstock. Figs. 6, 14–15: John Andrews. Figs. 7–10, 13: Courtesy of the Canadian Architectural Archives. Figs. 11, 21: Photo: Steve Rosenthal © Historic New England, from the Steve Rosenthal Collection of Commissioned Work at Historic New England. Fig. 12: Photo: Steve Rosenthal. Fig. 16: Photo: David Moore. Figs. 17, 19: James Stirling/Michael Wilford fonds, Canadian Centre for Architecture AP140.S2.SS1. D26.P5.4. Fig. 18: Photo: Steve Rosenthal, 1984; James Stirling/Michael Wilford fonds, Canadian Centre for Architecture AP140.S2.SS1.D58.P31.2. Fig. 20: Frances Loeb Library Special Collections, from the GSD History Collection: Administrative Affairs, Subseries EB: Building Services, Box EB023, 1972.

08: THE CAMERON OFFICES AND THE RETURN TO AUSTRALIA

Figs. 1–6: Courtesy of Canadian Architectural Archives. Figs. 7–8, 12: Photos PANDA Associates, courtesy of Canadian Architectural Archives. Figs. 9, 13, 15–19: Photos: David Moore. Figs. 10–11: Photos: Geoff Willing. Fig. 14: Photo: Paul Walker.

09: ANDREWS AS A PUBLIC ADVOCATE FOR DESIGN

Fig 1: *Architecture Australia*, 70:2 May 1981, cover photo: David Moore. Figs. 2, 10: Photos: David Moore. Fig. 3: Photo: Fairfax Syndication Photographs. Fig. 4: Zaha Hadid, 1982 © Zaha Hadid Foundation. Figs. 5–6: Photos: John Andrews, 1983. Figs. 7, 12–13: Leon Paroissien and Michael Griggs, *Old Continent, New Building: Contemporary Australian Architecture* (Sydney: David Ell Press, 1983) 8. Fig. 9: Michael Griggs and Craig McGregor, editors, *Australian Built: A Photographic Exhibition of Recent Australian Architecture* (Sydney: Design Arts Board of the Australia Council, 1982). Fig. 11: Taylor and Andrews, *John Andrews*, 168. Fig. 14: Photo: Peter Bennetts, 2011. Figs: 15–19: John Andrews.

10: ENVIRONMENTALISM AND THE QUEENSLAND PROJECTS

Figs. 1–2: photos: Knell & Chester. Fig. 3. Photo: Jill Gall. Fig. 4: AnupGandhe, CC BY SA 4.0, via Wikimedia Commons. Fig. 5: Taylor and Andrews, *John Andrews*, 31. Fig. 6: "Monarto City Centre Stage One Design Proposal," John Andrews International, 1975. Fig. 7: "RG2 Canberra College of Advanced Education," John Andrews International, 1973. Fig. 8: Photographer unknown. Figs. 9–10: Photos: David Moore. Fig. 11: Photographer unknown. Fig. 12: Photo: David Knell & Associates. Figs. 13: "Ipswich College of Technical and Further Education," John Andrews International, 1975. Figs. 14–15: Photos: Antony Moulis

11: TOWERS

Figs. 1, 6–8: Photos: PANDA Associates. Courtesy of Canadian Architectural Archives. Figs. 2–3: Photos: Michael Andrews. Fig. 4: Louis I. Kahn Collection, University of Pennsylvania and Pennsylvania Historical and Museum Commission. Fig. 5: *Canadian Architect* (July 1976). Fig. 9: Photo: David Moore. Fig. 10: John Andrews International, photographer unknown. Fig. 11: Photo: Milton Wordley & Associates. Figs. 12, 16: Photos: Eric Sierins. Figs. 13–15: John Andrews International. Fig. 18: Photo: Christopher Shain.

12: INTELSAT: A KIND OF CULMINATION

Figs. 1, 4–6, 12: Photos: Paul Walker, 2012. Figs. 2–3, 8–9, 11: John Andrews International. Fig. 7: , "Intelsat Project, Washington DC," John Andrews International, January 1980. Fig. 10: Herman Hertzberger. Figs. 13, 17: Photos: Geoff Willing. Fig. 14: "Monarto City Centre Stage One Design Proposal," John Andrews International, 1975. Fig. 15: "Intelsat Project, Washington DC, Section 4 Appendix: Annual Energy Consumption and Energy Design Aspects," John Andrews International, January 1980. Fig. 16: John Andrews International, photographer unknown.

13: CONVENTION CENTERS

Figs. 1–2: Photos: Milton Wordley & Associates. Figs. 3, 7–8: John Andrews International. Figs. 4, 6: Photos: John Gollings. Fig. 5: Photographer unknown. Fig. 9: Photo: Gary Ede. Figs. 10, 13–16: Photos: Peter Bennetts. Fig. 11: Photos: Max Dupain, 1986. Fig. 12: Photo: David Moore.

14: FINALE

Figs. 1, 3: Photos: Noritaka Minami. Figs. 2, 5: Photos: David Moore. Figs. 4, 7: Photos: Paul Walker. Fig. 6: Donaldytong, via Wikimedia Commons. Fig. 8: Stephen Byrnes, 2014.

CONTRIBUTORS

PHILIP GOAD is Redmond Barry Distinguished Professor, chair of architecture, and codirector of the Australian Centre for Architectural History, Urban and Cultural Heritage (ACAHUCH) at the University of Melbourne. He is a Fellow of the Australian Academy of Humanities. In 2019–2020 he was Gough Whitlam Malcom Fraser Chair of Australian Studies at Harvard University. An authority on modern Australian architecture, his research focuses on its national discourse, its buildings for health, education, and housing, and its place in Australasia and the Pan Pacific region. He is coauthor and coeditor of *Modern Times: The Untold Story of Modernism in Australia* (2008), *The Encyclopedia of Australian Architecture* (2012), *Bauhaus Diaspora and Beyond: Transforming Education through Art, Design, and Architecture* (2019), *Architecture and the Modern Hospital: Nosokomeion to Hygeia* (2019), and *Australia Modern: Architecture, Landscape, and Design, 1925–1975* (2019).

MARY LOU LOBSINGER is associate professor of architectural history and theory at the J. H. Daniels Faculty of Architecture, Landscape Architecture, and Design at the University of Toronto. Her architectural and urban research focuses on environmental issues, the political economy of institutions, media, and the historiography of architectural theory. She has published widely and held fellowships and received awards from the Canadian Centre for Architecture, the Graham Foundation for Advanced Studies in the Fine Arts, the Social Science and Humanities Research Council, the Canada Council for the Arts, the Toronto Arts Council, the Ontario Design Council, the Harvard Graduate School of Design, and the Harvard Graduate School of Arts and Sciences. Lobsinger's creative practice includes video- and text-based visual works and environments for multidisciplinary experiments as well as architectural practice.

NORITAKA MINAMI is an artist based in Chicago. He received an MFA in Studio Art from University of California, Irvine, and a BA in Art Practice from University of California, Berkeley. He is a recipient of grants from the Pollock-Krasner Foundation, the Graham Foundation for Advanced Studies in the Fine Arts, the Illinois Arts Council Agency, the Santo Foundation, and the Center for Cultural Innovation. In 2015, Kehrer Verlag published his monograph titled *1972: Nakagin Capsule Tower*, which received the 2015 Architectural Book Award from the Deutsches Architekturmuseum in Frankfurt, Germany. Solo exhibitions of his works have been held at FLXST Contemporary, Kana Kawanishi Gallery, SFO Museum, USC Roski School of Art and Design, UCLA Department of Architecture and Urban Design, UC Merced Art Gallery, and Griffin Museum of Photography. He has also participated in group exhibitions at the Aperture Foundation, Somerset House, Photo Basel, Las Cienegas Projects, New Wight Gallery, and Kearney Street Workshop. Minami's works are held in the collections of the San Francisco Museum of Modern Art, UCLA Architecture and Urban Design, Museum of Contemporary Photography Chicago, and Center for Photography at Woodstock. He is currently associate professor of photography at Loyola University Chicago.

ANTONY MOULIS is associate professor in the School of Architecture at the University of Queensland, where he researches architectural history, urbanism, and design. His recent works newly interpret the study of Le Corbusier. The solely authored book *Le Corbusier in the Antipodes: Art, Architecture and Urbanism* (Routledge, 2021) is a first account of the architect's reception, encounters, and global networks in Australasia, while the coedited four-volume anthology, *Le Corbusier: Critical Concepts in Architecture* (Routledge, 2018), is a detailed historiographic survey of writings on and by the architect from 1920 to the present. Moulis's collaborative design research investigates resilience and microurbanism in the contemporary city, with built and speculative projects featured in international journals such as *Architecture Australia*, *The Architectural Review*, *GA Houses*, and an invited installation at the 2021 Seoul Biennale of Architecture and Urbanism. Moulis's architectural writing and research spans professional and academic journals, including critical commentary on contemporary architecture.

PAOLO SCRIVANO is associate professor of history of architecture at the Politecnico di Milano. He received a PhD from the Politecnico di Torino and has taught at the University of Toronto, Boston University, and Xi'an Jiaotong-Liverpool University. He has widely published on 20th-century architecture, including the volumes *Storia di un'idea di architettura moderna, Henry-Russell Hitchcock e l'International Style* (2001), *Olivetti Builds: Modern Architecture in Ivrea* (2001, in coauthorship), and *Building Transatlantic Italy: Architectural Dialogues with Postwar America* (2013). He has been a visiting scholar at the Massachusetts Institute of Technology and at the Canadian Centre for Architecture as well as visiting fellow at the Center for the Advanced Study in the Visual Arts at the National Gallery of Art. Currently he is scientific coordinator of the research network "Mapping Architectural Criticism" based at the Université Rennes 2.

PETER SCRIVER is a Canadian architectural historian who now teaches in Australia, where he is a founding director of the Centre for Asian and Middle Eastern Architecture (CAMEA) at the University of Adelaide. He has published extensively on the architecture and planning history of colonial and contemporary South Asia (*After the Masters*, 1990; *India: Modern Architectures in History*, 2015), and has also contributed significantly to the critical historiography and theory of colonial design knowledge, its systems, and trans-colonial exchanges (*Colonial Modernities*, 2007; and *The Scaffolding of Empire*, 2007). Scriver's ongoing work focuses on the Indian Ocean Rim and the networks and exchanges of knowledge, labor, and materials between the building worlds of Asia, Africa, and Australasia that connect it. He has contributed critically to scholarship on the colonial-modern construction of the contemporary built environment, and the broader cultural, institutional, and political-economic frameworks of its production.

PAUL WALKER is a professor of architecture at the University of Melbourne where he teaches architectural history, theory, and design. He has written widely about modern and contemporary architecture in Australia and New Zealand and, through the frames of postcolonialism, about British colonial architecture in various locations. With Justine Clark, he is author of *Looking for the Local: Architecture and the New Zealand Modern* (2000), and with Julia Gatley, *Vertical Living: the Architectural Centre and the Remaking of Wellington* (2014). His work has appeared in the *Journal of Architecture*, *Fabrications*, *CLOG*, *Architecture Australia*, and *Volume*.

ACKNOWLEDGMENTS

The nature of John Andrews's multifaceted architecture career made it almost impossible for one person to document and analyze. For sharing the task, I am grateful to Antony Moulis, Peter Scriver, Philip Goad, Mary Lou Lobsinger, and Paolo Scrivano.

Resources for the book's initial research stemmed from a Discovery Project grant provided by the Australian Research Council. This funding allowed for a symposium to take place at the University of Melbourne in 2012, which featured John Andrews in full flight with former members of his Sydney office, including John Simpson, Arthur Robb, Doug McKay, Ian Bailey, and Tina Curtis. I am also grateful that John's old classmate Maurice Finegold, from the Harvard GSD Master of Architecture Class of 1958, joined us by video conference for the occasion. Also presenting were Mary Lou Lobsinger, Jared Bird, Philip Drew, and Jennifer Taylor. Taylor was, with Andrews, the coauthor of the only other book on Andrews's work, *John Andrews: Architecture, a Performing Art* (1982). I am grateful she gave her blessing to our work.

Late in 2012, I was able to travel to the United States and Canada to see Andrews's projects for the Miami Seaport Terminal, the Intelsat Headquarters, the Harvard GSD's Gund Hall, Scarborough College, and the University of Guelph's South Residences. My thanks to all those who made the visits possible. In Toronto I talked to Ed Galanyk and Roger du Toit, who worked in Andrews's Toronto office, and Peter Prangnell who oversaw curriculum reforms at the University of Toronto School of Architecture for which Andrews was responsible. Throughout the project I also interviewed Donovan Pinker, George Baird, and Geoff Willing.

Dr. Jane Grant worked assiduously as a research assistant on the project from 2012 to 2017. More recently, Dr. Jennifer Mitchelhill helped to organize images. I thank Tina Curtis for getting Andrews's Australian archive in order and making it accessible. I also thank all the photographers who allowed us to use their work. Various libraries and archives facilitated the use of historical images, notably the Canadian Architectural Archives at the University of Calgary, where Linda Fraser and Maggie Hunter have been very generous.

Ken Stewart and Marielle Suba of Harvard Design Press have been insightful and patient publishers, and Chad Kloepfer and Willis Kingery have devised a fitting and elegant design for the book. The publishers brought Noritaka Minami to the project, and his photographs are an outstanding addition.

The greatest thanks go to John Andrews and his family. John's son Lee has been consistently helpful with research and providing information. Rosemary ("Ro") Andrews has always been courteous and hospitable, even when I am sure she was perplexed to find me again on her doorstep. Finally, John Andrews himself was unstintingly generous in making himself available for visits, interviews, and phone calls over a period of 10 years. I am very sad that John, who died in March 2022, did not live to see this book complete, but he did read the first draft and reacted to it with enthusiasm characteristically mixed with exasperation at perceived misinterpretations. I have tried to correct all factual errors he pointed out. He also saw first proposals for the book's design and indicated his approval by suggesting improvements to the font featured on its cover. He was ever the designer.

Paul Walker

John Andrews: Architect of Uncommon Sense
Paul Walker, with contributions by Mary Lou Lobsinger, Peter Scriver, Antony Moulis, Philip Goad, Paolo Scrivano, and Noritaka Minami.

Published by Harvard Design Press at the Harvard University Graduate School of Design.

Dean and Josep Lluís Sert Professor of Architecture: Sarah M. Whiting
Assistant Dean and Director of Communications and Public Programs and Editor, Harvard Design Press: Ken Stewart
Editor, Harvard Design Press: Marielle Suba
Art Director: Chad Kloepfer
Designer: Willis Kingery
Copyeditors and proofreaders: Tyler Considine, Liz Janoff, and Rachel Holzman
Indexer: Kevin Broccoli
Publications Manager: Meghan Sandberg
Editorial Assistant: Taylor Davey
Printer: die Keure
Distributor: Harvard University Press

Typeset in Monument Grotesk, drawn by Kasper-Florio, 2018; and Archital, drawn by Willis Kingery in consultation with Craig and John Andrews, 2021.

ISBN 978-0-674278-56-1

© 2023 by the President and Fellows of Harvard College. All rights reserved. No part of this book may be reproduced in any form without prior written permission from the Harvard University Graduate School of Design.

Texts and images © their authors.

Every reasonable attempt has been made to identify owners of copyright. Errors or omissions will be corrected in subsequent editions.

Harvard University Graduate School of Design
48 Quincy Street
Cambridge, MA 02138
gsd.harvard.edu

Library of Congress Cataloging-in-Publication Data
Names: Walker, Paul, editor.
Title: John Andrews : architect of uncommon sense / edited by Paul Walker; with contributions by Mary Lou Lobsinger, Peter Scriver, Antony Moulis, Philip Goad, Paolo Scrivano, and Noritaka Minami.
Description: Cambridge, MA : Harvard University, Graduate School of Design, [2022]
Identifiers: LCCN 2022038048 | ISBN 9780674278561 (paperback)
Subjects: LCSH: Andrews, John, 1933-2022--Criticism and interpretation.
Classification: LCC NA1605.A5 J64 2022 | DDC 720.92--dc23/eng/20220824
LC record available at https://lccn.loc.gov/2022038048

Printed and bound in Belgium.

John Andrews   1933–2022